ALL THE RAGE

ALSO BY AARON MCGRUDER

The Boondocks: Because I Know You Don't Read the Newspaper

Fresh for '01 . . . You Suckas: A Boondocks Collection

A Right to Be Hostile: The Boondocks Treasury

Birth of a Nation: A Comic Novel
with Reginald Hudlin, illustrated by Kyle Baker

Public Enemy #2: An All-New Boondocks Collection

ALL THE RAGE

The Boondocks Past and Present

AARON McGRUDER

 THREE RIVERS PRESS • NEW YORK

Published in the United States by Three Rivers Press, an imprint of the Crown Publishing
Group, a division of Random House, Inc., New York.
www.crownpublishing.com

Three Rivers Press and the Tugboat design are registered trademarks of
Random House, Inc.

Library of Congress Cataloging-in-Publication Data

McGruder, Aaron.

      All the rage: The boondocks past and present / Aaron McGruder.—1st ed.

1. McGruder, Aaron. Boondocks. 2. Boondocks (Television program) I. Title.

PN6728.B633M34 2007

791.45'72—dc22   2007010386

ISBN 978-0-307-35266-8

Printed in the United States of America

Design by Maria Elias

10 9 8 7 6 5 4 3 2 1

First Edition

To my family and friends . . . whose names have been omitted
to throw off the haters

ACKNOWLEDGMENTS

Thanks to all these people for shouldering the burden of this book so I didn't have to worry about it one bit . . . Lydia Wills, Norman Aladjem, Yamara Taylor, Greg Melvin, Novena Wallach, Jason Yarn, Chris Jackson, Carrie Thornton, Brandi Bowles, Steve Ross, Philip Patrick, and Brian Ash.

Another big thanks to Lee Salem and Universal Press Syndicate for putting up with all this rage for so many years, and to Carl Jones for his tireless hard work and friendship.

CONTENTS

ALL THE RAGE

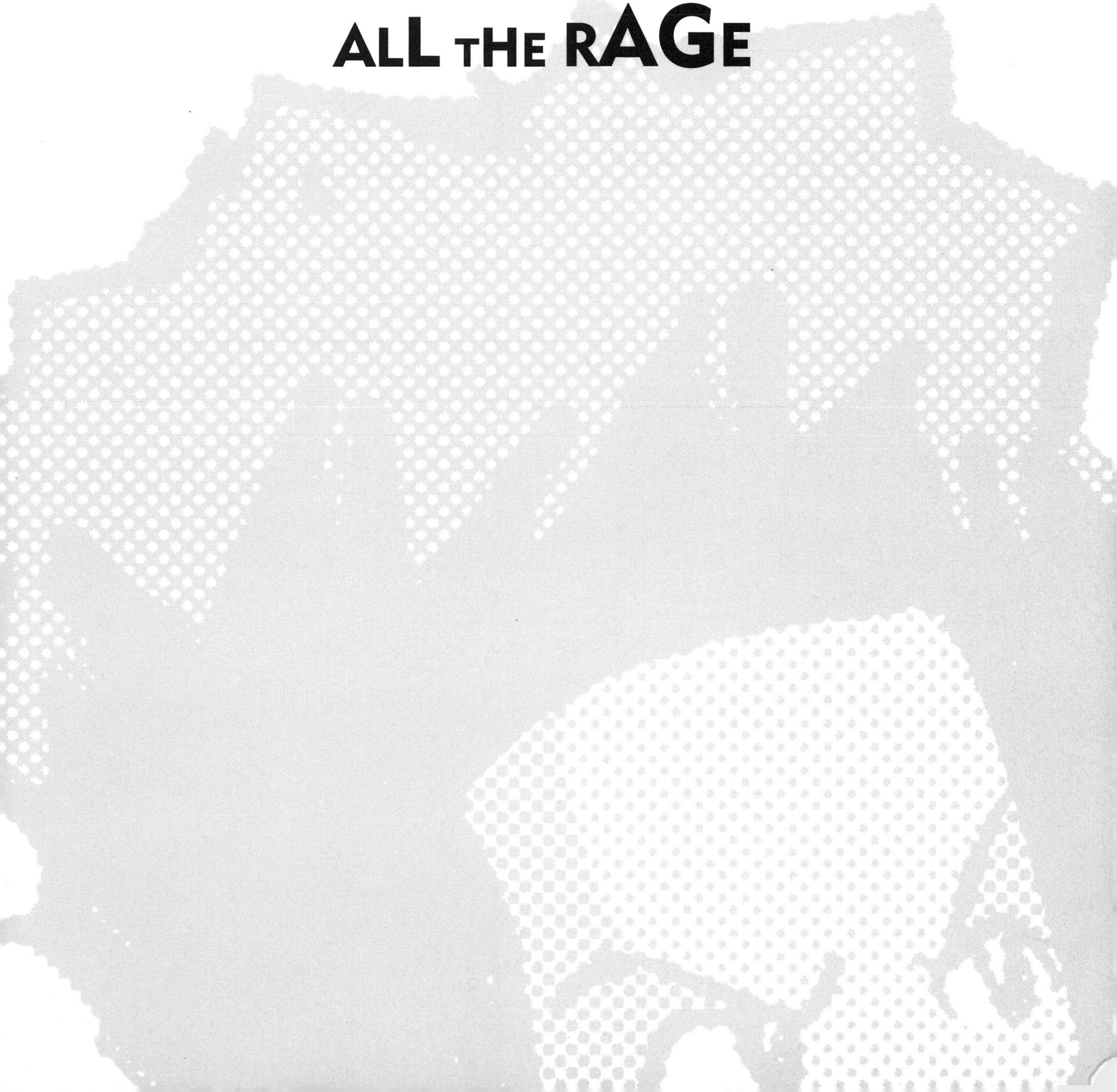

PART

I

THE STRIPS

It's not always fun being hated on.

I had been warned several times by the syndicate to tread carefully during the first year—which is like a probationary period when newspapers are quick to cancel new strips before they have a chance to find their audience. My editors encouraged balancing the hard-hitting racial and political humor with weeks of lighter stuff—jokes about movies or rappers or just having the kids act like kids. Made sense to me, and in an attempt to follow that advice, I swapped a week about Huey starting an armed, neighborhood Klan watch and replaced it with a week of strips involving Riley and plastic toy light sabers, offering up what I thought was a break from all the angry race stuff that might get me in trouble.

The toy light-saber strips ran, and much to everyone's surprise, all hell broke loose. Editors were panicking and readers were screaming bloody murder—somehow linking Riley's off-panel plastic rampage with the Columbine slayings. I sweated out the week while the syndicate did damage control and readers flooded papers with angry letters. My career as a cartoonist almost ended before it started. The Klan-watch strips that followed, by comparison, received very little attention.

I learned from that experience that controversy is an unstable element. It cannot be dependably controlled, contained, or predicted. It's dangerous to spend too much time trying to chase after it or trying to avoid it. Thankfully that first big crisis passed with my job and my client list intact, but many more near-catastrophes were waiting around the corner.

What I find remarkable about the strip was that no matter how much time had passed, people never stopped getting mad. Pretty soon the problems with newspapers over content became so frequent it became business as usual. We stopped panicking and started to deal with these annoyances as just another part of the workweek. If a strip was only banned in a paper or two, the syndicate wouldn't even bother telling me. Occasionally a fan would catch me on the street and say something like "I heard they banned you again in the *Post!*" as if hoping to set me off on a tirade against the oppressive newspaper industry and their fascist censors. Most of the time, I didn't even know which "Post" they were talking about or even the strips that had gotten me in trouble. Cartooning offers very little time to think about old strips once they're printed . . . there is always another week to worry about. The irony, of course, is how much all that hate also fuels the popularity of the strip. I have always been fortunate to have fans as vocal as my critics, as well as critics who seem to keep reading the strip no matter how much they claim to despise it.

The strips presented in this first part represent the end of a satisfying run in newspapers. You can see there was very little fear of reprisals for inappropriate content. I was deliberately trying to push the boundaries—but not in search of controversy, just some funnier jokes to tell.

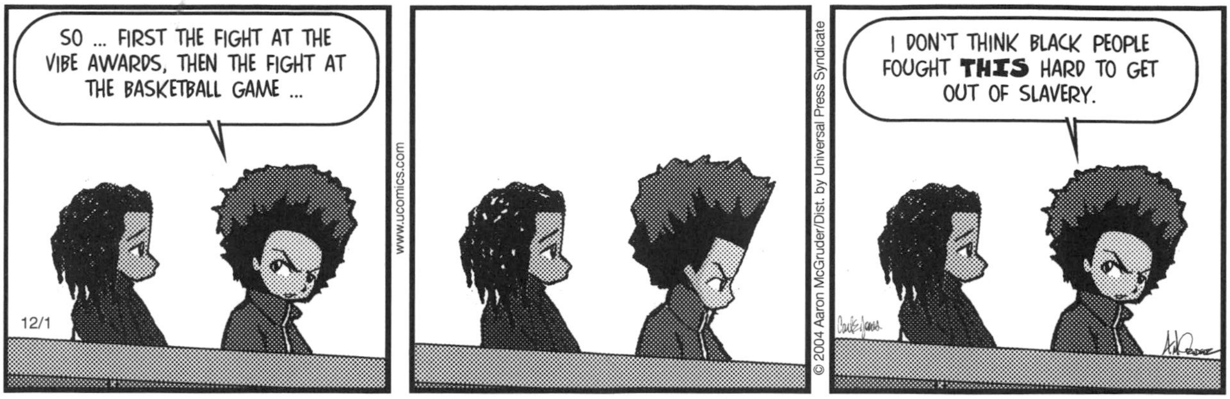
SO ... FIRST THE FIGHT AT THE VIBE AWARDS, THEN THE FIGHT AT THE BASKETBALL GAME ...
12/1
www.ucomics.com
© 2004 Aaron McGruder/Dist. by Universal Press Syndicate
I DON'T THINK BLACK PEOPLE FOUGHT THIS HARD TO GET OUT OF SLAVERY.

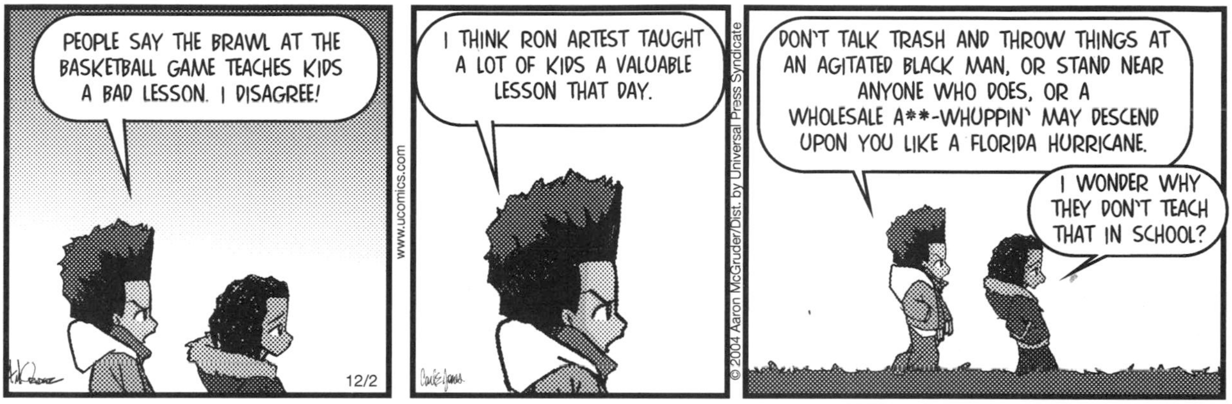
PEOPLE SAY THE BRAWL AT THE BASKETBALL GAME TEACHES KIDS A BAD LESSON. I DISAGREE!
12/2
www.ucomics.com
I THINK RON ARTEST TAUGHT A LOT OF KIDS A VALUABLE LESSON THAT DAY.
© 2004 Aaron McGruder/Dist. by Universal Press Syndicate
DON'T TALK TRASH AND THROW THINGS AT AN AGITATED BLACK MAN, OR STAND NEAR ANYONE WHO DOES, OR A WHOLESALE A**-WHUPPIN' MAY DESCEND UPON YOU LIKE A FLORIDA HURRICANE.
I WONDER WHY THEY DON'T TEACH THAT IN SCHOOL?

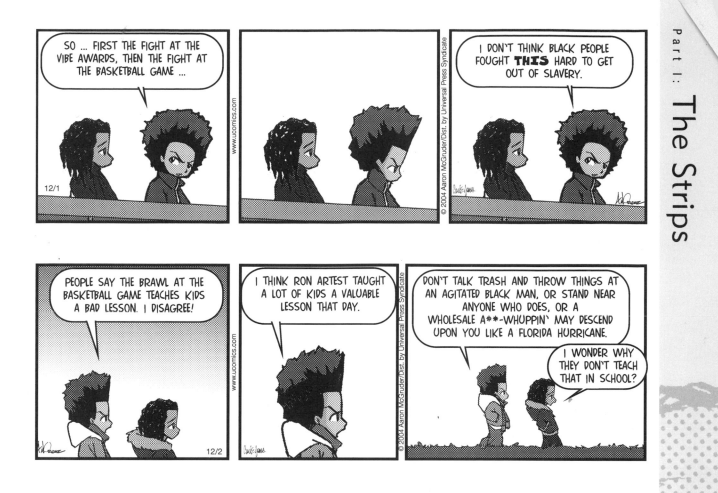

Step into the mind of a cartoon radical armed with a pen.

—*The Spokesman* (Morgan State University)

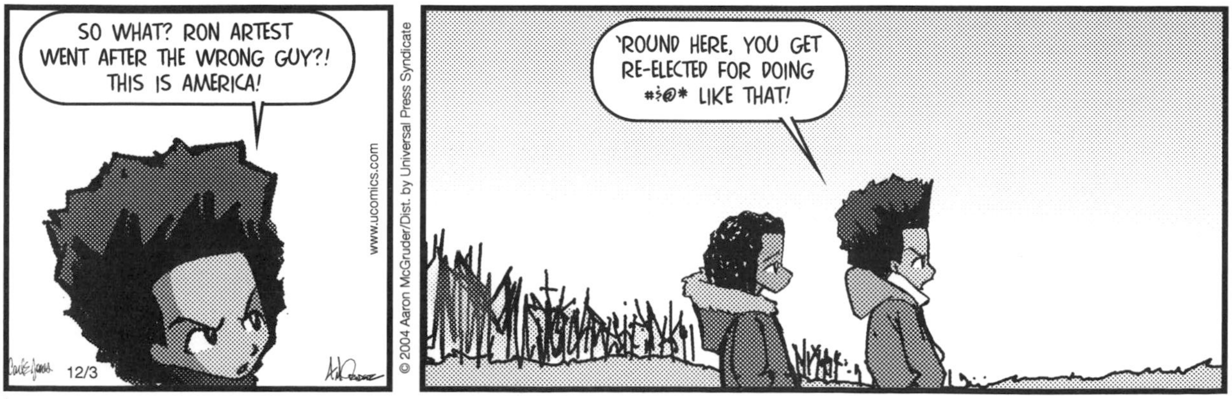
SO WHAT? RON ARTEST WENT AFTER THE WRONG GUY?! THIS IS AMERICA!
12/3
www.ucomics.com
© 2004 Aaron McGruder/Dist. by Universal Press Syndicate
'ROUND HERE, YOU GET RE-ELECTED FOR DOING #$@* LIKE THAT!

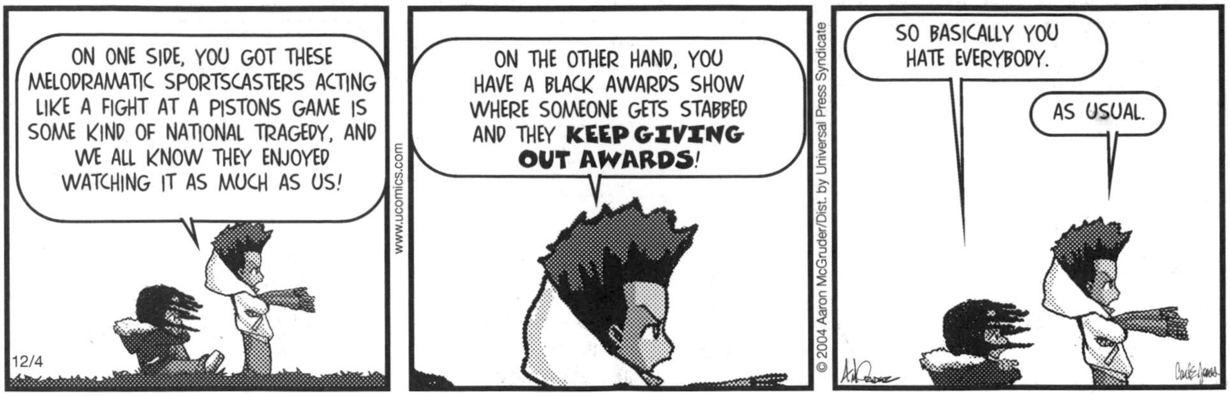
ON ONE SIDE, YOU GOT THESE MELODRAMATIC SPORTSCASTERS ACTING LIKE A FIGHT AT A PISTONS GAME IS SOME KIND OF NATIONAL TRAGEDY, AND WE ALL KNOW THEY ENJOYED WATCHING IT AS MUCH AS US!
12/4
www.ucomics.com
ON THE OTHER HAND, YOU HAVE A BLACK AWARDS SHOW WHERE SOMEONE GETS STABBED AND THEY **KEEP GIVING OUT AWARDS**!
© 2004 Aaron McGruder/Dist. by Universal Press Syndicate
SO BASICALLY YOU HATE EVERYBODY.
AS USUAL.

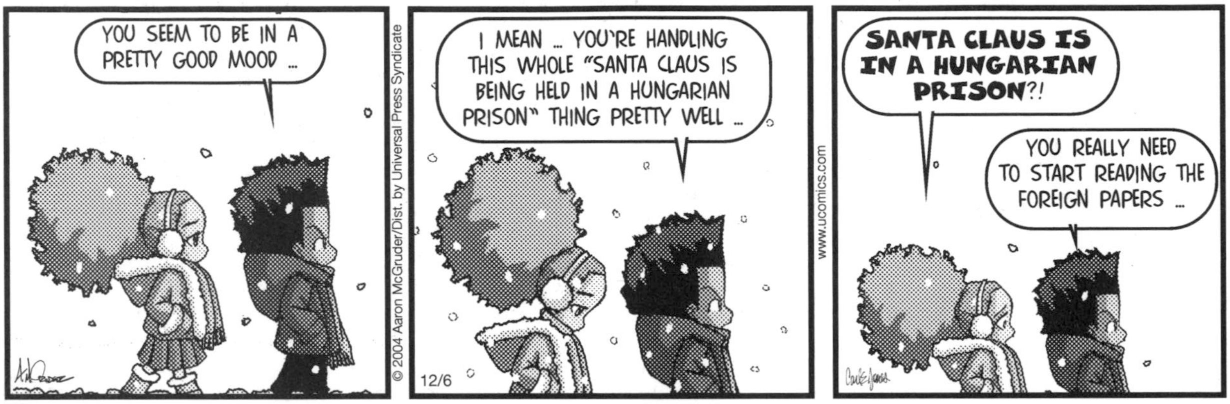
YOU SEEM TO BE IN A PRETTY GOOD MOOD ...
© 2004 Aaron McGruder/Dist. by Universal Press Syndicate
I MEAN ... YOU'RE HANDLING THIS WHOLE "SANTA CLAUS IS BEING HELD IN A HUNGARIAN PRISON" THING PRETTY WELL ...
12/6
www.ucomics.com
SANTA CLAUS IS IN A HUNGARIAN PRISON?!
YOU REALLY NEED TO START READING THE FOREIGN PAPERS ...

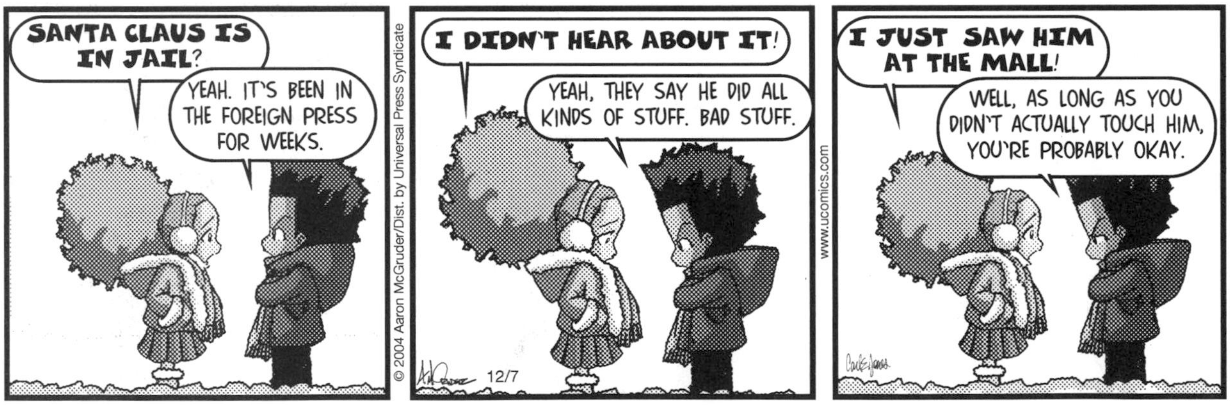
SANTA CLAUS IS IN JAIL?
YEAH. IT'S BEEN IN THE FOREIGN PRESS FOR WEEKS.
© 2004 Aaron McGruder/Dist. by Universal Press Syndicate
I DIDN'T HEAR ABOUT IT!
YEAH, THEY SAY HE DID ALL KINDS OF STUFF. BAD STUFF.
12/7
www.ucomics.com
I JUST SAW HIM AT THE MALL!
WELL, AS LONG AS YOU DIDN'T ACTUALLY TOUCH HIM, YOU'RE PROBABLY OKAY.

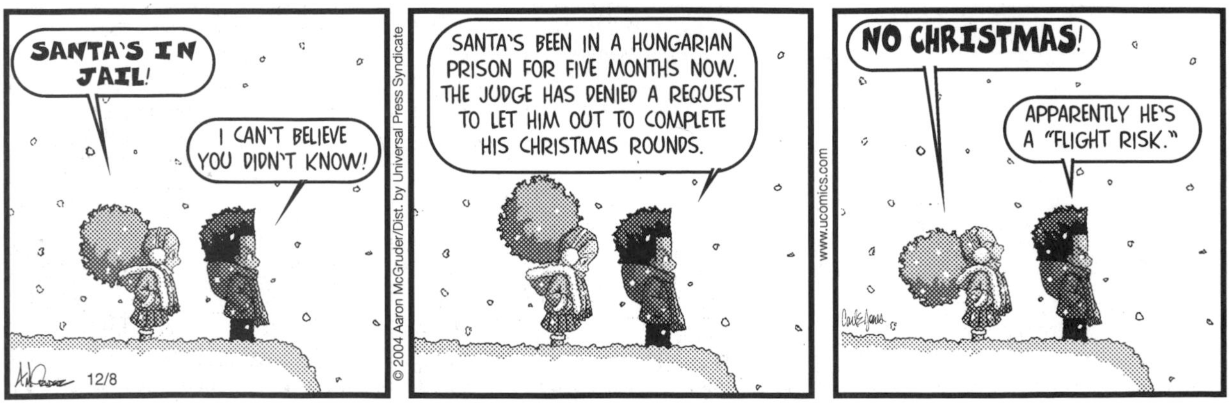
SANTA'S IN JAIL!
I CAN'T BELIEVE YOU DIDN'T KNOW!
12/8
© 2004 Aaron McGruder/Dist. by Universal Press Syndicate
SANTA'S BEEN IN A HUNGARIAN PRISON FOR FIVE MONTHS NOW. THE JUDGE HAS DENIED A REQUEST TO LET HIM OUT TO COMPLETE HIS CHRISTMAS ROUNDS.
www.ucomics.com
NO CHRISTMAS!
APPARENTLY HE'S A "FLIGHT RISK."

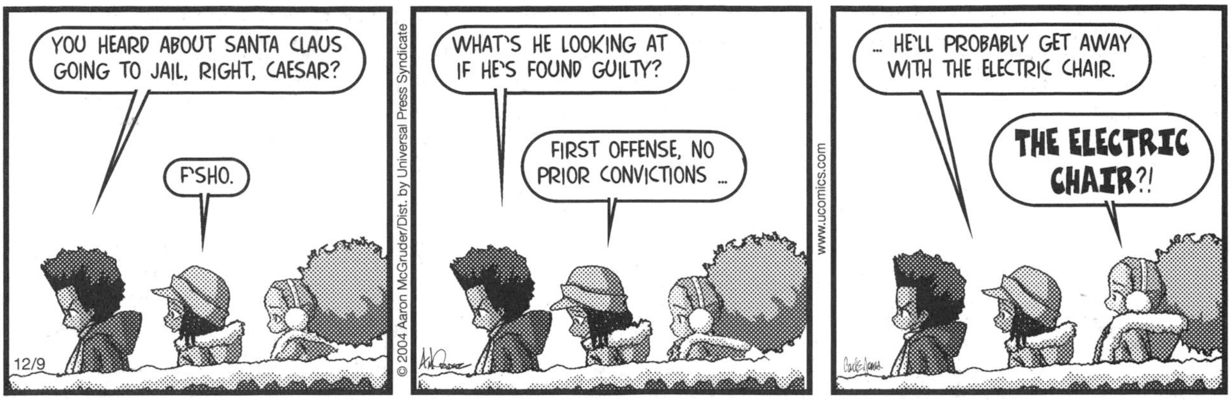
YOU HEARD ABOUT SANTA CLAUS GOING TO JAIL, RIGHT, CAESAR?
F'SHO.
12/9
WHAT'S HE LOOKING AT IF HE'S FOUND GUILTY?
FIRST OFFENSE, NO PRIOR CONVICTIONS ...
... HE'LL PROBABLY GET AWAY WITH THE ELECTRIC CHAIR.
THE ELECTRIC CHAIR?!
© 2004 Aaron McGruder/Dist. by Universal Press Syndicate
www.ucomics.com

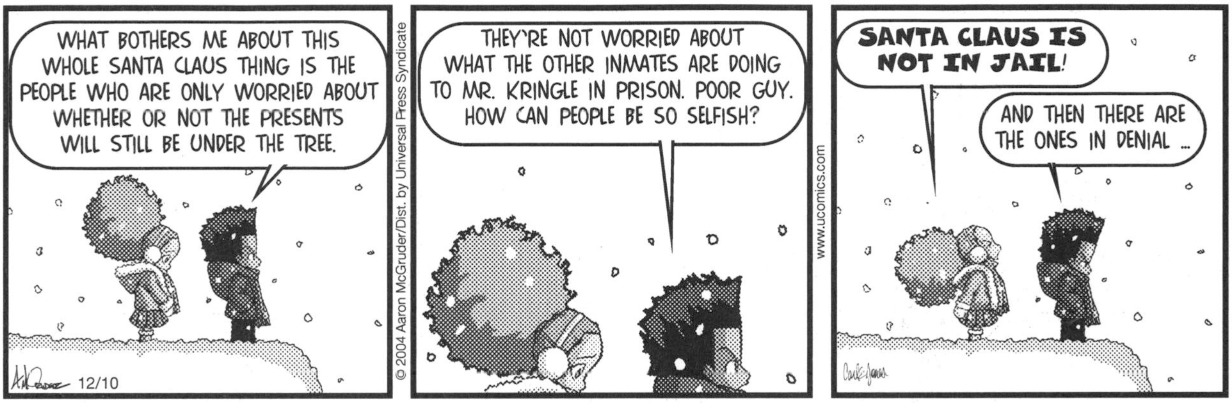
WHAT BOTHERS ME ABOUT THIS WHOLE SANTA CLAUS THING IS THE PEOPLE WHO ARE ONLY WORRIED ABOUT WHETHER OR NOT THE PRESENTS WILL STILL BE UNDER THE TREE.
12/10
THEY'RE NOT WORRIED ABOUT WHAT THE OTHER INMATES ARE DOING TO MR. KRINGLE IN PRISON. POOR GUY. HOW CAN PEOPLE BE SO SELFISH?
SANTA CLAUS IS NOT IN JAIL!
AND THEN THERE ARE THE ONES IN DENIAL ...
© 2004 Aaron McGruder/Dist. by Universal Press Syndicate
www.ucomics.com

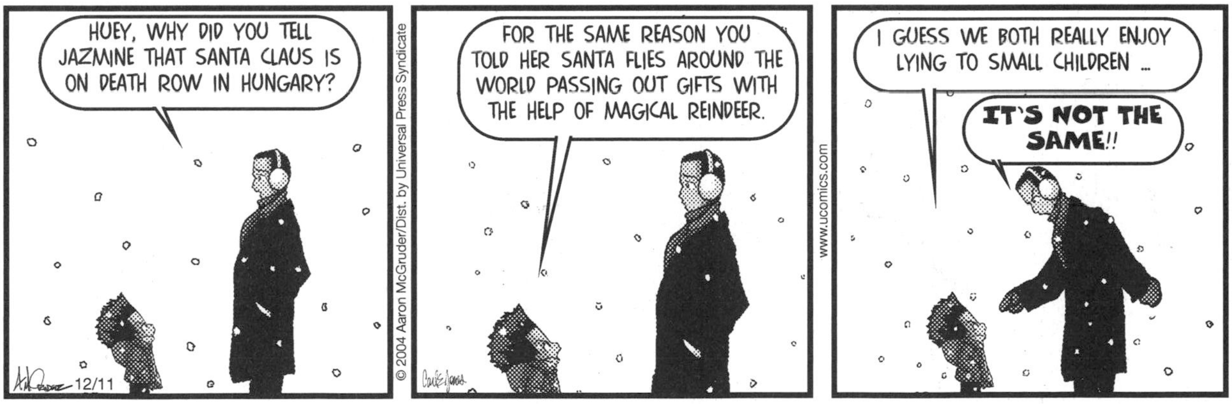
HUEY, WHY DID YOU TELL JAZMINE THAT SANTA CLAUS IS ON DEATH ROW IN HUNGARY?
12/11
FOR THE SAME REASON YOU TOLD HER SANTA FLIES AROUND THE WORLD PASSING OUT GIFTS WITH THE HELP OF MAGICAL REINDEER.
I GUESS WE BOTH REALLY ENJOY LYING TO SMALL CHILDREN ...
IT'S NOT THE SAME!!
© 2004 Aaron McGruder/Dist. by Universal Press Syndicate
www.ucomics.com

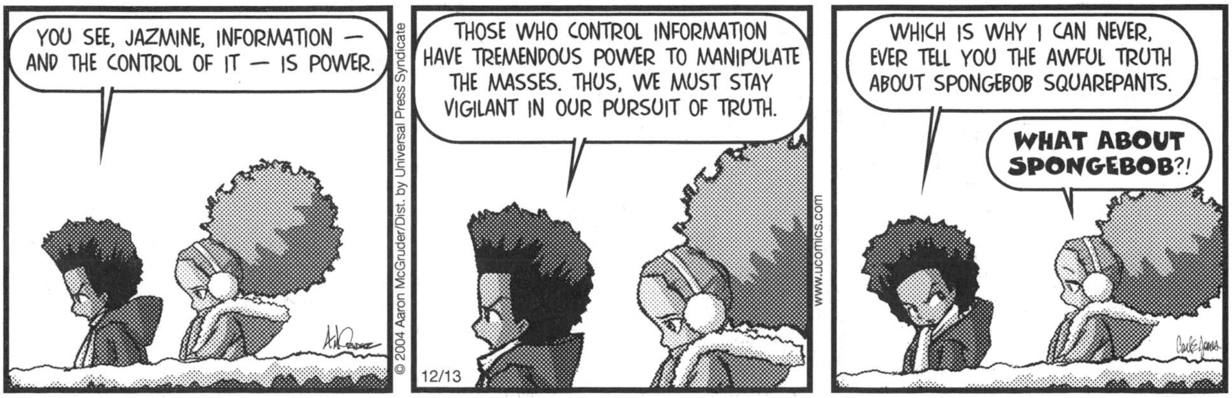
YOU SEE, JAZMINE, INFORMATION — AND THE CONTROL OF IT — IS POWER.
THOSE WHO CONTROL INFORMATION HAVE TREMENDOUS POWER TO MANIPULATE THE MASSES. THUS, WE MUST STAY VIGILANT IN OUR PURSUIT OF TRUTH.
12/13
WHICH IS WHY I CAN NEVER, EVER TELL YOU THE AWFUL TRUTH ABOUT SPONGEBOB SQUAREPANTS.
WHAT ABOUT SPONGEBOB?!
© 2004 Aaron McGruder/Dist. by Universal Press Syndicate
www.ucomics.com

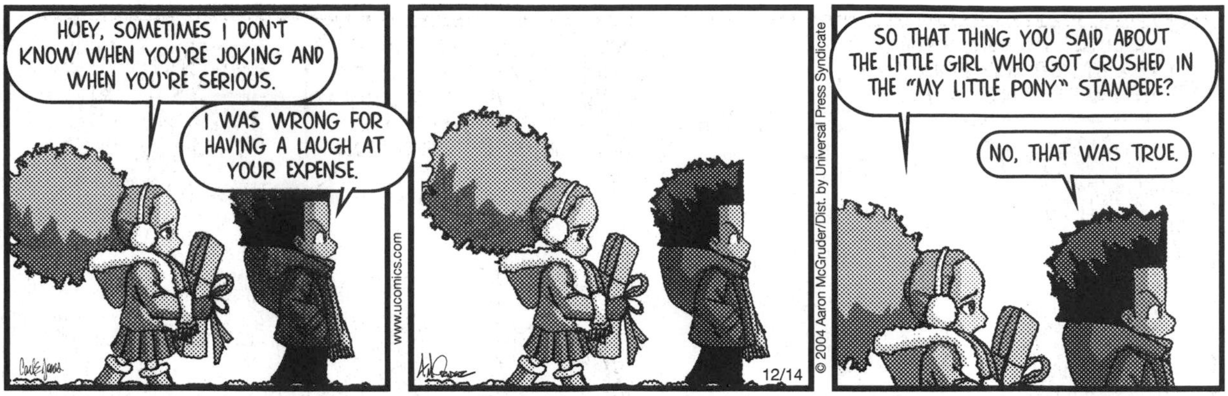
HUEY, SOMETIMES I DON'T KNOW WHEN YOU'RE JOKING AND WHEN YOU'RE SERIOUS.
I WAS WRONG FOR HAVING A LAUGH AT YOUR EXPENSE.
www.ucomics.com
12/14
© 2004 Aaron McGruder/Dist. by Universal Press Syndicate
SO THAT THING YOU SAID ABOUT THE LITTLE GIRL WHO GOT CRUSHED IN THE "MY LITTLE PONY" STAMPEDE?
NO, THAT WAS TRUE.

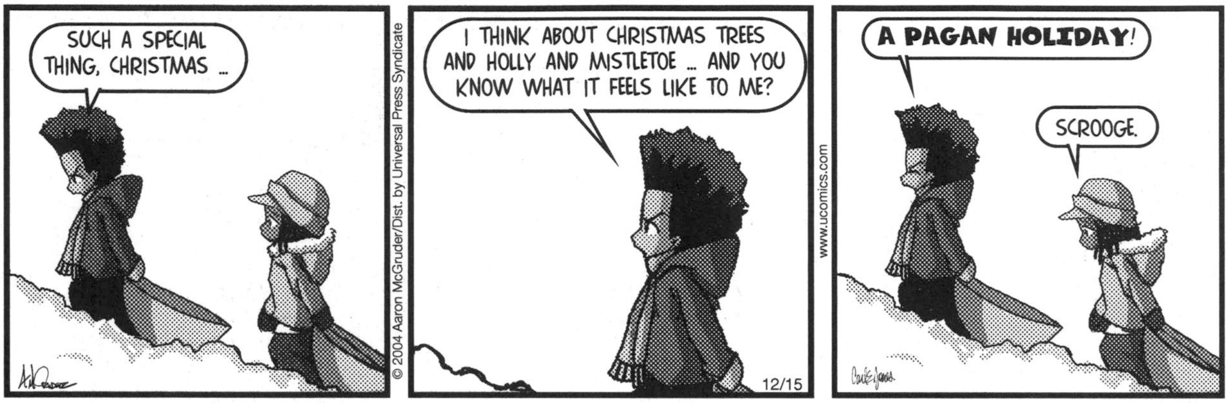
SUCH A SPECIAL THING, CHRISTMAS ...
© 2004 Aaron McGruder/Dist. by Universal Press Syndicate
I THINK ABOUT CHRISTMAS TREES AND HOLLY AND MISTLETOE ... AND YOU KNOW WHAT IT FEELS LIKE TO ME?
12/15
www.ucomics.com
A PAGAN HOLIDAY!
SCROOGE.

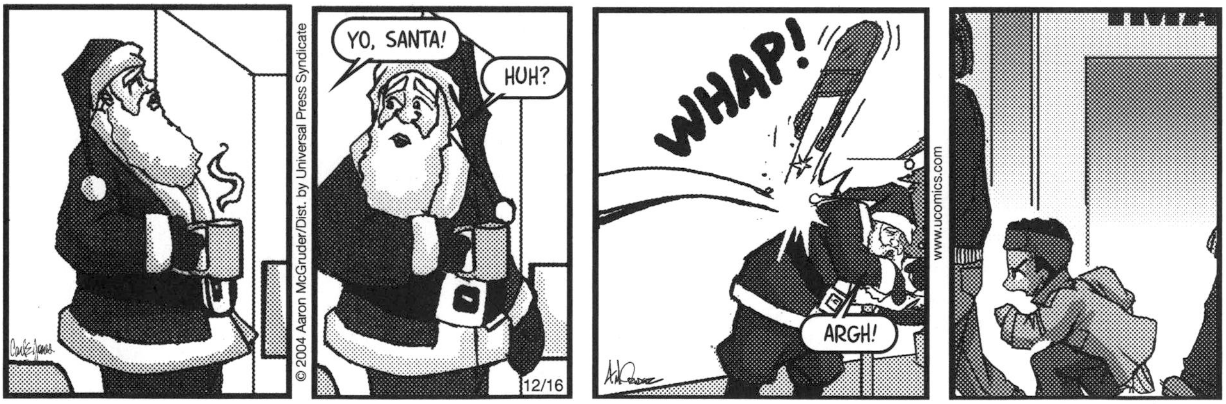
© 2004 Aaron McGruder/Dist. by Universal Press Syndicate
YO, SANTA!
HUH?
12/16
WHAP!
ARGH!
www.ucomics.com

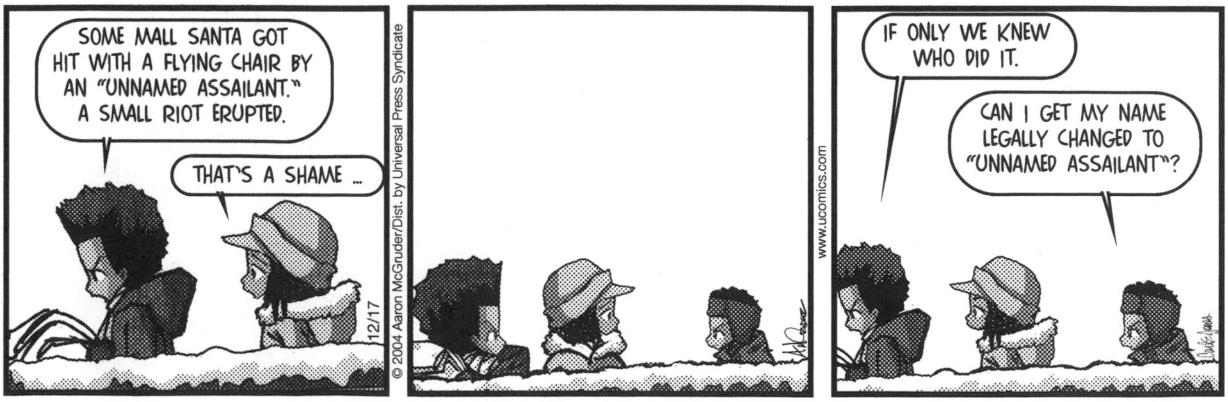
SOME MALL SANTA GOT HIT WITH A FLYING CHAIR BY AN "UNNAMED ASSAILANT." A SMALL RIOT ERUPTED.
THAT'S A SHAME ...
12/17
© 2004 Aaron McGruder/Dist. by Universal Press Syndicate
www.ucomics.com
IF ONLY WE KNEW WHO DID IT.
CAN I GET MY NAME LEGALLY CHANGED TO "UNNAMED ASSAILANT"?

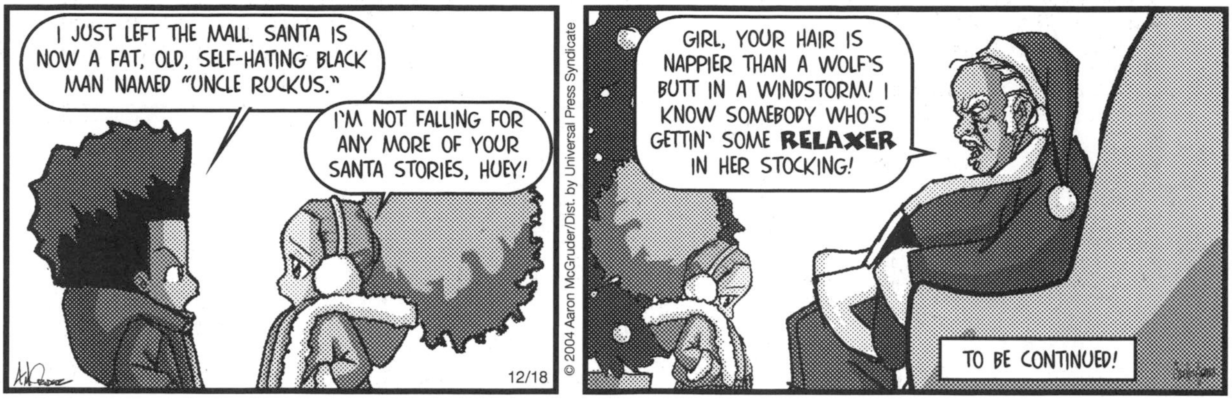
I JUST LEFT THE MALL. SANTA IS NOW A FAT, OLD, SELF-HATING BLACK MAN NAMED "UNCLE RUCKUS."
I'M NOT FALLING FOR ANY MORE OF YOUR SANTA STORIES, HUEY!
12/18
© 2004 Aaron McGruder/Dist. by Universal Press Syndicate
GIRL, YOUR HAIR IS NAPPIER THAN A WOLF'S BUTT IN A WINDSTORM! I KNOW SOMEBODY WHO'S GETTIN' SOME **RELAXER** IN HER STOCKING!
TO BE CONTINUED!

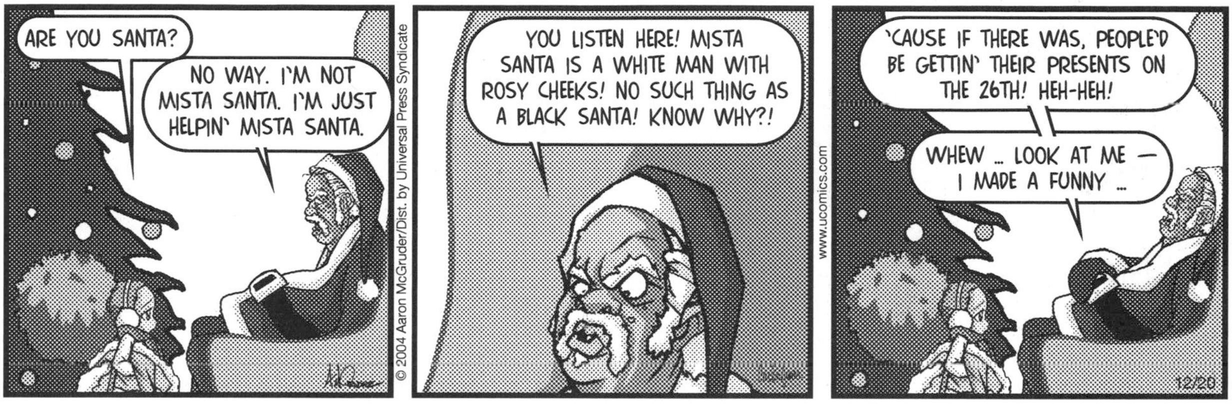
ARE YOU SANTA?
NO WAY. I'M NOT MISTA SANTA. I'M JUST HELPIN' MISTA SANTA.
© 2004 Aaron McGruder/Dist. by Universal Press Syndicate
YOU LISTEN HERE! MISTA SANTA IS A WHITE MAN WITH ROSY CHEEKS! NO SUCH THING AS A BLACK SANTA! KNOW WHY?!
www.ucomics.com
'CAUSE IF THERE WAS, PEOPLE'D BE GETTIN' THEIR PRESENTS ON THE 26TH! HEH-HEH!
WHEW ... LOOK AT ME — I MADE A FUNNY ...
12/20

As to McGruder's being allowed to say the things he says only because he is black, it would probably be more accurate to say that he is able to see the things he sees because he is black.

—Chicago Tribune

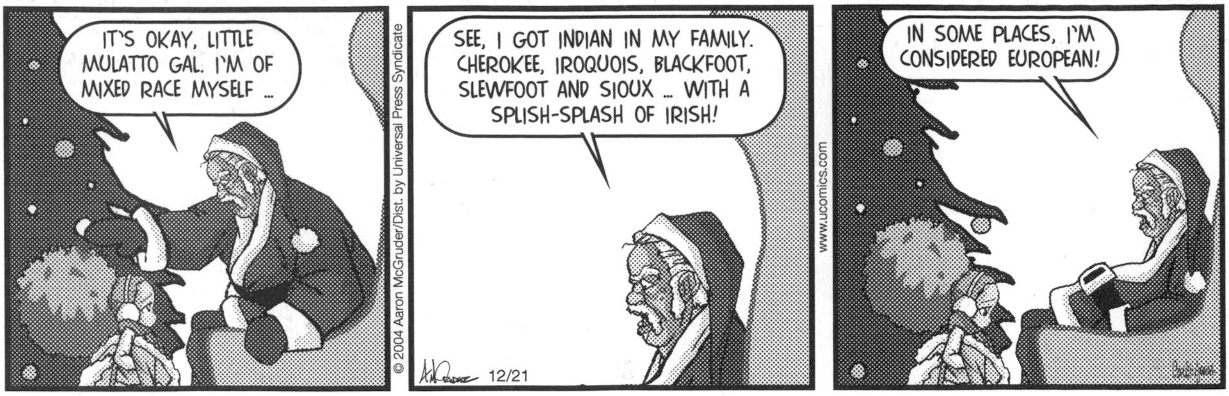
IT'S OKAY, LITTLE MULATTO GAL. I'M OF MIXED RACE MYSELF ...
© 2004 Aaron McGruder/Dist. by Universal Press Syndicate
SEE, I GOT INDIAN IN MY FAMILY. CHEROKEE, IROQUOIS, BLACKFOOT, SLEWFOOT AND SIOUX ... WITH A SPLISH-SPLASH OF IRISH!
12/21
www.ucomics.com
IN SOME PLACES, I'M CONSIDERED EUROPEAN!

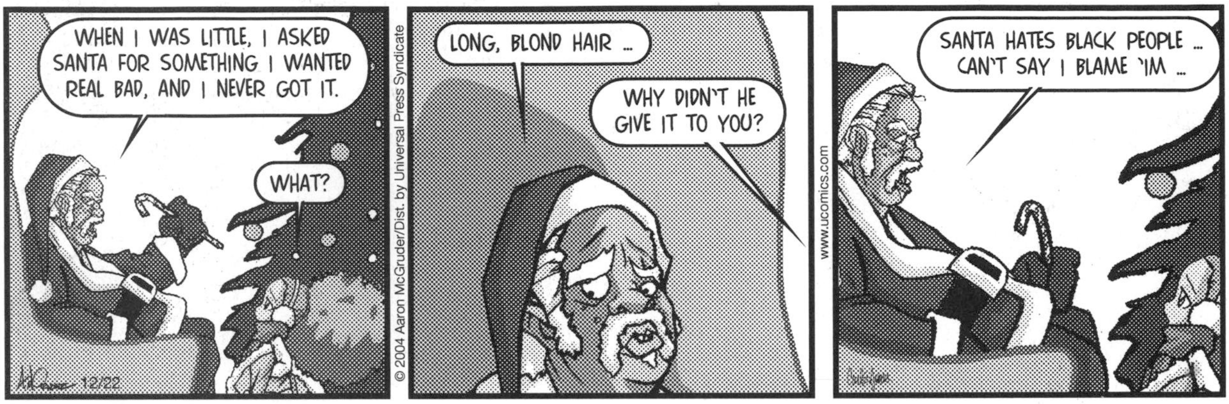
WHEN I WAS LITTLE, I ASKED SANTA FOR SOMETHING I WANTED REAL BAD, AND I NEVER GOT IT.
WHAT?
12/22
© 2004 Aaron McGruder/Dist. by Universal Press Syndicate
LONG, BLOND HAIR ...
WHY DIDN'T HE GIVE IT TO YOU?
www.ucomics.com
SANTA HATES BLACK PEOPLE ... CAN'T SAY I BLAME 'IM ...

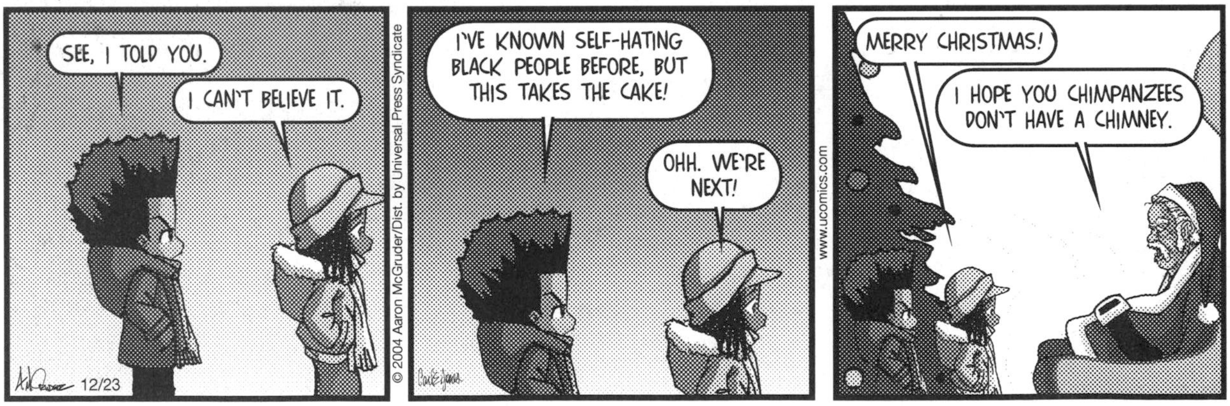
SEE, I TOLD YOU.
I CAN'T BELIEVE IT.
12/23
© 2004 Aaron McGruder/Dist. by Universal Press Syndicate
I'VE KNOWN SELF-HATING BLACK PEOPLE BEFORE, BUT THIS TAKES THE CAKE!
OHH. WE'RE NEXT!
www.ucomics.com
MERRY CHRISTMAS!
I HOPE YOU CHIMPANZEES DON'T HAVE A CHIMNEY.

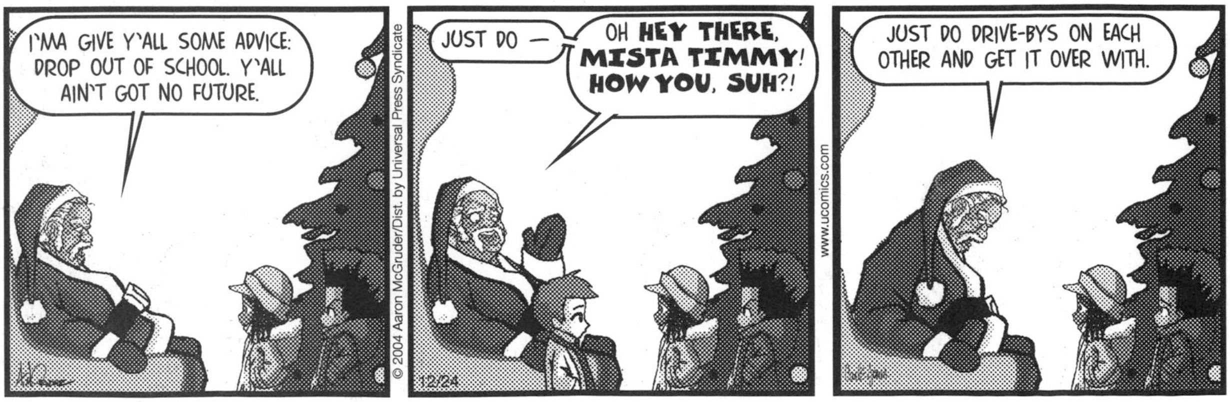
I'MA GIVE Y'ALL SOME ADVICE: DROP OUT OF SCHOOL. Y'ALL AIN'T GOT NO FUTURE.
© 2004 Aaron McGruder/Dist. by Universal Press Syndicate
JUST DO —
OH HEY THERE, MISTA TIMMY! HOW YOU, SUH?!
12/24
www.ucomics.com
JUST DO DRIVE-BYS ON EACH OTHER AND GET IT OVER WITH.

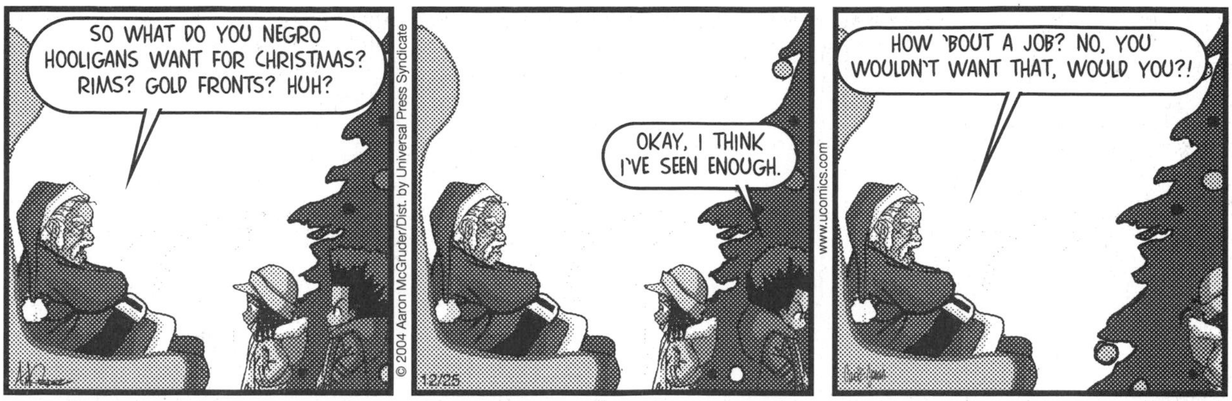
SO WHAT DO YOU NEGRO HOOLIGANS WANT FOR CHRISTMAS? RIMS? GOLD FRONTS? HUH?
© 2004 Aaron McGruder/Dist. by Universal Press Syndicate
12/25
OKAY, I THINK I'VE SEEN ENOUGH.
www.ucomics.com
HOW 'BOUT A JOB? NO, YOU WOULDN'T WANT THAT, WOULD YOU?!

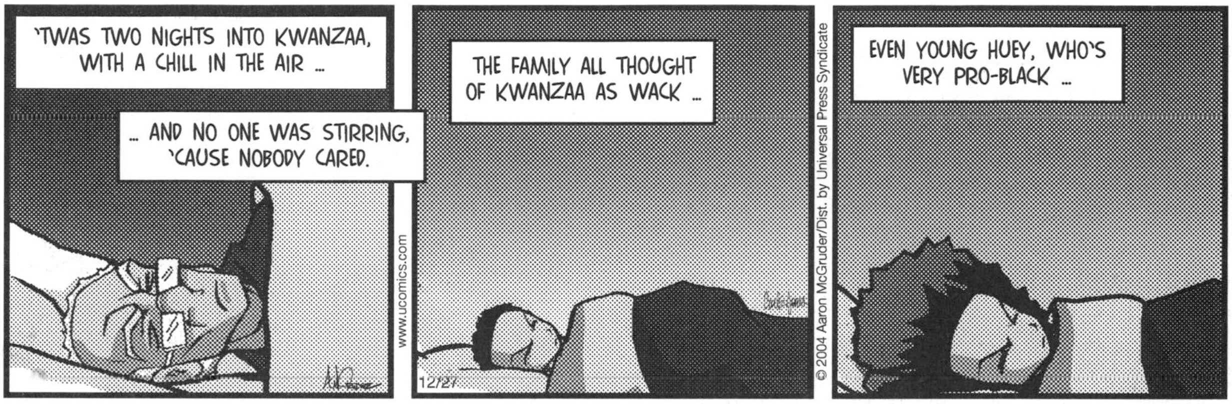
'TWAS TWO NIGHTS INTO KWANZAA, WITH A CHILL IN THE AIR ...
... AND NO ONE WAS STIRRING, 'CAUSE NOBODY CARED.
www.ucomics.com
THE FAMILY ALL THOUGHT OF KWANZAA AS WACK ...
12/27
© 2004 Aaron McGruder/Dist. by Universal Press Syndicate
EVEN YOUNG HUEY, WHO'S VERY PRO-BLACK ...

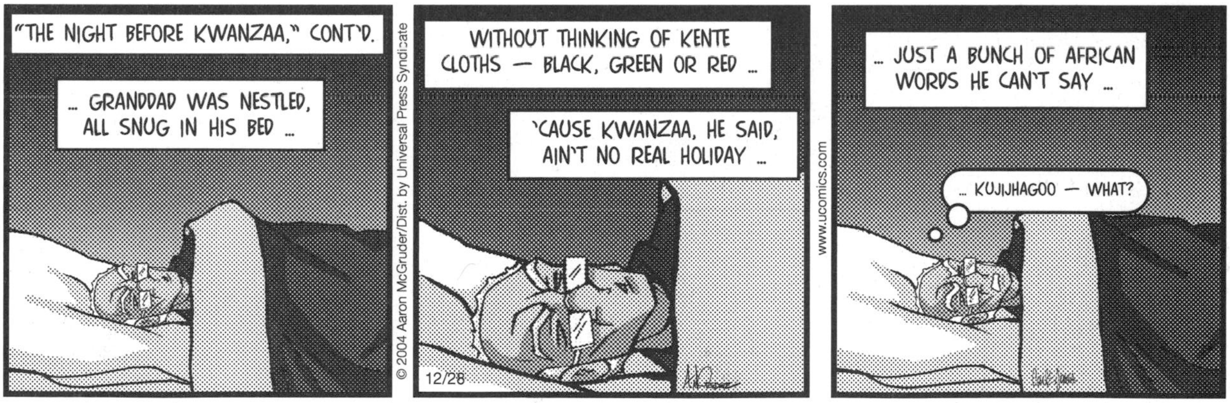
"THE NIGHT BEFORE KWANZAA," CONT'D.
... GRANDDAD WAS NESTLED, ALL SNUG IN HIS BED ...
© 2004 Aaron McGruder/Dist. by Universal Press Syndicate
WITHOUT THINKING OF KENTE CLOTHS — BLACK, GREEN OR RED ...
'CAUSE KWANZAA, HE SAID, AIN'T NO REAL HOLIDAY ...
12/28
www.ucomics.com
... JUST A BUNCH OF AFRICAN WORDS HE CAN'T SAY ...
... KUJIJHAGOO — WHAT?

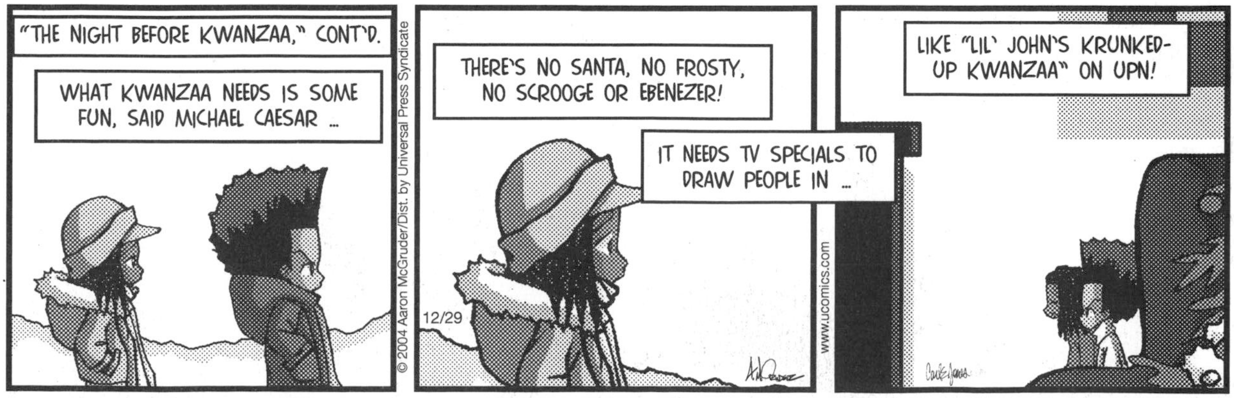
"THE NIGHT BEFORE KWANZAA," CONT'D.
WHAT KWANZAA NEEDS IS SOME FUN, SAID MICHAEL CAESAR ...
© 2004 Aaron McGruder/Dist. by Universal Press Syndicate
THERE'S NO SANTA, NO FROSTY, NO SCROOGE OR EBENEZER!
IT NEEDS TV SPECIALS TO DRAW PEOPLE IN ...
12/29
www.ucomics.com
LIKE "LIL' JOHN'S KRUNKED-UP KWANZAA" ON UPN!

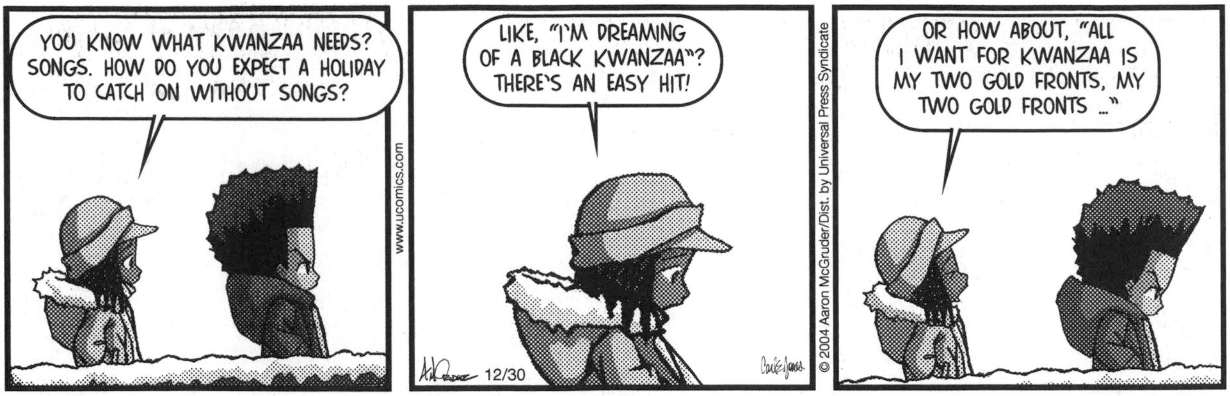
YOU KNOW WHAT KWANZAA NEEDS? SONGS. HOW DO YOU EXPECT A HOLIDAY TO CATCH ON WITHOUT SONGS?
LIKE, "I'M DREAMING OF A BLACK KWANZAA"? THERE'S AN EASY HIT!
OR HOW ABOUT, "ALL I WANT FOR KWANZAA IS MY TWO GOLD FRONTS, MY TWO GOLD FRONTS ..."
www.ucomics.com
12/30
© 2004 Aaron McGruder/Dist. by Universal Press Syndicate

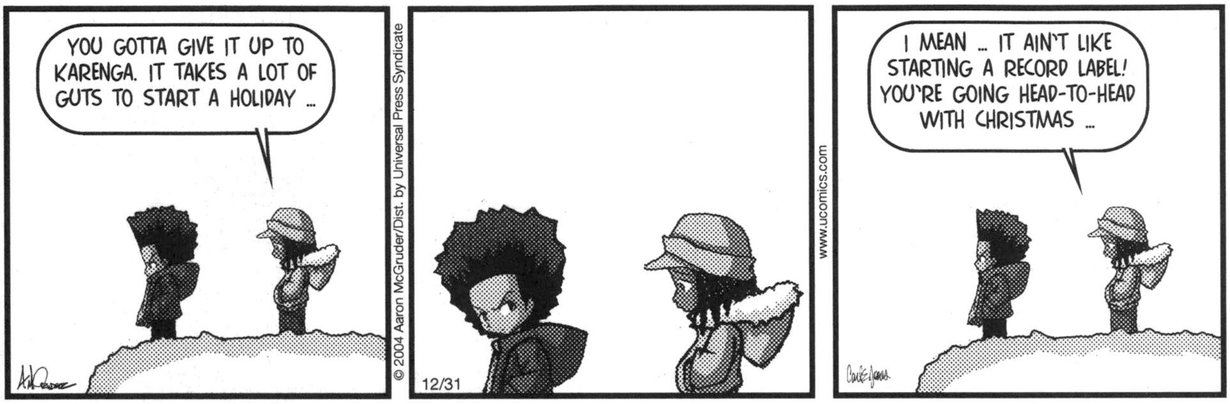
YOU GOTTA GIVE IT UP TO KARENGA. IT TAKES A LOT OF GUTS TO START A HOLIDAY ...
I MEAN ... IT AIN'T LIKE STARTING A RECORD LABEL! YOU'RE GOING HEAD-TO-HEAD WITH CHRISTMAS ...
© 2004 Aaron McGruder/Dist. by Universal Press Syndicate
12/31
www.ucomics.com

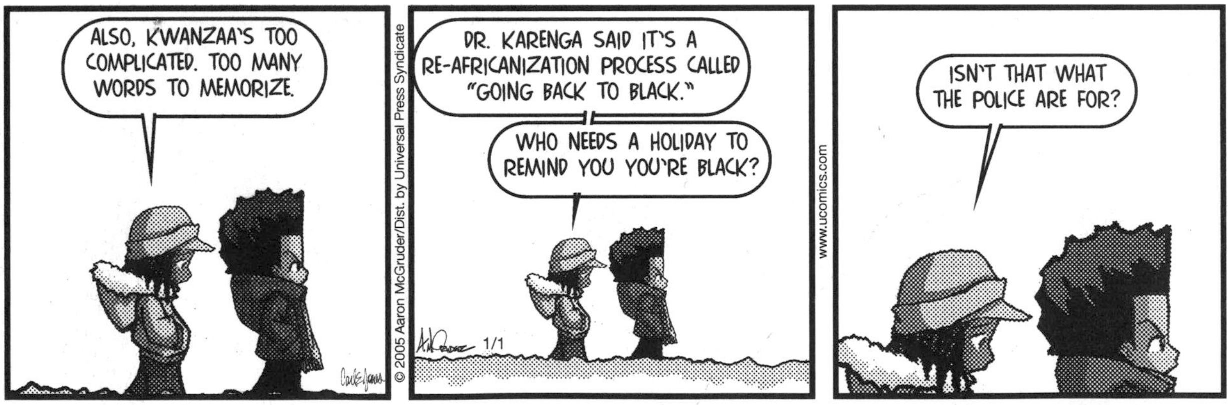
ALSO, KWANZAA'S TOO COMPLICATED. TOO MANY WORDS TO MEMORIZE.
DR. KARENGA SAID IT'S A RE-AFRICANIZATION PROCESS CALLED "GOING BACK TO BLACK."
WHO NEEDS A HOLIDAY TO REMIND YOU YOU'RE BLACK?
ISN'T THAT WHAT THE POLICE ARE FOR?
© 2005 Aaron McGruder/Dist. by Universal Press Syndicate
1/1
www.ucomics.com

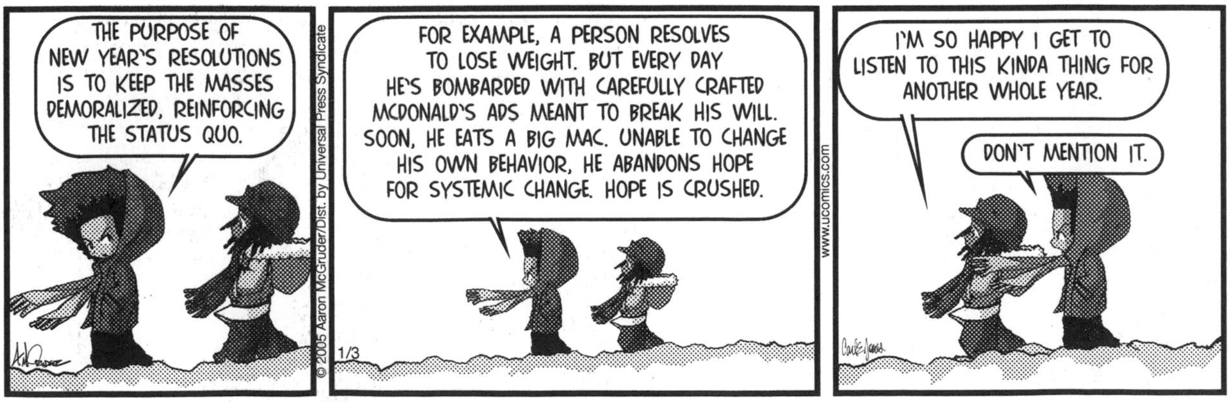
THE PURPOSE OF NEW YEAR'S RESOLUTIONS IS TO KEEP THE MASSES DEMORALIZED, REINFORCING THE STATUS QUO.
FOR EXAMPLE, A PERSON RESOLVES TO LOSE WEIGHT. BUT EVERY DAY HE'S BOMBARDED WITH CAREFULLY CRAFTED MCDONALD'S ADS MEANT TO BREAK HIS WILL. SOON, HE EATS A BIG MAC. UNABLE TO CHANGE HIS OWN BEHAVIOR, HE ABANDONS HOPE FOR SYSTEMIC CHANGE. HOPE IS CRUSHED.
I'M SO HAPPY I GET TO LISTEN TO THIS KINDA THING FOR ANOTHER WHOLE YEAR.
DON'T MENTION IT.
© 2005 Aaron McGruder/Dist. by Universal Press Syndicate
1/3
www.ucomics.com

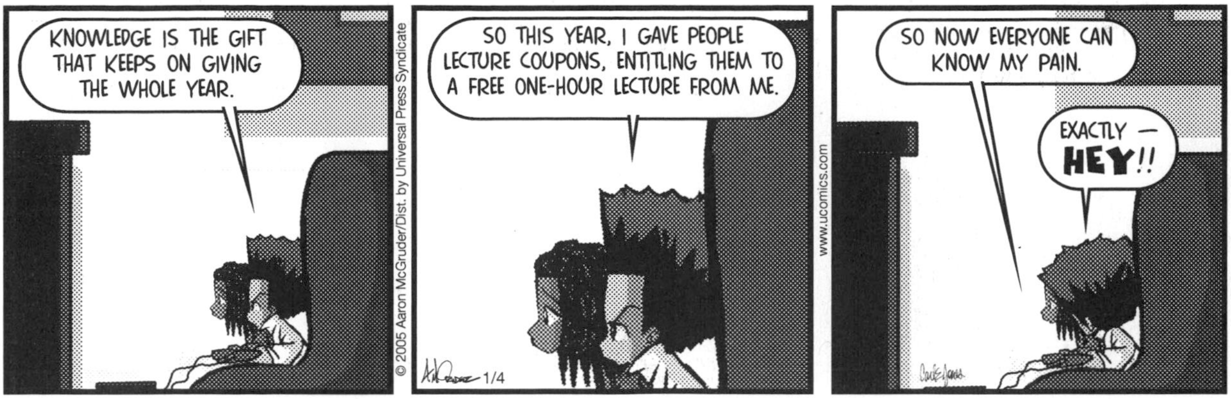
KNOWLEDGE IS THE GIFT THAT KEEPS ON GIVING THE WHOLE YEAR.
SO THIS YEAR, I GAVE PEOPLE LECTURE COUPONS, ENTITLING THEM TO A FREE ONE-HOUR LECTURE FROM ME.
SO NOW EVERYONE CAN KNOW MY PAIN.
EXACTLY — **HEY**!!
© 2005 Aaron McGruder/Dist. by Universal Press Syndicate
www.ucomics.com
1/4

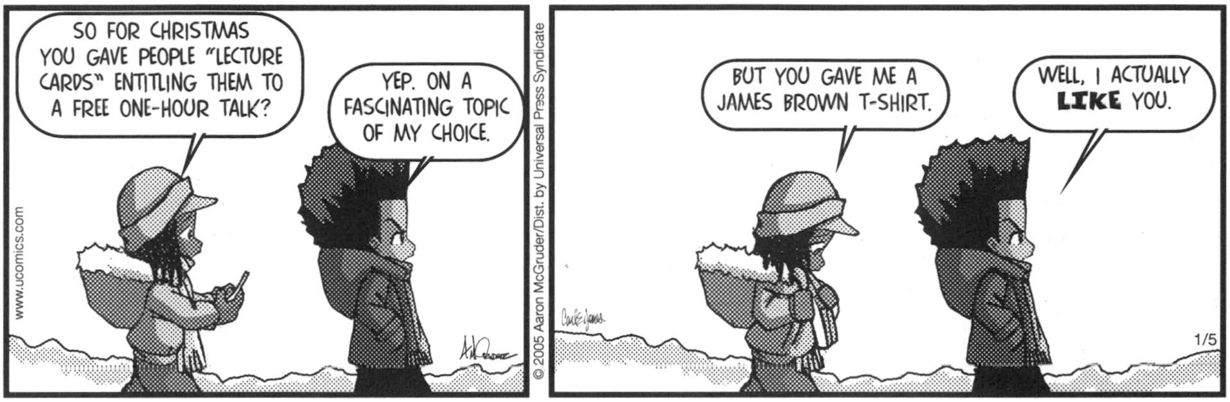
SO FOR CHRISTMAS YOU GAVE PEOPLE "LECTURE CARDS" ENTITLING THEM TO A FREE ONE-HOUR TALK?
YEP. ON A FASCINATING TOPIC OF MY CHOICE.
BUT YOU GAVE ME A JAMES BROWN T-SHIRT.
WELL, I ACTUALLY **LIKE** YOU.
www.ucomics.com
© 2005 Aaron McGruder/Dist. by Universal Press Syndicate
1/5

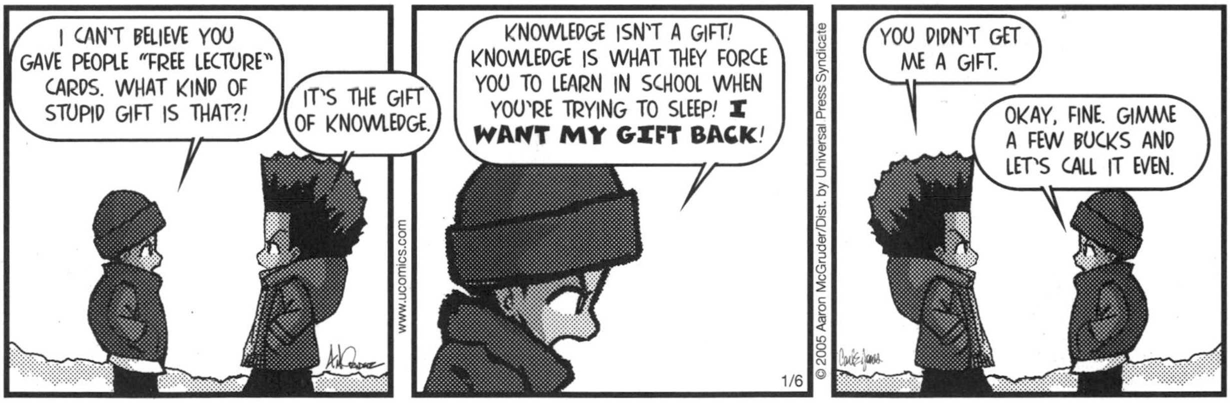
I CAN'T BELIEVE YOU GAVE PEOPLE "FREE LECTURE" CARDS. WHAT KIND OF STUPID GIFT IS THAT?!
IT'S THE GIFT OF KNOWLEDGE.
KNOWLEDGE ISN'T A GIFT! KNOWLEDGE IS WHAT THEY FORCE YOU TO LEARN IN SCHOOL WHEN YOU'RE TRYING TO SLEEP! **I WANT MY GIFT BACK**!
YOU DIDN'T GET ME A GIFT.
OKAY, FINE. GIMME A FEW BUCKS AND LET'S CALL IT EVEN.
www.ucomics.com
© 2005 Aaron McGruder/Dist. by Universal Press Syndicate
1/6

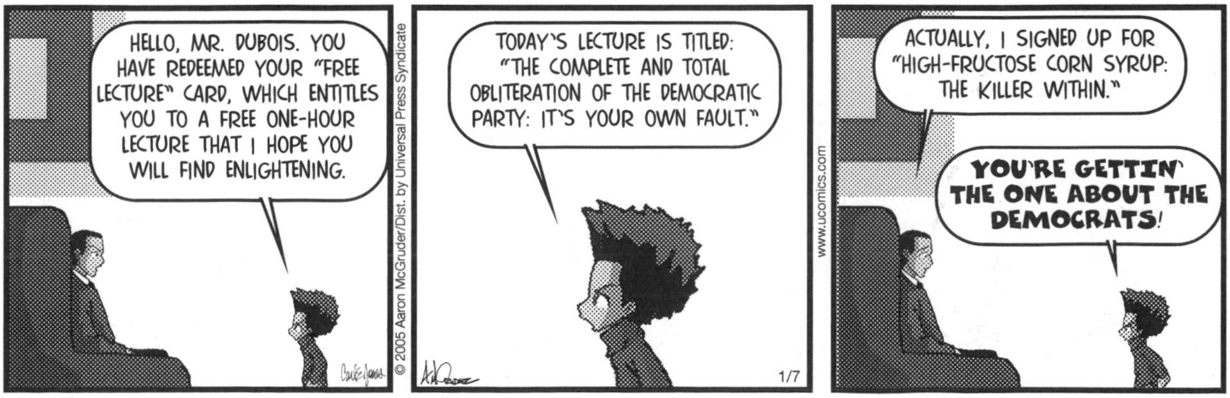
HELLO, MR. DUBOIS. YOU HAVE REDEEMED YOUR "FREE LECTURE" CARD, WHICH ENTITLES YOU TO A FREE ONE-HOUR LECTURE THAT I HOPE YOU WILL FIND ENLIGHTENING.
TODAY'S LECTURE IS TITLED: "THE COMPLETE AND TOTAL OBLITERATION OF THE DEMOCRATIC PARTY: IT'S YOUR OWN FAULT."
ACTUALLY, I SIGNED UP FOR "HIGH-FRUCTOSE CORN SYRUP: THE KILLER WITHIN."
YOU'RE GETTIN' THE ONE ABOUT THE DEMOCRATS!
© 2005 Aaron McGruder/Dist. by Universal Press Syndicate
www.ucomics.com
1/7

I think it's a lot of people who are quietly outraged at what's going on in the country, but who have no means to make their voice heard.

—Aaron McGruder, *Observer Magazine*

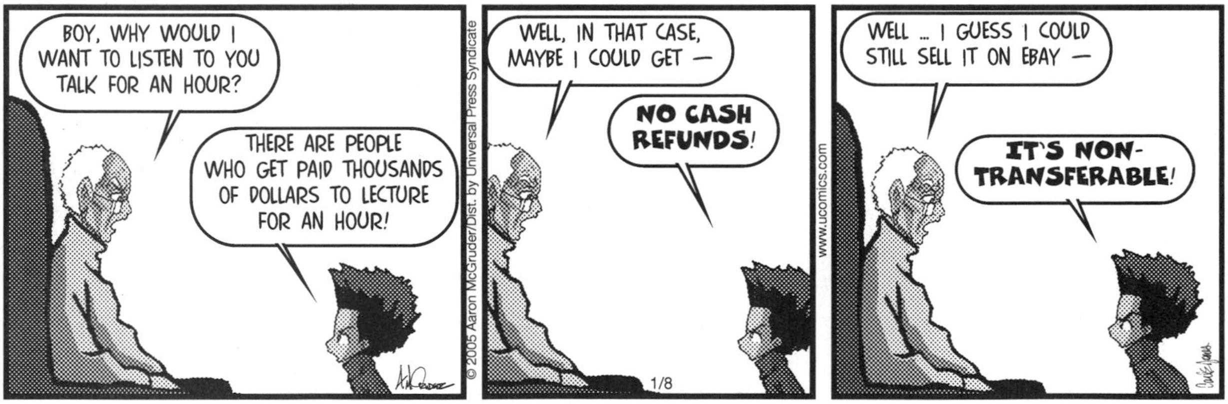
BOY, WHY WOULD I WANT TO LISTEN TO YOU TALK FOR AN HOUR?
THERE ARE PEOPLE WHO GET PAID THOUSANDS OF DOLLARS TO LECTURE FOR AN HOUR!
© 2005 Aaron McGruder/Dist. by Universal Press Syndicate
WELL, IN THAT CASE, MAYBE I COULD GET —
NO CASH REFUNDS!
1/8
www.ucomics.com
WELL ... I GUESS I COULD STILL SELL IT ON EBAY —
IT'S NON-TRANSFERABLE!

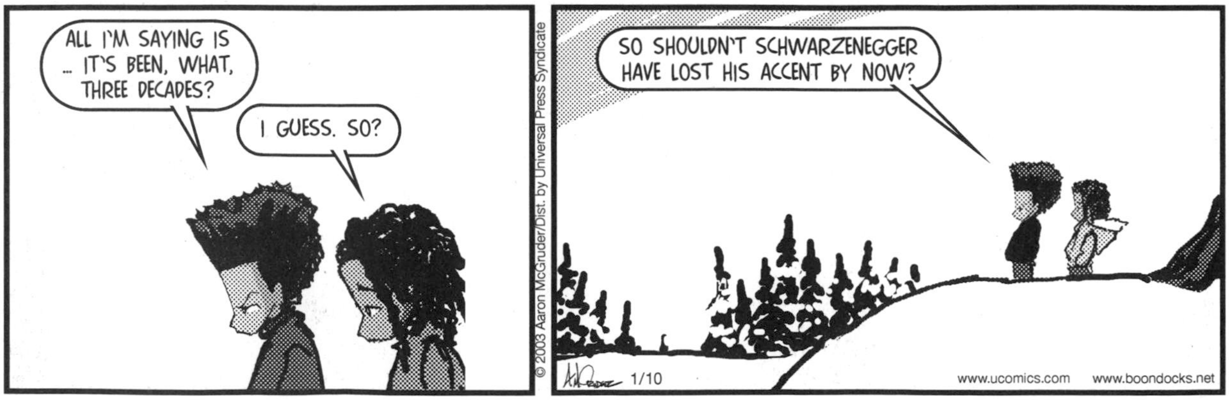
ALL I'M SAYING IS ... IT'S BEEN, WHAT, THREE DECADES?
I GUESS. SO?
© 2003 Aaron McGruder/Dist. by Universal Press Syndicate
SO SHOULDN'T SCHWARZENEGGER HAVE LOST HIS ACCENT BY NOW?
1/10
www.ucomics.com
www.boondocks.net

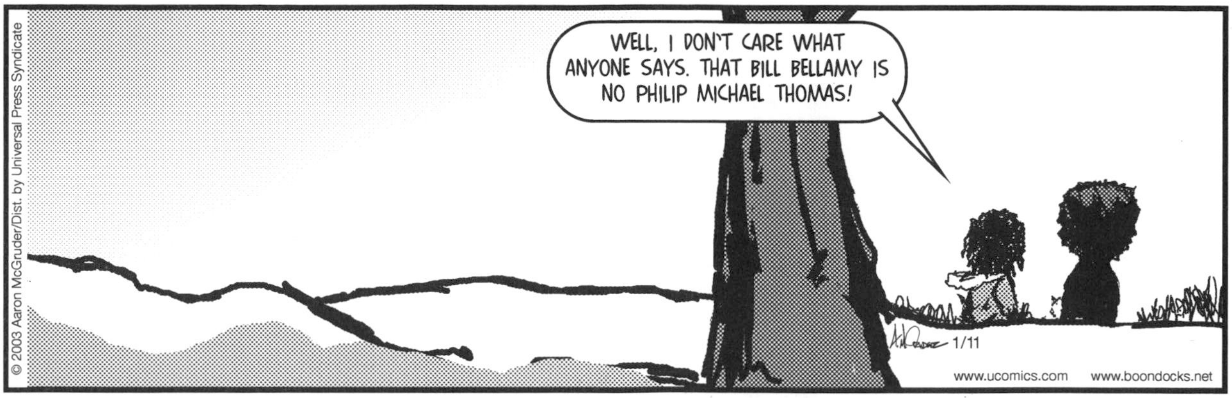
WELL, I DON'T CARE WHAT ANYONE SAYS. THAT BILL BELLAMY IS NO PHILIP MICHAEL THOMAS!
© 2003 Aaron McGruder/Dist. by Universal Press Syndicate
1/11
www.ucomics.com www.boondocks.net

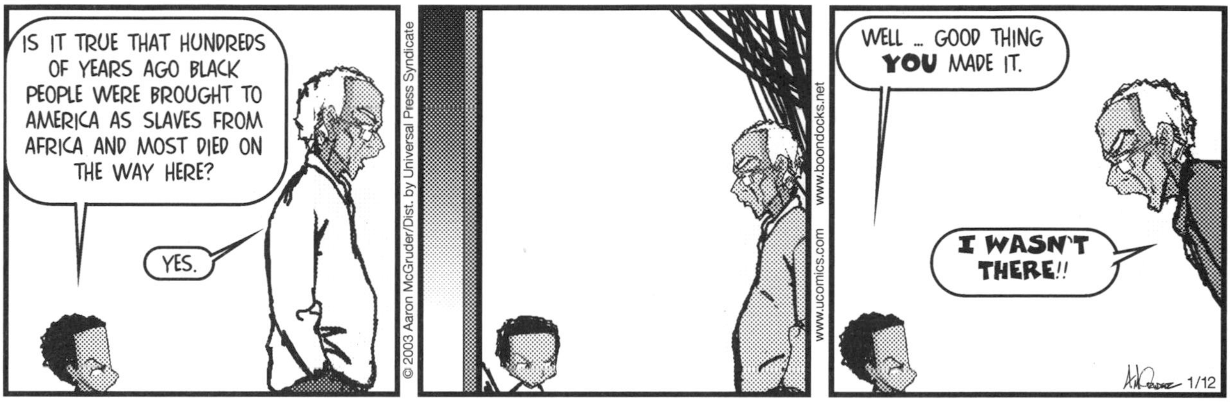
IS IT TRUE THAT HUNDREDS OF YEARS AGO BLACK PEOPLE WERE BROUGHT TO AMERICA AS SLAVES FROM AFRICA AND MOST DIED ON THE WAY HERE?
YES.
© 2003 Aaron McGruder/Dist. by Universal Press Syndicate
www.ucomics.com www.boondocks.net
WELL ... GOOD THING **YOU** MADE IT.
I WASN'T THERE!!
1/12

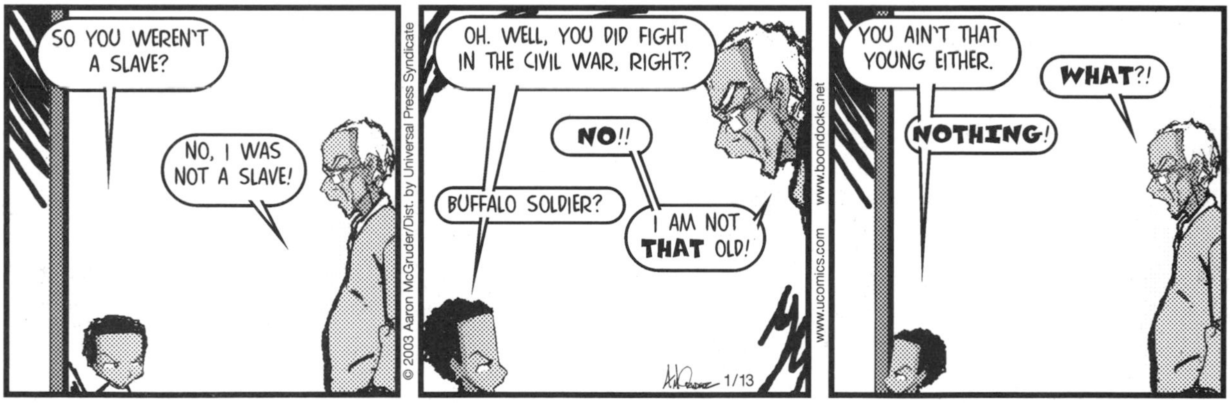
SO YOU WEREN'T A SLAVE?
NO, I WAS NOT A SLAVE!
© 2003 Aaron McGruder/Dist. by Universal Press Syndicate
OH. WELL, YOU DID FIGHT IN THE CIVIL WAR, RIGHT?
NO!!
BUFFALO SOLDIER?
I AM NOT **THAT** OLD!
1/13
www.ucomics.com www.boondocks.net
YOU AIN'T THAT YOUNG EITHER.
WHAT?!
NOTHING!

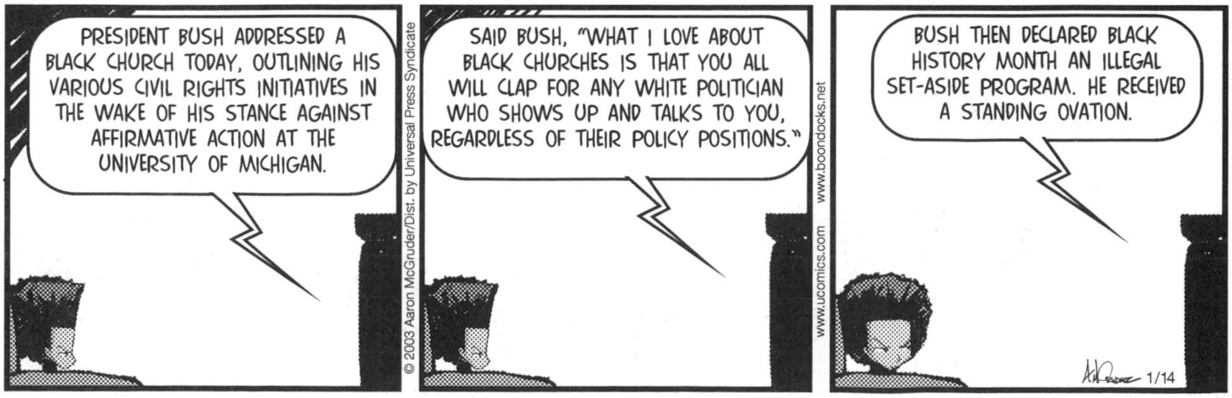
PRESIDENT BUSH ADDRESSED A BLACK CHURCH TODAY, OUTLINING HIS VARIOUS CIVIL RIGHTS INITIATIVES IN THE WAKE OF HIS STANCE AGAINST AFFIRMATIVE ACTION AT THE UNIVERSITY OF MICHIGAN.
© 2003 Aaron McGruder/Dist. by Universal Press Syndicate
SAID BUSH, "WHAT I LOVE ABOUT BLACK CHURCHES IS THAT YOU ALL WILL CLAP FOR ANY WHITE POLITICIAN WHO SHOWS UP AND TALKS TO YOU, REGARDLESS OF THEIR POLICY POSITIONS."
www.ucomics.com www.boondocks.net
BUSH THEN DECLARED BLACK HISTORY MONTH AN ILLEGAL SET-ASIDE PROGRAM. HE RECEIVED A STANDING OVATION.
1/14

Boondocks does more than attack the white establishment, however; it also trains its sights on blacks from across the political spectrum. "I don't feel like I have to overromanticize black people just to show that I care about them," McGruder says. "We need more voices to be critical."

—*New York Times Magazine*

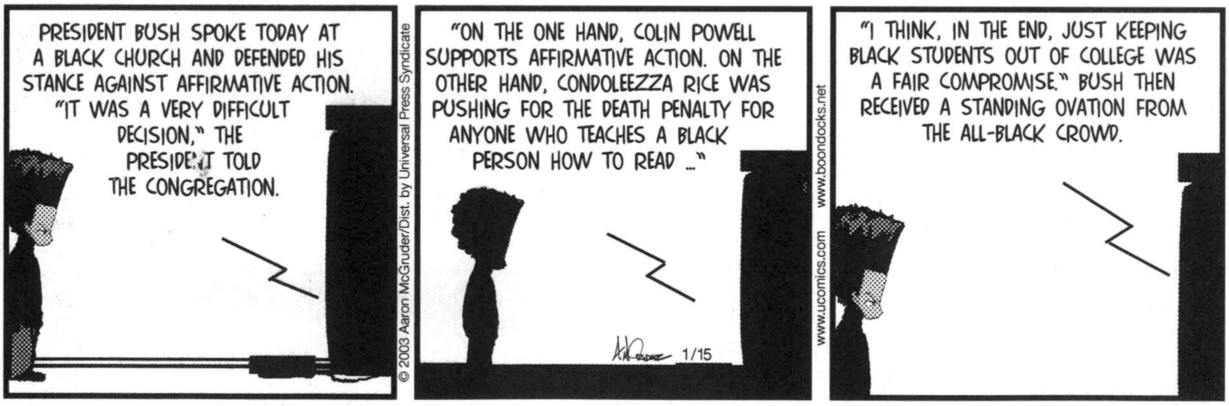
PRESIDENT BUSH SPOKE TODAY AT A BLACK CHURCH AND DEFENDED HIS STANCE AGAINST AFFIRMATIVE ACTION. "IT WAS A VERY DIFFICULT DECISION," THE PRESIDENT TOLD THE CONGREGATION.
© 2003 Aaron McGruder/Dist. by Universal Press Syndicate
"ON THE ONE HAND, COLIN POWELL SUPPORTS AFFIRMATIVE ACTION. ON THE OTHER HAND, CONDOLEEZZA RICE WAS PUSHING FOR THE DEATH PENALTY FOR ANYONE WHO TEACHES A BLACK PERSON HOW TO READ ..."
1/15
www.ucomics.com www.boondocks.net
"I THINK, IN THE END, JUST KEEPING BLACK STUDENTS OUT OF COLLEGE WAS A FAIR COMPROMISE." BUSH THEN RECEIVED A STANDING OVATION FROM THE ALL-BLACK CROWD.

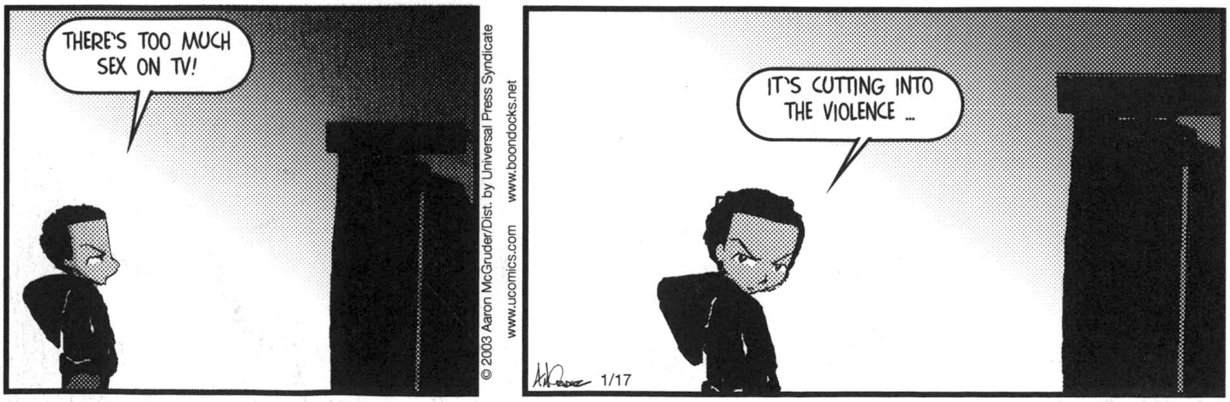
THERE'S TOO MUCH SEX ON TV!
© 2003 Aaron McGruder/Dist. by Universal Press Syndicate
www.ucomics.com www.boondocks.net
IT'S CUTTING INTO THE VIOLENCE ...
1/17

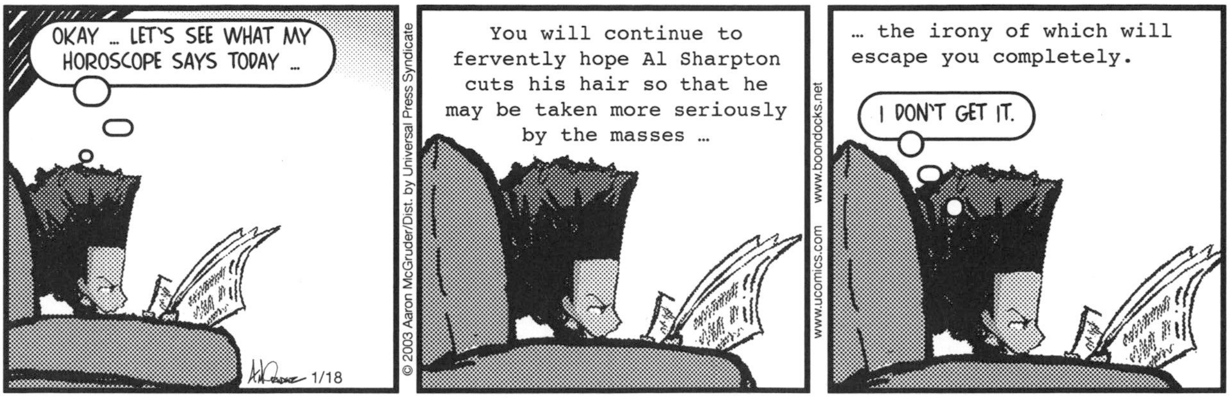
OKAY ... LET'S SEE WHAT MY HOROSCOPE SAYS TODAY ...
1/18
© 2003 Aaron McGruder/Dist. by Universal Press Syndicate
You will continue to fervently hope Al Sharpton cuts his hair so that he may be taken more seriously by the masses ...
www.ucomics.com www.boondocks.net
... the irony of which will escape you completely.
I DON'T GET IT.

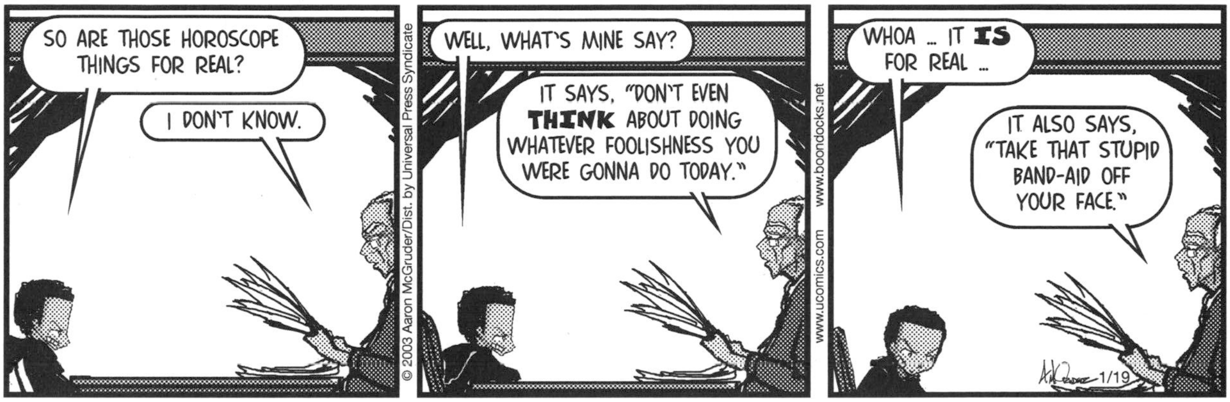
SO ARE THOSE HOROSCOPE THINGS FOR REAL?
I DON'T KNOW.
© 2003 Aaron McGruder/Dist. by Universal Press Syndicate
WELL, WHAT'S MINE SAY?
IT SAYS, "DON'T EVEN **THINK** ABOUT DOING WHATEVER FOOLISHNESS YOU WERE GONNA DO TODAY."
www.ucomics.com www.boondocks.net
WHOA ... IT **IS** FOR REAL ...
IT ALSO SAYS, "TAKE THAT STUPID BAND-AID OFF YOUR FACE."
1/19

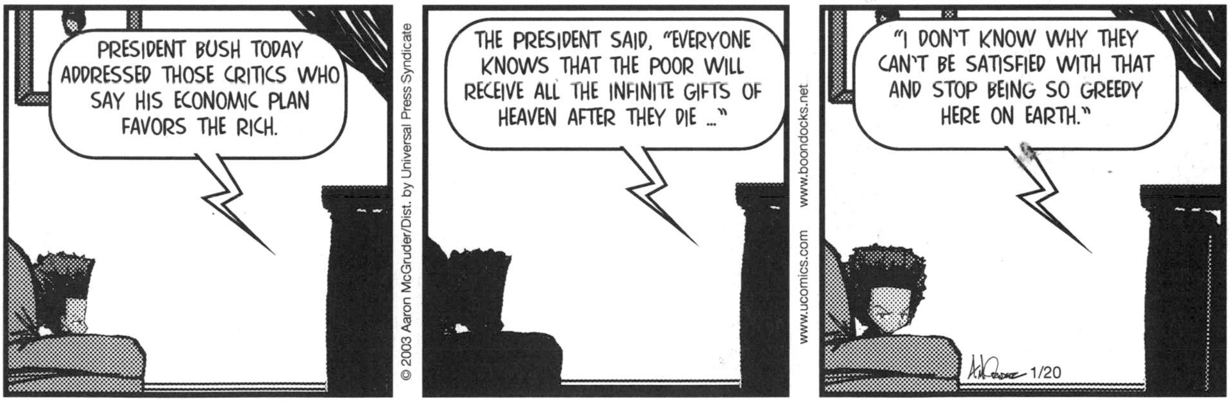
PRESIDENT BUSH TODAY ADDRESSED THOSE CRITICS WHO SAY HIS ECONOMIC PLAN FAVORS THE RICH.
© 2003 Aaron McGruder/Dist. by Universal Press Syndicate
THE PRESIDENT SAID, "EVERYONE KNOWS THAT THE POOR WILL RECEIVE ALL THE INFINITE GIFTS OF HEAVEN AFTER THEY DIE ..."
www.ucomics.com www.boondocks.net
"I DON'T KNOW WHY THEY CAN'T BE SATISFIED WITH THAT AND STOP BEING SO GREEDY HERE ON EARTH."
1/20

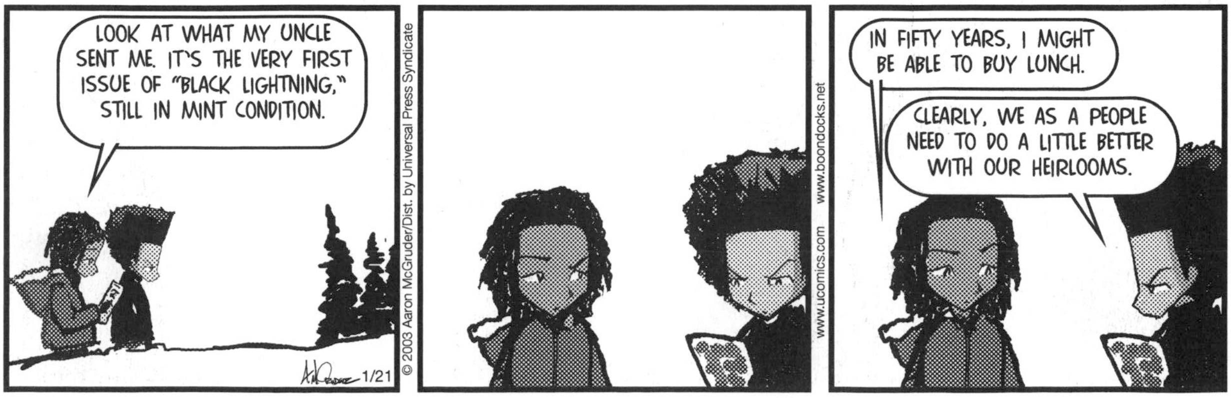
LOOK AT WHAT MY UNCLE SENT ME. IT'S THE VERY FIRST ISSUE OF "BLACK LIGHTNING," STILL IN MINT CONDITION.
1/21
© 2003 Aaron McGruder/Dist. by Universal Press Syndicate
www.ucomics.com www.boondocks.net
IN FIFTY YEARS, I MIGHT BE ABLE TO BUY LUNCH.
CLEARLY, WE AS A PEOPLE NEED TO DO A LITTLE BETTER WITH OUR HEIRLOOMS.

> Decades ago, the mark of a good reporter was how much dirt you could dig up. Like the Watergate scandal. . . . Now it's the exact opposite. Nobody wants to say anything that makes the government mad, and that's ridiculous.
>
> —Aaron McGruder, *Salon*

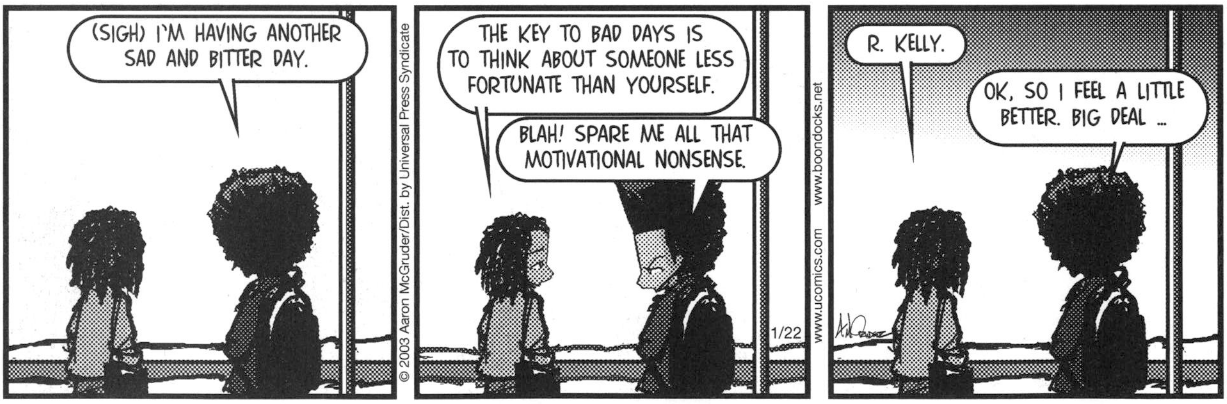
(SIGH) I'M HAVING ANOTHER SAD AND BITTER DAY.
THE KEY TO BAD DAYS IS TO THINK ABOUT SOMEONE LESS FORTUNATE THAN YOURSELF.
BLAH! SPARE ME ALL THAT MOTIVATIONAL NONSENSE.
1/22
R. KELLY.
OK, SO I FEEL A LITTLE BETTER. BIG DEAL ...
© 2003 Aaron McGruder/Dist. by Universal Press Syndicate
www.ucomics.com www.boondocks.net

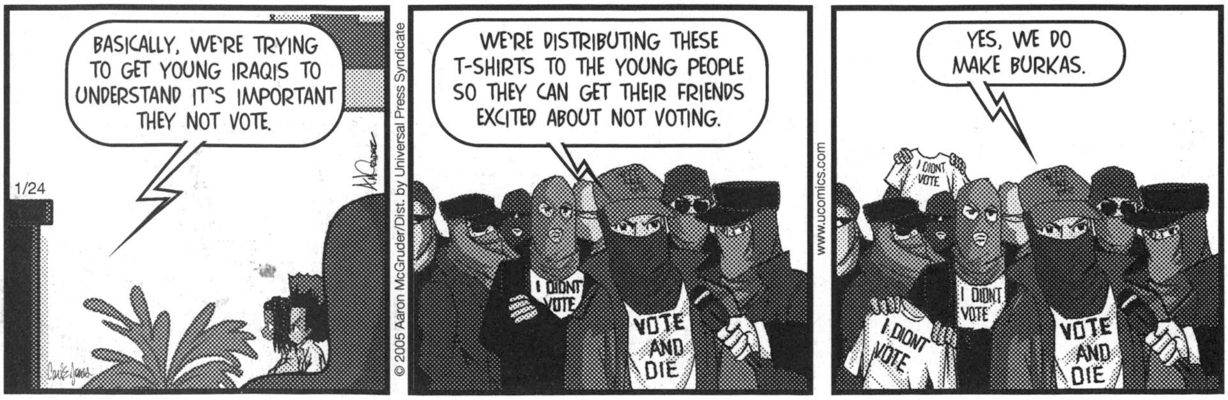
BASICALLY, WE'RE TRYING TO GET YOUNG IRAQIS TO UNDERSTAND IT'S IMPORTANT THEY NOT VOTE.
1/24
WE'RE DISTRIBUTING THESE T-SHIRTS TO THE YOUNG PEOPLE SO THEY CAN GET THEIR FRIENDS EXCITED ABOUT NOT VOTING.
I DIDNT VOTE
VOTE AND DIE
YES, WE DO MAKE BURKAS.
© 2005 Aaron McGruder/Dist. by Universal Press Syndicate
www.ucomics.com

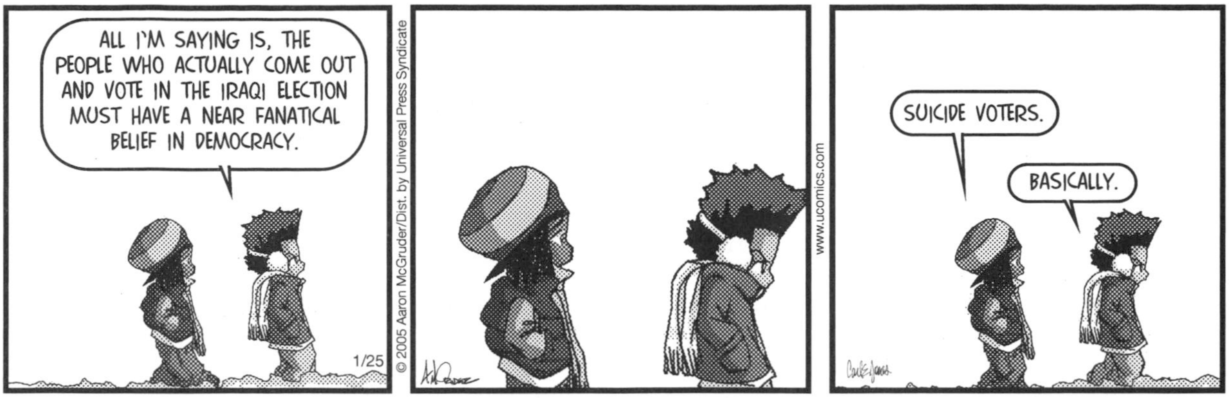
ALL I'M SAYING IS, THE PEOPLE WHO ACTUALLY COME OUT AND VOTE IN THE IRAQI ELECTION MUST HAVE A NEAR FANATICAL BELIEF IN DEMOCRACY.
1/25
© 2005 Aaron McGruder/Dist. by Universal Press Syndicate
www.ucomics.com
SUICIDE VOTERS.
BASICALLY.

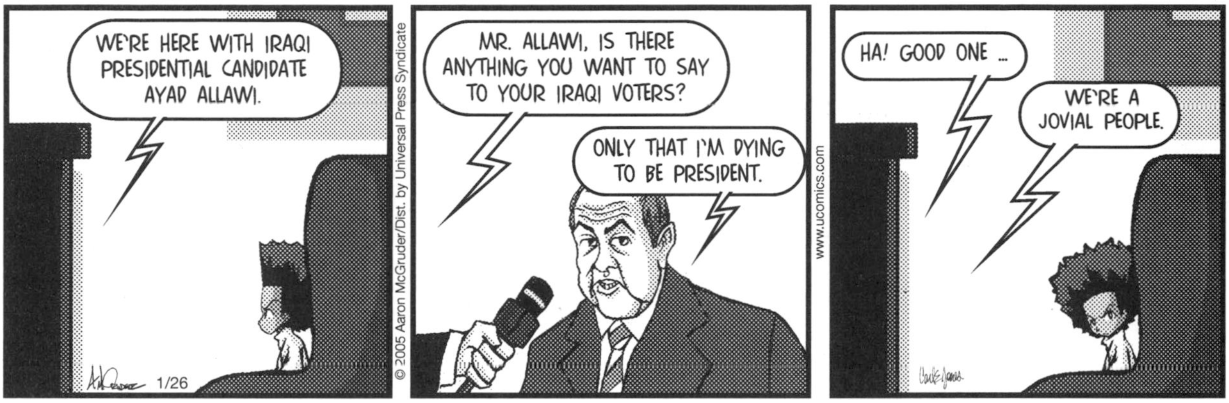
WE'RE HERE WITH IRAQI PRESIDENTIAL CANDIDATE AYAD ALLAWI.
1/26
© 2005 Aaron McGruder/Dist. by Universal Press Syndicate
MR. ALLAWI, IS THERE ANYTHING YOU WANT TO SAY TO YOUR IRAQI VOTERS?
ONLY THAT I'M DYING TO BE PRESIDENT.
www.ucomics.com
HA! GOOD ONE ...
WE'RE A JOVIAL PEOPLE.

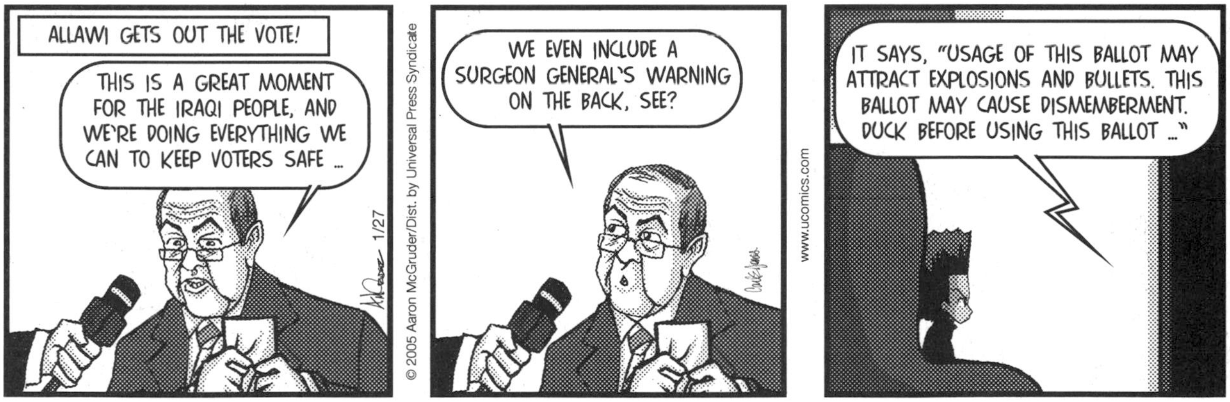
ALLAWI GETS OUT THE VOTE!
THIS IS A GREAT MOMENT FOR THE IRAQI PEOPLE, AND WE'RE DOING EVERYTHING WE CAN TO KEEP VOTERS SAFE ...
1/27
© 2005 Aaron McGruder/Dist. by Universal Press Syndicate
WE EVEN INCLUDE A SURGEON GENERAL'S WARNING ON THE BACK, SEE?
www.ucomics.com
IT SAYS, "USAGE OF THIS BALLOT MAY ATTRACT EXPLOSIONS AND BULLETS. THIS BALLOT MAY CAUSE DISMEMBERMENT. DUCK BEFORE USING THIS BALLOT ..."

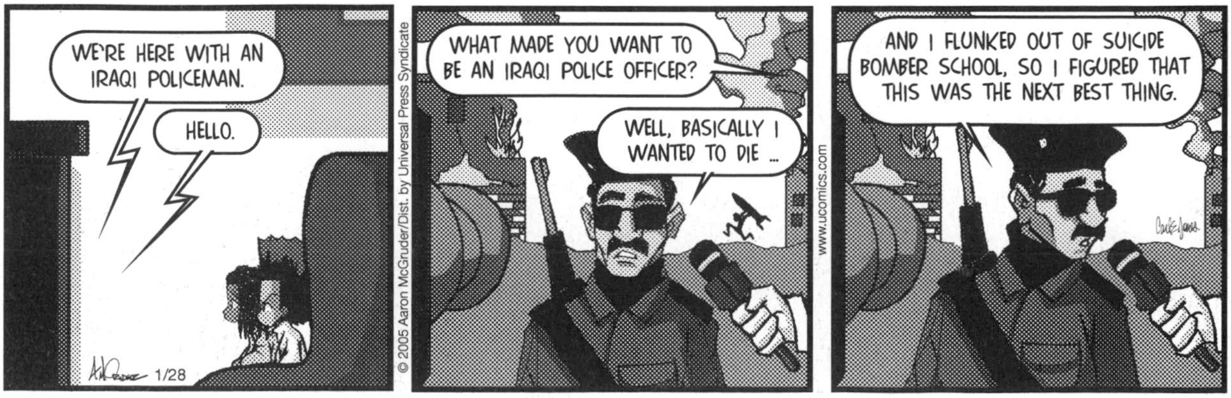
WE'RE HERE WITH AN IRAQI POLICEMAN.
HELLO.
1/28
© 2005 Aaron McGruder/Dist. by Universal Press Syndicate
WHAT MADE YOU WANT TO BE AN IRAQI POLICE OFFICER?
WELL, BASICALLY I WANTED TO DIE ...
www.ucomics.com
AND I FLUNKED OUT OF SUICIDE BOMBER SCHOOL, SO I FIGURED THAT THIS WAS THE NEXT BEST THING.

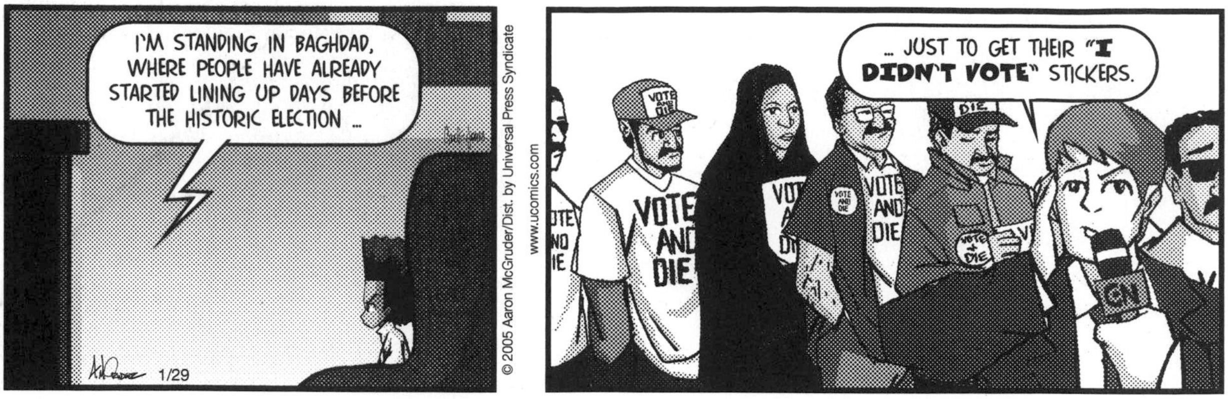
I'M STANDING IN BAGHDAD, WHERE PEOPLE HAVE ALREADY STARTED LINING UP DAYS BEFORE THE HISTORIC ELECTION ...
1/29
© 2005 Aaron McGruder/Dist. by Universal Press Syndicate
www.ucomics.com
... JUST TO GET THEIR "I DIDN'T VOTE" STICKERS.
VOTE AND DIE

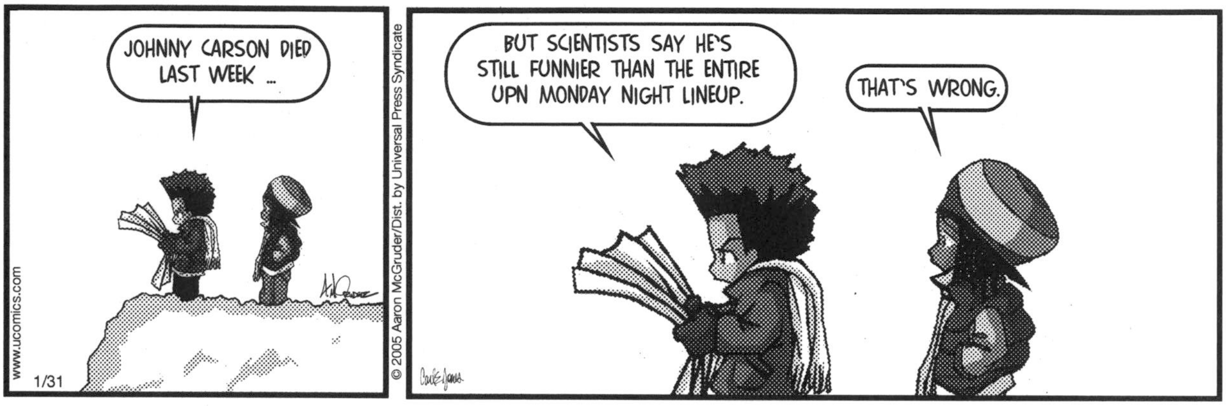
JOHNNY CARSON DIED LAST WEEK ...
www.ucomics.com
1/31
© 2005 Aaron McGruder/Dist. by Universal Press Syndicate
BUT SCIENTISTS SAY HE'S STILL FUNNIER THAN THE ENTIRE UPN MONDAY NIGHT LINEUP.
THAT'S WRONG.

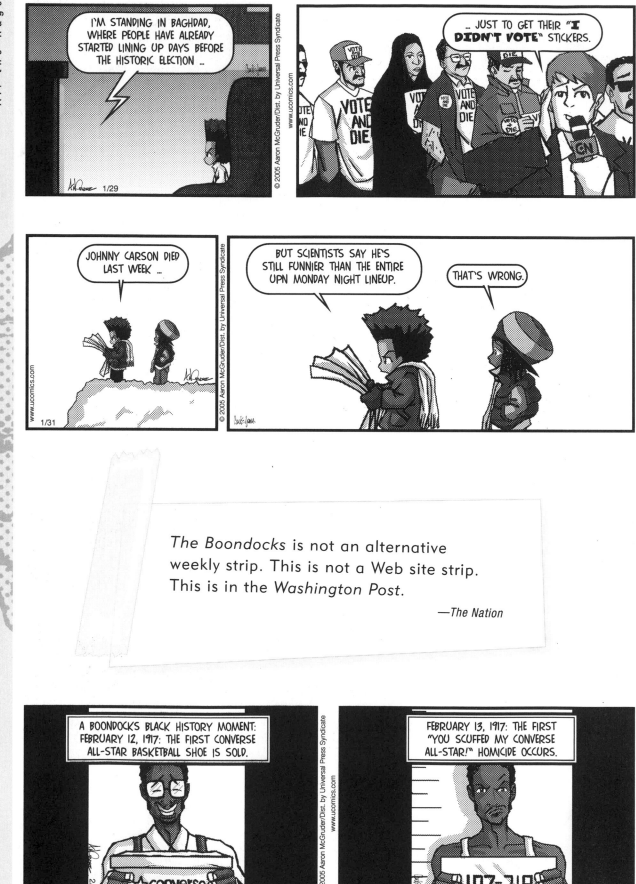

The Boondocks is not an alternative weekly strip. This is not a Web site strip. This is in the *Washington Post*.

—*The Nation*

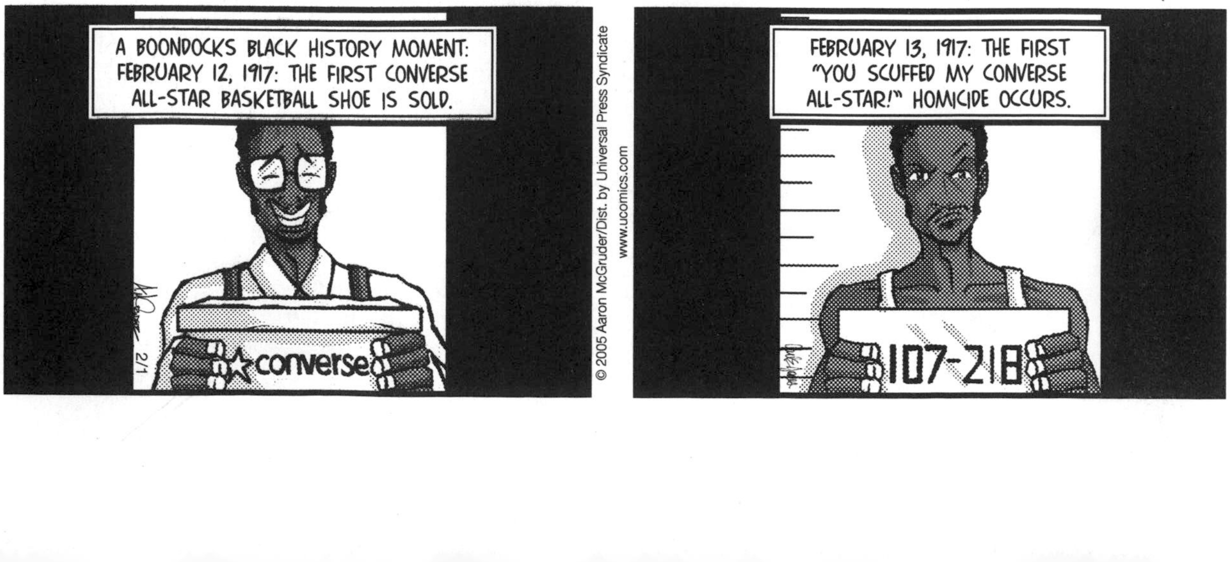
A BOONDOCKS BLACK HISTORY MOMENT: FEBRUARY 12, 1917: THE FIRST CONVERSE ALL-STAR BASKETBALL SHOE IS SOLD.
converse
2/1
© 2005 Aaron McGruder/Dist. by Universal Press Syndicate
www.ucomics.com
FEBRUARY 13, 1917: THE FIRST "YOU SCUFFED MY CONVERSE ALL-STAR!" HOMICIDE OCCURS.
107-218

THE BOONDOCKS ***BY AARON McGRUDER***

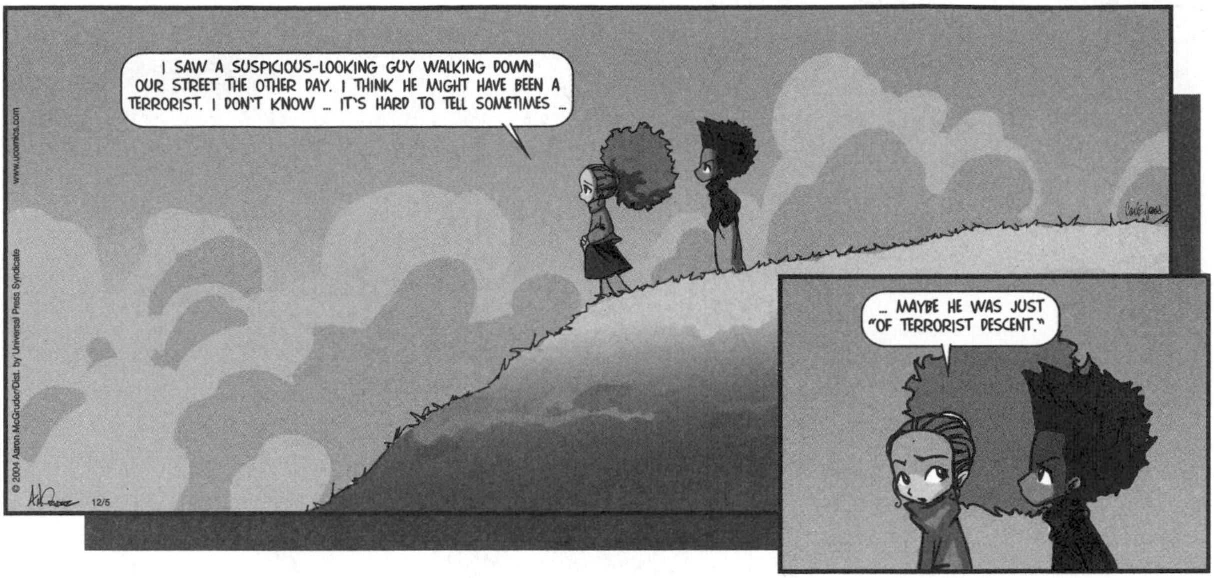
I SAW A SUSPICIOUS-LOOKING GUY WALKING DOWN OUR STREET THE OTHER DAY. I THINK HE MIGHT HAVE BEEN A TERRORIST. I DON'T KNOW ... IT'S HARD TO TELL SOMETIMES ...
... MAYBE HE WAS JUST "OF TERRORIST DESCENT."
© 2004 Aaron McGruder/Dist. by Universal Press Syndicate
www.ucomics.com
12/5

THE BOONDOCKS ***BY AARON McGRUDER***

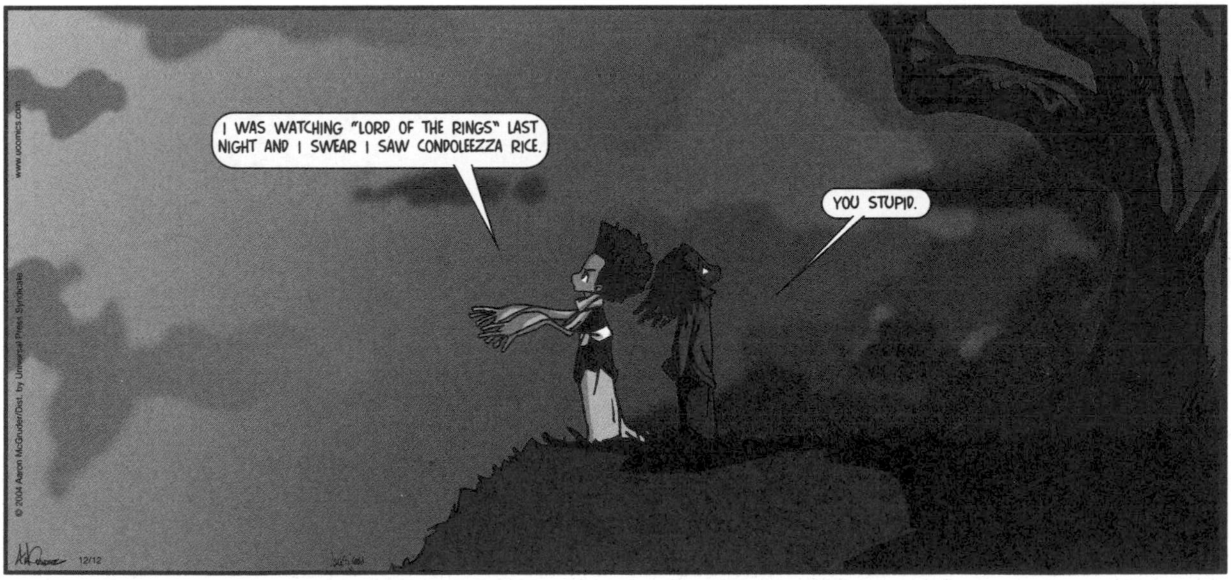
I WAS WATCHING "LORD OF THE RINGS" LAST NIGHT AND I SWEAR I SAW CONDOLEEZZA RICE.
YOU STUPID.
© 2004 Aaron McGruder/Dist. by Universal Press Syndicate
www.ucomics.com
12/12

THE BOONDOCKS

BY AARON McGRUDER

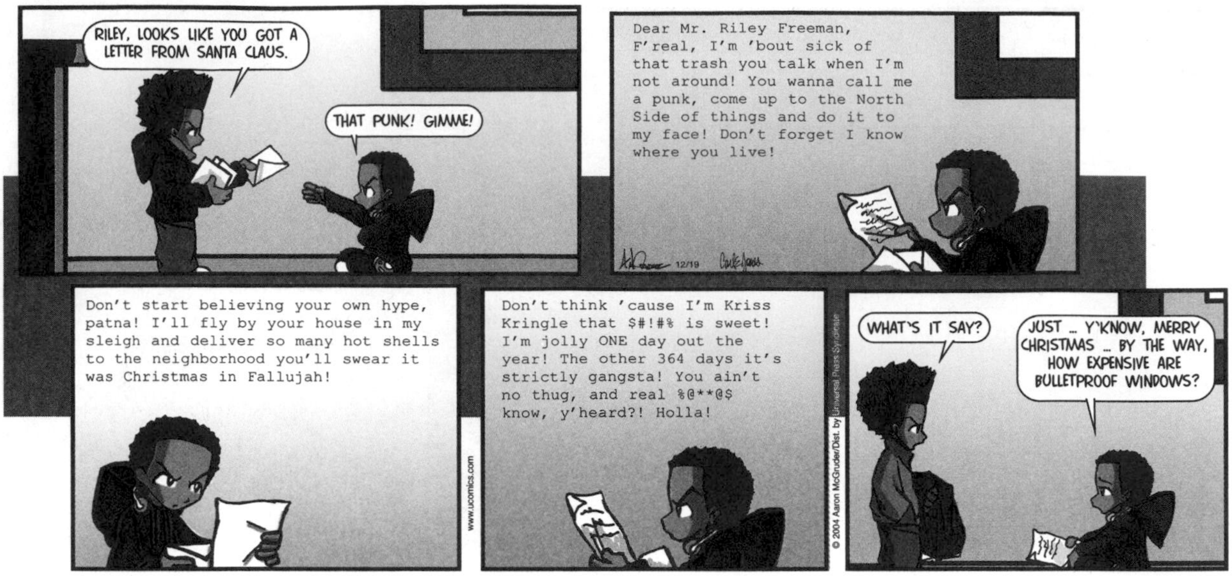
RILEY, LOOKS LIKE YOU GOT A LETTER FROM SANTA CLAUS.
THAT PUNK! GIMME!
Dear Mr. Riley Freeman, F'real, I'm 'bout sick of that trash you talk when I'm not around! You wanna call me a punk, come up to the North Side of things and do it to my face! Don't forget I know where you live!
12/19
Don't start believing your own hype, patna! I'll fly by your house in my sleigh and deliver so many hot shells to the neighborhood you'll swear it was Christmas in Fallujah!
www.ucomics.com
Don't think 'cause I'm Kriss Kringle that $#!#% is sweet! I'm jolly ONE day out the year! The other 364 days it's strictly gangsta! You ain't no thug, and real %@**@$ know, y'heard?! Holla!
© 2004 Aaron McGruder/Dist. by Universal Press Syndicate
WHAT'S IT SAY?
JUST ... Y'KNOW, MERRY CHRISTMAS ... BY THE WAY, HOW EXPENSIVE ARE BULLETPROOF WINDOWS?

THE BOONDOCKS

BY AARON McGRUDER

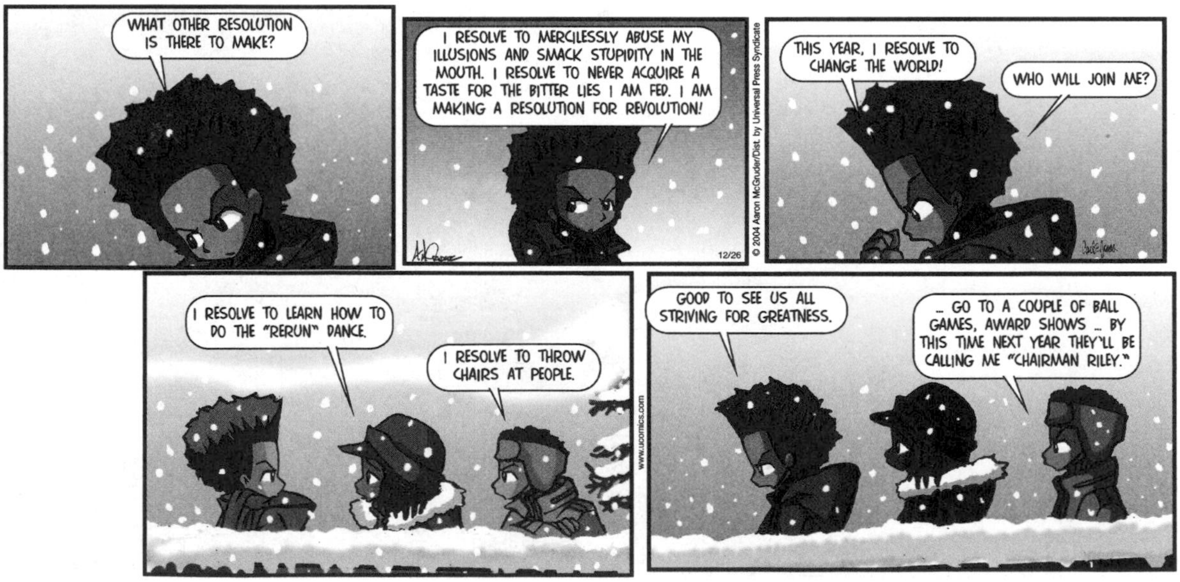
WHAT OTHER RESOLUTION IS THERE TO MAKE?
I RESOLVE TO MERCILESSLY ABUSE MY ILLUSIONS AND SMACK STUPIDITY IN THE MOUTH. I RESOLVE TO NEVER ACQUIRE A TASTE FOR THE BITTER LIES I AM FED. I AM MAKING A RESOLUTION FOR REVOLUTION!
12/26
© 2004 Aaron McGruder/Dist. by Universal Press Syndicate
THIS YEAR, I RESOLVE TO CHANGE THE WORLD!
WHO WILL JOIN ME?
I RESOLVE TO LEARN HOW TO DO THE "RERUN" DANCE.
I RESOLVE TO THROW CHAIRS AT PEOPLE.
www.ucomics.com
GOOD TO SEE US ALL STRIVING FOR GREATNESS.
... GO TO A COUPLE OF BALL GAMES, AWARD SHOWS ... BY THIS TIME NEXT YEAR THEY'LL BE CALLING ME "CHAIRMAN RILEY."

THE BOONDOCKS BY AARON McGRUDER

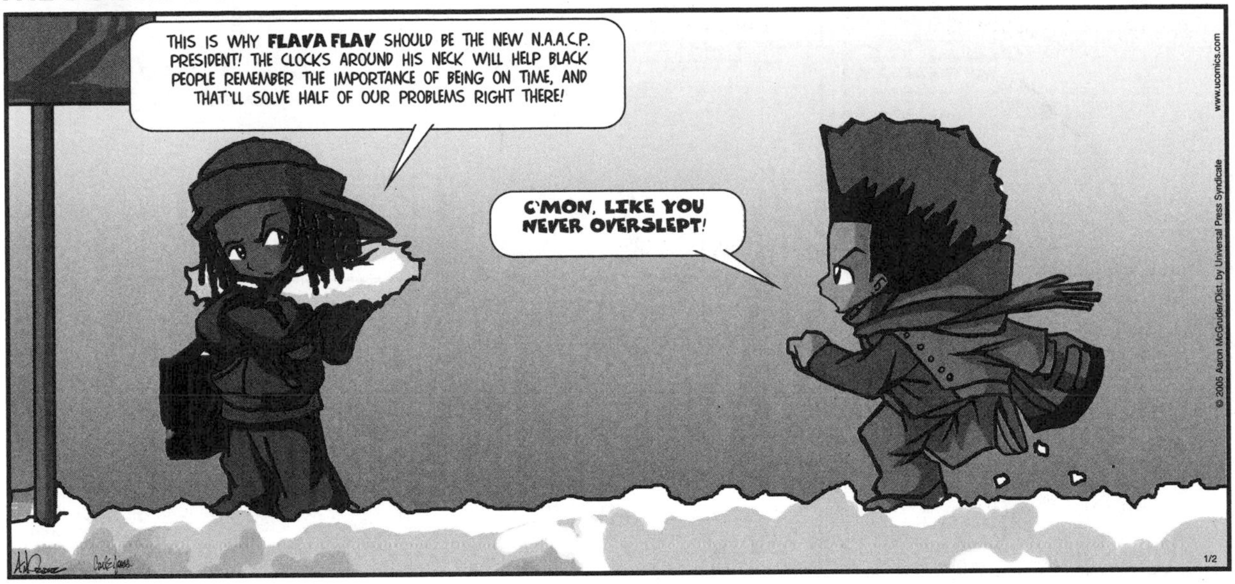
THIS IS WHY FLAVA FLAV SHOULD BE THE NEW N.A.A.C.P. PRESIDENT! THE CLOCKS AROUND HIS NECK WILL HELP BLACK PEOPLE REMEMBER THE IMPORTANCE OF BEING ON TIME, AND THAT'LL SOLVE HALF OF OUR PROBLEMS RIGHT THERE!
C'MON, LIKE YOU NEVER OVERSLEPT!
© 2005 Aaron McGruder/Dist. by Universal Press Syndicate
www.ucomics.com
1/2

THE BOONDOCKS BY AARON McGRUDER

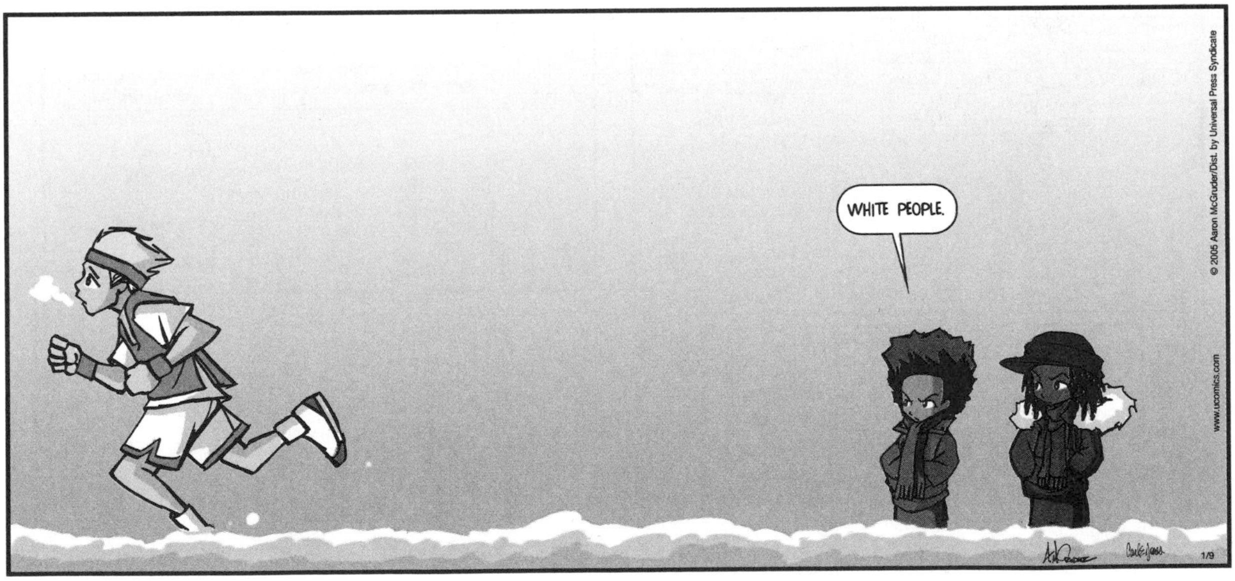
WHITE PEOPLE.
© 2005 Aaron McGruder/Dist. by Universal Press Syndicate
www.ucomics.com
1/9

THE BOONDOCKS

BY AARON McGRUDER

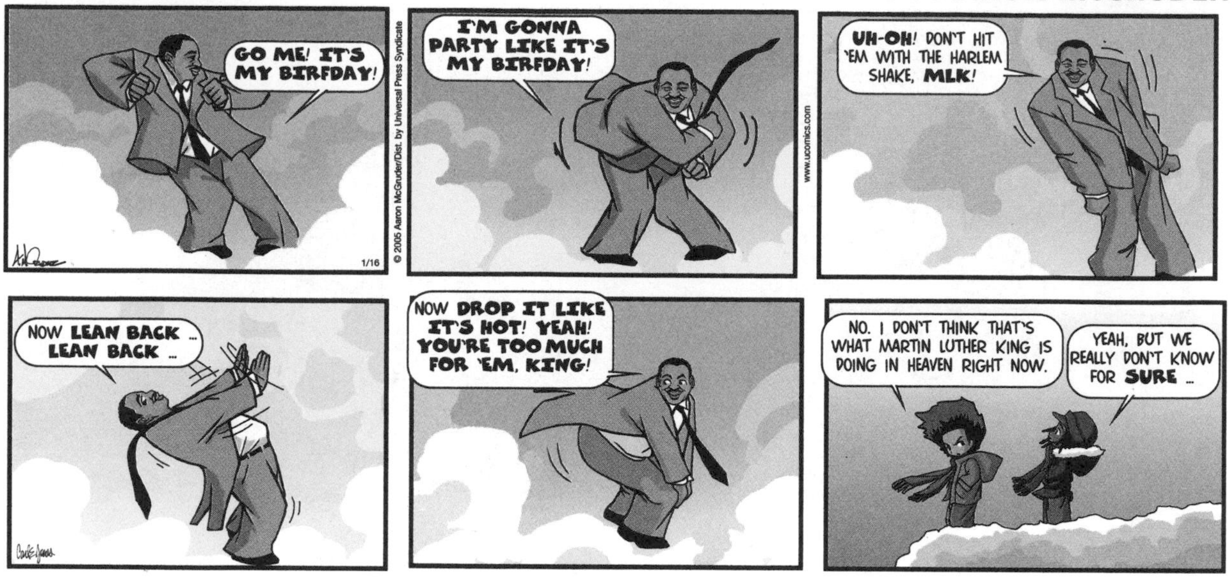
GO ME! IT'S MY BIRFDAY!
1/16
© 2005 Aaron McGruder/Dist. by Universal Press Syndicate
I'M GONNA PARTY LIKE IT'S MY BIRFDAY!
www.ucomics.com
UH-OH! DON'T HIT 'EM WITH THE HARLEM SHAKE, MLK!
NOW LEAN BACK ... LEAN BACK ...
NOW DROP IT LIKE IT'S HOT! YEAH! YOU'RE TOO MUCH FOR 'EM, KING!
NO. I DON'T THINK THAT'S WHAT MARTIN LUTHER KING IS DOING IN HEAVEN RIGHT NOW.
YEAH, BUT WE REALLY DON'T KNOW FOR SURE ...

THE BOONDOCKS

BY AARON McGRUDER

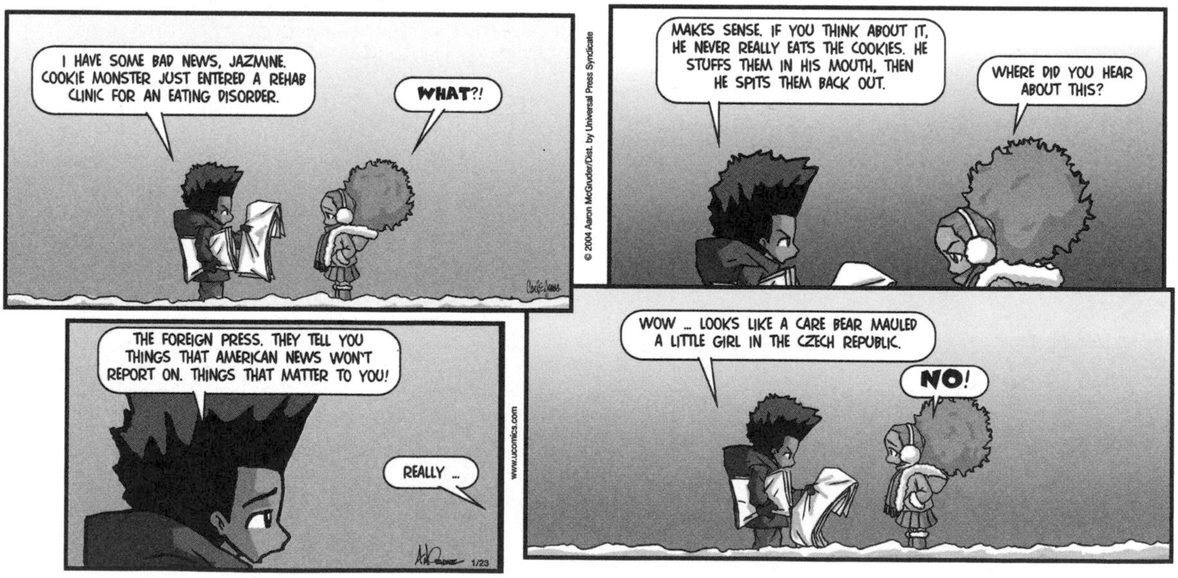
I HAVE SOME BAD NEWS, JAZMINE. COOKIE MONSTER JUST ENTERED A REHAB CLINIC FOR AN EATING DISORDER.
WHAT?!
© 2004 Aaron McGruder/Dist. by Universal Press Syndicate
MAKES SENSE. IF YOU THINK ABOUT IT, HE NEVER REALLY EATS THE COOKIES. HE STUFFS THEM IN HIS MOUTH, THEN HE SPITS THEM BACK OUT.
WHERE DID YOU HEAR ABOUT THIS?
THE FOREIGN PRESS. THEY TELL YOU THINGS THAT AMERICAN NEWS WON'T REPORT ON. THINGS THAT MATTER TO YOU!
REALLY ...
1/23
www.ucomics.com
WOW ... LOOKS LIKE A CARE BEAR MAULED A LITTLE GIRL IN THE CZECH REPUBLIC.
NO!

THE BOONDOCKS **BY AARON McGRUDER**

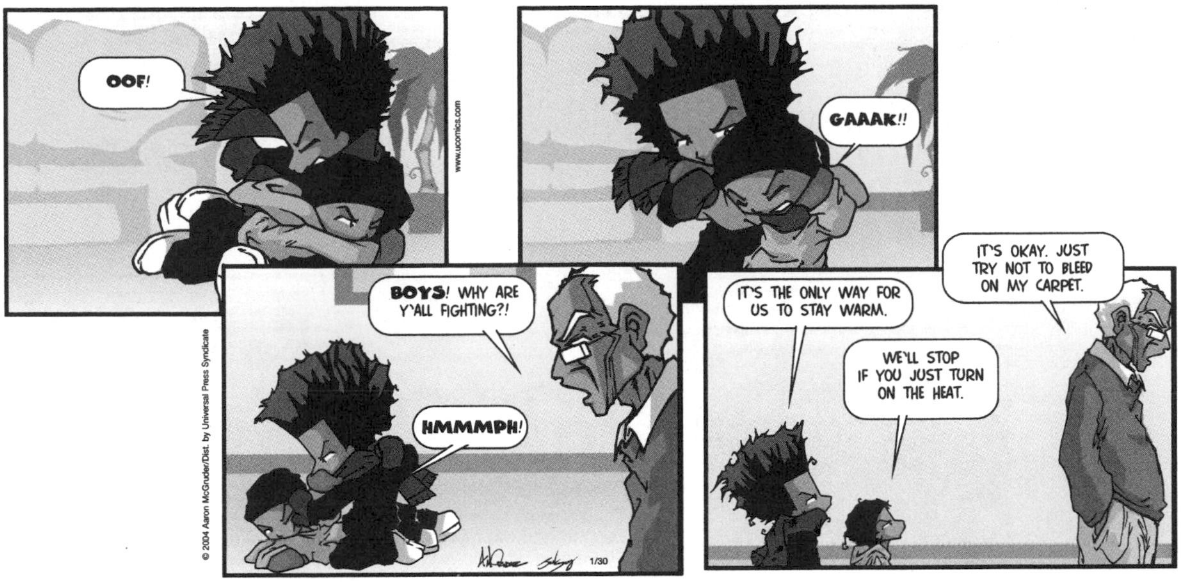
OOF!
GAAAK!!
BOYS! WHY ARE Y'ALL FIGHTING?!
HMMMPH!
IT'S THE ONLY WAY FOR US TO STAY WARM.
WE'LL STOP IF YOU JUST TURN ON THE HEAT.
IT'S OKAY. JUST TRY NOT TO BLEED ON MY CARPET.
www.ucomics.com
© 2004 Aaron McGruder/Dist. by Universal Press Syndicate
1/30

THE BOONDOCKS **BY AARON McGRUDER**

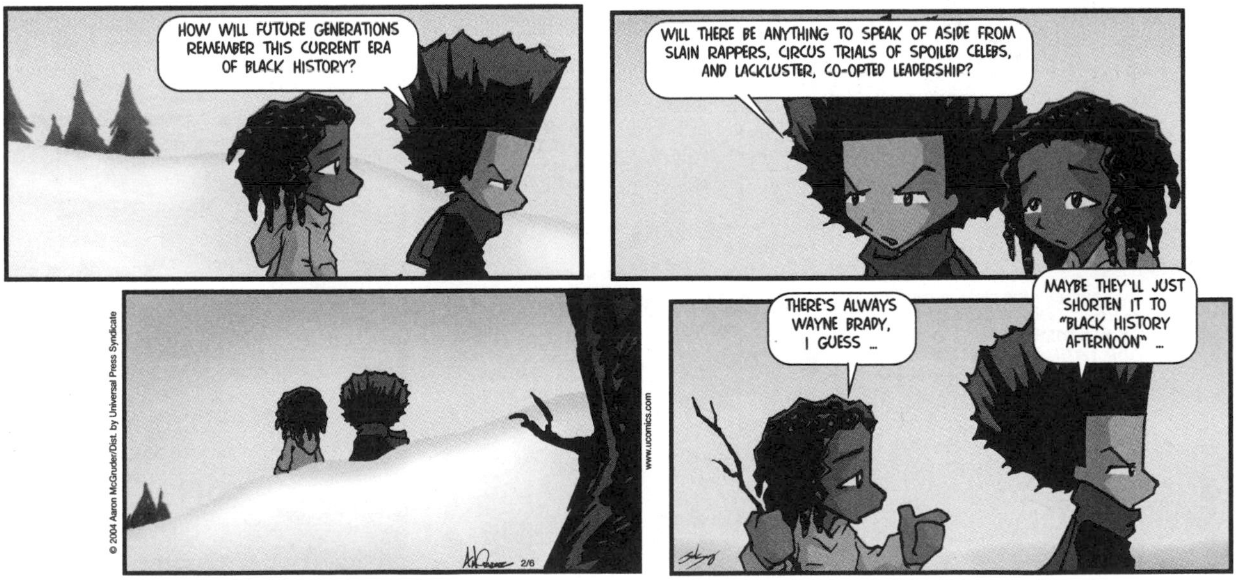
HOW WILL FUTURE GENERATIONS REMEMBER THIS CURRENT ERA OF BLACK HISTORY?
WILL THERE BE ANYTHING TO SPEAK OF ASIDE FROM SLAIN RAPPERS, CIRCUS TRIALS OF SPOILED CELEBS, AND LACKLUSTER, CO-OPTED LEADERSHIP?
© 2004 Aaron McGruder/Dist. by Universal Press Syndicate
2/6
www.ucomics.com
THERE'S ALWAYS WAYNE BRADY, I GUESS ...
MAYBE THEY'LL JUST SHORTEN IT TO "BLACK HISTORY AFTERNOON" ...

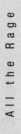

THE BOONDOCKS BY AARON McGRUDER

LATRELL SPREWELL GAINED HIS PLACE IN BLACK HISTORY WHEN HE BECAME THE FIRST NBA ATHLETE TO DO WHAT NO OTHER WOULD DARE DO BEFORE HIM ...
BUT HIS CONTRIBUTION TO BLACK HISTORY DIDN'T STOP THERE. LATRELL SPREWELL WANTED TO REVOLUTIONIZE CHROME RIMS.
PEOPLE SAID IT COULDN'T BE DONE. THEY SAID, "YOU'RE CRAZY, SPREWELL! RIMS ONLY SPIN WHEN THE CAR IS MOVING!"
BUT HE PROVED THE HATERS WRONG.
AND HE DIDN'T STOP THERE. SPREWELL HAD A DREAM THAT ONE DAY EVERYTHING WOULD MOVE WITHOUT GOING ANYWHERE.
SO HE INVENTED THE WORLD'S FIRST SPINNING-RIM SNEAKER.
BLACK HISTORY
INAPPROPRIATE?! THIS IS THE GEORGE WASHINGTON CARVER OF RIMS!
© 2005 Aaron McGruder/Dist. by Universal Press Syndicate
www.ucomics.com

THE BOONDOCKS BY AARON McGRUDER

HUEY! C'MERE, BOY!
HOLD ON!
DON'T GIMME NO "HOLD ON." GET IN HERE!!!
I'M KINDA DOING SOMETHING!
I DON'T CARE WHAT YOU'RE DOING!
IS IT IMPORTANT?!
EVERY TIME I CALL YOU IT'S IMPORTANT! GET YOUR TAIL IN HERE! NOW!!
OK ... I'M COMING ...
HURRY UP!
YES, GRANDDAD?
DID 50 CENT LOSE HIS HAND WHEN IT GOT CAUGHT IN A CAR DOOR?
IT WAS A RUMOR, GRANDDAD!
© 2005 Aaron McGruder/Dist. by Universal Press Syndicate
www.ucomics.com

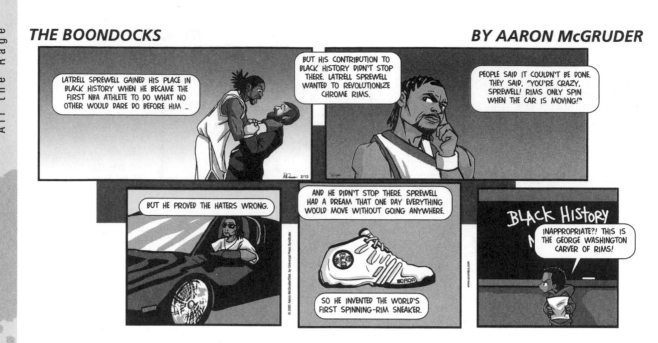

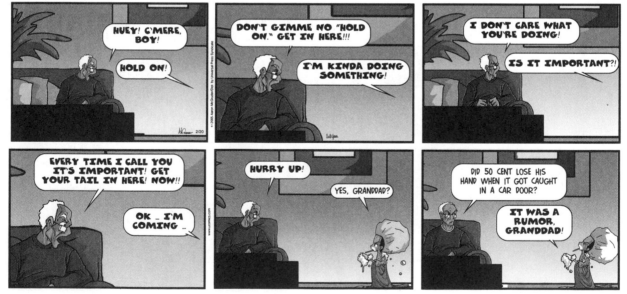

THE BOONDOCKS ***BY AARON McGRUDER***

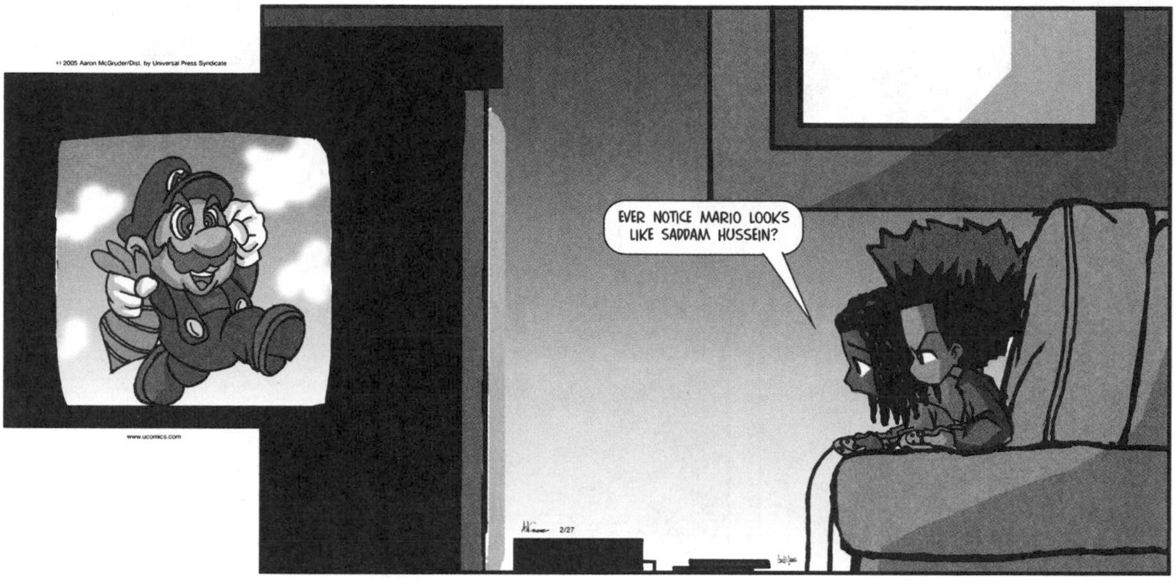
© 2005 Aaron McGruder/Dist. by Universal Press Syndicate
www.ucomics.com
EVER NOTICE MARIO LOOKS LIKE SADDAM HUSSEIN?

THE BOONDOCKS ***BY AARON McGRUDER***

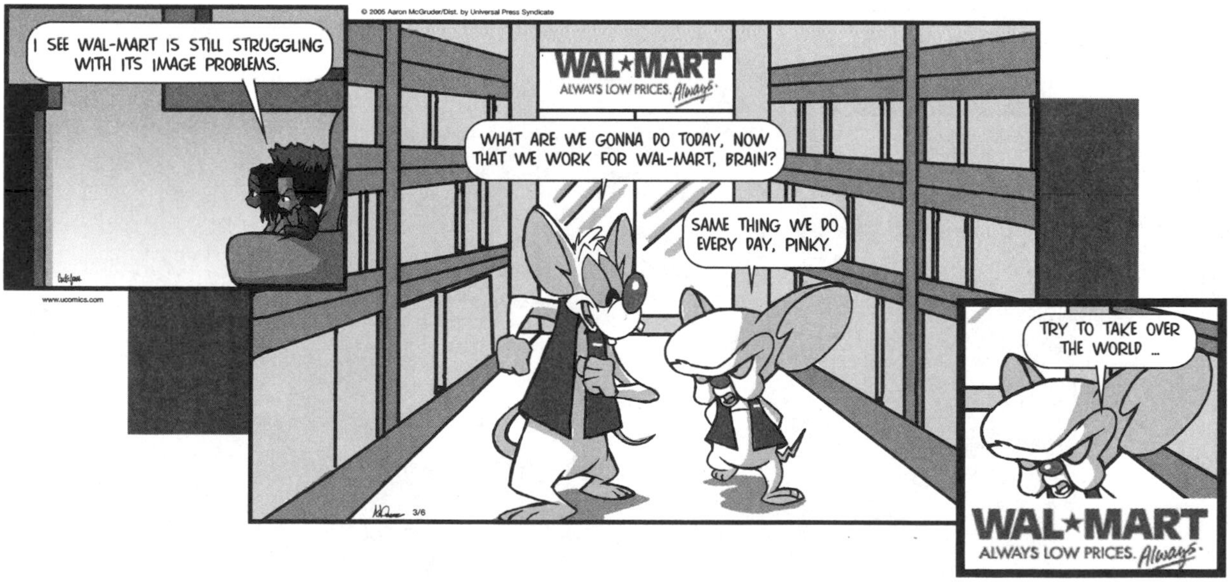
© 2005 Aaron McGruder/Dist. by Universal Press Syndicate
I SEE WAL-MART IS STILL STRUGGLING WITH ITS IMAGE PROBLEMS.
www.ucomics.com
WAL★MART
ALWAYS LOW PRICES. Always.
WHAT ARE WE GONNA DO TODAY, NOW THAT WE WORK FOR WAL-MART, BRAIN?
SAME THING WE DO EVERY DAY, PINKY.
TRY TO TAKE OVER THE WORLD ...
WAL★MART
ALWAYS LOW PRICES. Always.

THE BOONDOCKS BY AARON McGRUDER

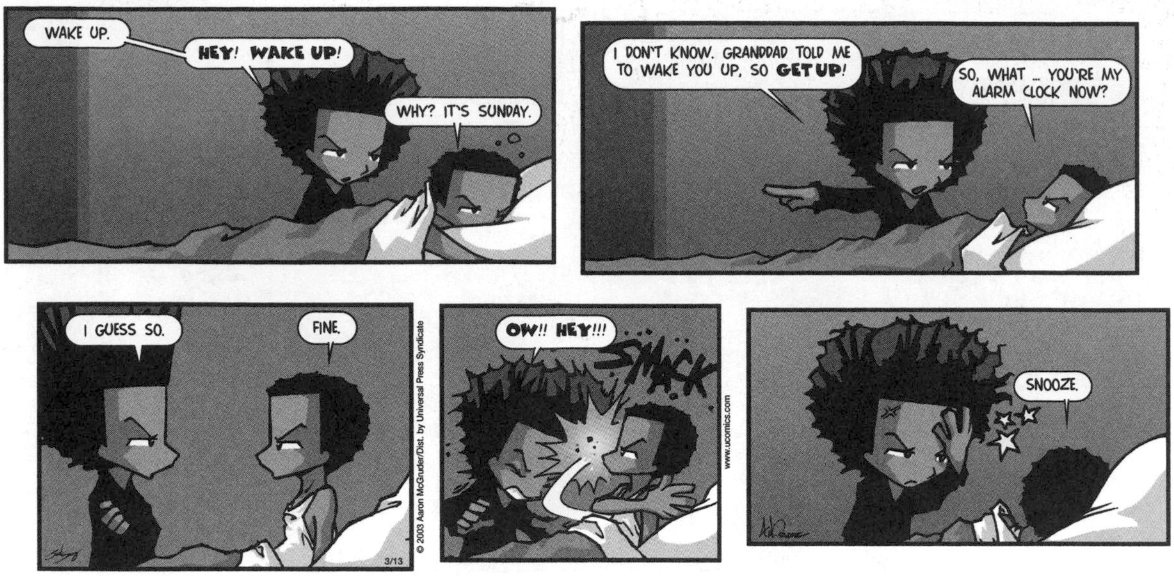
WAKE UP.
HEY! WAKE UP!
WHY? IT'S SUNDAY.
I DON'T KNOW. GRANDDAD TOLD ME TO WAKE YOU UP, SO GET UP!
SO, WHAT ... YOU'RE MY ALARM CLOCK NOW?
I GUESS SO.
FINE.
3/13
© 2003 Aaron McGruder/Dist. by Universal Press Syndicate
OW!! HEY!!!
SMACK
www.ucomics.com
SNOOZE.

THE BOONDOCKS BY AARON McGRUDER

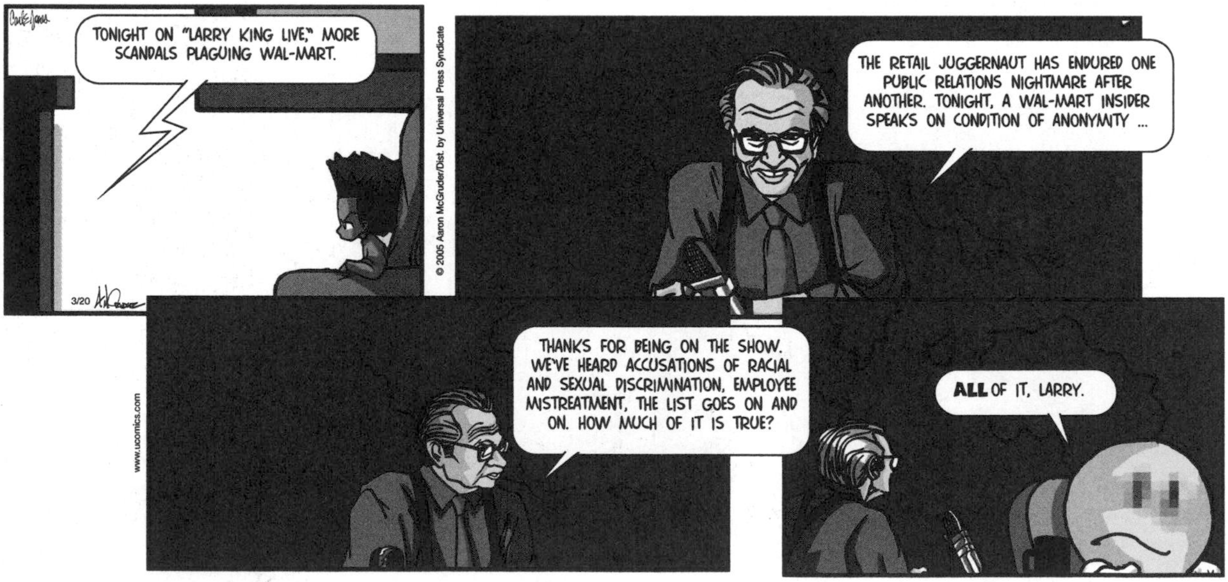
TONIGHT ON "LARRY KING LIVE," MORE SCANDALS PLAGUING WAL-MART.
3/20
© 2005 Aaron McGruder/Dist. by Universal Press Syndicate
THE RETAIL JUGGERNAUT HAS ENDURED ONE PUBLIC RELATIONS NIGHTMARE AFTER ANOTHER. TONIGHT, A WAL-MART INSIDER SPEAKS ON CONDITION OF ANONYMITY ...
www.ucomics.com
THANKS FOR BEING ON THE SHOW. WE'VE HEARD ACCUSATIONS OF RACIAL AND SEXUAL DISCRIMINATION, EMPLOYEE MISTREATMENT, THE LIST GOES ON AND ON. HOW MUCH OF IT IS TRUE?
ALL OF IT, LARRY.

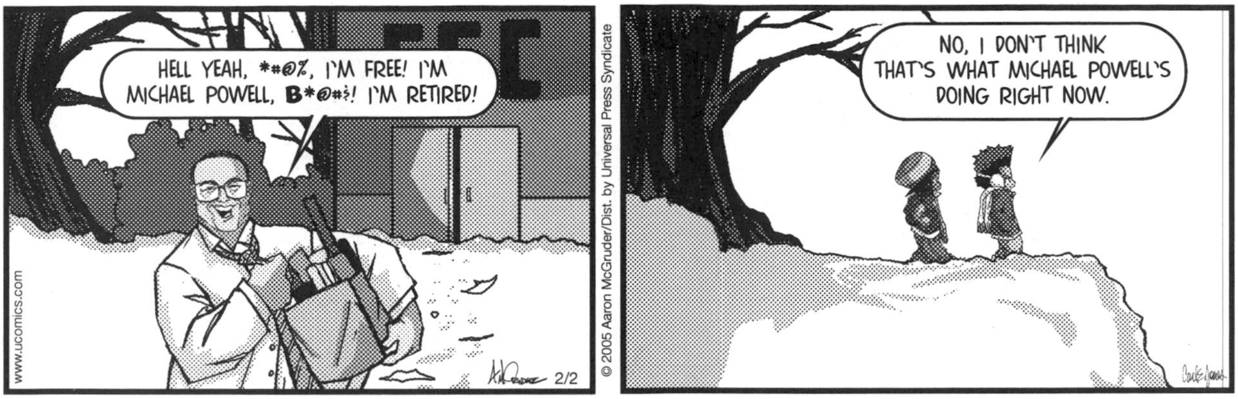
HELL YEAH, *#@%, I'M FREE! I'M MICHAEL POWELL, B*@#$! I'M RETIRED!
NO, I DON'T THINK THAT'S WHAT MICHAEL POWELL'S DOING RIGHT NOW.
2/2
www.ucomics.com
© 2005 Aaron McGruder/Dist. by Universal Press Syndicate

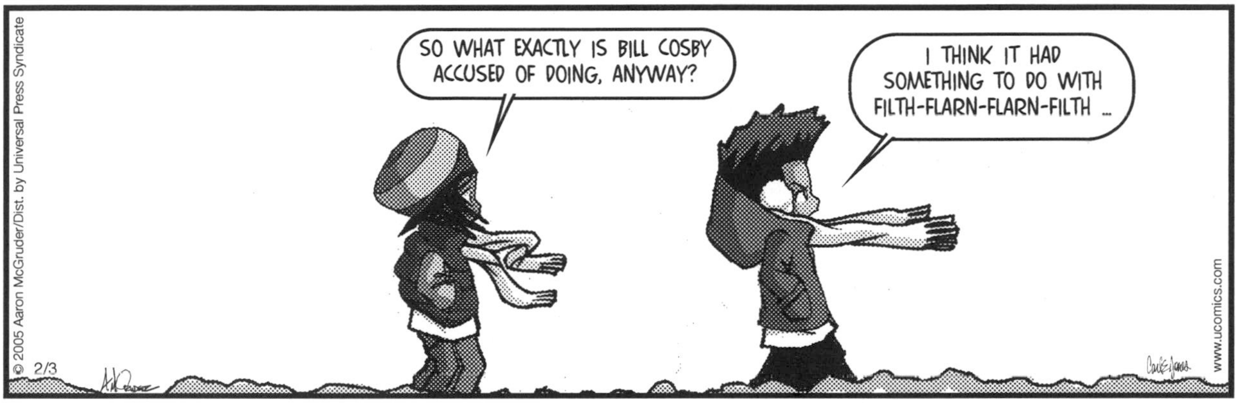
SO WHAT EXACTLY IS BILL COSBY ACCUSED OF DOING, ANYWAY?
I THINK IT HAD SOMETHING TO DO WITH FILTH-FLARN-FLARN-FILTH ...
2/3
© 2005 Aaron McGruder/Dist. by Universal Press Syndicate
www.ucomics.com

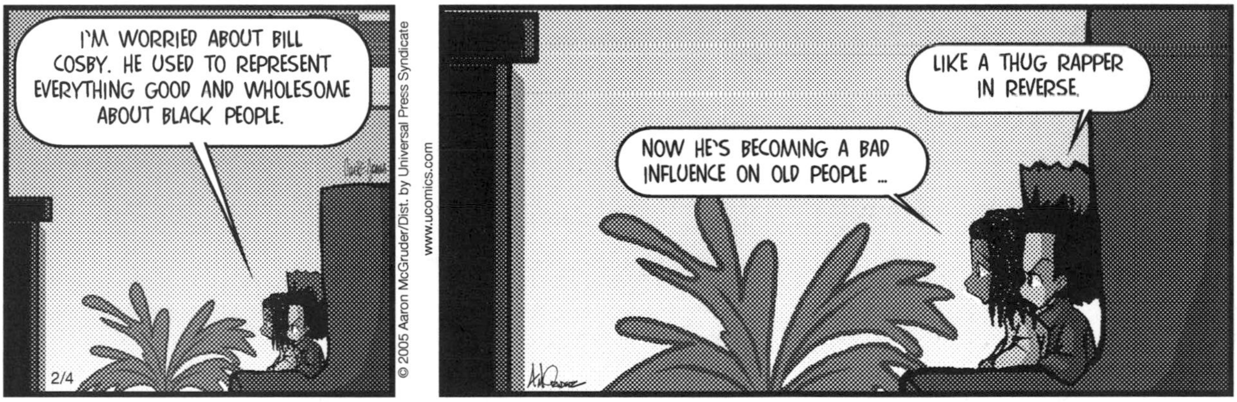
I'M WORRIED ABOUT BILL COSBY. HE USED TO REPRESENT EVERYTHING GOOD AND WHOLESOME ABOUT BLACK PEOPLE.
NOW HE'S BECOMING A BAD INFLUENCE ON OLD PEOPLE ...
LIKE A THUG RAPPER IN REVERSE.
2/4
© 2005 Aaron McGruder/Dist. by Universal Press Syndicate
www.ucomics.com

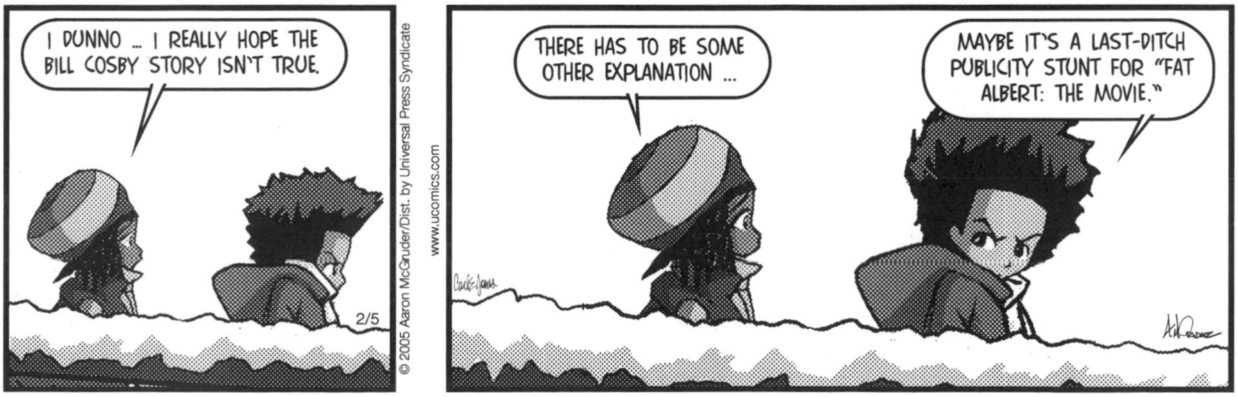
I DUNNO ... I REALLY HOPE THE BILL COSBY STORY ISN'T TRUE.
THERE HAS TO BE SOME OTHER EXPLANATION ...
MAYBE IT'S A LAST-DITCH PUBLICITY STUNT FOR "FAT ALBERT: THE MOVIE."
2/5
© 2005 Aaron McGruder/Dist. by Universal Press Syndicate
www.ucomics.com

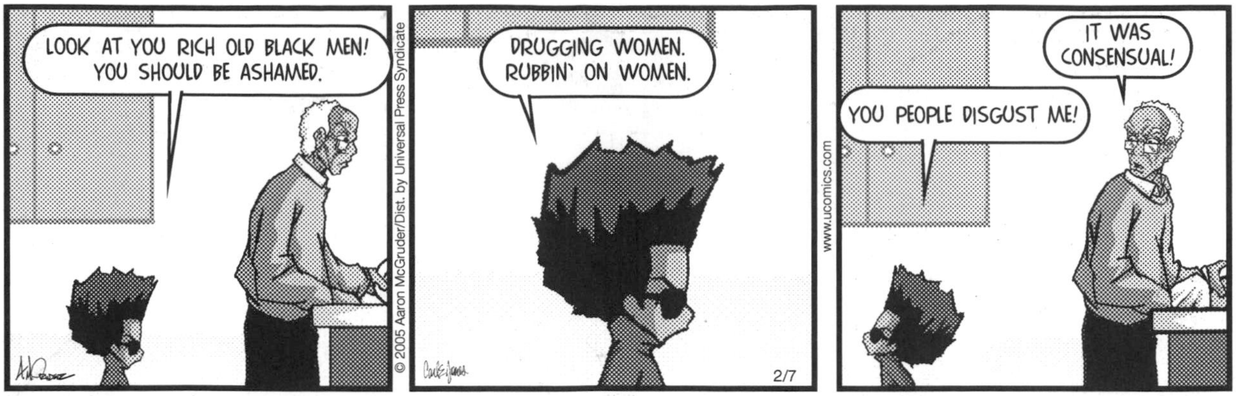
LOOK AT YOU RICH OLD BLACK MEN! YOU SHOULD BE ASHAMED.
© 2005 Aaron McGruder/Dist. by Universal Press Syndicate
DRUGGING WOMEN. RUBBIN' ON WOMEN.
2/7
www.ucomics.com
IT WAS CONSENSUAL!
YOU PEOPLE DISGUST ME!

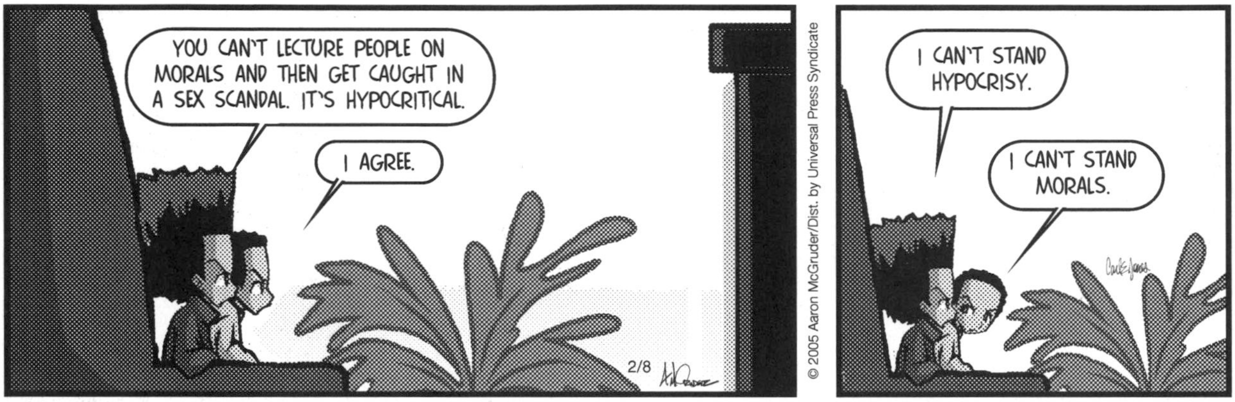
YOU CAN'T LECTURE PEOPLE ON MORALS AND THEN GET CAUGHT IN A SEX SCANDAL. IT'S HYPOCRITICAL.
I AGREE.
2/8
© 2005 Aaron McGruder/Dist. by Universal Press Syndicate
I CAN'T STAND HYPOCRISY.
I CAN'T STAND MORALS.

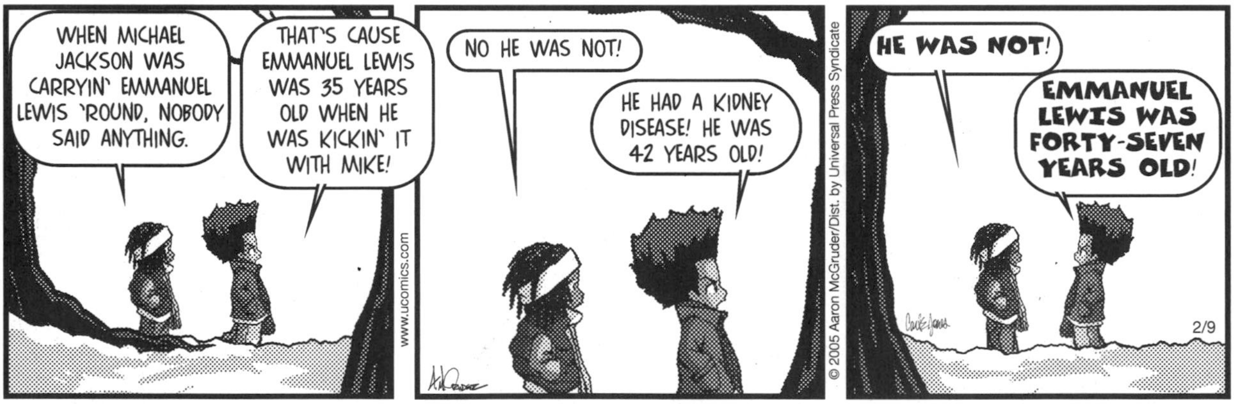
WHEN MICHAEL JACKSON WAS CARRYIN' EMMANUEL LEWIS 'ROUND, NOBODY SAID ANYTHING.
THAT'S CAUSE EMMANUEL LEWIS WAS 35 YEARS OLD WHEN HE WAS KICKIN' IT WITH MIKE!
www.ucomics.com
NO HE WAS NOT!
HE HAD A KIDNEY DISEASE! HE WAS 42 YEARS OLD!
© 2005 Aaron McGruder/Dist. by Universal Press Syndicate
HE WAS NOT!
EMMANUEL LEWIS WAS FORTY-SEVEN YEARS OLD!
2/9

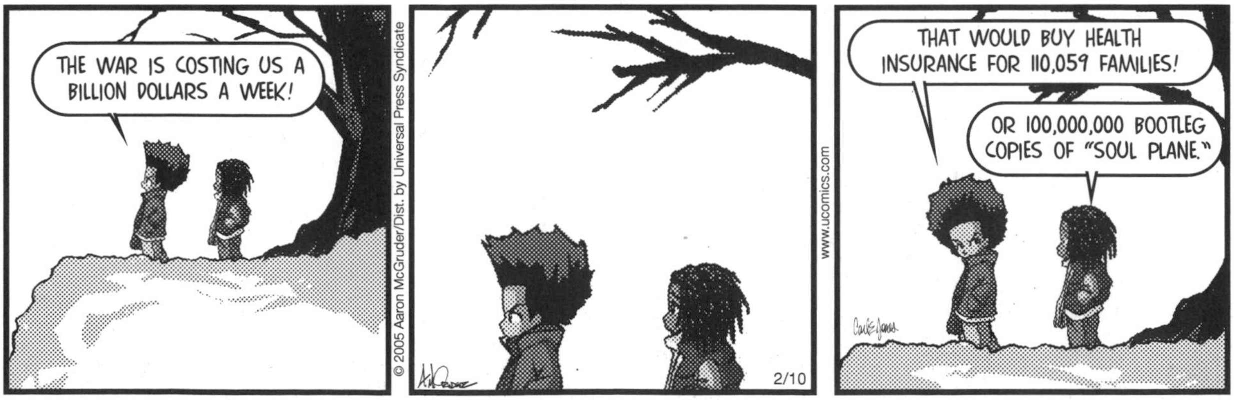
THE WAR IS COSTING US A BILLION DOLLARS A WEEK!
© 2005 Aaron McGruder/Dist. by Universal Press Syndicate
2/10
www.ucomics.com
THAT WOULD BUY HEALTH INSURANCE FOR 110,059 FAMILIES!
OR 100,000,000 BOOTLEG COPIES OF "SOUL PLANE."

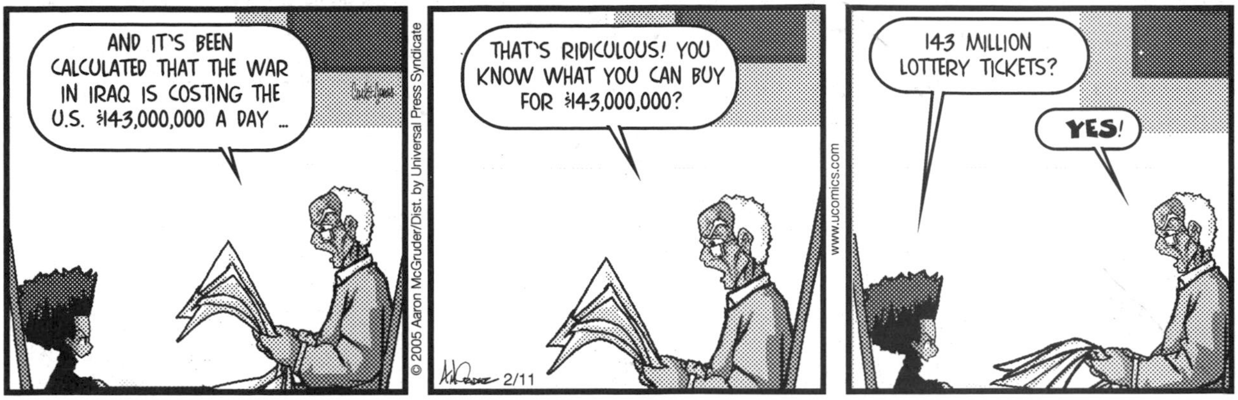
AND IT'S BEEN CALCULATED THAT THE WAR IN IRAQ IS COSTING THE U.S. $143,000,000 A DAY ...
© 2005 Aaron McGruder/Dist. by Universal Press Syndicate
THAT'S RIDICULOUS! YOU KNOW WHAT YOU CAN BUY FOR $143,000,000?
2/11
www.ucomics.com
143 MILLION LOTTERY TICKETS?
YES!

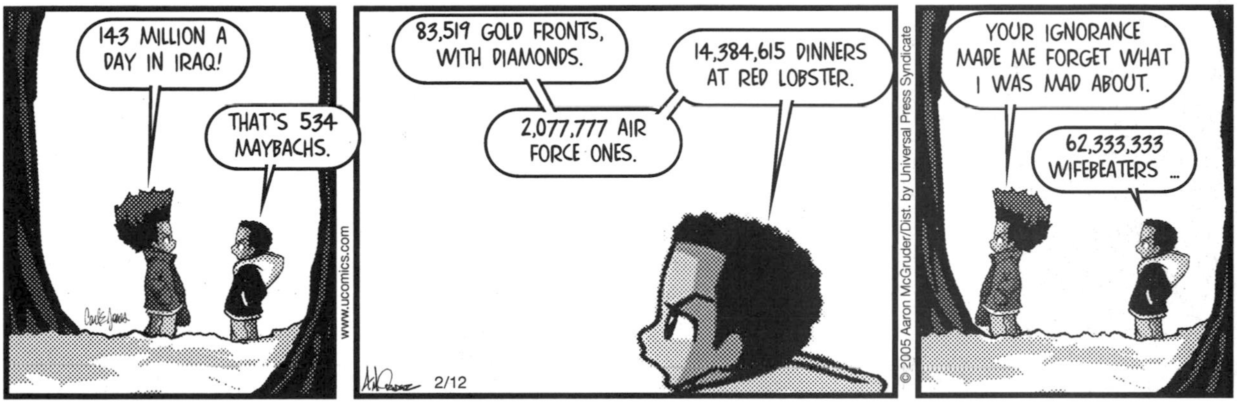
143 MILLION A DAY IN IRAQ!
THAT'S 534 MAYBACHS.
www.ucomics.com
83,519 GOLD FRONTS, WITH DIAMONDS.
2,077,777 AIR FORCE ONES.
14,384,615 DINNERS AT RED LOBSTER.
2/12
© 2005 Aaron McGruder/Dist. by Universal Press Syndicate
YOUR IGNORANCE MADE ME FORGET WHAT I WAS MAD ABOUT.
62,333,333 WIFEBEATERS ...

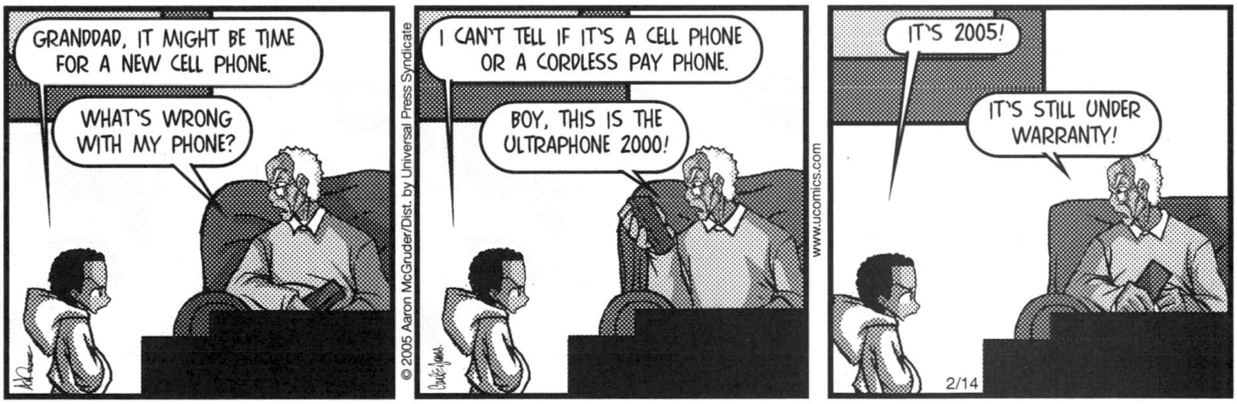
GRANDDAD, IT MIGHT BE TIME FOR A NEW CELL PHONE.
WHAT'S WRONG WITH MY PHONE?
© 2005 Aaron McGruder/Dist. by Universal Press Syndicate
I CAN'T TELL IF IT'S A CELL PHONE OR A CORDLESS PAY PHONE.
BOY, THIS IS THE ULTRAPHONE 2000!
www.ucomics.com
IT'S 2005!
IT'S STILL UNDER WARRANTY!
2/14

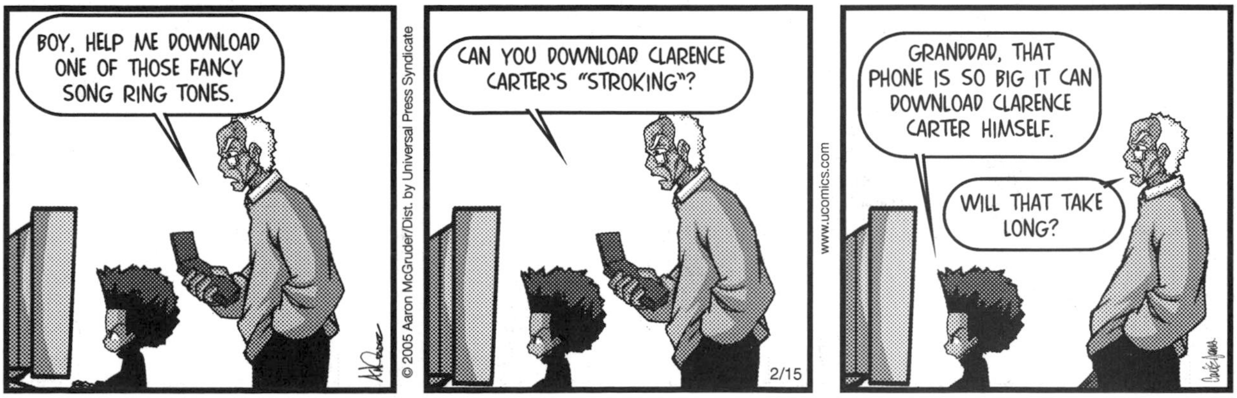
BOY, HELP ME DOWNLOAD ONE OF THOSE FANCY SONG RING TONES.
© 2005 Aaron McGruder/Dist. by Universal Press Syndicate
CAN YOU DOWNLOAD CLARENCE CARTER'S "STROKING"?
2/15
www.ucomics.com
GRANDDAD, THAT PHONE IS SO BIG IT CAN DOWNLOAD CLARENCE CARTER HIMSELF.
WILL THAT TAKE LONG?

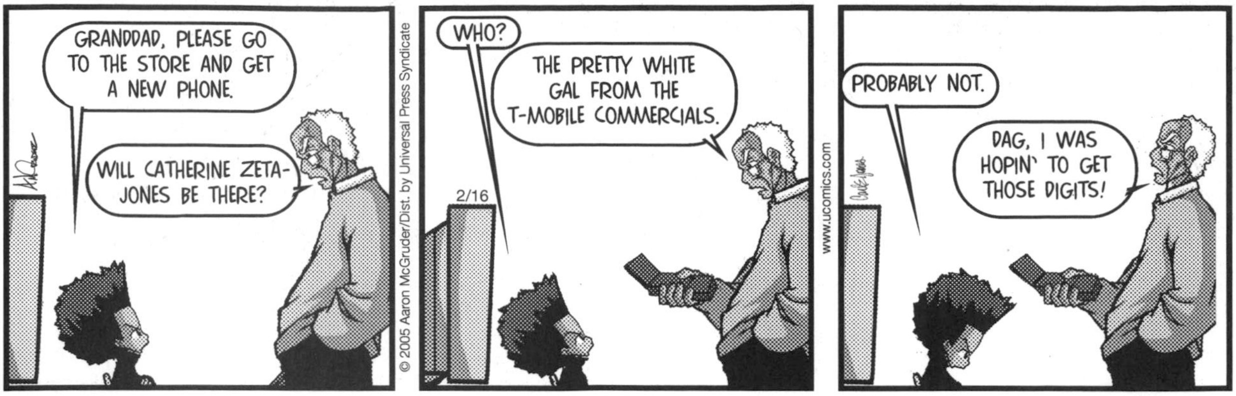
GRANDDAD, PLEASE GO TO THE STORE AND GET A NEW PHONE.
WILL CATHERINE ZETA-JONES BE THERE?
© 2005 Aaron McGruder/Dist. by Universal Press Syndicate
2/16
WHO?
THE PRETTY WHITE GAL FROM THE T-MOBILE COMMERCIALS.
www.ucomics.com
PROBABLY NOT.
DAG, I WAS HOPIN' TO GET THOSE DIGITS!

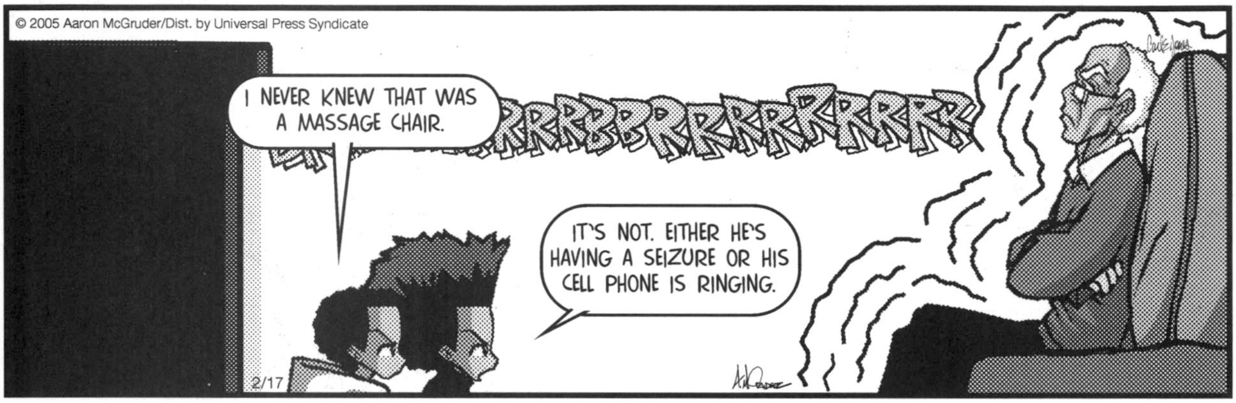
© 2005 Aaron McGruder/Dist. by Universal Press Syndicate
I NEVER KNEW THAT WAS A MASSAGE CHAIR.
IT'S NOT. EITHER HE'S HAVING A SEIZURE OR HIS CELL PHONE IS RINGING.
2/17

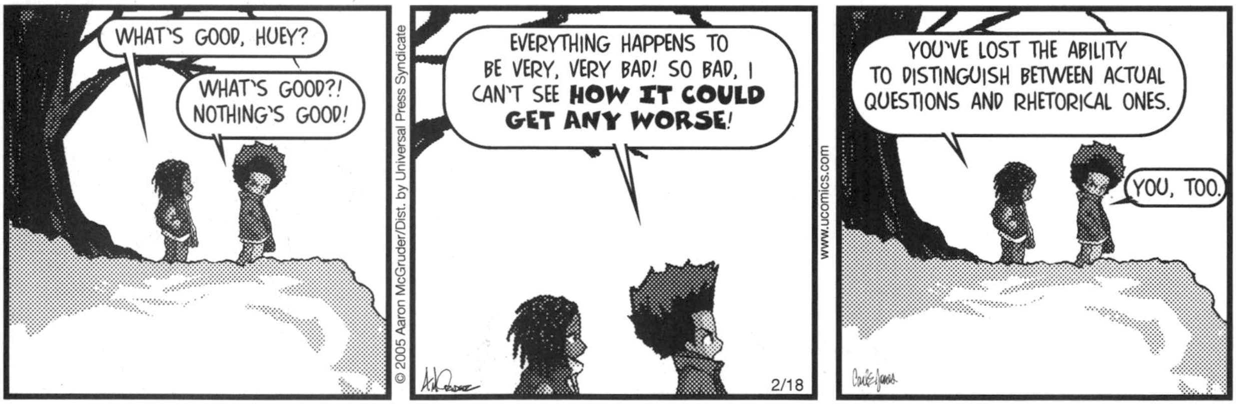
WHAT'S GOOD, HUEY?
WHAT'S GOOD?! NOTHING'S GOOD!
© 2005 Aaron McGruder/Dist. by Universal Press Syndicate
EVERYTHING HAPPENS TO BE VERY, VERY BAD! SO BAD, I CAN'T SEE **HOW IT COULD GET ANY WORSE**!
2/18
www.ucomics.com
YOU'VE LOST THE ABILITY TO DISTINGUISH BETWEEN ACTUAL QUESTIONS AND RHETORICAL ONES.
YOU, TOO.

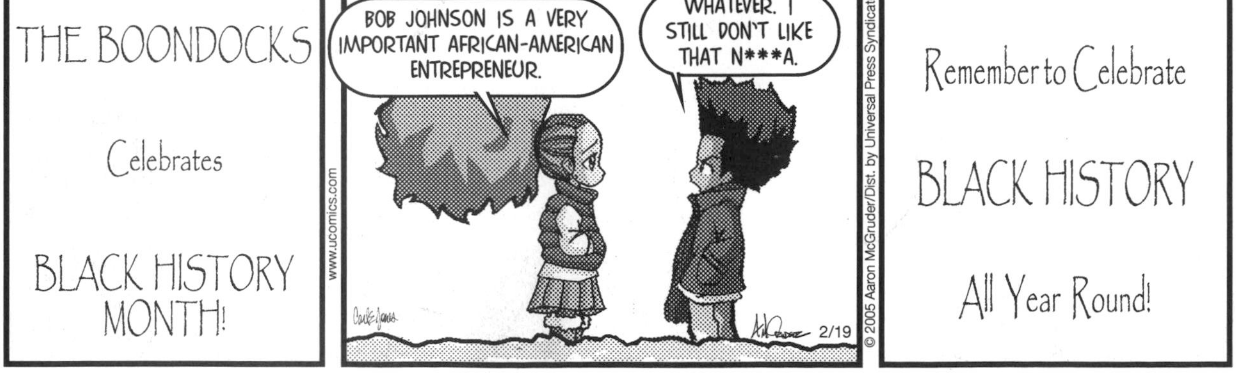
THE BOONDOCKS
Celebrates
BLACK HISTORY MONTH!
www.ucomics.com
BOB JOHNSON IS A VERY IMPORTANT AFRICAN-AMERICAN ENTREPRENEUR.
WHATEVER. I STILL DON'T LIKE THAT N***A.
2/19
© 2005 Aaron McGruder/Dist. by Universal Press Syndicate
Remember to Celebrate
BLACK HISTORY
All Year Round!

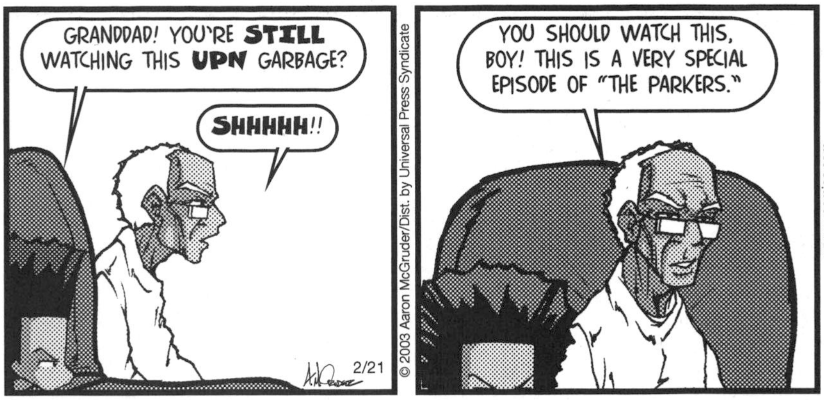
GRANDDAD! YOU'RE **STILL** WATCHING THIS **UPN** GARBAGE?
SHHHHH!!
2/21
© 2003 Aaron McGruder/Dist. by Universal Press Syndicate
YOU SHOULD WATCH THIS, BOY! THIS IS A VERY SPECIAL EPISODE OF "THE PARKERS."
www.ucomics.com
COUNTESS VAUGHN AND MO'NIQUE ARE STUCK IN THE KITCHEN DOORWAY AFTER A RACE FOR A CHEESEBURGER GOES TERRIBLY WRONG!
GOOD GRIEF!

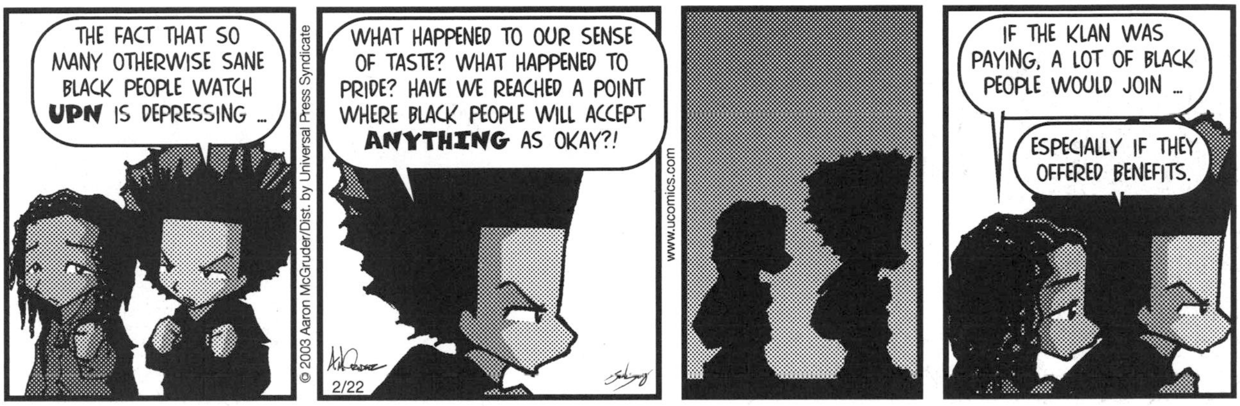
THE FACT THAT SO MANY OTHERWISE SANE BLACK PEOPLE WATCH **UPN** IS DEPRESSING ...
© 2003 Aaron McGruder/Dist. by Universal Press Syndicate
WHAT HAPPENED TO OUR SENSE OF TASTE? WHAT HAPPENED TO PRIDE? HAVE WE REACHED A POINT WHERE BLACK PEOPLE WILL ACCEPT **ANYTHING** AS OKAY?!
2/22
www.ucomics.com
IF THE KLAN WAS PAYING, A LOT OF BLACK PEOPLE WOULD JOIN ...
ESPECIALLY IF THEY OFFERED BENEFITS.

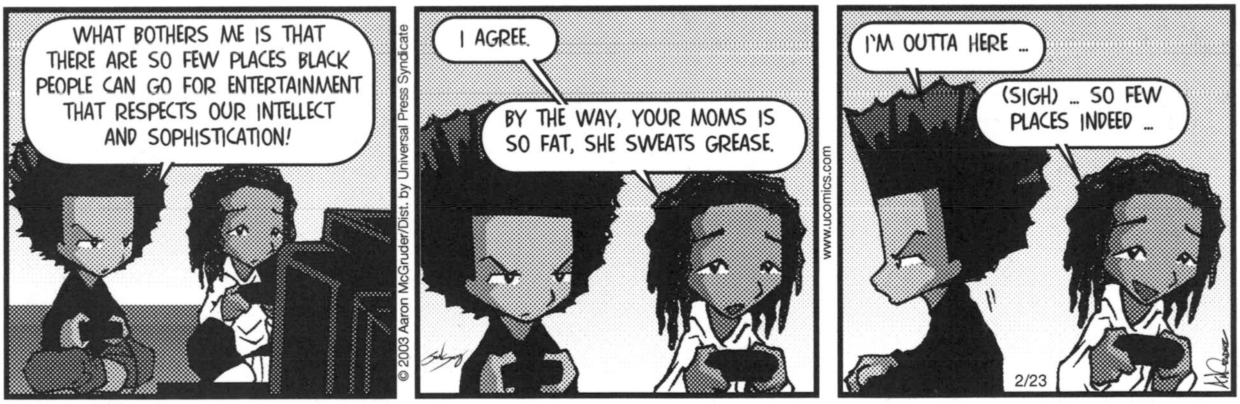
WHAT BOTHERS ME IS THAT THERE ARE SO FEW PLACES BLACK PEOPLE CAN GO FOR ENTERTAINMENT THAT RESPECTS OUR INTELLECT AND SOPHISTICATION!
© 2003 Aaron McGruder/Dist. by Universal Press Syndicate
I AGREE.
BY THE WAY, YOUR MOMS IS SO FAT, SHE SWEATS GREASE.
www.ucomics.com
I'M OUTTA HERE ...
(SIGH) ... SO FEW PLACES INDEED ...
2/23

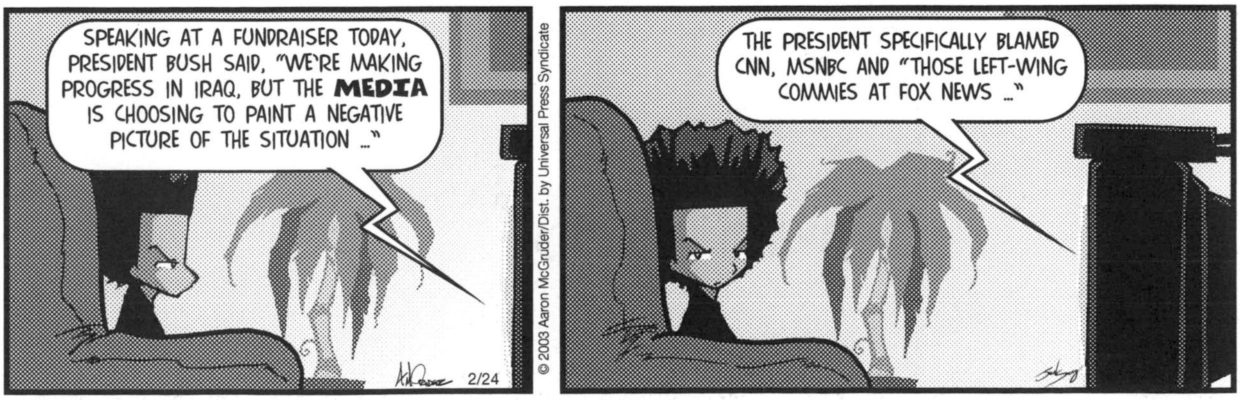
SPEAKING AT A FUNDRAISER TODAY, PRESIDENT BUSH SAID, "WE'RE MAKING PROGRESS IN IRAQ, BUT THE **MEDIA** IS CHOOSING TO PAINT A NEGATIVE PICTURE OF THE SITUATION ..."
2/24
© 2003 Aaron McGruder/Dist. by Universal Press Syndicate
THE PRESIDENT SPECIFICALLY BLAMED CNN, MSNBC AND "THOSE LEFT-WING COMMIES AT FOX NEWS ..."

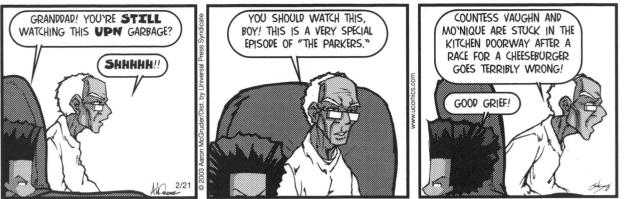

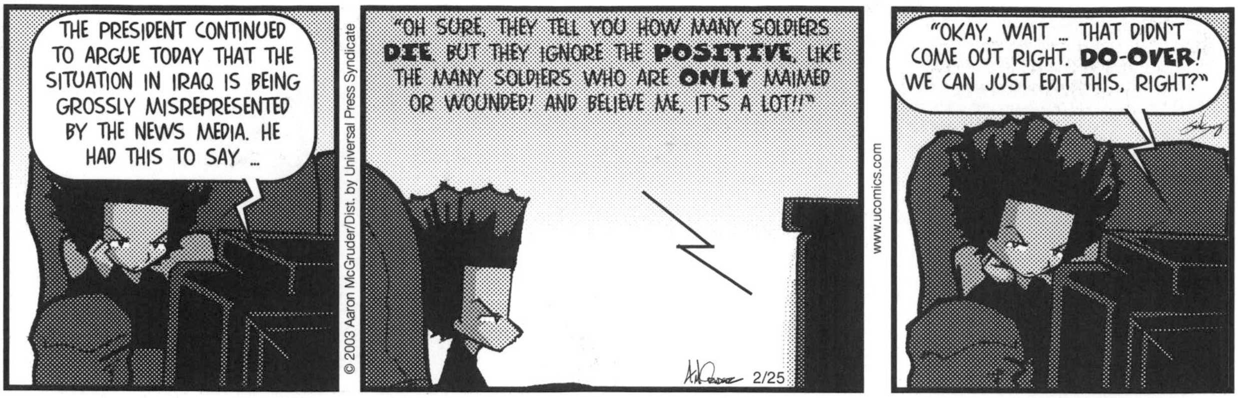
THE PRESIDENT CONTINUED TO ARGUE TODAY THAT THE SITUATION IN IRAQ IS BEING GROSSLY MISREPRESENTED BY THE NEWS MEDIA. HE HAD THIS TO SAY ...
© 2003 Aaron McGruder/Dist. by Universal Press Syndicate
"OH SURE, THEY TELL YOU HOW MANY SOLDIERS **DIE**, BUT THEY IGNORE THE **POSITIVE**, LIKE THE MANY SOLDIERS WHO ARE **ONLY** MAIMED OR WOUNDED! AND BELIEVE ME, IT'S A LOT!!"
2/25
www.ucomics.com
"OKAY, WAIT ... THAT DIDN'T COME OUT RIGHT. **DO-OVER**! WE CAN JUST EDIT THIS, RIGHT?"

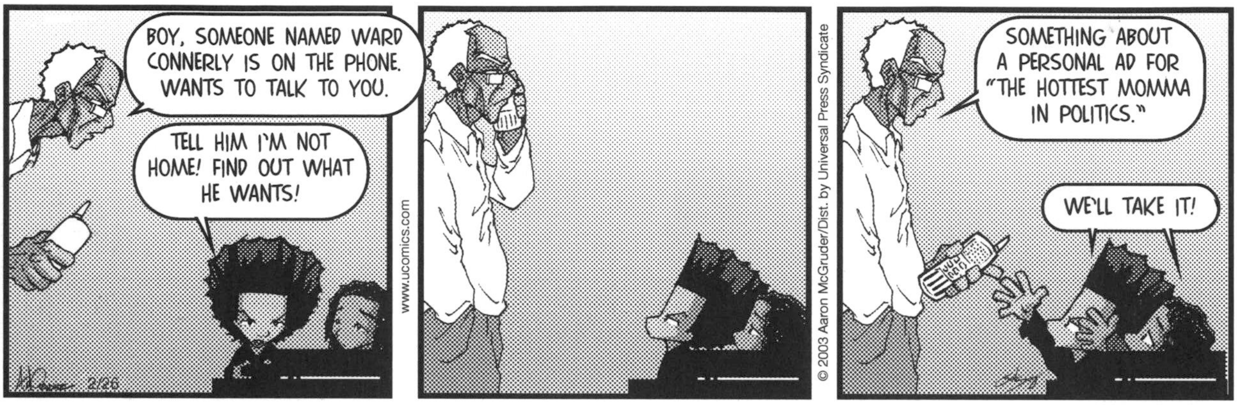
BOY, SOMEONE NAMED WARD CONNERLY IS ON THE PHONE. WANTS TO TALK TO YOU.
TELL HIM I'M NOT HOME! FIND OUT WHAT HE WANTS!
2/26
www.ucomics.com
© 2003 Aaron McGruder/Dist. by Universal Press Syndicate
SOMETHING ABOUT A PERSONAL AD FOR "THE HOTTEST MOMMA IN POLITICS."
WE'LL TAKE IT!

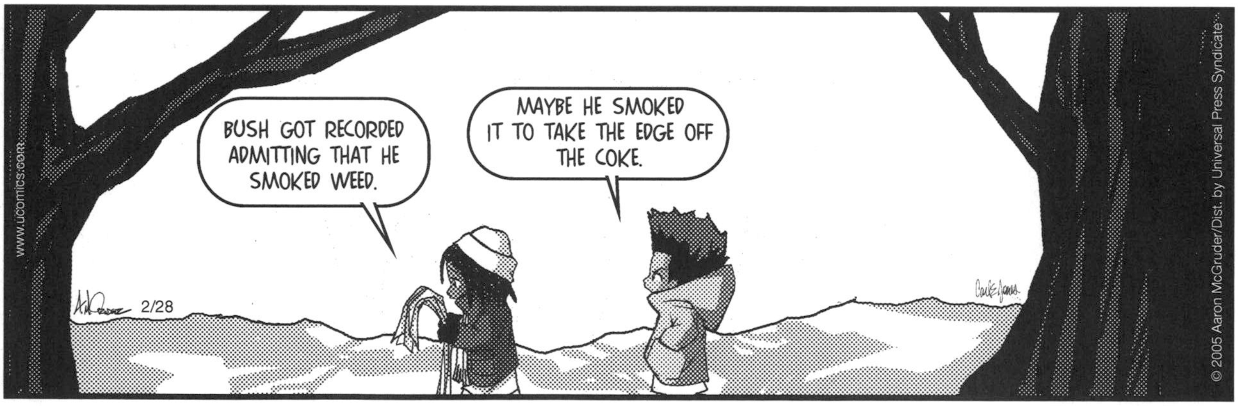
www.ucomics.com
BUSH GOT RECORDED ADMITTING THAT HE SMOKED WEED.
MAYBE HE SMOKED IT TO TAKE THE EDGE OFF THE COKE.
2/28
© 2005 Aaron McGruder/Dist. by Universal Press Syndicate

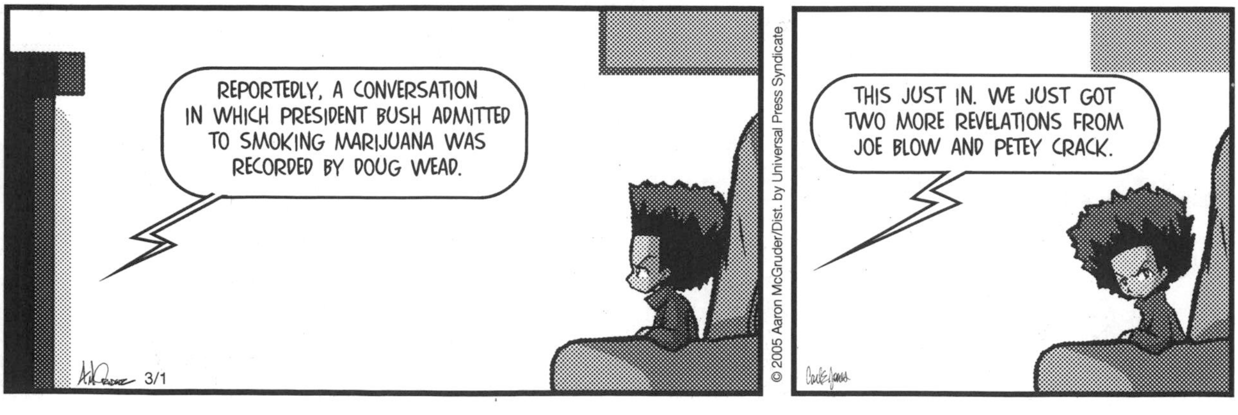
REPORTEDLY, A CONVERSATION IN WHICH PRESIDENT BUSH ADMITTED TO SMOKING MARIJUANA WAS RECORDED BY DOUG WEAD.
3/1
© 2005 Aaron McGruder/Dist. by Universal Press Syndicate
THIS JUST IN. WE JUST GOT TWO MORE REVELATIONS FROM JOE BLOW AND PETEY CRACK.

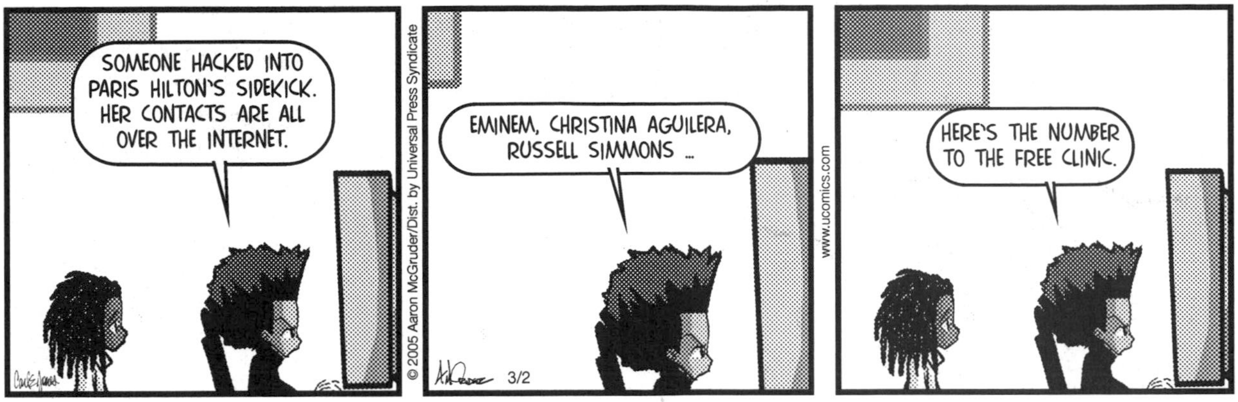
SOMEONE HACKED INTO PARIS HILTON'S SIDEKICK. HER CONTACTS ARE ALL OVER THE INTERNET.
© 2005 Aaron McGruder/Dist. by Universal Press Syndicate
EMINEM, CHRISTINA AGUILERA, RUSSELL SIMMONS ...
3/2
www.ucomics.com
HERE'S THE NUMBER TO THE FREE CLINIC.

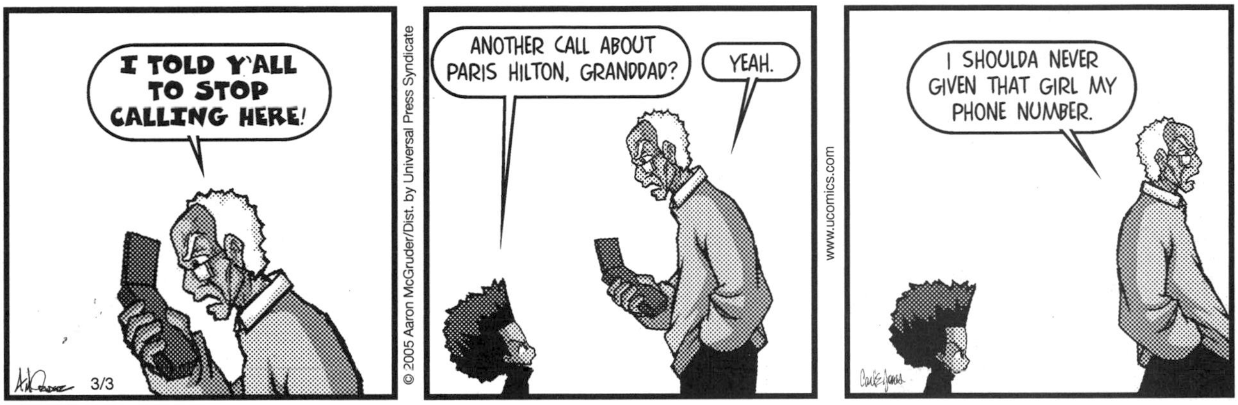
I TOLD Y'ALL TO STOP CALLING HERE!
3/3
© 2005 Aaron McGruder/Dist. by Universal Press Syndicate
ANOTHER CALL ABOUT PARIS HILTON, GRANDDAD?
YEAH.
www.ucomics.com
I SHOULDA NEVER GIVEN THAT GIRL MY PHONE NUMBER.

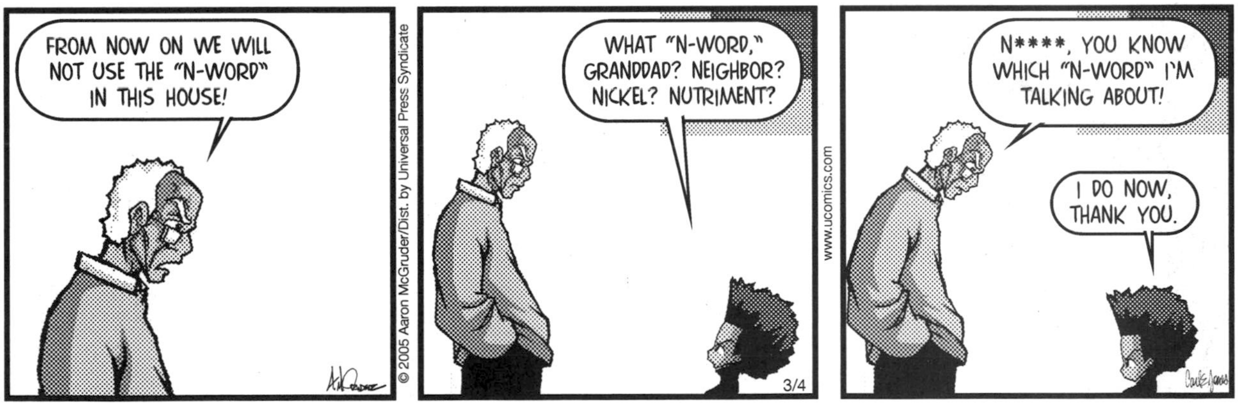
FROM NOW ON WE WILL NOT USE THE "N-WORD" IN THIS HOUSE!
© 2005 Aaron McGruder/Dist. by Universal Press Syndicate
WHAT "N-WORD," GRANDDAD? NEIGHBOR? NICKEL? NUTRIMENT?
3/4
www.ucomics.com
N****, YOU KNOW WHICH "N-WORD" I'M TALKING ABOUT!
I DO NOW, THANK YOU.

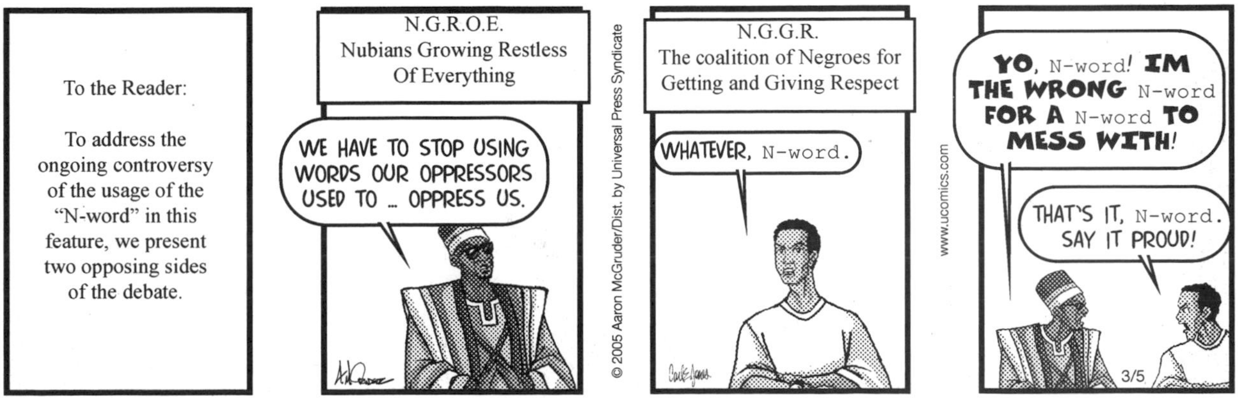
To the Reader:
To address the ongoing controversy of the usage of the "N-word" in this feature, we present two opposing sides of the debate.
N.G.R.O.E. Nubians Growing Restless Of Everything
WE HAVE TO STOP USING WORDS OUR OPPRESSORS USED TO ... OPPRESS US.
© 2005 Aaron McGruder/Dist. by Universal Press Syndicate
N.G.G.R. The coalition of Negroes for Getting and Giving Respect
WHATEVER, N-word.
www.ucomics.com
YO, N-word! IM THE WRONG N-word FOR A N-word TO MESS WITH!
THAT'S IT, N-word. SAY IT PROUD!
3/5

We are totally offended by the continuous use of the "N" word . . . If we don't receive an apology, we will picket the corporate headquarters.

—Al Sharpton

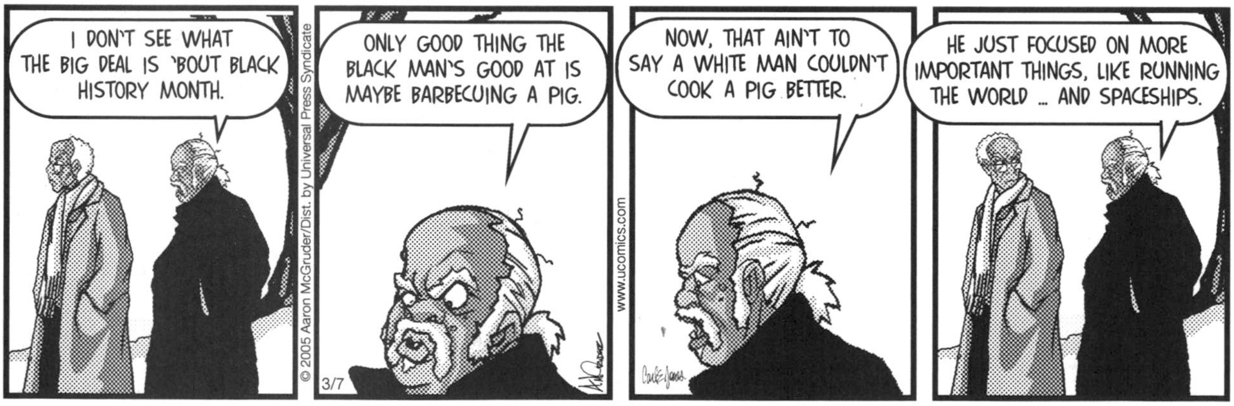
I DON'T SEE WHAT THE BIG DEAL IS 'BOUT BLACK HISTORY MONTH.
© 2005 Aaron McGruder/Dist. by Universal Press Syndicate
ONLY GOOD THING THE BLACK MAN'S GOOD AT IS MAYBE BARBECUING A PIG.
3/7
www.ucomics.com
NOW, THAT AIN'T TO SAY A WHITE MAN COULDN'T COOK A PIG BETTER.
HE JUST FOCUSED ON MORE IMPORTANT THINGS, LIKE RUNNING THE WORLD ... AND SPACESHIPS.

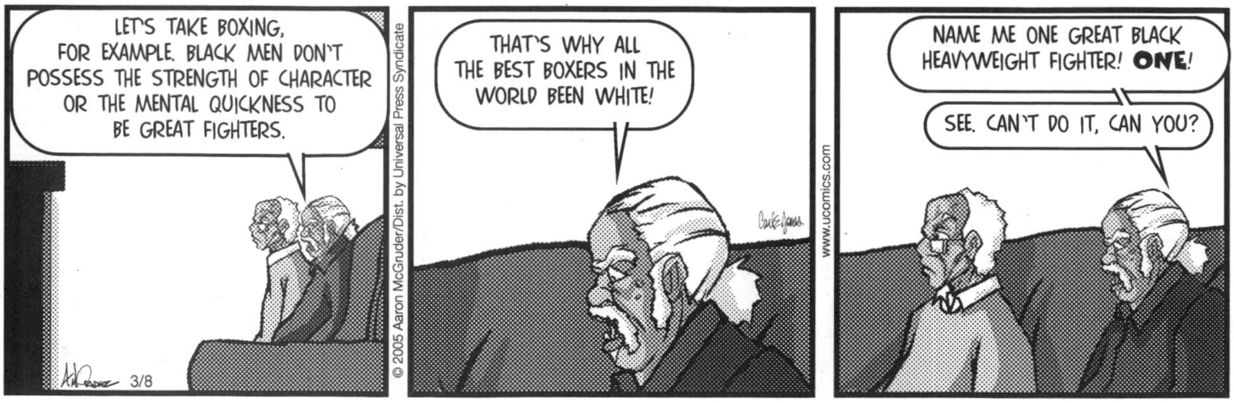
LET'S TAKE BOXING, FOR EXAMPLE. BLACK MEN DON'T POSSESS THE STRENGTH OF CHARACTER OR THE MENTAL QUICKNESS TO BE GREAT FIGHTERS.
3/8
© 2005 Aaron McGruder/Dist. by Universal Press Syndicate
THAT'S WHY ALL THE BEST BOXERS IN THE WORLD BEEN WHITE!
www.ucomics.com
NAME ME ONE GREAT BLACK HEAVYWEIGHT FIGHTER! **ONE**!
SEE. CAN'T DO IT, CAN YOU?

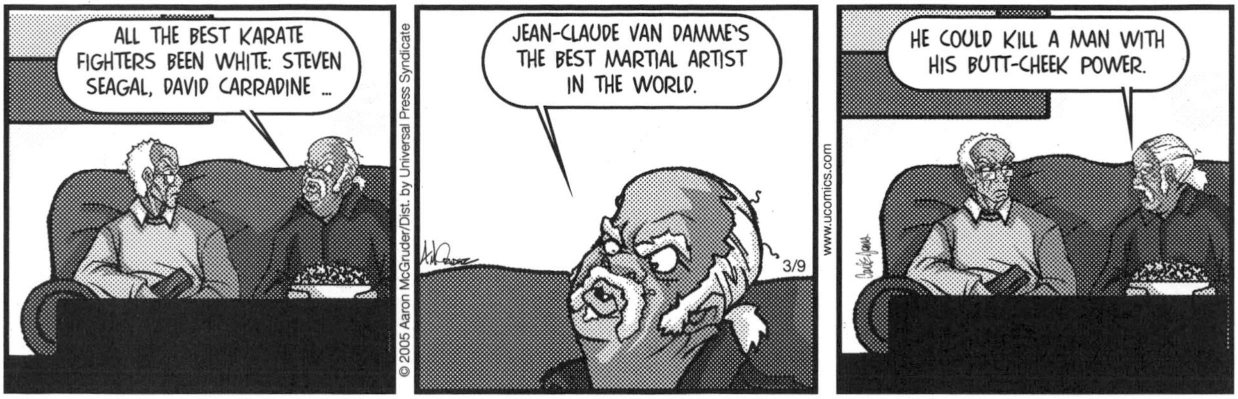
ALL THE BEST KARATE FIGHTERS BEEN WHITE: STEVEN SEAGAL, DAVID CARRADINE ...
JEAN-CLAUDE VAN DAMME'S THE BEST MARTIAL ARTIST IN THE WORLD.
HE COULD KILL A MAN WITH HIS BUTT-CHEEK POWER.
© 2005 Aaron McGruder/Dist. by Universal Press Syndicate
3/9
www.ucomics.com

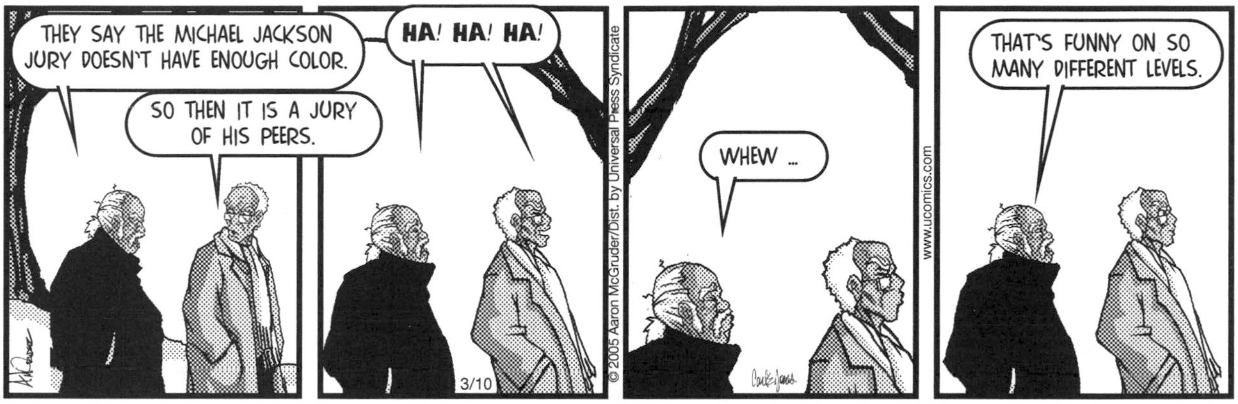
THEY SAY THE MICHAEL JACKSON JURY DOESN'T HAVE ENOUGH COLOR.
SO THEN IT IS A JURY OF HIS PEERS.
HA! HA! HA!
WHEW ...
THAT'S FUNNY ON SO MANY DIFFERENT LEVELS.
3/10
© 2005 Aaron McGruder/Dist. by Universal Press Syndicate
www.ucomics.com

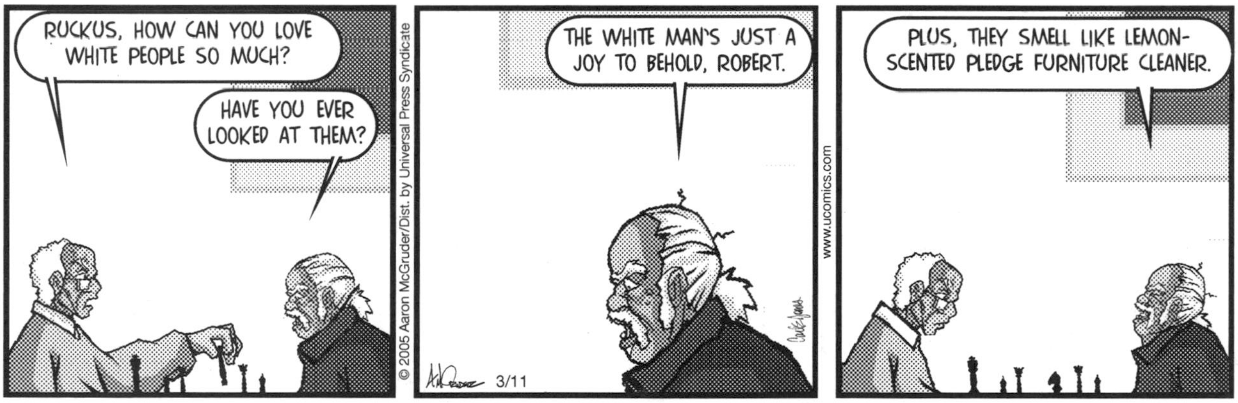
RUCKUS, HOW CAN YOU LOVE WHITE PEOPLE SO MUCH?
HAVE YOU EVER LOOKED AT THEM?
THE WHITE MAN'S JUST A JOY TO BEHOLD, ROBERT.
PLUS, THEY SMELL LIKE LEMON-SCENTED PLEDGE FURNITURE CLEANER.
© 2005 Aaron McGruder/Dist. by Universal Press Syndicate
3/11
www.ucomics.com

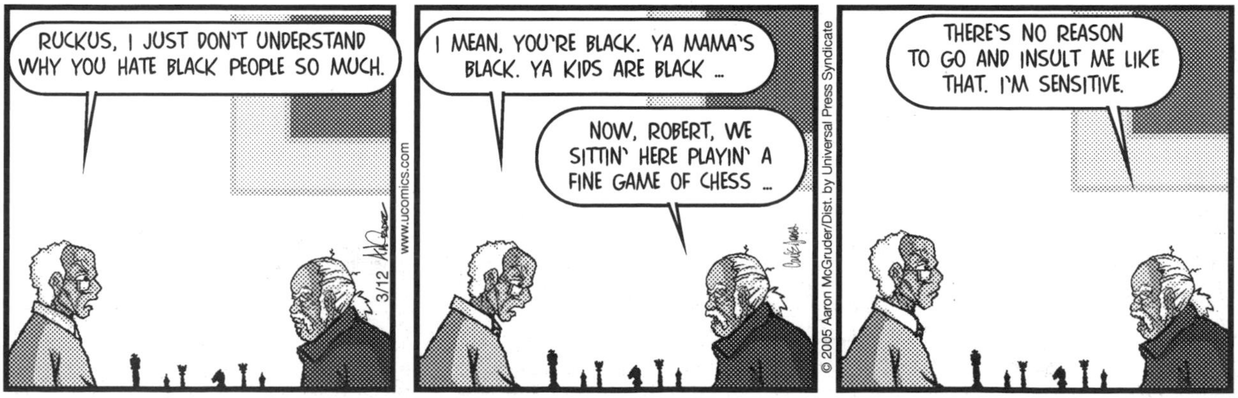
RUCKUS, I JUST DON'T UNDERSTAND WHY YOU HATE BLACK PEOPLE SO MUCH.
I MEAN, YOU'RE BLACK. YA MAMA'S BLACK. YA KIDS ARE BLACK ...
NOW, ROBERT, WE SITTIN' HERE PLAYIN' A FINE GAME OF CHESS ...
THERE'S NO REASON TO GO AND INSULT ME LIKE THAT. I'M SENSITIVE.
www.ucomics.com
3/12
© 2005 Aaron McGruder/Dist. by Universal Press Syndicate

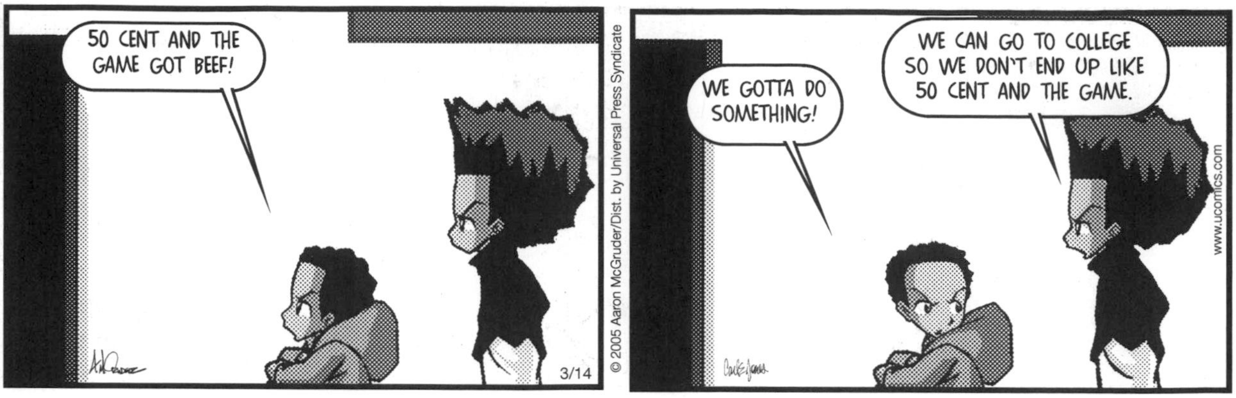
50 CENT AND THE GAME GOT BEEF!
3/14
© 2005 Aaron McGruder/Dist. by Universal Press Syndicate
WE GOTTA DO SOMETHING!
WE CAN GO TO COLLEGE SO WE DON'T END UP LIKE 50 CENT AND THE GAME.
www.ucomics.com

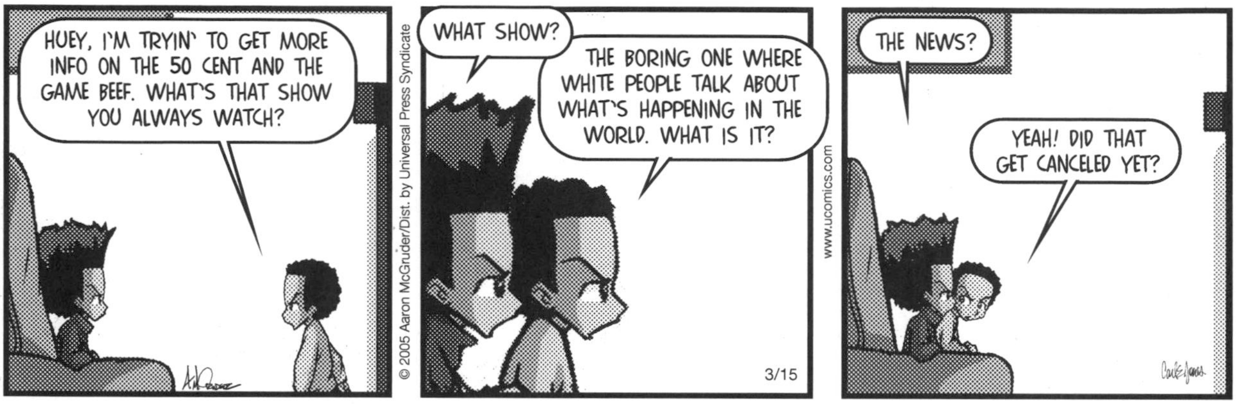
HUEY, I'M TRYIN' TO GET MORE INFO ON THE 50 CENT AND THE GAME BEEF. WHAT'S THAT SHOW YOU ALWAYS WATCH?
© 2005 Aaron McGruder/Dist. by Universal Press Syndicate
WHAT SHOW?
THE BORING ONE WHERE WHITE PEOPLE TALK ABOUT WHAT'S HAPPENING IN THE WORLD. WHAT IS IT?
3/15
www.ucomics.com
THE NEWS?
YEAH! DID THAT GET CANCELED YET?

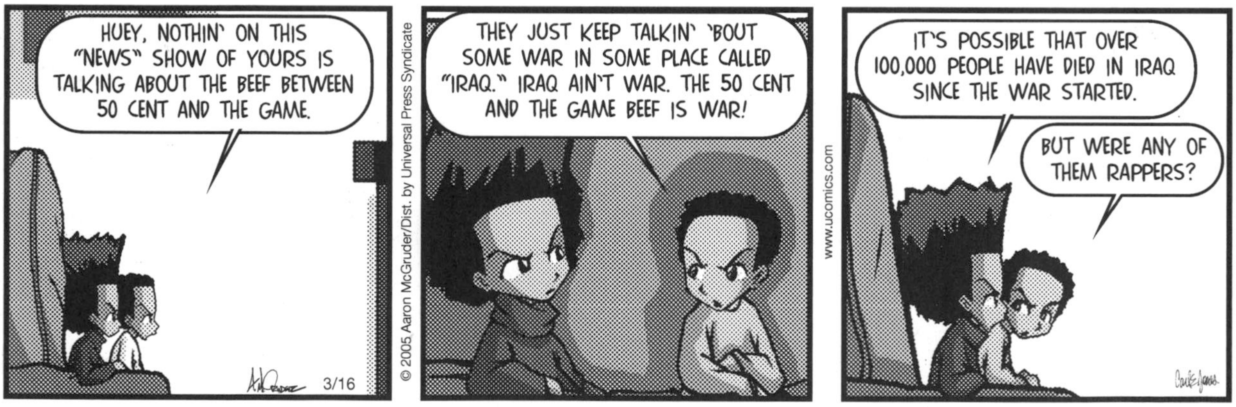
HUEY, NOTHIN' ON THIS "NEWS" SHOW OF YOURS IS TALKING ABOUT THE BEEF BETWEEN 50 CENT AND THE GAME.
3/16
© 2005 Aaron McGruder/Dist. by Universal Press Syndicate
THEY JUST KEEP TALKIN' 'BOUT SOME WAR IN SOME PLACE CALLED "IRAQ." IRAQ AIN'T WAR. THE 50 CENT AND THE GAME BEEF IS WAR!
www.ucomics.com
IT'S POSSIBLE THAT OVER 100,000 PEOPLE HAVE DIED IN IRAQ SINCE THE WAR STARTED.
BUT WERE ANY OF THEM RAPPERS?

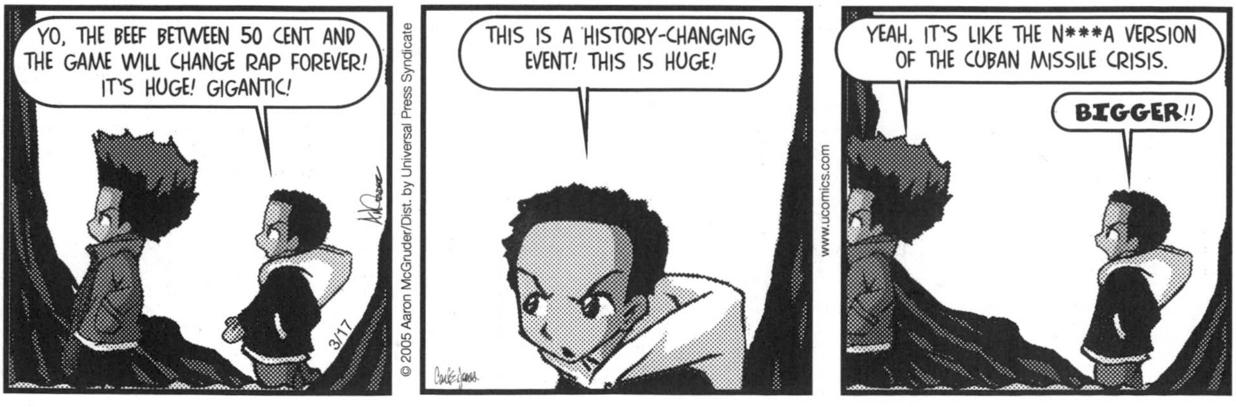
YO, THE BEEF BETWEEN 50 CENT AND THE GAME WILL CHANGE RAP FOREVER! IT'S HUGE! GIGANTIC!
3/17
© 2005 Aaron McGruder/Dist. by Universal Press Syndicate
THIS IS A HISTORY-CHANGING EVENT! THIS IS HUGE!
www.ucomics.com
YEAH, IT'S LIKE THE N***A VERSION OF THE CUBAN MISSILE CRISIS.
BIGGER!!

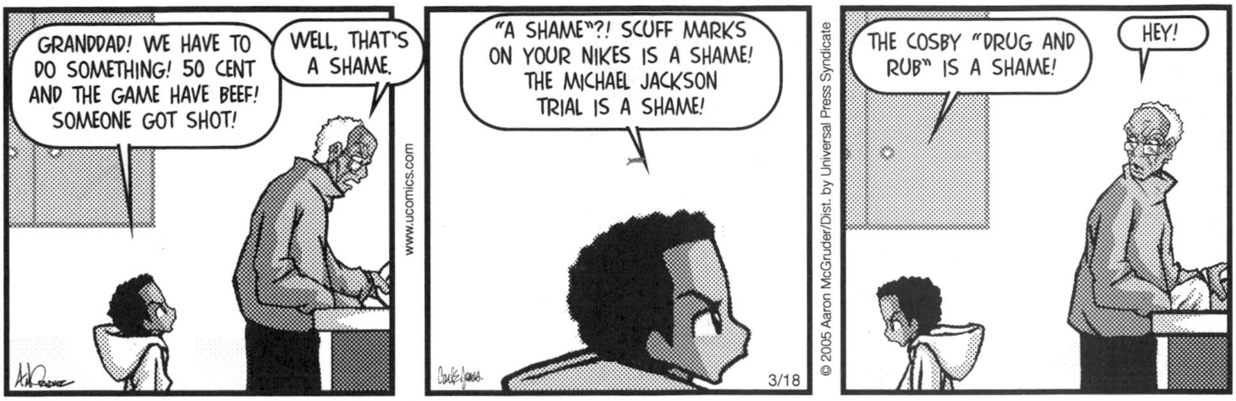
GRANDDAD! WE HAVE TO DO SOMETHING! 50 CENT AND THE GAME HAVE BEEF! SOMEONE GOT SHOT!
WELL, THAT'S A SHAME.
www.ucomics.com
"A SHAME"?! SCUFF MARKS ON YOUR NIKES IS A SHAME! THE MICHAEL JACKSON TRIAL IS A SHAME!
3/18
© 2005 Aaron McGruder/Dist. by Universal Press Syndicate
THE COSBY "DRUG AND RUB" IS A SHAME!
HEY!

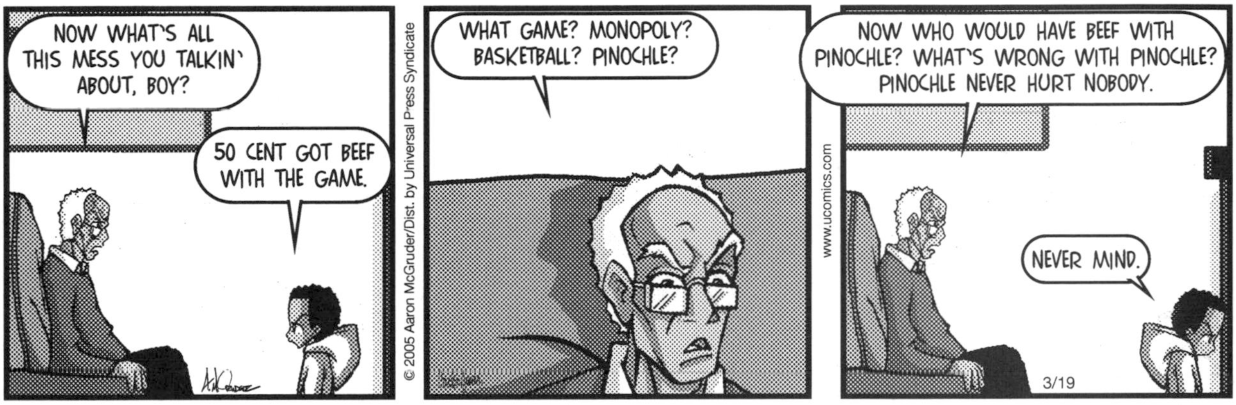
NOW WHAT'S ALL THIS MESS YOU TALKIN' ABOUT, BOY?
50 CENT GOT BEEF WITH THE GAME.
© 2005 Aaron McGruder/Dist. by Universal Press Syndicate
WHAT GAME? MONOPOLY? BASKETBALL? PINOCHLE?
NOW WHO WOULD HAVE BEEF WITH PINOCHLE? WHAT'S WRONG WITH PINOCHLE? PINOCHLE NEVER HURT NOBODY.
www.ucomics.com
NEVER MIND.
3/19

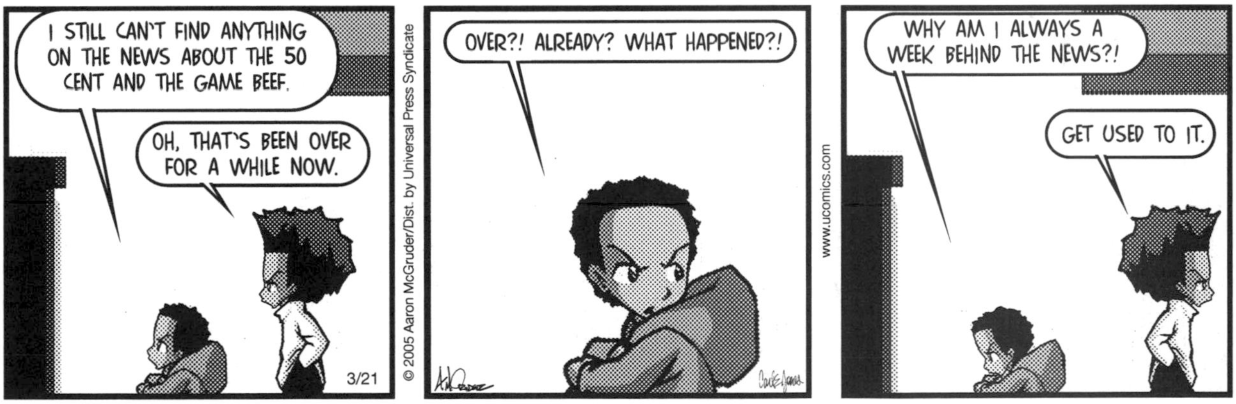
I STILL CAN'T FIND ANYTHING ON THE NEWS ABOUT THE 50 CENT AND THE GAME BEEF.
OH, THAT'S BEEN OVER FOR A WHILE NOW.
3/21
© 2005 Aaron McGruder/Dist. by Universal Press Syndicate
OVER?! ALREADY? WHAT HAPPENED?!
www.ucomics.com
WHY AM I ALWAYS A WEEK BEHIND THE NEWS?!
GET USED TO IT.

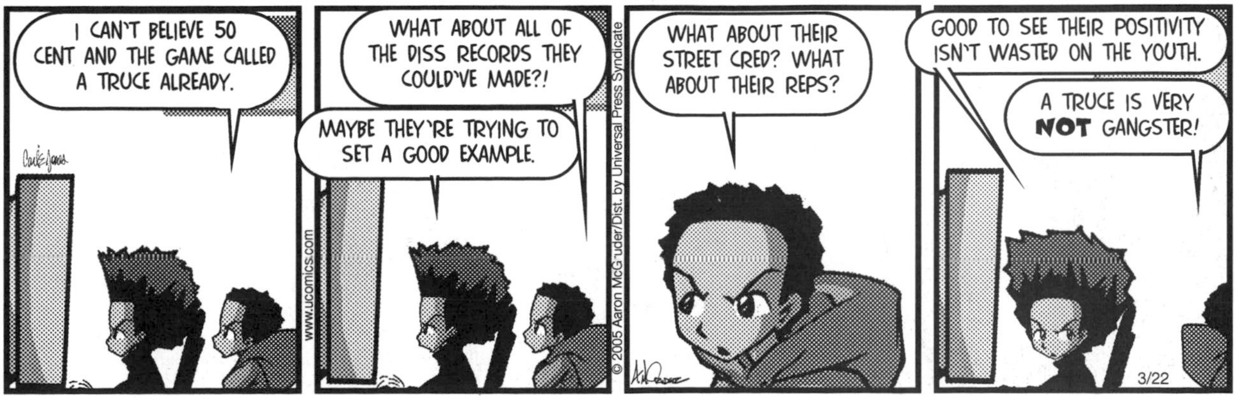
I CAN'T BELIEVE 50 CENT AND THE GAME CALLED A TRUCE ALREADY.
www.ucomics.com
WHAT ABOUT ALL OF THE DISS RECORDS THEY COULD'VE MADE?!
MAYBE THEY'RE TRYING TO SET A GOOD EXAMPLE.
© 2005 Aaron McGruder/Dist. by Universal Press Syndicate
WHAT ABOUT THEIR STREET CRED? WHAT ABOUT THEIR REPS?
GOOD TO SEE THEIR POSITIVITY ISN'T WASTED ON THE YOUTH.
A TRUCE IS VERY NOT GANGSTER!
3/22

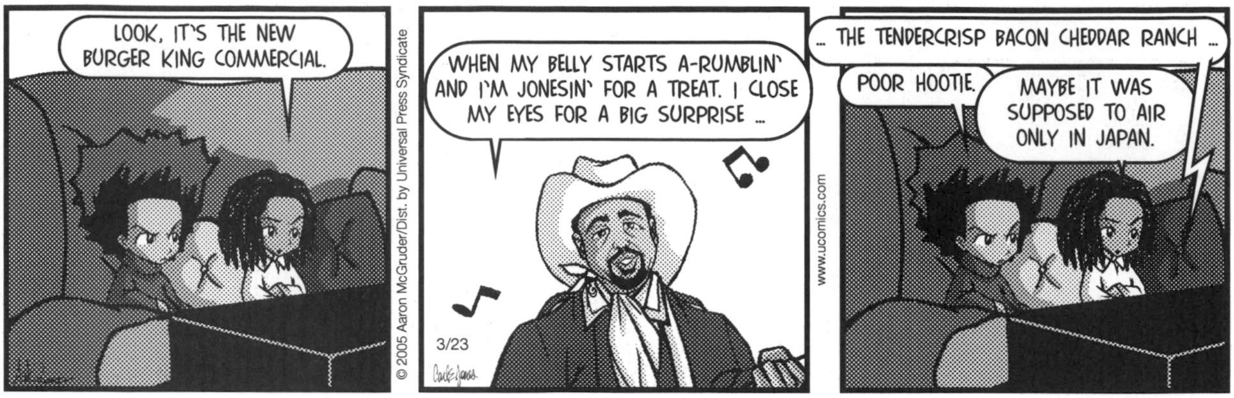
LOOK, IT'S THE NEW BURGER KING COMMERCIAL.
WHEN MY BELLY STARTS A-RUMBLIN' AND I'M JONESIN' FOR A TREAT. I CLOSE MY EYES FOR A BIG SURPRISE ...
© 2005 Aaron McGruder/Dist. by Universal Press Syndicate
3/23
... THE TENDERCRISP BACON CHEDDAR RANCH ...
POOR HOOTIE.
MAYBE IT WAS SUPPOSED TO AIR ONLY IN JAPAN.
www.ucomics.com

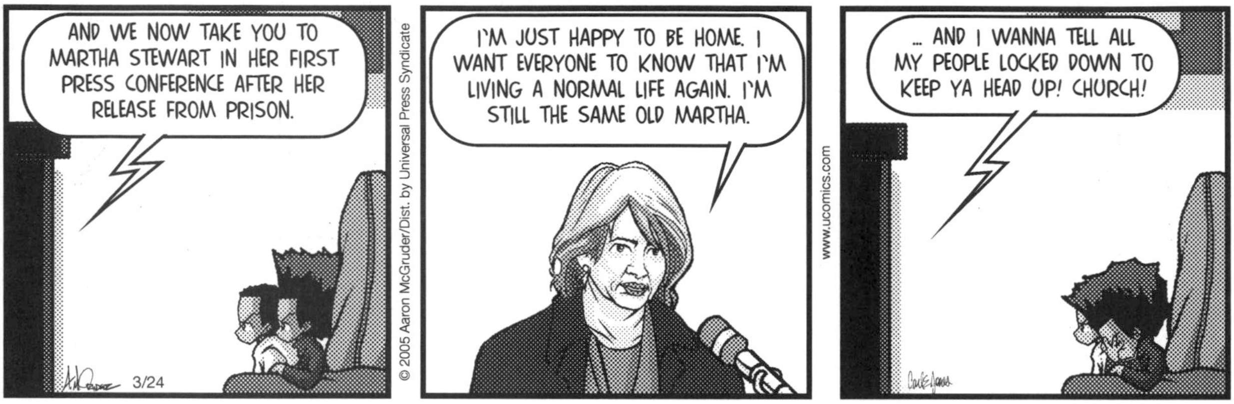
AND WE NOW TAKE YOU TO MARTHA STEWART IN HER FIRST PRESS CONFERENCE AFTER HER RELEASE FROM PRISON.
3/24
© 2005 Aaron McGruder/Dist. by Universal Press Syndicate
I'M JUST HAPPY TO BE HOME. I WANT EVERYONE TO KNOW THAT I'M LIVING A NORMAL LIFE AGAIN. I'M STILL THE SAME OLD MARTHA.
www.ucomics.com
... AND I WANNA TELL ALL MY PEOPLE LOCKED DOWN TO KEEP YA HEAD UP! CHURCH!

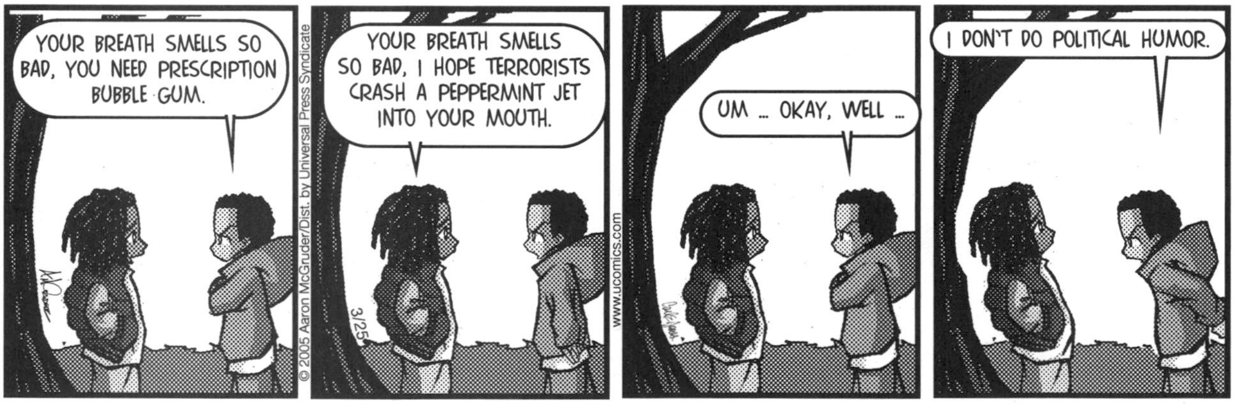
YOUR BREATH SMELLS SO BAD, YOU NEED PRESCRIPTION BUBBLE GUM.
© 2005 Aaron McGruder/Dist. by Universal Press Syndicate
YOUR BREATH SMELLS SO BAD, I HOPE TERRORISTS CRASH A PEPPERMINT JET INTO YOUR MOUTH.
3/25
www.ucomics.com
UM ... OKAY, WELL ...
I DON'T DO POLITICAL HUMOR.

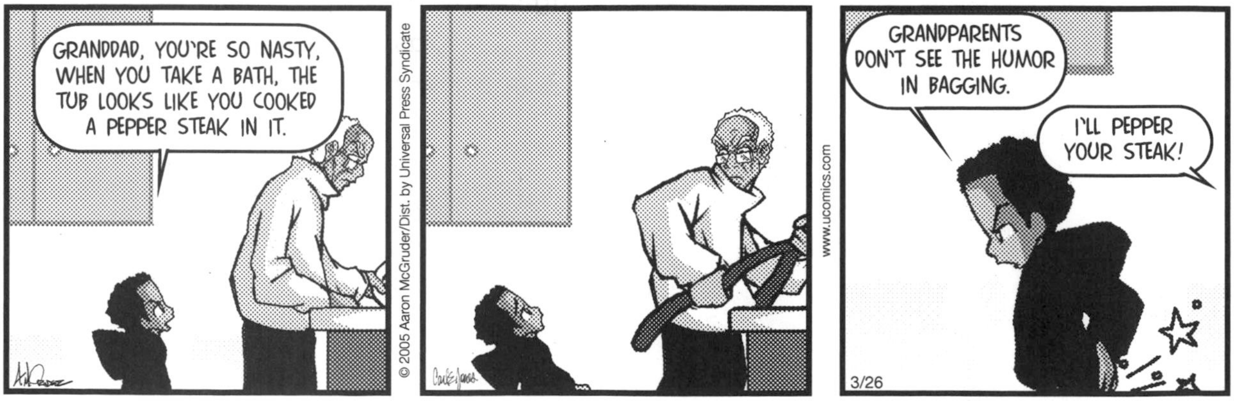
GRANDDAD, YOU'RE SO NASTY, WHEN YOU TAKE A BATH, THE TUB LOOKS LIKE YOU COOKED A PEPPER STEAK IN IT.
© 2005 Aaron McGruder/Dist. by Universal Press Syndicate
www.ucomics.com
GRANDPARENTS DON'T SEE THE HUMOR IN BAGGING.
I'LL PEPPER YOUR STEAK!
3/26

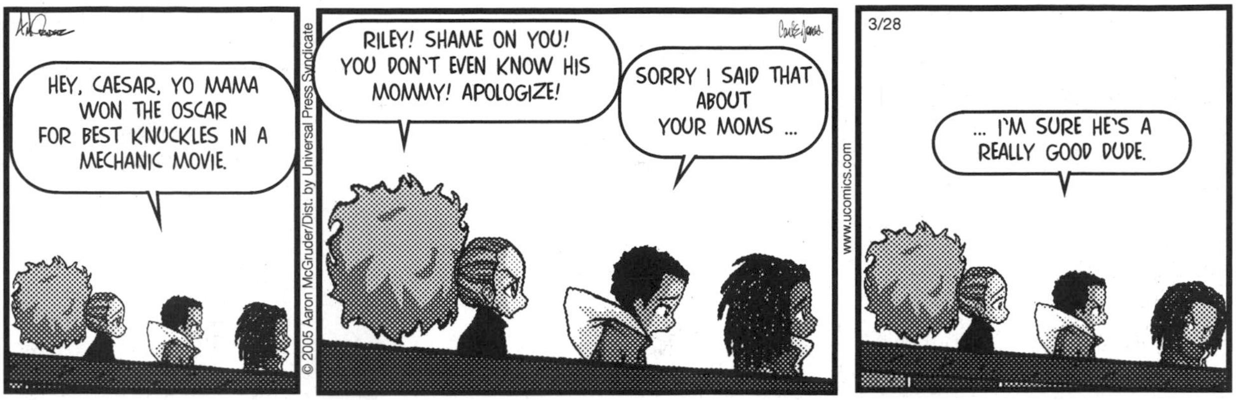
HEY, CAESAR, YO MAMA WON THE OSCAR FOR BEST KNUCKLES IN A MECHANIC MOVIE.
© 2005 Aaron McGruder/Dist. by Universal Press Syndicate
RILEY! SHAME ON YOU! YOU DON'T EVEN KNOW HIS MOMMY! APOLOGIZE!
SORRY I SAID THAT ABOUT YOUR MOMS ...
www.ucomics.com
3/28
... I'M SURE HE'S A REALLY GOOD DUDE.

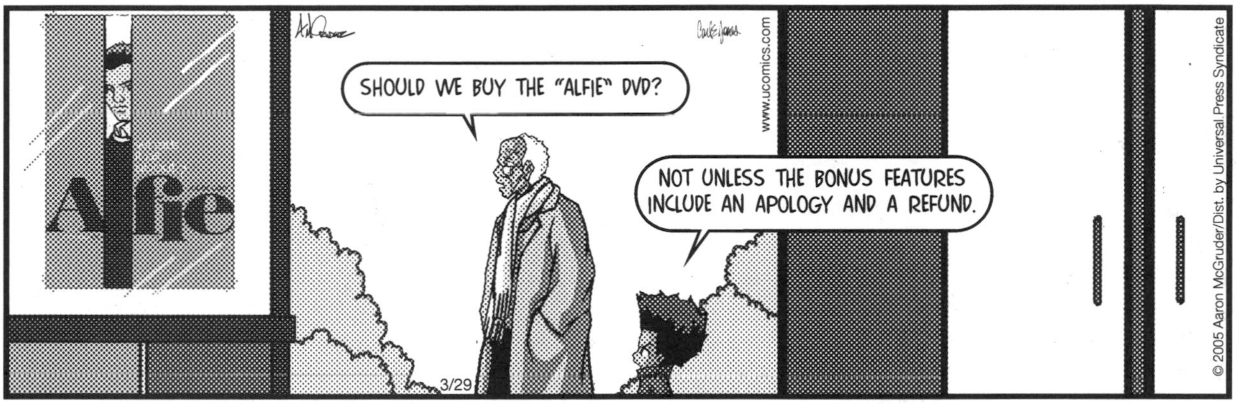
Alfie
SHOULD WE BUY THE "ALFIE" DVD?
www.ucomics.com
NOT UNLESS THE BONUS FEATURES INCLUDE AN APOLOGY AND A REFUND.
3/29
© 2005 Aaron McGruder/Dist. by Universal Press Syndicate

What did you like to read and were there any favorite cartoons you liked to watch?

I was always into Peanuts stuff, Speed Racer, Transformers. I was always a huge *Star Wars* fan. I even played Dungeons & Dragons. I was into everything nerdy. Whatever nerd stuff was out there, I was in it.

—Aaron McGruder, *The Spokesman* (Morgan State University)

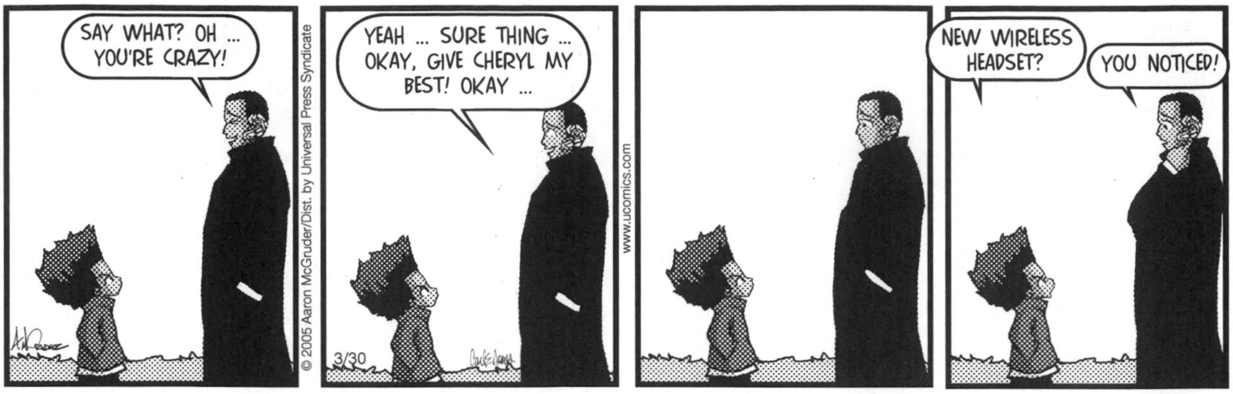
SAY WHAT? OH ... YOU'RE CRAZY!
© 2005 Aaron McGruder/Dist. by Universal Press Syndicate
3/30
YEAH ... SURE THING ... OKAY, GIVE CHERYL MY BEST! OKAY ...
www.ucomics.com
NEW WIRELESS HEADSET?
YOU NOTICED!

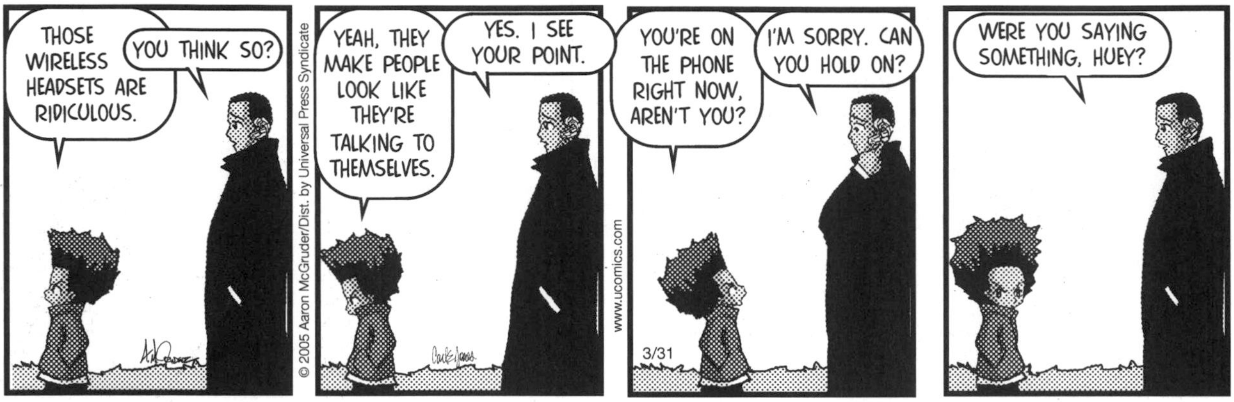
THOSE WIRELESS HEADSETS ARE RIDICULOUS.
YOU THINK SO?
© 2005 Aaron McGruder/Dist. by Universal Press Syndicate
YEAH, THEY MAKE PEOPLE LOOK LIKE THEY'RE TALKING TO THEMSELVES.
YES. I SEE YOUR POINT.
www.ucomics.com
YOU'RE ON THE PHONE RIGHT NOW, AREN'T YOU?
I'M SORRY. CAN YOU HOLD ON?
3/31
WERE YOU SAYING SOMETHING, HUEY?

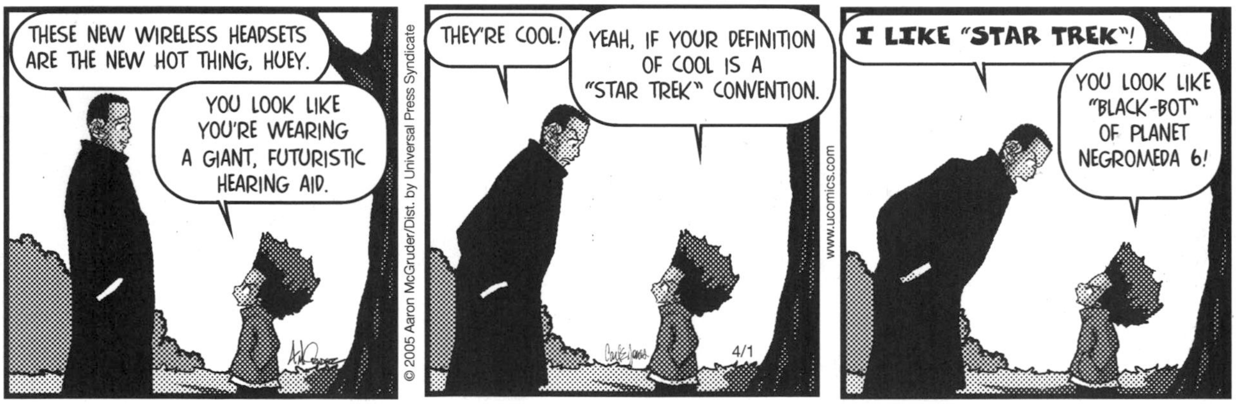
THESE NEW WIRELESS HEADSETS ARE THE NEW HOT THING, HUEY.
YOU LOOK LIKE YOU'RE WEARING A GIANT, FUTURISTIC HEARING AID.
© 2005 Aaron McGruder/Dist. by Universal Press Syndicate
THEY'RE COOL!
YEAH, IF YOUR DEFINITION OF COOL IS A "STAR TREK" CONVENTION.
4/1
www.ucomics.com
I LIKE "STAR TREK"!
YOU LOOK LIKE "BLACK-BOT" OF PLANET NEGROMEDA 6!

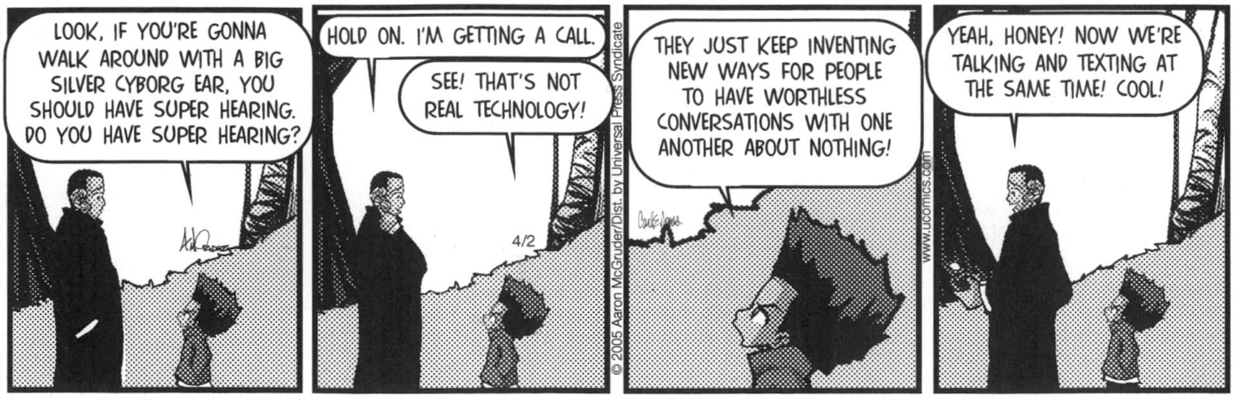
LOOK, IF YOU'RE GONNA WALK AROUND WITH A BIG SILVER CYBORG EAR, YOU SHOULD HAVE SUPER HEARING. DO YOU HAVE SUPER HEARING?
HOLD ON. I'M GETTING A CALL.
SEE! THAT'S NOT REAL TECHNOLOGY!
4/2
© 2005 Aaron McGruder/Dist. by Universal Press Syndicate
THEY JUST KEEP INVENTING NEW WAYS FOR PEOPLE TO HAVE WORTHLESS CONVERSATIONS WITH ONE ANOTHER ABOUT NOTHING!
www.ucomics.com
YEAH, HONEY! NOW WE'RE TALKING AND TEXTING AT THE SAME TIME! COOL!

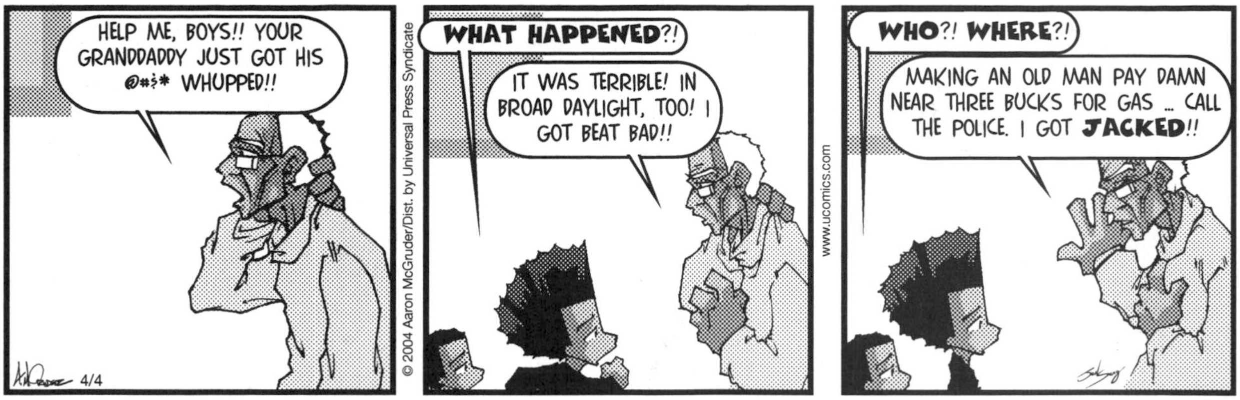
HELP ME, BOYS!! YOUR GRANDDADDY JUST GOT HIS @#$* WHUPPED!!
4/4
WHAT HAPPENED?!
IT WAS TERRIBLE! IN BROAD DAYLIGHT, TOO! I GOT BEAT BAD!!
WHO?! WHERE?!
MAKING AN OLD MAN PAY DAMN NEAR THREE BUCKS FOR GAS ... CALL THE POLICE. I GOT **JACKED**!!
© 2004 Aaron McGruder/Dist. by Universal Press Syndicate
www.ucomics.com

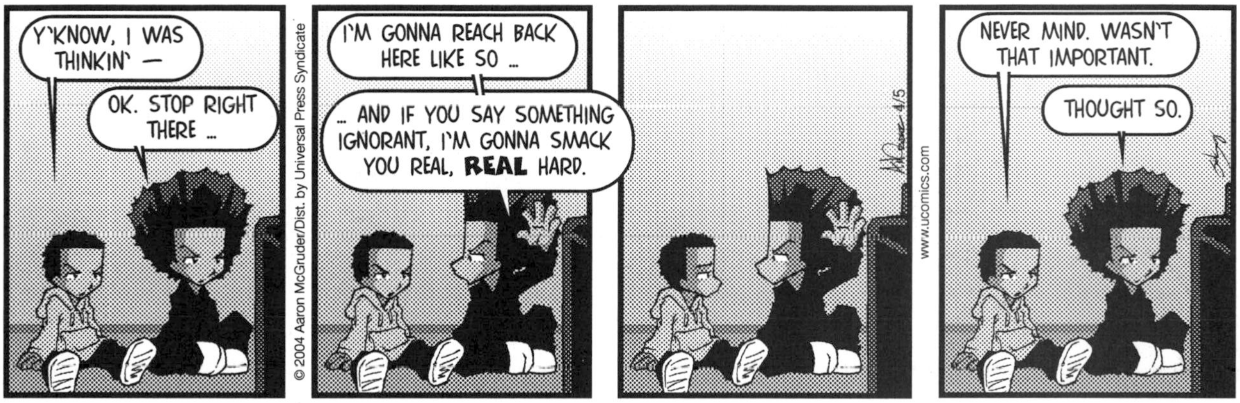
Y'KNOW, I WAS THINKIN' —
OK. STOP RIGHT THERE ...
I'M GONNA REACH BACK HERE LIKE SO ...
... AND IF YOU SAY SOMETHING IGNORANT, I'M GONNA SMACK YOU REAL, **REAL** HARD.
4/5
NEVER MIND. WASN'T THAT IMPORTANT.
THOUGHT SO.
© 2004 Aaron McGruder/Dist. by Universal Press Syndicate
www.ucomics.com

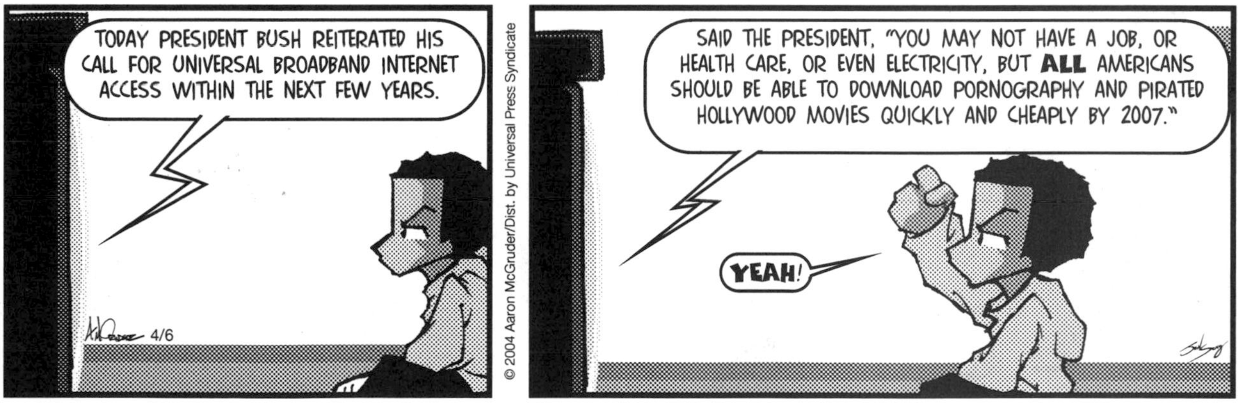
TODAY PRESIDENT BUSH REITERATED HIS CALL FOR UNIVERSAL BROADBAND INTERNET ACCESS WITHIN THE NEXT FEW YEARS.
4/6
SAID THE PRESIDENT, "YOU MAY NOT HAVE A JOB, OR HEALTH CARE, OR EVEN ELECTRICITY, BUT **ALL** AMERICANS SHOULD BE ABLE TO DOWNLOAD PORNOGRAPHY AND PIRATED HOLLYWOOD MOVIES QUICKLY AND CHEAPLY BY 2007."
YEAH!
© 2004 Aaron McGruder/Dist. by Universal Press Syndicate

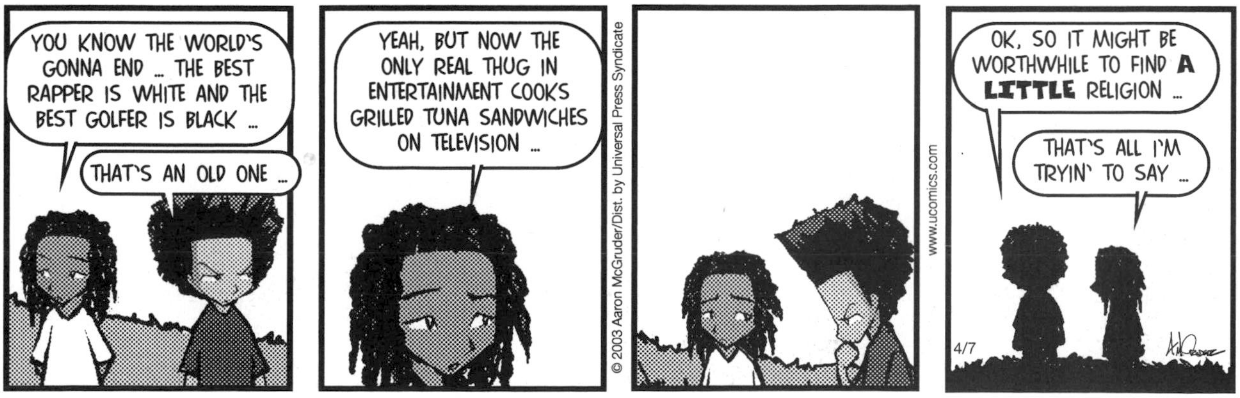
YOU KNOW THE WORLD'S GONNA END ... THE BEST RAPPER IS WHITE AND THE BEST GOLFER IS BLACK ...
THAT'S AN OLD ONE ...
YEAH, BUT NOW THE ONLY REAL THUG IN ENTERTAINMENT COOKS GRILLED TUNA SANDWICHES ON TELEVISION ...
OK, SO IT MIGHT BE WORTHWHILE TO FIND **A LITTLE** RELIGION ...
THAT'S ALL I'M TRYIN' TO SAY ...
4/7
© 2003 Aaron McGruder/Dist. by Universal Press Syndicate
www.ucomics.com

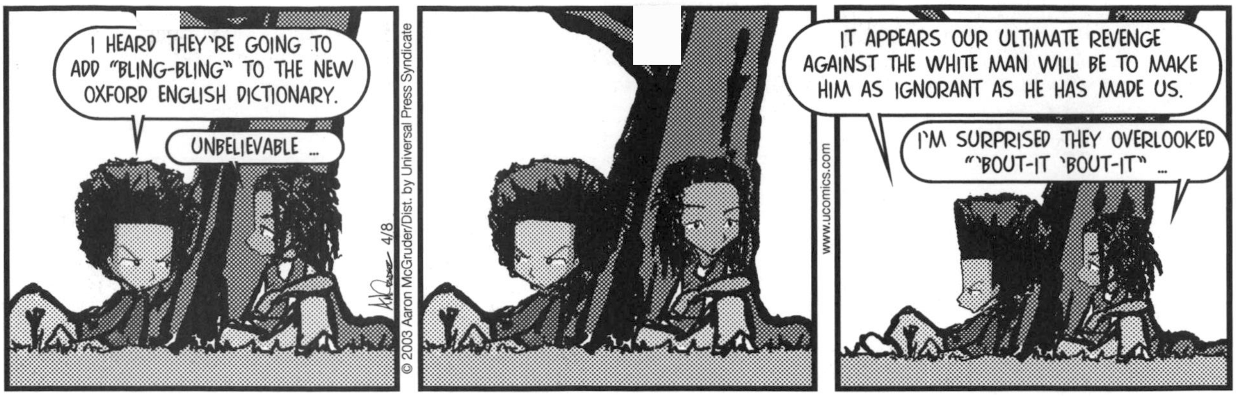
I HEARD THEY'RE GOING TO ADD "BLING-BLING" TO THE NEW OXFORD ENGLISH DICTIONARY.
UNBELIEVABLE ...
4/8
© 2003 Aaron McGruder/Dist. by Universal Press Syndicate
www.ucomics.com
IT APPEARS OUR ULTIMATE REVENGE AGAINST THE WHITE MAN WILL BE TO MAKE HIM AS IGNORANT AS HE HAS MADE US.
I'M SURPRISED THEY OVERLOOKED "'BOUT-IT 'BOUT-IT" ...

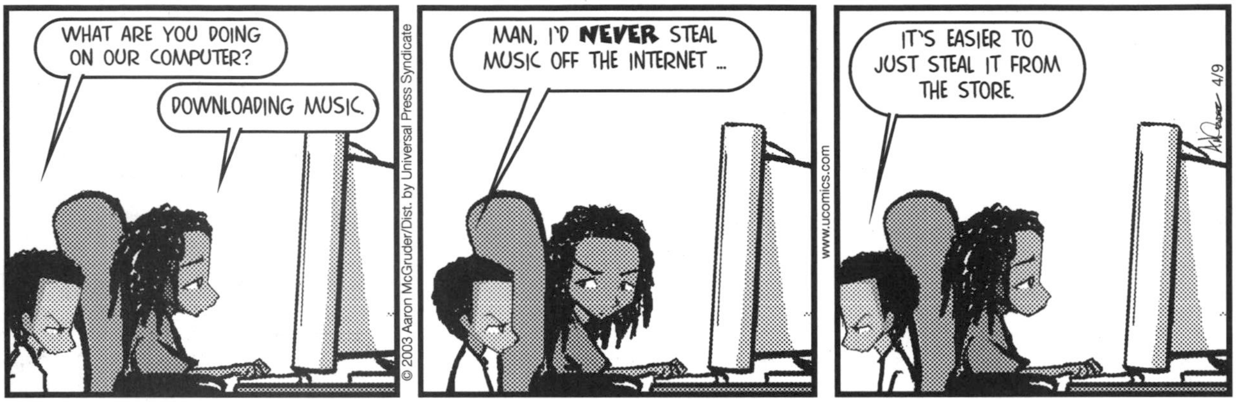
WHAT ARE YOU DOING ON OUR COMPUTER?
DOWNLOADING MUSIC.
© 2003 Aaron McGruder/Dist. by Universal Press Syndicate
MAN, I'D NEVER STEAL MUSIC OFF THE INTERNET ...
www.ucomics.com
IT'S EASIER TO JUST STEAL IT FROM THE STORE.
4/9

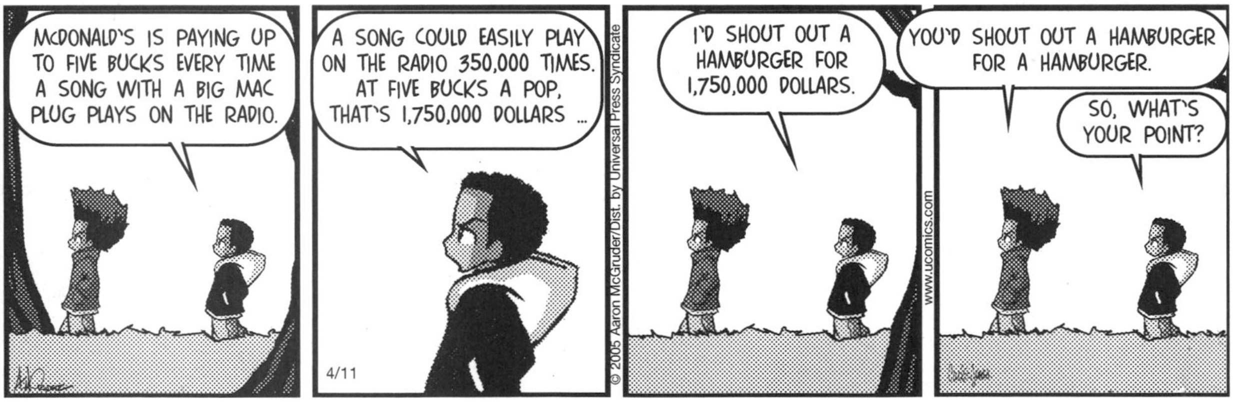
McDONALD'S IS PAYING UP TO FIVE BUCKS EVERY TIME A SONG WITH A BIG MAC PLUG PLAYS ON THE RADIO.
A SONG COULD EASILY PLAY ON THE RADIO 350,000 TIMES. AT FIVE BUCKS A POP, THAT'S 1,750,000 DOLLARS ...
4/11
© 2005 Aaron McGruder/Dist. by Universal Press Syndicate
I'D SHOUT OUT A HAMBURGER FOR 1,750,000 DOLLARS.
www.ucomics.com
YOU'D SHOUT OUT A HAMBURGER FOR A HAMBURGER.
SO, WHAT'S YOUR POINT?

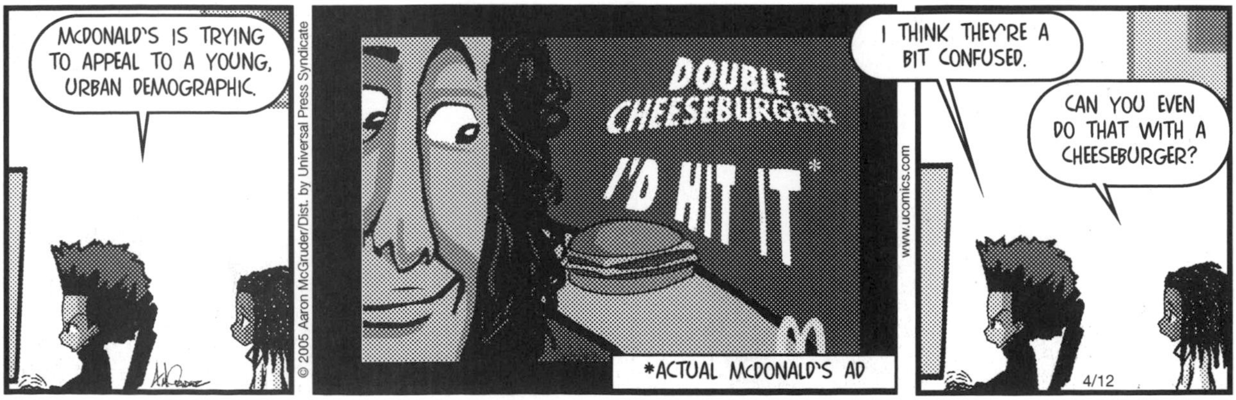
McDONALD'S IS TRYING TO APPEAL TO A YOUNG, URBAN DEMOGRAPHIC.
© 2005 Aaron McGruder/Dist. by Universal Press Syndicate
DOUBLE CHEESEBURGER?
I'D HIT IT*
*ACTUAL McDONALD'S AD
www.ucomics.com
I THINK THEY'RE A BIT CONFUSED.
CAN YOU EVEN DO THAT WITH A CHEESEBURGER?
4/12

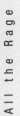

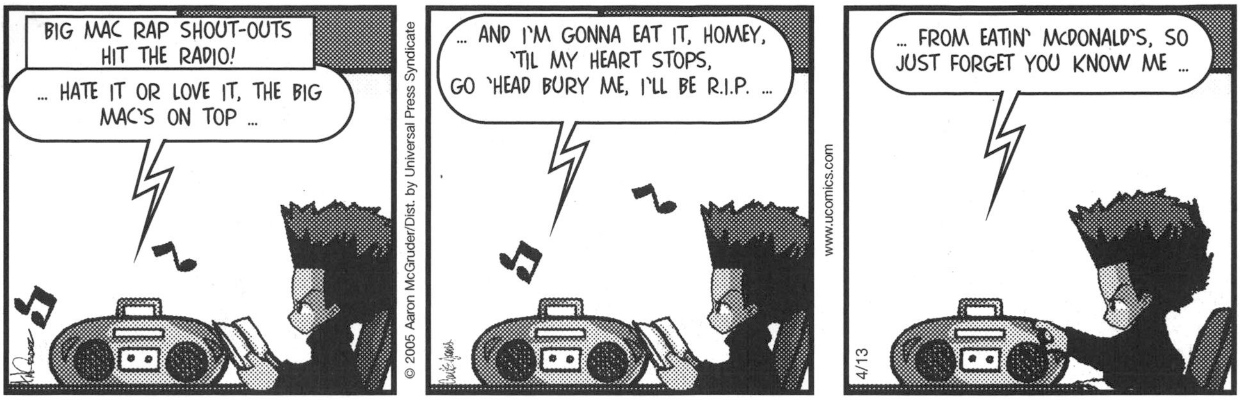
BIG MAC RAP SHOUT-OUTS HIT THE RADIO!
... HATE IT OR LOVE IT, THE BIG MAC'S ON TOP ...
© 2005 Aaron McGruder/Dist. by Universal Press Syndicate
... AND I'M GONNA EAT IT, HOMEY, 'TIL MY HEART STOPS, GO 'HEAD BURY ME, I'LL BE R.I.P. ...
www.ucomics.com
... FROM EATIN' McDONALD'S, SO JUST FORGET YOU KNOW ME ...
4/13

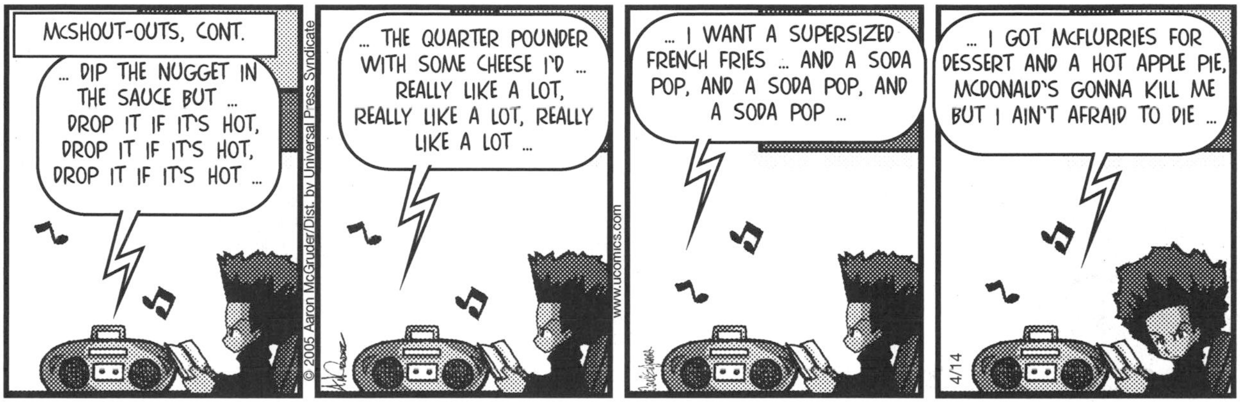
McSHOUT-OUTS, CONT.
... DIP THE NUGGET IN THE SAUCE BUT ... DROP IT IF IT'S HOT, DROP IT IF IT'S HOT, DROP IT IF IT'S HOT ...
© 2005 Aaron McGruder/Dist. by Universal Press Syndicate
... THE QUARTER POUNDER WITH SOME CHEESE I'D ... REALLY LIKE A LOT, REALLY LIKE A LOT, REALLY LIKE A LOT ...
www.ucomics.com
... I WANT A SUPERSIZED FRENCH FRIES ... AND A SODA POP, AND A SODA POP, AND A SODA POP ...
... I GOT McFLURRIES FOR DESSERT AND A HOT APPLE PIE, McDONALD'S GONNA KILL ME BUT I AIN'T AFRAID TO DIE ...
4/14

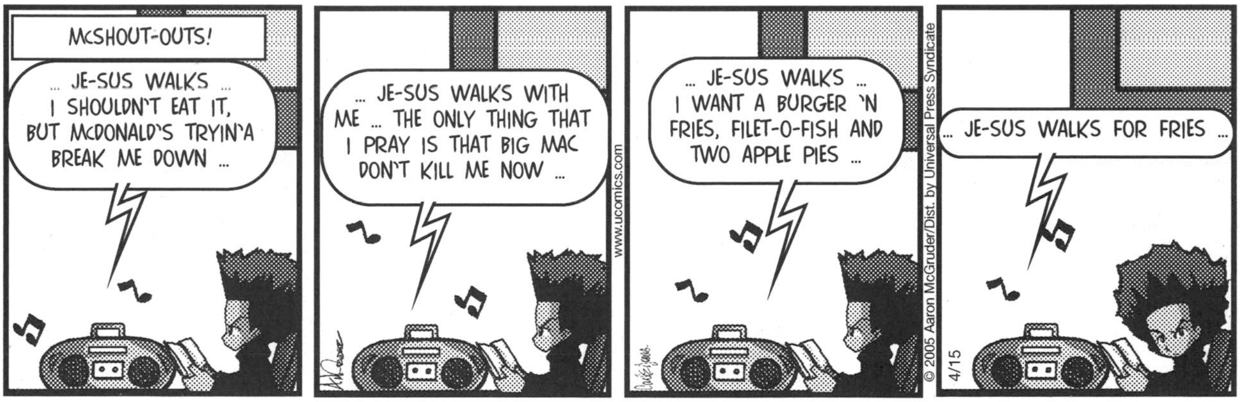
McSHOUT-OUTS!
... JE-SUS WALKS ... I SHOULDN'T EAT IT, BUT McDONALD'S TRYIN'A BREAK ME DOWN ...
... JE-SUS WALKS WITH ME ... THE ONLY THING THAT I PRAY IS THAT BIG MAC DON'T KILL ME NOW ...
www.ucomics.com
... JE-SUS WALKS ... I WANT A BURGER 'N FRIES, FILET-O-FISH AND TWO APPLE PIES ...
© 2005 Aaron McGruder/Dist. by Universal Press Syndicate
... JE-SUS WALKS FOR FRIES ...
4/15

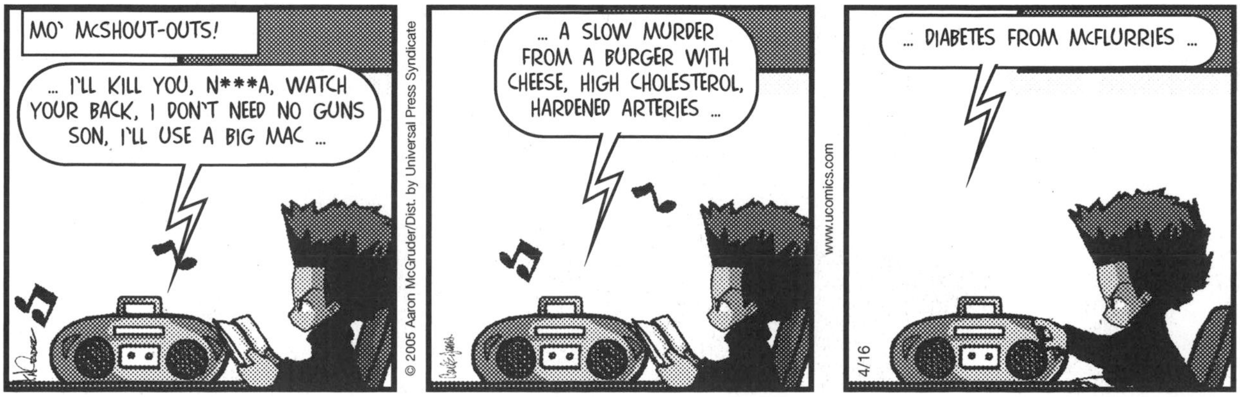
MO' McSHOUT-OUTS!
... I'LL KILL YOU, N***A, WATCH YOUR BACK, I DON'T NEED NO GUNS SON, I'LL USE A BIG MAC ...
© 2005 Aaron McGruder/Dist. by Universal Press Syndicate
... A SLOW MURDER FROM A BURGER WITH CHEESE, HIGH CHOLESTEROL, HARDENED ARTERIES ...
www.ucomics.com
... DIABETES FROM McFLURRIES ...
4/16

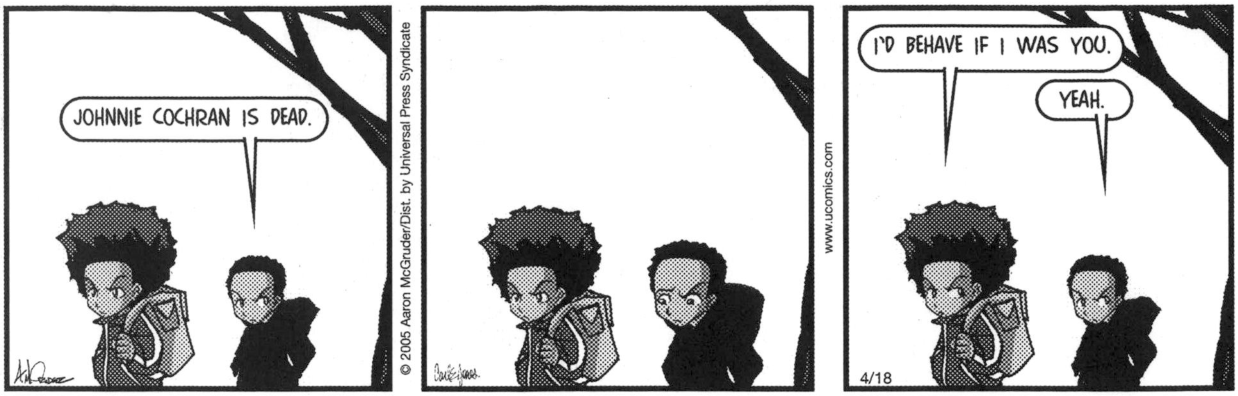
JOHNNIE COCHRAN IS DEAD.
© 2005 Aaron McGruder/Dist. by Universal Press Syndicate
I'D BEHAVE IF I WAS YOU.
YEAH.
www.ucomics.com
4/18

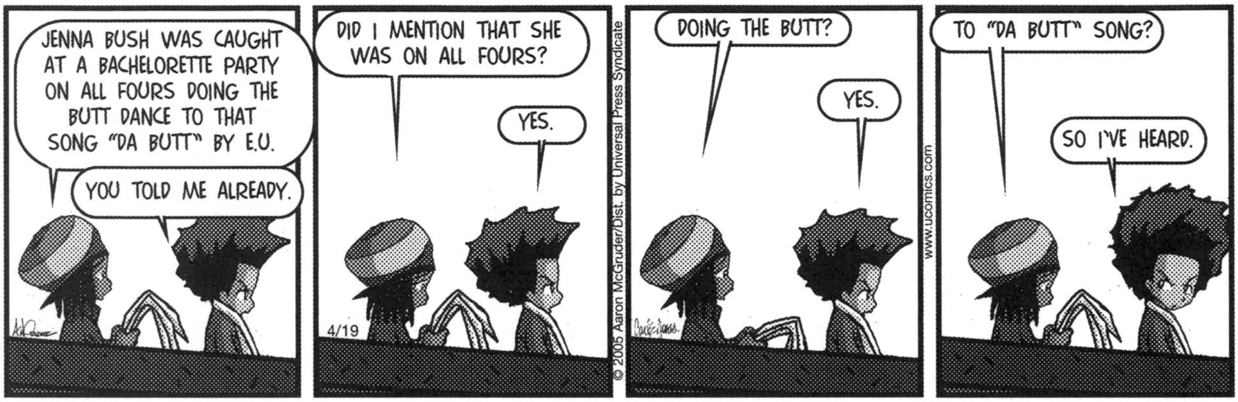
JENNA BUSH WAS CAUGHT AT A BACHELORETTE PARTY ON ALL FOURS DOING THE BUTT DANCE TO THAT SONG "DA BUTT" BY E.U.
YOU TOLD ME ALREADY.
DID I MENTION THAT SHE WAS ON ALL FOURS?
YES.
4/19
© 2005 Aaron McGruder/Dist. by Universal Press Syndicate
DOING THE BUTT?
YES.
www.ucomics.com
TO "DA BUTT" SONG?
SO I'VE HEARD.

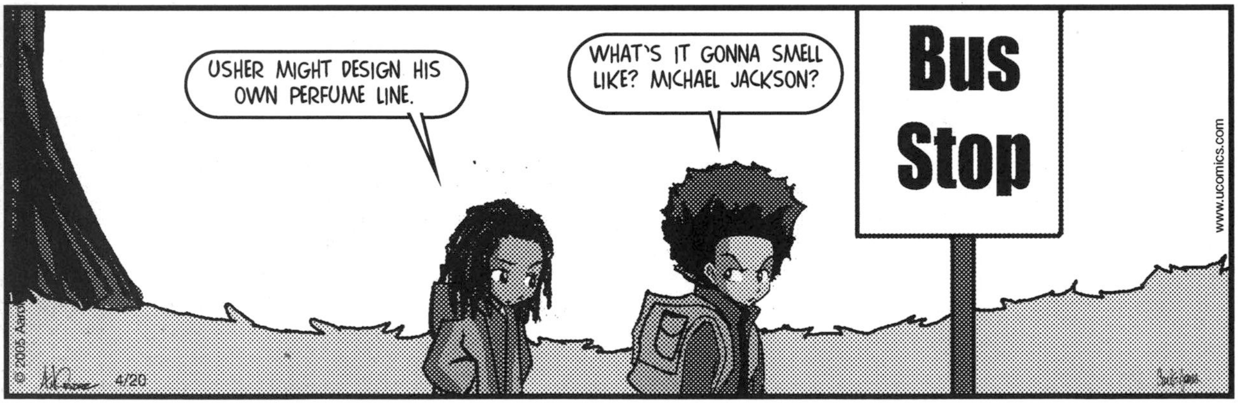
USHER MIGHT DESIGN HIS OWN PERFUME LINE.
WHAT'S IT GONNA SMELL LIKE? MICHAEL JACKSON?
Bus Stop
www.ucomics.com
4/20

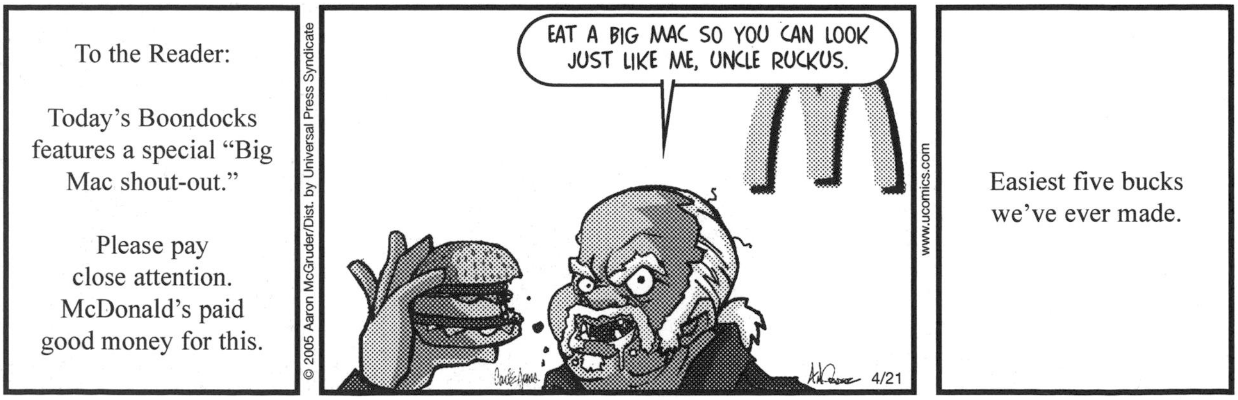
To the Reader:
Today's Boondocks features a special "Big Mac shout-out."
Please pay close attention. McDonald's paid good money for this.
© 2005 Aaron McGruder/Dist. by Universal Press Syndicate
EAT A BIG MAC SO YOU CAN LOOK JUST LIKE ME, UNCLE RUCKUS.
www.ucomics.com
4/21
Easiest five bucks we've ever made.

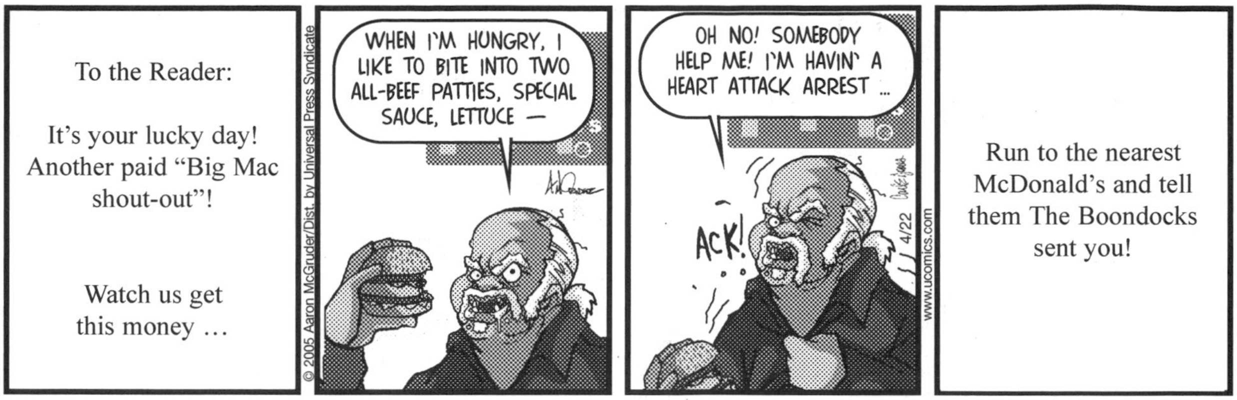
To the Reader:
It's your lucky day! Another paid "Big Mac shout-out"!
Watch us get this money …
© 2005 Aaron McGruder/Dist. by Universal Press Syndicate
WHEN I'M HUNGRY, I LIKE TO BITE INTO TWO ALL-BEEF PATTIES, SPECIAL SAUCE, LETTUCE —
OH NO! SOMEBODY HELP ME! I'M HAVIN' A HEART ATTACK ARREST …
ACK!
4/22
www.ucomics.com
Run to the nearest McDonald's and tell them The Boondocks sent you!

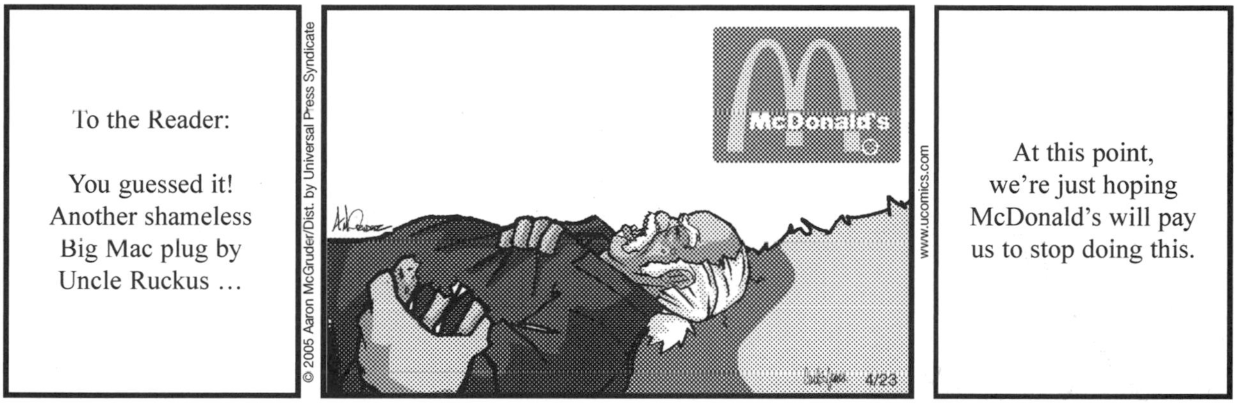
To the Reader:
You guessed it! Another shameless Big Mac plug by Uncle Ruckus …
© 2005 Aaron McGruder/Dist. by Universal Press Syndicate
McDonald's
4/23
www.ucomics.com
At this point, we're just hoping McDonald's will pay us to stop doing this.

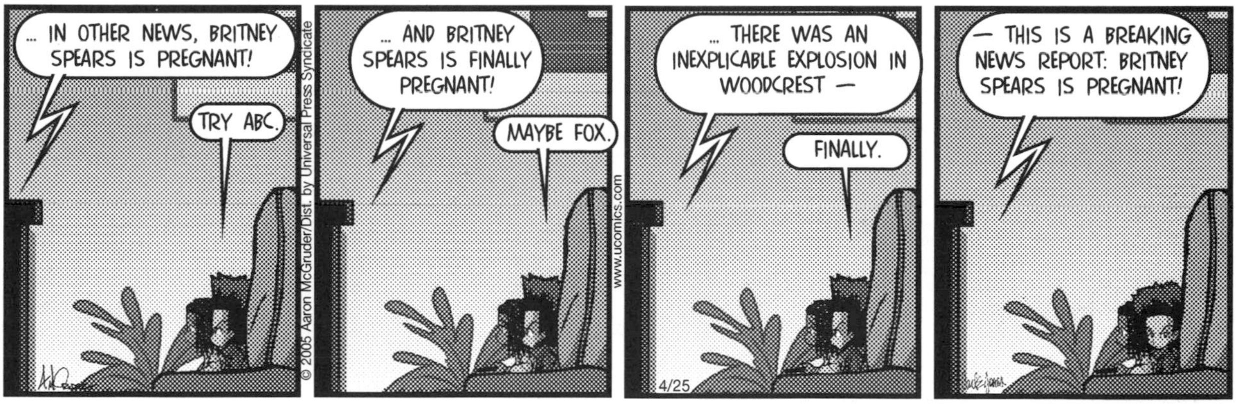
… IN OTHER NEWS, BRITNEY SPEARS IS PREGNANT!
TRY ABC.
© 2005 Aaron McGruder/Dist. by Universal Press Syndicate
… AND BRITNEY SPEARS IS FINALLY PREGNANT!
MAYBE FOX.
www.ucomics.com
… THERE WAS AN INEXPLICABLE EXPLOSION IN WOODCREST —
FINALLY.
4/25
— THIS IS A BREAKING NEWS REPORT: BRITNEY SPEARS IS PREGNANT!

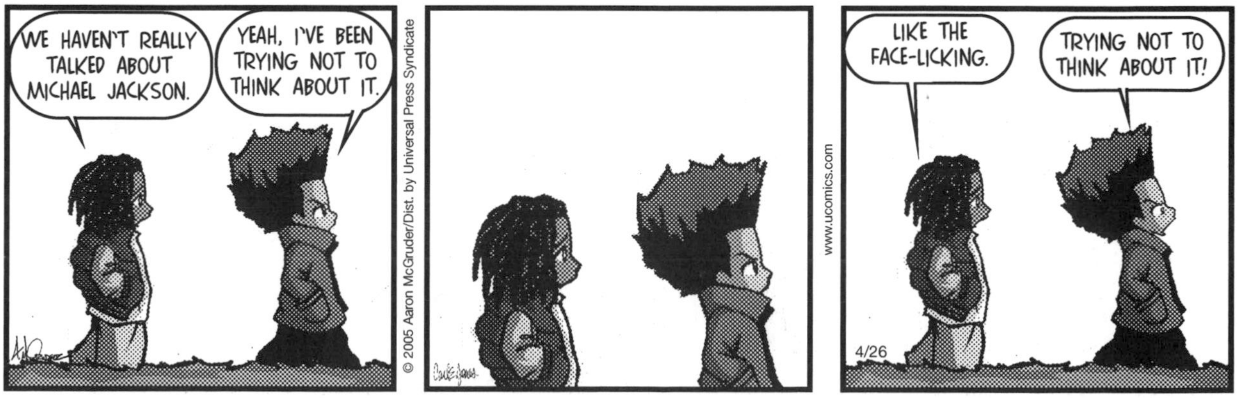
WE HAVEN'T REALLY TALKED ABOUT MICHAEL JACKSON.
YEAH, I'VE BEEN TRYING NOT TO THINK ABOUT IT.
© 2005 Aaron McGruder/Dist. by Universal Press Syndicate
www.ucomics.com
LIKE THE FACE-LICKING.
TRYING NOT TO THINK ABOUT IT!
4/26

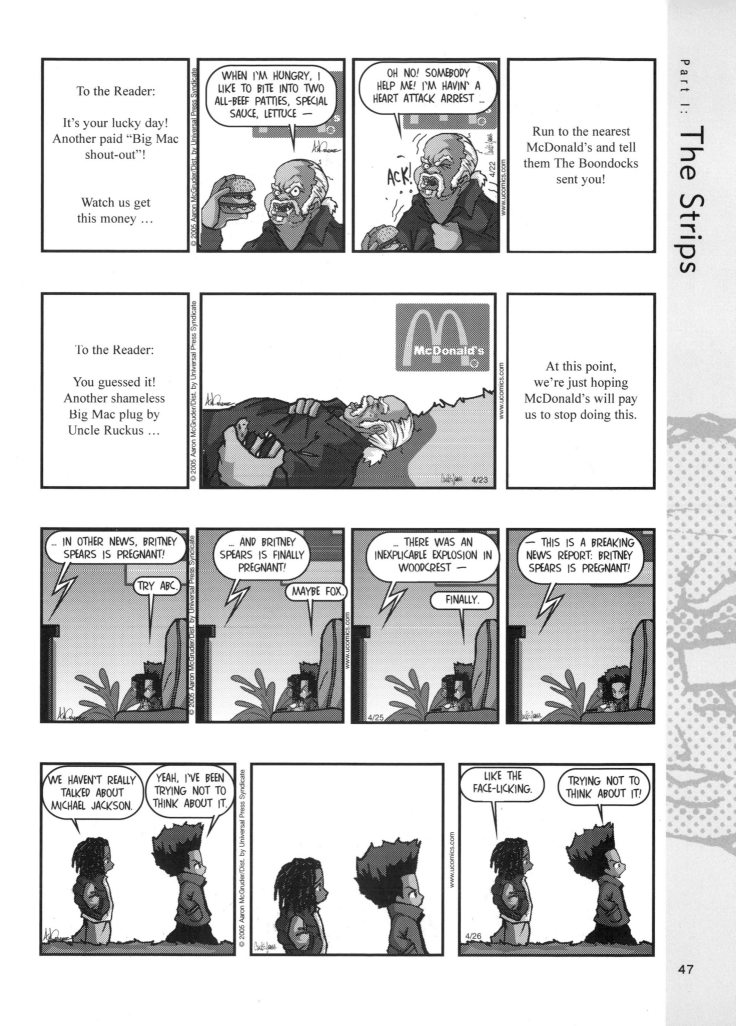

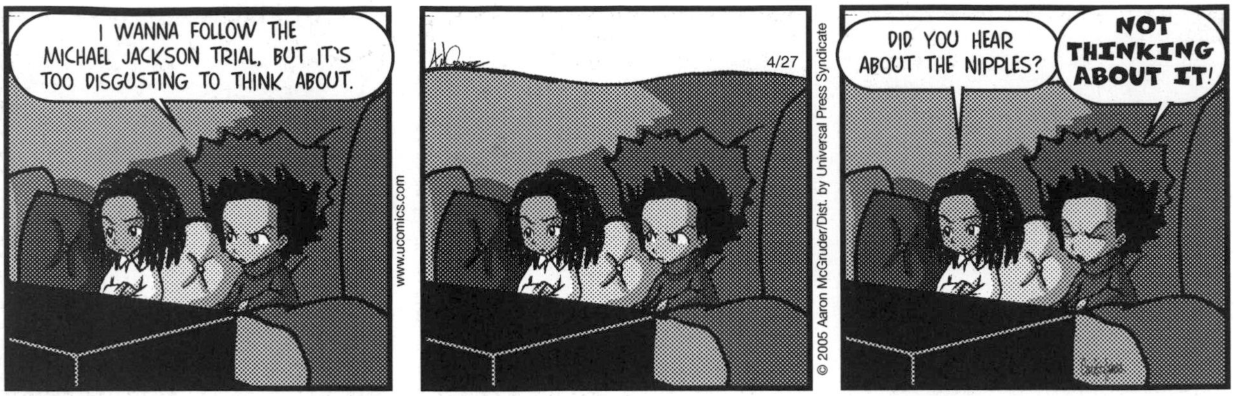
I WANNA FOLLOW THE MICHAEL JACKSON TRIAL, BUT IT'S TOO DISGUSTING TO THINK ABOUT.
DID YOU HEAR ABOUT THE NIPPLES?
NOT THINKING ABOUT IT!

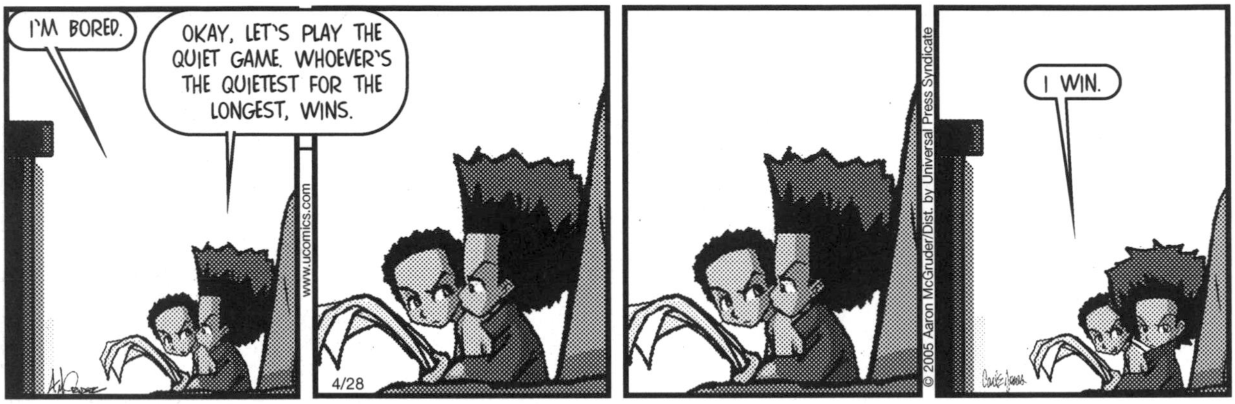
I'M BORED.
OKAY, LET'S PLAY THE QUIET GAME. WHOEVER'S THE QUIETEST FOR THE LONGEST, WINS.
I WIN.

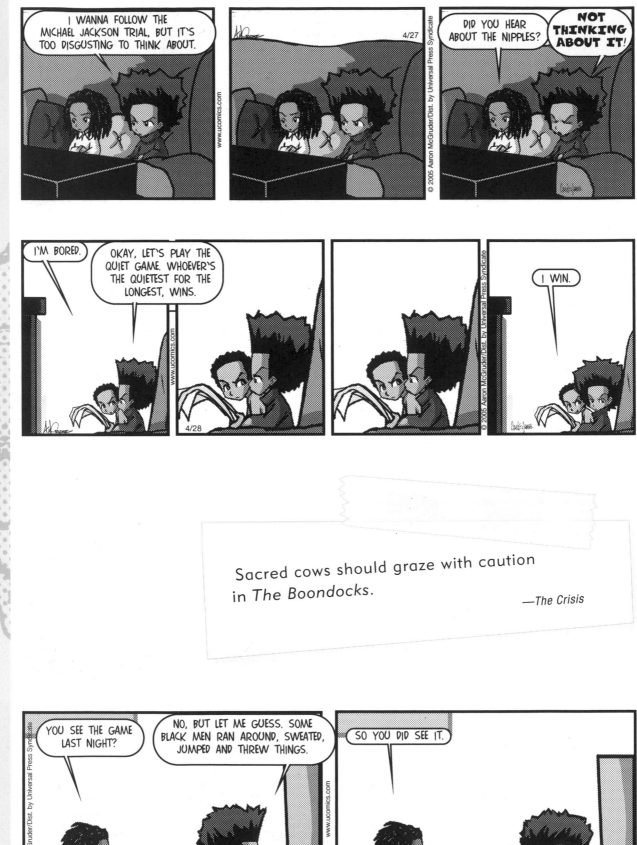

Sacred cows should graze with caution in *The Boondocks*.

—*The Crisis*

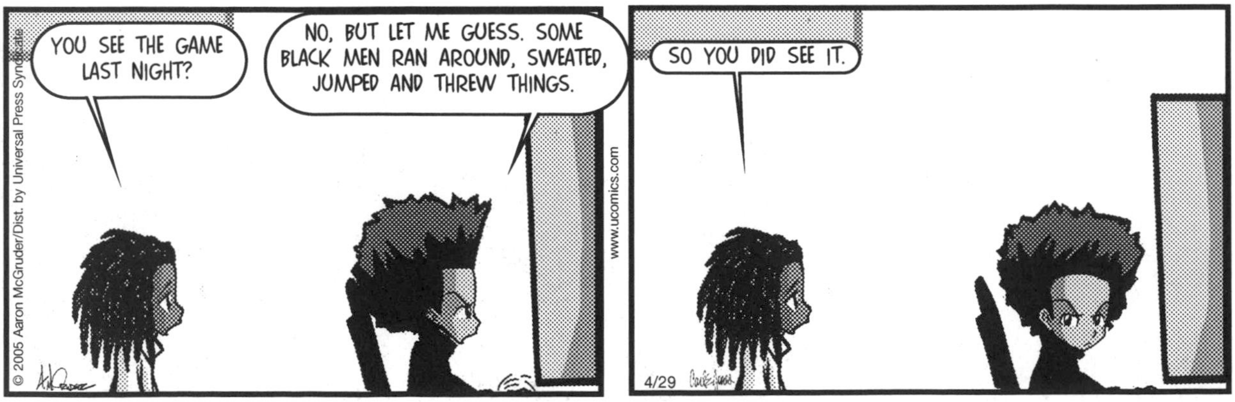
YOU SEE THE GAME LAST NIGHT?
NO, BUT LET ME GUESS. SOME BLACK MEN RAN AROUND, SWEATED, JUMPED AND THREW THINGS.
SO YOU DID SEE IT.

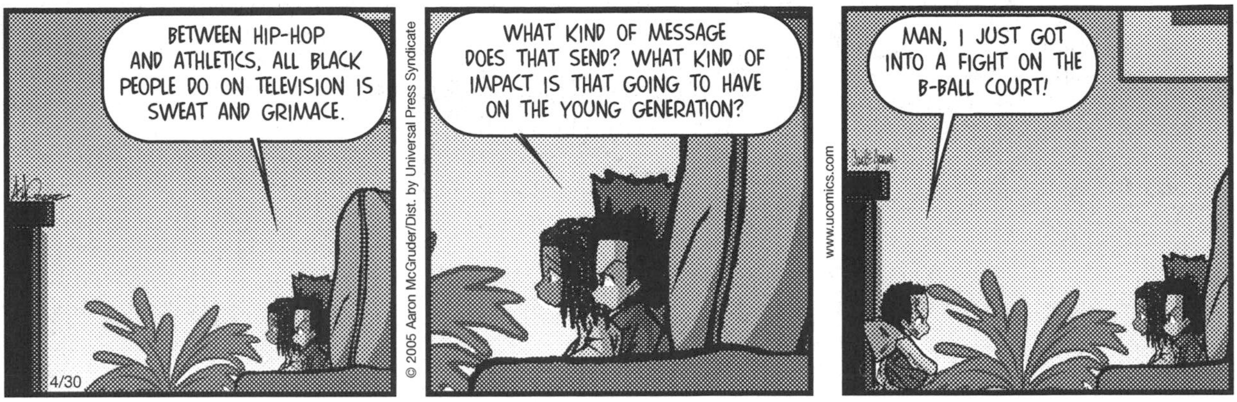
BETWEEN HIP-HOP AND ATHLETICS, ALL BLACK PEOPLE DO ON TELEVISION IS SWEAT AND GRIMACE.
4/30
© 2005 Aaron McGruder/Dist. by Universal Press Syndicate
WHAT KIND OF MESSAGE DOES THAT SEND? WHAT KIND OF IMPACT IS THAT GOING TO HAVE ON THE YOUNG GENERATION?
www.ucomics.com
MAN, I JUST GOT INTO A FIGHT ON THE B-BALL COURT!

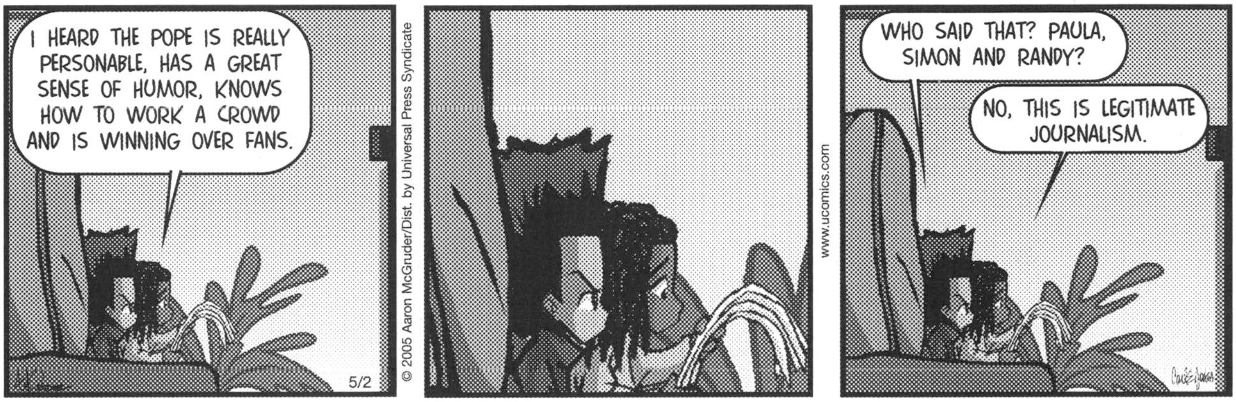
I HEARD THE POPE IS REALLY PERSONABLE, HAS A GREAT SENSE OF HUMOR, KNOWS HOW TO WORK A CROWD AND IS WINNING OVER FANS.
5/2
© 2005 Aaron McGruder/Dist. by Universal Press Syndicate
www.ucomics.com
WHO SAID THAT? PAULA, SIMON AND RANDY?
NO, THIS IS LEGITIMATE JOURNALISM.

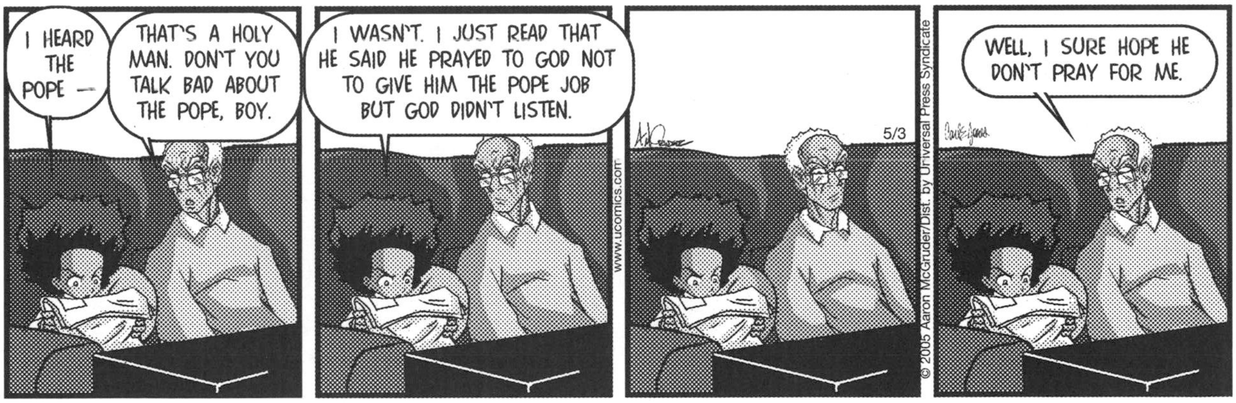
I HEARD THE POPE —
THAT'S A HOLY MAN. DON'T YOU TALK BAD ABOUT THE POPE, BOY.
I WASN'T. I JUST READ THAT HE SAID HE PRAYED TO GOD NOT TO GIVE HIM THE POPE JOB BUT GOD DIDN'T LISTEN.
www.ucomics.com
5/3
© 2005 Aaron McGruder/Dist. by Universal Press Syndicate
WELL, I SURE HOPE HE DON'T PRAY FOR ME.

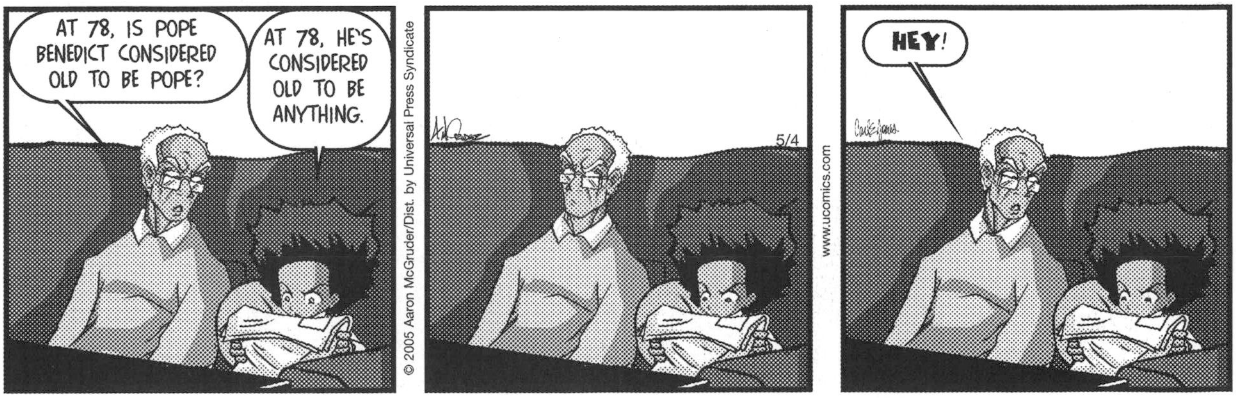
AT 78, IS POPE BENEDICT CONSIDERED OLD TO BE POPE?
AT 78, HE'S CONSIDERED OLD TO BE ANYTHING.
© 2005 Aaron McGruder/Dist. by Universal Press Syndicate
5/4
www.ucomics.com
HEY!

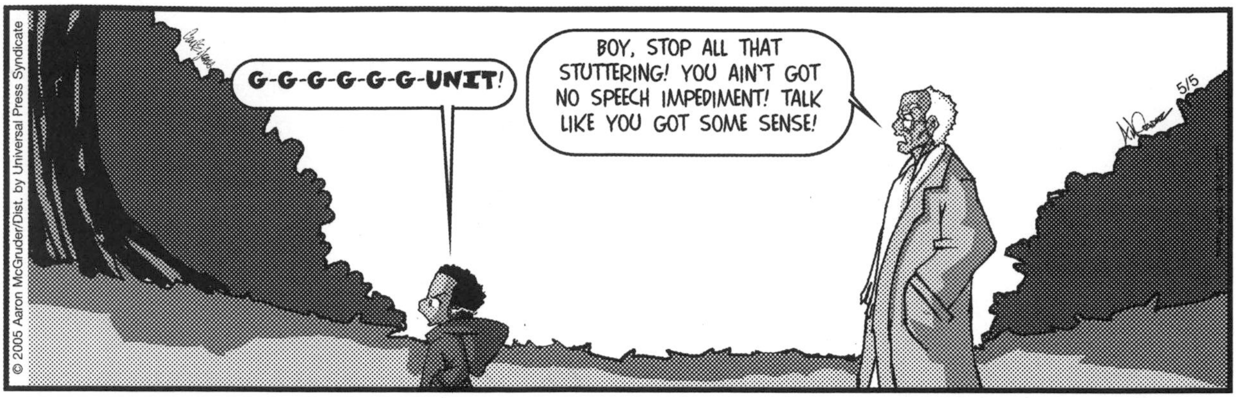
© 2005 Aaron McGruder/Dist. by Universal Press Syndicate
G-G-G-G-G-G-UNIT!
BOY, STOP ALL THAT STUTTERING! YOU AIN'T GOT NO SPEECH IMPEDIMENT! TALK LIKE YOU GOT SOME SENSE!
5/5

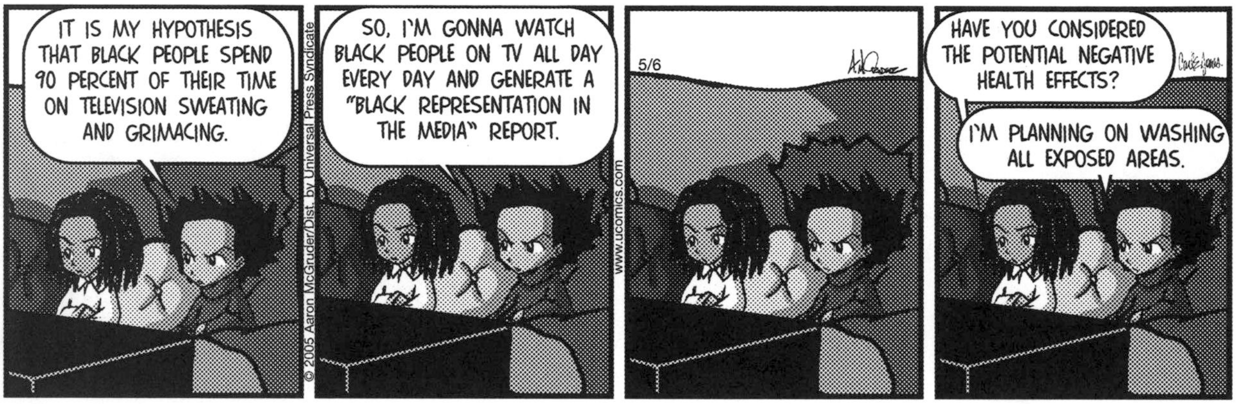
IT IS MY HYPOTHESIS THAT BLACK PEOPLE SPEND 90 PERCENT OF THEIR TIME ON TELEVISION SWEATING AND GRIMACING.
© 2005 Aaron McGruder/Dist. by Universal Press Syndicate
SO, I'M GONNA WATCH BLACK PEOPLE ON TV ALL DAY EVERY DAY AND GENERATE A "BLACK REPRESENTATION IN THE MEDIA" REPORT.
www.ucomics.com
5/6
HAVE YOU CONSIDERED THE POTENTIAL NEGATIVE HEALTH EFFECTS?
I'M PLANNING ON WASHING ALL EXPOSED AREAS.

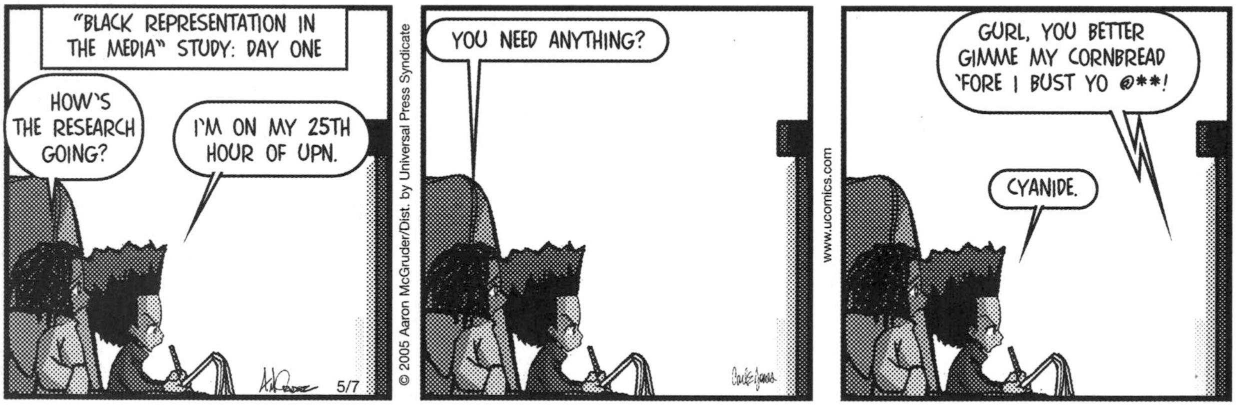
"BLACK REPRESENTATION IN THE MEDIA" STUDY: DAY ONE
HOW'S THE RESEARCH GOING?
I'M ON MY 25TH HOUR OF UPN.
5/7
© 2005 Aaron McGruder/Dist. by Universal Press Syndicate
YOU NEED ANYTHING?
www.ucomics.com
GURL, YOU BETTER GIMME MY CORNBREAD 'FORE I BUST YO @**!
CYANIDE.

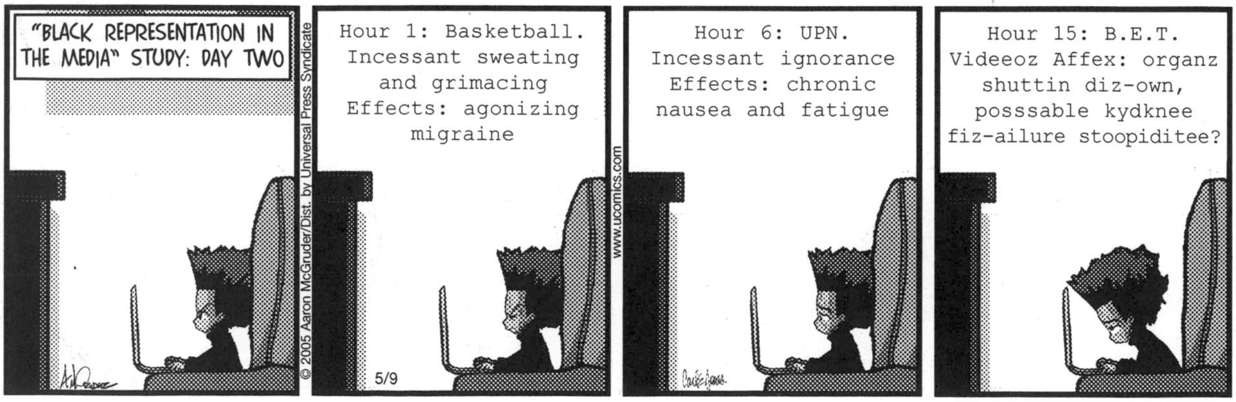
"BLACK REPRESENTATION IN THE MEDIA" STUDY: DAY TWO
© 2005 Aaron McGruder/Dist. by Universal Press Syndicate
Hour 1: Basketball. Incessant sweating and grimacing Effects: agonizing migraine
5/9
www.ucomics.com
Hour 6: UPN. Incessant ignorance Effects: chronic nausea and fatigue
Hour 15: B.E.T. Videeoz Affex: organz shuttin diz-own, posssable kydknee fiz-ailure stoopiditee?

> Since Universal Press Syndicate began syndicating *The Boondocks* in 1999, the 29-year-old free thinker has had something to say, and an audience of more than 20 million to say it to. And McGruder has not been shy.
>
> —*The Crisis*

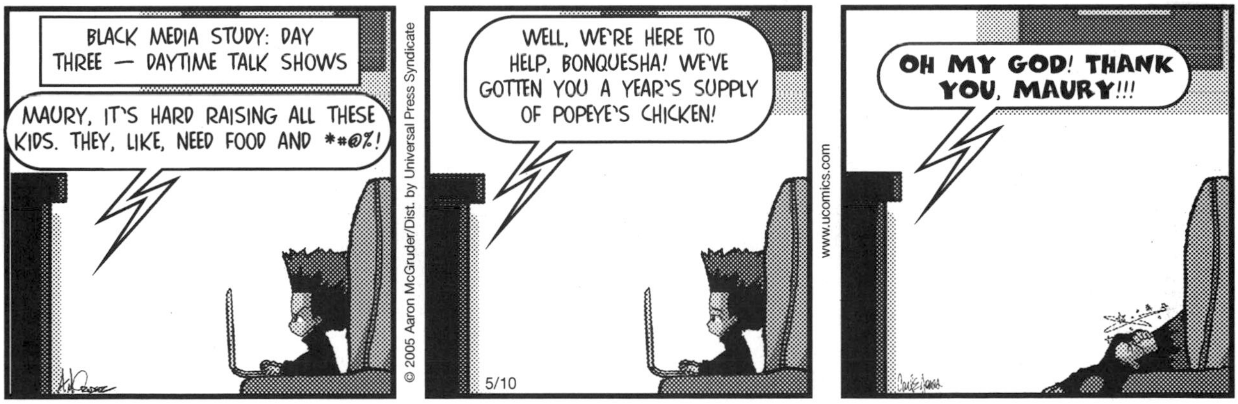
BLACK MEDIA STUDY: DAY THREE — DAYTIME TALK SHOWS
MAURY, IT'S HARD RAISING ALL THESE KIDS. THEY, LIKE, NEED FOOD AND *#@%!
© 2005 Aaron McGruder/Dist. by Universal Press Syndicate
WELL, WE'RE HERE TO HELP, BONQUESHA! WE'VE GOTTEN YOU A YEAR'S SUPPLY OF POPEYE'S CHICKEN!
5/10
www.ucomics.com
OH MY GOD! THANK YOU, MAURY!!!

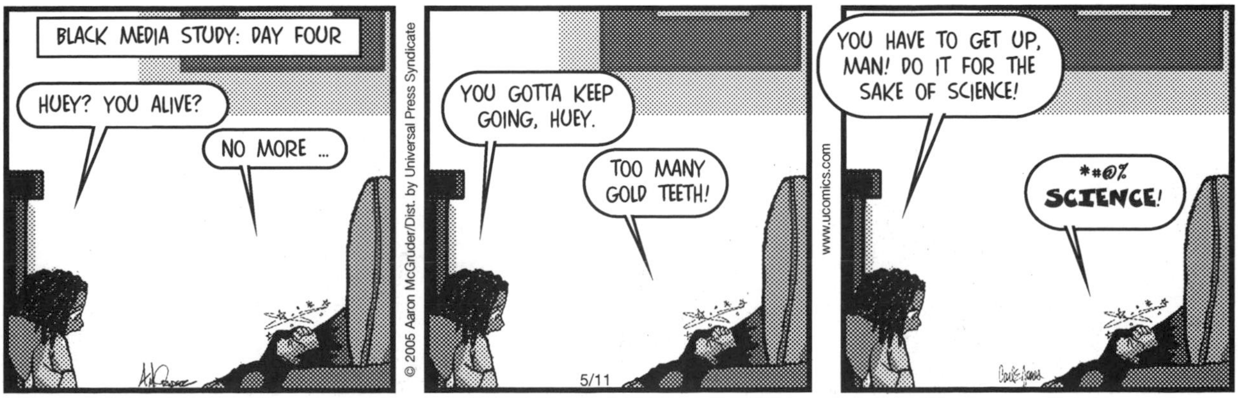
BLACK MEDIA STUDY: DAY FOUR
HUEY? YOU ALIVE?
NO MORE ...
© 2005 Aaron McGruder/Dist. by Universal Press Syndicate
YOU GOTTA KEEP GOING, HUEY.
TOO MANY GOLD TEETH!
5/11
www.ucomics.com
YOU HAVE TO GET UP, MAN! DO IT FOR THE SAKE OF SCIENCE!
*#@% SCIENCE!

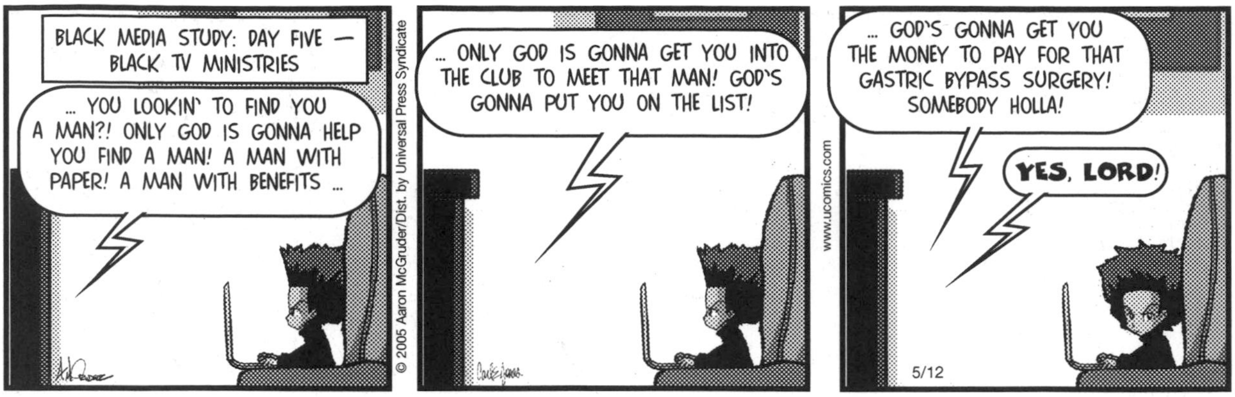
BLACK MEDIA STUDY: DAY FIVE — BLACK TV MINISTRIES
... YOU LOOKIN' TO FIND YOU A MAN?! ONLY GOD IS GONNA HELP YOU FIND A MAN! A MAN WITH PAPER! A MAN WITH BENEFITS ...
© 2005 Aaron McGruder/Dist. by Universal Press Syndicate
... ONLY GOD IS GONNA GET YOU INTO THE CLUB TO MEET THAT MAN! GOD'S GONNA PUT YOU ON THE LIST!
www.ucomics.com
... GOD'S GONNA GET YOU THE MONEY TO PAY FOR THAT GASTRIC BYPASS SURGERY! SOMEBODY HOLLA!
YES, LORD!
5/12

The biting comic is as irreverent as Richard Pryor and as controversial as Spike Lee.

—Philadelphia Inquirer

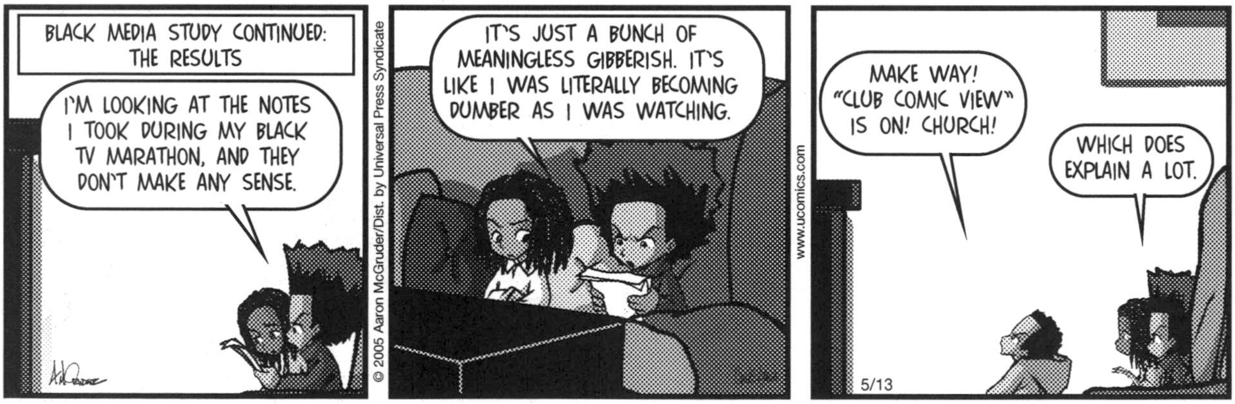
BLACK MEDIA STUDY CONTINUED: THE RESULTS
I'M LOOKING AT THE NOTES I TOOK DURING MY BLACK TV MARATHON, AND THEY DON'T MAKE ANY SENSE.
© 2005 Aaron McGruder/Dist. by Universal Press Syndicate
IT'S JUST A BUNCH OF MEANINGLESS GIBBERISH. IT'S LIKE I WAS LITERALLY BECOMING DUMBER AS I WAS WATCHING.
www.ucomics.com
MAKE WAY! "CLUB COMIC VIEW" IS ON! CHURCH!
WHICH DOES EXPLAIN A LOT.
5/13

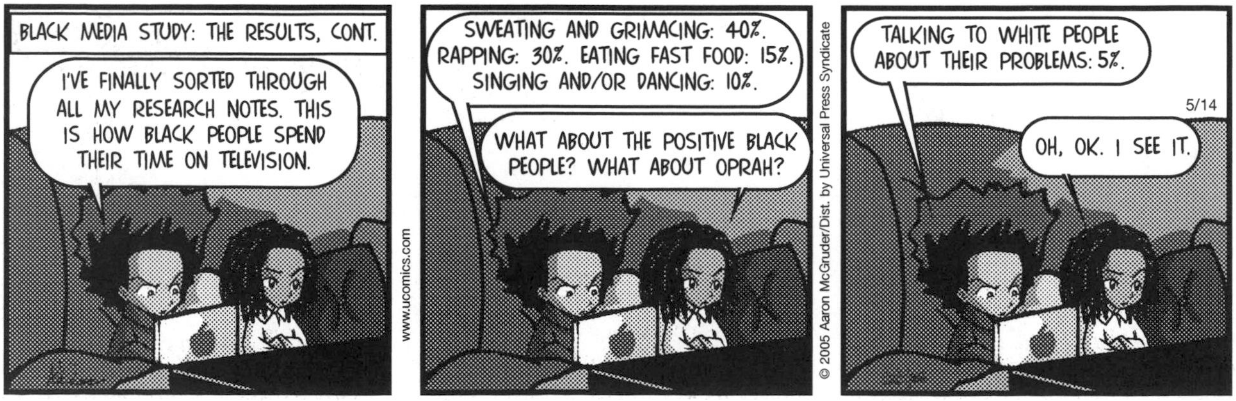
BLACK MEDIA STUDY: THE RESULTS, CONT.
I'VE FINALLY SORTED THROUGH ALL MY RESEARCH NOTES. THIS IS HOW BLACK PEOPLE SPEND THEIR TIME ON TELEVISION.
www.ucomics.com
SWEATING AND GRIMACING: 40%. RAPPING: 30%. EATING FAST FOOD: 15%. SINGING AND/OR DANCING: 10%.
WHAT ABOUT THE POSITIVE BLACK PEOPLE? WHAT ABOUT OPRAH?
© 2005 Aaron McGruder/Dist. by Universal Press Syndicate
TALKING TO WHITE PEOPLE ABOUT THEIR PROBLEMS: 5%.
5/14
OH, OK. I SEE IT.

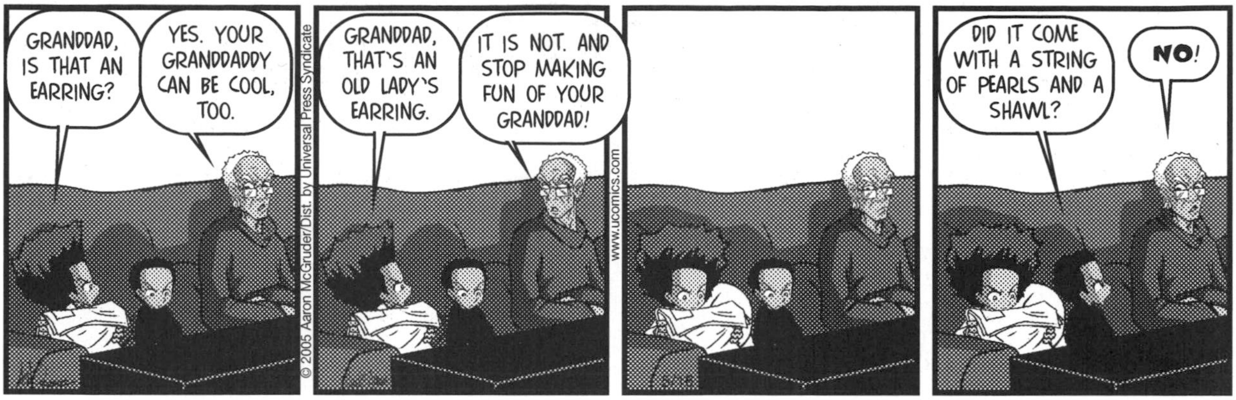
GRANDDAD, IS THAT AN EARRING?
YES. YOUR GRANDDADDY CAN BE COOL, TOO.
© 2005 Aaron McGruder/Dist. by Universal Press Syndicate
GRANDDAD, THAT'S AN OLD LADY'S EARRING.
IT IS NOT. AND STOP MAKING FUN OF YOUR GRANDDAD!
www.ucomics.com
DID IT COME WITH A STRING OF PEARLS AND A SHAWL?
NO!

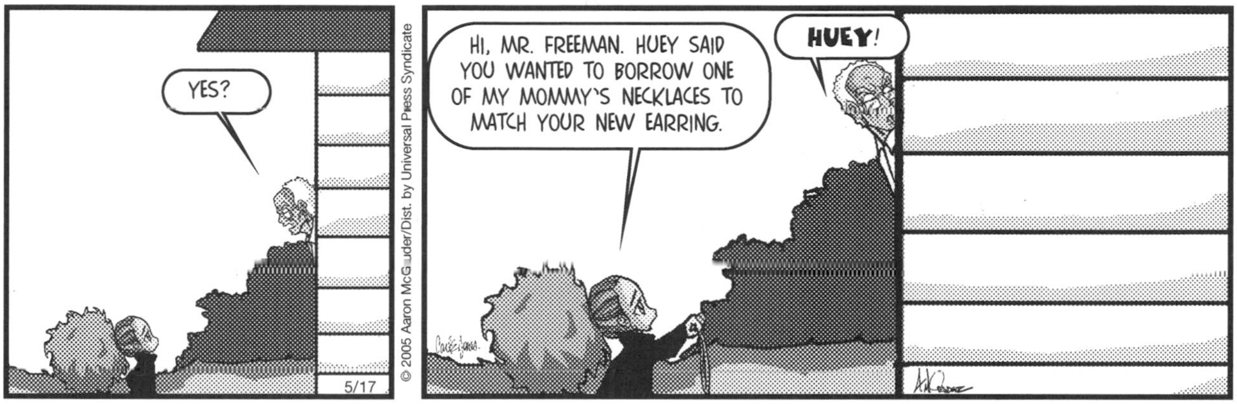
YES?
5/17
© 2005 Aaron McGruder/Dist. by Universal Press Syndicate
HI, MR. FREEMAN. HUEY SAID YOU WANTED TO BORROW ONE OF MY MOMMY'S NECKLACES TO MATCH YOUR NEW EARRING.
HUEY!

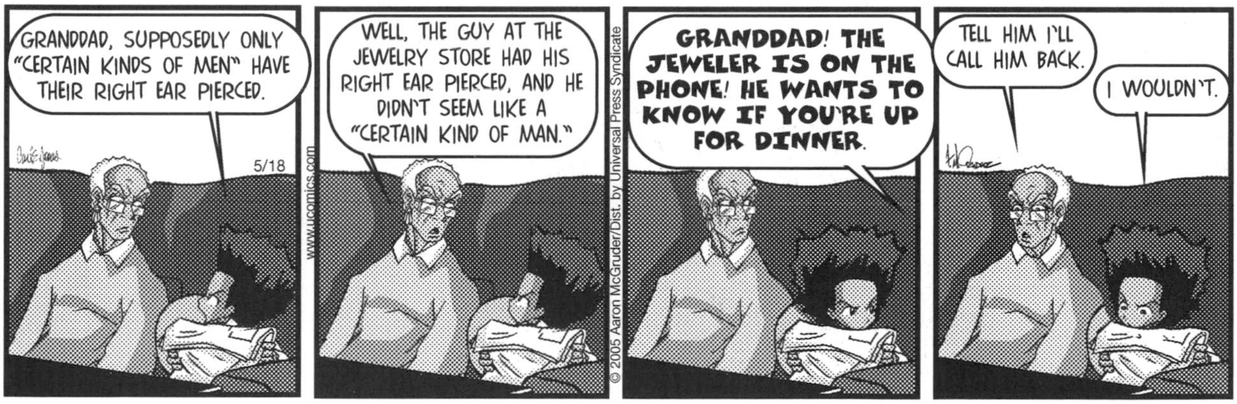
GRANDDAD, SUPPOSEDLY ONLY "CERTAIN KINDS OF MEN" HAVE THEIR RIGHT EAR PIERCED.
5/18
www.ucomics.com
WELL, THE GUY AT THE JEWELRY STORE HAD HIS RIGHT EAR PIERCED, AND HE DIDN'T SEEM LIKE A "CERTAIN KIND OF MAN."
© 2005 Aaron McGruder/Dist. by Universal Press Syndicate
GRANDDAD! THE JEWELER IS ON THE PHONE! HE WANTS TO KNOW IF YOU'RE UP FOR DINNER.
TELL HIM I'LL CALL HIM BACK.
I WOULDN'T.

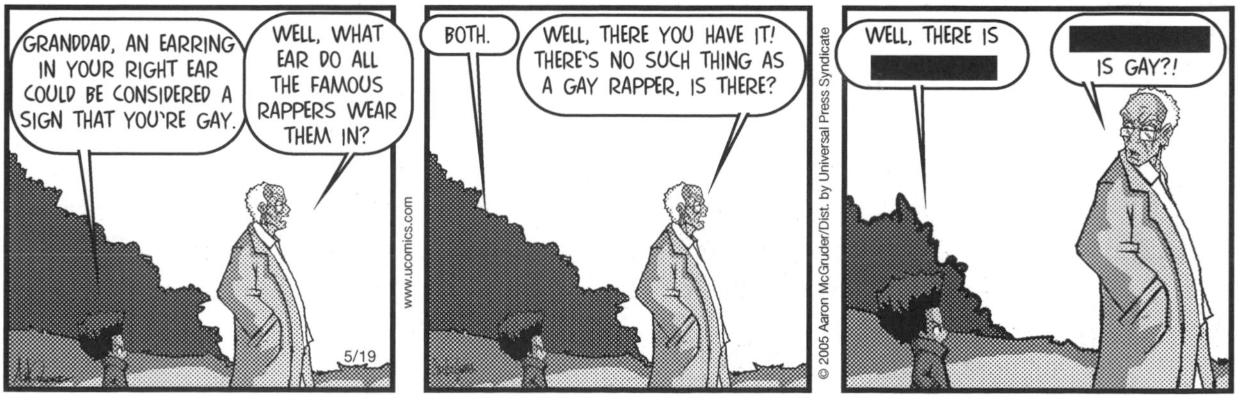
GRANDDAD, AN EARRING IN YOUR RIGHT EAR COULD BE CONSIDERED A SIGN THAT YOU'RE GAY.
WELL, WHAT EAR DO ALL THE FAMOUS RAPPERS WEAR THEM IN?
5/19
www.ucomics.com
BOTH.
WELL, THERE YOU HAVE IT! THERE'S NO SUCH THING AS A GAY RAPPER, IS THERE?
© 2005 Aaron McGruder/Dist. by Universal Press Syndicate
WELL, THERE IS [redacted]
[redacted] IS GAY?!

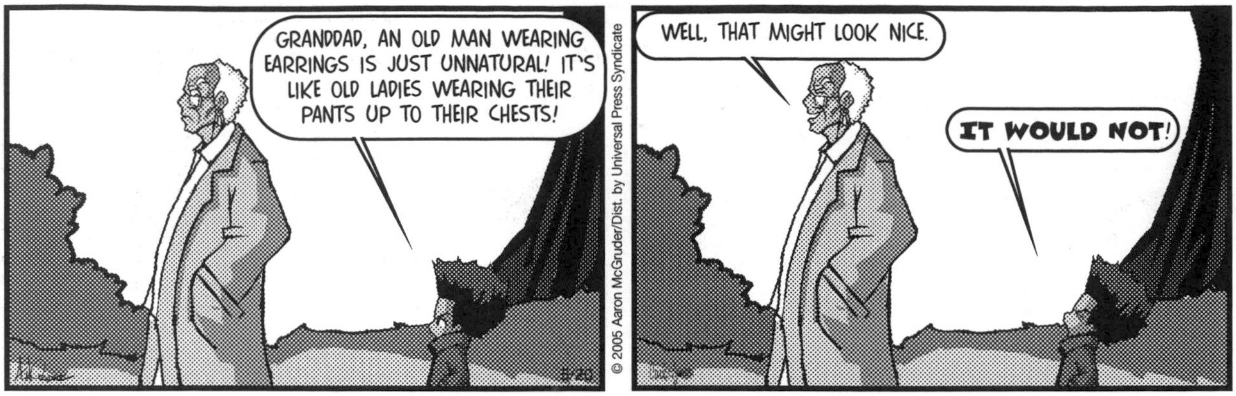
GRANDDAD, AN OLD MAN WEARING EARRINGS IS JUST UNNATURAL! IT'S LIKE OLD LADIES WEARING THEIR PANTS UP TO THEIR CHESTS!
5/20
© 2005 Aaron McGruder/Dist. by Universal Press Syndicate
WELL, THAT MIGHT LOOK NICE.
IT WOULD NOT!

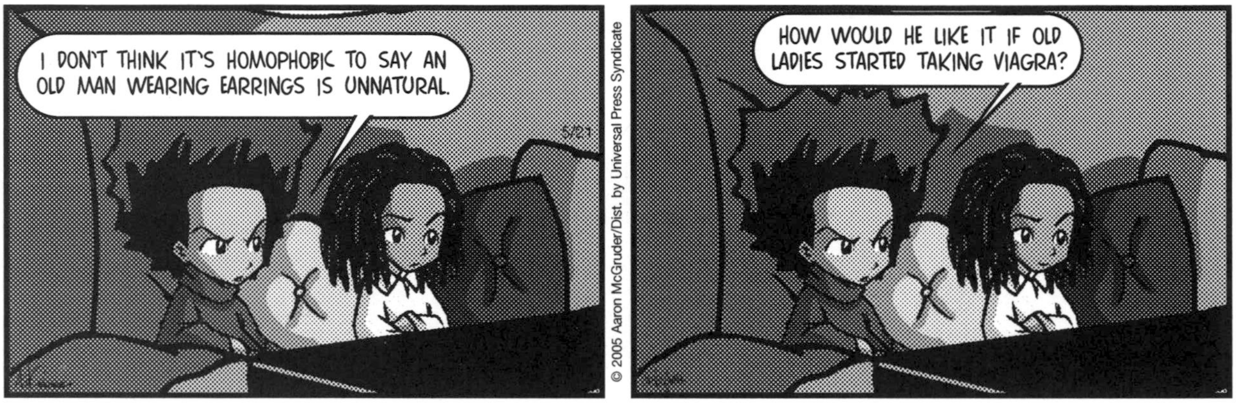
I DON'T THINK IT'S HOMOPHOBIC TO SAY AN OLD MAN WEARING EARRINGS IS UNNATURAL.
5/21
© 2005 Aaron McGruder/Dist. by Universal Press Syndicate
HOW WOULD HE LIKE IT IF OLD LADIES STARTED TAKING VIAGRA?

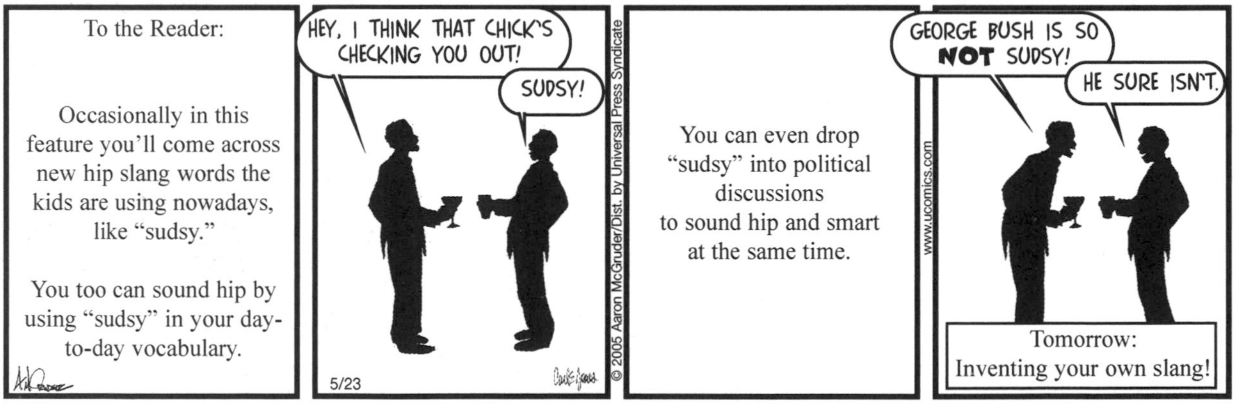
To the Reader:
Occasionally in this feature you'll come across new hip slang words the kids are using nowadays, like "sudsy."
You too can sound hip by using "sudsy" in your day-to-day vocabulary.
HEY, I THINK THAT CHICK'S CHECKING YOU OUT!
SUDSY!
5/23
© 2005 Aaron McGruder/Dist. by Universal Press Syndicate
You can even drop "sudsy" into political discussions to sound hip and smart at the same time.
GEORGE BUSH IS SO **NOT** SUDSY!
HE SURE ISN'T.
www.ucomics.com
Tomorrow: Inventing your own slang!

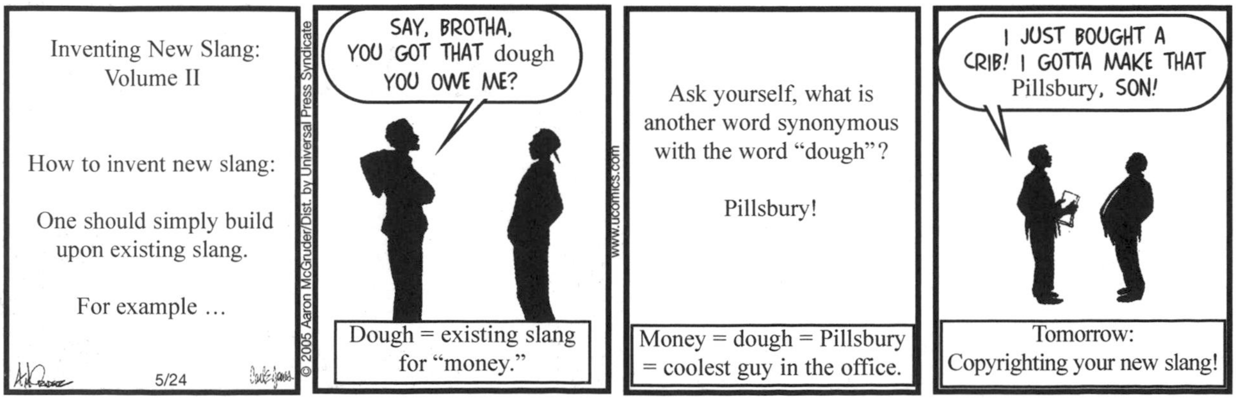
Inventing New Slang: Volume II
How to invent new slang:
One should simply build upon existing slang.
For example …
5/24
© 2005 Aaron McGruder/Dist. by Universal Press Syndicate
SAY, BROTHA, YOU GOT THAT dough YOU OWE ME?
Dough = existing slang for "money."
www.ucomics.com
Ask yourself, what is another word synonymous with the word "dough"?
Pillsbury!
Money = dough = Pillsbury = coolest guy in the office.
I JUST BOUGHT A CRIB! I GOTTA MAKE THAT Pillsbury, SON!
Tomorrow: Copyrighting your new slang!

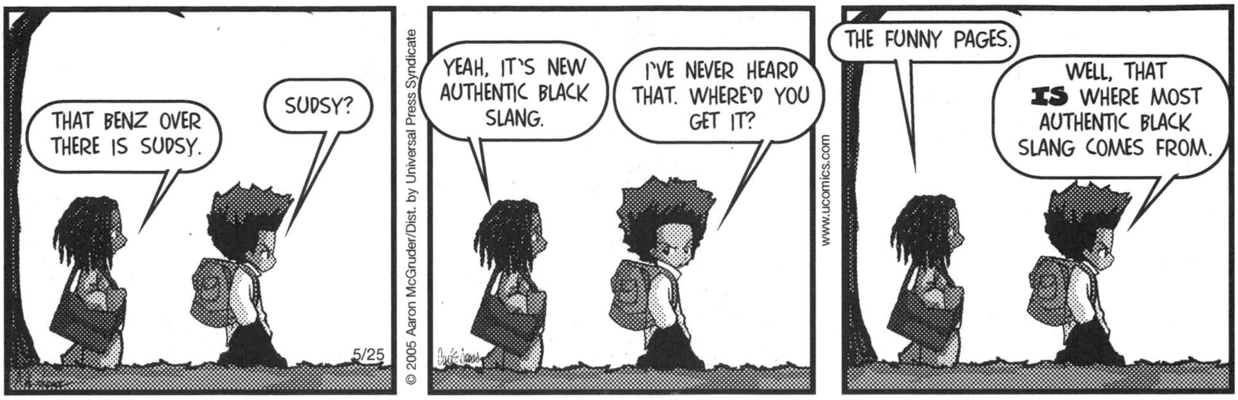
THAT BENZ OVER THERE IS SUDSY.
SUDSY?
5/25
© 2005 Aaron McGruder/Dist. by Universal Press Syndicate
YEAH, IT'S NEW AUTHENTIC BLACK SLANG.
I'VE NEVER HEARD THAT. WHERE'D YOU GET IT?
www.ucomics.com
THE FUNNY PAGES.
WELL, THAT **IS** WHERE MOST AUTHENTIC BLACK SLANG COMES FROM.

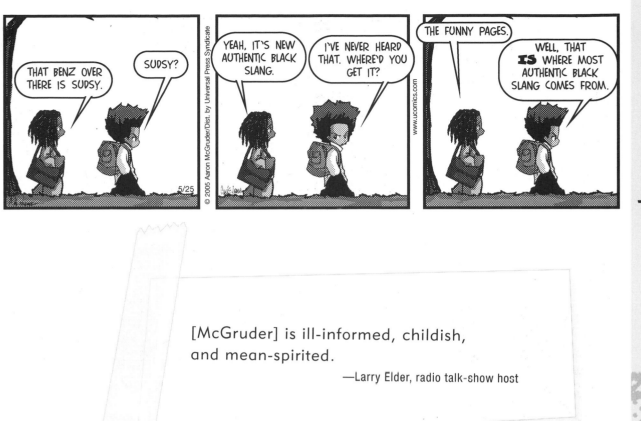

[McGruder] is ill-informed, childish, and mean-spirited.

—Larry Elder, radio talk-show host

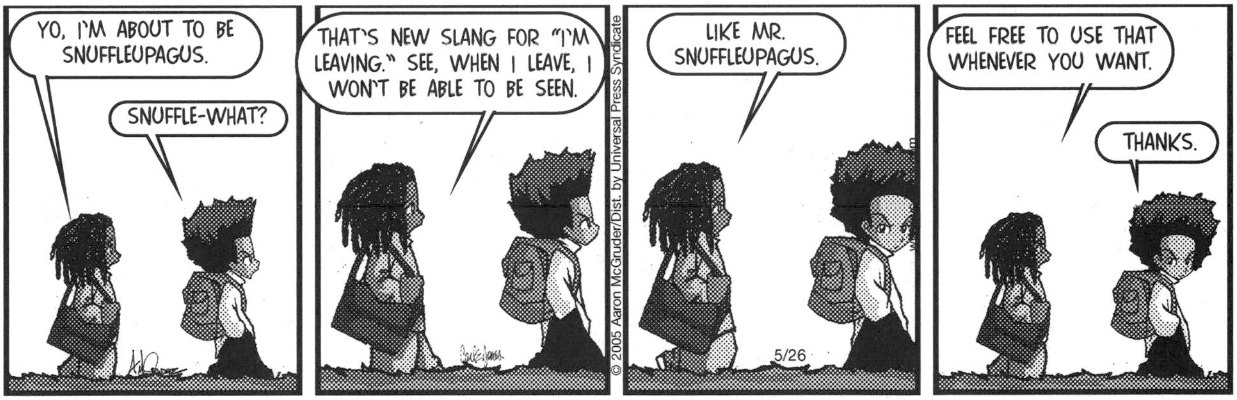
YO, I'M ABOUT TO BE SNUFFLEUPAGUS.
SNUFFLE-WHAT?
THAT'S NEW SLANG FOR "I'M LEAVING." SEE, WHEN I LEAVE, I WON'T BE ABLE TO BE SEEN.
© 2005 Aaron McGruder/Dist. by Universal Press Syndicate
LIKE MR. SNUFFLEUPAGUS.
5/26
FEEL FREE TO USE THAT WHENEVER YOU WANT.
THANKS.

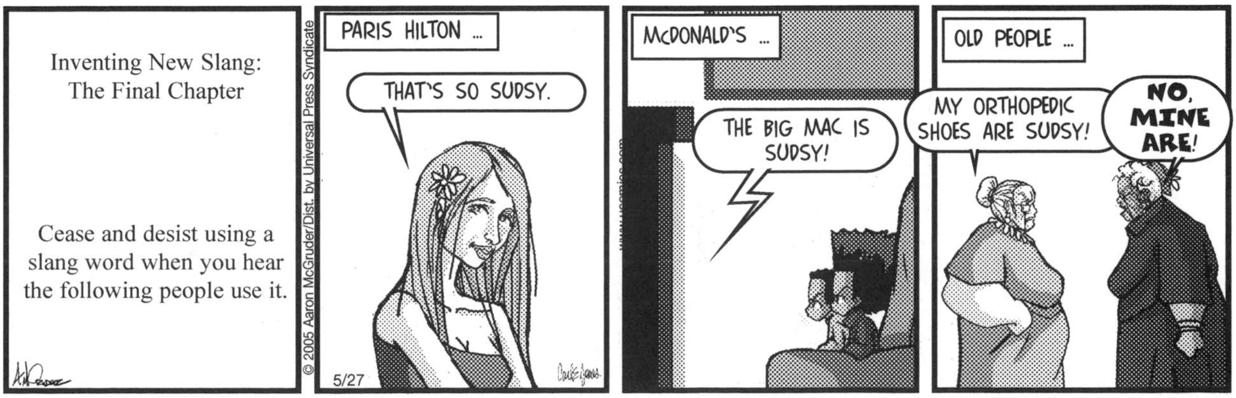
Inventing New Slang: The Final Chapter
Cease and desist using a slang word when you hear the following people use it.
© 2005 Aaron McGruder/Dist. by Universal Press Syndicate
PARIS HILTON ...
THAT'S SO SUDSY.
5/27
McDONALD'S ...
THE BIG MAC IS SUDSY!
OLD PEOPLE ...
MY ORTHOPEDIC SHOES ARE SUDSY!
NO, MINE ARE!

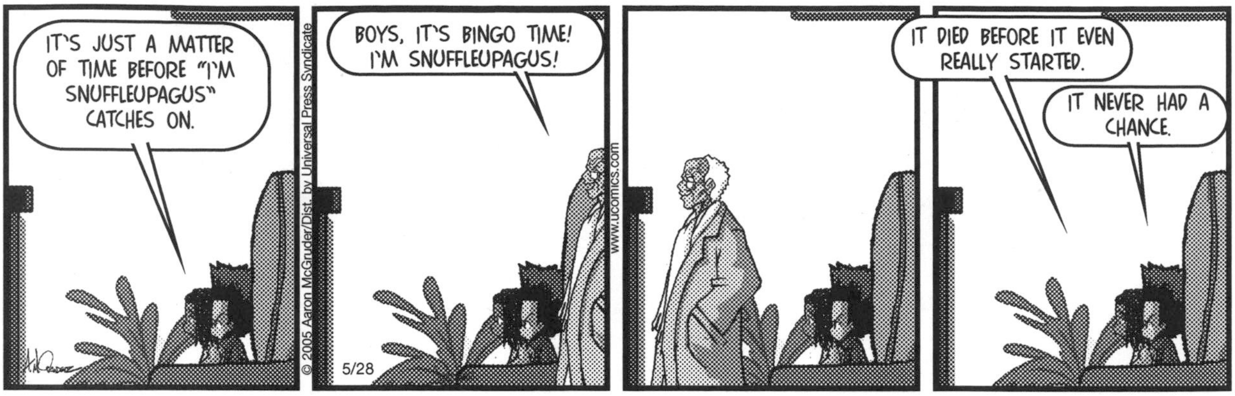
IT'S JUST A MATTER OF TIME BEFORE "I'M SNUFFLEUPAGUS" CATCHES ON.
© 2005 Aaron McGruder/Dist. by Universal Press Syndicate
5/28
BOYS, IT'S BINGO TIME! I'M SNUFFLEUPAGUS!
www.ucomics.com
IT DIED BEFORE IT EVEN REALLY STARTED.
IT NEVER HAD A CHANCE.

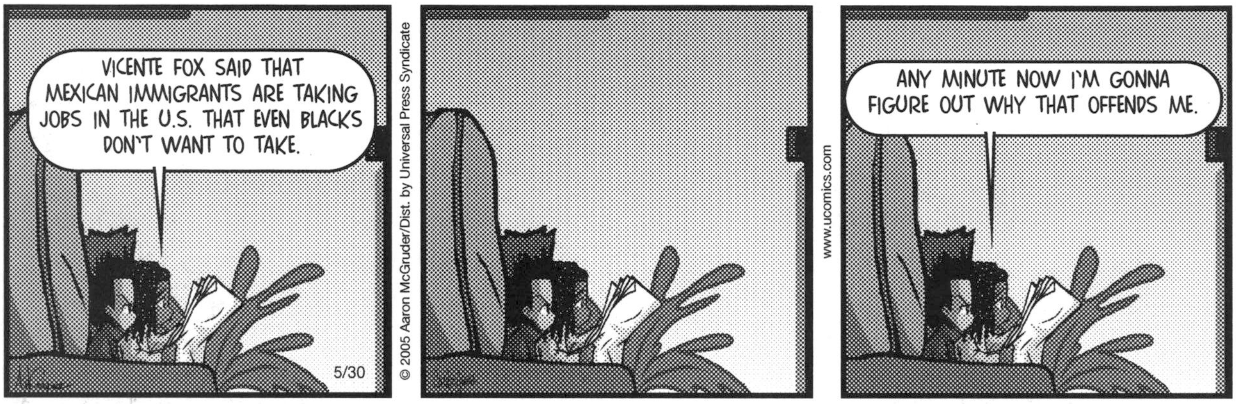
VICENTE FOX SAID THAT MEXICAN IMMIGRANTS ARE TAKING JOBS IN THE U.S. THAT EVEN BLACKS DON'T WANT TO TAKE.
5/30
© 2005 Aaron McGruder/Dist. by Universal Press Syndicate
www.ucomics.com
ANY MINUTE NOW I'M GONNA FIGURE OUT WHY THAT OFFENDS ME.

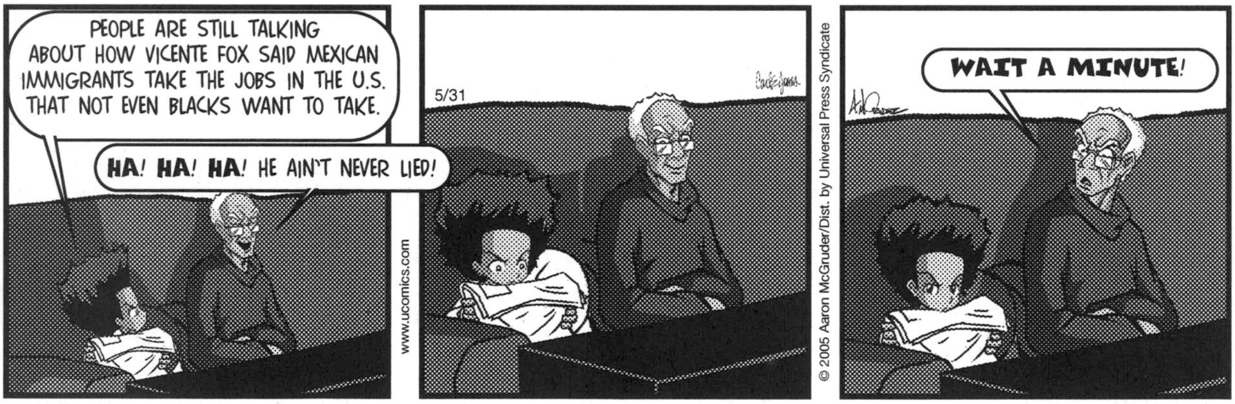
PEOPLE ARE STILL TALKING ABOUT HOW VICENTE FOX SAID MEXICAN IMMIGRANTS TAKE THE JOBS IN THE U.S. THAT NOT EVEN BLACKS WANT TO TAKE.
HA! HA! HA! HE AIN'T NEVER LIED!
www.ucomics.com
5/31
© 2005 Aaron McGruder/Dist. by Universal Press Syndicate
WAIT A MINUTE!

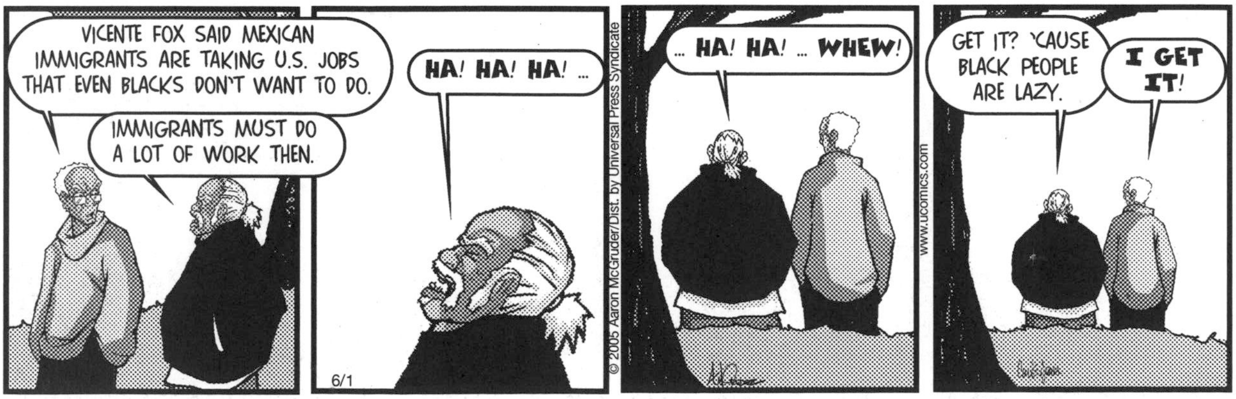
VICENTE FOX SAID MEXICAN IMMIGRANTS ARE TAKING U.S. JOBS THAT EVEN BLACKS DON'T WANT TO DO.
IMMIGRANTS MUST DO A LOT OF WORK THEN.
HA! HA! HA! ...
6/1
© 2005 Aaron McGruder/Dist. by Universal Press Syndicate
... HA! HA! ... WHEW!
GET IT? 'CAUSE BLACK PEOPLE ARE LAZY.
I GET IT!
www.ucomics.com

Today folks charge *The Boondocks* with being racist and demeaning. Maybe they aren't prepared for what Aaron McGruder has to say.

—*Baltimore Sun*

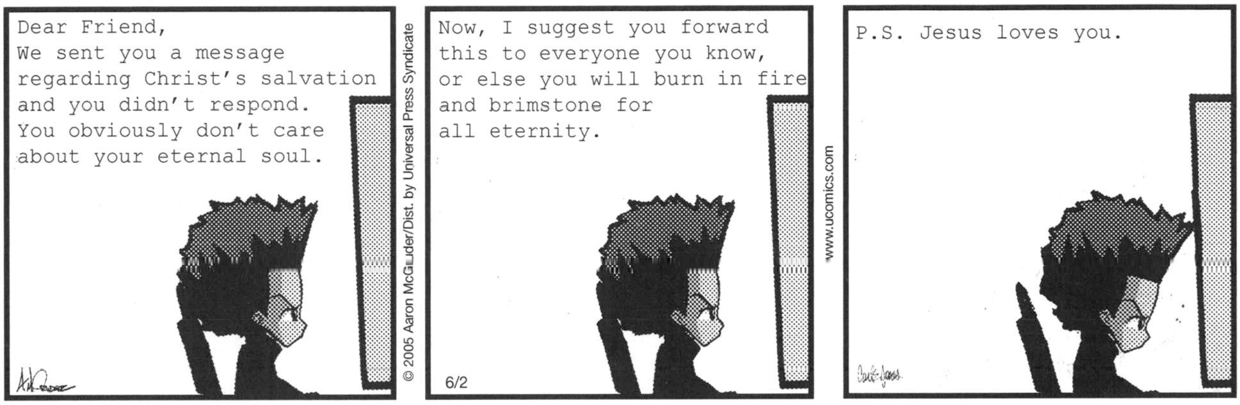
Dear Friend,
We sent you a message regarding Christ's salvation and you didn't respond. You obviously don't care about your eternal soul.
© 2005 Aaron McGruder/Dist. by Universal Press Syndicate
Now, I suggest you forward this to everyone you know, or else you will burn in fire and brimstone for all eternity.
6/2
www.ucomics.com
P.S. Jesus loves you.

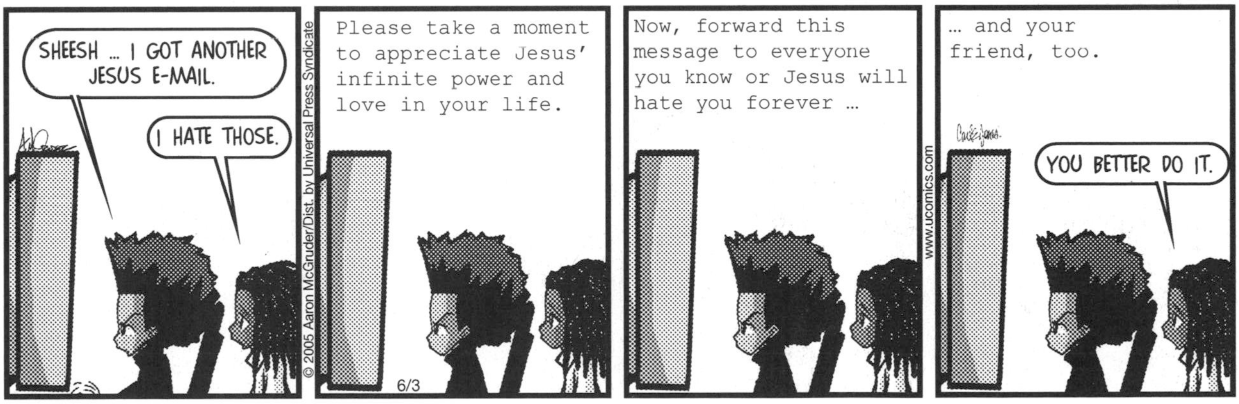
SHEESH … I GOT ANOTHER JESUS E-MAIL.
I HATE THOSE.
© 2005 Aaron McGruder/Dist. by Universal Press Syndicate
Please take a moment to appreciate Jesus' infinite power and love in your life.
6/3
Now, forward this message to everyone you know or Jesus will hate you forever …
www.ucomics.com
… and your friend, too.
YOU BETTER DO IT.

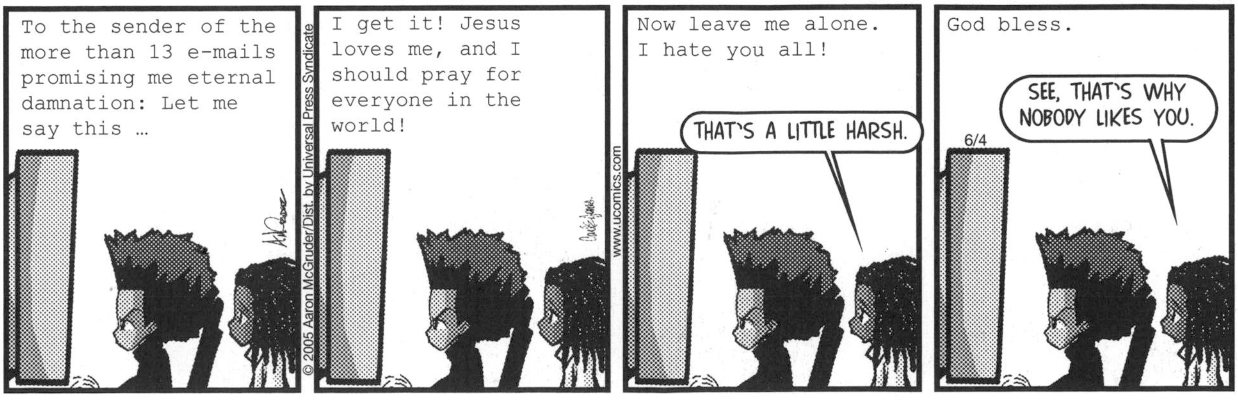
To the sender of the more than 13 e-mails promising me eternal damnation: Let me say this …
© 2005 Aaron McGruder/Dist. by Universal Press Syndicate
I get it! Jesus loves me, and I should pray for everyone in the world!
www.ucomics.com
Now leave me alone. I hate you all!
THAT'S A LITTLE HARSH.
God bless.
6/4
SEE, THAT'S WHY NOBODY LIKES YOU.

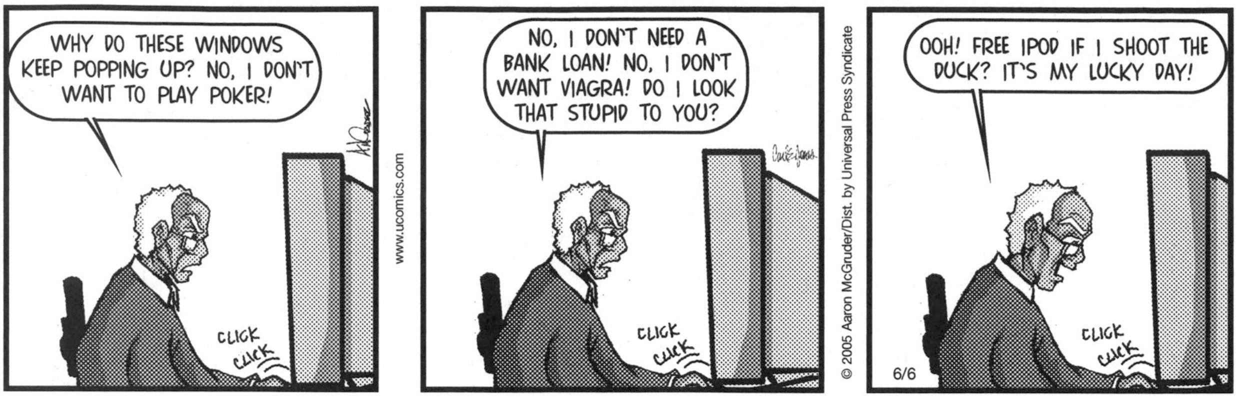

WHY DO THESE WINDOWS KEEP POPPING UP? NO, I DON'T WANT TO PLAY POKER!
CLICK CLICK
NO, I DON'T NEED A BANK LOAN! NO, I DON'T WANT VIAGRA! DO I LOOK THAT STUPID TO YOU?
CLICK CLICK
OOH! FREE IPOD IF I SHOOT THE DUCK? IT'S MY LUCKY DAY!
CLICK CLICK
6/6
www.ucomics.com
© 2005 Aaron McGruder/Dist. by Universal Press Syndicate

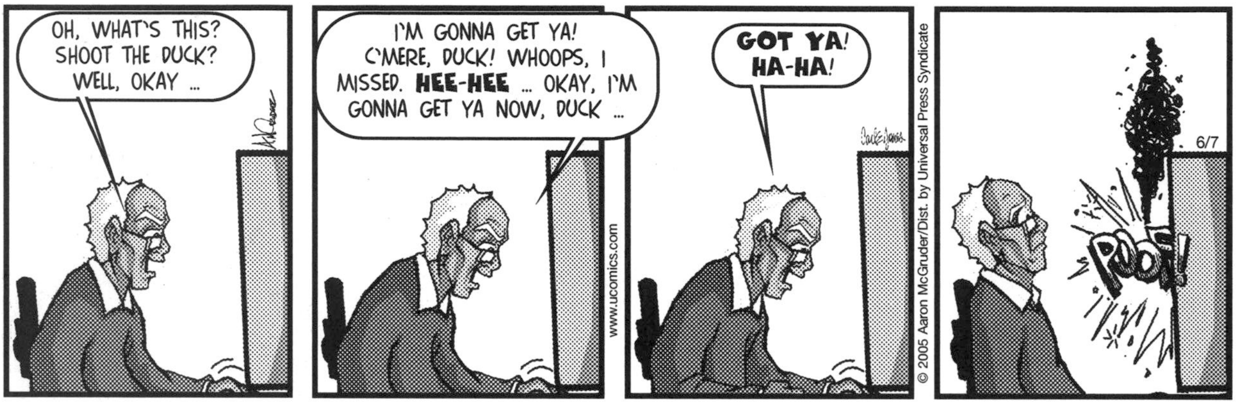

OH, WHAT'S THIS? SHOOT THE DUCK? WELL, OKAY ...
I'M GONNA GET YA! C'MERE, DUCK! WHOOPS, I MISSED. HEE-HEE ... OKAY, I'M GONNA GET YA NOW, DUCK ...
GOT YA! HA-HA!
POOF!
6/7
www.ucomics.com
© 2005 Aaron McGruder/Dist. by Universal Press Syndicate

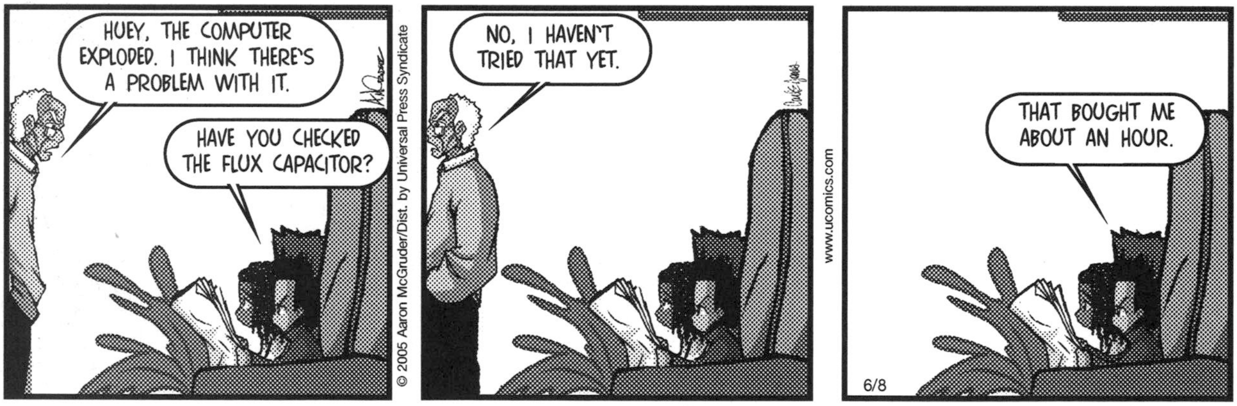

HUEY, THE COMPUTER EXPLODED. I THINK THERE'S A PROBLEM WITH IT.
HAVE YOU CHECKED THE FLUX CAPACITOR?
NO, I HAVEN'T TRIED THAT YET.
THAT BOUGHT ME ABOUT AN HOUR.
6/8
© 2005 Aaron McGruder/Dist. by Universal Press Syndicate
www.ucomics.com

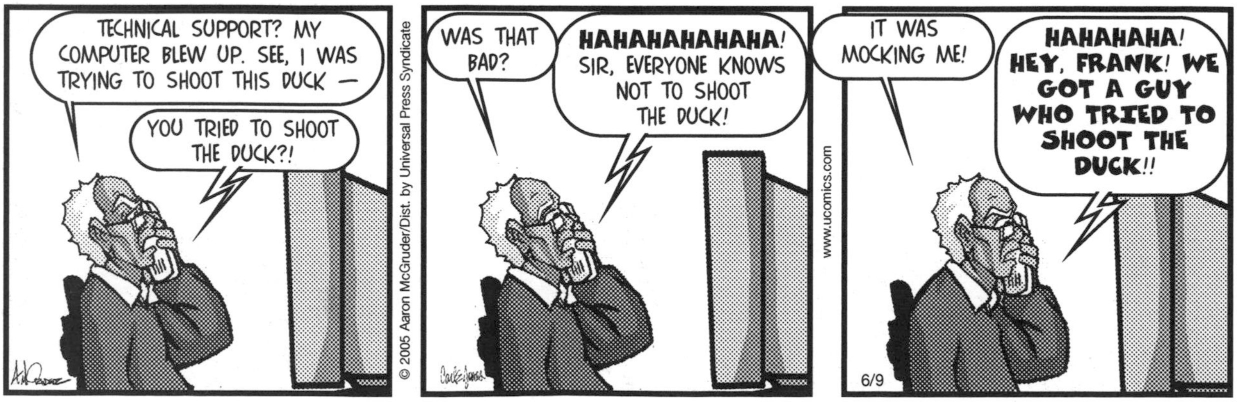

TECHNICAL SUPPORT? MY COMPUTER BLEW UP. SEE, I WAS TRYING TO SHOOT THIS DUCK —
YOU TRIED TO SHOOT THE DUCK?!
WAS THAT BAD?
HAHAHAHAHAHA! SIR, EVERYONE KNOWS NOT TO SHOOT THE DUCK!
IT WAS MOCKING ME!
HAHAHAHA! HEY, FRANK! WE GOT A GUY WHO TRIED TO SHOOT THE DUCK!!
6/9
© 2005 Aaron McGruder/Dist. by Universal Press Syndicate
www.ucomics.com

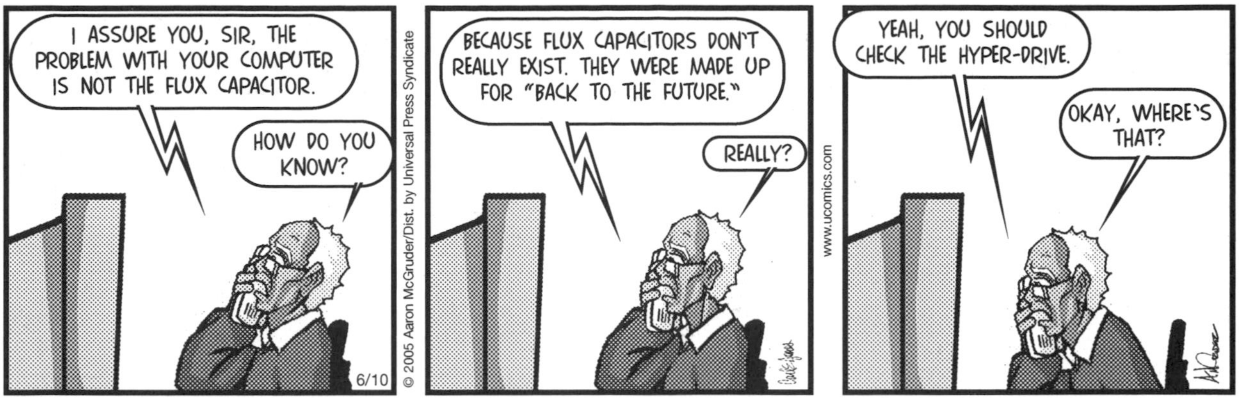
I ASSURE YOU, SIR, THE PROBLEM WITH YOUR COMPUTER IS NOT THE FLUX CAPACITOR.
HOW DO YOU KNOW?
6/10
© 2005 Aaron McGruder/Dist. by Universal Press Syndicate
BECAUSE FLUX CAPACITORS DON'T REALLY EXIST. THEY WERE MADE UP FOR "BACK TO THE FUTURE."
REALLY?
www.ucomics.com
YEAH, YOU SHOULD CHECK THE HYPER-DRIVE.
OKAY, WHERE'S THAT?

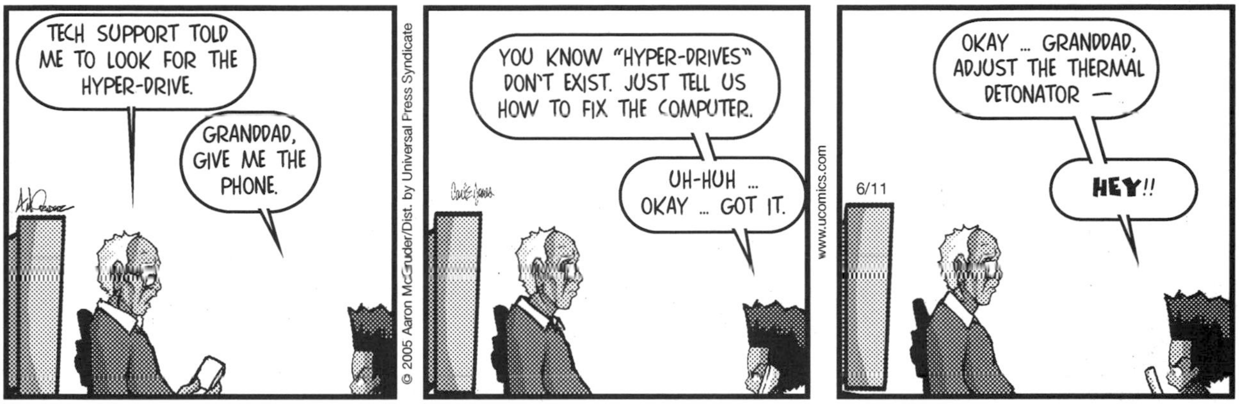
TECH SUPPORT TOLD ME TO LOOK FOR THE HYPER-DRIVE.
GRANDDAD, GIVE ME THE PHONE.
© 2005 Aaron McGruder/Dist. by Universal Press Syndicate
YOU KNOW "HYPER-DRIVES" DON'T EXIST. JUST TELL US HOW TO FIX THE COMPUTER.
UH-HUH ... OKAY ... GOT IT.
www.ucomics.com
6/11
OKAY ... GRANDDAD, ADJUST THE THERMAL DETONATOR —
HEY!!

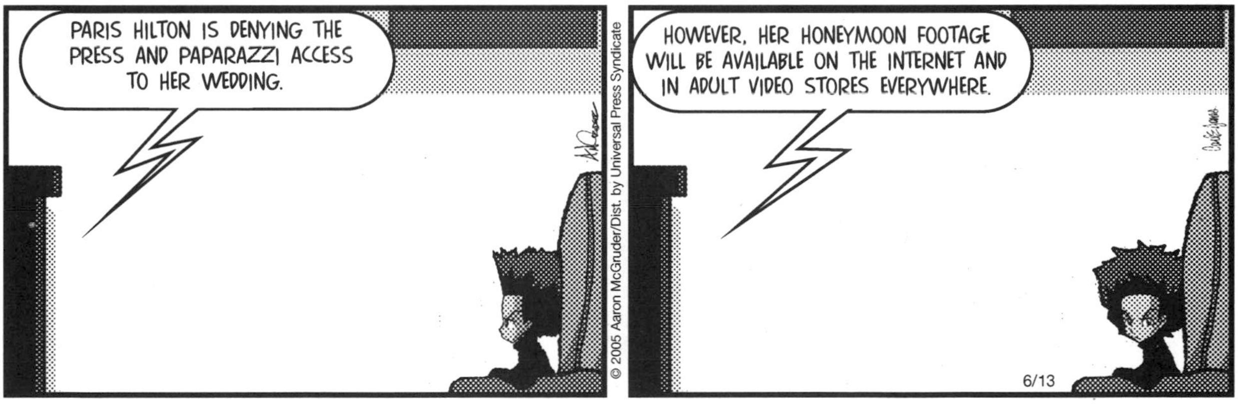
PARIS HILTON IS DENYING THE PRESS AND PAPARAZZI ACCESS TO HER WEDDING.
© 2005 Aaron McGruder/Dist. by Universal Press Syndicate
HOWEVER, HER HONEYMOON FOOTAGE WILL BE AVAILABLE ON THE INTERNET AND IN ADULT VIDEO STORES EVERYWHERE.
6/13

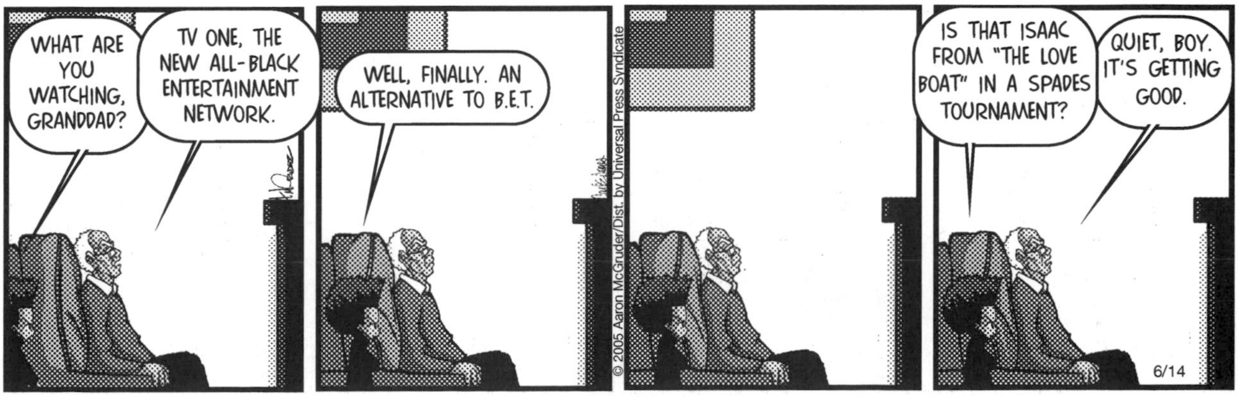
WHAT ARE YOU WATCHING, GRANDDAD?
TV ONE, THE NEW ALL-BLACK ENTERTAINMENT NETWORK.
WELL, FINALLY. AN ALTERNATIVE TO B.E.T.
© 2005 Aaron McGruder/Dist. by Universal Press Syndicate
IS THAT ISAAC FROM "THE LOVE BOAT" IN A SPADES TOURNAMENT?
QUIET, BOY. IT'S GETTING GOOD.
6/14

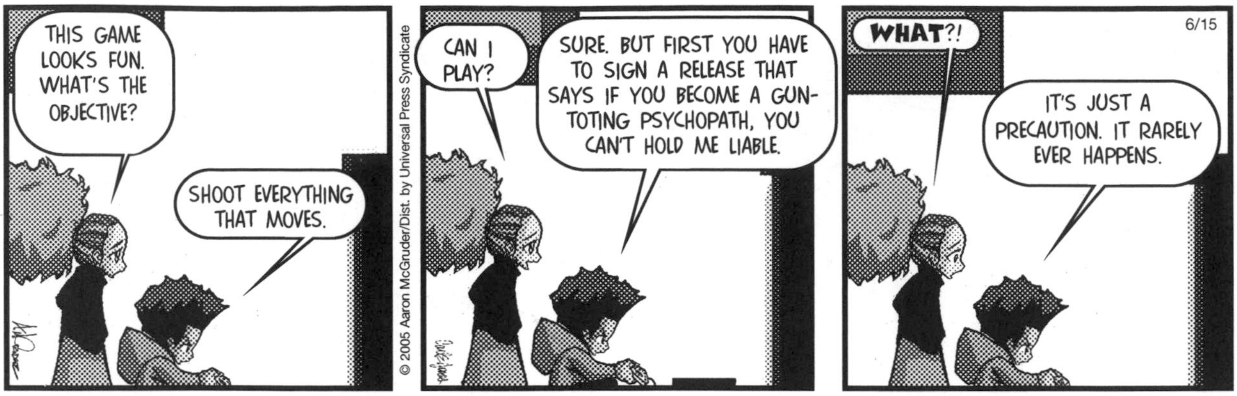
THIS GAME LOOKS FUN. WHAT'S THE OBJECTIVE?
SHOOT EVERYTHING THAT MOVES.
© 2005 Aaron McGruder/Dist. by Universal Press Syndicate
CAN I PLAY?
SURE. BUT FIRST YOU HAVE TO SIGN A RELEASE THAT SAYS IF YOU BECOME A GUN-TOTING PSYCHOPATH, YOU CAN'T HOLD ME LIABLE.
6/15
WHAT?!
IT'S JUST A PRECAUTION. IT RARELY EVER HAPPENS.

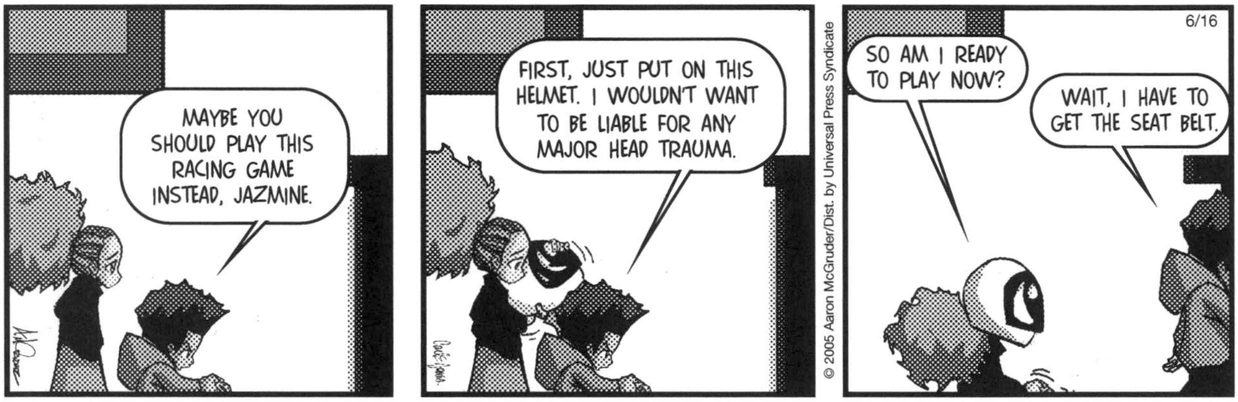
MAYBE YOU SHOULD PLAY THIS RACING GAME INSTEAD, JAZMINE.
FIRST, JUST PUT ON THIS HELMET. I WOULDN'T WANT TO BE LIABLE FOR ANY MAJOR HEAD TRAUMA.
© 2005 Aaron McGruder/Dist. by Universal Press Syndicate
6/16
SO AM I READY TO PLAY NOW?
WAIT, I HAVE TO GET THE SEAT BELT.

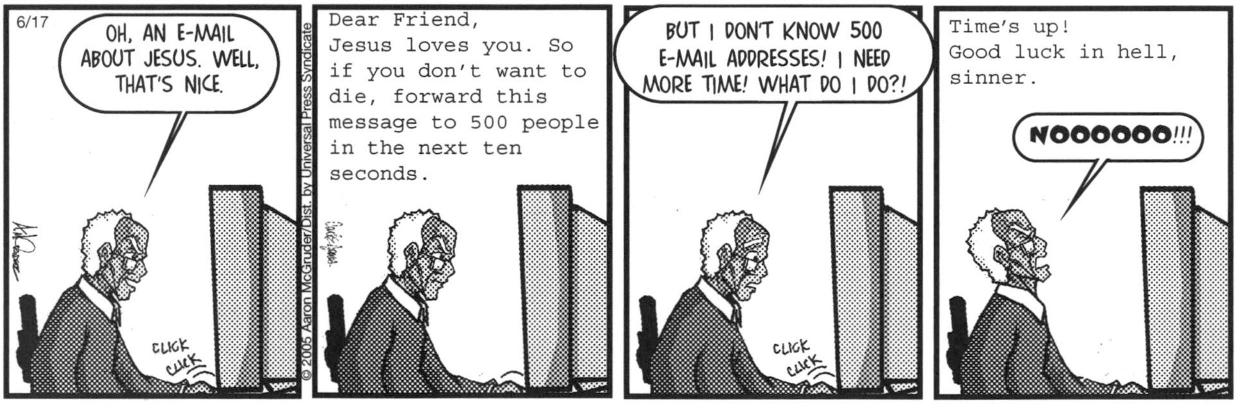
6/17
OH, AN E-MAIL ABOUT JESUS. WELL, THAT'S NICE.
CLICK CLICK
© 2005 Aaron McGruder/Dist. by Universal Press Syndicate
Dear Friend,
Jesus loves you. So if you don't want to die, forward this message to 500 people in the next ten seconds.
BUT I DON'T KNOW 500 E-MAIL ADDRESSES! I NEED MORE TIME! WHAT DO I DO?!
CLICK CLICK
Time's up!
Good luck in hell, sinner.
NOOOOOO!!!

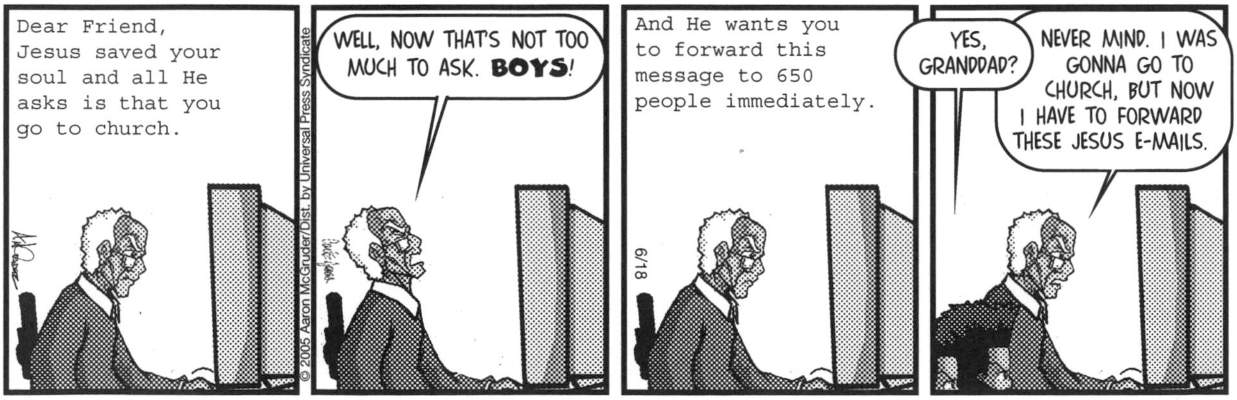
Dear Friend,
Jesus saved your soul and all He asks is that you go to church.
© 2005 Aaron McGruder/Dist. by Universal Press Syndicate
WELL, NOW THAT'S NOT TOO MUCH TO ASK. BOYS!
And He wants you to forward this message to 650 people immediately.
6/18
YES, GRANDDAD?
NEVER MIND. I WAS GONNA GO TO CHURCH, BUT NOW I HAVE TO FORWARD THESE JESUS E-MAILS.

THE BOONDOCKS **BY AARON McGRUDER**

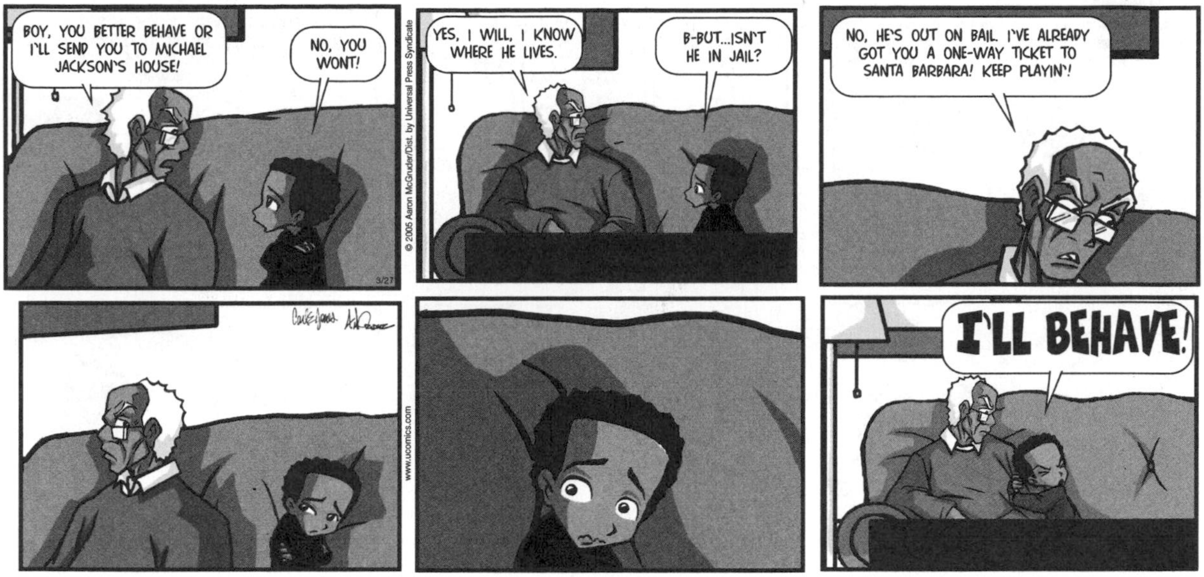
BOY, YOU BETTER BEHAVE OR I'LL SEND YOU TO MICHAEL JACKSON'S HOUSE!
NO, YOU WONT!
YES, I WILL, I KNOW WHERE HE LIVES.
B-BUT...ISN'T HE IN JAIL?
NO, HE'S OUT ON BAIL. I'VE ALREADY GOT YOU A ONE-WAY TICKET TO SANTA BARBARA! KEEP PLAYIN'!
I'LL BEHAVE!
© 2005 Aaron McGruder/Dist. by Universal Press Syndicate
www.ucomics.com

THE BOONDOCKS **BY AARON McGRUDER**

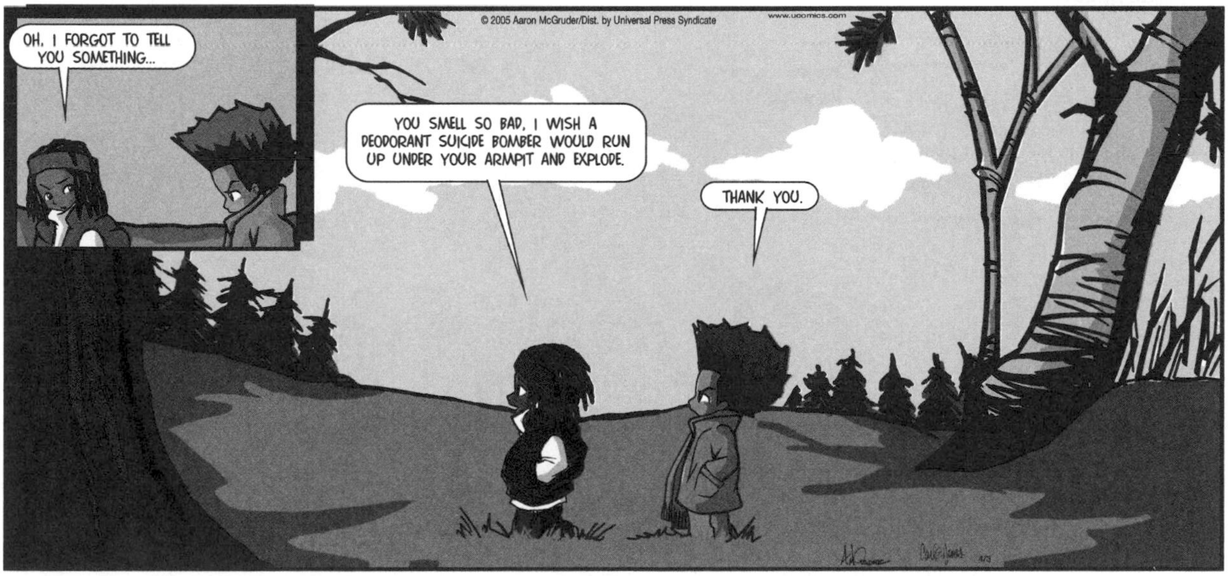
OH, I FORGOT TO TELL YOU SOMETHING...
YOU SMELL SO BAD, I WISH A DEODORANT SUICIDE BOMBER WOULD RUN UP UNDER YOUR ARMPIT AND EXPLODE.
THANK YOU.
© 2005 Aaron McGruder/Dist. by Universal Press Syndicate
www.ucomics.com

THE BOONDOCKS **BY AARON McGRUDER**

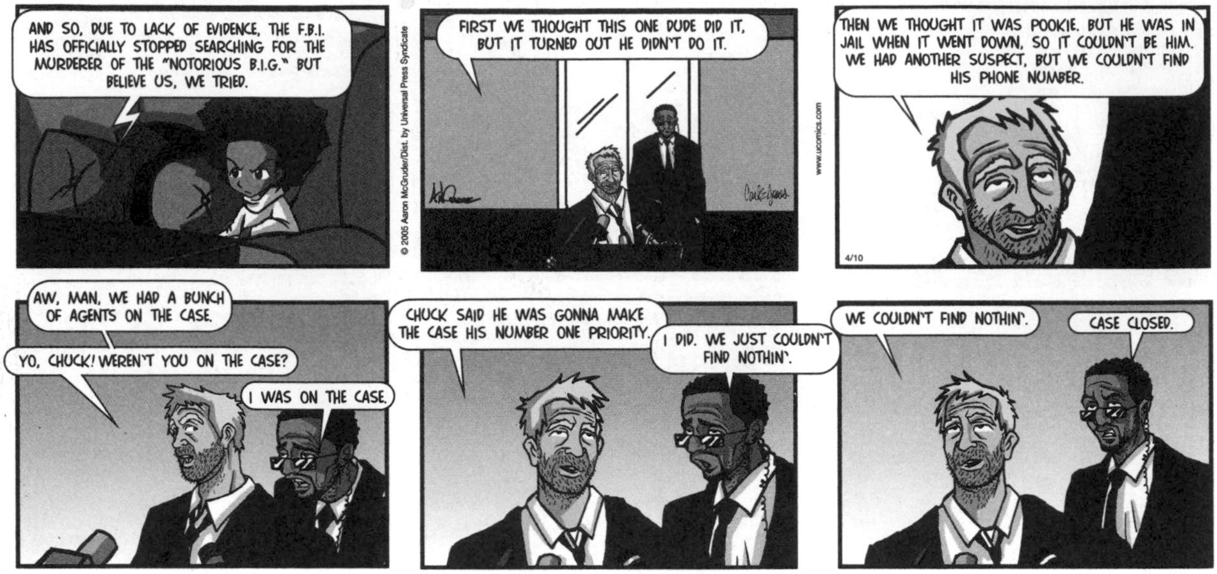
AND SO, DUE TO LACK OF EVIDENCE, THE F.B.I. HAS OFFICIALLY STOPPED SEARCHING FOR THE MURDERER OF THE "NOTORIOUS B.I.G." BUT BELIEVE US, WE TRIED.
© 2005 Aaron McGruder/Dist. by Universal Press Syndicate
FIRST WE THOUGHT THIS ONE DUDE DID IT, BUT IT TURNED OUT HE DIDN'T DO IT.
www.ucomics.com
THEN WE THOUGHT IT WAS POOKIE. BUT HE WAS IN JAIL WHEN IT WENT DOWN, SO IT COULDN'T BE HIM. WE HAD ANOTHER SUSPECT, BUT WE COULDN'T FIND HIS PHONE NUMBER.
4/10
AW, MAN, WE HAD A BUNCH OF AGENTS ON THE CASE.
YO, CHUCK! WEREN'T YOU ON THE CASE?
I WAS ON THE CASE.
CHUCK SAID HE WAS GONNA MAKE THE CASE HIS NUMBER ONE PRIORITY.
I DID. WE JUST COULDN'T FIND NOTHIN'.
WE COULDN'T FIND NOTHIN'.
CASE CLOSED.

THE BOONDOCKS **BY AARON McGRUDER**

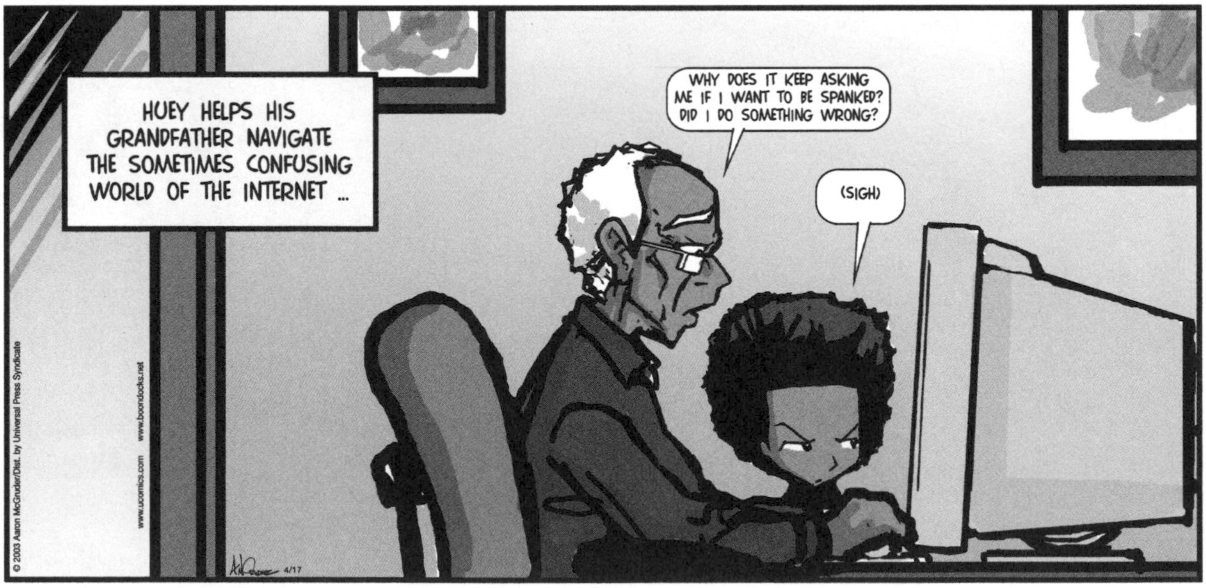
HUEY HELPS HIS GRANDFATHER NAVIGATE THE SOMETIMES CONFUSING WORLD OF THE INTERNET ...
WHY DOES IT KEEP ASKING ME IF I WANT TO BE SPANKED? DID I DO SOMETHING WRONG?
(SIGH)
© 2003 Aaron McGruder/Dist. by Universal Press Syndicate
www.ucomics.com
www.boondocks.net
4/17

THE BOONDOCKS **BY AARON McGRUDER**

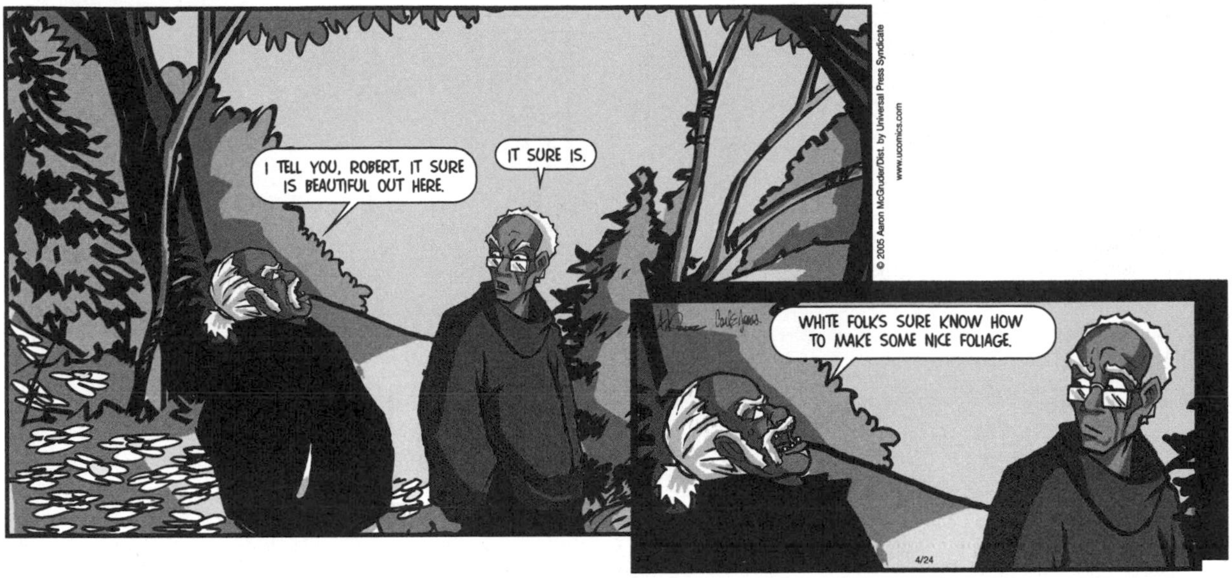
I TELL YOU, ROBERT, IT SURE IS BEAUTIFUL OUT HERE.
IT SURE IS.
WHITE FOLKS SURE KNOW HOW TO MAKE SOME NICE FOLIAGE.
© 2005 Aaron McGruder/Dist. by Universal Press Syndicate www.ucomics.com
4/24

THE BOONDOCKS **BY AARON McGRUDER**

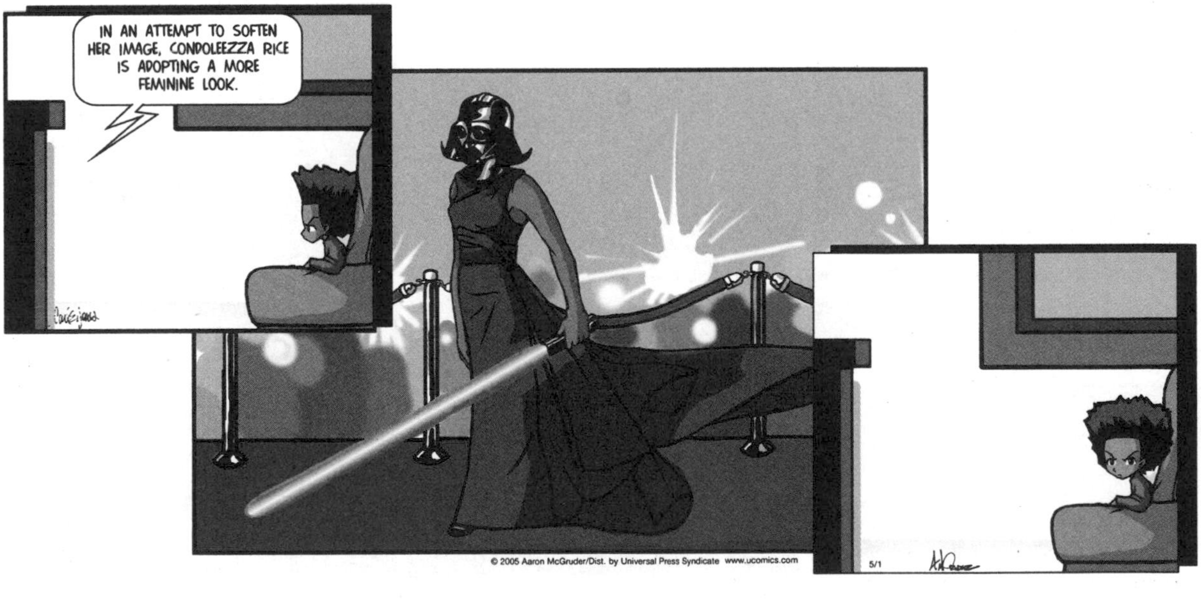
IN AN ATTEMPT TO SOFTEN HER IMAGE, CONDOLEEZZA RICE IS ADOPTING A MORE FEMININE LOOK.
© 2005 Aaron McGruder/Dist. by Universal Press Syndicate www.ucomics.com
5/1

THE BOONDOCKS **BY AARON McGRUDER**

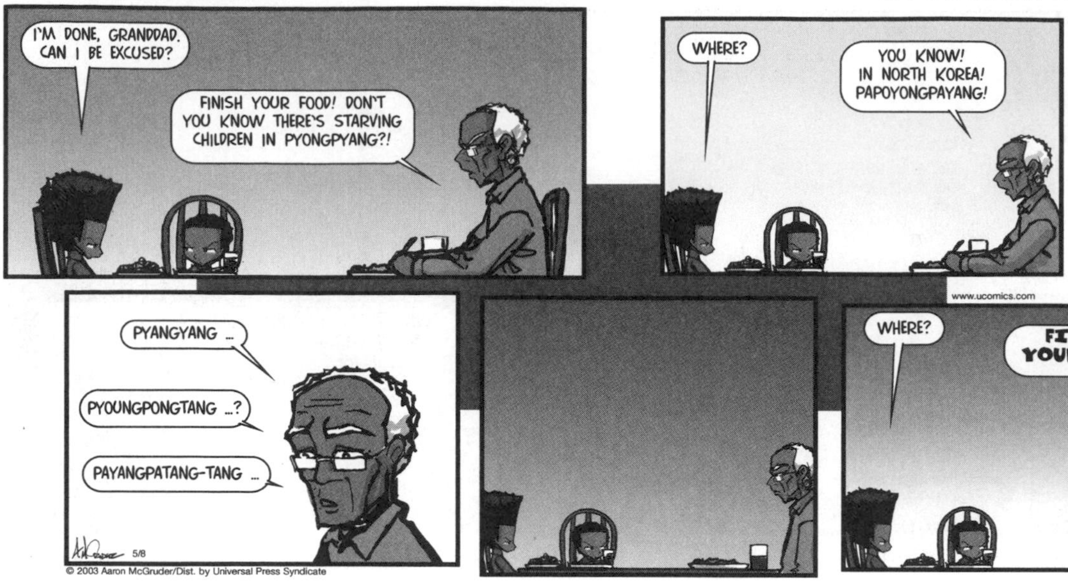
I'M DONE, GRANDDAD. CAN I BE EXCUSED?
FINISH YOUR FOOD! DON'T YOU KNOW THERE'S STARVING CHILDREN IN PYONGPYANG?!
WHERE?
YOU KNOW! IN NORTH KOREA! PAPOYONGPAYANG!
www.ucomics.com
PYANGYANG ...
PYOUNGPONGTANG ...?
PAYANGPATANG-TANG ...
5/8
© 2003 Aaron McGruder/Dist. by Universal Press Syndicate
WHERE?
FINISH YOUR FOOD!

THE BOONDOCKS **BY AARON McGRUDER**

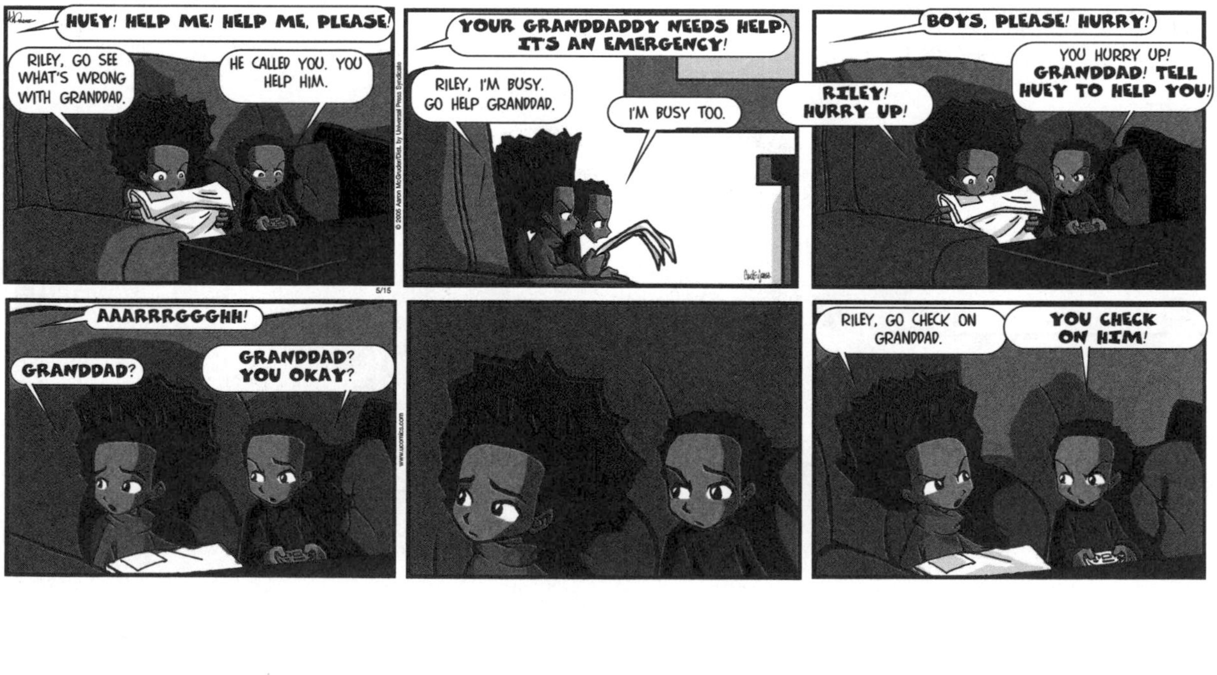
HUEY! HELP ME! HELP ME, PLEASE!
RILEY, GO SEE WHAT'S WRONG WITH GRANDDAD.
HE CALLED YOU. YOU HELP HIM.
5/15
YOUR GRANDDADDY NEEDS HELP! IT'S AN EMERGENCY!
RILEY, I'M BUSY. GO HELP GRANDDAD.
I'M BUSY TOO.
BOYS, PLEASE! HURRY!
RILEY! HURRY UP!
YOU HURRY UP! GRANDDAD! TELL HUEY TO HELP YOU!
AAARRRGGGHH!
GRANDDAD?
GRANDDAD? YOU OKAY?
RILEY, GO CHECK ON GRANDDAD.
YOU CHECK ON HIM!

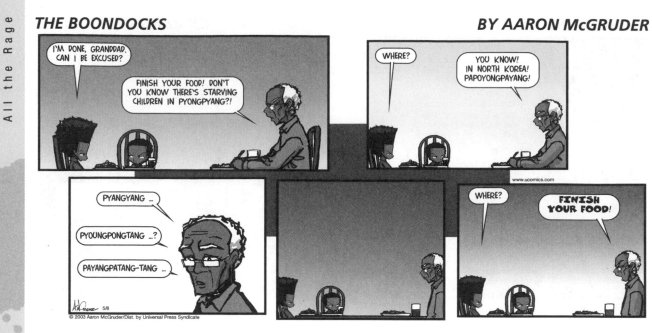

THE BOONDOCKS **BY AARON McGRUDER**

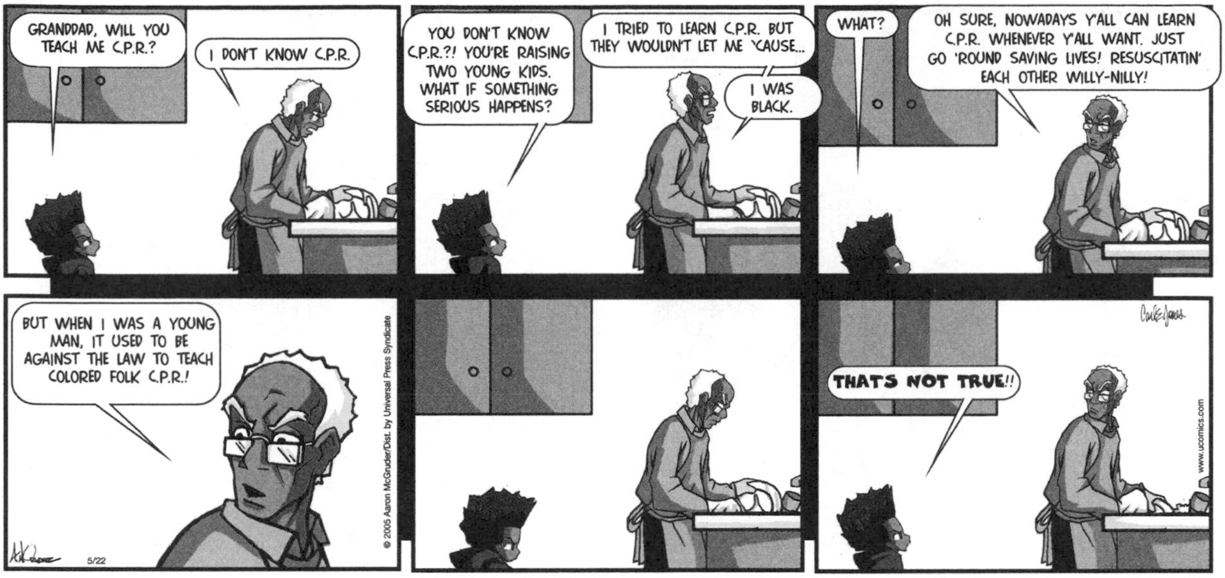
GRANDDAD, WILL YOU TEACH ME C.P.R.?
I DON'T KNOW C.P.R.
YOU DON'T KNOW C.P.R.?! YOU'RE RAISING TWO YOUNG KIDS. WHAT IF SOMETHING SERIOUS HAPPENS?
I TRIED TO LEARN C.P.R. BUT THEY WOULDN'T LET ME 'CAUSE...
I WAS BLACK.
WHAT?
OH SURE, NOWADAYS Y'ALL CAN LEARN C.P.R. WHENEVER Y'ALL WANT. JUST GO 'ROUND SAVING LIVES! RESUSCITATIN' EACH OTHER WILLY-NILLY!
BUT WHEN I WAS A YOUNG MAN, IT USED TO BE AGAINST THE LAW TO TEACH COLORED FOLK C.P.R.!
© 2005 Aaron McGruder/Dist. by Universal Press Syndicate
5/22
THAT'S NOT TRUE!!
www.ucomics.com

THE BOONDOCKS **BY AARON McGRUDER**

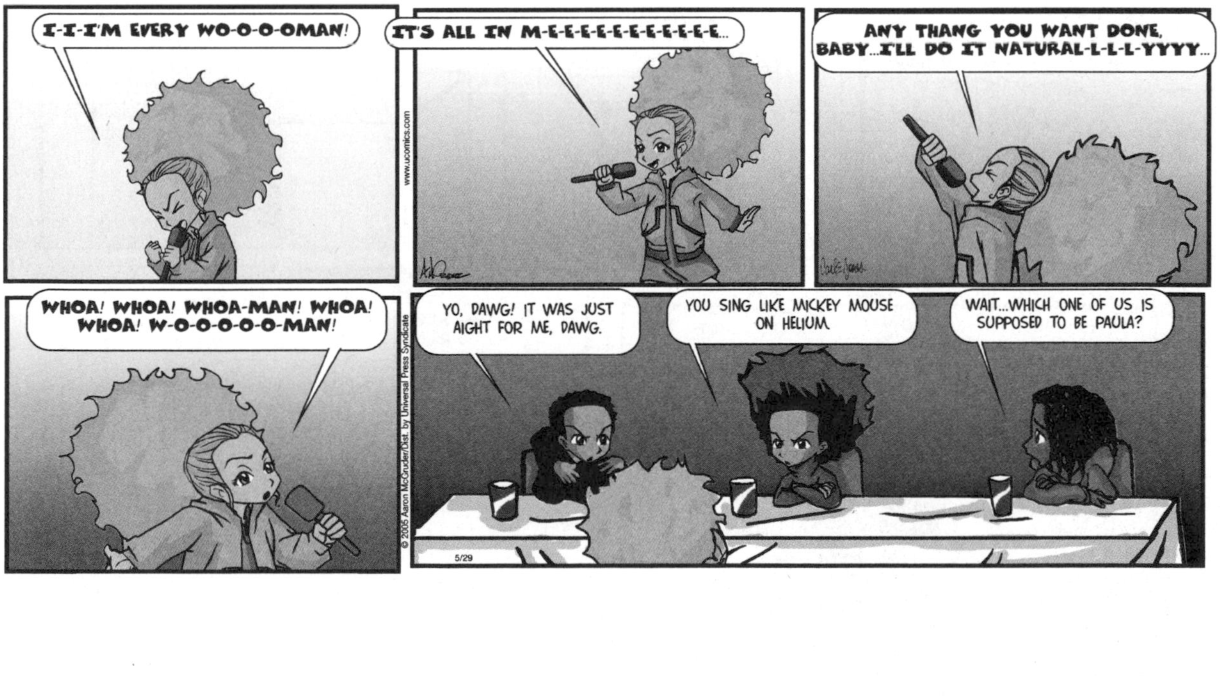
I-I-I'M EVERY WO-O-O-OMAN!
IT'S ALL IN M-E-E-E-E-E-E-E-E-E-E-E...
www.ucomics.com
ANY THANG YOU WANT DONE, BABY...I'LL DO IT NATURAL-L-L-L-YYYY...
WHOA! WHOA! WHOA-MAN! WHOA! WHOA! W-O-O-O-O-O-MAN!
© 2005 Aaron McGruder/Dist. by Universal Press Syndicate
YO, DAWG! IT WAS JUST AIGHT FOR ME, DAWG.
YOU SING LIKE MICKEY MOUSE ON HELIUM.
WAIT...WHICH ONE OF US IS SUPPOSED TO BE PAULA?
5/29

THE BOONDOCKS BY AARON McGRUDER

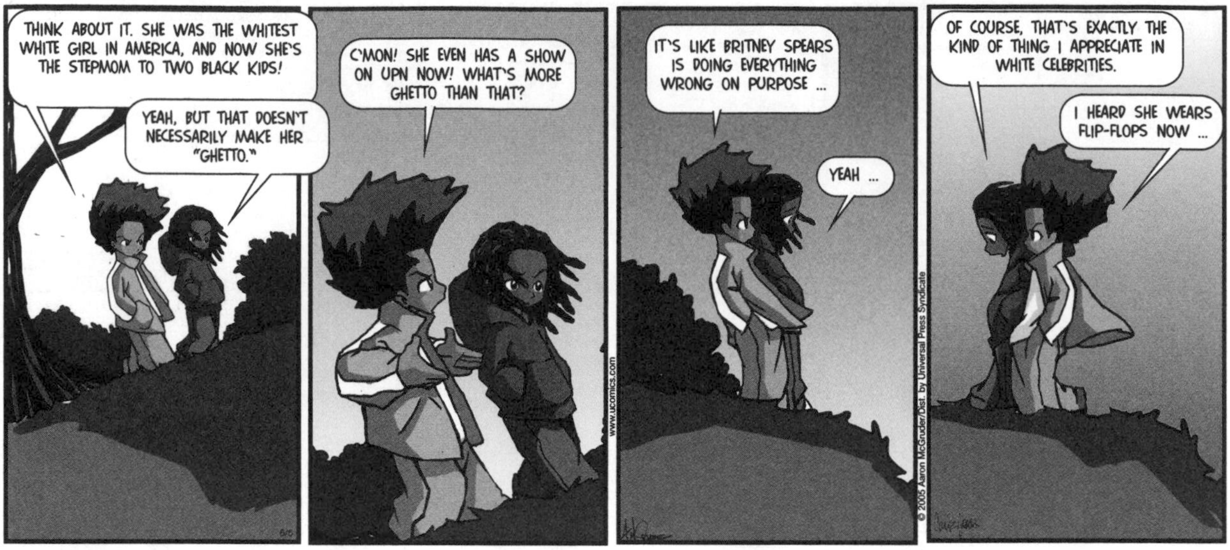
THINK ABOUT IT. SHE WAS THE WHITEST WHITE GIRL IN AMERICA, AND NOW SHE'S THE STEPMOM TO TWO BLACK KIDS!
YEAH, BUT THAT DOESN'T NECESSARILY MAKE HER "GHETTO."
C'MON! SHE EVEN HAS A SHOW ON UPN NOW! WHAT'S MORE GHETTO THAN THAT?
www.ucomics.com
IT'S LIKE BRITNEY SPEARS IS DOING EVERYTHING WRONG ON PURPOSE ...
YEAH ...
© 2005 Aaron McGruder/Dist. by Universal Press Syndicate
OF COURSE, THAT'S EXACTLY THE KIND OF THING I APPRECIATE IN WHITE CELEBRITIES.
I HEARD SHE WEARS FLIP-FLOPS NOW ...

THE BOONDOCKS BY AARON McGRUDER

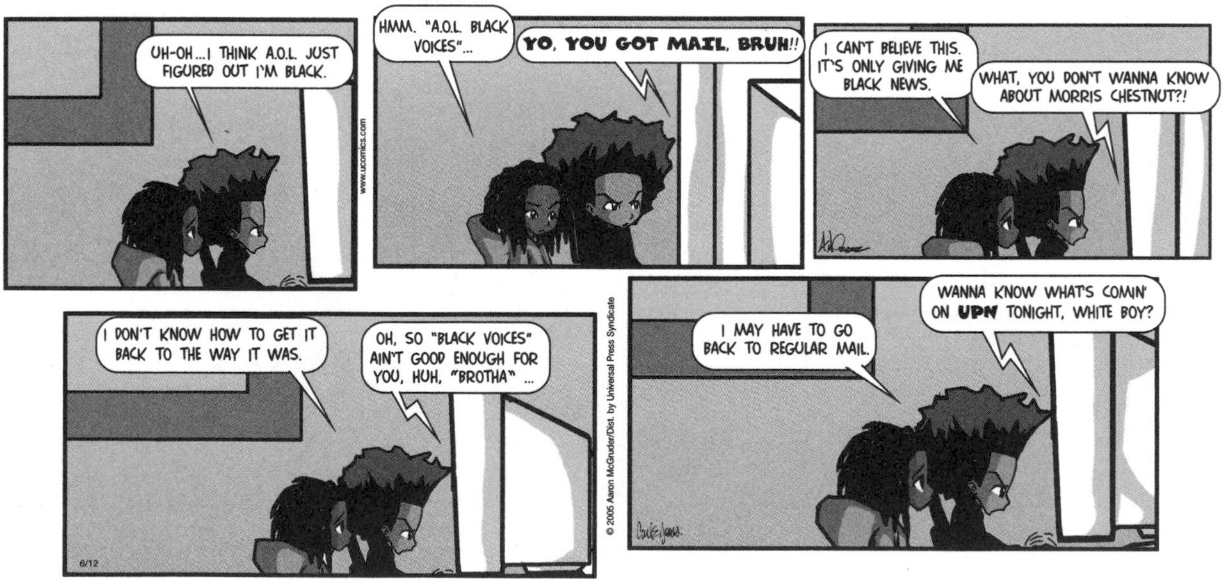
UH-OH... I THINK A.O.L. JUST FIGURED OUT I'M BLACK.
www.ucomics.com
HMM. "A.O.L. BLACK VOICES"...
YO, YOU GOT MAIL, BRUH!!
I CAN'T BELIEVE THIS. IT'S ONLY GIVING ME BLACK NEWS.
WHAT, YOU DON'T WANNA KNOW ABOUT MORRIS CHESTNUT?!
I DON'T KNOW HOW TO GET IT BACK TO THE WAY IT WAS.
OH, SO "BLACK VOICES" AIN'T GOOD ENOUGH FOR YOU, HUH, "BROTHA" ...
6/12
© 2005 Aaron McGruder/Dist. by Universal Press Syndicate
I MAY HAVE TO GO BACK TO REGULAR MAIL.
WANNA KNOW WHAT'S COMIN' ON UPN TONIGHT, WHITE BOY?

THE BOONDOCKS BY AARON McGRUDER

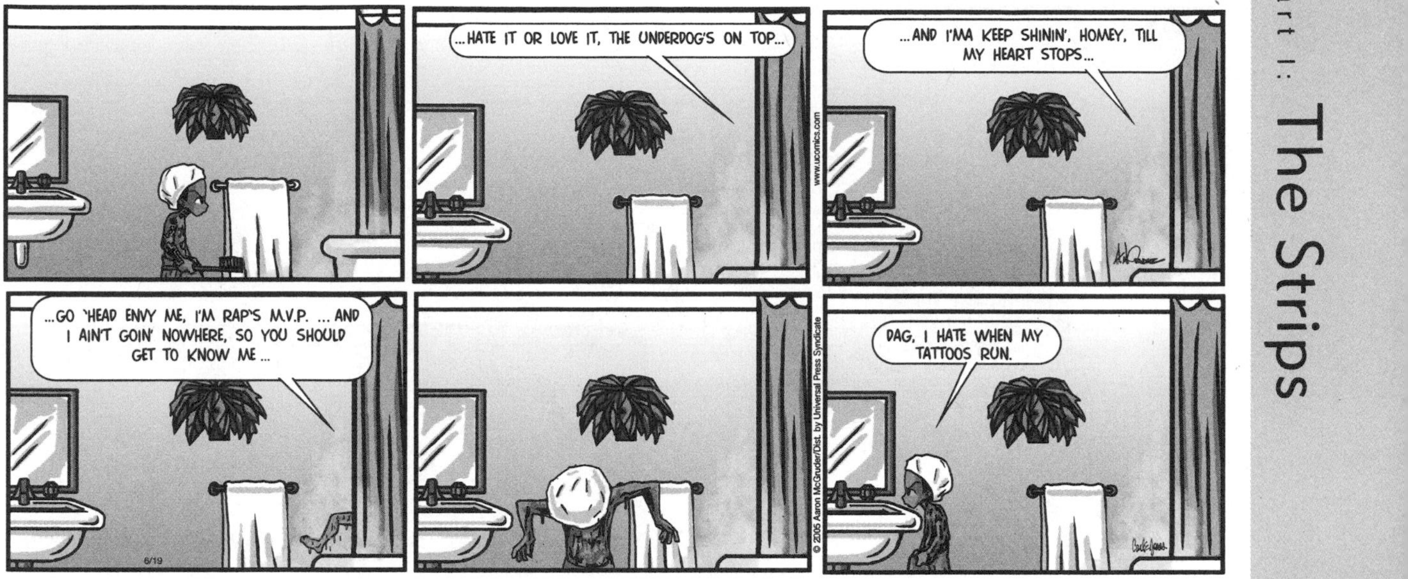
...HATE IT OR LOVE IT, THE UNDERDOG'S ON TOP...
...AND I'MA KEEP SHININ', HOMEY, TILL MY HEART STOPS...
...GO 'HEAD ENVY ME, I'M RAP'S M.V.P. ... AND I AIN'T GOIN' NOWHERE, SO YOU SHOULD GET TO KNOW ME ...
DAG, I HATE WHEN MY TATTOOS RUN.
6/19
www.ucomics.com
© 2005 Aaron McGruder/Dist. by Universal Press Syndicate

THE BOONDOCKS BY AARON McGRUDER

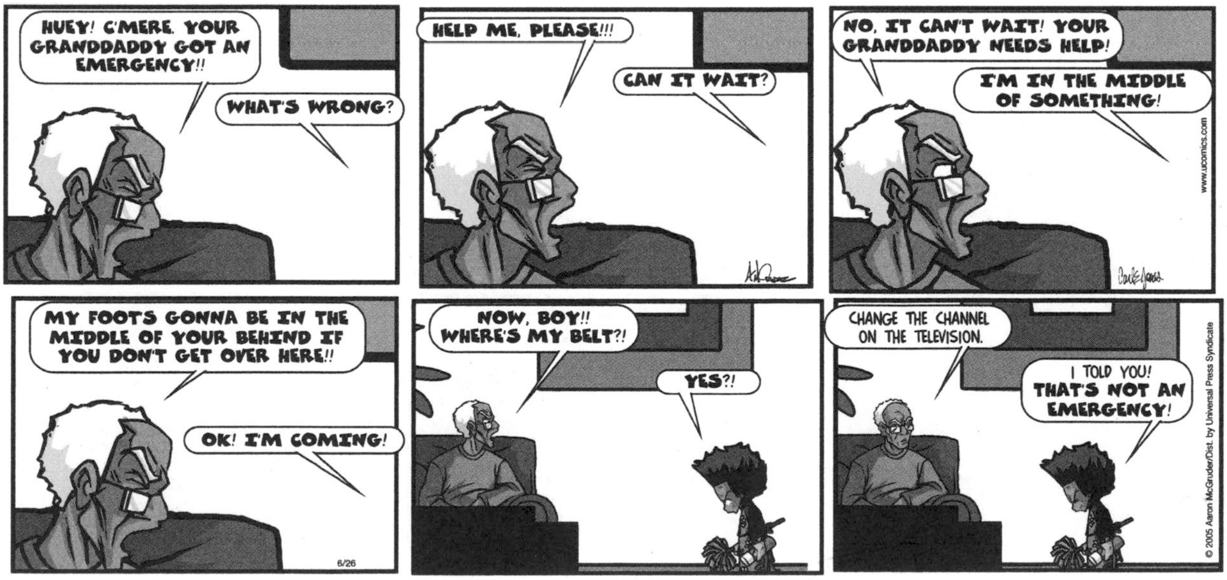
HUEY! C'MERE. YOUR GRANDDADDY GOT AN EMERGENCY!!
WHAT'S WRONG?
HELP ME, PLEASE!!!
CAN IT WAIT?
NO, IT CAN'T WAIT! YOUR GRANDDADDY NEEDS HELP!
I'M IN THE MIDDLE OF SOMETHING!
MY FOOTS GONNA BE IN THE MIDDLE OF YOUR BEHIND IF YOU DON'T GET OVER HERE!!
OK! I'M COMING!
6/26
NOW, BOY!! WHERE'S MY BELT?!
YES?!
CHANGE THE CHANNEL ON THE TELEVISION.
I TOLD YOU! THAT'S NOT AN EMERGENCY!
www.ucomics.com
© 2005 Aaron McGruder/Dist. by Universal Press Syndicate

THE BOONDOCKS

BY AARON McGRUDER

GRANDDAD, REMEMBER WHEN WE AGREED THAT I WOULDN'T PLAY WITH FIREWORKS?
YES...
UM...THE COPS ARE HERE. SOMETHING ABOUT THE NEIGHBOR'S DOG EXPLODING.
GET BACK HERE, BOY!
TOO LATE. THAT'S OUR STORY AND WE'RE STICKING TO IT.
© 2005 Aaron McGruder/Dist. by Universal Press Syndicate
www.ucomics.com
7/3

THE BOONDOCKS

BY AARON McGRUDER

FIXIN' THE COMPUTER, HUH? YOU KNOW, I'M PRETTY HANDY MYSELF. MAYBE YOU SHOULD..UH...REBOOT THE RAM.
THANKS, GRANDDAD, BUT I GOT IT.
© 2005 Aaron McGruder/Dist. by Universal Press Syndicate
DID YOU CHECK THE MEGABYTE? IT COULD BE THE MEGABYTE.
IT'S NOT THE MEGABYTE, GRANDDAD.
JIGGLE THE NETWORK, BOY!
GRANDDAD, I SAID I GOT IT.
SORRY...I'LL LEAVE YOU ALONE.
THANK YOU.
www.ucomics.com
7/10
I BET YOU HAVE TO REPROGRAM THE FLUX CAPACITOR.
GRANDDAD! THAT DOESN'T EXIST!

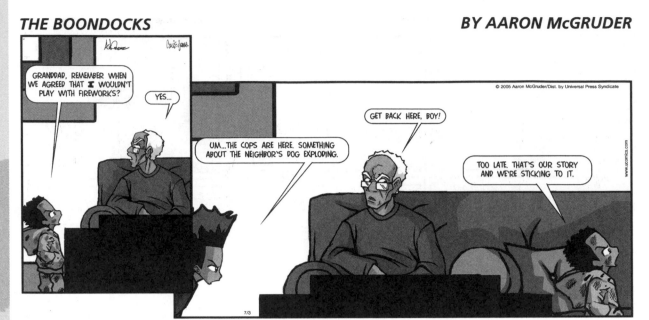

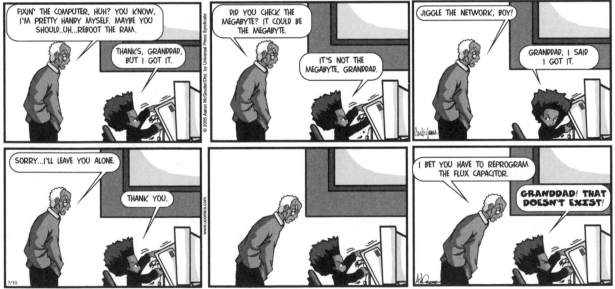

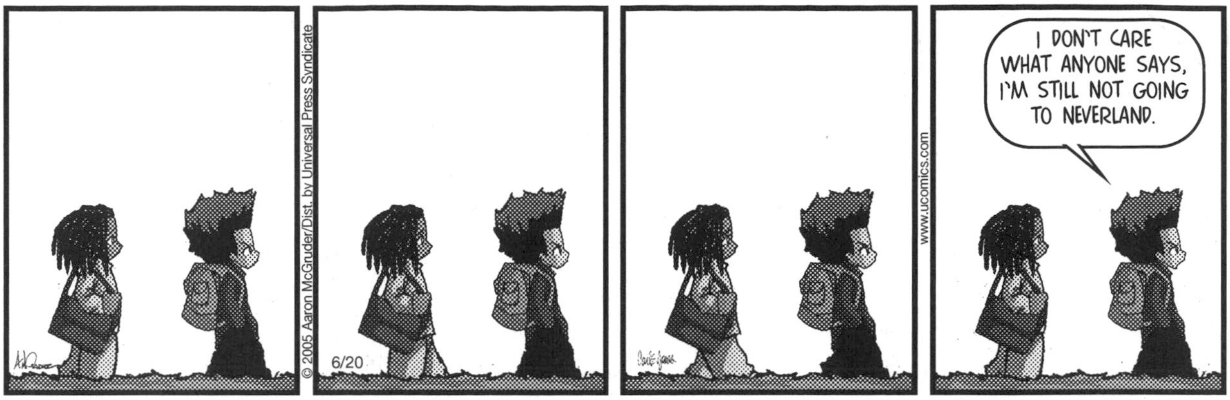

© 2005 Aaron McGruder/Dist. by Universal Press Syndicate
6/20
www.ucomics.com
I DON'T CARE WHAT ANYONE SAYS, I'M STILL NOT GOING TO NEVERLAND.

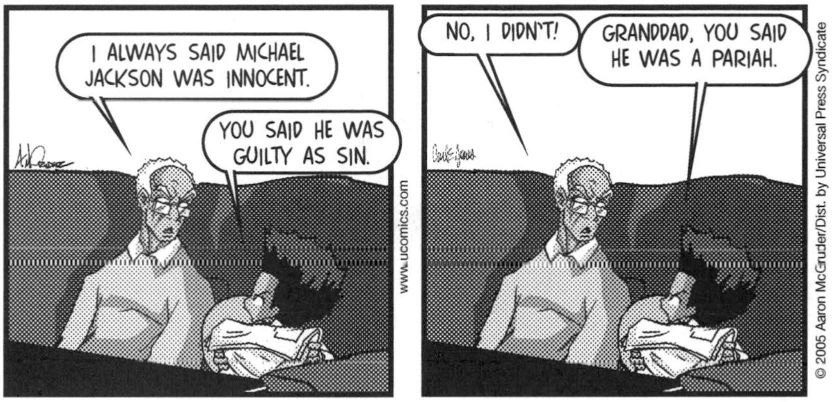

I ALWAYS SAID MICHAEL JACKSON WAS INNOCENT.
YOU SAID HE WAS GUILTY AS SIN.
www.ucomics.com
NO, I DIDN'T!
GRANDDAD, YOU SAID HE WAS A PARIAH.
© 2005 Aaron McGruder/Dist. by Universal Press Syndicate
NO, NO, I SAID HE WAS LIKE MARIAH ... A LITTLE CRAZY, BUT VERY TALENTED.
6/21

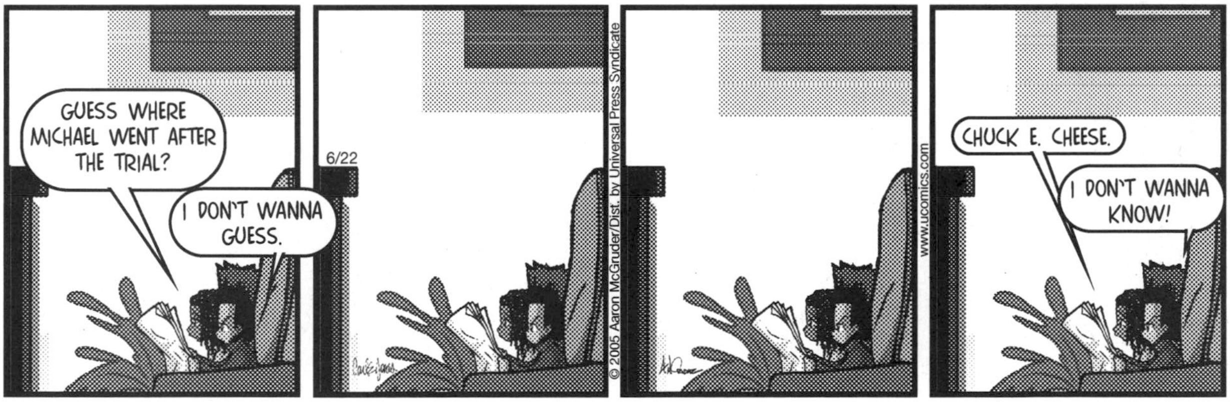

GUESS WHERE MICHAEL WENT AFTER THE TRIAL?
I DON'T WANNA GUESS.
6/22
© 2005 Aaron McGruder/Dist. by Universal Press Syndicate
www.ucomics.com
CHUCK E. CHEESE.
I DON'T WANNA KNOW!

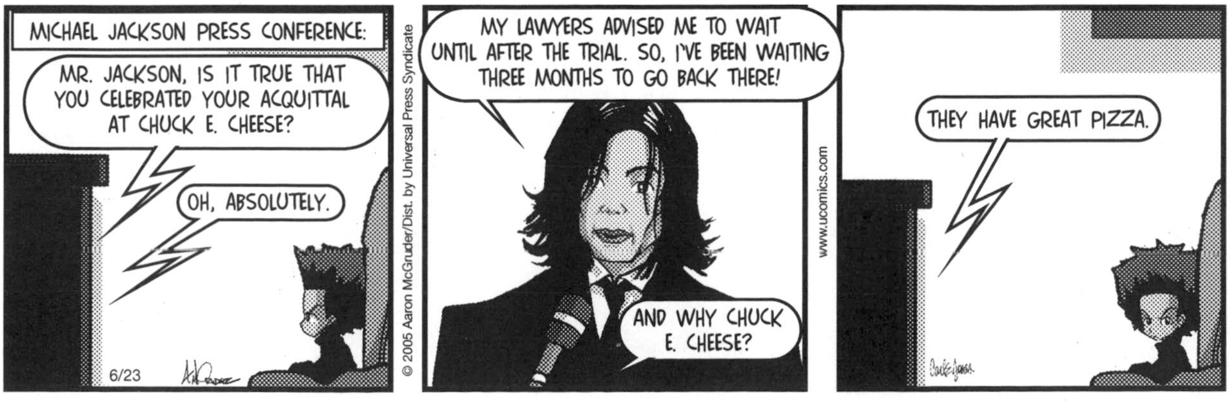

MICHAEL JACKSON PRESS CONFERENCE:
MR. JACKSON, IS IT TRUE THAT YOU CELEBRATED YOUR ACQUITTAL AT CHUCK E. CHEESE?
OH, ABSOLUTELY.
6/23
© 2005 Aaron McGruder/Dist. by Universal Press Syndicate
MY LAWYERS ADVISED ME TO WAIT UNTIL AFTER THE TRIAL. SO, I'VE BEEN WAITING THREE MONTHS TO GO BACK THERE!
AND WHY CHUCK E. CHEESE?
www.ucomics.com
THEY HAVE GREAT PIZZA.

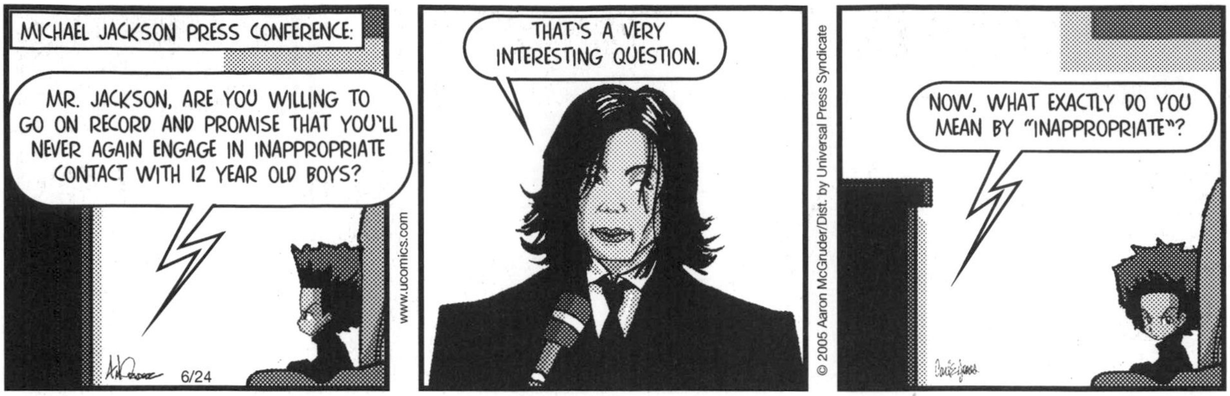
MICHAEL JACKSON PRESS CONFERENCE:
MR. JACKSON, ARE YOU WILLING TO GO ON RECORD AND PROMISE THAT YOU'LL NEVER AGAIN ENGAGE IN INAPPROPRIATE CONTACT WITH 12 YEAR OLD BOYS?
6/24
www.ucomics.com
THAT'S A VERY INTERESTING QUESTION.
© 2005 Aaron McGruder/Dist. by Universal Press Syndicate
NOW, WHAT EXACTLY DO YOU MEAN BY "INAPPROPRIATE"?

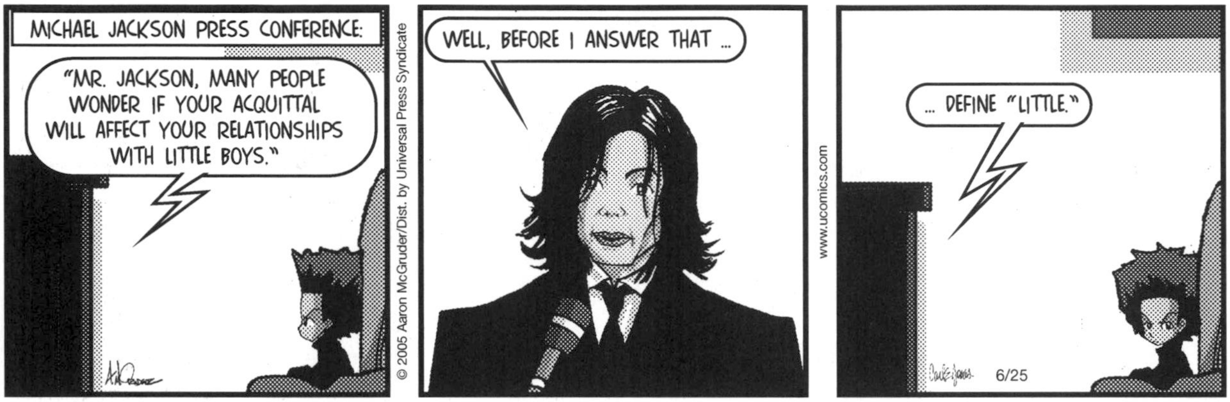
MICHAEL JACKSON PRESS CONFERENCE:
"MR. JACKSON, MANY PEOPLE WONDER IF YOUR ACQUITTAL WILL AFFECT YOUR RELATIONSHIPS WITH LITTLE BOYS."
© 2005 Aaron McGruder/Dist. by Universal Press Syndicate
WELL, BEFORE I ANSWER THAT ...
www.ucomics.com
... DEFINE "LITTLE."
6/25

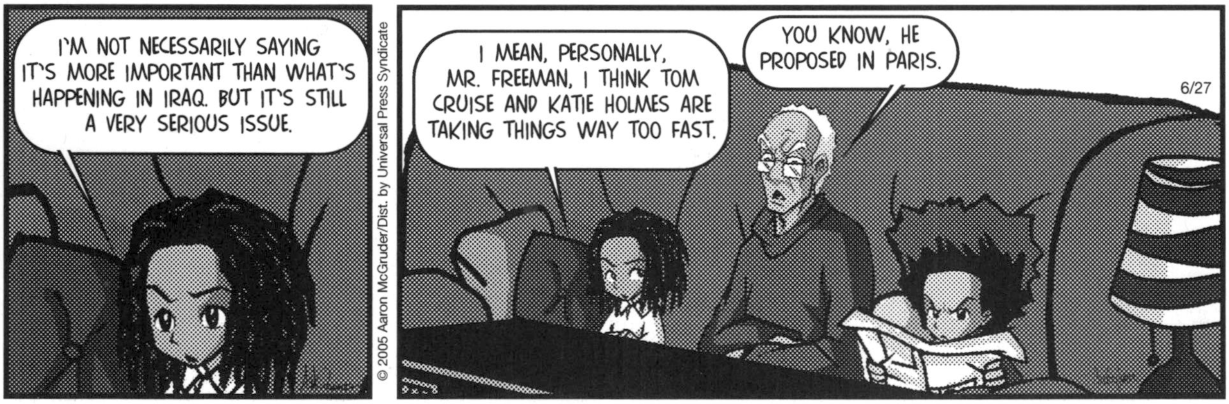
I'M NOT NECESSARILY SAYING IT'S MORE IMPORTANT THAN WHAT'S HAPPENING IN IRAQ. BUT IT'S STILL A VERY SERIOUS ISSUE.
© 2005 Aaron McGruder/Dist. by Universal Press Syndicate
I MEAN, PERSONALLY, MR. FREEMAN, I THINK TOM CRUISE AND KATIE HOLMES ARE TAKING THINGS WAY TOO FAST.
YOU KNOW, HE PROPOSED IN PARIS.
6/27

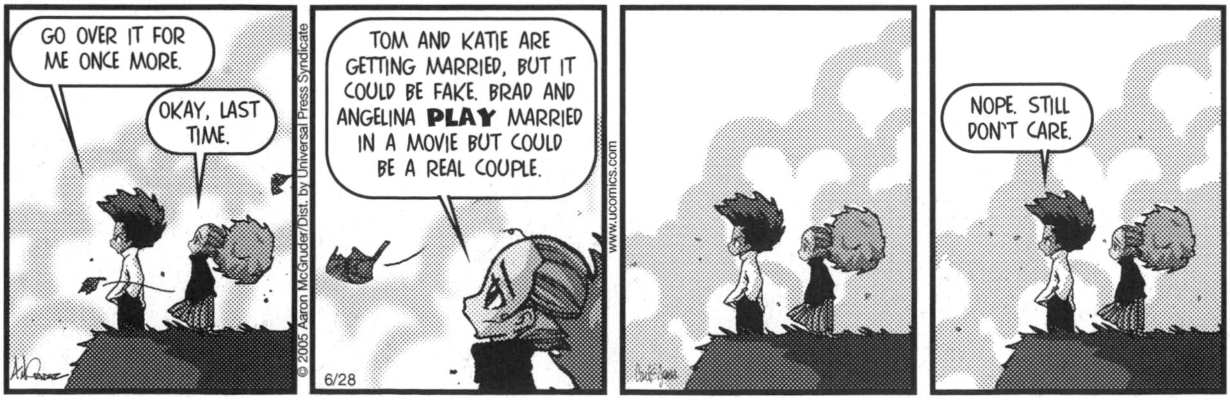
GO OVER IT FOR ME ONCE MORE.
OKAY, LAST TIME.
© 2005 Aaron McGruder/Dist. by Universal Press Syndicate
TOM AND KATIE ARE GETTING MARRIED, BUT IT COULD BE FAKE. BRAD AND ANGELINA **PLAY** MARRIED IN A MOVIE BUT COULD BE A REAL COUPLE.
6/28
www.ucomics.com
NOPE. STILL DON'T CARE.

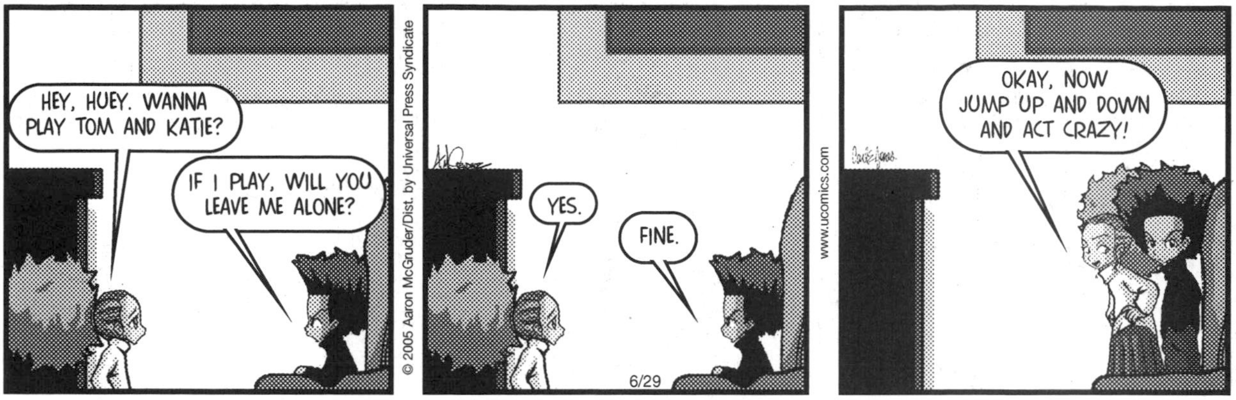
HEY, HUEY. WANNA PLAY TOM AND KATIE?
IF I PLAY, WILL YOU LEAVE ME ALONE?
© 2005 Aaron McGruder/Dist. by Universal Press Syndicate
YES.
FINE.
6/29
www.ucomics.com
OKAY, NOW JUMP UP AND DOWN AND ACT CRAZY!

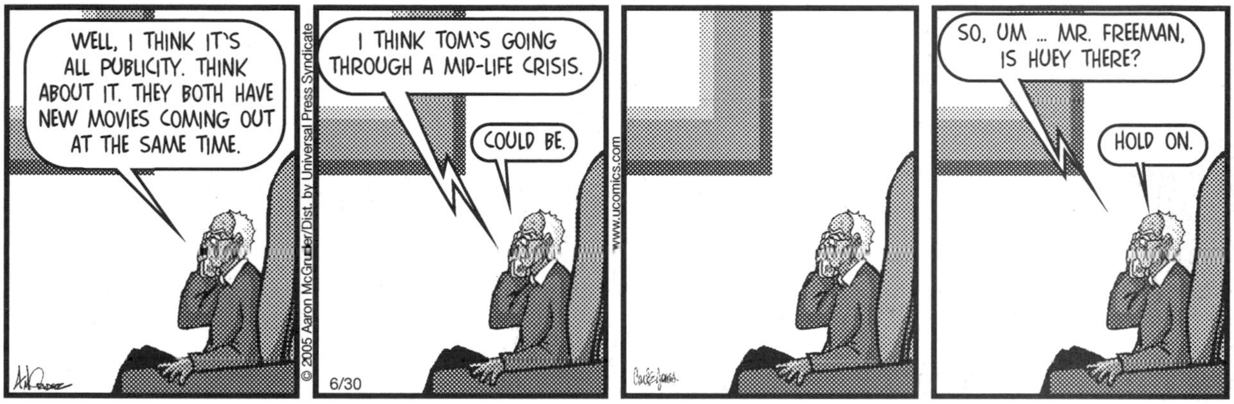
WELL, I THINK IT'S ALL PUBLICITY. THINK ABOUT IT. THEY BOTH HAVE NEW MOVIES COMING OUT AT THE SAME TIME.
© 2005 Aaron McGruder/Dist. by Universal Press Syndicate
6/30
I THINK TOM'S GOING THROUGH A MID-LIFE CRISIS.
COULD BE.
www.ucomics.com
SO, UM ... MR. FREEMAN, IS HUEY THERE?
HOLD ON.

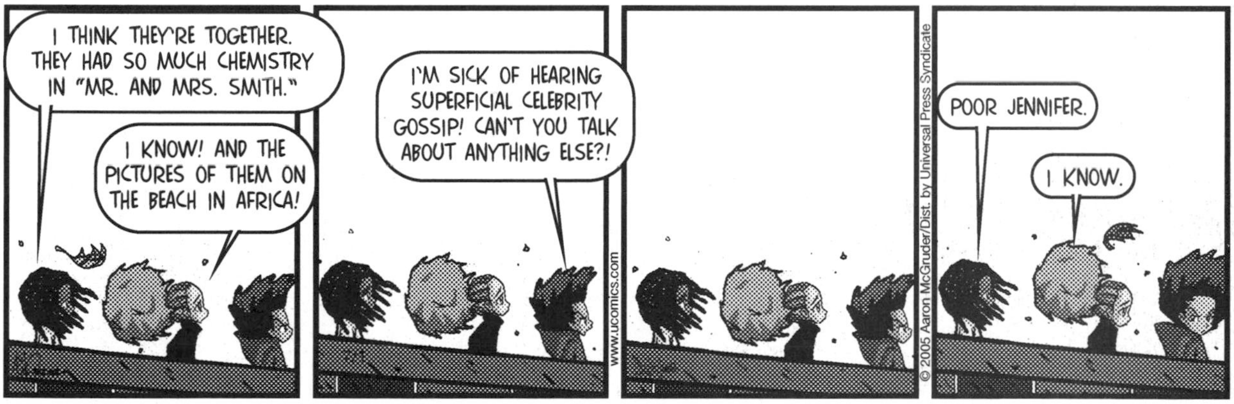
I THINK THEY'RE TOGETHER. THEY HAD SO MUCH CHEMISTRY IN "MR. AND MRS. SMITH."
I KNOW! AND THE PICTURES OF THEM ON THE BEACH IN AFRICA!
I'M SICK OF HEARING SUPERFICIAL CELEBRITY GOSSIP! CAN'T YOU TALK ABOUT ANYTHING ELSE?!
www.ucomics.com
© 2005 Aaron McGruder/Dist. by Universal Press Syndicate
POOR JENNIFER.
I KNOW.

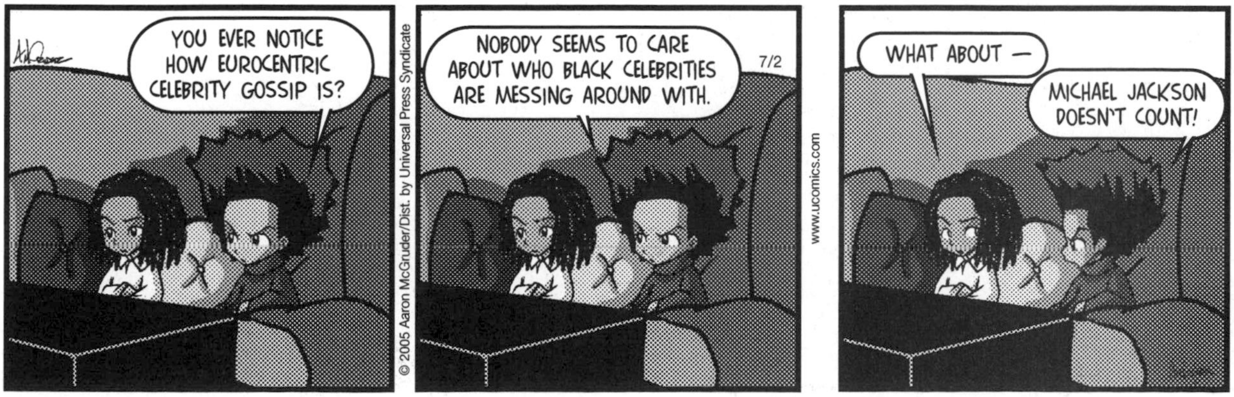
YOU EVER NOTICE HOW EUROCENTRIC CELEBRITY GOSSIP IS?
© 2005 Aaron McGruder/Dist. by Universal Press Syndicate
NOBODY SEEMS TO CARE ABOUT WHO BLACK CELEBRITIES ARE MESSING AROUND WITH.
7/2
www.ucomics.com
WHAT ABOUT —
MICHAEL JACKSON DOESN'T COUNT!

McGruder's made his mark and earned his readers by representing the hip-hop generation.

—*Los Angeles Magazine*

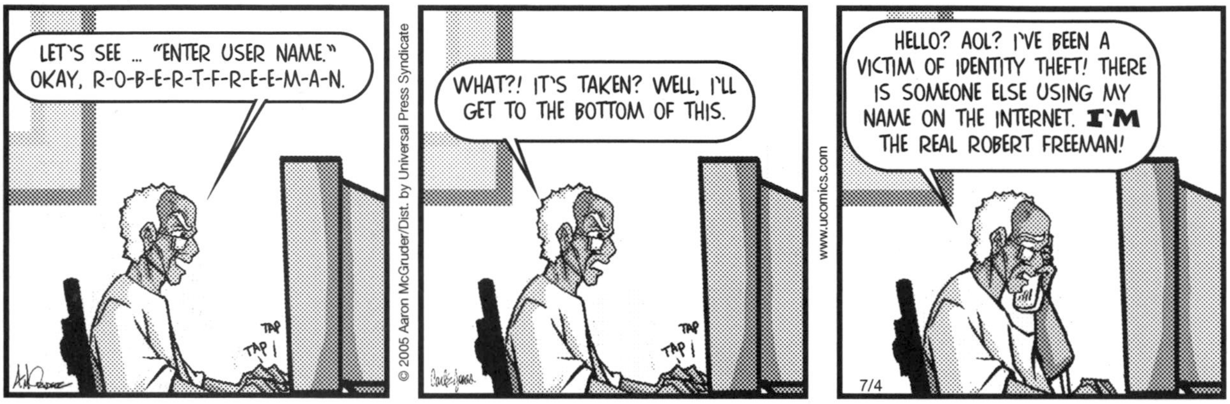
LET'S SEE ... "ENTER USER NAME." OKAY, R-O-B-E-R-T-F-R-E-E-M-A-N.
TAP TAP
© 2005 Aaron McGruder/Dist. by Universal Press Syndicate
WHAT?! IT'S TAKEN? WELL, I'LL GET TO THE BOTTOM OF THIS.
TAP TAP
www.ucomics.com
HELLO? AOL? I'VE BEEN A VICTIM OF IDENTITY THEFT! THERE IS SOMEONE ELSE USING MY NAME ON THE INTERNET. I'M THE REAL ROBERT FREEMAN!
7/4

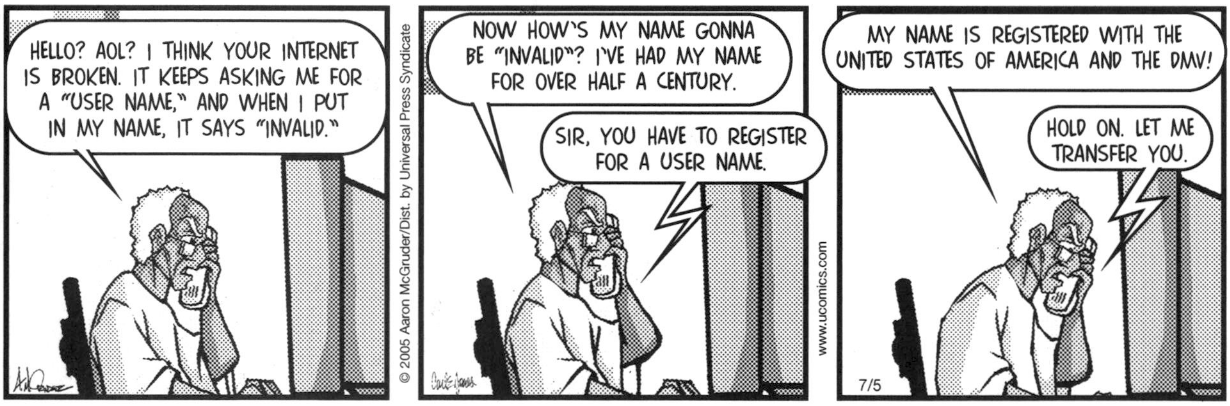
HELLO? AOL? I THINK YOUR INTERNET IS BROKEN. IT KEEPS ASKING ME FOR A "USER NAME," AND WHEN I PUT IN MY NAME, IT SAYS "INVALID."
© 2005 Aaron McGruder/Dist. by Universal Press Syndicate
NOW HOW'S MY NAME GONNA BE "INVALID"? I'VE HAD MY NAME FOR OVER HALF A CENTURY.
SIR, YOU HAVE TO REGISTER FOR A USER NAME.
www.ucomics.com
MY NAME IS REGISTERED WITH THE UNITED STATES OF AMERICA AND THE DMV!
HOLD ON. LET ME TRANSFER YOU.
7/5

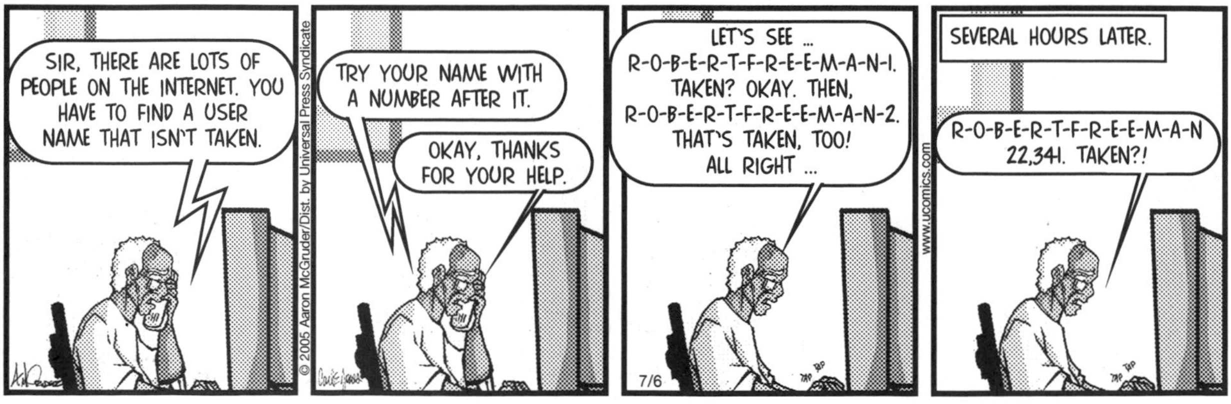
SIR, THERE ARE LOTS OF PEOPLE ON THE INTERNET. YOU HAVE TO FIND A USER NAME THAT ISN'T TAKEN.
© 2005 Aaron McGruder/Dist. by Universal Press Syndicate
TRY YOUR NAME WITH A NUMBER AFTER IT.
OKAY, THANKS FOR YOUR HELP.
LET'S SEE ... R-O-B-E-R-T-F-R-E-E-M-A-N-1. TAKEN? OKAY. THEN, R-O-B-E-R-T-F-R-E-E-M-A-N-2. THAT'S TAKEN, TOO! ALL RIGHT ...
7/6
www.ucomics.com
SEVERAL HOURS LATER.
R-O-B-E-R-T-F-R-E-E-M-A-N 22,341. TAKEN?!

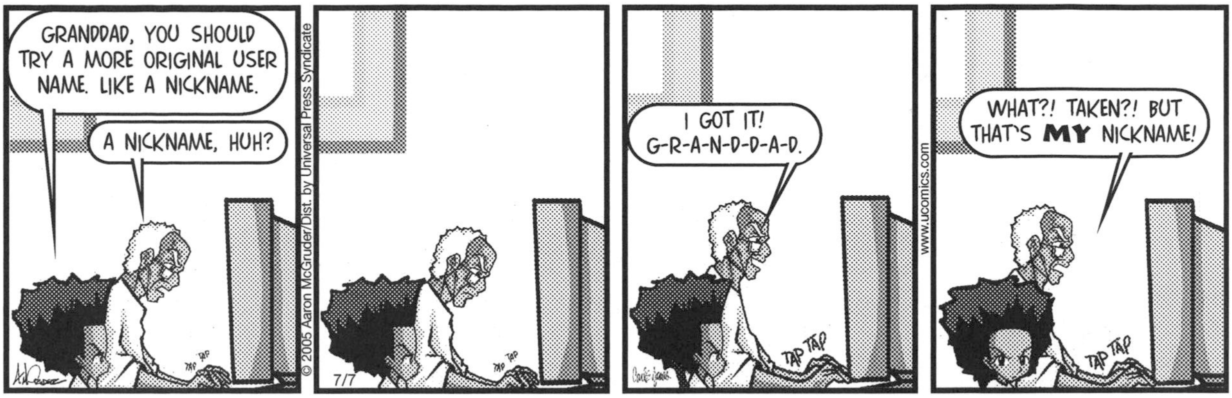
GRANDDAD, YOU SHOULD TRY A MORE ORIGINAL USER NAME. LIKE A NICKNAME.
A NICKNAME, HUH?
TAP TAP
© 2005 Aaron McGruder/Dist. by Universal Press Syndicate
7/7
TAP TAP
I GOT IT! G-R-A-N-D-D-A-D.
TAP TAP
www.ucomics.com
WHAT?! TAKEN?! BUT THAT'S **MY** NICKNAME!
TAP TAP

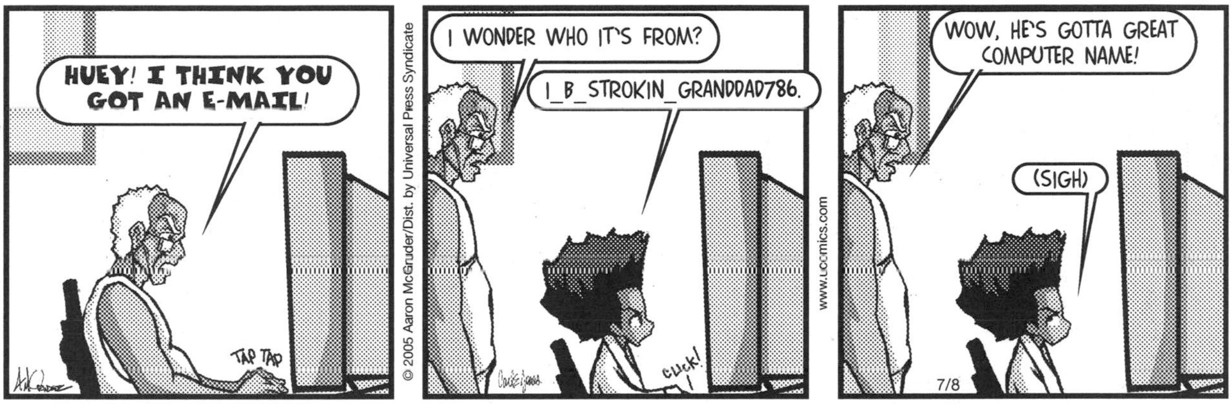
HUEY! I THINK YOU GOT AN E-MAIL!
TAP TAP
© 2005 Aaron McGruder/Dist. by Universal Press Syndicate
I WONDER WHO IT'S FROM?
I_B_STROKIN_GRANDDAD786.
CLICK!
www.ucomics.com
WOW, HE'S GOTTA GREAT COMPUTER NAME!
(SIGH)
7/8

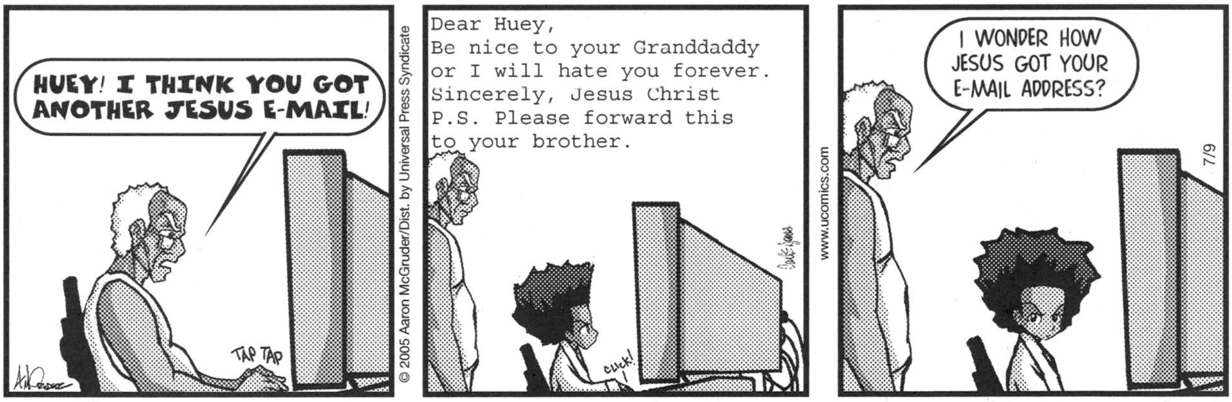
HUEY! I THINK YOU GOT ANOTHER JESUS E-MAIL!
TAP TAP
© 2005 Aaron McGruder/Dist. by Universal Press Syndicate
Dear Huey,
Be nice to your Granddaddy
or I will hate you forever.
Sincerely, Jesus Christ
P.S. Please forward this
to your brother.
CLICK!
www.ucomics.com
I WONDER HOW JESUS GOT YOUR E-MAIL ADDRESS?
7/9

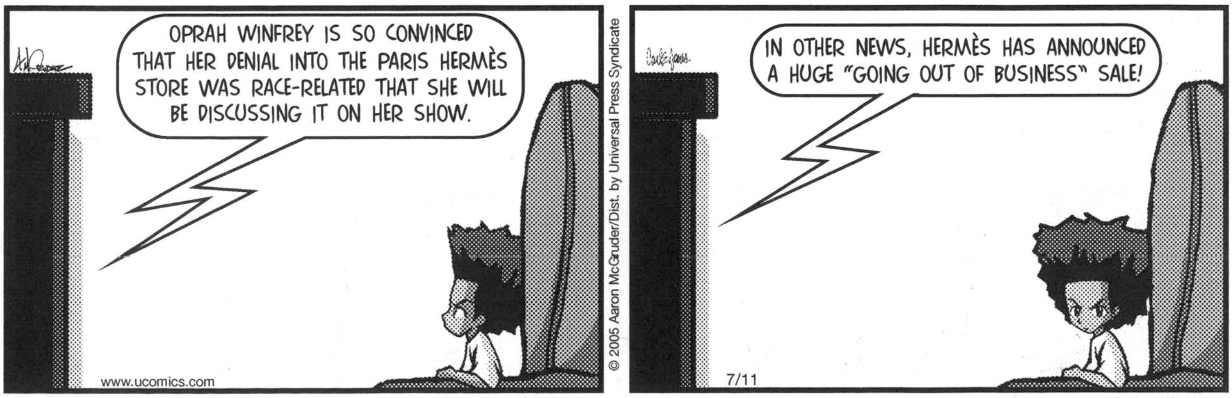
OPRAH WINFREY IS SO CONVINCED THAT HER DENIAL INTO THE PARIS HERMÈS STORE WAS RACE-RELATED THAT SHE WILL BE DISCUSSING IT ON HER SHOW.
www.ucomics.com
© 2005 Aaron McGruder/Dist. by Universal Press Syndicate
IN OTHER NEWS, HERMÈS HAS ANNOUNCED A HUGE "GOING OUT OF BUSINESS" SALE!
7/11

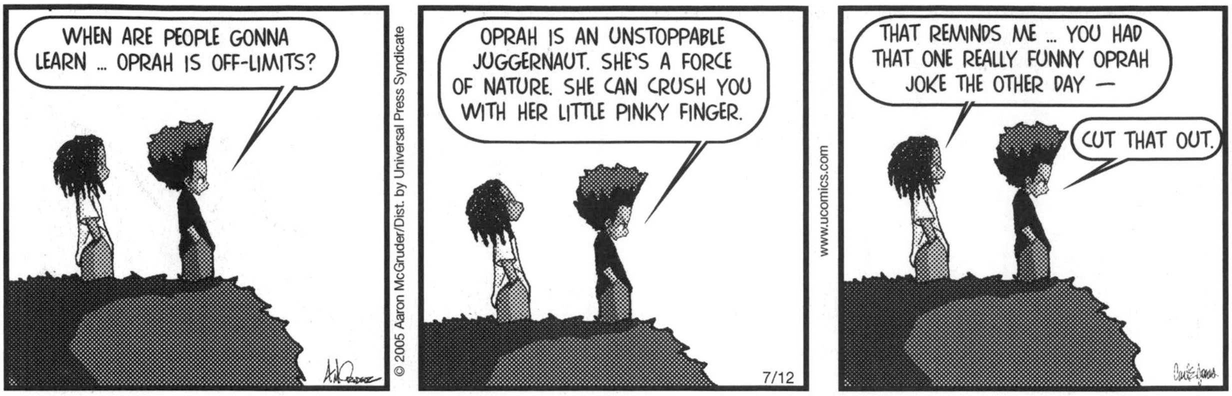
WHEN ARE PEOPLE GONNA LEARN ... OPRAH IS OFF-LIMITS?
OPRAH IS AN UNSTOPPABLE JUGGERNAUT. SHE'S A FORCE OF NATURE. SHE CAN CRUSH YOU WITH HER LITTLE PINKY FINGER.
THAT REMINDS ME ... YOU HAD THAT ONE REALLY FUNNY OPRAH JOKE THE OTHER DAY —
CUT THAT OUT.
© 2005 Aaron McGruder/Dist. by Universal Press Syndicate
www.ucomics.com
7/12

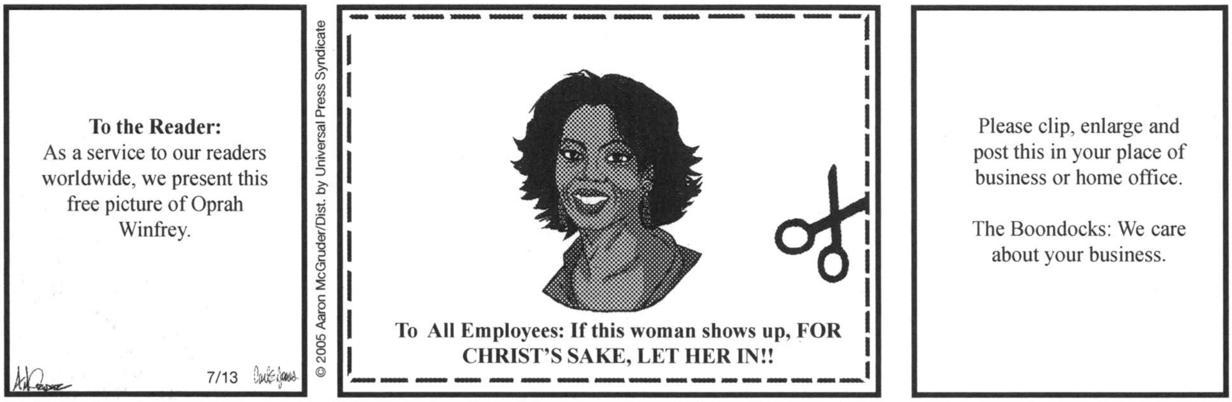
To the Reader:
As a service to our readers worldwide, we present this free picture of Oprah Winfrey.
7/13
© 2005 Aaron McGruder/Dist. by Universal Press Syndicate
To All Employees: If this woman shows up, FOR CHRIST'S SAKE, LET HER IN!!
Please clip, enlarge and post this in your place of business or home office.
The Boondocks: We care about your business.

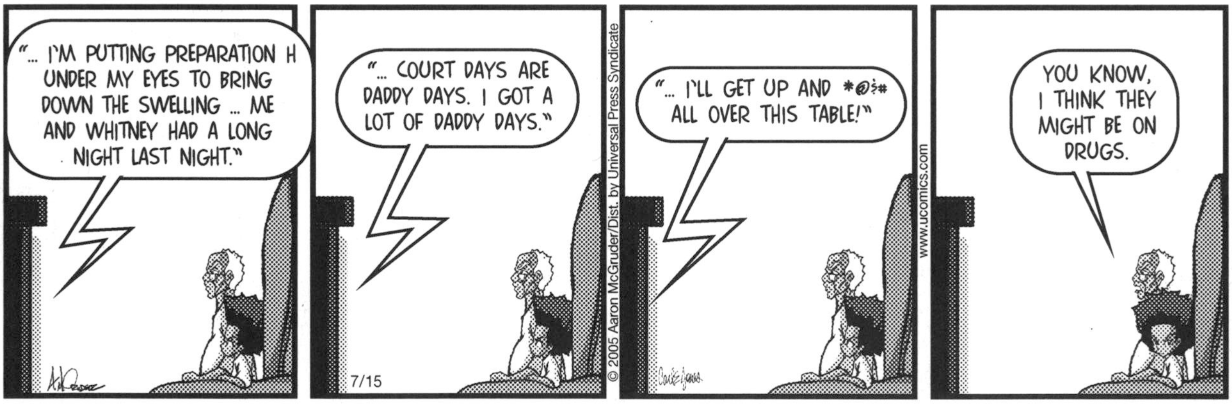
"... I'M PUTTING PREPARATION H UNDER MY EYES TO BRING DOWN THE SWELLING ... ME AND WHITNEY HAD A LONG NIGHT LAST NIGHT."
"... COURT DAYS ARE DADDY DAYS. I GOT A LOT OF DADDY DAYS."
7/15
© 2005 Aaron McGruder/Dist. by Universal Press Syndicate
"... I'LL GET UP AND *@$# ALL OVER THIS TABLE!"
www.ucomics.com
YOU KNOW, I THINK THEY MIGHT BE ON DRUGS.

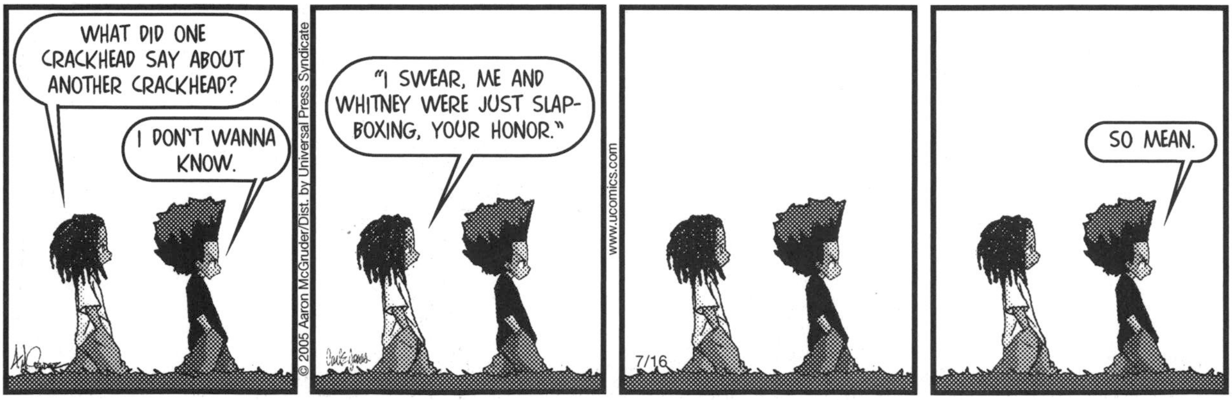
WHAT DID ONE CRACKHEAD SAY ABOUT ANOTHER CRACKHEAD?
I DON'T WANNA KNOW.
© 2005 Aaron McGruder/Dist. by Universal Press Syndicate
"I SWEAR, ME AND WHITNEY WERE JUST SLAP-BOXING, YOUR HONOR."
www.ucomics.com
7/16
SO MEAN.

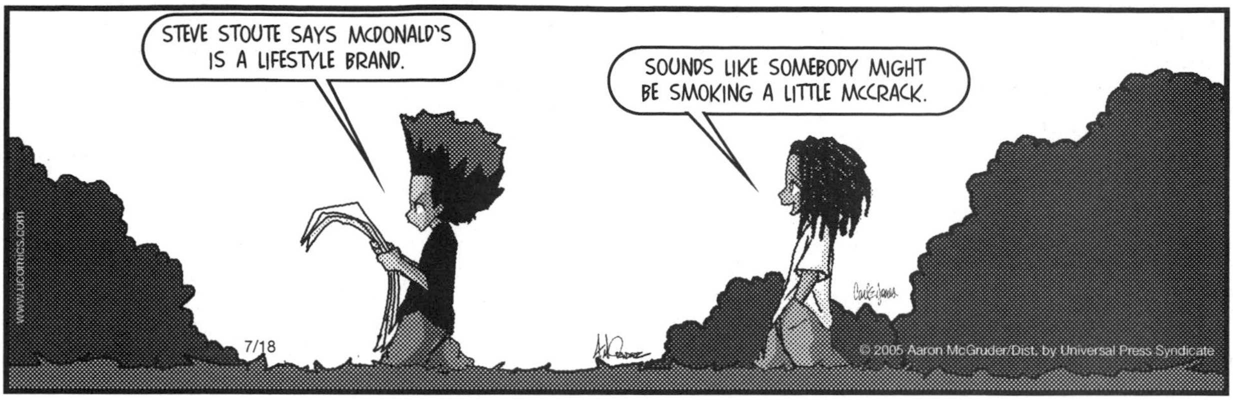
STEVE STOUTE SAYS McDONALD'S IS A LIFESTYLE BRAND.
SOUNDS LIKE SOMEBODY MIGHT BE SMOKING A LITTLE McCRACK.
7/18
www.ucomics.com
© 2005 Aaron McGruder/Dist. by Universal Press Syndicate

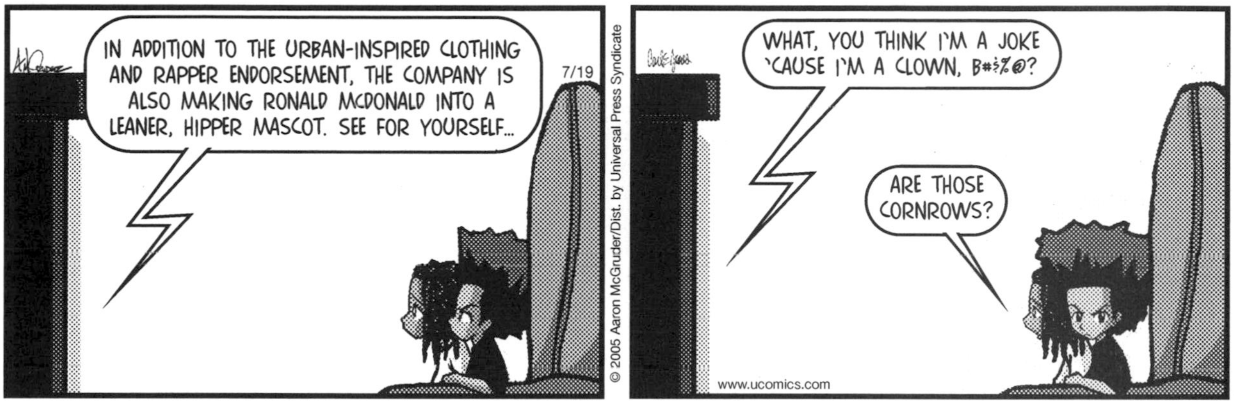
IN ADDITION TO THE URBAN-INSPIRED CLOTHING AND RAPPER ENDORSEMENT, THE COMPANY IS ALSO MAKING RONALD McDONALD INTO A LEANER, HIPPER MASCOT. SEE FOR YOURSELF...
7/19
© 2005 Aaron McGruder/Dist. by Universal Press Syndicate
WHAT, YOU THINK I'M A JOKE 'CAUSE I'M A CLOWN, B#$%@?
ARE THOSE CORNROWS?
www.ucomics.com

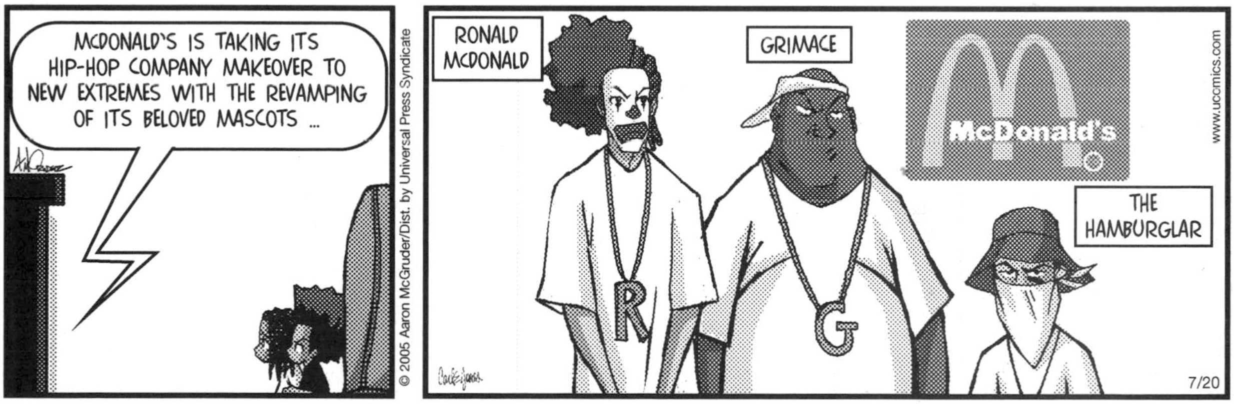
McDONALD'S IS TAKING ITS HIP-HOP COMPANY MAKEOVER TO NEW EXTREMES WITH THE REVAMPING OF ITS BELOVED MASCOTS ...
© 2005 Aaron McGruder/Dist. by Universal Press Syndicate
RONALD McDONALD
GRIMACE
McDonald's
THE HAMBURGLAR
www.ucomics.com
7/20

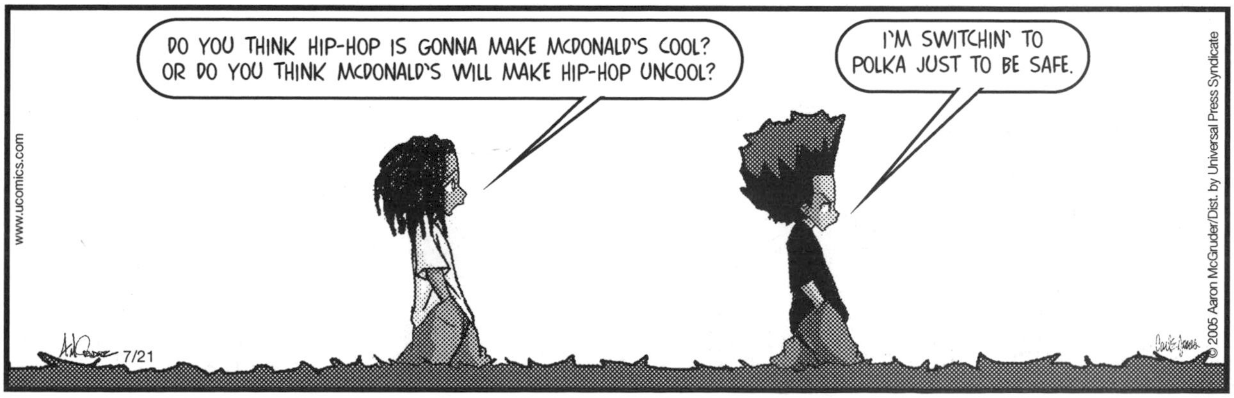
DO YOU THINK HIP-HOP IS GONNA MAKE McDONALD'S COOL? OR DO YOU THINK McDONALD'S WILL MAKE HIP-HOP UNCOOL?
I'M SWITCHIN' TO POLKA JUST TO BE SAFE.
www.ucomics.com
7/21
© 2005 Aaron McGruder/Dist. by Universal Press Syndicate

Unhappy readers have criticized McGruder . . . for inflaming racial tensions, advocating violence, and misrepresenting the truth.

—*Kansas City Star*

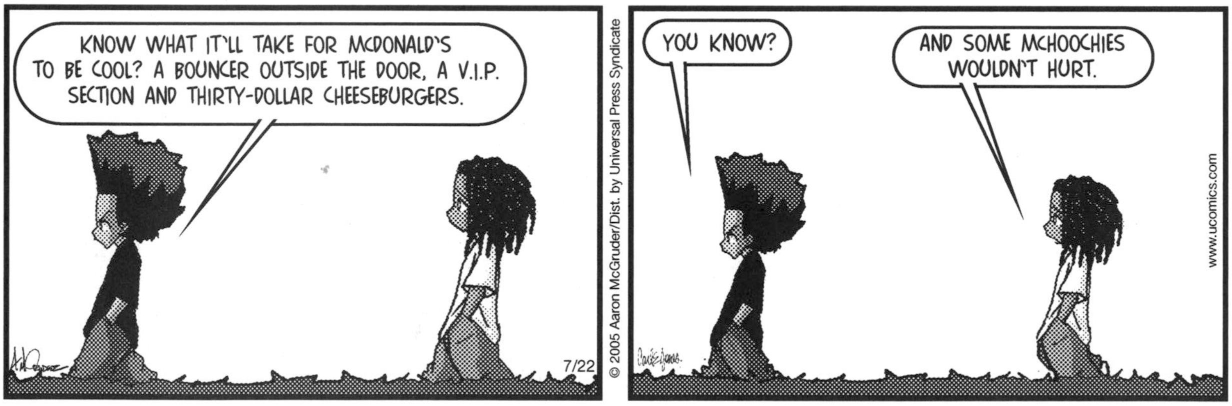
KNOW WHAT IT'LL TAKE FOR MCDONALD'S TO BE COOL? A BOUNCER OUTSIDE THE DOOR, A V.I.P. SECTION AND THIRTY-DOLLAR CHEESEBURGERS.
7/22
© 2005 Aaron McGruder/Dist. by Universal Press Syndicate
YOU KNOW?
AND SOME MCHOOCHIES WOULDN'T HURT.
www.ucomics.com

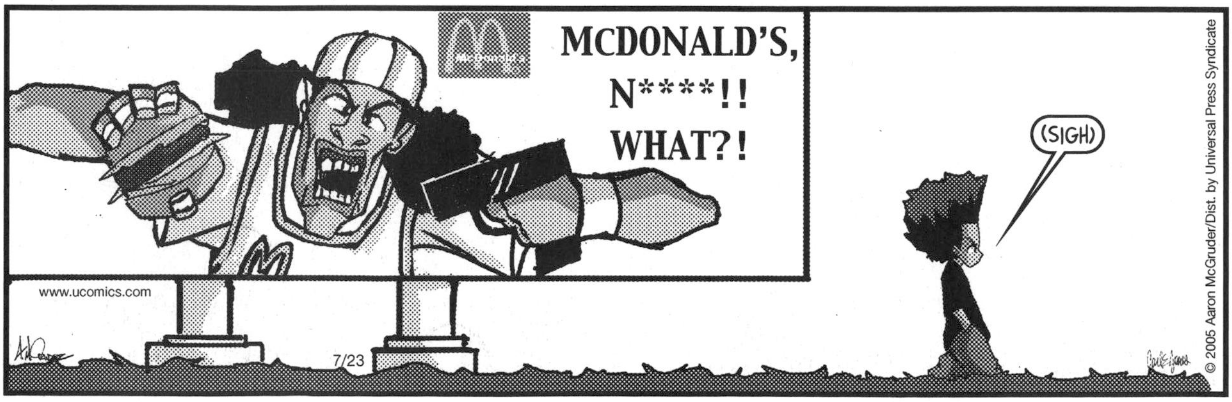
MCDONALD'S, N****!! WHAT?!
(SIGH)
www.ucomics.com
7/23
© 2005 Aaron McGruder/Dist. by Universal Press Syndicate

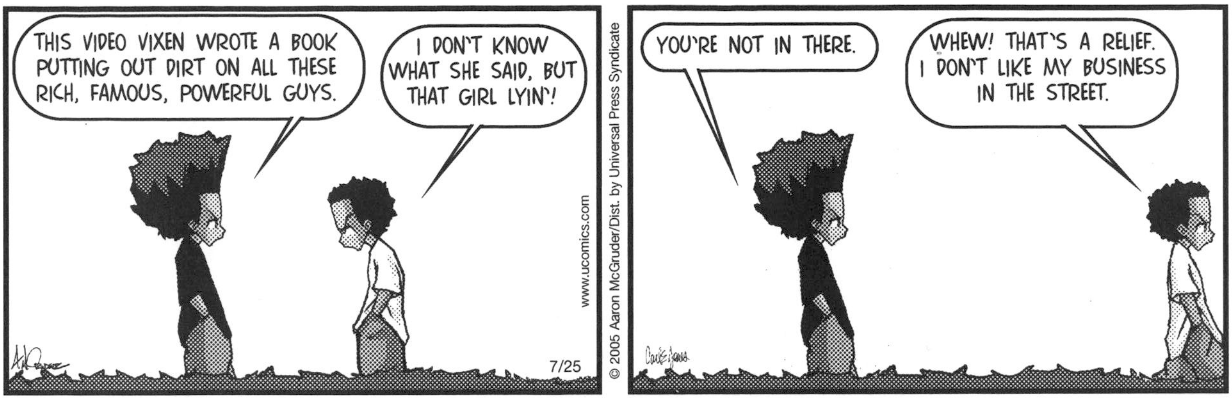
THIS VIDEO VIXEN WROTE A BOOK PUTTING OUT DIRT ON ALL THESE RICH, FAMOUS, POWERFUL GUYS.
I DON'T KNOW WHAT SHE SAID, BUT THAT GIRL LYIN'!
7/25
www.ucomics.com
© 2005 Aaron McGruder/Dist. by Universal Press Syndicate
YOU'RE NOT IN THERE.
WHEW! THAT'S A RELIEF. I DON'T LIKE MY BUSINESS IN THE STREET.

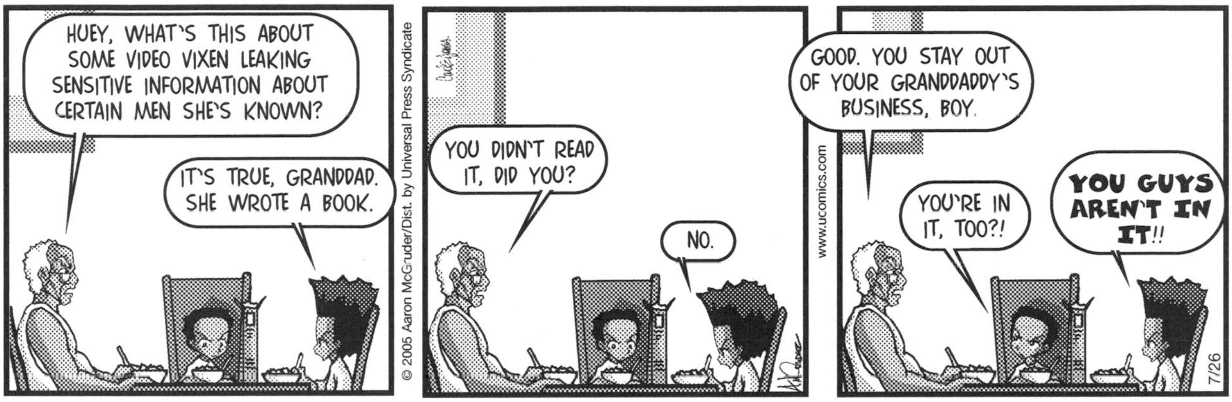
HUEY, WHAT'S THIS ABOUT SOME VIDEO VIXEN LEAKING SENSITIVE INFORMATION ABOUT CERTAIN MEN SHE'S KNOWN?
IT'S TRUE, GRANDDAD. SHE WROTE A BOOK.
© 2005 Aaron McGruder/Dist. by Universal Press Syndicate
YOU DIDN'T READ IT, DID YOU?
NO.
www.ucomics.com
GOOD. YOU STAY OUT OF YOUR GRANDDADDY'S BUSINESS, BOY.
YOU'RE IN IT, TOO?!
YOU GUYS AREN'T IN IT!!
7/26

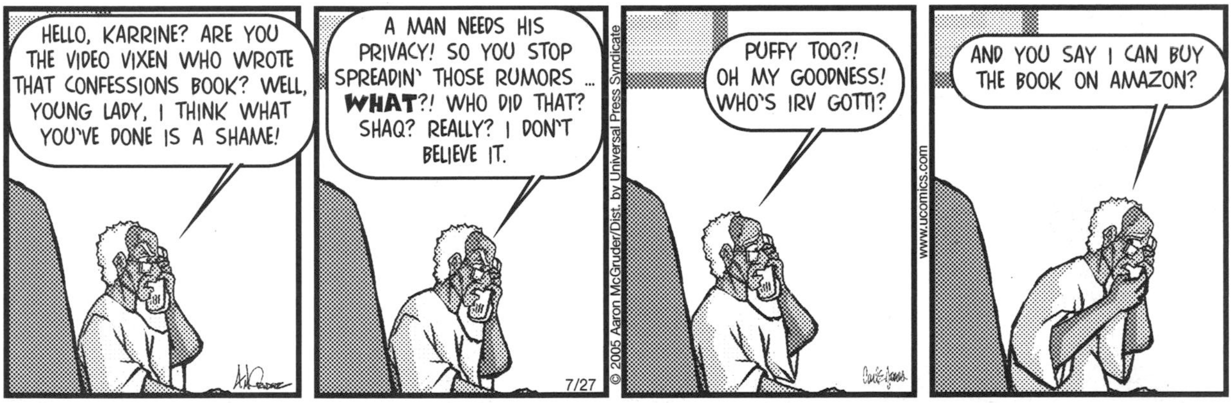
HELLO, KARRINE? ARE YOU THE VIDEO VIXEN WHO WROTE THAT CONFESSIONS BOOK? WELL, YOUNG LADY, I THINK WHAT YOU'VE DONE IS A SHAME!
A MAN NEEDS HIS PRIVACY! SO YOU STOP SPREADIN' THOSE RUMORS ... WHAT?! WHO DID THAT? SHAQ? REALLY? I DON'T BELIEVE IT.
7/27
© 2005 Aaron McGruder/Dist. by Universal Press Syndicate
PUFFY TOO?! OH MY GOODNESS! WHO'S IRV GOTTI?
www.ucomics.com
AND YOU SAY I CAN BUY THE BOOK ON AMAZON?

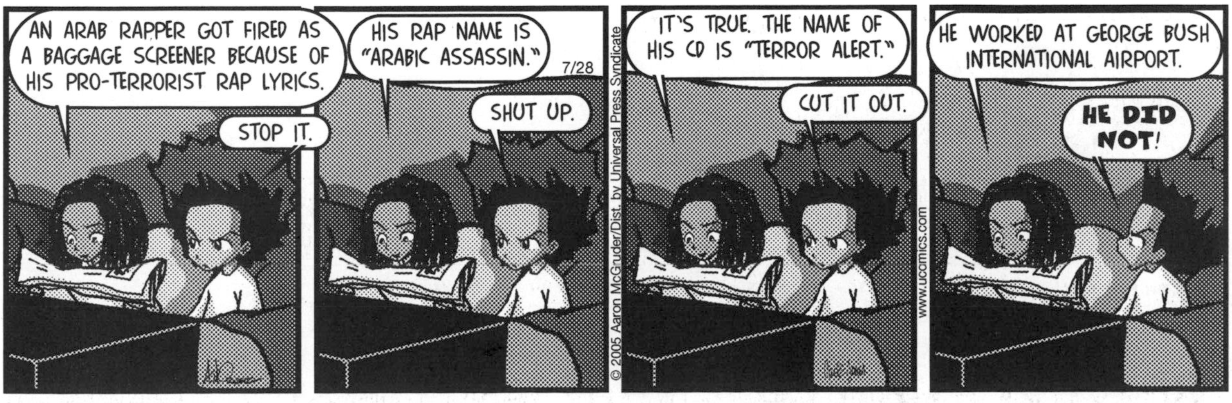
AN ARAB RAPPER GOT FIRED AS A BAGGAGE SCREENER BECAUSE OF HIS PRO-TERRORIST RAP LYRICS.
STOP IT.
HIS RAP NAME IS "ARABIC ASSASSIN."
7/28
SHUT UP.
© 2005 Aaron McGruder/Dist. by Universal Press Syndicate
IT'S TRUE. THE NAME OF HIS CD IS "TERROR ALERT."
CUT IT OUT.
www.ucomics.com
HE WORKED AT GEORGE BUSH INTERNATIONAL AIRPORT.
HE DID NOT!

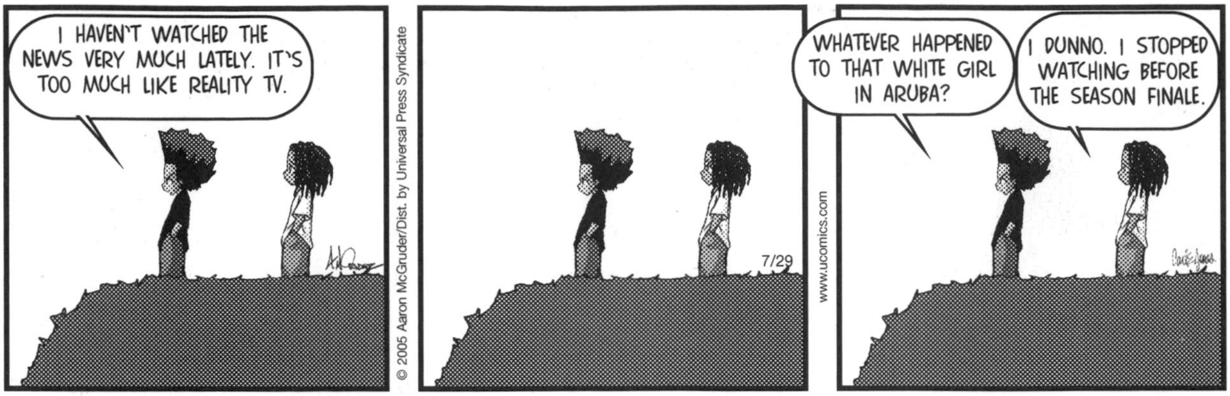
I HAVEN'T WATCHED THE NEWS VERY MUCH LATELY. IT'S TOO MUCH LIKE REALITY TV.
© 2005 Aaron McGruder/Dist. by Universal Press Syndicate
7/29
www.ucomics.com
WHATEVER HAPPENED TO THAT WHITE GIRL IN ARUBA?
I DUNNO. I STOPPED WATCHING BEFORE THE SEASON FINALE.

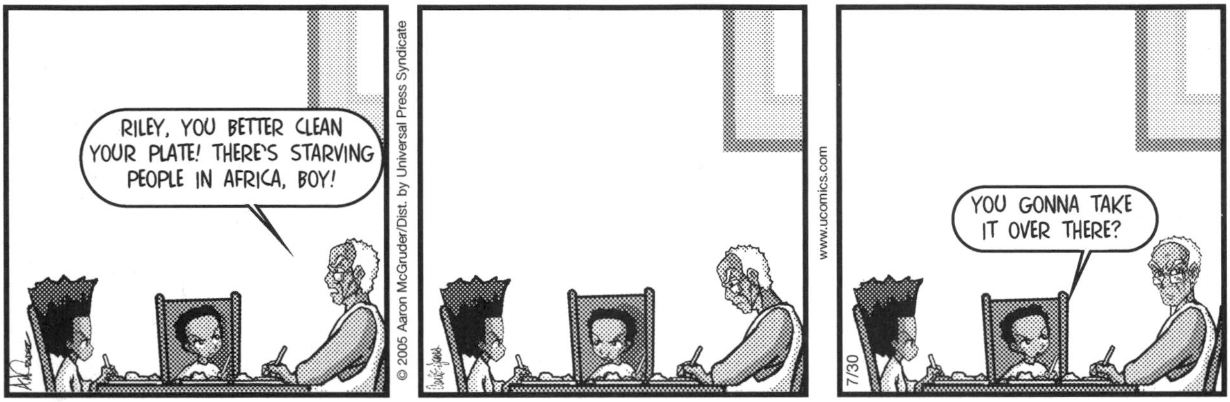
RILEY, YOU BETTER CLEAN YOUR PLATE! THERE'S STARVING PEOPLE IN AFRICA, BOY!
© 2005 Aaron McGruder/Dist. by Universal Press Syndicate
www.ucomics.com
7/30
YOU GONNA TAKE IT OVER THERE?

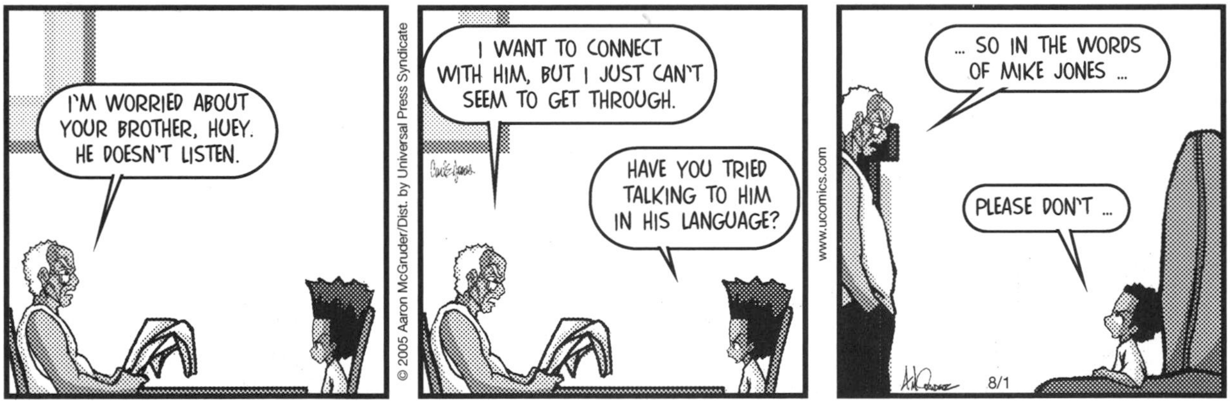
I'M WORRIED ABOUT YOUR BROTHER, HUEY. HE DOESN'T LISTEN.
© 2005 Aaron McGruder/Dist. by Universal Press Syndicate
I WANT TO CONNECT WITH HIM, BUT I JUST CAN'T SEEM TO GET THROUGH.
HAVE YOU TRIED TALKING TO HIM IN HIS LANGUAGE?
www.ucomics.com
... SO IN THE WORDS OF MIKE JONES ...
PLEASE DON'T ...
8/1

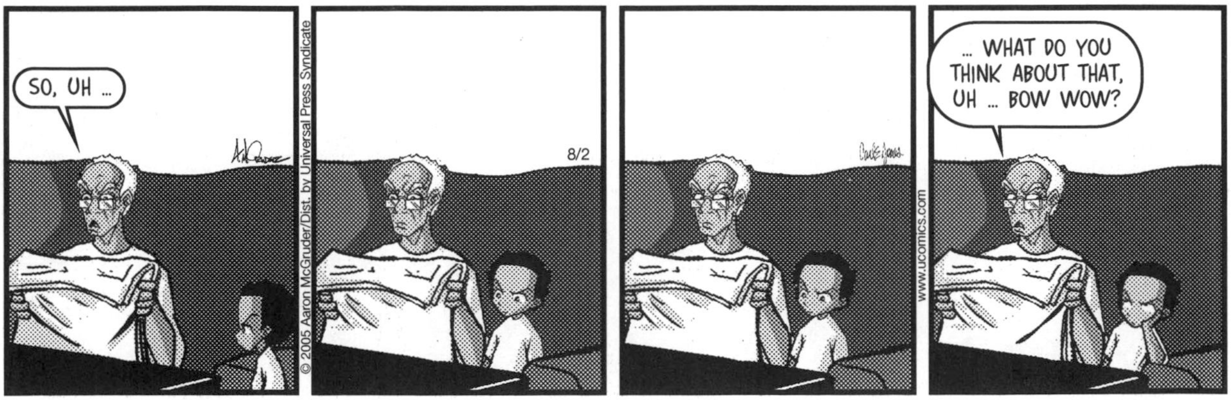
SO, UH ...
© 2005 Aaron McGruder/Dist. by Universal Press Syndicate
8/2
www.ucomics.com
... WHAT DO YOU THINK ABOUT THAT, UH ... BOW WOW?

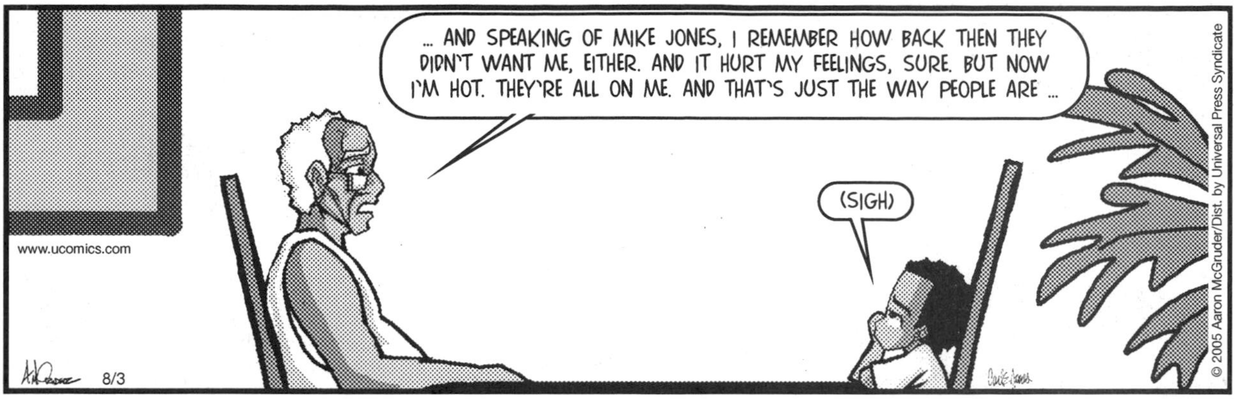
... AND SPEAKING OF MIKE JONES, I REMEMBER HOW BACK THEN THEY DIDN'T WANT ME, EITHER. AND IT HURT MY FEELINGS, SURE. BUT NOW I'M HOT. THEY'RE ALL ON ME. AND THAT'S JUST THE WAY PEOPLE ARE ...
(SIGH)
www.ucomics.com
8/3
© 2005 Aaron McGruder/Dist. by Universal Press Syndicate

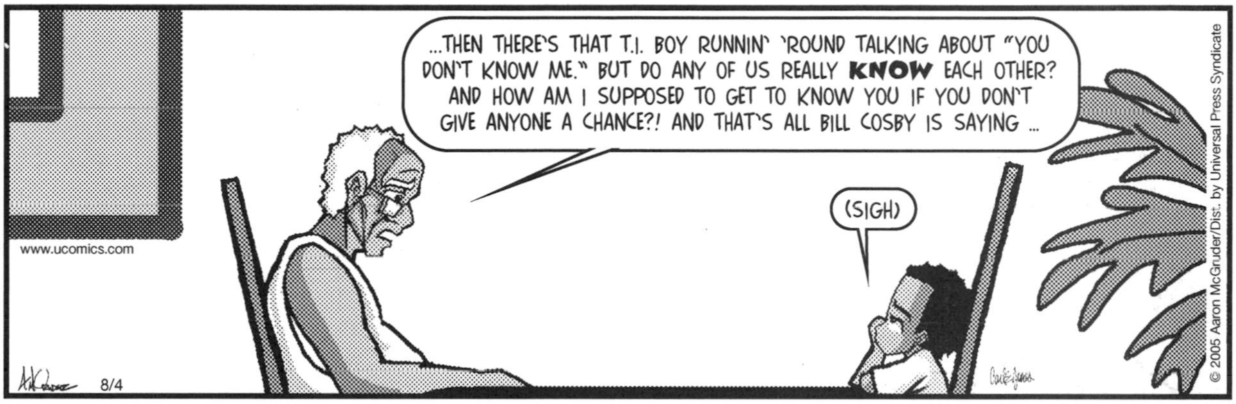
...THEN THERE'S THAT T.I. BOY RUNNIN' 'ROUND TALKING ABOUT "YOU DON'T KNOW ME." BUT DO ANY OF US REALLY **KNOW** EACH OTHER? AND HOW AM I SUPPOSED TO GET TO KNOW YOU IF YOU DON'T GIVE ANYONE A CHANCE?! AND THAT'S ALL BILL COSBY IS SAYING ...
(SIGH)
www.ucomics.com
8/4
© 2005 Aaron McGruder/Dist. by Universal Press Syndicate

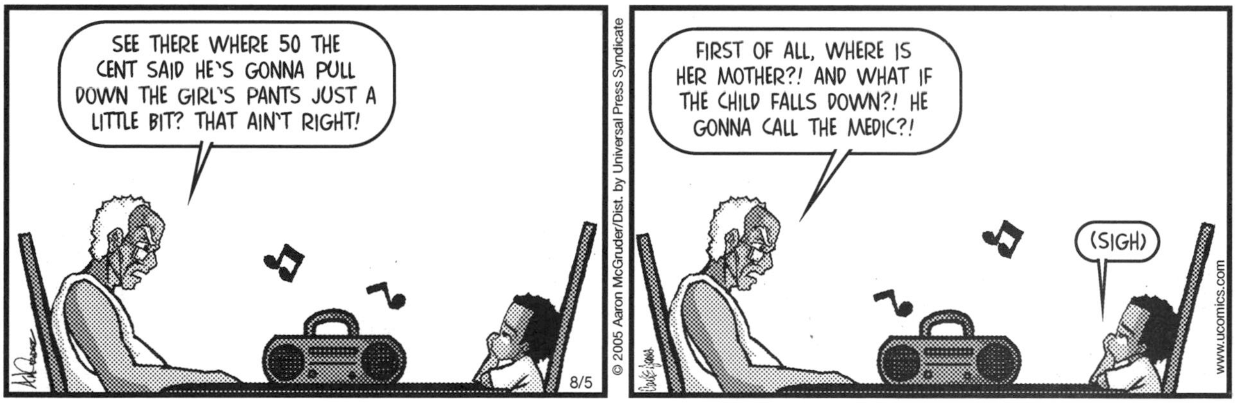
SEE THERE WHERE 50 THE CENT SAID HE'S GONNA PULL DOWN THE GIRL'S PANTS JUST A LITTLE BIT? THAT AIN'T RIGHT!
8/5
© 2005 Aaron McGruder/Dist. by Universal Press Syndicate
FIRST OF ALL, WHERE IS HER MOTHER?! AND WHAT IF THE CHILD FALLS DOWN?! HE GONNA CALL THE MEDIC?!
(SIGH)
www.ucomics.com

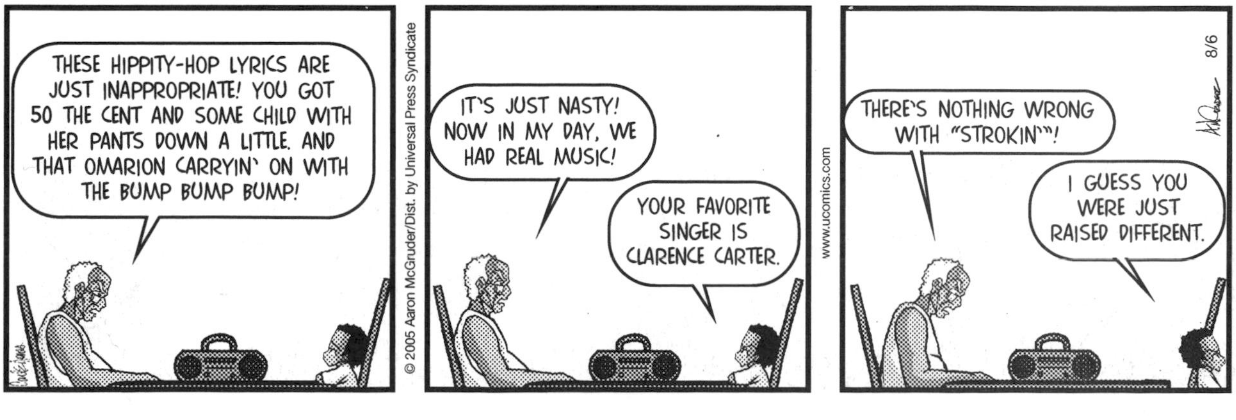
THESE HIPPITY-HOP LYRICS ARE JUST INAPPROPRIATE! YOU GOT 50 THE CENT AND SOME CHILD WITH HER PANTS DOWN A LITTLE. AND THAT OMARION CARRYIN' ON WITH THE BUMP BUMP BUMP!
© 2005 Aaron McGruder/Dist. by Universal Press Syndicate
IT'S JUST NASTY! NOW IN MY DAY, WE HAD REAL MUSIC!
YOUR FAVORITE SINGER IS CLARENCE CARTER.
www.ucomics.com
8/6
THERE'S NOTHING WRONG WITH "STROKIN'"!
I GUESS YOU WERE JUST RAISED DIFFERENT.

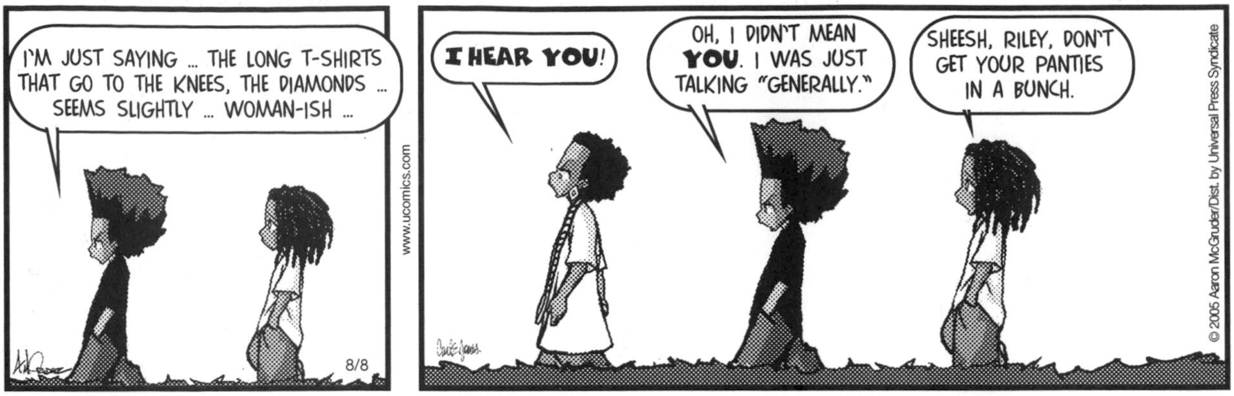
I'M JUST SAYING ... THE LONG T-SHIRTS THAT GO TO THE KNEES, THE DIAMONDS ... SEEMS SLIGHTLY ... WOMAN-ISH ...
8/8
www.ucomics.com
I HEAR YOU!
OH, I DIDN'T MEAN YOU. I WAS JUST TALKING "GENERALLY."
SHEESH, RILEY, DON'T GET YOUR PANTIES IN A BUNCH.
© 2005 Aaron McGruder/Dist. by Universal Press Syndicate

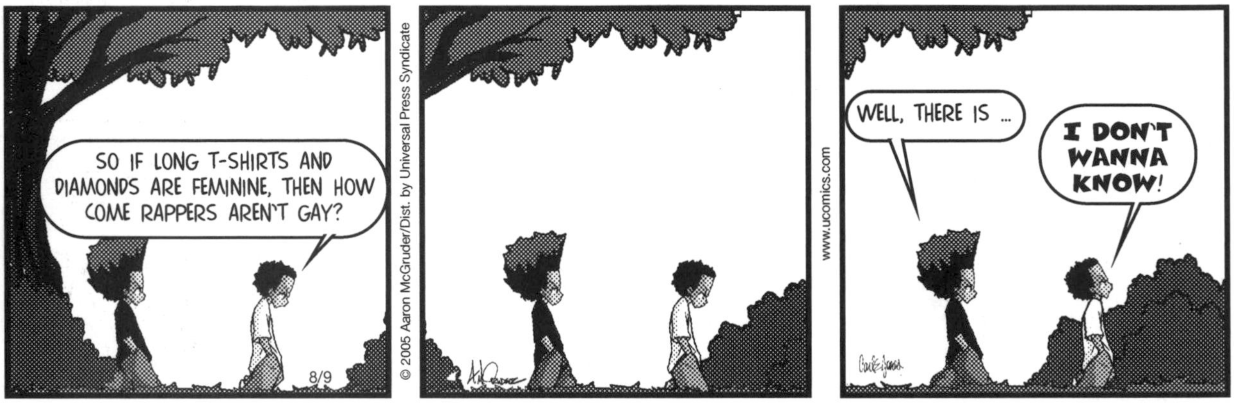
SO IF LONG T-SHIRTS AND DIAMONDS ARE FEMININE, THEN HOW COME RAPPERS AREN'T GAY?
8/9
© 2005 Aaron McGruder/Dist. by Universal Press Syndicate
www.ucomics.com
WELL, THERE IS ...
I DON'T WANNA KNOW!

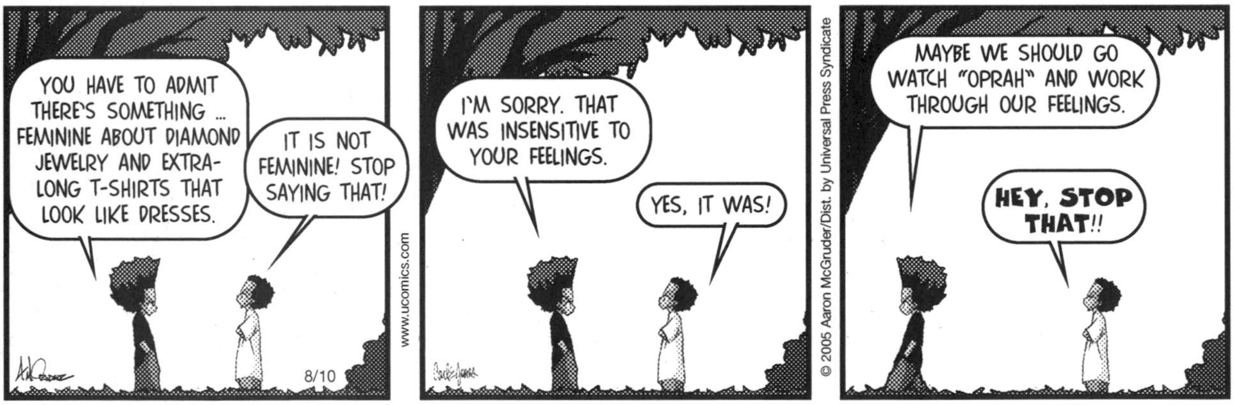
YOU HAVE TO ADMIT THERE'S SOMETHING ... FEMININE ABOUT DIAMOND JEWELRY AND EXTRA-LONG T-SHIRTS THAT LOOK LIKE DRESSES.
IT IS NOT FEMININE! STOP SAYING THAT!
8/10
www.ucomics.com
I'M SORRY. THAT WAS INSENSITIVE TO YOUR FEELINGS.
YES, IT WAS!
© 2005 Aaron McGruder/Dist. by Universal Press Syndicate
MAYBE WE SHOULD GO WATCH "OPRAH" AND WORK THROUGH OUR FEELINGS.
HEY, STOP THAT!!

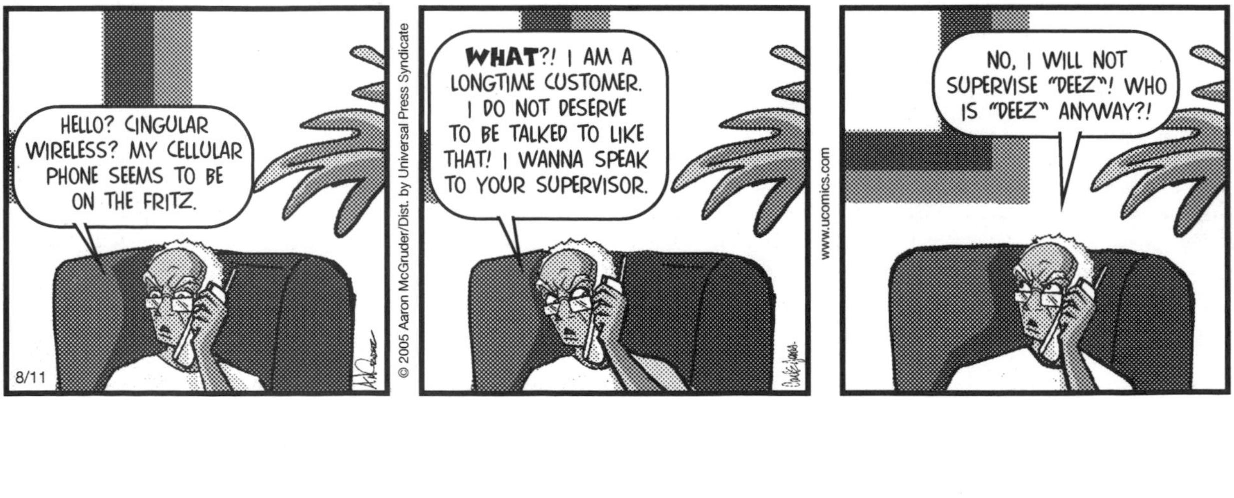
HELLO? CINGULAR WIRELESS? MY CELLULAR PHONE SEEMS TO BE ON THE FRITZ.
8/11
© 2005 Aaron McGruder/Dist. by Universal Press Syndicate
WHAT?! I AM A LONGTIME CUSTOMER. I DO NOT DESERVE TO BE TALKED TO LIKE THAT! I WANNA SPEAK TO YOUR SUPERVISOR.
www.ucomics.com
NO, I WILL NOT SUPERVISE "DEEZ"! WHO IS "DEEZ" ANYWAY?!

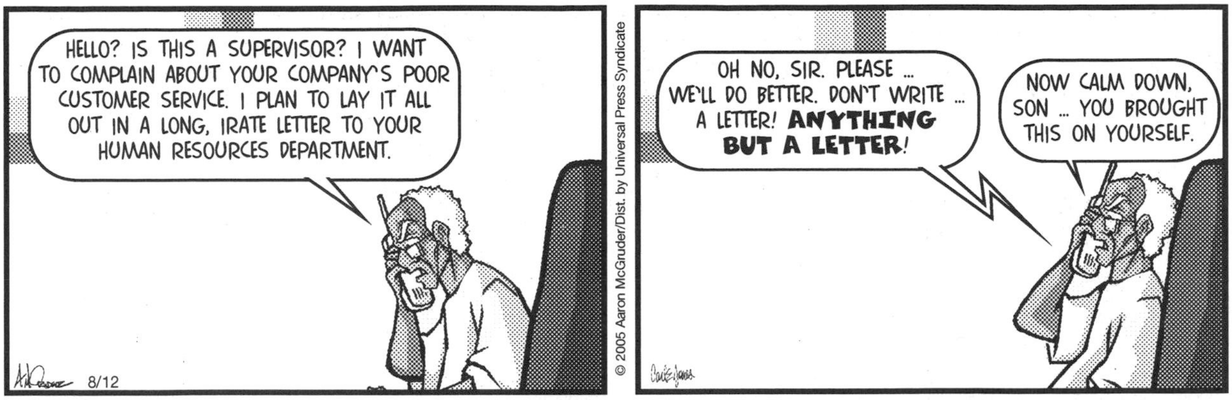
HELLO? IS THIS A SUPERVISOR? I WANT TO COMPLAIN ABOUT YOUR COMPANY'S POOR CUSTOMER SERVICE. I PLAN TO LAY IT ALL OUT IN A LONG, IRATE LETTER TO YOUR HUMAN RESOURCES DEPARTMENT.
8/12
© 2005 Aaron McGruder/Dist. by Universal Press Syndicate
OH NO, SIR. PLEASE ... WE'LL DO BETTER. DON'T WRITE ... A LETTER! **ANYTHING BUT A LETTER!**
NOW CALM DOWN, SON ... YOU BROUGHT THIS ON YOURSELF.

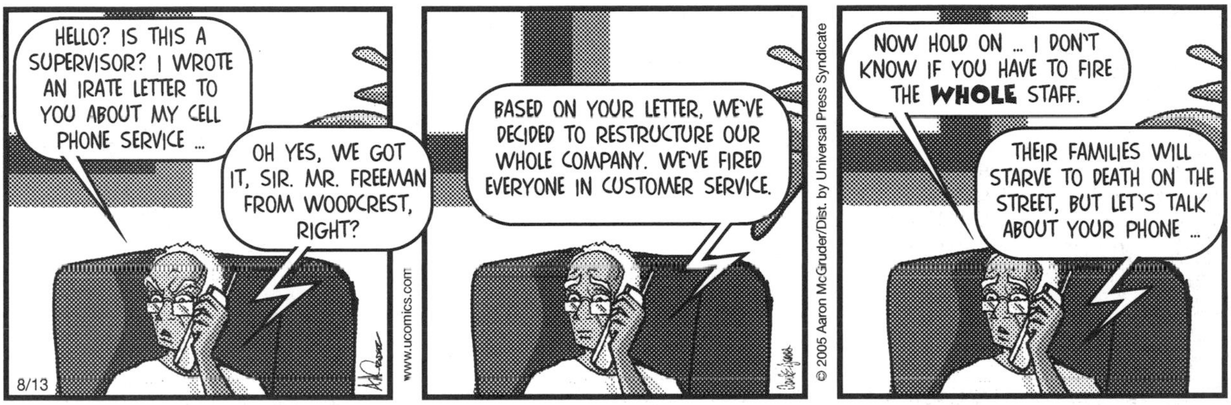
HELLO? IS THIS A SUPERVISOR? I WROTE AN IRATE LETTER TO YOU ABOUT MY CELL PHONE SERVICE ...
OH YES, WE GOT IT, SIR. MR. FREEMAN FROM WOODCREST, RIGHT?
8/13
www.ucomics.com
BASED ON YOUR LETTER, WE'VE DECIDED TO RESTRUCTURE OUR WHOLE COMPANY. WE'VE FIRED EVERYONE IN CUSTOMER SERVICE.
© 2005 Aaron McGruder/Dist. by Universal Press Syndicate
NOW HOLD ON ... I DON'T KNOW IF YOU HAVE TO FIRE THE **WHOLE** STAFF.
THEIR FAMILIES WILL STARVE TO DEATH ON THE STREET, BUT LET'S TALK ABOUT YOUR PHONE ...

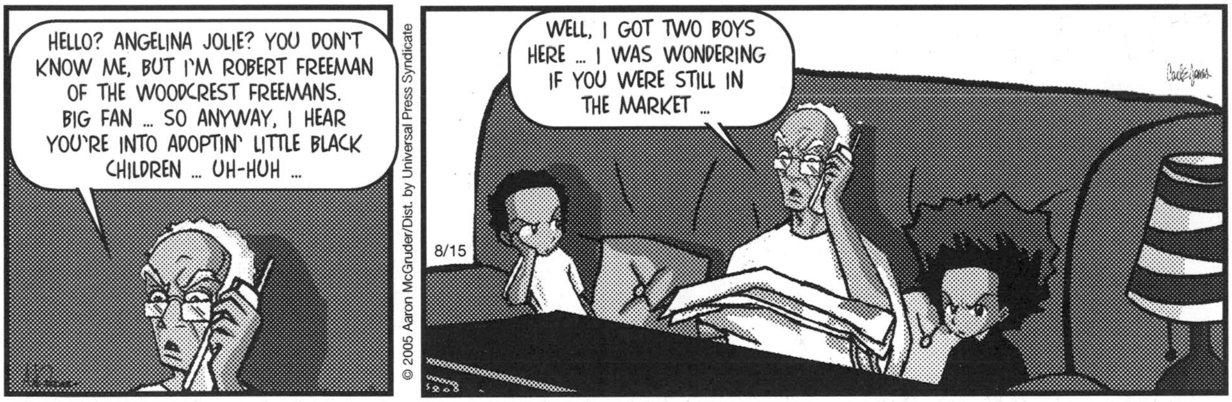
HELLO? ANGELINA JOLIE? YOU DON'T KNOW ME, BUT I'M ROBERT FREEMAN OF THE WOODCREST FREEMANS. BIG FAN ... SO ANYWAY, I HEAR YOU'RE INTO ADOPTIN' LITTLE BLACK CHILDREN ... UH-HUH ...
© 2005 Aaron McGruder/Dist. by Universal Press Syndicate
WELL, I GOT TWO BOYS HERE ... I WAS WONDERING IF YOU WERE STILL IN THE MARKET ...
8/15

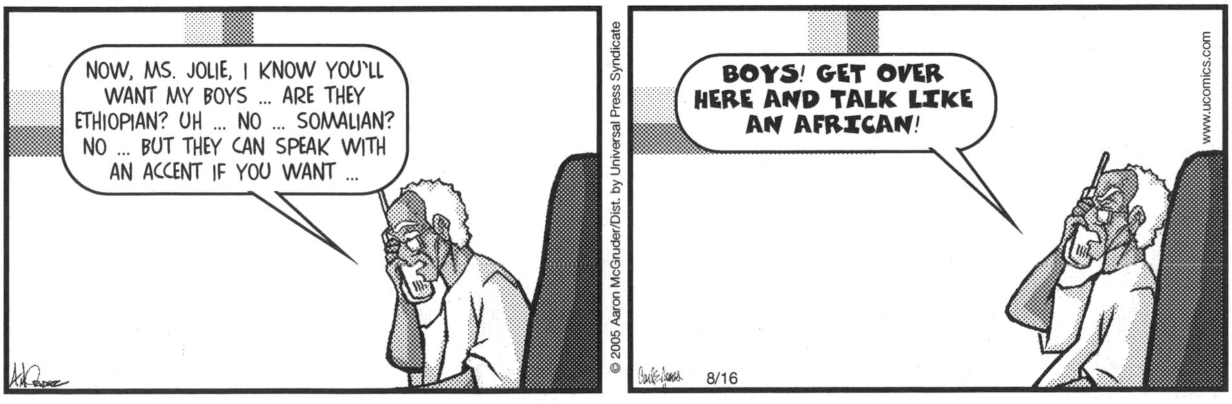
NOW, MS. JOLIE, I KNOW YOU'LL WANT MY BOYS ... ARE THEY ETHIOPIAN? UH ... NO ... SOMALIAN? NO ... BUT THEY CAN SPEAK WITH AN ACCENT IF YOU WANT ...
© 2005 Aaron McGruder/Dist. by Universal Press Syndicate
BOYS! GET OVER HERE AND TALK LIKE AN AFRICAN!
8/16
www.ucomics.com

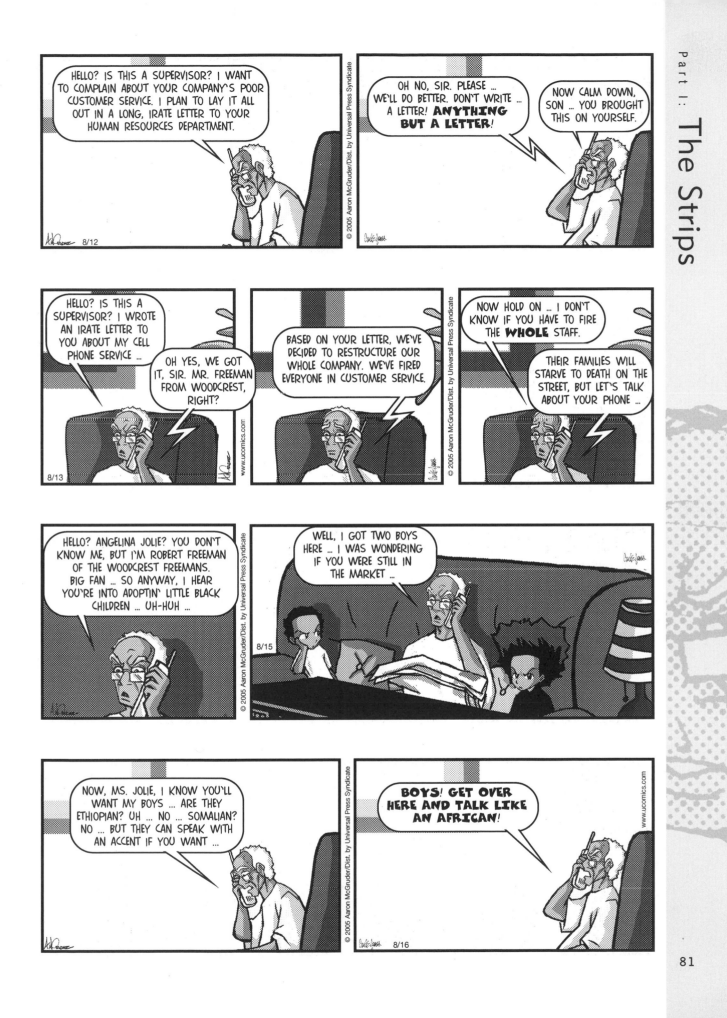

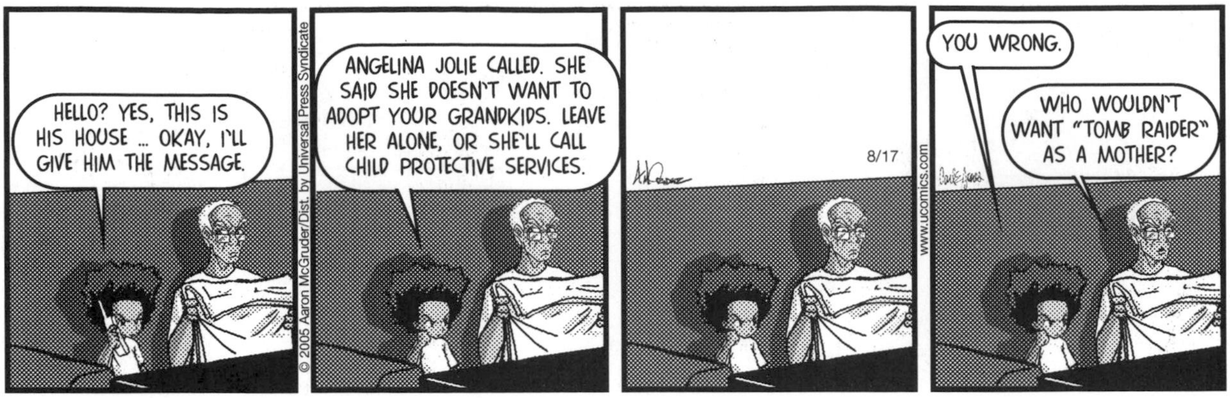
HELLO? YES, THIS IS HIS HOUSE ... OKAY, I'LL GIVE HIM THE MESSAGE.
© 2005 Aaron McGruder/Dist. by Universal Press Syndicate
ANGELINA JOLIE CALLED. SHE SAID SHE DOESN'T WANT TO ADOPT YOUR GRANDKIDS. LEAVE HER ALONE, OR SHE'LL CALL CHILD PROTECTIVE SERVICES.
8/17
www.ucomics.com
YOU WRONG.
WHO WOULDN'T WANT "TOMB RAIDER" AS A MOTHER?

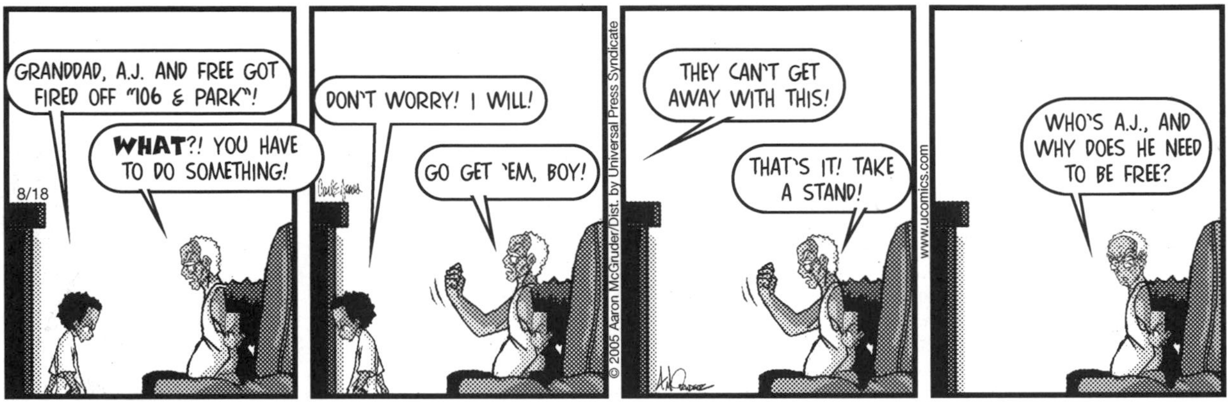
GRANDDAD, A.J. AND FREE GOT FIRED OFF "106 & PARK"!
WHAT?! YOU HAVE TO DO SOMETHING!
8/18
DON'T WORRY! I WILL!
GO GET 'EM, BOY!
© 2005 Aaron McGruder/Dist. by Universal Press Syndicate
THEY CAN'T GET AWAY WITH THIS!
THAT'S IT! TAKE A STAND!
www.ucomics.com
WHO'S A.J., AND WHY DOES HE NEED TO BE FREE?

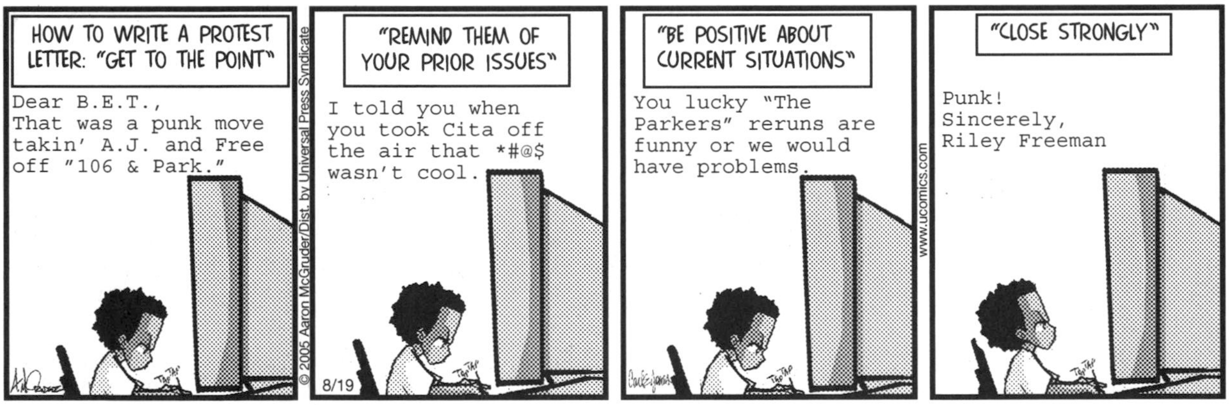
HOW TO WRITE A PROTEST LETTER: "GET TO THE POINT"
Dear B.E.T.,
That was a punk move takin' A.J. and Free off "106 & Park."
© 2005 Aaron McGruder/Dist. by Universal Press Syndicate
"REMIND THEM OF YOUR PRIOR ISSUES"
I told you when you took Cita off the air that *#@$ wasn't cool.
8/19
"BE POSITIVE ABOUT CURRENT SITUATIONS"
You lucky "The Parkers" reruns are funny or we would have problems.
www.ucomics.com
"CLOSE STRONGLY"
Punk!
Sincerely,
Riley Freeman

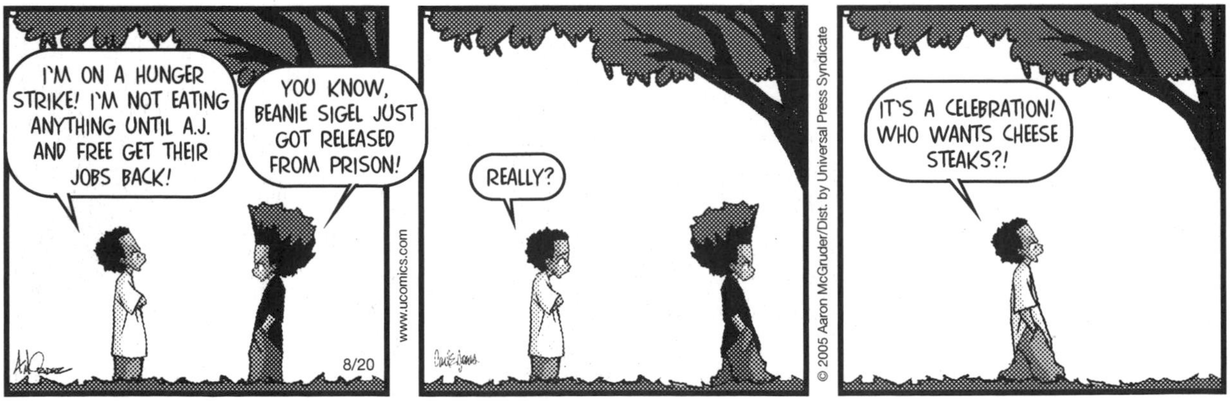
I'M ON A HUNGER STRIKE! I'M NOT EATING ANYTHING UNTIL A.J. AND FREE GET THEIR JOBS BACK!
YOU KNOW, BEANIE SIGEL JUST GOT RELEASED FROM PRISON!
8/20
www.ucomics.com
REALLY?
© 2005 Aaron McGruder/Dist. by Universal Press Syndicate
IT'S A CELEBRATION! WHO WANTS CHEESE STEAKS?!

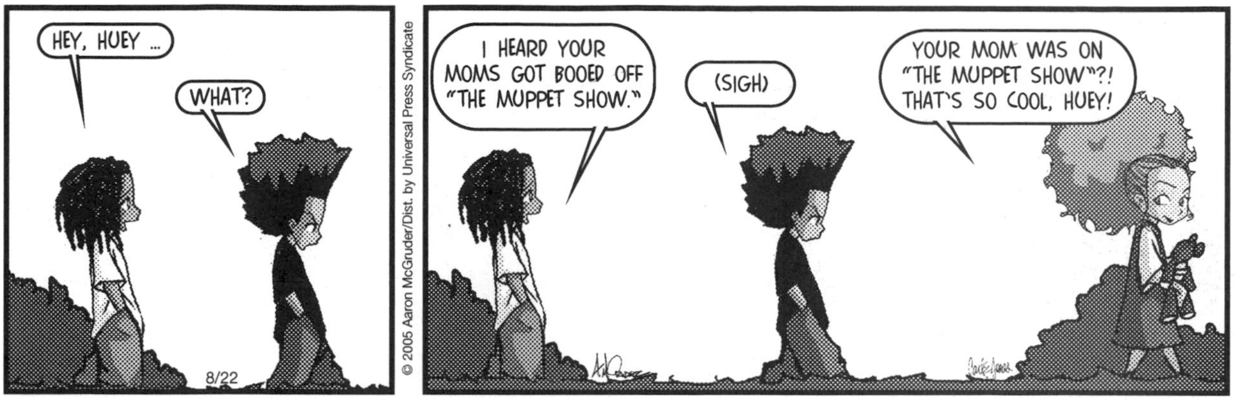
HEY, HUEY ...
WHAT?
8/22
© 2005 Aaron McGruder/Dist. by Universal Press Syndicate
I HEARD YOUR MOMS GOT BOOED OFF "THE MUPPET SHOW."
(SIGH)
YOUR MOM WAS ON "THE MUPPET SHOW"?! THAT'S SO COOL, HUEY!

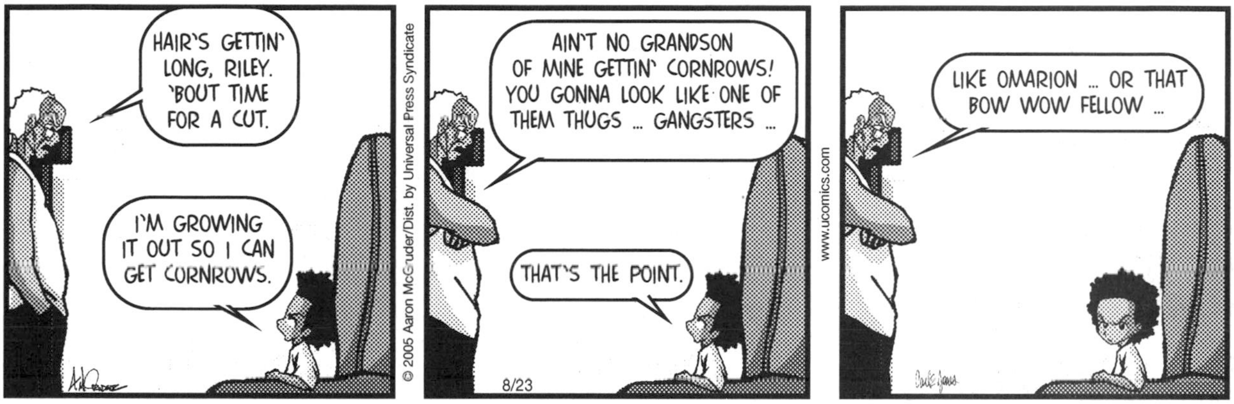
HAIR'S GETTIN' LONG, RILEY. 'BOUT TIME FOR A CUT.
I'M GROWING IT OUT SO I CAN GET CORNROWS.
© 2005 Aaron McGruder/Dist. by Universal Press Syndicate
AIN'T NO GRANDSON OF MINE GETTIN' CORNROWS! YOU GONNA LOOK LIKE ONE OF THEM THUGS ... GANGSTERS ...
THAT'S THE POINT.
8/23
www.ucomics.com
LIKE OMARION ... OR THAT BOW WOW FELLOW ...

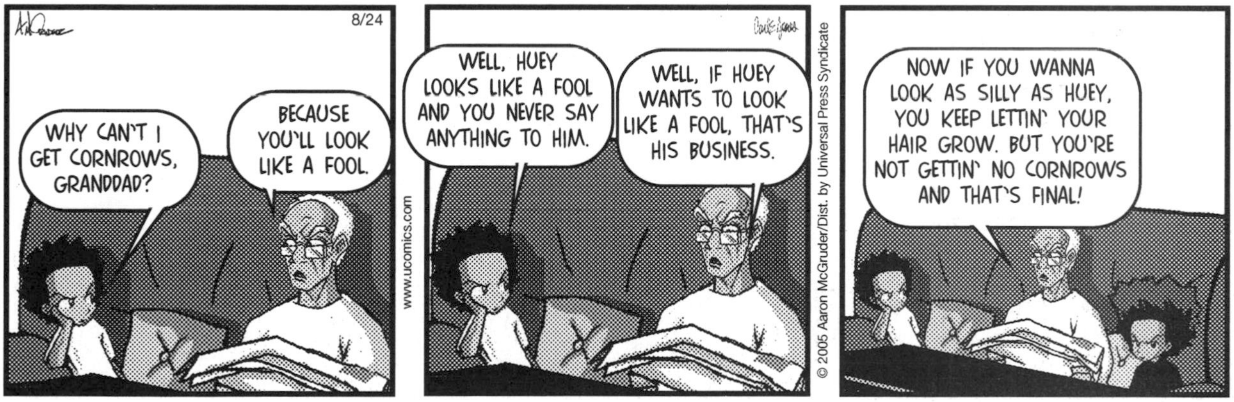
8/24
WHY CAN'T I GET CORNROWS, GRANDDAD?
BECAUSE YOU'LL LOOK LIKE A FOOL.
www.ucomics.com
WELL, HUEY LOOKS LIKE A FOOL AND YOU NEVER SAY ANYTHING TO HIM.
WELL, IF HUEY WANTS TO LOOK LIKE A FOOL, THAT'S HIS BUSINESS.
© 2005 Aaron McGruder/Dist. by Universal Press Syndicate
NOW IF YOU WANNA LOOK AS SILLY AS HUEY, YOU KEEP LETTIN' YOUR HAIR GROW. BUT YOU'RE NOT GETTIN' NO CORNROWS AND THAT'S FINAL!

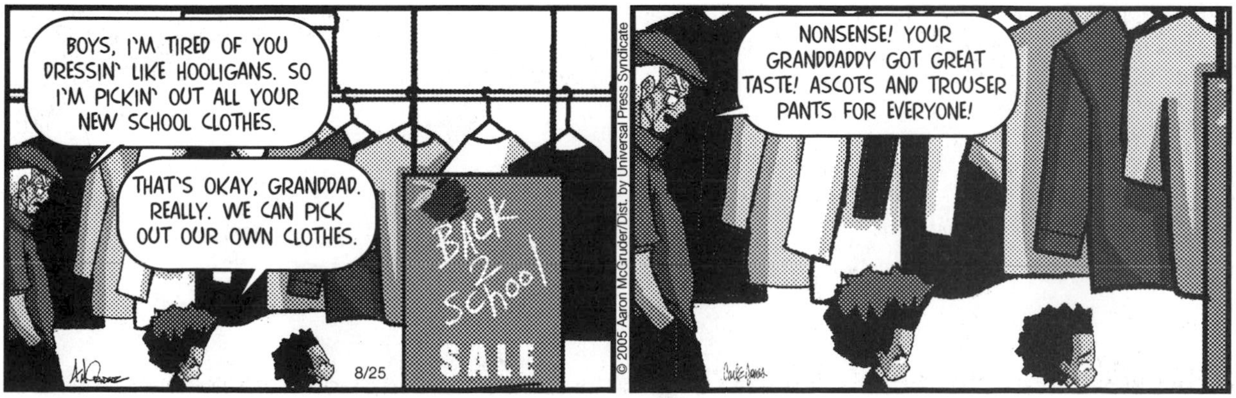
BOYS, I'M TIRED OF YOU DRESSIN' LIKE HOOLIGANS. SO I'M PICKIN' OUT ALL YOUR NEW SCHOOL CLOTHES.
THAT'S OKAY, GRANDDAD. REALLY. WE CAN PICK OUT OUR OWN CLOTHES.
BACK 2 School
SALE
8/25
© 2005 Aaron McGruder/Dist. by Universal Press Syndicate
NONSENSE! YOUR GRANDDADDY GOT GREAT TASTE! ASCOTS AND TROUSER PANTS FOR EVERYONE!

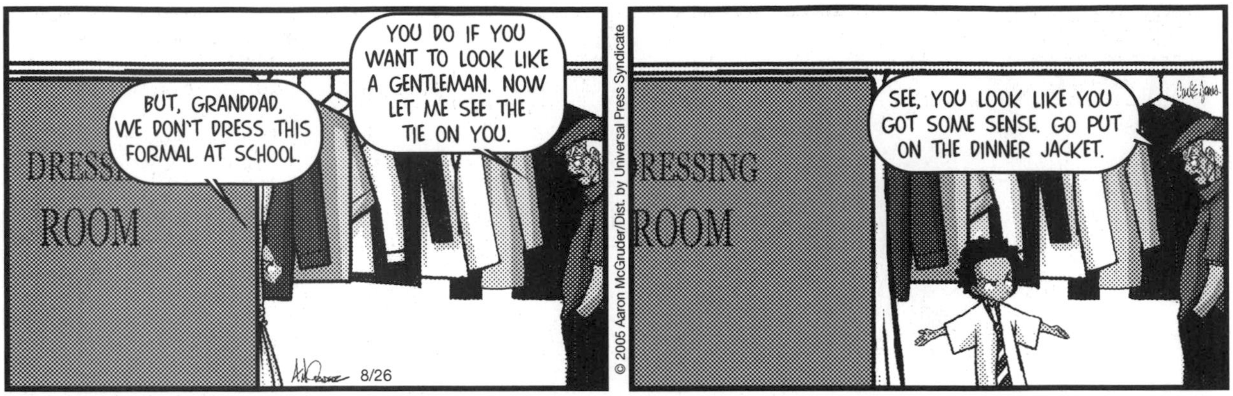
BUT, GRANDDAD, WE DON'T DRESS THIS FORMAL AT SCHOOL.
YOU DO IF YOU WANT TO LOOK LIKE A GENTLEMAN. NOW LET ME SEE THE TIE ON YOU.
DRESSING ROOM
8/26
© 2005 Aaron McGruder/Dist. by Universal Press Syndicate
SEE, YOU LOOK LIKE YOU GOT SOME SENSE. GO PUT ON THE DINNER JACKET.

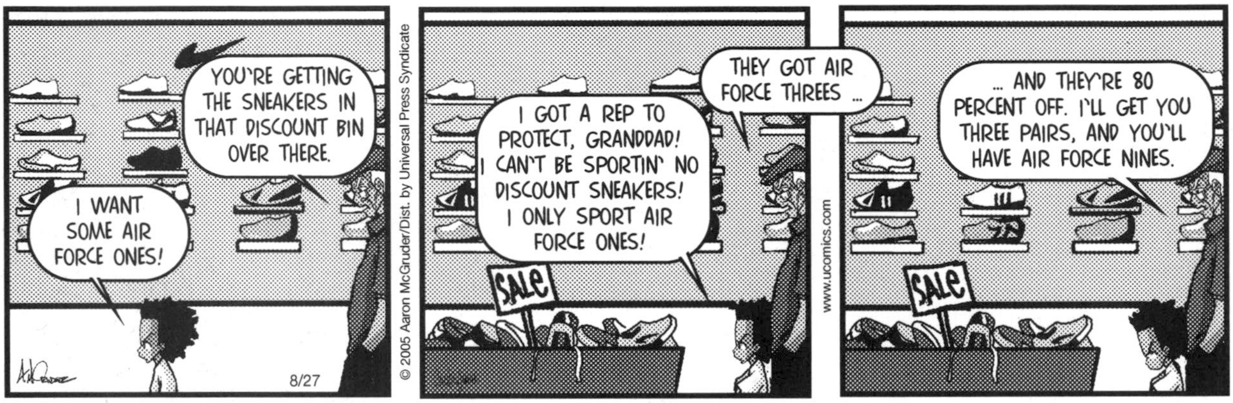
I WANT SOME AIR FORCE ONES!
YOU'RE GETTING THE SNEAKERS IN THAT DISCOUNT BIN OVER THERE.
8/27
© 2005 Aaron McGruder/Dist. by Universal Press Syndicate
I GOT A REP TO PROTECT, GRANDDAD! I CAN'T BE SPORTIN' NO DISCOUNT SNEAKERS! I ONLY SPORT AIR FORCE ONES!
THEY GOT AIR FORCE THREES ...
SALE
www.ucomics.com
... AND THEY'RE 80 PERCENT OFF. I'LL GET YOU THREE PAIRS, AND YOU'LL HAVE AIR FORCE NINES.
SALE

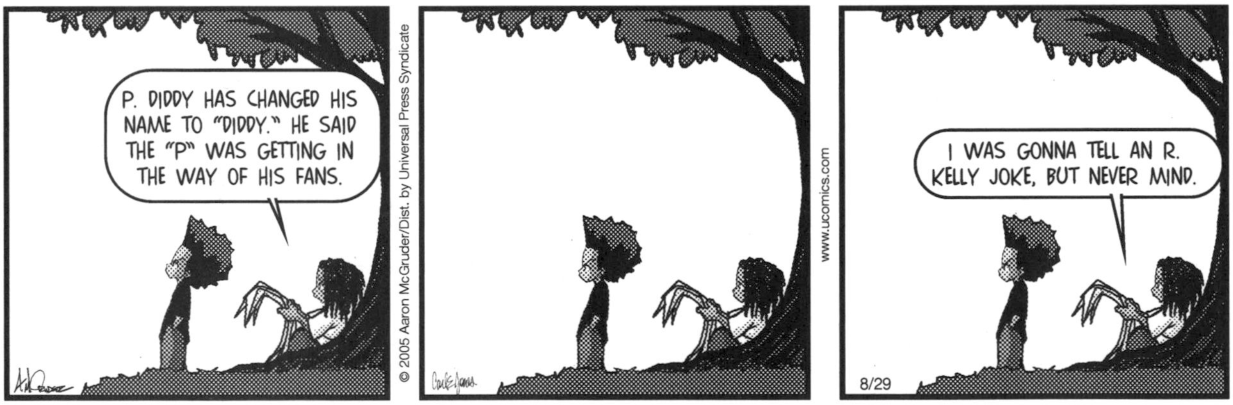
P. DIDDY HAS CHANGED HIS NAME TO "DIDDY." HE SAID THE "P" WAS GETTING IN THE WAY OF HIS FANS.
© 2005 Aaron McGruder/Dist. by Universal Press Syndicate
www.ucomics.com
I WAS GONNA TELL AN R. KELLY JOKE, BUT NEVER MIND.
8/29

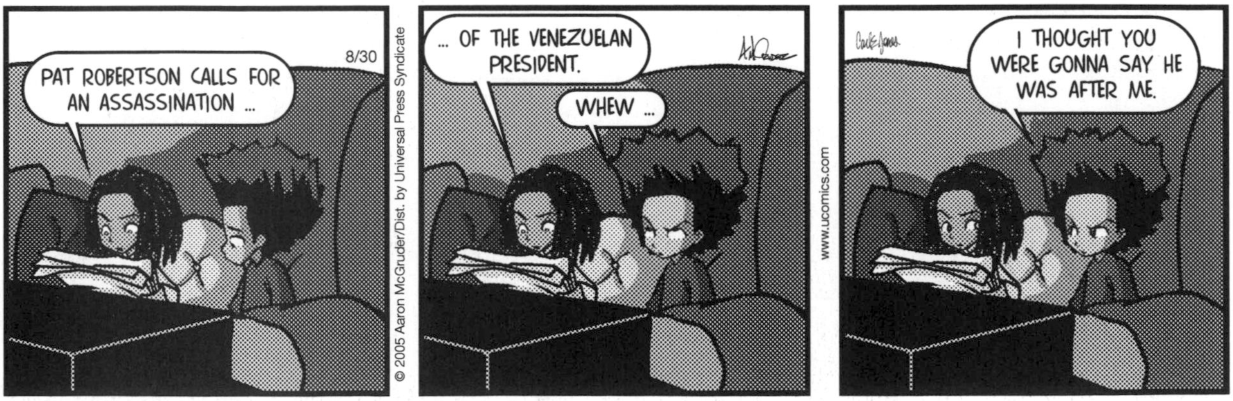
PAT ROBERTSON CALLS FOR AN ASSASSINATION ...
8/30
© 2005 Aaron McGruder/Dist. by Universal Press Syndicate
... OF THE VENEZUELAN PRESIDENT.
WHEW ...
www.ucomics.com
I THOUGHT YOU WERE GONNA SAY HE WAS AFTER ME.

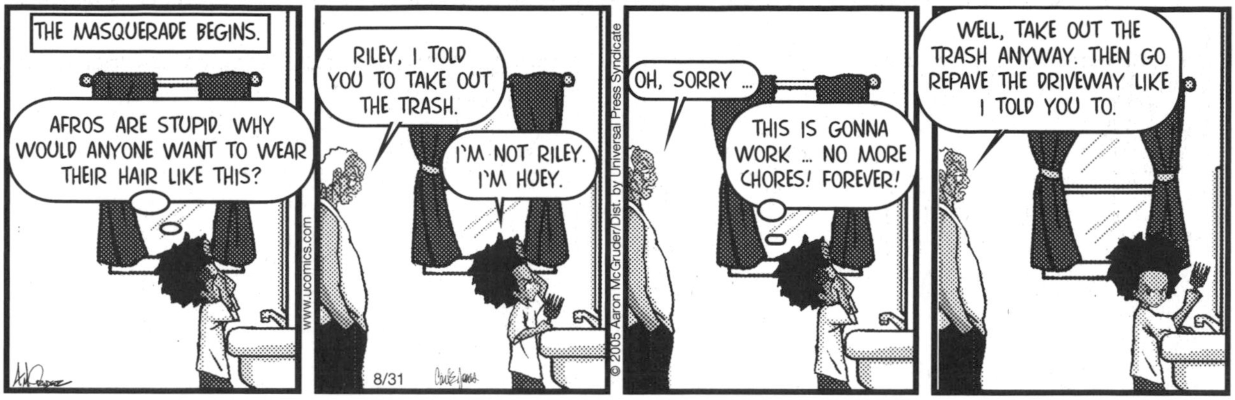
THE MASQUERADE BEGINS.
AFROS ARE STUPID. WHY WOULD ANYONE WANT TO WEAR THEIR HAIR LIKE THIS?
www.ucomics.com
RILEY, I TOLD YOU TO TAKE OUT THE TRASH.
I'M NOT RILEY. I'M HUEY.
8/31
© 2005 Aaron McGruder/Dist. by Universal Press Syndicate
OH, SORRY ...
THIS IS GONNA WORK ... NO MORE CHORES! FOREVER!
WELL, TAKE OUT THE TRASH ANYWAY. THEN GO REPAVE THE DRIVEWAY LIKE I TOLD YOU TO.

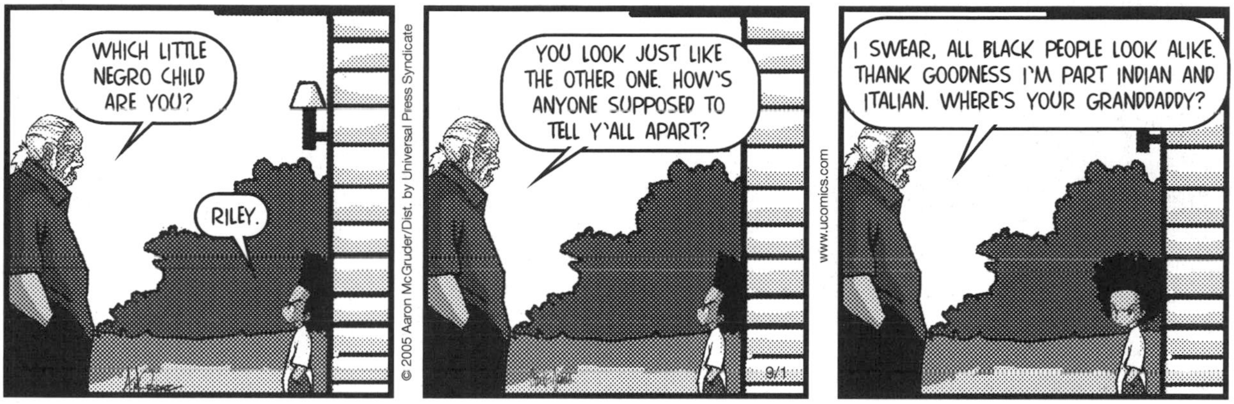
WHICH LITTLE NEGRO CHILD ARE YOU?
RILEY.
© 2005 Aaron McGruder/Dist. by Universal Press Syndicate
YOU LOOK JUST LIKE THE OTHER ONE. HOW'S ANYONE SUPPOSED TO TELL Y'ALL APART?
9/1
www.ucomics.com
I SWEAR, ALL BLACK PEOPLE LOOK ALIKE. THANK GOODNESS I'M PART INDIAN AND ITALIAN. WHERE'S YOUR GRANDDADDY?

[Readers] like it because it's different—very different—from the other white-bread comics that dominate North American comics pages.

—Montreal Gazette

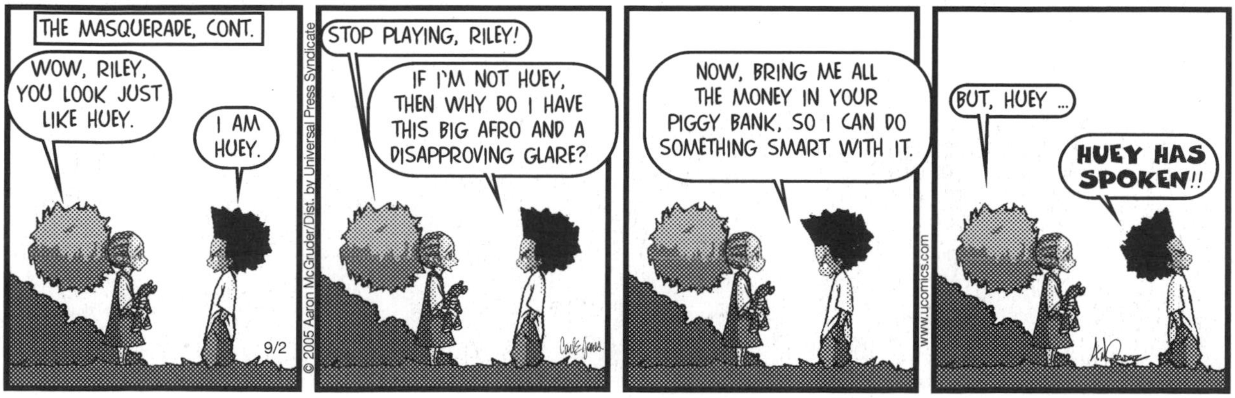
THE MASQUERADE, CONT.
WOW, RILEY, YOU LOOK JUST LIKE HUEY.
I AM HUEY.
9/2
© 2005 Aaron McGruder/Dist. by Universal Press Syndicate
STOP PLAYING, RILEY!
IF I'M NOT HUEY, THEN WHY DO I HAVE THIS BIG AFRO AND A DISAPPROVING GLARE?
NOW, BRING ME ALL THE MONEY IN YOUR PIGGY BANK, SO I CAN DO SOMETHING SMART WITH IT.
www.ucomics.com
BUT, HUEY ...
HUEY HAS SPOKEN!!

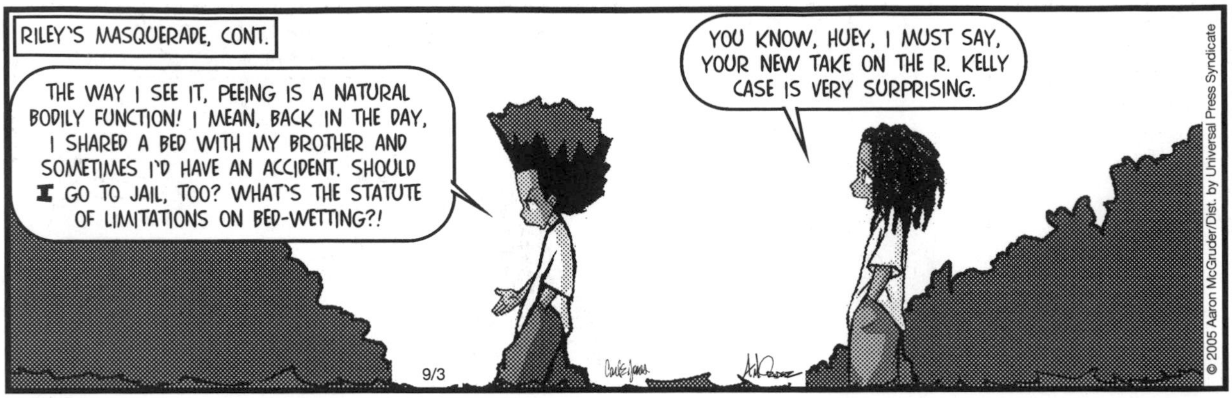
RILEY'S MASQUERADE, CONT.
THE WAY I SEE IT, PEEING IS A NATURAL BODILY FUNCTION! I MEAN, BACK IN THE DAY, I SHARED A BED WITH MY BROTHER AND SOMETIMES I'D HAVE AN ACCIDENT. SHOULD **I** GO TO JAIL, TOO? WHAT'S THE STATUTE OF LIMITATIONS ON BED-WETTING?!
YOU KNOW, HUEY, I MUST SAY, YOUR NEW TAKE ON THE R. KELLY CASE IS VERY SURPRISING.
9/3
© 2005 Aaron McGruder/Dist. by Universal Press Syndicate

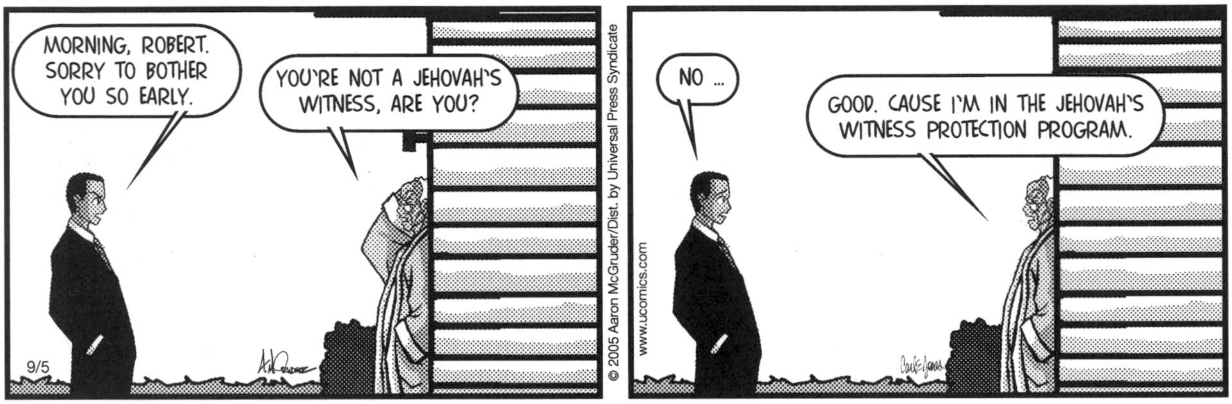
MORNING, ROBERT. SORRY TO BOTHER YOU SO EARLY.
YOU'RE NOT A JEHOVAH'S WITNESS, ARE YOU?
9/5
© 2005 Aaron McGruder/Dist. by Universal Press Syndicate
www.ucomics.com
NO ...
GOOD. CAUSE I'M IN THE JEHOVAH'S WITNESS PROTECTION PROGRAM.

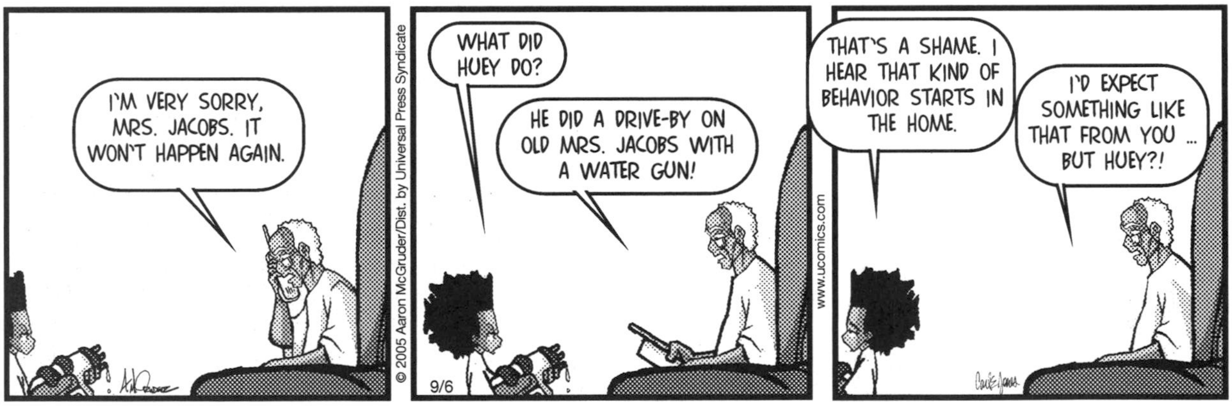
I'M VERY SORRY, MRS. JACOBS. IT WON'T HAPPEN AGAIN.
© 2005 Aaron McGruder/Dist. by Universal Press Syndicate
WHAT DID HUEY DO?
HE DID A DRIVE-BY ON OLD MRS. JACOBS WITH A WATER GUN!
9/6
www.ucomics.com
THAT'S A SHAME. I HEAR THAT KIND OF BEHAVIOR STARTS IN THE HOME.
I'D EXPECT SOMETHING LIKE THAT FROM YOU ... BUT HUEY?!

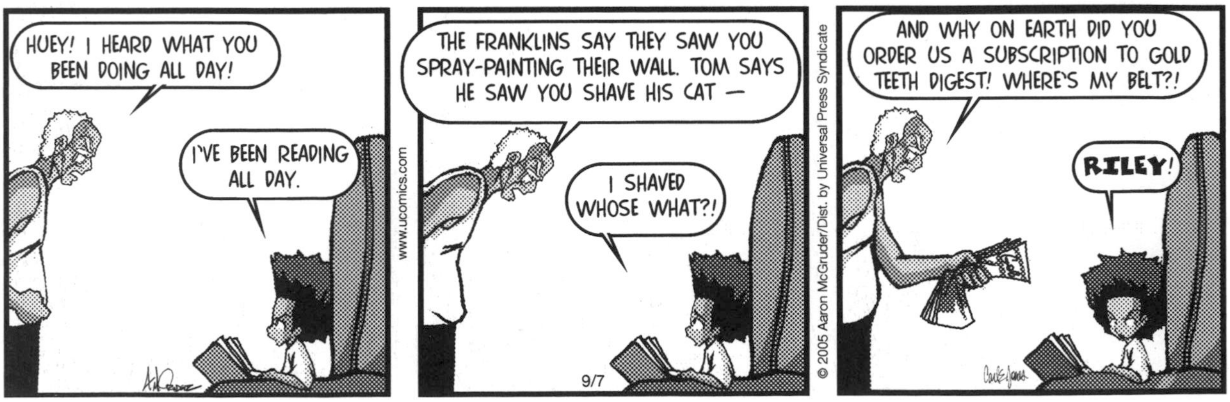
HUEY! I HEARD WHAT YOU BEEN DOING ALL DAY!
I'VE BEEN READING ALL DAY.
www.ucomics.com
THE FRANKLINS SAY THEY SAW YOU SPRAY-PAINTING THEIR WALL. TOM SAYS HE SAW YOU SHAVE HIS CAT —
I SHAVED WHOSE WHAT?!
9/7
© 2005 Aaron McGruder/Dist. by Universal Press Syndicate
AND WHY ON EARTH DID YOU ORDER US A SUBSCRIPTION TO GOLD TEETH DIGEST! WHERE'S MY BELT?!
RILEY!

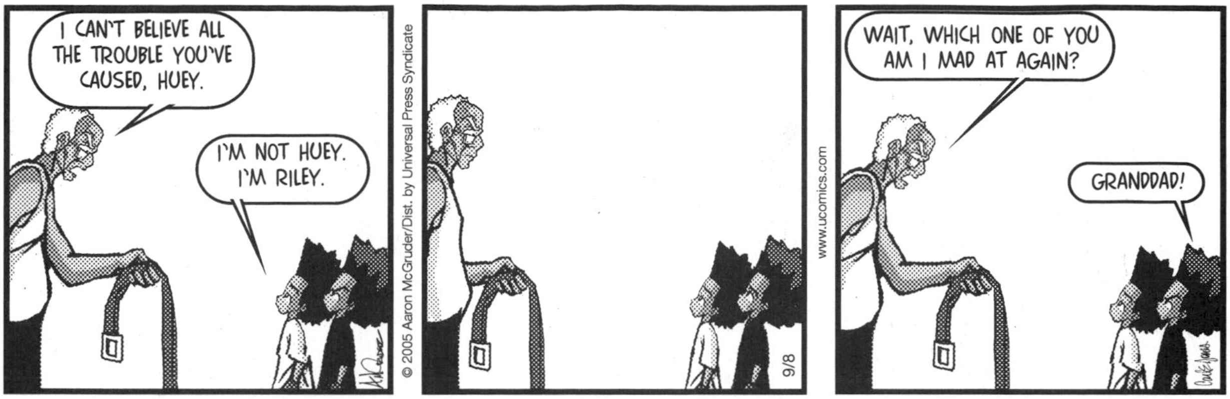
I CAN'T BELIEVE ALL THE TROUBLE YOU'VE CAUSED, HUEY.
I'M NOT HUEY. I'M RILEY.
© 2005 Aaron McGruder/Dist. by Universal Press Syndicate
www.ucomics.com
9/8
WAIT, WHICH ONE OF YOU AM I MAD AT AGAIN?
GRANDDAD!

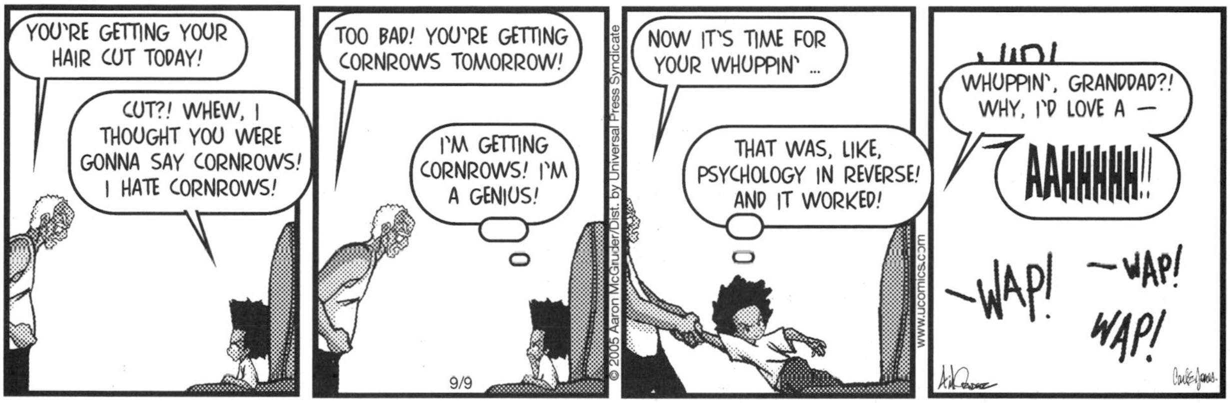
YOU'RE GETTING YOUR HAIR CUT TODAY!
CUT?! WHEW, I THOUGHT YOU WERE GONNA SAY CORNROWS! I HATE CORNROWS!
TOO BAD! YOU'RE GETTING CORNROWS TOMORROW!
I'M GETTING CORNROWS! I'M A GENIUS!
9/9
© 2005 Aaron McGruder/Dist. by Universal Press Syndicate
NOW IT'S TIME FOR YOUR WHUPPIN' ...
THAT WAS, LIKE, PSYCHOLOGY IN REVERSE! AND IT WORKED!
www.ucomics.com
WHUPPIN', GRANDDAD?! WHY, I'D LOVE A —
AAHHHHH!!
-WAP!
-WAP!
WAP!

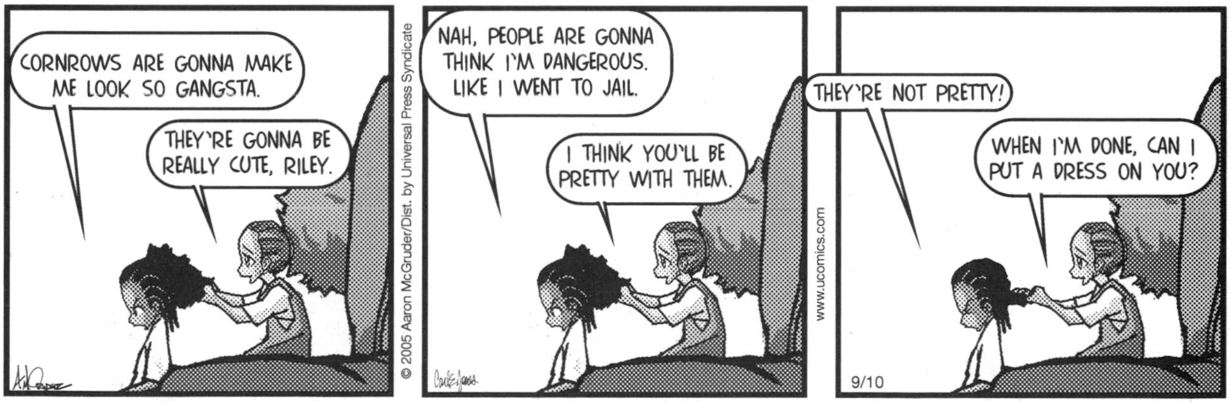
CORNROWS ARE GONNA MAKE ME LOOK SO GANGSTA.
THEY'RE GONNA BE REALLY CUTE, RILEY.
© 2005 Aaron McGruder/Dist. by Universal Press Syndicate
NAH, PEOPLE ARE GONNA THINK I'M DANGEROUS. LIKE I WENT TO JAIL.
I THINK YOU'LL BE PRETTY WITH THEM.
www.ucomics.com
THEY'RE NOT PRETTY!
WHEN I'M DONE, CAN I PUT A DRESS ON YOU?
9/10

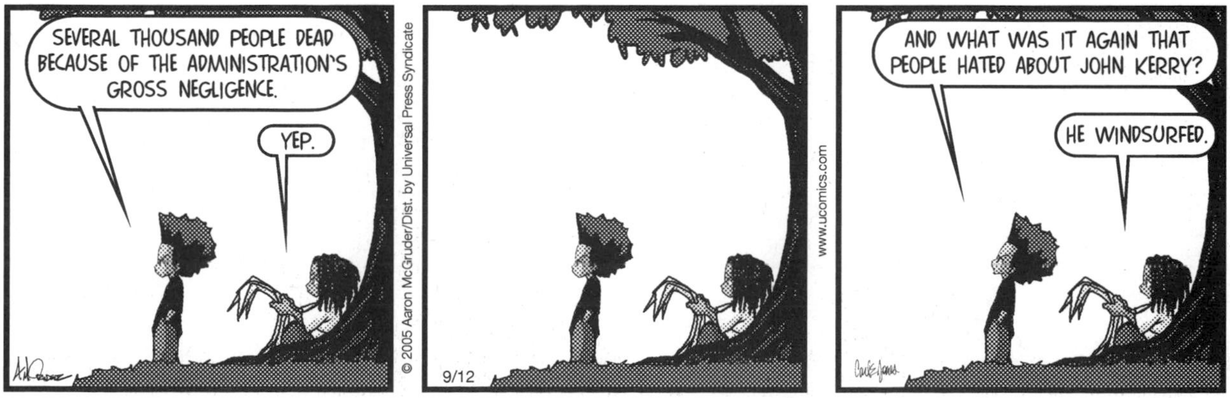
SEVERAL THOUSAND PEOPLE DEAD BECAUSE OF THE ADMINISTRATION'S GROSS NEGLIGENCE.
YEP.
© 2005 Aaron McGruder/Dist. by Universal Press Syndicate
9/12
www.ucomics.com
AND WHAT WAS IT AGAIN THAT PEOPLE HATED ABOUT JOHN KERRY?
HE WINDSURFED.

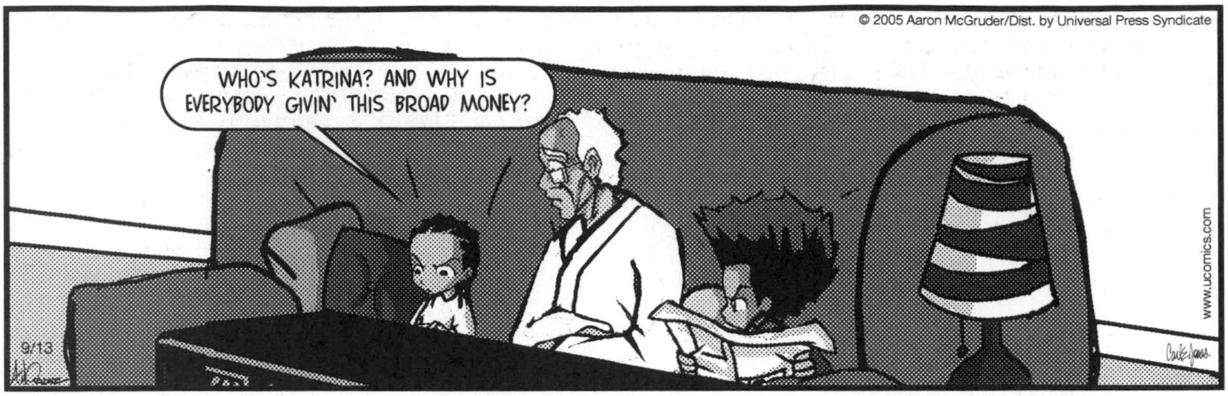
© 2005 Aaron McGruder/Dist. by Universal Press Syndicate
WHO'S KATRINA? AND WHY IS EVERYBODY GIVIN' THIS BROAD MONEY?
www.ucomics.com
9/13

A.V. Club: You almost have a nostalgia for a time when the government was better at deceiving people, and was better . . .

Aaron McGruder: Yeah, we call those the Clinton years.

—*A.V. Club*

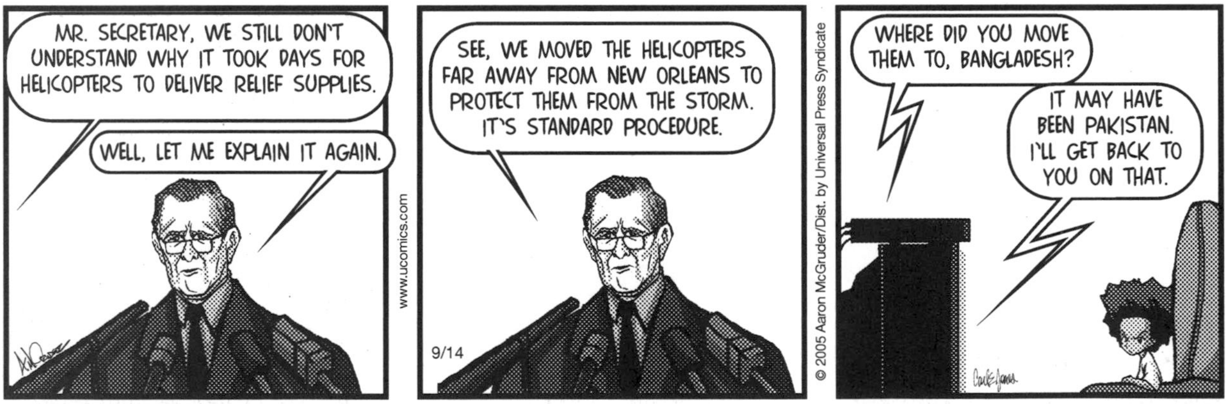
MR. SECRETARY, WE STILL DON'T UNDERSTAND WHY IT TOOK DAYS FOR HELICOPTERS TO DELIVER RELIEF SUPPLIES.
WELL, LET ME EXPLAIN IT AGAIN.
www.ucomics.com
SEE, WE MOVED THE HELICOPTERS FAR AWAY FROM NEW ORLEANS TO PROTECT THEM FROM THE STORM. IT'S STANDARD PROCEDURE.
9/14
© 2005 Aaron McGruder/Dist. by Universal Press Syndicate
WHERE DID YOU MOVE THEM TO, BANGLADESH?
IT MAY HAVE BEEN PAKISTAN. I'LL GET BACK TO YOU ON THAT.

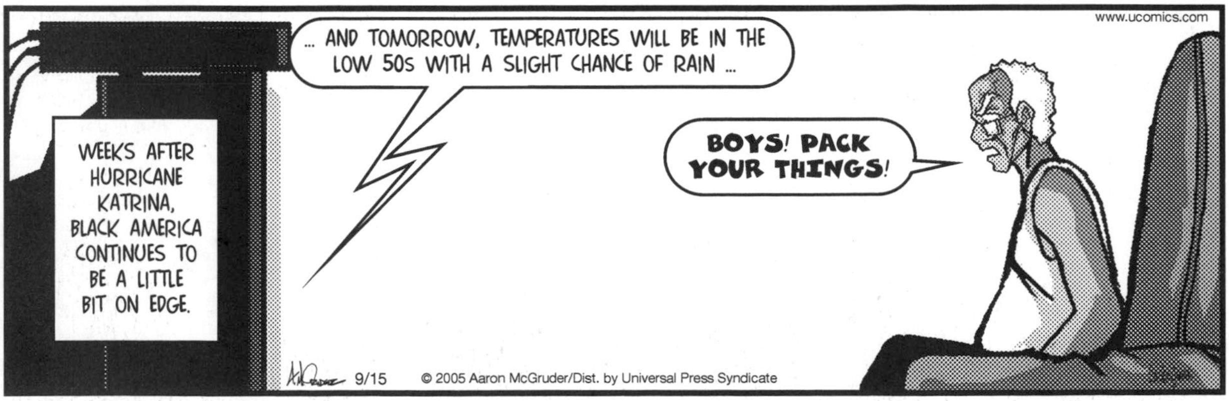
www.ucomics.com
... AND TOMORROW, TEMPERATURES WILL BE IN THE LOW 50s WITH A SLIGHT CHANCE OF RAIN ...
WEEKS AFTER HURRICANE KATRINA, BLACK AMERICA CONTINUES TO BE A LITTLE BIT ON EDGE.
BOYS! PACK YOUR THINGS!
9/15
© 2005 Aaron McGruder/Dist. by Universal Press Syndicate

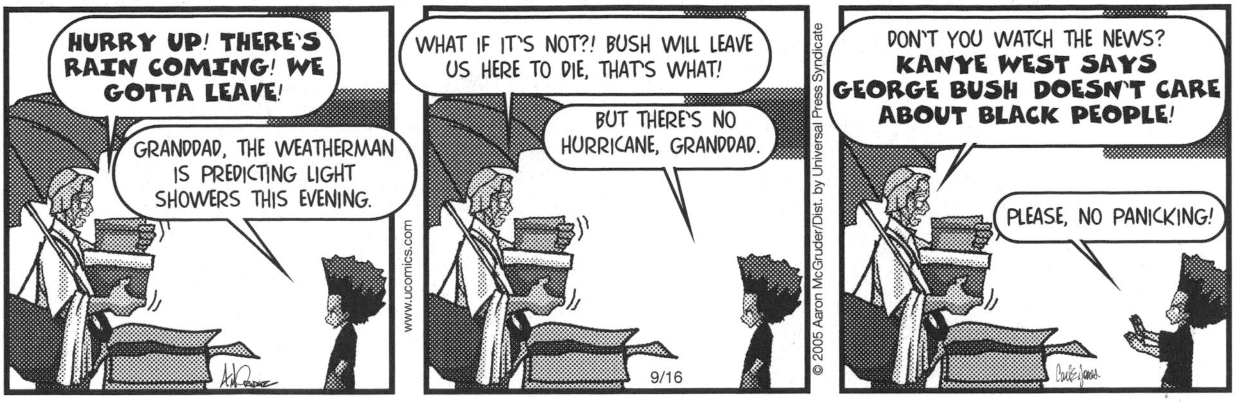
HURRY UP! THERE'S RAIN COMING! WE GOTTA LEAVE!
GRANDDAD, THE WEATHERMAN IS PREDICTING LIGHT SHOWERS THIS EVENING.
www.ucomics.com
WHAT IF IT'S NOT?! BUSH WILL LEAVE US HERE TO DIE, THAT'S WHAT!
BUT THERE'S NO HURRICANE, GRANDDAD.
9/16
© 2005 Aaron McGruder/Dist. by Universal Press Syndicate
DON'T YOU WATCH THE NEWS? KANYE WEST SAYS GEORGE BUSH DOESN'T CARE ABOUT BLACK PEOPLE!
PLEASE, NO PANICKING!

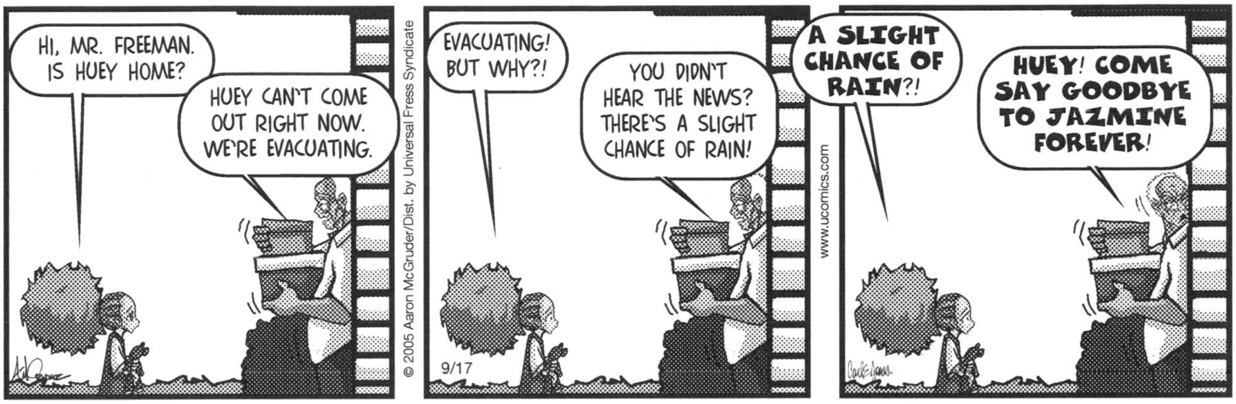
HI, MR. FREEMAN. IS HUEY HOME?
HUEY CAN'T COME OUT RIGHT NOW. WE'RE EVACUATING.
© 2005 Aaron McGruder/Dist. by Universal Press Syndicate
EVACUATING! BUT WHY?!
YOU DIDN'T HEAR THE NEWS? THERE'S A SLIGHT CHANCE OF RAIN!
9/17
www.ucomics.com
A SLIGHT CHANCE OF RAIN?!
HUEY! COME SAY GOODBYE TO JAZMINE FOREVER!

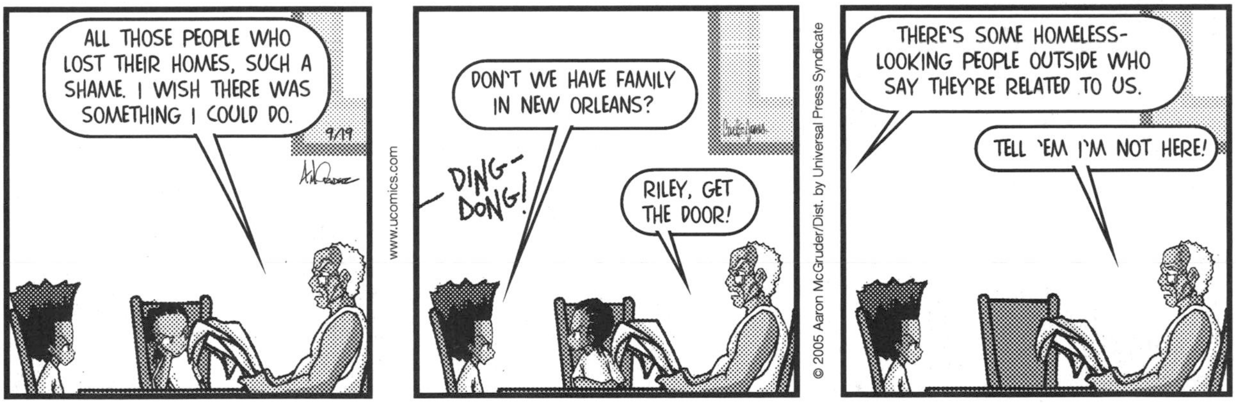
ALL THOSE PEOPLE WHO LOST THEIR HOMES, SUCH A SHAME. I WISH THERE WAS SOMETHING I COULD DO.
9/19
www.ucomics.com
DON'T WE HAVE FAMILY IN NEW ORLEANS?
DING-DONG!
RILEY, GET THE DOOR!
© 2005 Aaron McGruder/Dist. by Universal Press Syndicate
THERE'S SOME HOMELESS-LOOKING PEOPLE OUTSIDE WHO SAY THEY'RE RELATED TO US.
TELL 'EM I'M NOT HERE!

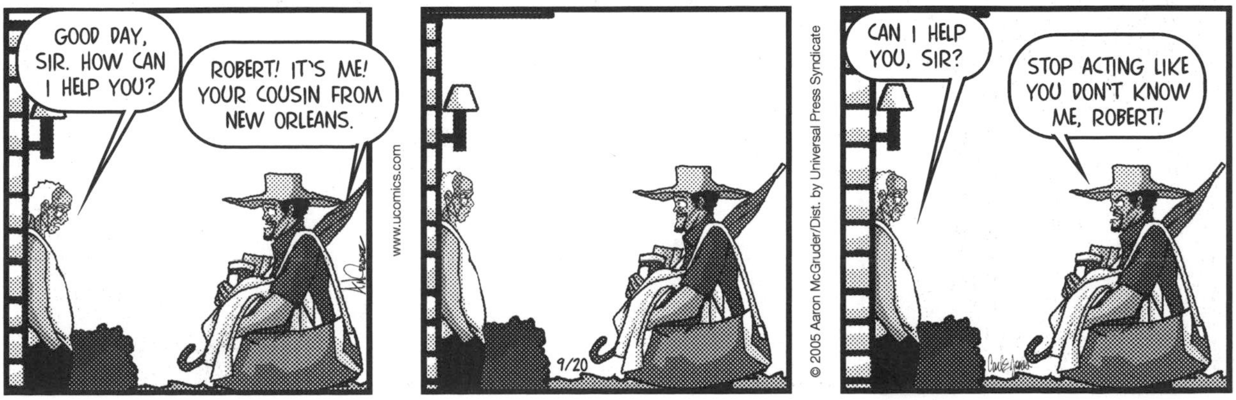
GOOD DAY, SIR. HOW CAN I HELP YOU?
ROBERT! IT'S ME! YOUR COUSIN FROM NEW ORLEANS.
www.ucomics.com
9/20
© 2005 Aaron McGruder/Dist. by Universal Press Syndicate
CAN I HELP YOU, SIR?
STOP ACTING LIKE YOU DON'T KNOW ME, ROBERT!

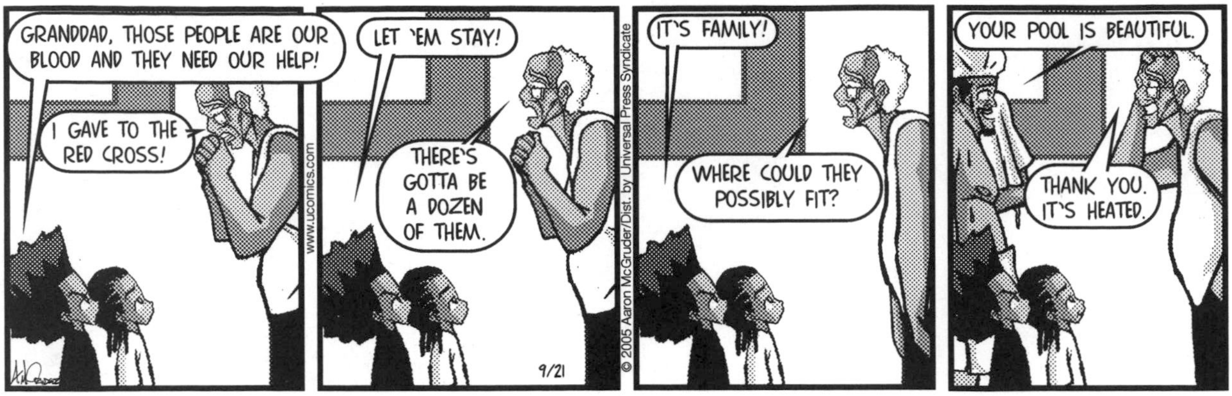
GRANDDAD, THOSE PEOPLE ARE OUR BLOOD AND THEY NEED OUR HELP!
I GAVE TO THE RED CROSS!
www.ucomics.com
LET 'EM STAY!
THERE'S GOTTA BE A DOZEN OF THEM.
9/21
© 2005 Aaron McGruder/Dist. by Universal Press Syndicate
IT'S FAMILY!
WHERE COULD THEY POSSIBLY FIT?
YOUR POOL IS BEAUTIFUL.
THANK YOU. IT'S HEATED.

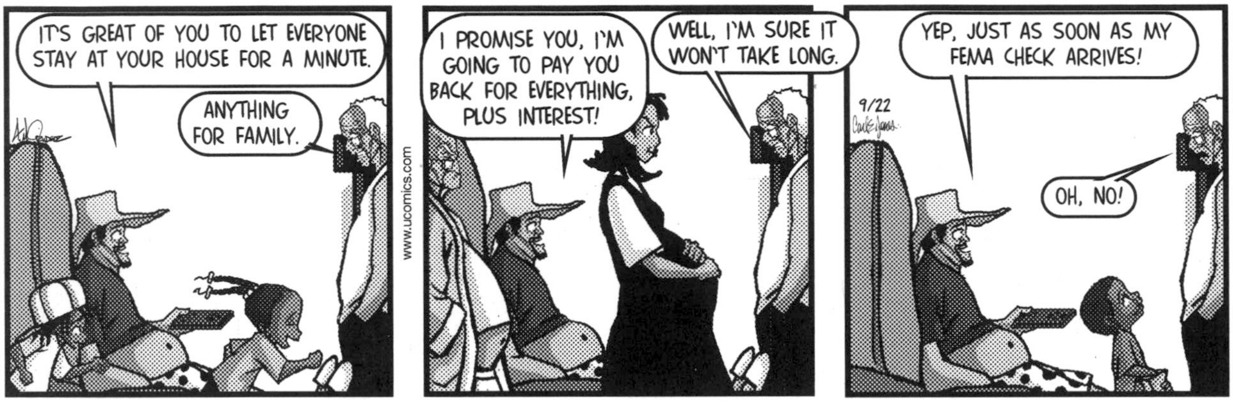
IT'S GREAT OF YOU TO LET EVERYONE STAY AT YOUR HOUSE FOR A MINUTE.
ANYTHING FOR FAMILY.
www.ucomics.com
I PROMISE YOU, I'M GOING TO PAY YOU BACK FOR EVERYTHING, PLUS INTEREST!
WELL, I'M SURE IT WON'T TAKE LONG.
9/22
YEP, JUST AS SOON AS MY FEMA CHECK ARRIVES!
OH, NO!

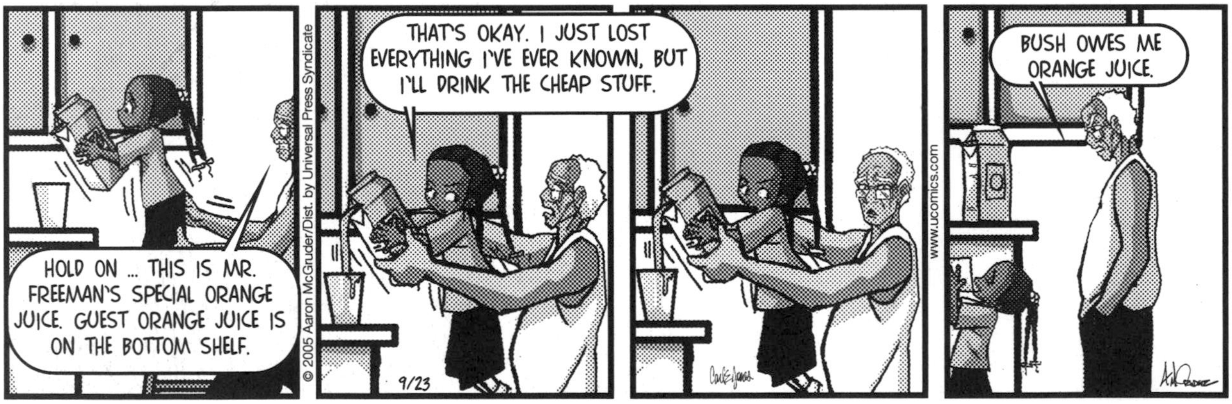
HOLD ON ... THIS IS MR. FREEMAN'S SPECIAL ORANGE JUICE. GUEST ORANGE JUICE IS ON THE BOTTOM SHELF.
© 2005 Aaron McGruder/Dist. by Universal Press Syndicate
THAT'S OKAY. I JUST LOST EVERYTHING I'VE EVER KNOWN, BUT I'LL DRINK THE CHEAP STUFF.
9/23
www.ucomics.com
BUSH OWES ME ORANGE JUICE.

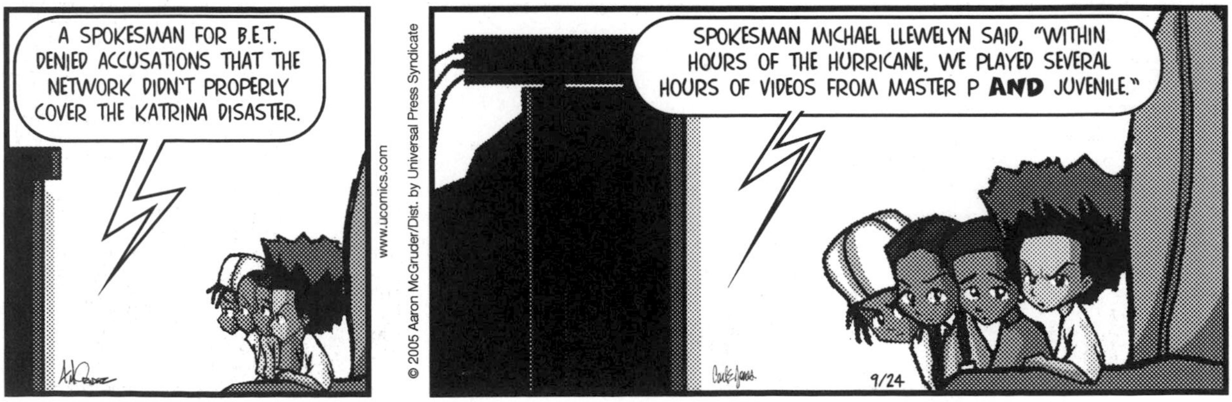
A SPOKESMAN FOR B.E.T. DENIED ACCUSATIONS THAT THE NETWORK DIDN'T PROPERLY COVER THE KATRINA DISASTER.
www.ucomics.com
© 2005 Aaron McGruder/Dist. by Universal Press Syndicate
SPOKESMAN MICHAEL LLEWELYN SAID, "WITHIN HOURS OF THE HURRICANE, WE PLAYED SEVERAL HOURS OF VIDEOS FROM MASTER P **AND** JUVENILE."
9/24

> [My employees] do more in one day to serve the interests of African Americans than this young man has done in his entire life.
>
> —Robert Johnson, founder and CEO of Black Entertainment Television

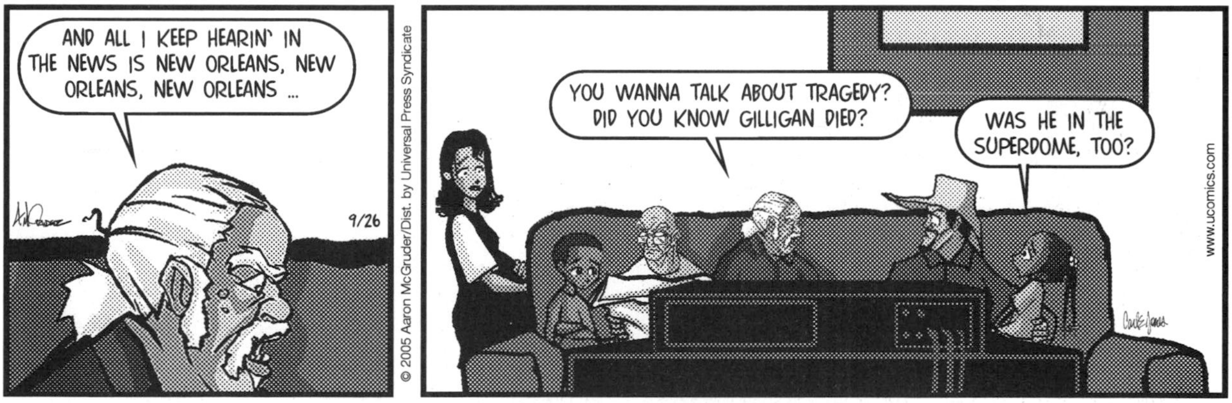
AND ALL I KEEP HEARIN' IN THE NEWS IS NEW ORLEANS, NEW ORLEANS, NEW ORLEANS ...
9/26
© 2005 Aaron McGruder/Dist. by Universal Press Syndicate
YOU WANNA TALK ABOUT TRAGEDY? DID YOU KNOW GILLIGAN DIED?
WAS HE IN THE SUPERDOME, TOO?
www.ucomics.com

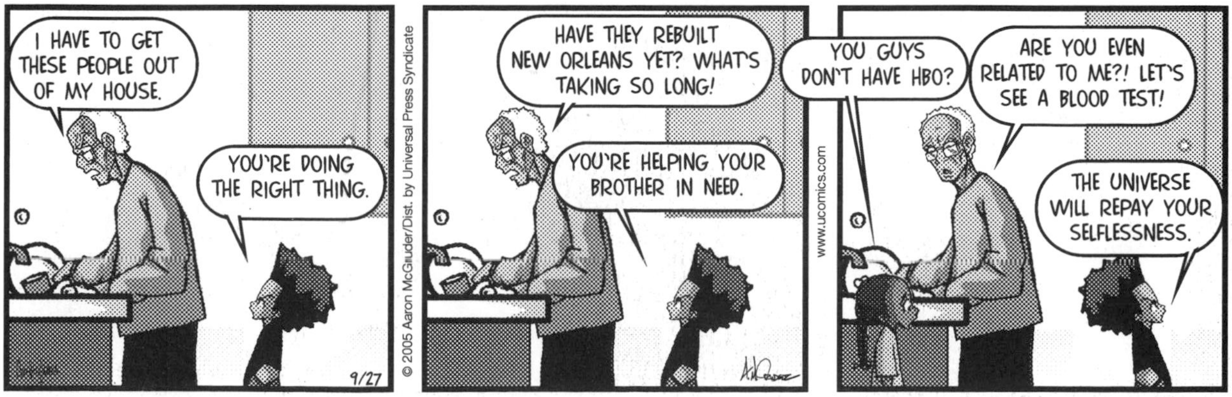
I HAVE TO GET THESE PEOPLE OUT OF MY HOUSE.
YOU'RE DOING THE RIGHT THING.
9/27
© 2005 Aaron McGruder/Dist. by Universal Press Syndicate
HAVE THEY REBUILT NEW ORLEANS YET? WHAT'S TAKING SO LONG!
YOU'RE HELPING YOUR BROTHER IN NEED.
www.ucomics.com
YOU GUYS DON'T HAVE HBO?
ARE YOU EVEN RELATED TO ME?! LET'S SEE A BLOOD TEST!
THE UNIVERSE WILL REPAY YOUR SELFLESSNESS.

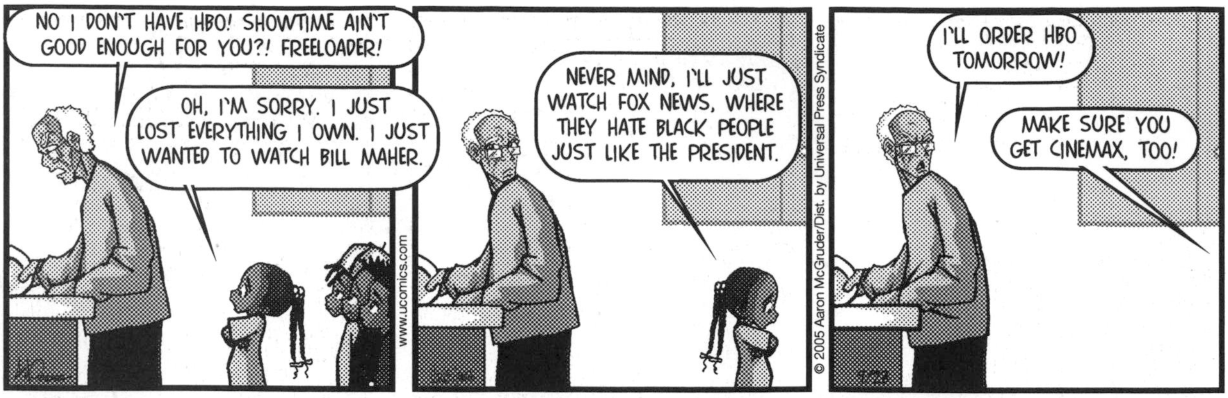
NO I DON'T HAVE HBO! SHOWTIME AIN'T GOOD ENOUGH FOR YOU?! FREELOADER!
OH, I'M SORRY. I JUST LOST EVERYTHING I OWN. I JUST WANTED TO WATCH BILL MAHER.
www.ucomics.com
NEVER MIND, I'LL JUST WATCH FOX NEWS, WHERE THEY HATE BLACK PEOPLE JUST LIKE THE PRESIDENT.
© 2005 Aaron McGruder/Dist. by Universal Press Syndicate
I'LL ORDER HBO TOMORROW!
MAKE SURE YOU GET CINEMAX, TOO!

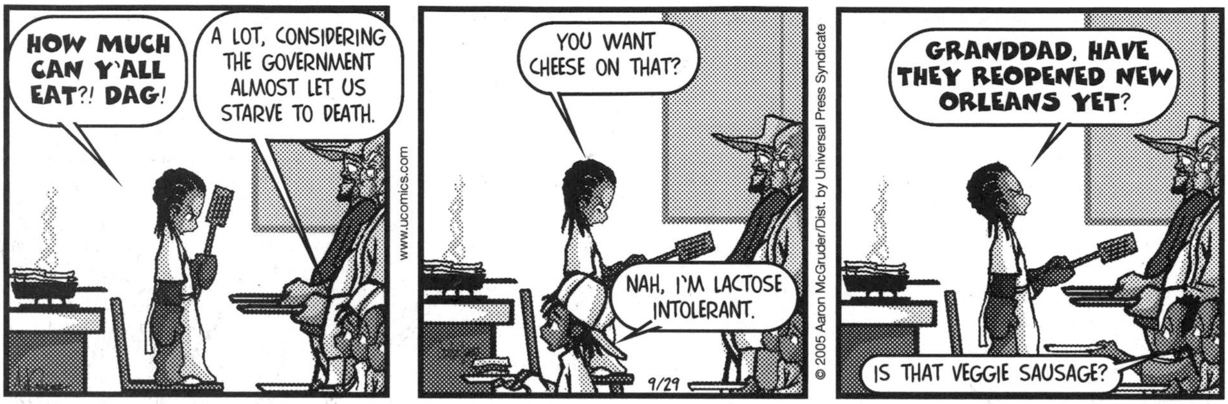
HOW MUCH CAN Y'ALL EAT?! DAG!
A LOT, CONSIDERING THE GOVERNMENT ALMOST LET US STARVE TO DEATH.
www.ucomics.com
YOU WANT CHEESE ON THAT?
NAH, I'M LACTOSE INTOLERANT.
9/29
© 2005 Aaron McGruder/Dist. by Universal Press Syndicate
GRANDDAD, HAVE THEY REOPENED NEW ORLEANS YET?
IS THAT VEGGIE SAUSAGE?

I'm interested in telling stories, stories that aren't being told.

—Aaron McGruder, *NBC News*

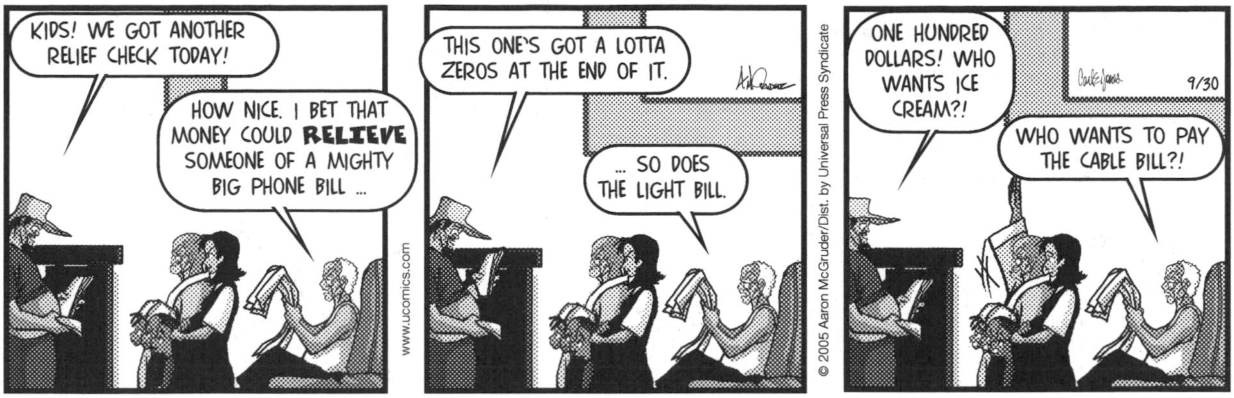
KIDS! WE GOT ANOTHER RELIEF CHECK TODAY!
HOW NICE. I BET THAT MONEY COULD **RELIEVE** SOMEONE OF A MIGHTY BIG PHONE BILL ...
www.ucomics.com
THIS ONE'S GOT A LOTTA ZEROS AT THE END OF IT.
... SO DOES THE LIGHT BILL.
© 2005 Aaron McGruder/Dist. by Universal Press Syndicate
ONE HUNDRED DOLLARS! WHO WANTS ICE CREAM?!
9/30
WHO WANTS TO PAY THE CABLE BILL?!

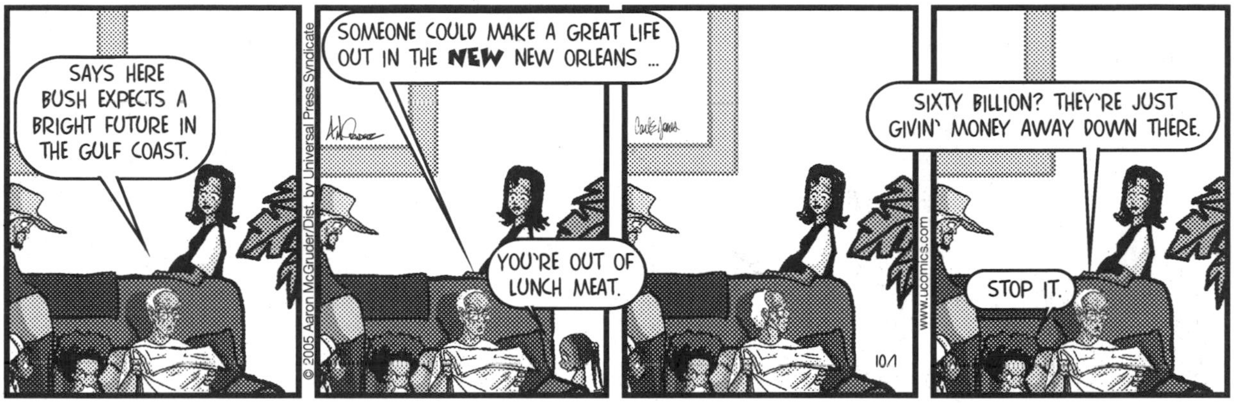
SAYS HERE BUSH EXPECTS A BRIGHT FUTURE IN THE GULF COAST.
© 2005 Aaron McGruder/Dist. by Universal Press Syndicate
SOMEONE COULD MAKE A GREAT LIFE OUT IN THE **NEW** NEW ORLEANS ...
YOU'RE OUT OF LUNCH MEAT.
10/1
www.ucomics.com
SIXTY BILLION? THEY'RE JUST GIVIN' MONEY AWAY DOWN THERE.
STOP IT.

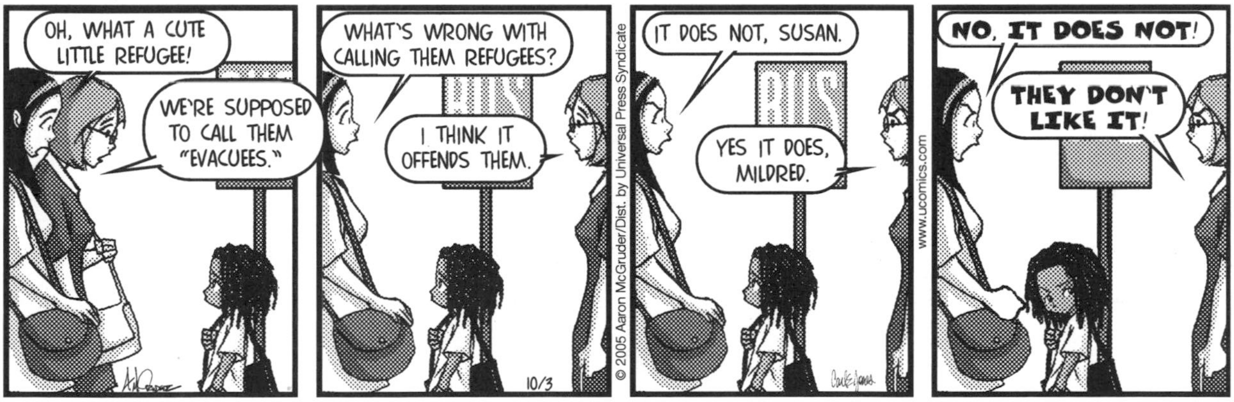
OH, WHAT A CUTE LITTLE REFUGEE!
WE'RE SUPPOSED TO CALL THEM "EVACUEES."
WHAT'S WRONG WITH CALLING THEM REFUGEES?
I THINK IT OFFENDS THEM.
10/3
© 2005 Aaron McGruder/Dist. by Universal Press Syndicate
IT DOES NOT, SUSAN.
YES IT DOES, MILDRED.
www.ucomics.com
NO, IT DOES NOT!
THEY DON'T LIKE IT!

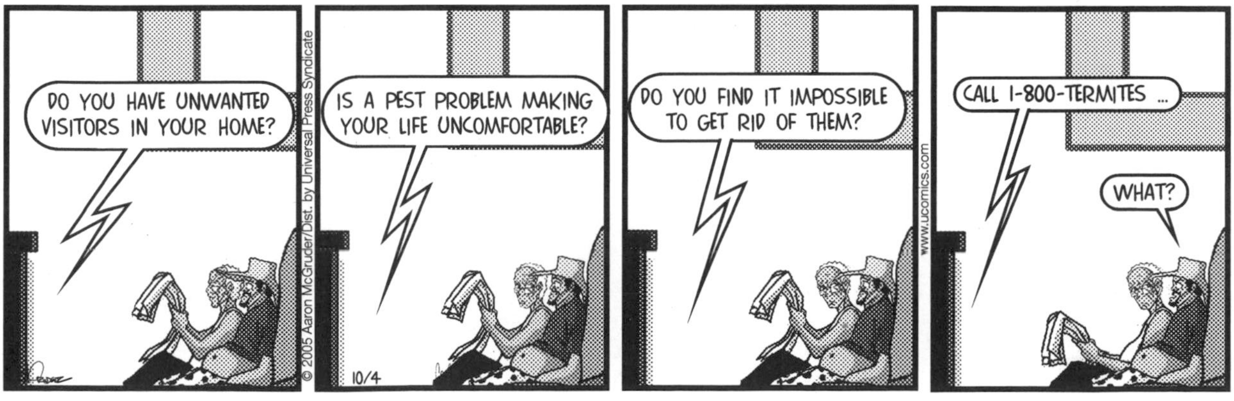
DO YOU HAVE UNWANTED VISITORS IN YOUR HOME?
© 2005 Aaron McGruder/Dist. by Universal Press Syndicate
IS A PEST PROBLEM MAKING YOUR LIFE UNCOMFORTABLE?
10/4
DO YOU FIND IT IMPOSSIBLE TO GET RID OF THEM?
www.ucomics.com
CALL 1-800-TERMITES ...
WHAT?

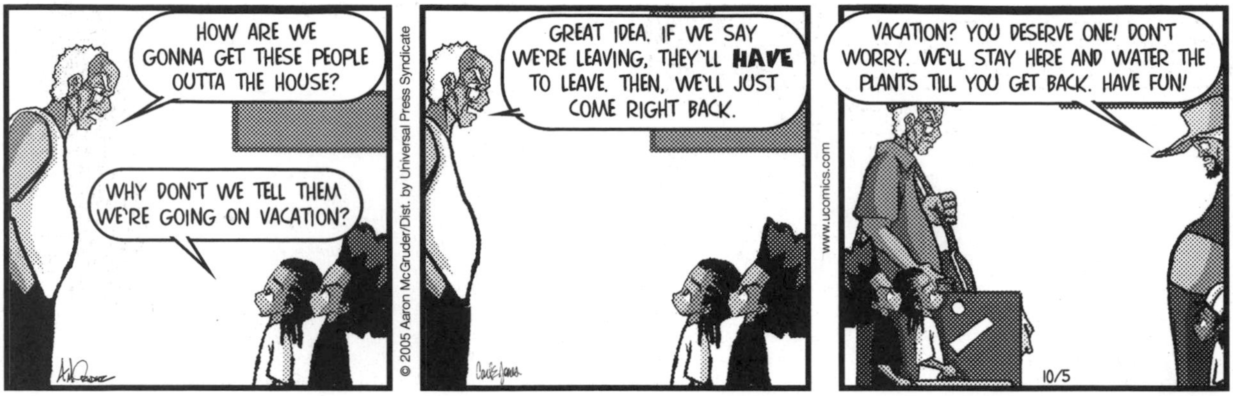
HOW ARE WE GONNA GET THESE PEOPLE OUTTA THE HOUSE?
WHY DON'T WE TELL THEM WE'RE GOING ON VACATION?
© 2005 Aaron McGruder/Dist. by Universal Press Syndicate
GREAT IDEA. IF WE SAY WE'RE LEAVING, THEY'LL **HAVE** TO LEAVE. THEN, WE'LL JUST COME RIGHT BACK.
www.ucomics.com
VACATION? YOU DESERVE ONE! DON'T WORRY. WE'LL STAY HERE AND WATER THE PLANTS TILL YOU GET BACK. HAVE FUN!
10/5

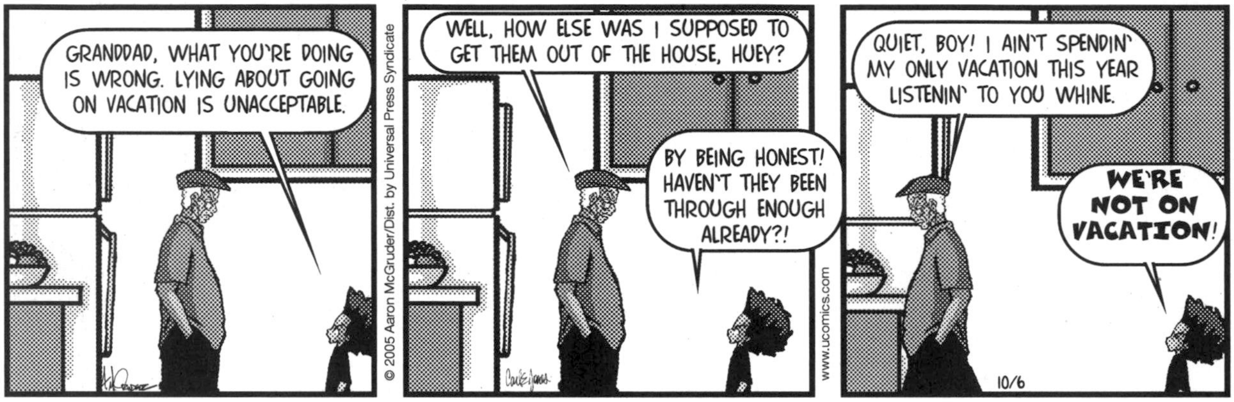
GRANDDAD, WHAT YOU'RE DOING IS WRONG. LYING ABOUT GOING ON VACATION IS UNACCEPTABLE.
© 2005 Aaron McGruder/Dist. by Universal Press Syndicate
WELL, HOW ELSE WAS I SUPPOSED TO GET THEM OUT OF THE HOUSE, HUEY?
BY BEING HONEST! HAVEN'T THEY BEEN THROUGH ENOUGH ALREADY?!
www.ucomics.com
QUIET, BOY! I AIN'T SPENDIN' MY ONLY VACATION THIS YEAR LISTENIN' TO YOU WHINE.
WE'RE NOT ON VACATION!
10/6

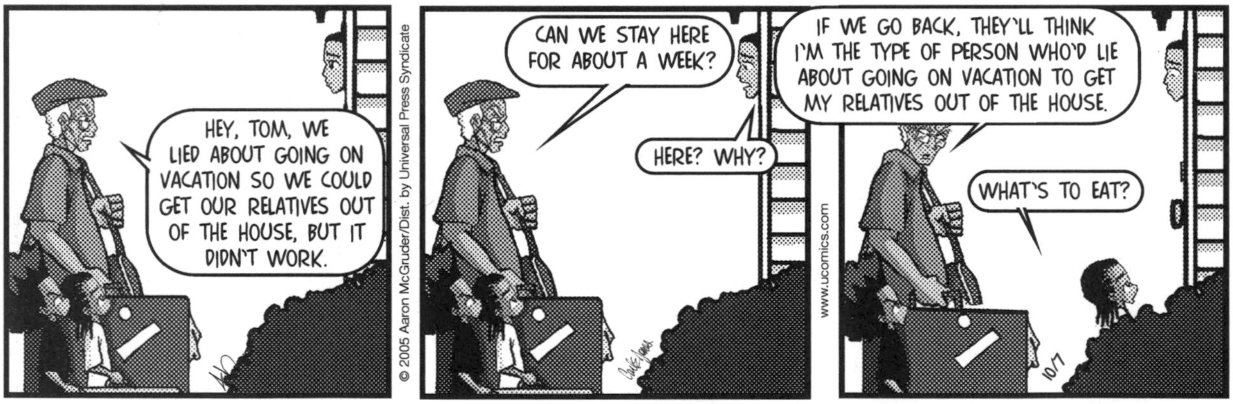
HEY, TOM, WE LIED ABOUT GOING ON VACATION SO WE COULD GET OUR RELATIVES OUT OF THE HOUSE, BUT IT DIDN'T WORK.
© 2005 Aaron McGruder/Dist. by Universal Press Syndicate
CAN WE STAY HERE FOR ABOUT A WEEK?
HERE? WHY?
www.ucomics.com
IF WE GO BACK, THEY'LL THINK I'M THE TYPE OF PERSON WHO'D LIE ABOUT GOING ON VACATION TO GET MY RELATIVES OUT OF THE HOUSE.
WHAT'S TO EAT?
10/7

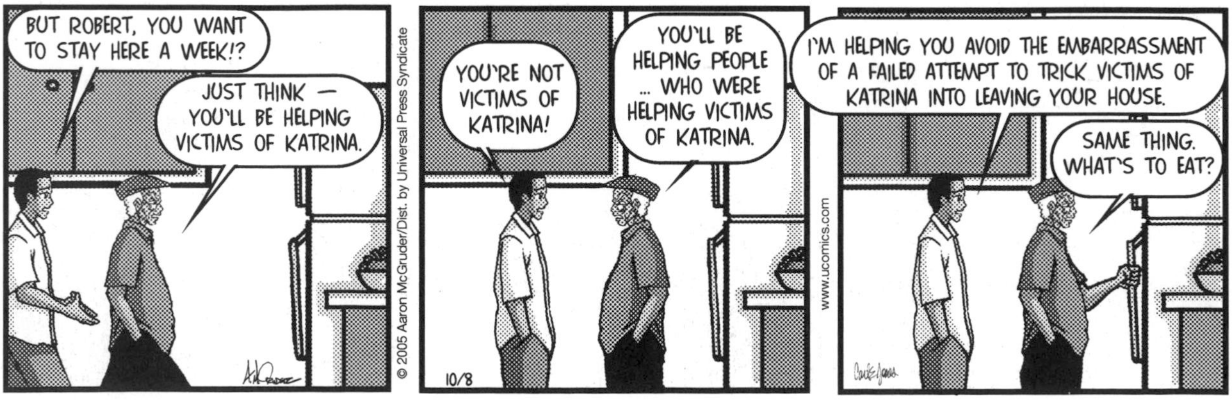
BUT ROBERT, YOU WANT TO STAY HERE A WEEK!?
JUST THINK — YOU'LL BE HELPING VICTIMS OF KATRINA.
© 2005 Aaron McGruder/Dist. by Universal Press Syndicate
YOU'RE NOT VICTIMS OF KATRINA!
YOU'LL BE HELPING PEOPLE ... WHO WERE HELPING VICTIMS OF KATRINA.
10/8
www.ucomics.com
I'M HELPING YOU AVOID THE EMBARRASSMENT OF A FAILED ATTEMPT TO TRICK VICTIMS OF KATRINA INTO LEAVING YOUR HOUSE.
SAME THING. WHAT'S TO EAT?

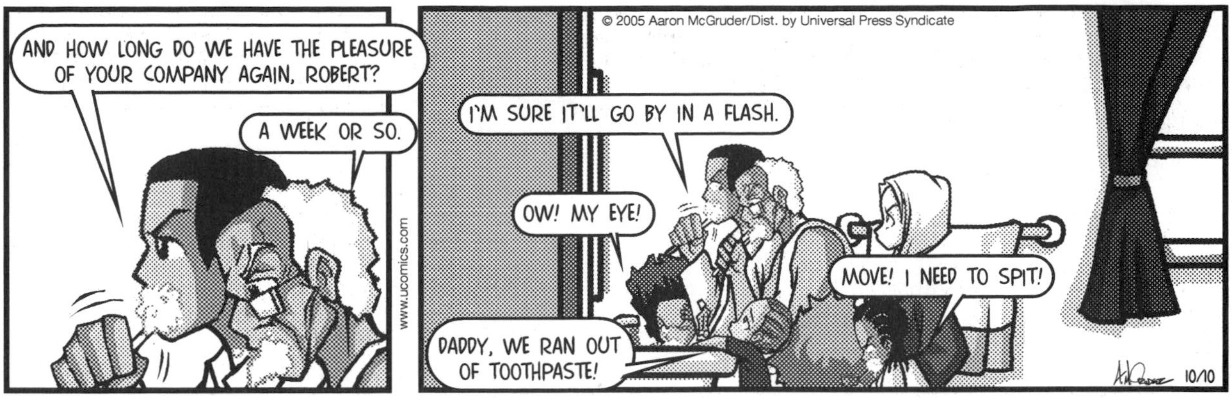
AND HOW LONG DO WE HAVE THE PLEASURE OF YOUR COMPANY AGAIN, ROBERT?
A WEEK OR SO.
www.ucomics.com
© 2005 Aaron McGruder/Dist. by Universal Press Syndicate
I'M SURE IT'LL GO BY IN A FLASH.
OW! MY EYE!
MOVE! I NEED TO SPIT!
DADDY, WE RAN OUT OF TOOTHPASTE!
10/10

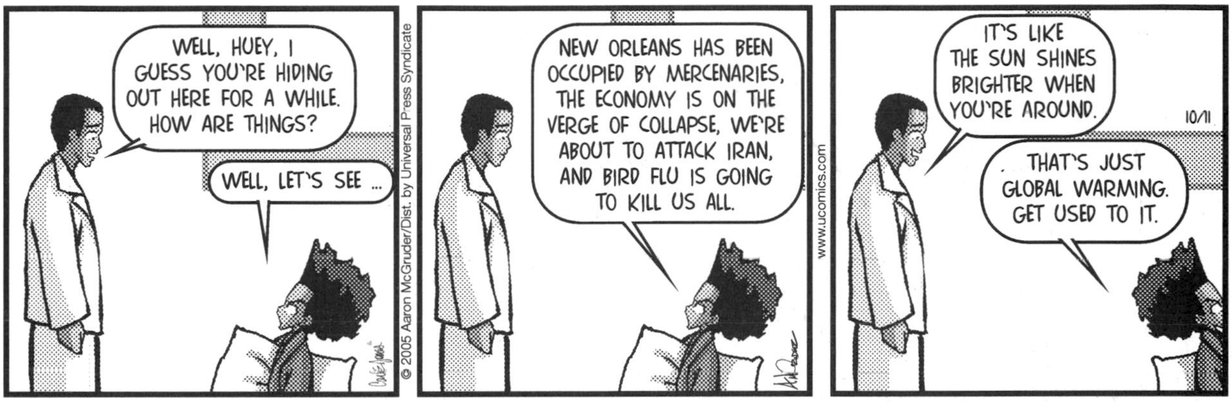
WELL, HUEY, I GUESS YOU'RE HIDING OUT HERE FOR A WHILE. HOW ARE THINGS?
WELL, LET'S SEE ...
© 2005 Aaron McGruder/Dist. by Universal Press Syndicate
NEW ORLEANS HAS BEEN OCCUPIED BY MERCENARIES, THE ECONOMY IS ON THE VERGE OF COLLAPSE, WE'RE ABOUT TO ATTACK IRAN, AND BIRD FLU IS GOING TO KILL US ALL.
www.ucomics.com
IT'S LIKE THE SUN SHINES BRIGHTER WHEN YOU'RE AROUND.
10/11
THAT'S JUST GLOBAL WARMING. GET USED TO IT.

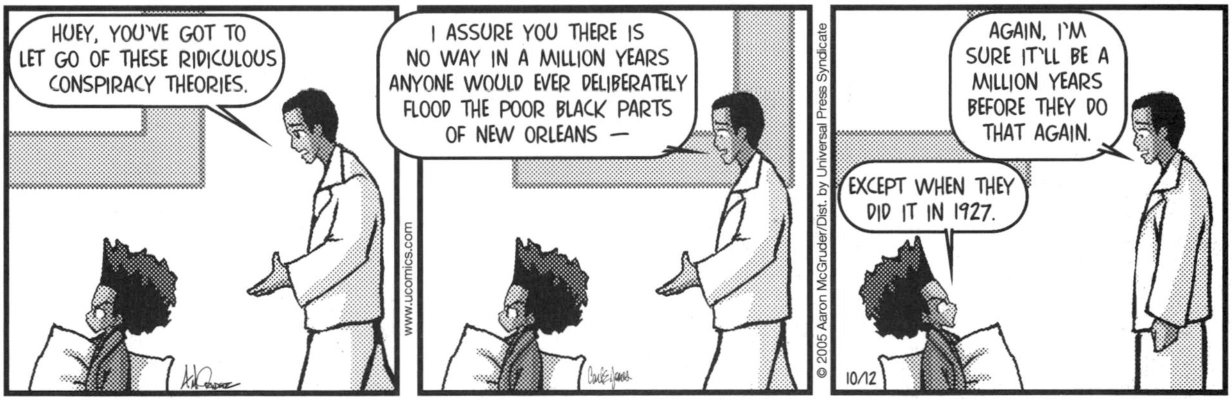
HUEY, YOU'VE GOT TO LET GO OF THESE RIDICULOUS CONSPIRACY THEORIES.
www.ucomics.com
I ASSURE YOU THERE IS NO WAY IN A MILLION YEARS ANYONE WOULD EVER DELIBERATELY FLOOD THE POOR BLACK PARTS OF NEW ORLEANS —
© 2005 Aaron McGruder/Dist. by Universal Press Syndicate
AGAIN, I'M SURE IT'LL BE A MILLION YEARS BEFORE THEY DO THAT AGAIN.
EXCEPT WHEN THEY DID IT IN 1927.
10/12

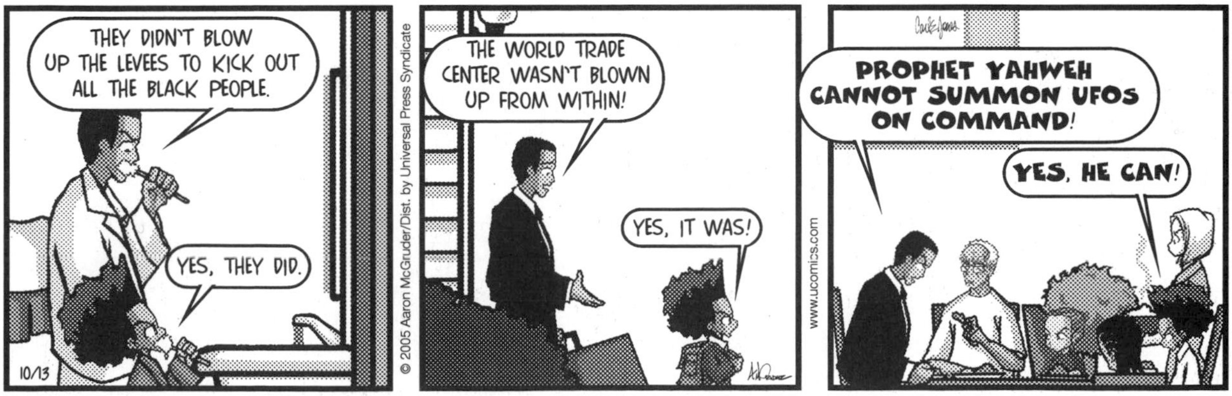
THEY DIDN'T BLOW UP THE LEVEES TO KICK OUT ALL THE BLACK PEOPLE.
YES, THEY DID.
10/13
© 2005 Aaron McGruder/Dist. by Universal Press Syndicate
THE WORLD TRADE CENTER WASN'T BLOWN UP FROM WITHIN!
YES, IT WAS!
www.ucomics.com
PROPHET YAHWEH CANNOT SUMMON UFOS ON COMMAND!
YES, HE CAN!

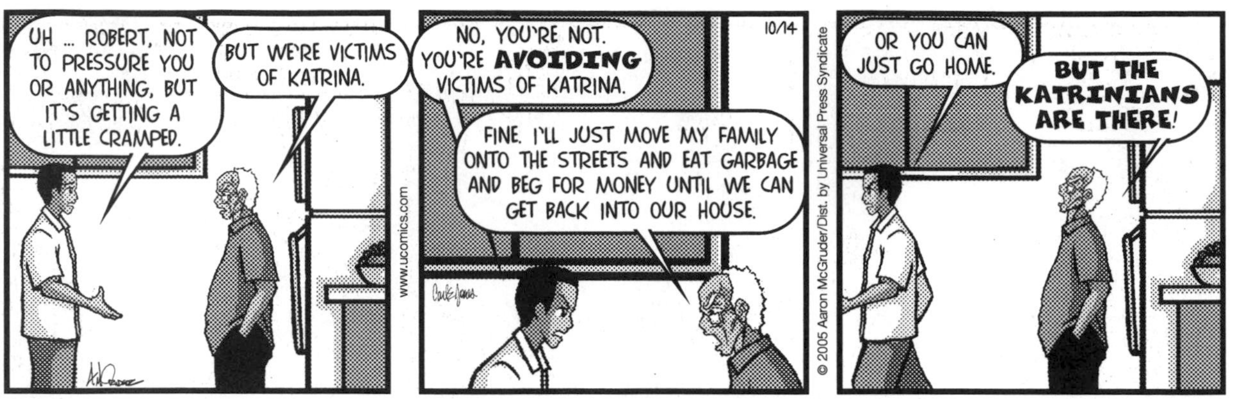
UH ... ROBERT, NOT TO PRESSURE YOU OR ANYTHING, BUT IT'S GETTING A LITTLE CRAMPED.
BUT WE'RE VICTIMS OF KATRINA.
www.ucomics.com
10/14
NO, YOU'RE NOT. YOU'RE AVOIDING VICTIMS OF KATRINA.
FINE. I'LL JUST MOVE MY FAMILY ONTO THE STREETS AND EAT GARBAGE AND BEG FOR MONEY UNTIL WE CAN GET BACK INTO OUR HOUSE.
© 2005 Aaron McGruder/Dist. by Universal Press Syndicate
OR YOU CAN JUST GO HOME.
BUT THE KATRINIANS ARE THERE!

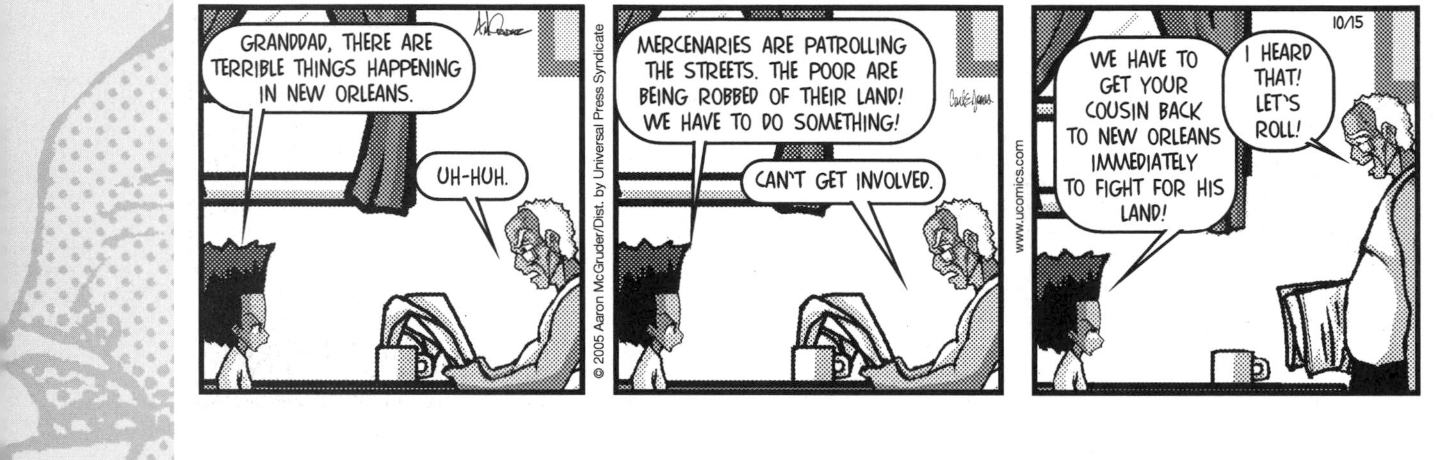
GRANDDAD, THERE ARE TERRIBLE THINGS HAPPENING IN NEW ORLEANS.
UH-HUH.
© 2005 Aaron McGruder/Dist. by Universal Press Syndicate
MERCENARIES ARE PATROLLING THE STREETS. THE POOR ARE BEING ROBBED OF THEIR LAND! WE HAVE TO DO SOMETHING!
CAN'T GET INVOLVED.
www.ucomics.com
10/15
WE HAVE TO GET YOUR COUSIN BACK TO NEW ORLEANS IMMEDIATELY TO FIGHT FOR HIS LAND!
I HEARD THAT! LET'S ROLL!

Sometimes, I do look around and say to myself, 'Gee, I'm the only one saying some of these things.' That can make you a little paranoid. But I don't think that's a reflection on me so much as it is a reflection on how narrow the discussion has become in most of the media today.

—Aaron McGruder, *The Nation*

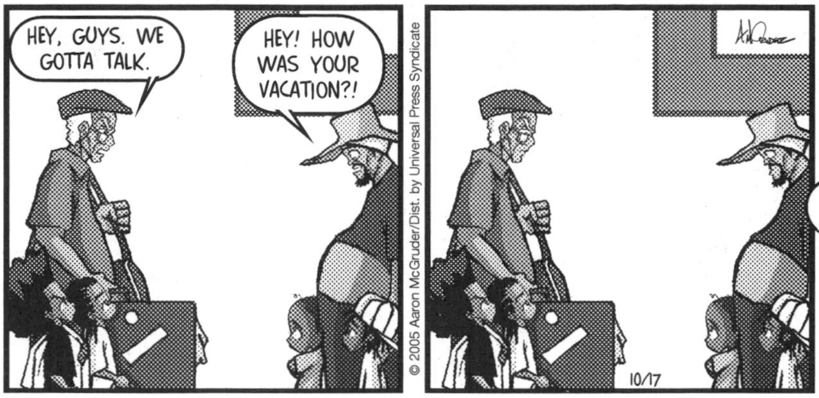
HEY, GUYS. WE GOTTA TALK.
HEY! HOW WAS YOUR VACATION?!
© 2005 Aaron McGruder/Dist. by Universal Press Syndicate
10/17
www.ucomics.com
OH, RIGHT. OUR VACATION. UH ... IT WAS GREAT, YOU KNOW...
GOT A SUNTAN.
TOOK SOME PICTURES.

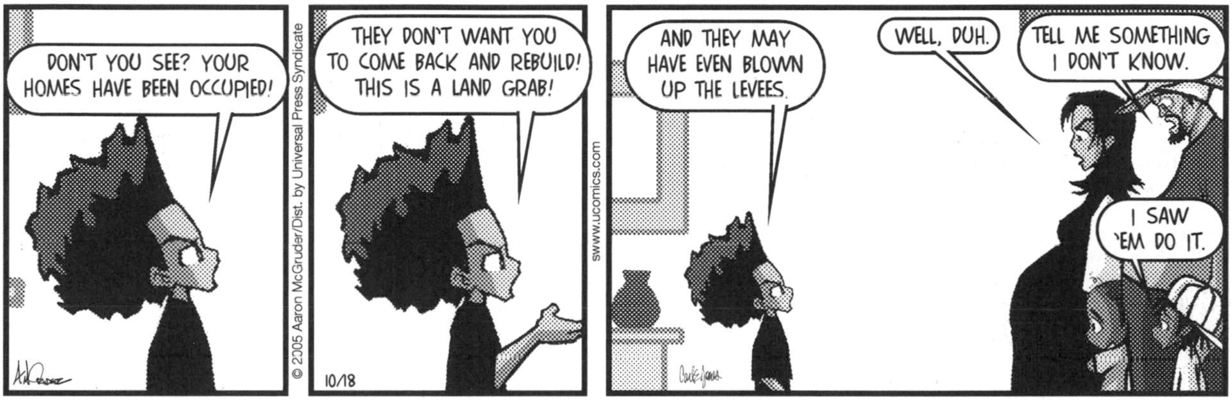
DON'T YOU SEE? YOUR HOMES HAVE BEEN OCCUPIED!
© 2005 Aaron McGruder/Dist. by Universal Press Syndicate
THEY DON'T WANT YOU TO COME BACK AND REBUILD! THIS IS A LAND GRAB!
10/18
swww.ucomics.com
AND THEY MAY HAVE EVEN BLOWN UP THE LEVEES.
WELL, DUH.
TELL ME SOMETHING I DON'T KNOW.
I SAW 'EM DO IT.

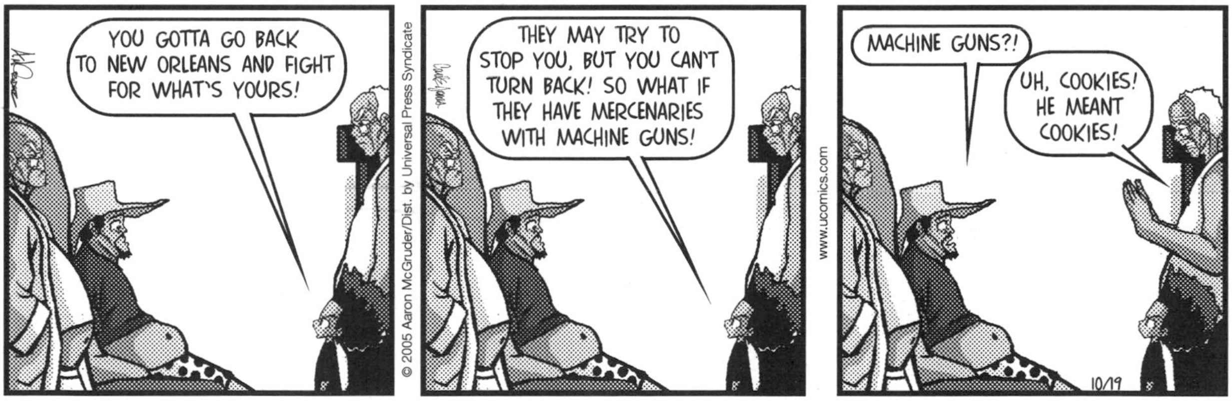
YOU GOTTA GO BACK TO NEW ORLEANS AND FIGHT FOR WHAT'S YOURS!
© 2005 Aaron McGruder/Dist. by Universal Press Syndicate
THEY MAY TRY TO STOP YOU, BUT YOU CAN'T TURN BACK! SO WHAT IF THEY HAVE MERCENARIES WITH MACHINE GUNS!
www.ucomics.com
MACHINE GUNS?!
UH, COOKIES! HE MEANT COOKIES!
10/19

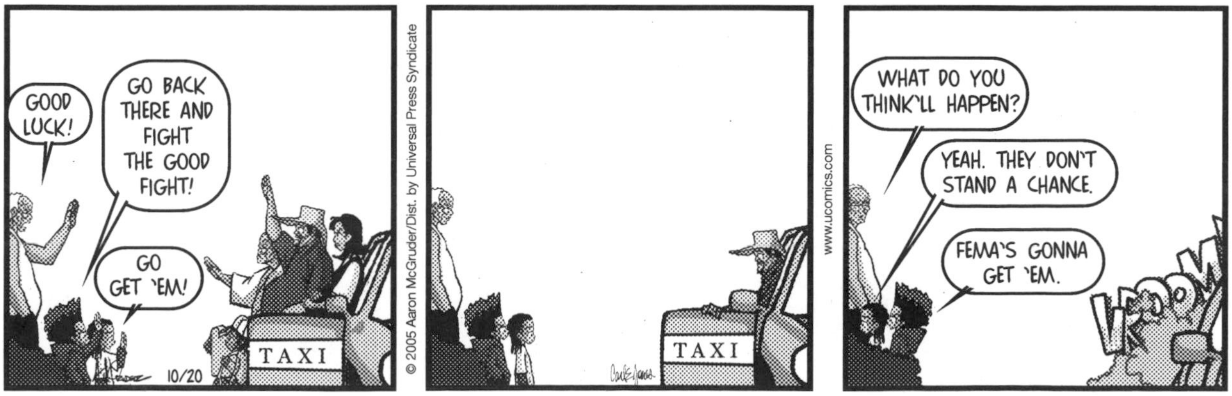
GOOD LUCK!
GO BACK THERE AND FIGHT THE GOOD FIGHT!
GO GET 'EM!
TAXI
10/20
© 2005 Aaron McGruder/Dist. by Universal Press Syndicate
TAXI
www.ucomics.com
WHAT DO YOU THINK'LL HAPPEN?
YEAH. THEY DON'T STAND A CHANCE.
FEMA'S GONNA GET 'EM.
VROOM

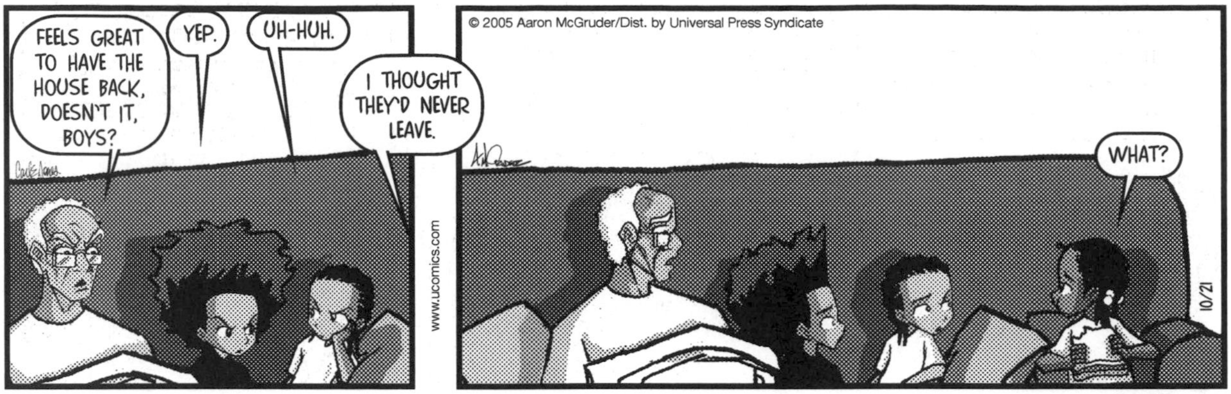
FEELS GREAT TO HAVE THE HOUSE BACK, DOESN'T IT, BOYS?
YEP.
UH-HUH.
I THOUGHT THEY'D NEVER LEAVE.
www.ucomics.com
© 2005 Aaron McGruder/Dist. by Universal Press Syndicate
WHAT?
10/21

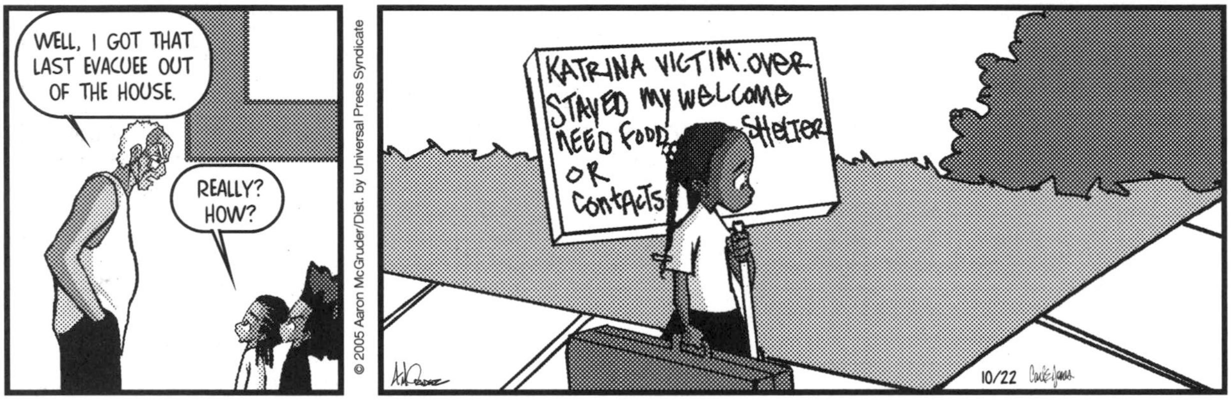
WELL, I GOT THAT LAST EVACUEE OUT OF THE HOUSE.
REALLY? HOW?
© 2005 Aaron McGruder/Dist. by Universal Press Syndicate
KATRINA VICTIM: OVER
STAYED MY WELCOME
NEED FOOD, SHELTER
OR
CONTACTS
10/22

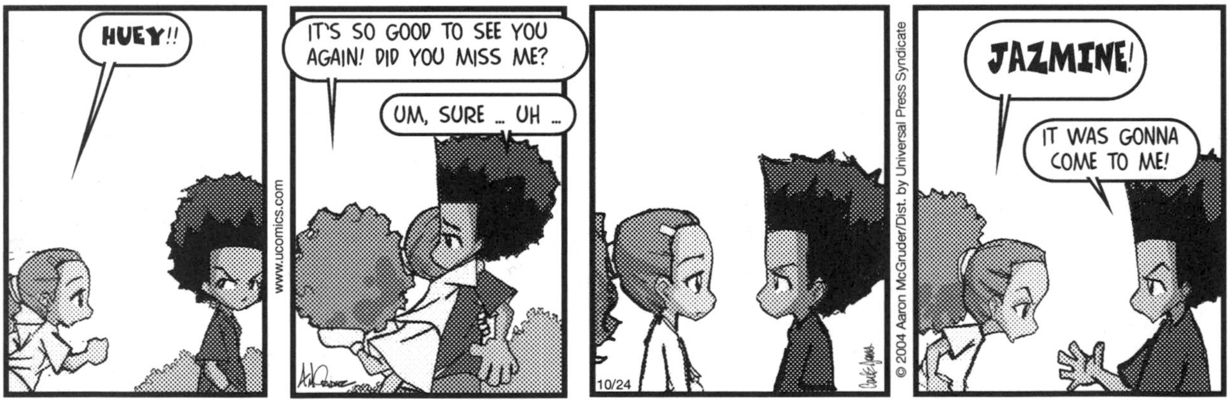
HUEY!!
www.ucomics.com
IT'S SO GOOD TO SEE YOU AGAIN! DID YOU MISS ME?
UM, SURE ... UH ...
10/24
© 2004 Aaron McGruder/Dist. by Universal Press Syndicate
JAZMINE!
IT WAS GONNA COME TO ME!

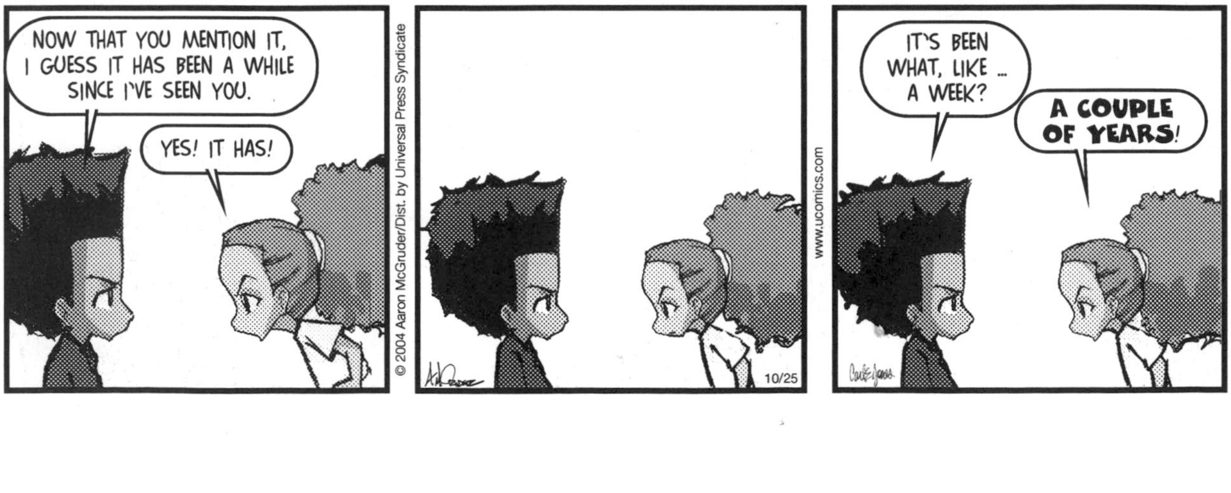
NOW THAT YOU MENTION IT, I GUESS IT HAS BEEN A WHILE SINCE I'VE SEEN YOU.
YES! IT HAS!
© 2004 Aaron McGruder/Dist. by Universal Press Syndicate
10/25
www.ucomics.com
IT'S BEEN WHAT, LIKE ... A WEEK?
A COUPLE OF YEARS!

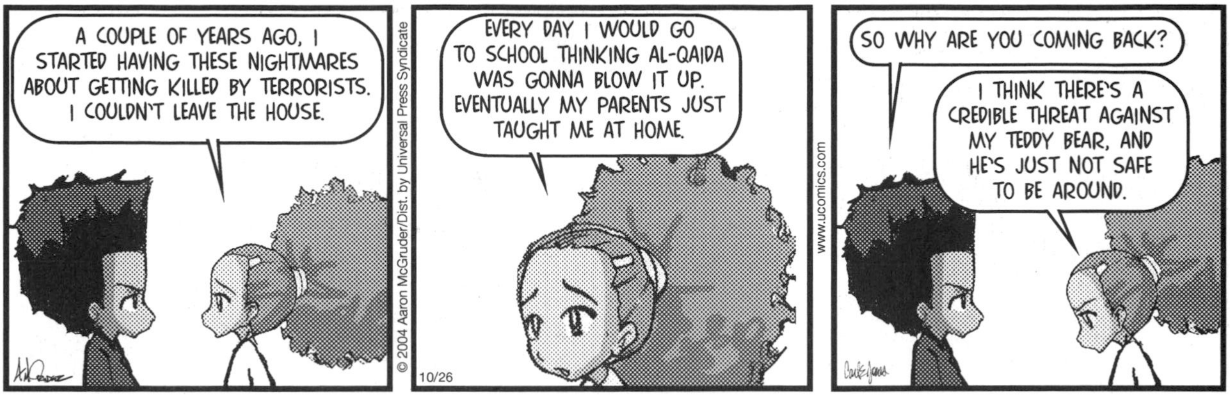
A COUPLE OF YEARS AGO, I STARTED HAVING THESE NIGHTMARES ABOUT GETTING KILLED BY TERRORISTS. I COULDN'T LEAVE THE HOUSE.
© 2004 Aaron McGruder/Dist. by Universal Press Syndicate
10/26
EVERY DAY I WOULD GO TO SCHOOL THINKING AL-QAIDA WAS GONNA BLOW IT UP. EVENTUALLY MY PARENTS JUST TAUGHT ME AT HOME.
www.ucomics.com
SO WHY ARE YOU COMING BACK?
I THINK THERE'S A CREDIBLE THREAT AGAINST MY TEDDY BEAR, AND HE'S JUST NOT SAFE TO BE AROUND.

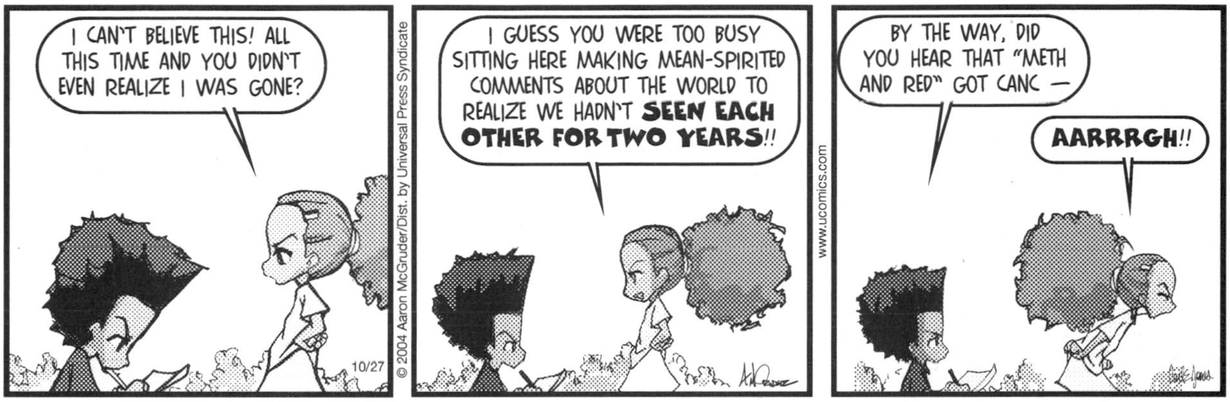
I CAN'T BELIEVE THIS! ALL THIS TIME AND YOU DIDN'T EVEN REALIZE I WAS GONE?
10/27
© 2004 Aaron McGruder/Dist. by Universal Press Syndicate
I GUESS YOU WERE TOO BUSY SITTING HERE MAKING MEAN-SPIRITED COMMENTS ABOUT THE WORLD TO REALIZE WE HADN'T SEEN EACH OTHER FOR TWO YEARS!!
www.ucomics.com
BY THE WAY, DID YOU HEAR THAT "METH AND RED" GOT CANC —
AARRRGH!!

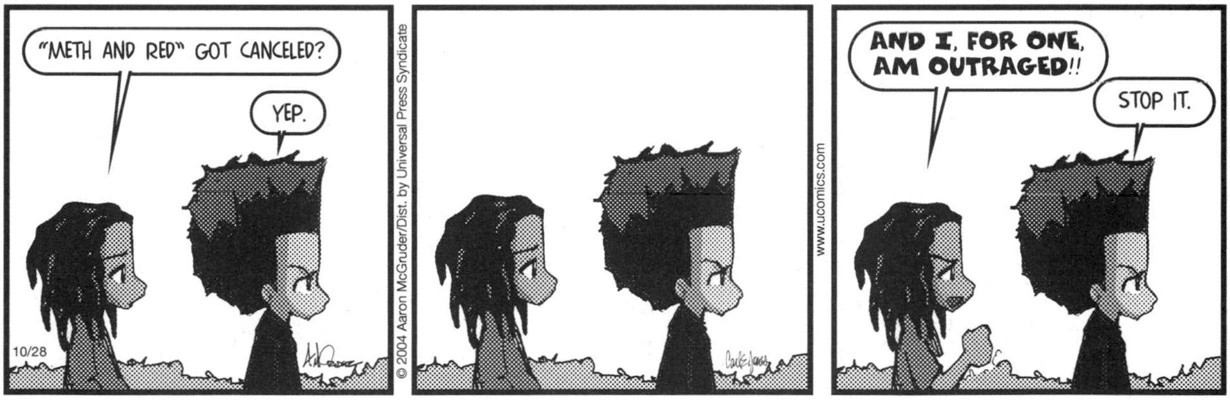
"METH AND RED" GOT CANCELED?
YEP.
10/28
© 2004 Aaron McGruder/Dist. by Universal Press Syndicate
www.ucomics.com
AND I, FOR ONE, AM OUTRAGED!!
STOP IT.

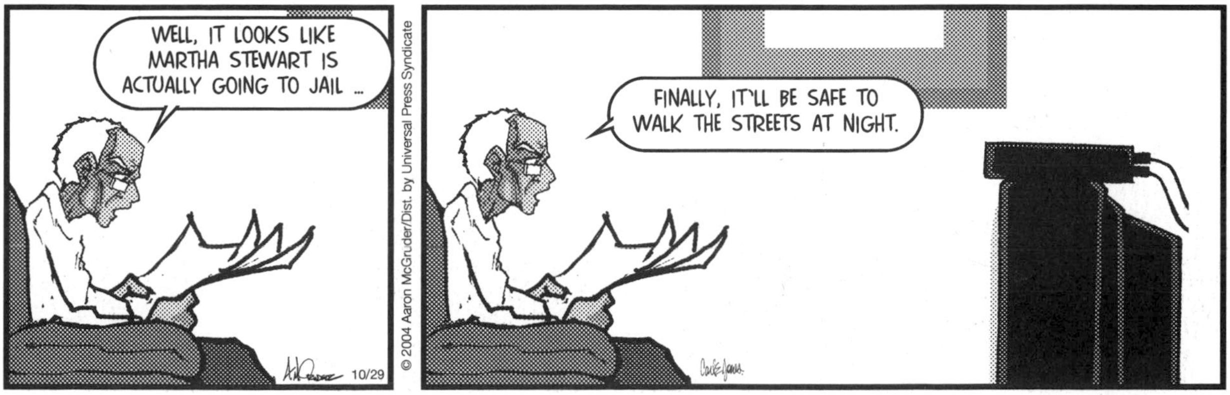
WELL, IT LOOKS LIKE MARTHA STEWART IS ACTUALLY GOING TO JAIL ...
10/29
© 2004 Aaron McGruder/Dist. by Universal Press Syndicate
FINALLY, IT'LL BE SAFE TO WALK THE STREETS AT NIGHT.

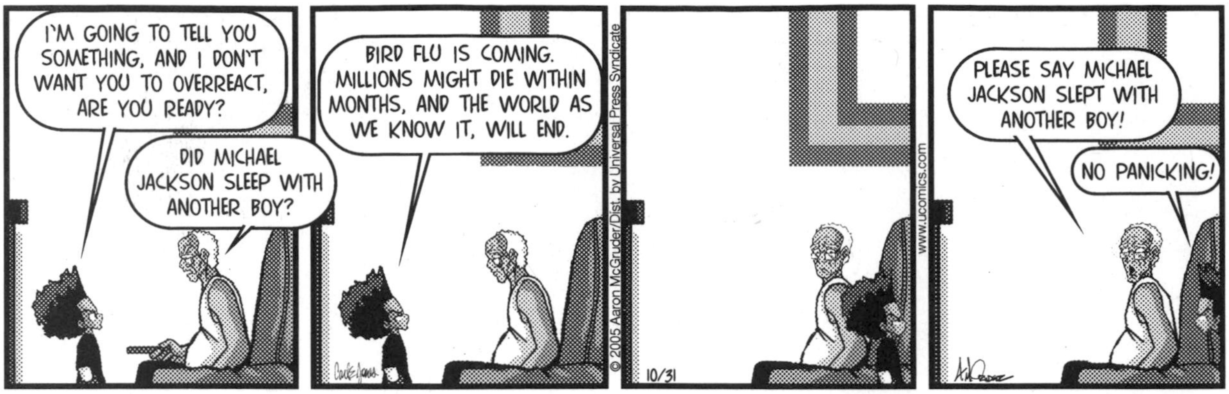
I'M GOING TO TELL YOU SOMETHING, AND I DON'T WANT YOU TO OVERREACT, ARE YOU READY?
DID MICHAEL JACKSON SLEEP WITH ANOTHER BOY?
BIRD FLU IS COMING. MILLIONS MIGHT DIE WITHIN MONTHS, AND THE WORLD AS WE KNOW IT, WILL END.
© 2005 Aaron McGruder/Dist. by Universal Press Syndicate
10/31
www.ucomics.com
PLEASE SAY MICHAEL JACKSON SLEPT WITH ANOTHER BOY!
NO PANICKING!

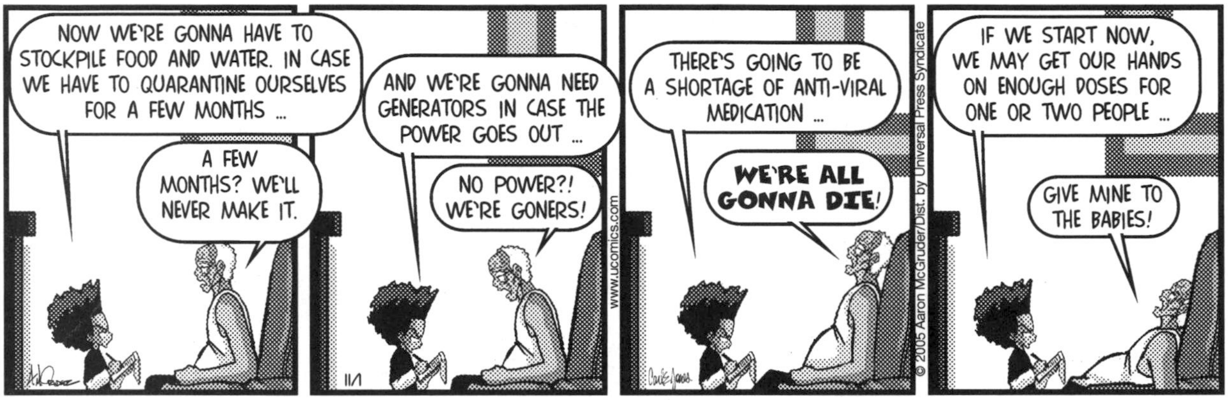
NOW WE'RE GONNA HAVE TO STOCKPILE FOOD AND WATER. IN CASE WE HAVE TO QUARANTINE OURSELVES FOR A FEW MONTHS ...
A FEW MONTHS? WE'LL NEVER MAKE IT.
AND WE'RE GONNA NEED GENERATORS IN CASE THE POWER GOES OUT ...
NO POWER?! WE'RE GONERS!
11/1
www.ucomics.com
THERE'S GOING TO BE A SHORTAGE OF ANTI-VIRAL MEDICATION ...
WE'RE ALL GONNA DIE!
© 2005 Aaron McGruder/Dist. by Universal Press Syndicate
IF WE START NOW, WE MAY GET OUR HANDS ON ENOUGH DOSES FOR ONE OR TWO PEOPLE ...
GIVE MINE TO THE BABIES!

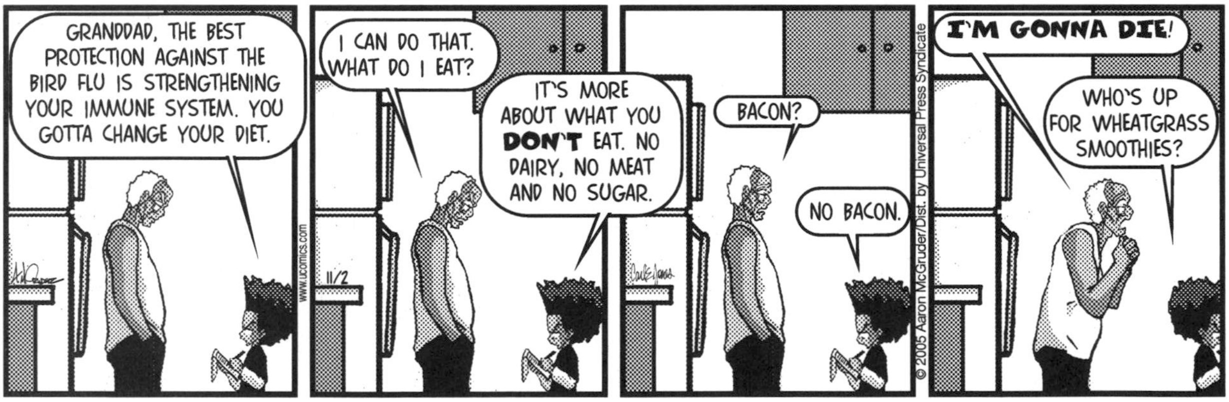
GRANDDAD, THE BEST PROTECTION AGAINST THE BIRD FLU IS STRENGTHENING YOUR IMMUNE SYSTEM. YOU GOTTA CHANGE YOUR DIET.
www.ucomics.com
I CAN DO THAT. WHAT DO I EAT?
IT'S MORE ABOUT WHAT YOU DON'T EAT. NO DAIRY, NO MEAT AND NO SUGAR.
11/2
BACON?
NO BACON.
© 2005 Aaron McGruder/Dist. by Universal Press Syndicate
I'M GONNA DIE!
WHO'S UP FOR WHEATGRASS SMOOTHIES?

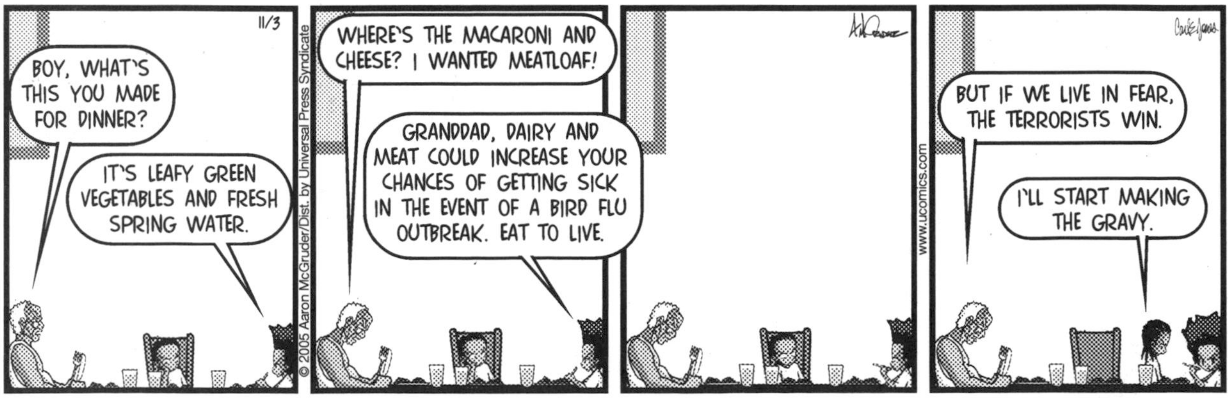
11/3
BOY, WHAT'S THIS YOU MADE FOR DINNER?
IT'S LEAFY GREEN VEGETABLES AND FRESH SPRING WATER.
© 2005 Aaron McGruder/Dist. by Universal Press Syndicate
WHERE'S THE MACARONI AND CHEESE? I WANTED MEATLOAF!
GRANDDAD, DAIRY AND MEAT COULD INCREASE YOUR CHANCES OF GETTING SICK IN THE EVENT OF A BIRD FLU OUTBREAK. EAT TO LIVE.
www.ucomics.com
BUT IF WE LIVE IN FEAR, THE TERRORISTS WIN.
I'LL START MAKING THE GRAVY.

THE BOONDOCKS BY AARON McGRUDER

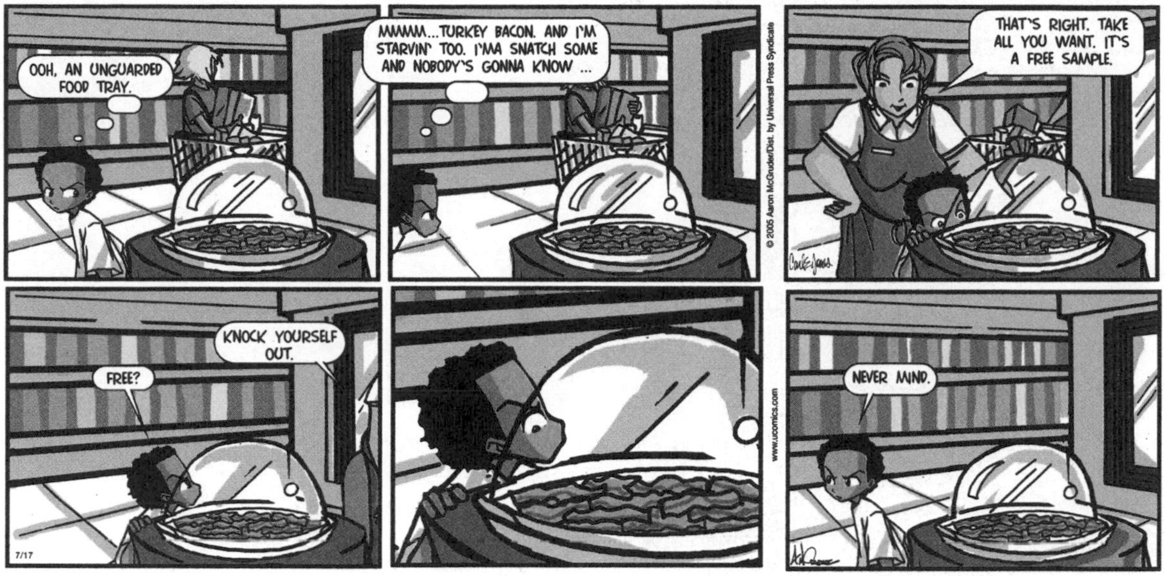
OOH, AN UNGUARDED FOOD TRAY.
MMMM...TURKEY BACON. AND I'M STARVIN' TOO. I'MA SNATCH SOME AND NOBODY'S GONNA KNOW ...
THAT'S RIGHT. TAKE ALL YOU WANT. IT'S A FREE SAMPLE.
© 2005 Aaron McGruder/Dist. by Universal Press Syndicate
FREE?
KNOCK YOURSELF OUT.
www.ucomics.com
NEVER MIND.
7/17

THE BOONDOCKS BY AARON McGRUDER

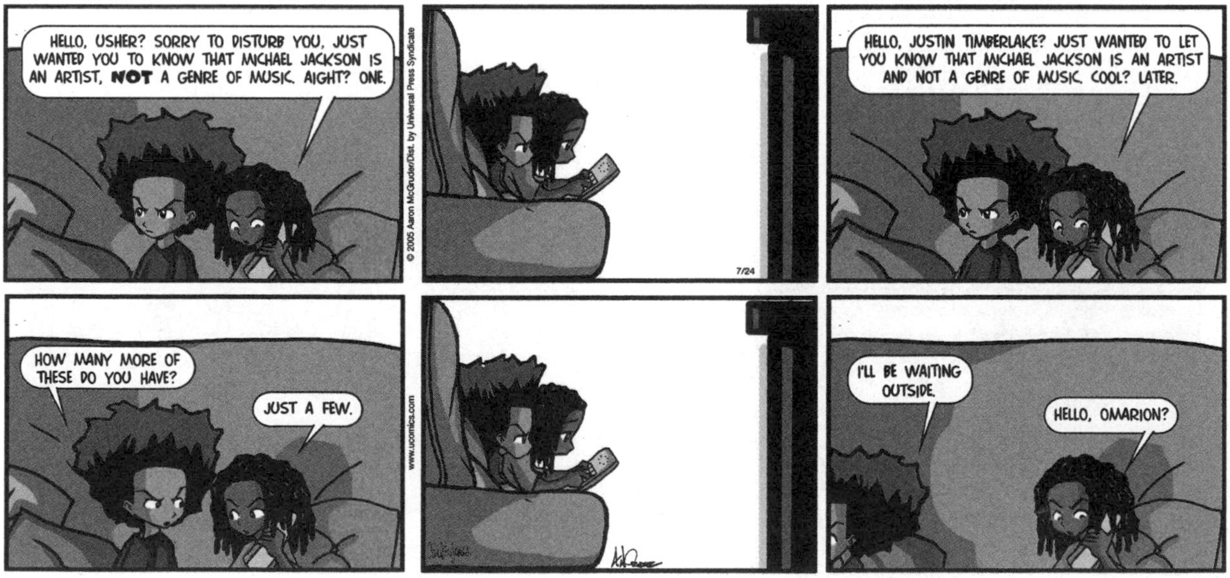
HELLO, USHER? SORRY TO DISTURB YOU. JUST WANTED YOU TO KNOW THAT MICHAEL JACKSON IS AN ARTIST, NOT A GENRE OF MUSIC. AIGHT? ONE.
© 2005 Aaron McGruder/Dist. by Universal Press Syndicate
7/24
HELLO, JUSTIN TIMBERLAKE? JUST WANTED TO LET YOU KNOW THAT MICHAEL JACKSON IS AN ARTIST AND NOT A GENRE OF MUSIC. COOL? LATER.
HOW MANY MORE OF THESE DO YOU HAVE?
JUST A FEW.
www.ucomics.com
I'LL BE WAITING OUTSIDE.
HELLO, OMARION?

THE BOONDOCKS BY AARON McGRUDER

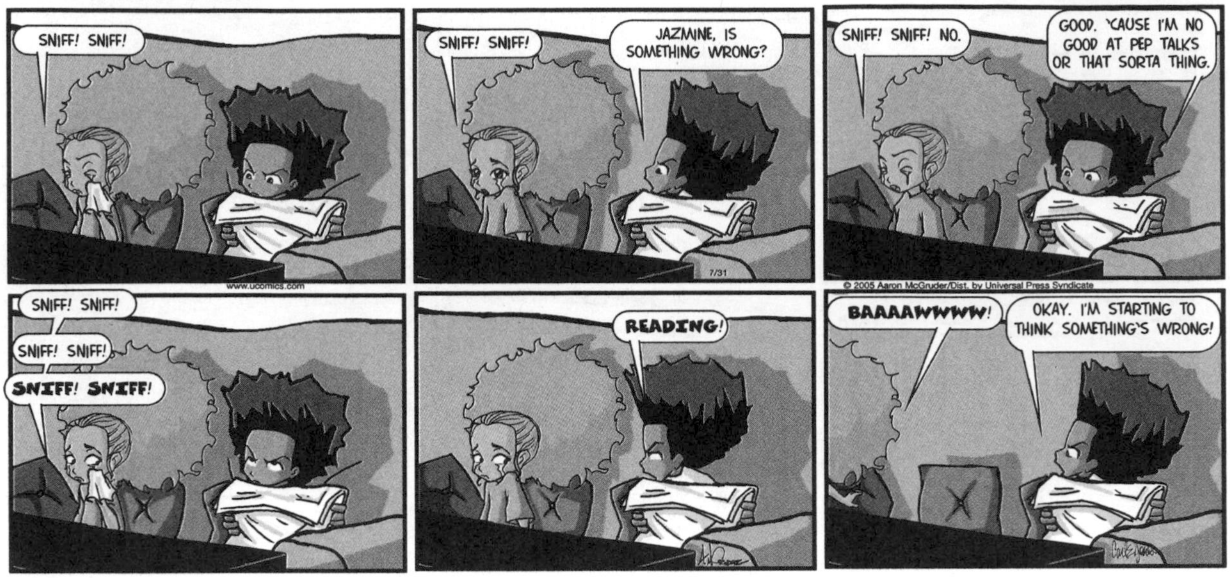
SNIFF! SNIFF!
SNIFF! SNIFF!
JAZMINE, IS SOMETHING WRONG?
SNIFF! SNIFF! NO.
GOOD. 'CAUSE I'M NO GOOD AT PEP TALKS OR THAT SORTA THING.
SNIFF! SNIFF!
SNIFF! SNIFF!
SNIFF! SNIFF!
READING!
BAAAAWWWW!
OKAY. I'M STARTING TO THINK SOMETHING'S WRONG!
www.ucomics.com
7/31
© 2005 Aaron McGruder/Dist. by Universal Press Syndicate

THE BOONDOCKS BY AARON McGRUDER

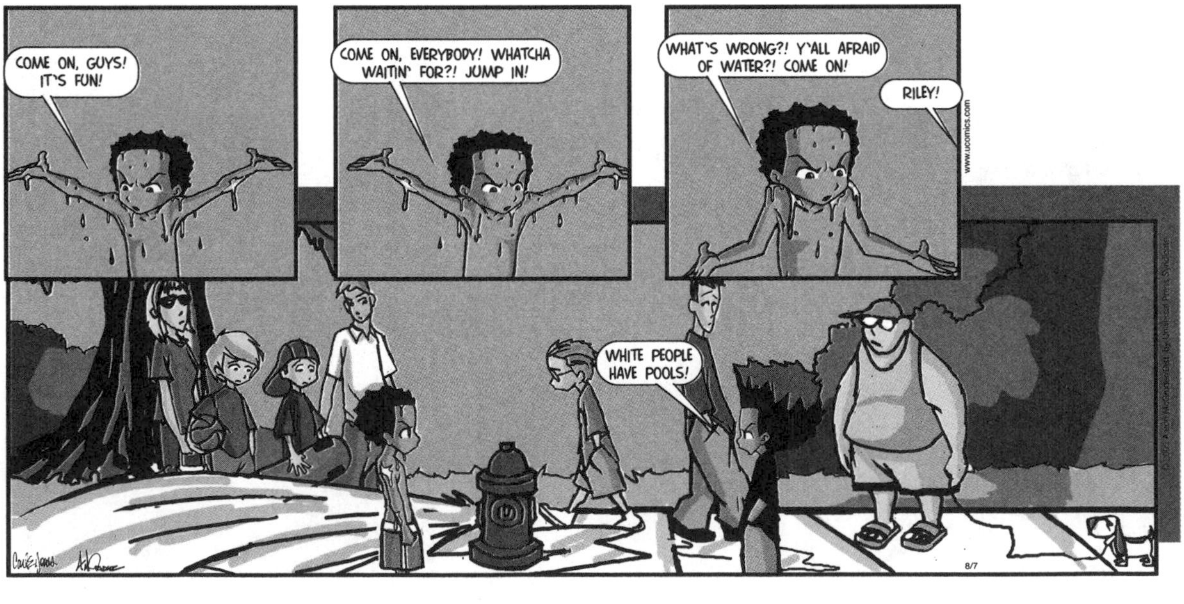
COME ON, GUYS! IT'S FUN!
COME ON, EVERYBODY! WHATCHA WAITIN' FOR?! JUMP IN!
WHAT'S WRONG?! Y'ALL AFRAID OF WATER?! COME ON!
RILEY!
WHITE PEOPLE HAVE POOLS!
www.ucomics.com
8/7

THE BOONDOCKS **BY AARON McGRUDER**

SIR, I'M SPREADING A TRUTH THAT'LL TEAR YOUR WORLD ASUNDER. ARE YOU READY FOR THAT?
YOU BETCHA! LET'S HEAR IT.
TRUTH
DID YOU KNOW THAT PROZAC CAN LEAD TO SUICIDE?
SURE DIDN'T.
THE GOVERNMENT WANTS YOU DEAD BY 62 SO YOU CAN'T COLLECT ON SOCIAL SECURITY.
MAKES SENSE. ANYTHING ELSE?
UM... FLUORIDE FOUND IN YOUR TOOTHPASTE IS TOXIC?
AND PAMELA ANDERSON AND TOMMY LEE ARE BACK TOGETHER.
NO!!!!!!
© 2005 Aaron McGruder/Dist. by Universal Press Syndicate
www.ucomics.com
8/14

THE BOONDOCKS **BY AARON McGRUDER**

I BET THE WATER IN YOUR LEMONADE HAS FLUORIDE IN IT, WHICH IS MORE TOXIC THAN LEAD.
Lemonade
DO YOU GUYS HAVE ... UM ...
THAT'S ALL I GOT IS 15 CENT! MAKE IT WORK! I'M THIRSTY!
IT'S A DOLLAR, RILEY!
DO YOU USE HIGH-FRUCTOSE CORN SYRUP? THAT'LL KILL YOU, TOO.
LOOK, I AIN'T GOT A DOLLAR! JUST HOOK ME UP! ALL THE MONEY I SPENT IN THIS PLACE?!
LEMONADE IS ONE DOLLAR!!
UH ... DO YOU GUYS HAVE ANYTHING OTHER THAN LEMONADE?
© 2005 Aaron McGruder/Dist. by Universal Press Syndicate
www.ucomics.com
8/21

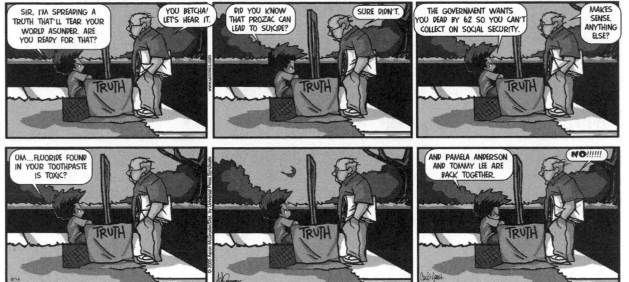

THE BOONDOCKS BY AARON McGRUDER

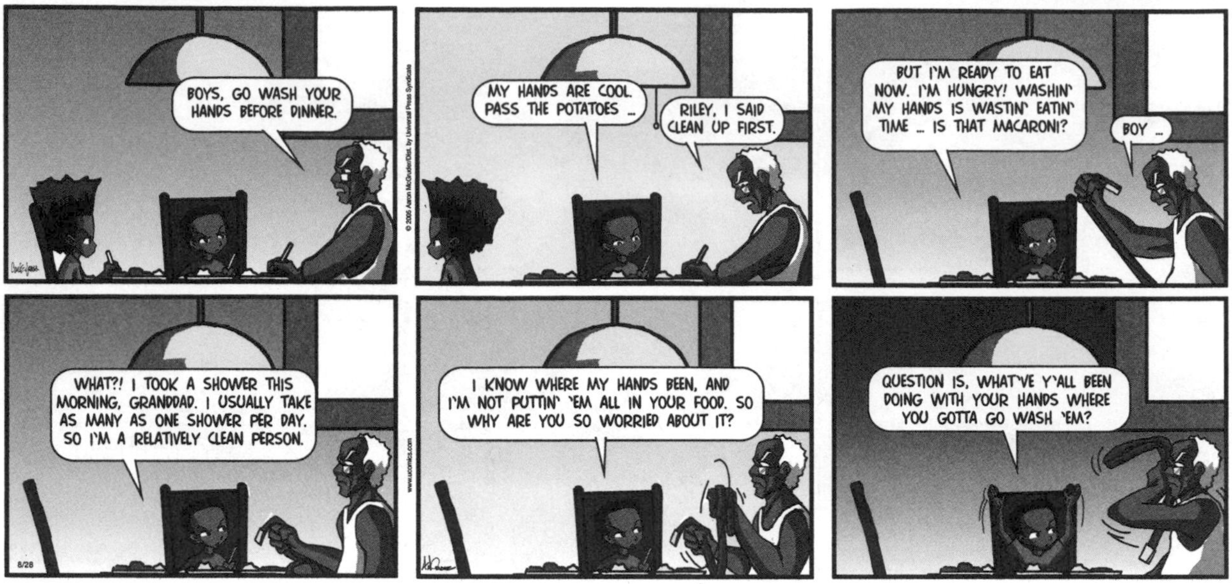
BOYS, GO WASH YOUR HANDS BEFORE DINNER.
MY HANDS ARE COOL. PASS THE POTATOES ...
RILEY, I SAID CLEAN UP FIRST.
BUT I'M READY TO EAT NOW. I'M HUNGRY! WASHIN' MY HANDS IS WASTIN' EATIN' TIME ... IS THAT MACARONI?
BOY ...
WHAT?! I TOOK A SHOWER THIS MORNING, GRANDDAD. I USUALLY TAKE AS MANY AS ONE SHOWER PER DAY. SO I'M A RELATIVELY CLEAN PERSON.
I KNOW WHERE MY HANDS BEEN, AND I'M NOT PUTTIN' 'EM ALL IN YOUR FOOD. SO WHY ARE YOU SO WORRIED ABOUT IT?
QUESTION IS, WHAT'VE Y'ALL BEEN DOING WITH YOUR HANDS WHERE YOU GOTTA GO WASH 'EM?

THE BOONDOCKS BY AARON McGRUDER

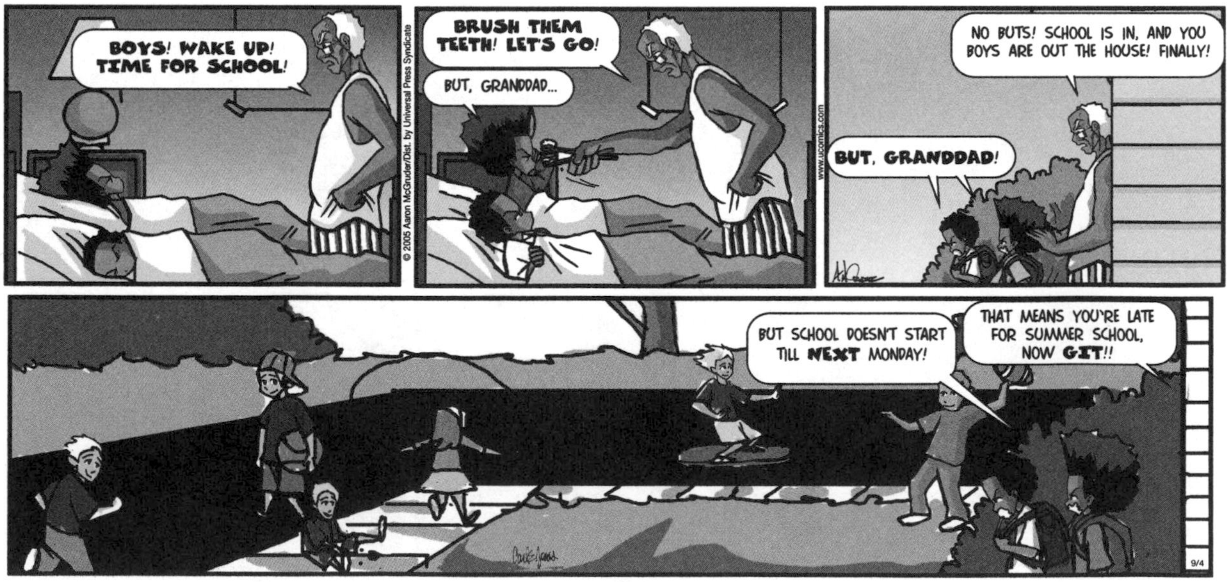
BOYS! WAKE UP! TIME FOR SCHOOL!
BRUSH THEM TEETH! LET'S GO!
BUT, GRANDDAD...
© 2005 Aaron McGruder/Dist. by Universal Press Syndicate
NO BUTS! SCHOOL IS IN, AND YOU BOYS ARE OUT THE HOUSE! FINALLY!
BUT, GRANDDAD!
www.ucomics.com
BUT SCHOOL DOESN'T START TILL NEXT MONDAY!
THAT MEANS YOU'RE LATE FOR SUMMER SCHOOL, NOW GIT!!
9/4

THE BOONDOCKS BY AARON McGRUDER

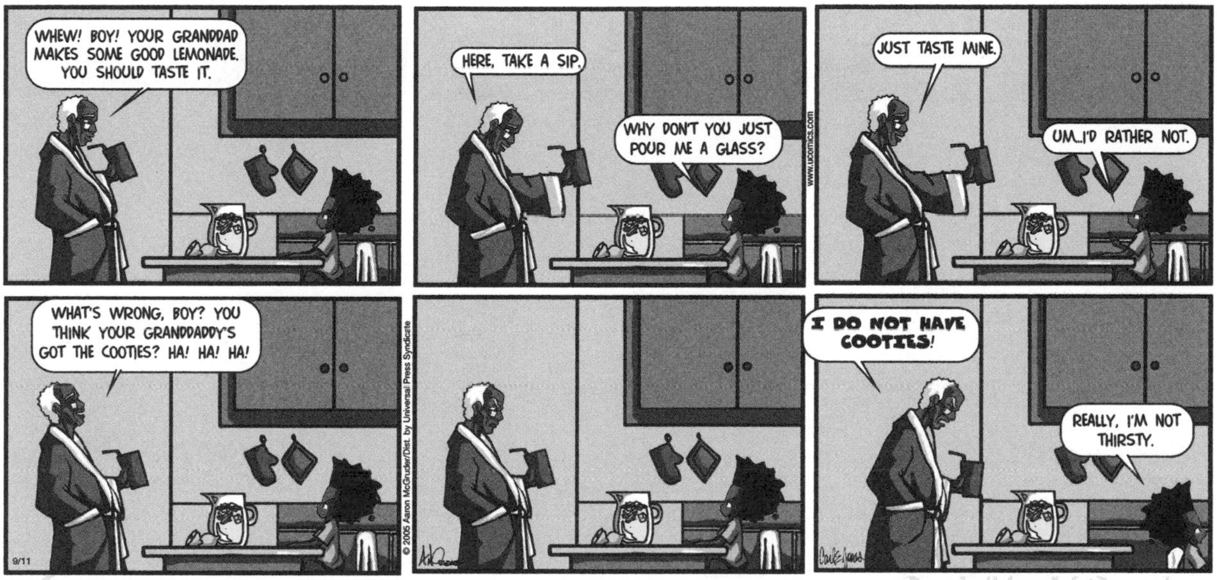
WHEW! BOY! YOUR GRANDDAD MAKES SOME GOOD LEMONADE. YOU SHOULD TASTE IT.
HERE, TAKE A SIP.
WHY DON'T YOU JUST POUR ME A GLASS?
www.ucomics.com
JUST TASTE MINE.
UM...I'D RATHER NOT.
WHAT'S WRONG, BOY? YOU THINK YOUR GRANDDADDY'S GOT THE COOTIES? HA! HA! HA!
9/11
© 2005 Aaron McGruder/Dist. by Universal Press Syndicate
I DO NOT HAVE COOTIES!
REALLY, I'M NOT THIRSTY.

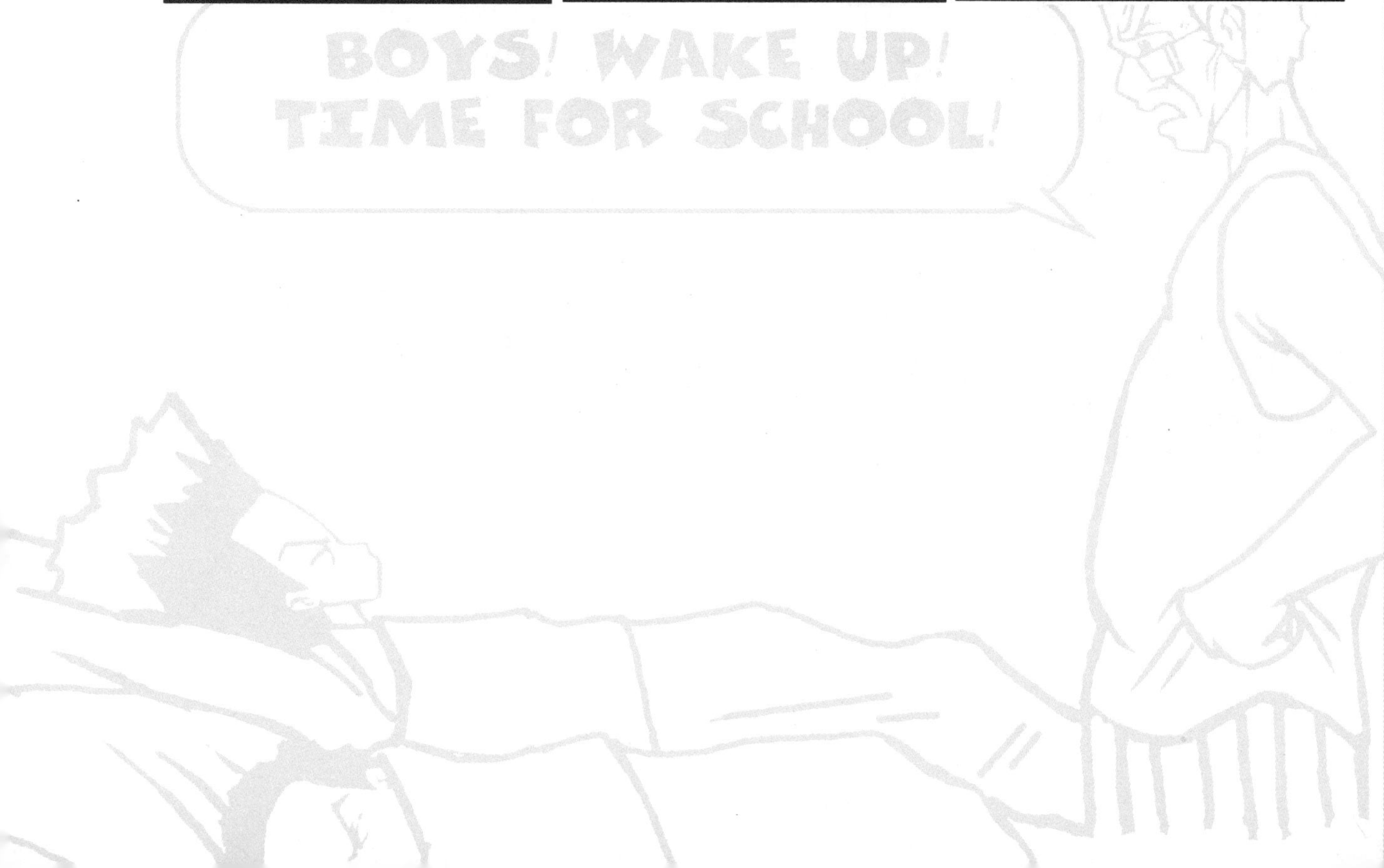
BOYS! WAKE UP! TIME FOR SCHOOL!

THE BOONDOCKS BY AARON McGRUDER

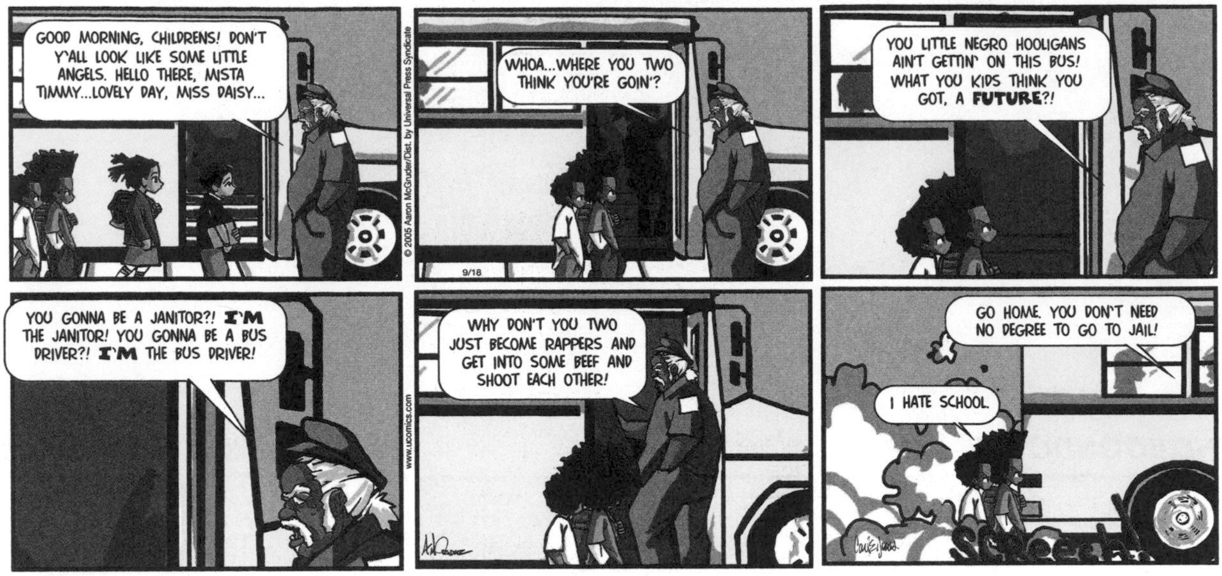
GOOD MORNING, CHILDRENS! DON'T Y'ALL LOOK LIKE SOME LITTLE ANGELS. HELLO THERE, MISTA TIMMY...LOVELY DAY, MISS DAISY...
© 2005 Aaron McGruder/Dist. by Universal Press Syndicate
WHOA...WHERE YOU TWO THINK YOU'RE GOIN'?
9/18
YOU LITTLE NEGRO HOOLIGANS AIN'T GETTIN' ON THIS BUS! WHAT YOU KIDS THINK YOU GOT, A **FUTURE**?!
YOU GONNA BE A JANITOR?! **I'M** THE JANITOR! YOU GONNA BE A BUS DRIVER?! **I'M** THE BUS DRIVER!
www.ucomics.com
WHY DON'T YOU TWO JUST BECOME RAPPERS AND GET INTO SOME BEEF AND SHOOT EACH OTHER!
GO HOME. YOU DON'T NEED NO DEGREE TO GO TO JAIL!
I HATE SCHOOL.

THE BOONDOCKS BY AARON McGRUDER

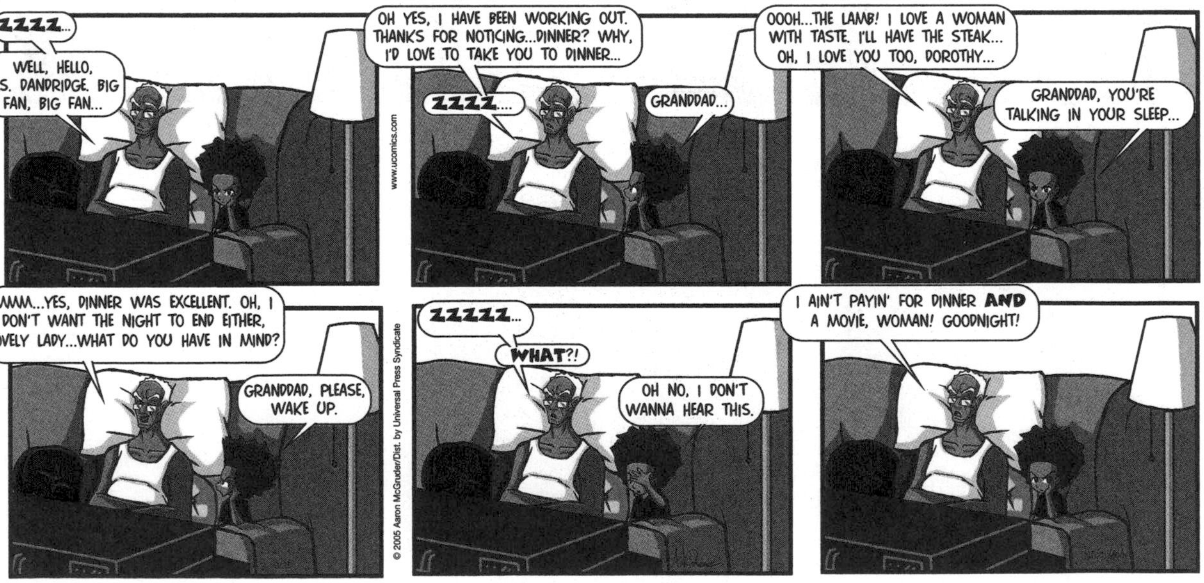
ZZZZ...
WELL, HELLO, MS. DANDRIDGE. BIG FAN, BIG FAN...
OH YES, I HAVE BEEN WORKING OUT. THANKS FOR NOTICING...DINNER? WHY, I'D LOVE TO TAKE YOU TO DINNER...
ZZZZ...
GRANDDAD...
www.ucomics.com
OOOH...THE LAMB! I LOVE A WOMAN WITH TASTE. I'LL HAVE THE STEAK... OH, I LOVE YOU TOO, DOROTHY...
GRANDDAD, YOU'RE TALKING IN YOUR SLEEP...
MMM...YES, DINNER WAS EXCELLENT. OH, I DON'T WANT THE NIGHT TO END EITHER, LOVELY LADY...WHAT DO YOU HAVE IN MIND?
GRANDDAD, PLEASE, WAKE UP.
© 2005 Aaron McGruder/Dist. by Universal Press Syndicate
ZZZZZ...
WHAT?!
OH NO, I DON'T WANNA HEAR THIS.
I AIN'T PAYIN' FOR DINNER **AND** A MOVIE, WOMAN! GOODNIGHT!

THE BOONDOCKS BY AARON McGRUDER

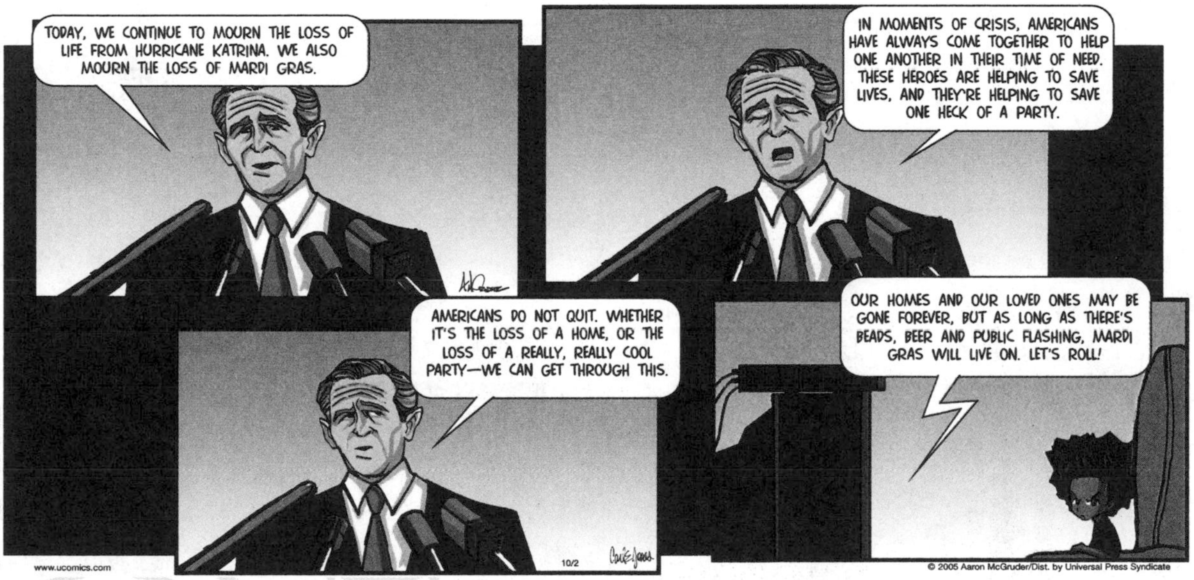
TODAY, WE CONTINUE TO MOURN THE LOSS OF LIFE FROM HURRICANE KATRINA. WE ALSO MOURN THE LOSS OF MARDI GRAS.
IN MOMENTS OF CRISIS, AMERICANS HAVE ALWAYS COME TOGETHER TO HELP ONE ANOTHER IN THEIR TIME OF NEED. THESE HEROES ARE HELPING TO SAVE LIVES, AND THEY'RE HELPING TO SAVE ONE HECK OF A PARTY.
AMERICANS DO NOT QUIT. WHETHER IT'S THE LOSS OF A HOME, OR THE LOSS OF A REALLY, REALLY COOL PARTY—WE CAN GET THROUGH THIS.
OUR HOMES AND OUR LOVED ONES MAY BE GONE FOREVER, BUT AS LONG AS THERE'S BEADS, BEER AND PUBLIC FLASHING, MARDI GRAS WILL LIVE ON. LET'S ROLL!
www.ucomics.com
10/2
© 2005 Aaron McGruder/Dist. by Universal Press Syndicate

THE BOONDOCKS

BY AARON McGRUDER

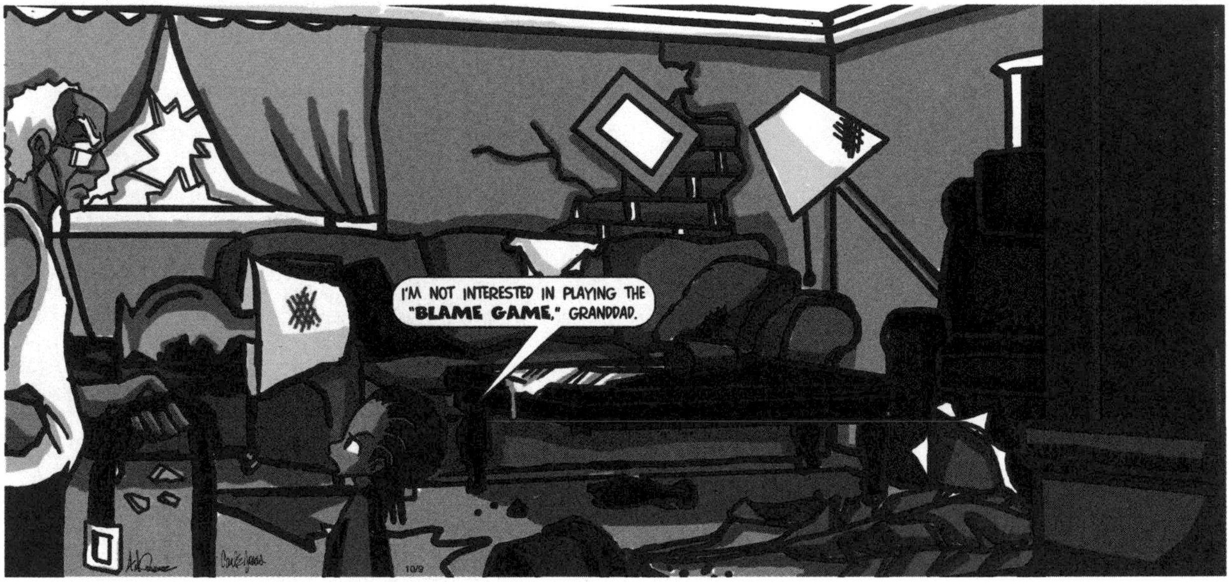
I'M NOT INTERESTED IN PLAYING THE "BLAME GAME," GRANDDAD.
10/9

THE BOONDOCKS **BY AARON McGRUDER**

GRANDDAD, I JUST WANT YOU TO KNOW I TAKE FULL RESPONSIBILITY.

THE BOONDOCKS

BY AARON McGRUDER

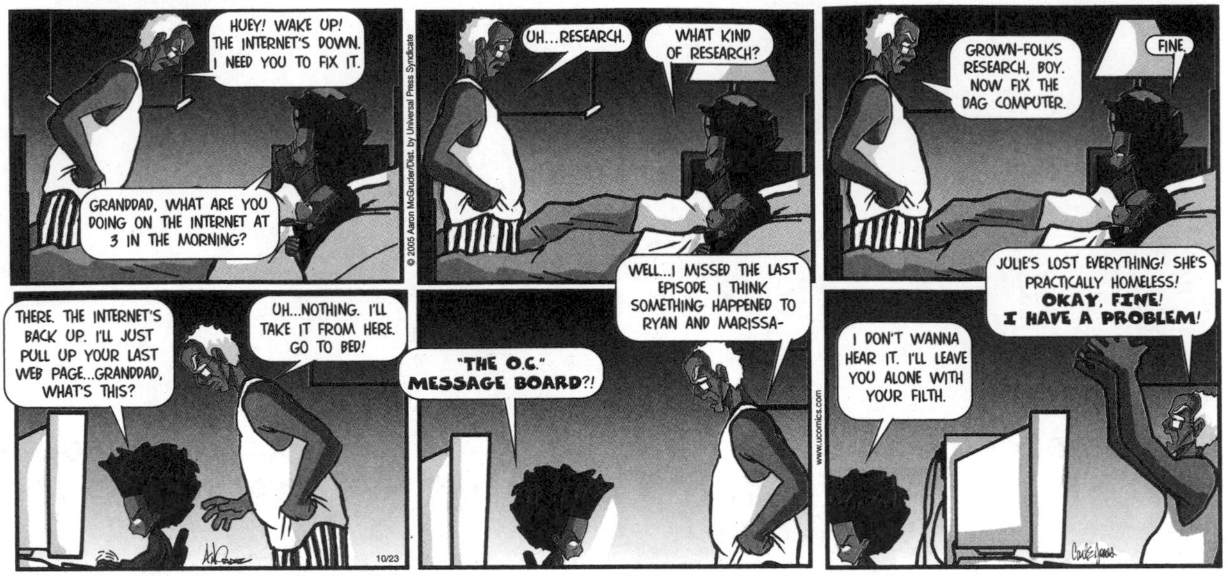
HUEY! WAKE UP! THE INTERNET'S DOWN. I NEED YOU TO FIX IT.
GRANDDAD, WHAT ARE YOU DOING ON THE INTERNET AT 3 IN THE MORNING?
© 2005 Aaron McGruder/Dist. by Universal Press Syndicate
UH...RESEARCH.
WHAT KIND OF RESEARCH?
GROWN-FOLKS RESEARCH, BOY. NOW FIX THE DAG COMPUTER.
FINE.
THERE. THE INTERNET'S BACK UP. I'LL JUST PULL UP YOUR LAST WEB PAGE...GRANDDAD, WHAT'S THIS?
UH...NOTHING. I'LL TAKE IT FROM HERE. GO TO BED!
10/23
"THE O.C." MESSAGE BOARD?!
WELL...I MISSED THE LAST EPISODE. I THINK SOMETHING HAPPENED TO RYAN AND MARISSA-
www.ucomics.com
I DON'T WANNA HEAR IT. I'LL LEAVE YOU ALONE WITH YOUR FILTH.
JULIE'S LOST EVERYTHING! SHE'S PRACTICALLY HOMELESS! OKAY, FINE! I HAVE A PROBLEM!

THE BOONDOCKS

BY AARON McGRUDER

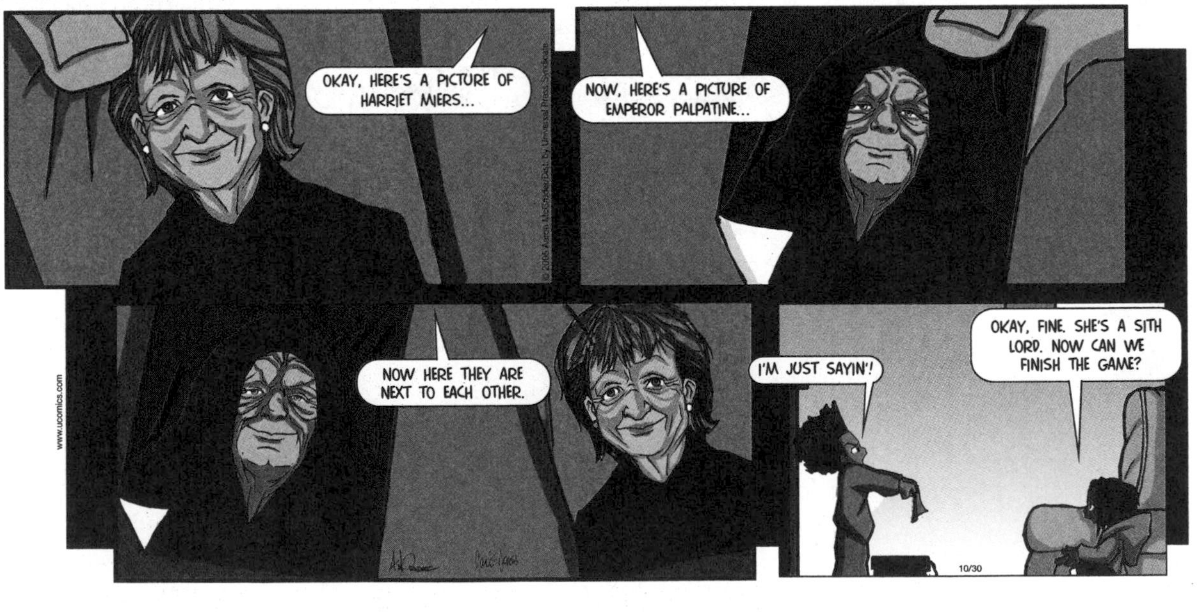
OKAY, HERE'S A PICTURE OF HARRIET MIERS...
NOW, HERE'S A PICTURE OF EMPEROR PALPATINE...
www.ucomics.com
NOW HERE THEY ARE NEXT TO EACH OTHER.
I'M JUST SAYIN'!
OKAY, FINE. SHE'S A SITH LORD. NOW CAN WE FINISH THE GAME?
10/30

THE BOONDOCKS **BY AARON McGRUDER**

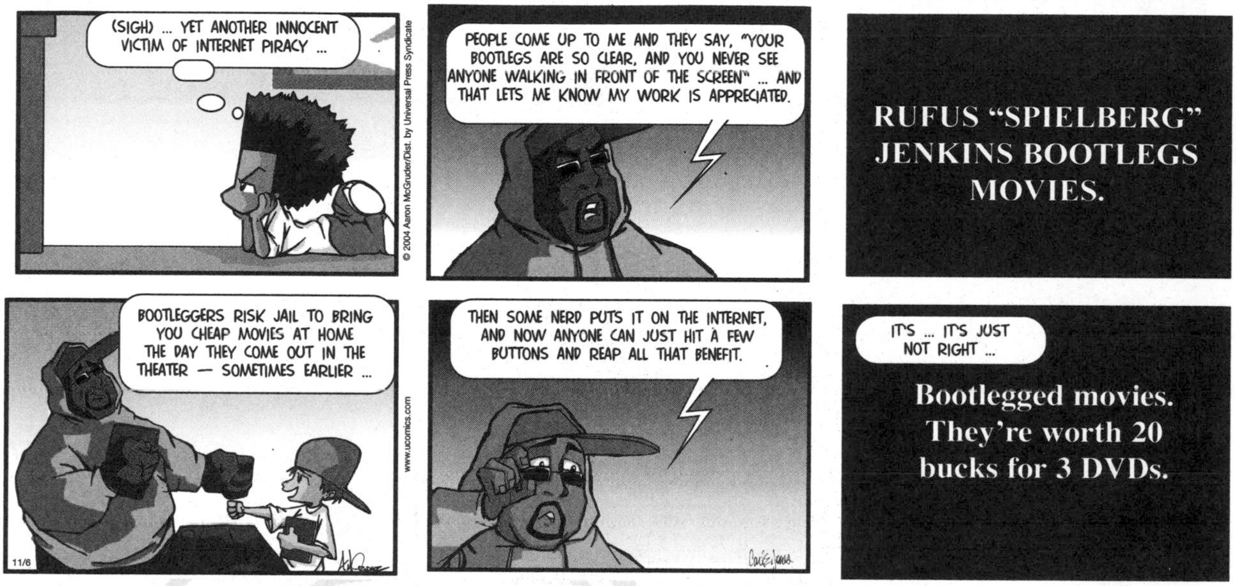
(SIGH) ... YET ANOTHER INNOCENT VICTIM OF INTERNET PIRACY ...
PEOPLE COME UP TO ME AND THEY SAY, "YOUR BOOTLEGS ARE SO CLEAR, AND YOU NEVER SEE ANYONE WALKING IN FRONT OF THE SCREEN" ... AND THAT LETS ME KNOW MY WORK IS APPRECIATED.
RUFUS "SPIELBERG" JENKINS BOOTLEGS MOVIES.
BOOTLEGGERS RISK JAIL TO BRING YOU CHEAP MOVIES AT HOME THE DAY THEY COME OUT IN THE THEATER — SOMETIMES EARLIER ...
THEN SOME NERD PUTS IT ON THE INTERNET, AND NOW ANYONE CAN JUST HIT A FEW BUTTONS AND REAP ALL THAT BENEFIT.
IT'S ... IT'S JUST NOT RIGHT ...
Bootlegged movies. They're worth 20 bucks for 3 DVDs.
© 2004 Aaron McGruder/Dist. by Universal Press Syndicate
www.ucomics.com
11/6

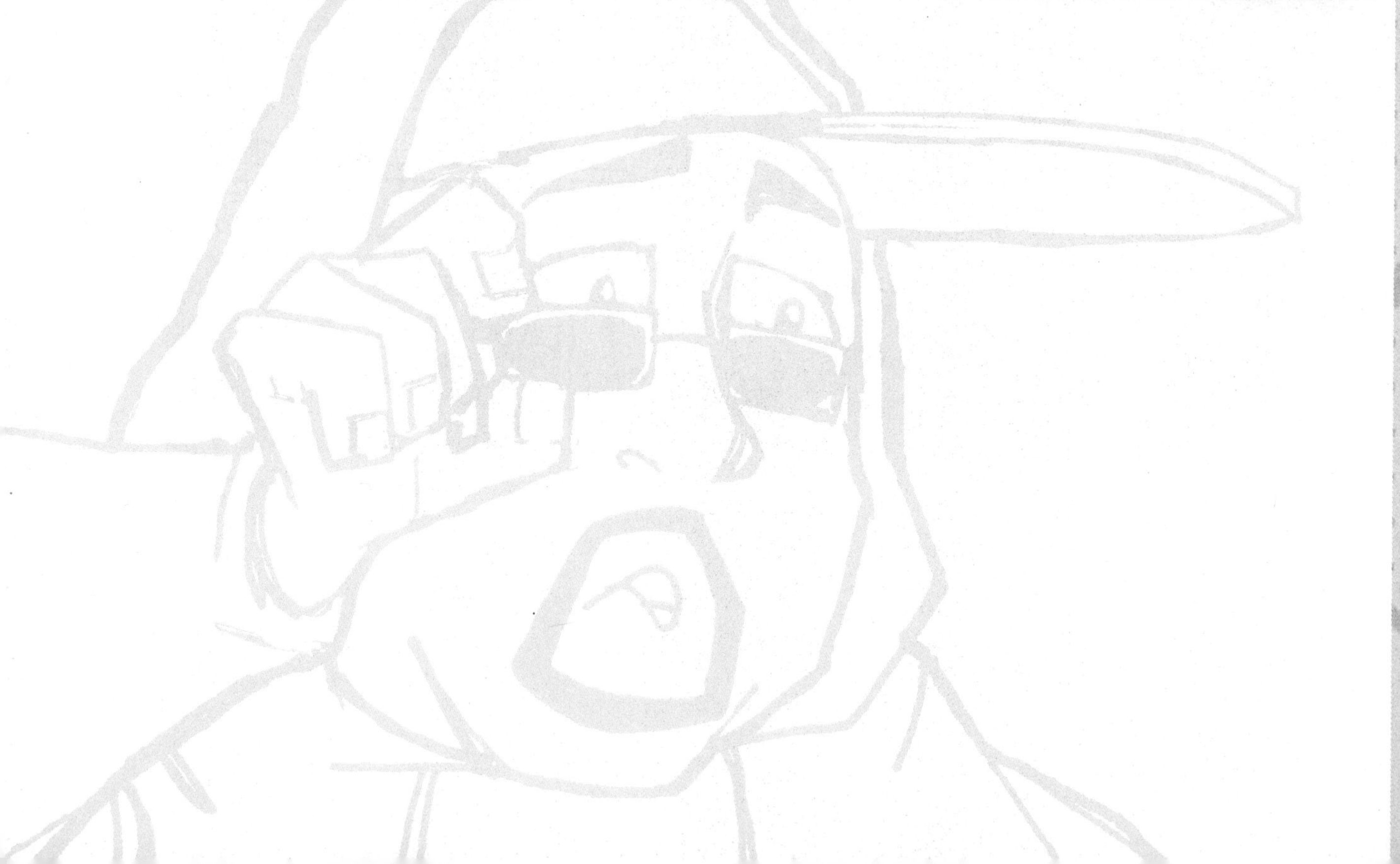

THE BOONDOCKS

BY AARON McGRUDER

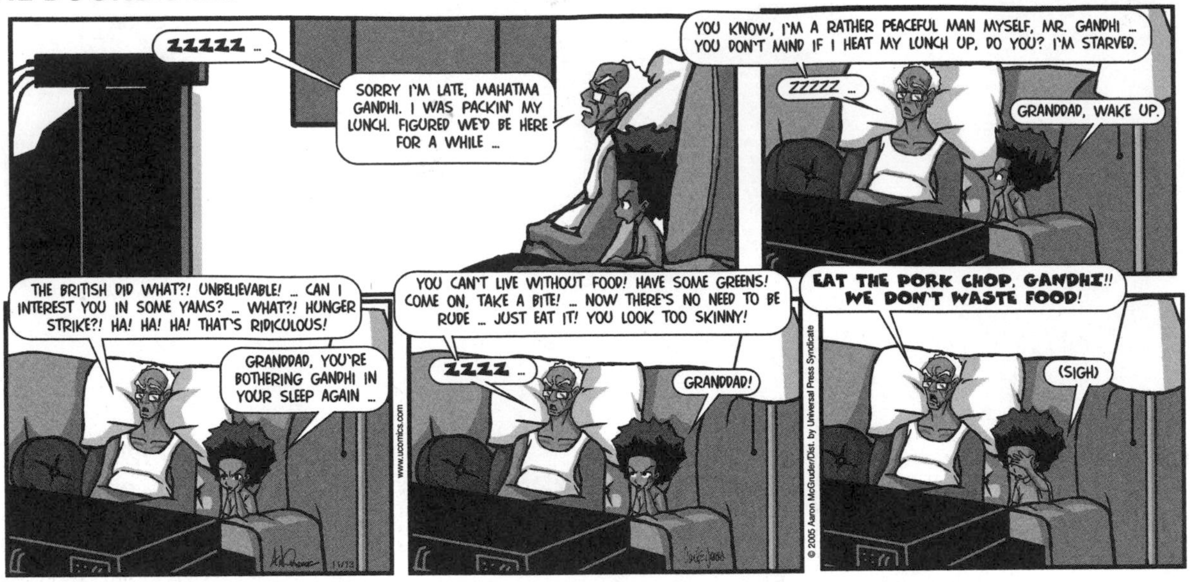
ZZZZZ ...
SORRY I'M LATE, MAHATMA GANDHI. I WAS PACKIN' MY LUNCH. FIGURED WE'D BE HERE FOR A WHILE ...
YOU KNOW, I'M A RATHER PEACEFUL MAN MYSELF, MR. GANDHI ... YOU DON'T MIND IF I HEAT MY LUNCH UP, DO YOU? I'M STARVED.
ZZZZZ ...
GRANDDAD, WAKE UP.
THE BRITISH DID WHAT?! UNBELIEVABLE! ... CAN I INTEREST YOU IN SOME YAMS? ... WHAT?! HUNGER STRIKE?! HA! HA! HA! THAT'S RIDICULOUS!
GRANDDAD, YOU'RE BOTHERING GANDHI IN YOUR SLEEP AGAIN ...
www.ucomics.com
YOU CAN'T LIVE WITHOUT FOOD! HAVE SOME GREENS! COME ON, TAKE A BITE! ... NOW THERE'S NO NEED TO BE RUDE ... JUST EAT IT! YOU LOOK TOO SKINNY!
ZZZZ ...
GRANDDAD!
© 2005 Aaron McGruder/Dist. by Universal Press Syndicate
EAT THE PORK CHOP, GANDHI!! WE DON'T WASTE FOOD!
(SIGH)

THE BOONDOCKS

BY AARON McGRUDER

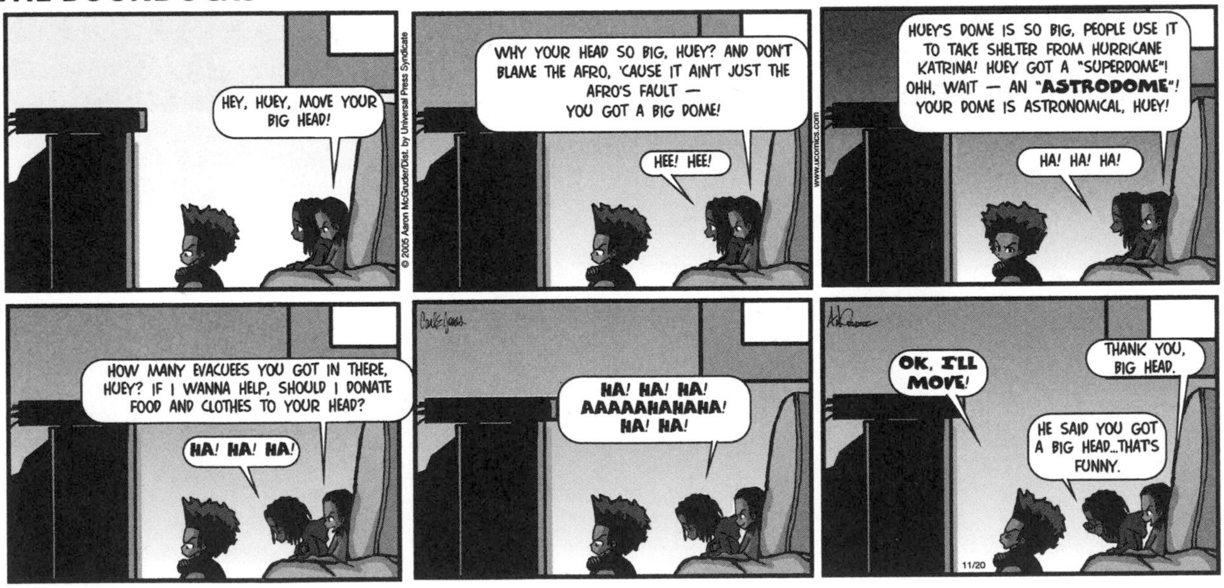
HEY, HUEY, MOVE YOUR BIG HEAD!
© 2005 Aaron McGruder/Dist. by Universal Press Syndicate
WHY YOUR HEAD SO BIG, HUEY? AND DON'T BLAME THE AFRO, 'CAUSE IT AIN'T JUST THE AFRO'S FAULT — YOU GOT A BIG DOME!
HEE! HEE!
www.ucomics.com
HUEY'S DOME IS SO BIG, PEOPLE USE IT TO TAKE SHELTER FROM HURRICANE KATRINA! HUEY GOT A "SUPERDOME"! OHH, WAIT — AN "ASTRODOME"! YOUR DOME IS ASTRONOMICAL, HUEY!
HA! HA! HA!
HOW MANY EVACUEES YOU GOT IN THERE, HUEY? IF I WANNA HELP, SHOULD I DONATE FOOD AND CLOTHES TO YOUR HEAD?
HA! HA! HA!
HA! HA! HA! AAAAAHAHAHA! HA! HA!
OK, I'LL MOVE!
THANK YOU, BIG HEAD.
HE SAID YOU GOT A BIG HEAD...THAT'S FUNNY.
11/20

THE BOONDOCKS **BY AARON McGRUDER**

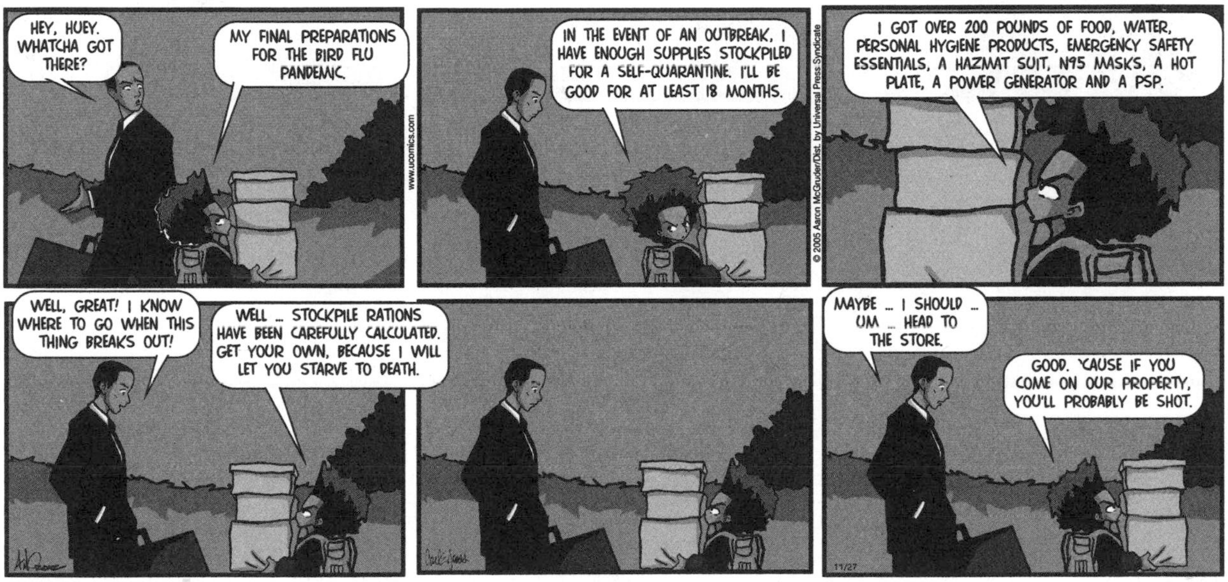
HEY, HUEY. WHATCHA GOT THERE?
MY FINAL PREPARATIONS FOR THE BIRD FLU PANDEMIC.
www.ucomics.com
IN THE EVENT OF AN OUTBREAK, I HAVE ENOUGH SUPPLIES STOCKPILED FOR A SELF-QUARANTINE. I'LL BE GOOD FOR AT LEAST 18 MONTHS.
© 2005 Aaron McGruder/Dist. by Universal Press Syndicate
I GOT OVER 200 POUNDS OF FOOD, WATER, PERSONAL HYGIENE PRODUCTS, EMERGENCY SAFETY ESSENTIALS, A HAZMAT SUIT, N95 MASKS, A HOT PLATE, A POWER GENERATOR AND A PSP.
WELL, GREAT! I KNOW WHERE TO GO WHEN THIS THING BREAKS OUT!
WELL ... STOCKPILE RATIONS HAVE BEEN CAREFULLY CALCULATED. GET YOUR OWN, BECAUSE I WILL LET YOU STARVE TO DEATH.
MAYBE ... I SHOULD ... UM ... HEAD TO THE STORE.
GOOD. 'CAUSE IF YOU COME ON OUR PROPERTY, YOU'LL PROBABLY BE SHOT.
11/27

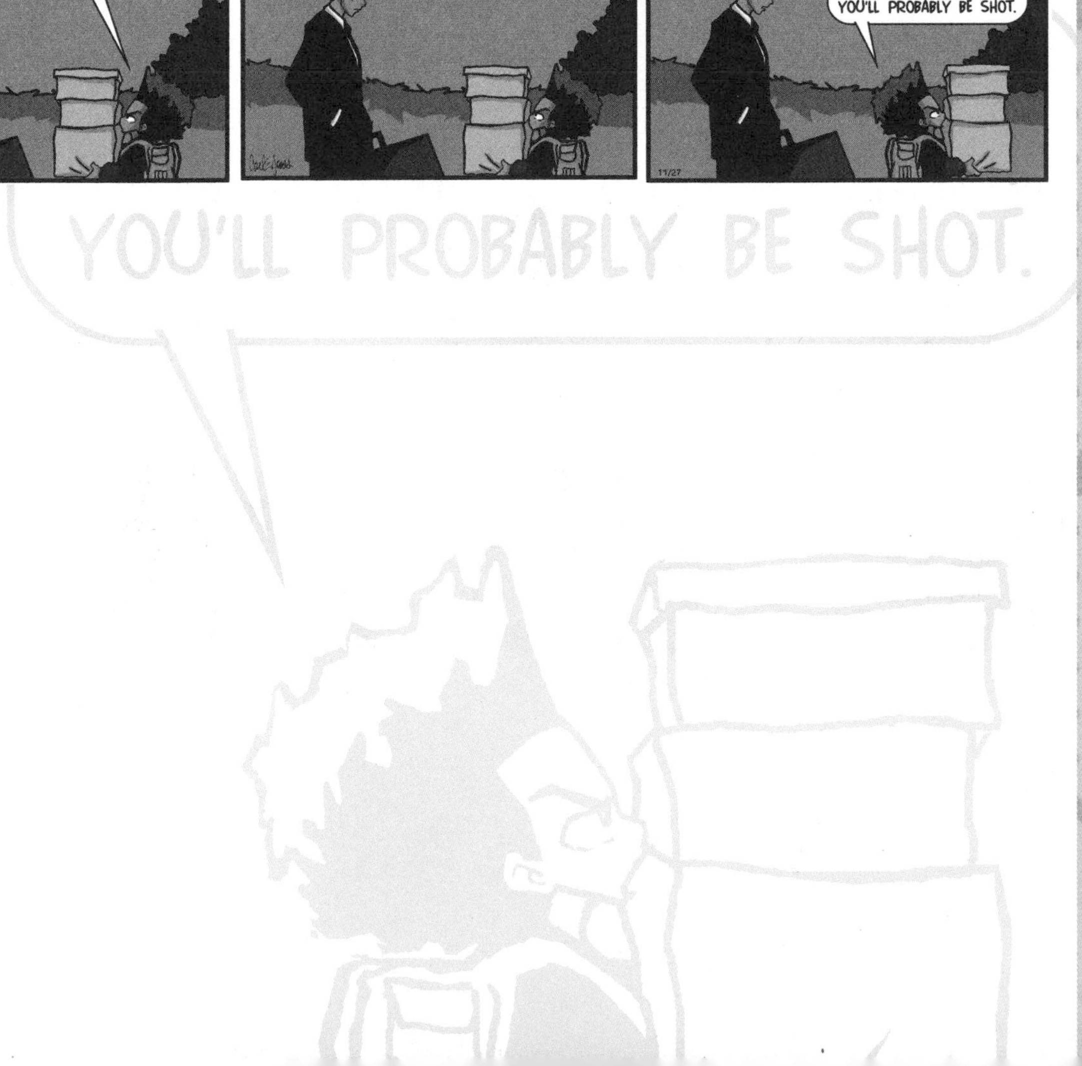
YOU'LL PROBABLY BE SHOT.

THE BOONDOCKS BY AARON McGRUDER

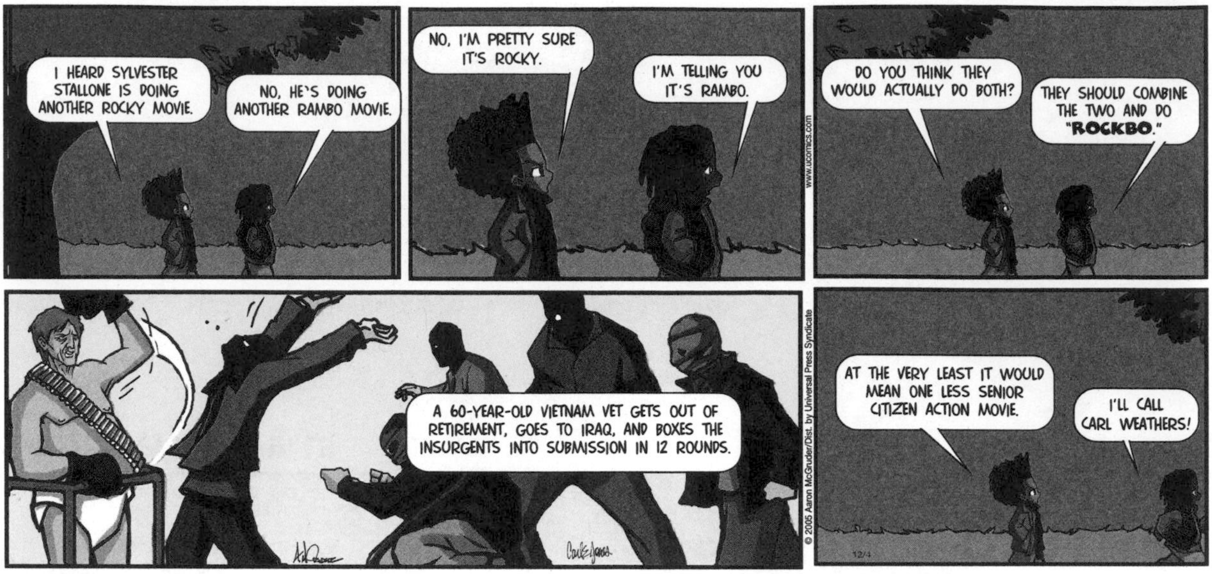
I HEARD SYLVESTER STALLONE IS DOING ANOTHER ROCKY MOVIE.
NO, HE'S DOING ANOTHER RAMBO MOVIE.
NO, I'M PRETTY SURE IT'S ROCKY.
I'M TELLING YOU IT'S RAMBO.
www.ucomics.com
DO YOU THINK THEY WOULD ACTUALLY DO BOTH?
THEY SHOULD COMBINE THE TWO AND DO "ROCKBO."
A 60-YEAR-OLD VIETNAM VET GETS OUT OF RETIREMENT, GOES TO IRAQ, AND BOXES THE INSURGENTS INTO SUBMISSION IN 12 ROUNDS.
© 2005 Aaron McGruder/Dist. by Universal Press Syndicate
AT THE VERY LEAST IT WOULD MEAN ONE LESS SENIOR CITIZEN ACTION MOVIE.
I'LL CALL CARL WEATHERS!
12/4

THE BOONDOCKS BY AARON McGRUDER

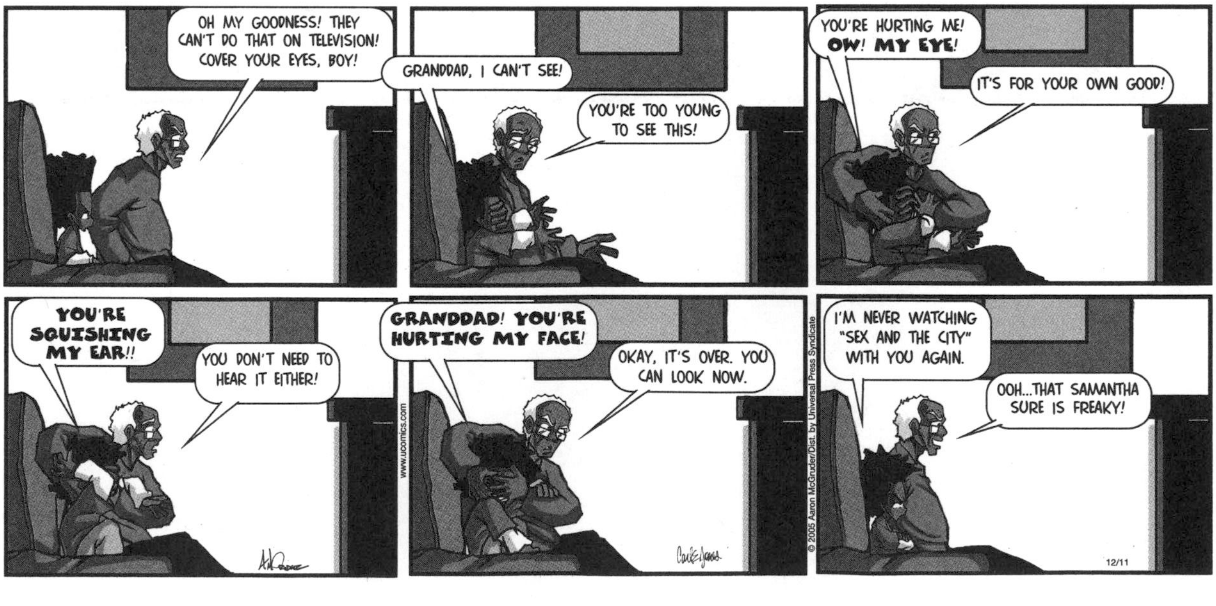
OH MY GOODNESS! THEY CAN'T DO THAT ON TELEVISION! COVER YOUR EYES, BOY!
GRANDDAD, I CAN'T SEE!
YOU'RE TOO YOUNG TO SEE THIS!
YOU'RE HURTING ME! OW! MY EYE!
IT'S FOR YOUR OWN GOOD!
YOU'RE SQUISHING MY EAR!!
YOU DON'T NEED TO HEAR IT EITHER!
www.ucomics.com
GRANDDAD! YOU'RE HURTING MY FACE!
OKAY, IT'S OVER. YOU CAN LOOK NOW.
© 2005 Aaron McGruder/Dist. by Universal Press Syndicate
I'M NEVER WATCHING "SEX AND THE CITY" WITH YOU AGAIN.
OOH...THAT SAMANTHA SURE IS FREAKY!
12/11

THE BOONDOCKS **BY AARON McGRUDER**

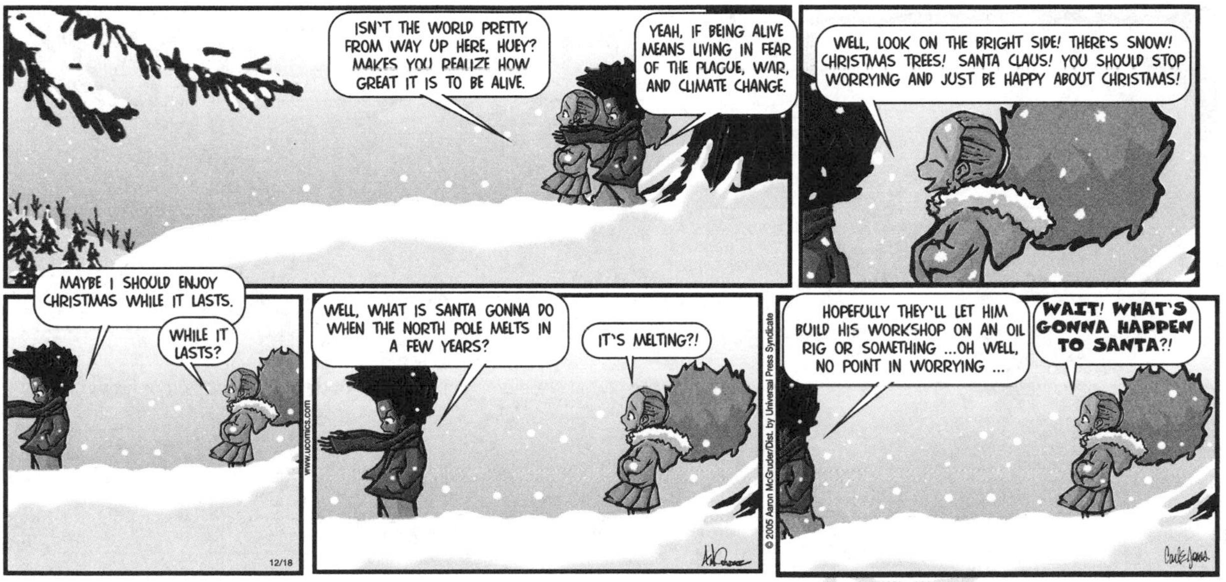
ISN'T THE WORLD PRETTY FROM WAY UP HERE, HUEY? MAKES YOU REALIZE HOW GREAT IT IS TO BE ALIVE.
YEAH, IF BEING ALIVE MEANS LIVING IN FEAR OF THE PLAGUE, WAR, AND CLIMATE CHANGE.
WELL, LOOK ON THE BRIGHT SIDE! THERE'S SNOW! CHRISTMAS TREES! SANTA CLAUS! YOU SHOULD STOP WORRYING AND JUST BE HAPPY ABOUT CHRISTMAS!
MAYBE I SHOULD ENJOY CHRISTMAS WHILE IT LASTS.
WHILE IT LASTS?
www.ucomics.com
12/18
WELL, WHAT IS SANTA GONNA DO WHEN THE NORTH POLE MELTS IN A FEW YEARS?
IT'S MELTING?!
© 2005 Aaron McGruder/Dist. by Universal Press Syndicate
HOPEFULLY THEY'LL LET HIM BUILD HIS WORKSHOP ON AN OIL RIG OR SOMETHING ...OH WELL, NO POINT IN WORRYING ...
WAIT! WHAT'S GONNA HAPPEN TO SANTA?!

THE BOONDOCKS BY AARON McGRUDER

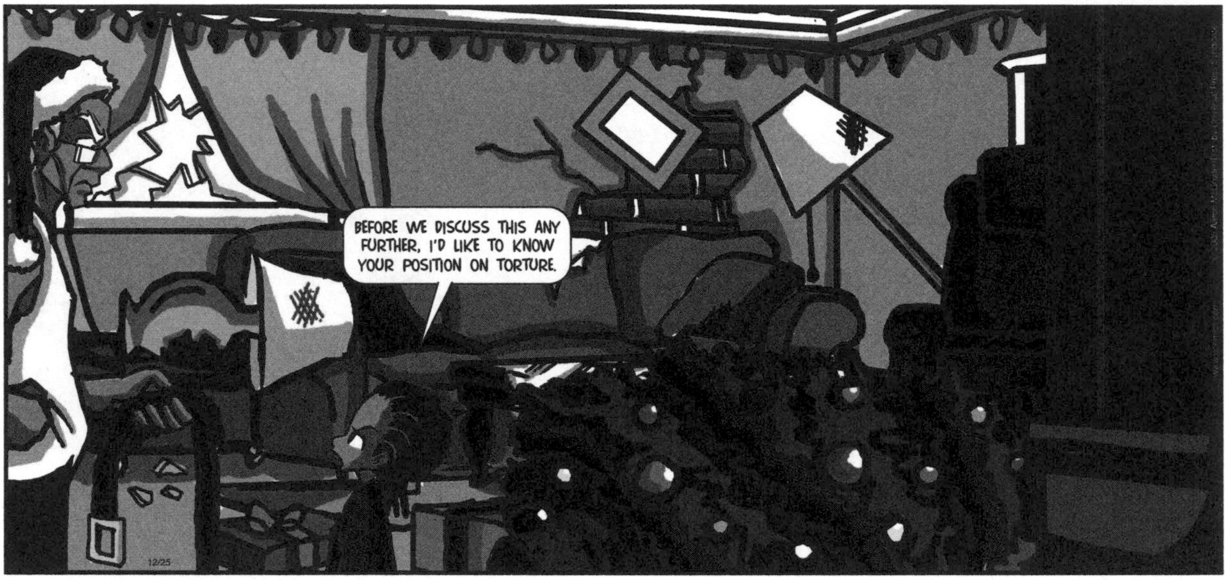
BEFORE WE DISCUSS THIS ANY FURTHER, I'D LIKE TO KNOW YOUR POSITION ON TORTURE.

> It is not funny in the way that *Calvin and Hobbes* was funny; it's usually not funny at all.
>
> —*San Francisco Chronicle*

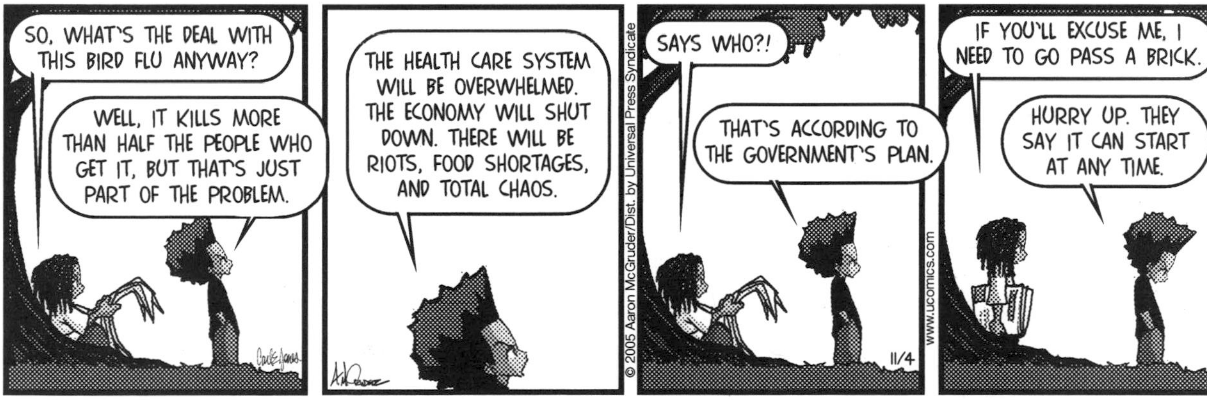
SO, WHAT'S THE DEAL WITH THIS BIRD FLU ANYWAY?
WELL, IT KILLS MORE THAN HALF THE PEOPLE WHO GET IT, BUT THAT'S JUST PART OF THE PROBLEM.
THE HEALTH CARE SYSTEM WILL BE OVERWHELMED. THE ECONOMY WILL SHUT DOWN. THERE WILL BE RIOTS, FOOD SHORTAGES, AND TOTAL CHAOS.
© 2005 Aaron McGruder/Dist. by Universal Press Syndicate
SAYS WHO?!
THAT'S ACCORDING TO THE GOVERNMENT'S PLAN.
www.ucomics.com
11/4
IF YOU'LL EXCUSE ME, I NEED TO GO PASS A BRICK.
HURRY UP. THEY SAY IT CAN START AT ANY TIME.

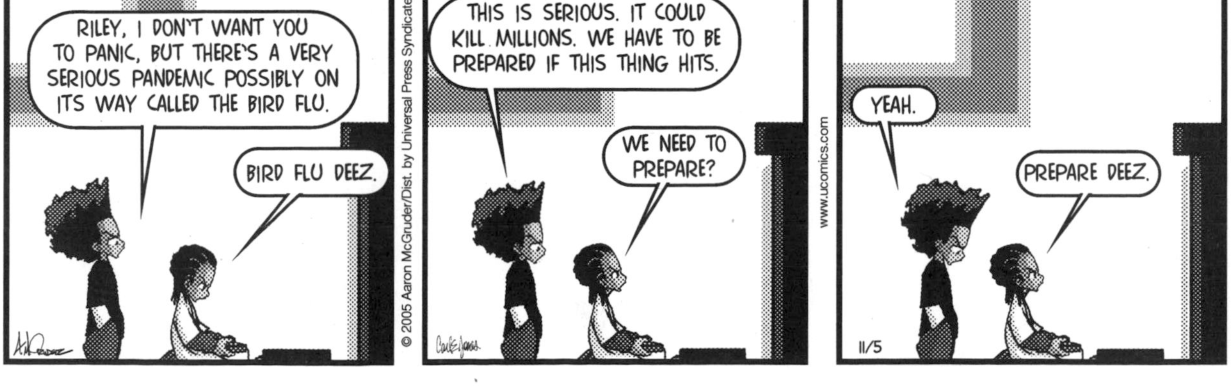
RILEY, I DON'T WANT YOU TO PANIC, BUT THERE'S A VERY SERIOUS PANDEMIC POSSIBLY ON ITS WAY CALLED THE BIRD FLU.
BIRD FLU DEEZ.
© 2005 Aaron McGruder/Dist. by Universal Press Syndicate
THIS IS SERIOUS. IT COULD KILL MILLIONS. WE HAVE TO BE PREPARED IF THIS THING HITS.
WE NEED TO PREPARE?
www.ucomics.com
YEAH.
PREPARE DEEZ.
11/5

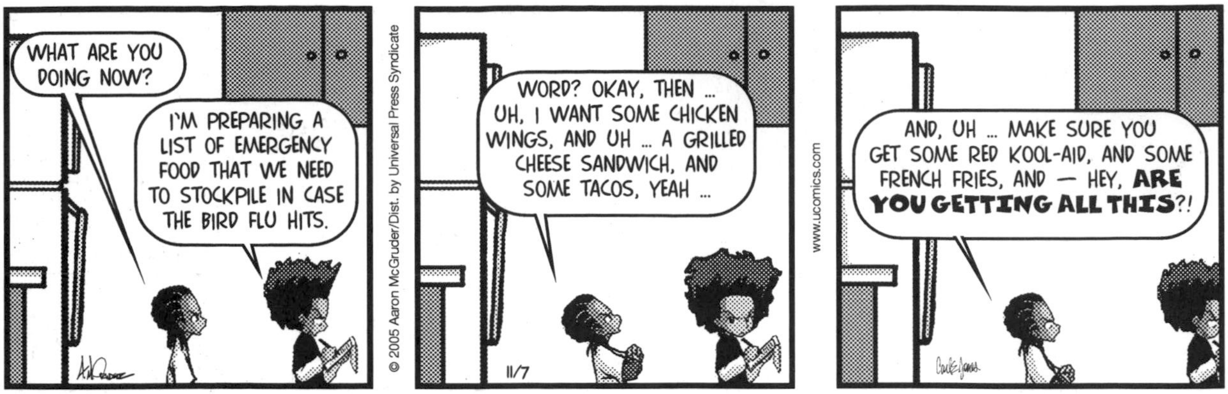
WHAT ARE YOU DOING NOW?
I'M PREPARING A LIST OF EMERGENCY FOOD THAT WE NEED TO STOCKPILE IN CASE THE BIRD FLU HITS.
© 2005 Aaron McGruder/Dist. by Universal Press Syndicate
WORD? OKAY, THEN ... UH, I WANT SOME CHICKEN WINGS, AND UH ... A GRILLED CHEESE SANDWICH, AND SOME TACOS, YEAH ...
11/7
www.ucomics.com
AND, UH ... MAKE SURE YOU GET SOME RED KOOL-AID, AND SOME FRENCH FRIES, AND — HEY, **ARE YOU GETTING ALL THIS**?!

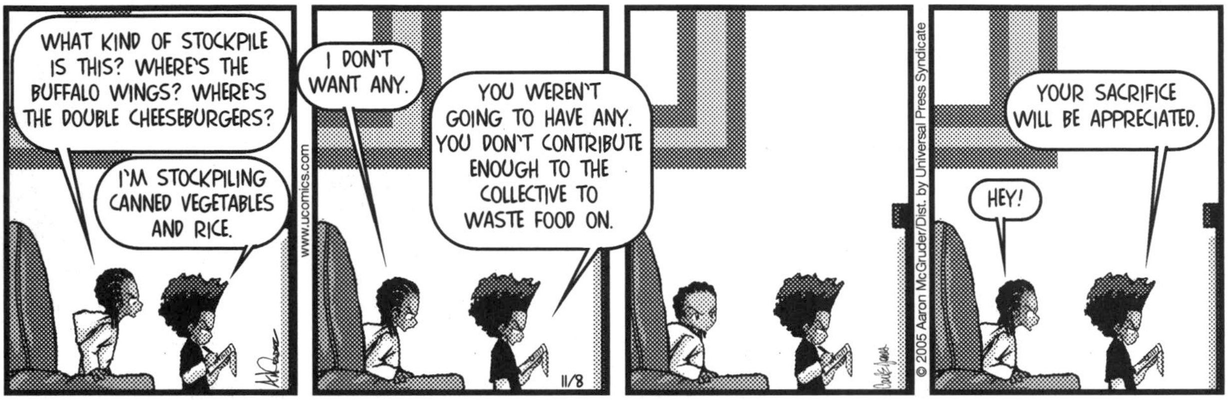
WHAT KIND OF STOCKPILE IS THIS? WHERE'S THE BUFFALO WINGS? WHERE'S THE DOUBLE CHEESEBURGERS?
I'M STOCKPILING CANNED VEGETABLES AND RICE.
www.ucomics.com
I DON'T WANT ANY.
YOU WEREN'T GOING TO HAVE ANY. YOU DON'T CONTRIBUTE ENOUGH TO THE COLLECTIVE TO WASTE FOOD ON.
11/8
© 2005 Aaron McGruder/Dist. by Universal Press Syndicate
HEY!
YOUR SACRIFICE WILL BE APPRECIATED.

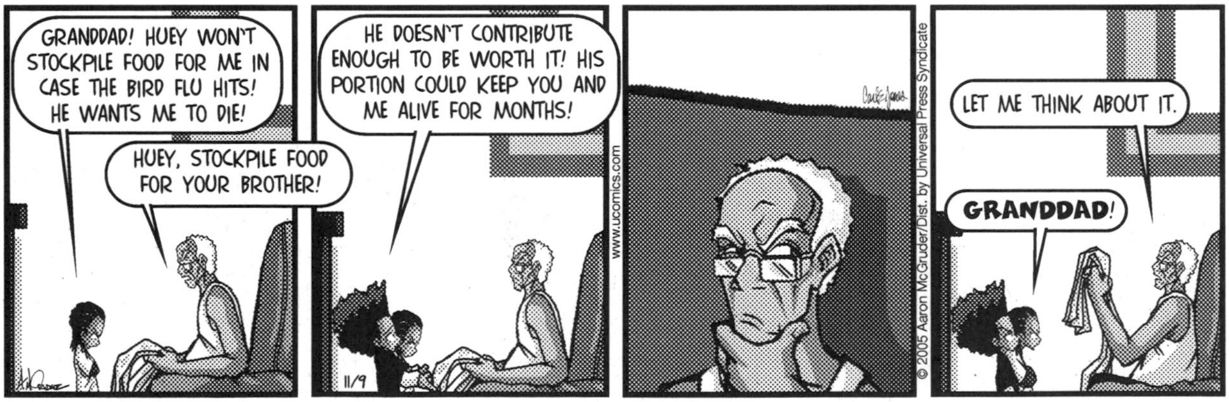
GRANDDAD! HUEY WON'T STOCKPILE FOOD FOR ME IN CASE THE BIRD FLU HITS! HE WANTS ME TO DIE!
HUEY, STOCKPILE FOOD FOR YOUR BROTHER!
HE DOESN'T CONTRIBUTE ENOUGH TO BE WORTH IT! HIS PORTION COULD KEEP YOU AND ME ALIVE FOR MONTHS!
11/9
www.ucomics.com
© 2005 Aaron McGruder/Dist. by Universal Press Syndicate
LET ME THINK ABOUT IT.
GRANDDAD!

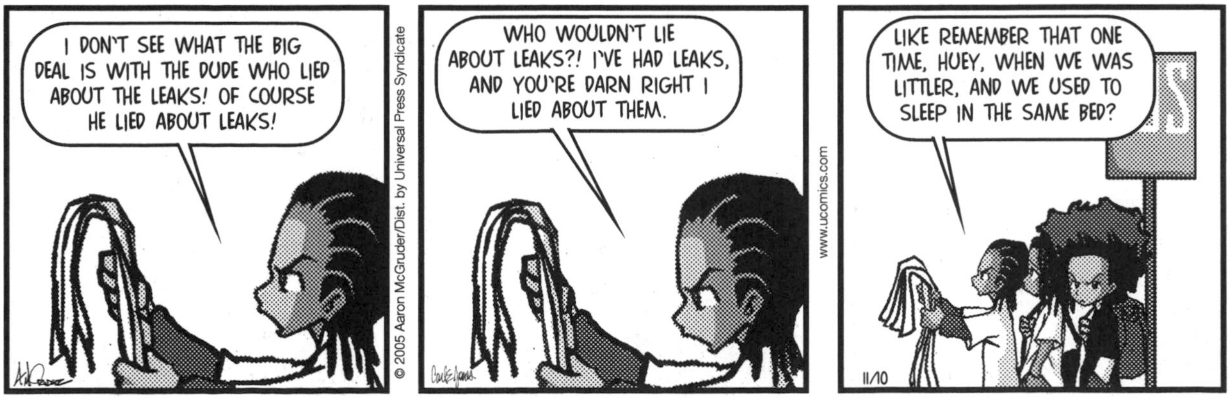
I DON'T SEE WHAT THE BIG DEAL IS WITH THE DUDE WHO LIED ABOUT THE LEAKS! OF COURSE HE LIED ABOUT LEAKS!
© 2005 Aaron McGruder/Dist. by Universal Press Syndicate
WHO WOULDN'T LIE ABOUT LEAKS?! I'VE HAD LEAKS, AND YOU'RE DARN RIGHT I LIED ABOUT THEM.
www.ucomics.com
LIKE REMEMBER THAT ONE TIME, HUEY, WHEN WE WAS LITTLER, AND WE USED TO SLEEP IN THE SAME BED?
11/10

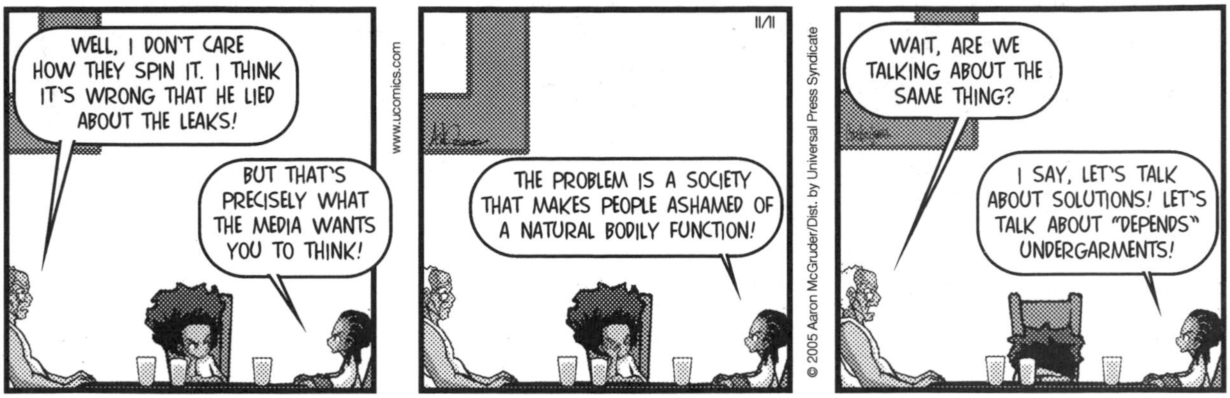
WELL, I DON'T CARE HOW THEY SPIN IT. I THINK IT'S WRONG THAT HE LIED ABOUT THE LEAKS!
BUT THAT'S PRECISELY WHAT THE MEDIA WANTS YOU TO THINK!
www.ucomics.com
11/11
THE PROBLEM IS A SOCIETY THAT MAKES PEOPLE ASHAMED OF A NATURAL BODILY FUNCTION!
© 2005 Aaron McGruder/Dist. by Universal Press Syndicate
WAIT, ARE WE TALKING ABOUT THE SAME THING?
I SAY, LET'S TALK ABOUT SOLUTIONS! LET'S TALK ABOUT "DEPENDS" UNDERGARMENTS!

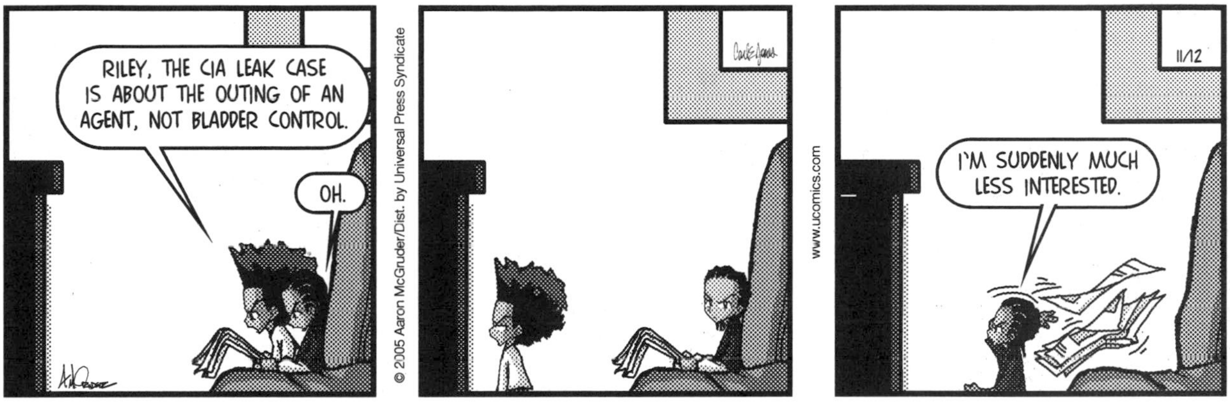
RILEY, THE CIA LEAK CASE IS ABOUT THE OUTING OF AN AGENT, NOT BLADDER CONTROL.
OH.
© 2005 Aaron McGruder/Dist. by Universal Press Syndicate
www.ucomics.com
11/12
I'M SUDDENLY MUCH LESS INTERESTED.

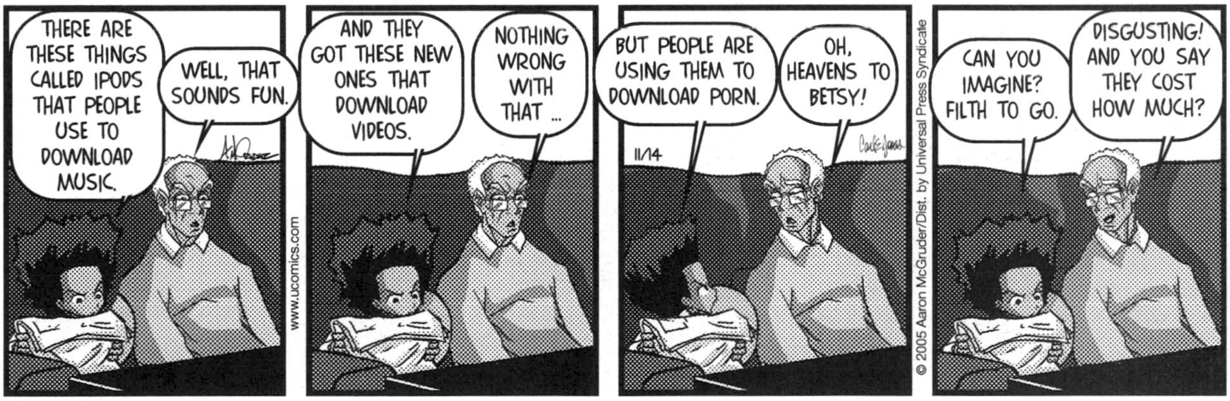
THERE ARE THESE THINGS CALLED IPODS THAT PEOPLE USE TO DOWNLOAD MUSIC.
WELL, THAT SOUNDS FUN.
www.ucomics.com
AND THEY GOT THESE NEW ONES THAT DOWNLOAD VIDEOS.
NOTHING WRONG WITH THAT ...
BUT PEOPLE ARE USING THEM TO DOWNLOAD PORN.
OH, HEAVENS TO BETSY!
11/14
© 2005 Aaron McGruder/Dist. by Universal Press Syndicate
CAN YOU IMAGINE? FILTH TO GO.
DISGUSTING! AND YOU SAY THEY COST HOW MUCH?

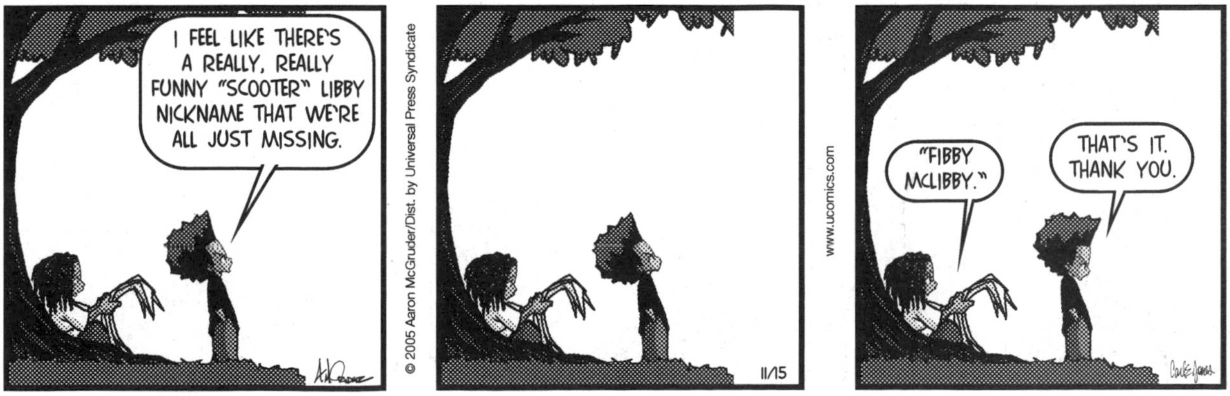
I FEEL LIKE THERE'S A REALLY, REALLY FUNNY "SCOOTER" LIBBY NICKNAME THAT WE'RE ALL JUST MISSING.
© 2005 Aaron McGruder/Dist. by Universal Press Syndicate
11/15
www.ucomics.com
"FIBBY MCLIBBY."
THAT'S IT. THANK YOU.

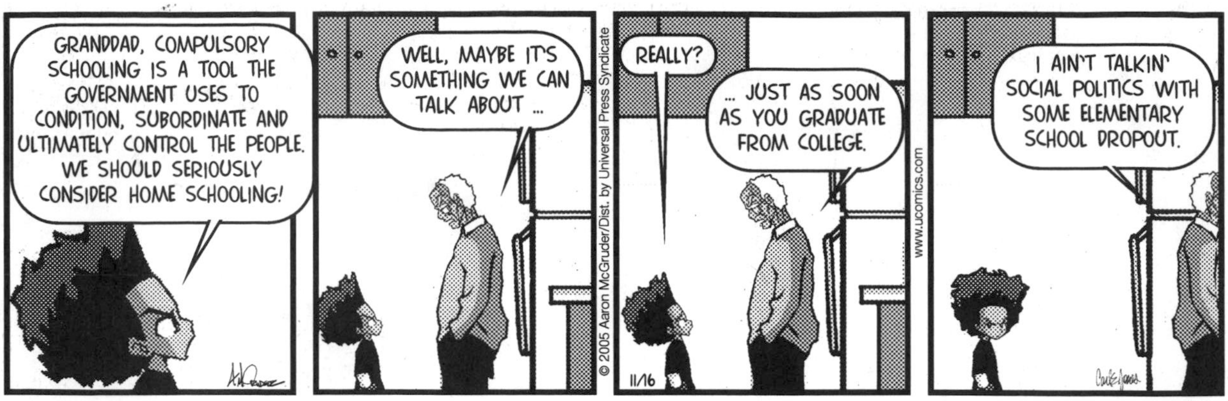
GRANDDAD, COMPULSORY SCHOOLING IS A TOOL THE GOVERNMENT USES TO CONDITION, SUBORDINATE AND ULTIMATELY CONTROL THE PEOPLE. WE SHOULD SERIOUSLY CONSIDER HOME SCHOOLING!
WELL, MAYBE IT'S SOMETHING WE CAN TALK ABOUT ...
© 2005 Aaron McGruder/Dist. by Universal Press Syndicate
REALLY?
... JUST AS SOON AS YOU GRADUATE FROM COLLEGE.
11/16
www.ucomics.com
I AIN'T TALKIN' SOCIAL POLITICS WITH SOME ELEMENTARY SCHOOL DROPOUT.

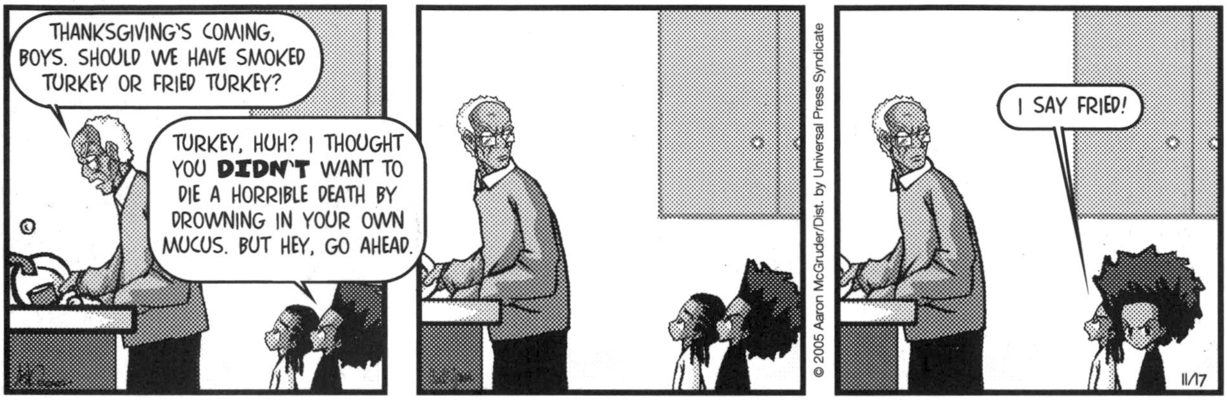
THANKSGIVING'S COMING, BOYS. SHOULD WE HAVE SMOKED TURKEY OR FRIED TURKEY?
TURKEY, HUH? I THOUGHT YOU **DIDN'T** WANT TO DIE A HORRIBLE DEATH BY DROWNING IN YOUR OWN MUCUS. BUT HEY, GO AHEAD.
© 2005 Aaron McGruder/Dist. by Universal Press Syndicate
I SAY FRIED!
11/17

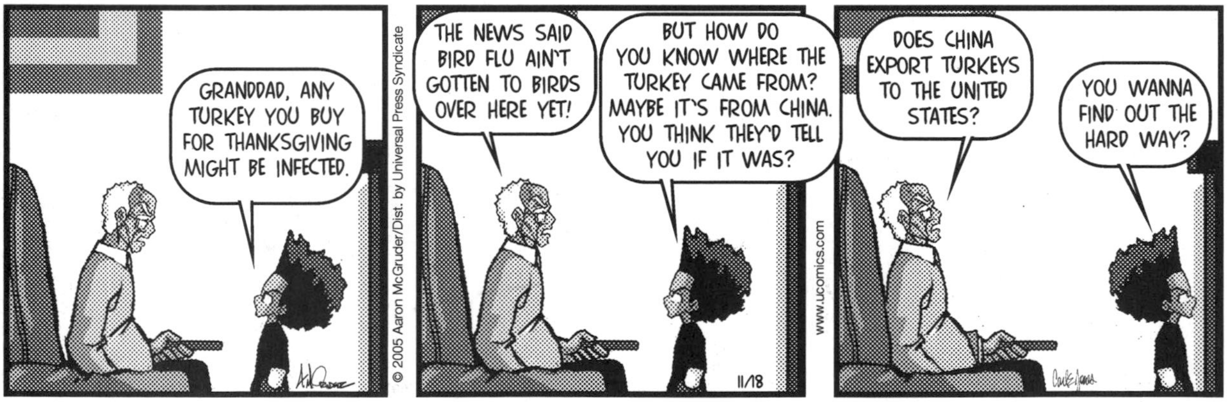
GRANDDAD, ANY TURKEY YOU BUY FOR THANKSGIVING MIGHT BE INFECTED.
© 2005 Aaron McGruder/Dist. by Universal Press Syndicate
THE NEWS SAID BIRD FLU AIN'T GOTTEN TO BIRDS OVER HERE YET!
BUT HOW DO YOU KNOW WHERE THE TURKEY CAME FROM? MAYBE IT'S FROM CHINA. YOU THINK THEY'D TELL YOU IF IT WAS?
11/18
www.ucomics.com
DOES CHINA EXPORT TURKEYS TO THE UNITED STATES?
YOU WANNA FIND OUT THE HARD WAY?

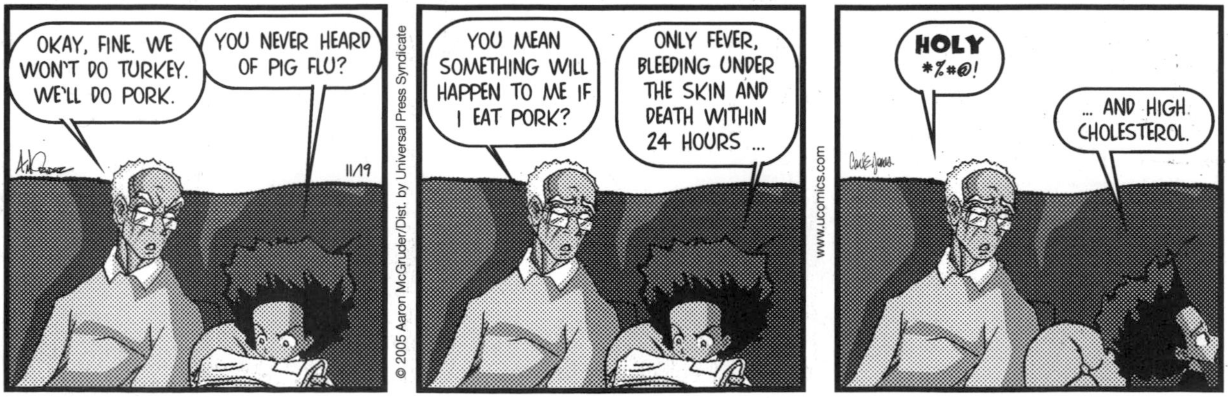
OKAY, FINE. WE WON'T DO TURKEY. WE'LL DO PORK.
YOU NEVER HEARD OF PIG FLU?
11/19
© 2005 Aaron McGruder/Dist. by Universal Press Syndicate
YOU MEAN SOMETHING WILL HAPPEN TO ME IF I EAT PORK?
ONLY FEVER, BLEEDING UNDER THE SKIN AND DEATH WITHIN 24 HOURS ...
www.ucomics.com
HOLY *%#@!
... AND HIGH CHOLESTEROL.

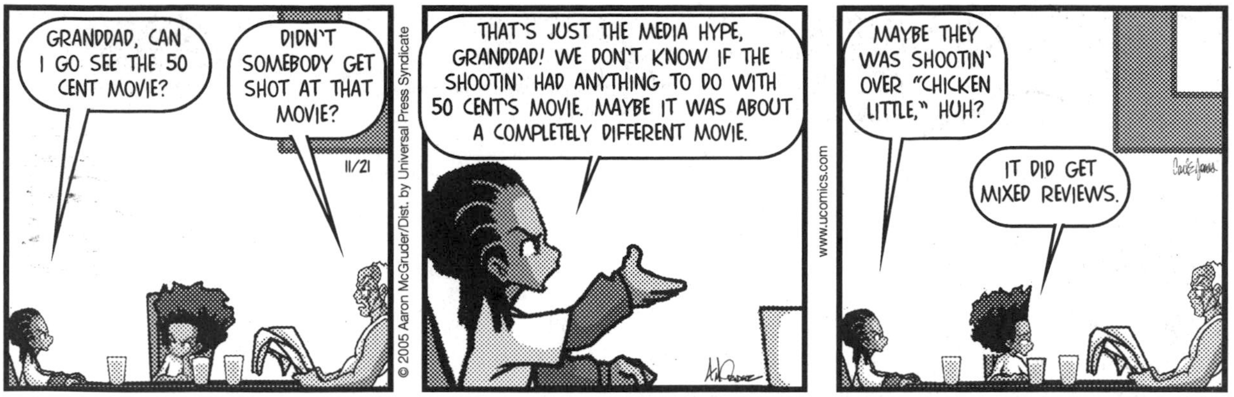
GRANDDAD, CAN I GO SEE THE 50 CENT MOVIE?
DIDN'T SOMEBODY GET SHOT AT THAT MOVIE?
11/21
© 2005 Aaron McGruder/Dist. by Universal Press Syndicate
THAT'S JUST THE MEDIA HYPE, GRANDDAD! WE DON'T KNOW IF THE SHOOTIN' HAD ANYTHING TO DO WITH 50 CENT'S MOVIE. MAYBE IT WAS ABOUT A COMPLETELY DIFFERENT MOVIE.
www.ucomics.com
MAYBE THEY WAS SHOOTIN' OVER "CHICKEN LITTLE," HUH?
IT DID GET MIXED REVIEWS.

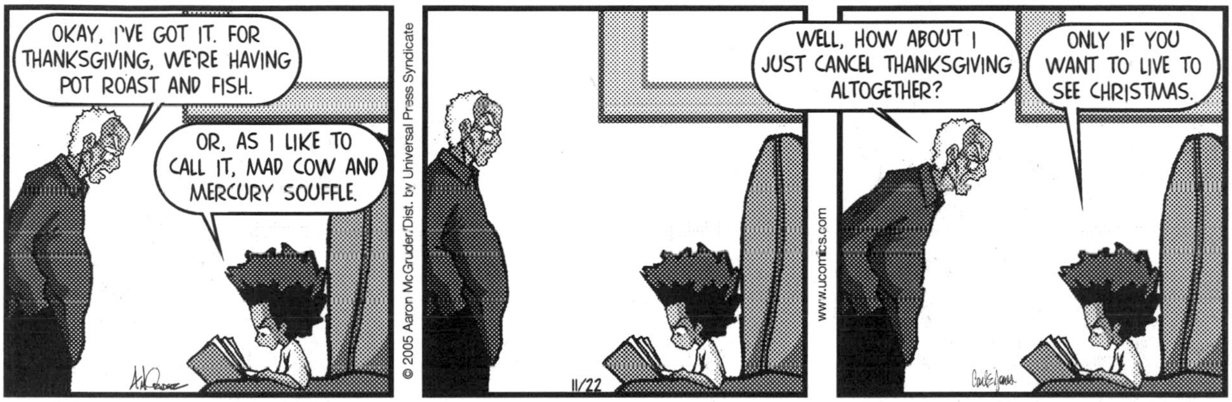
OKAY, I'VE GOT IT. FOR THANKSGIVING, WE'RE HAVING POT ROAST AND FISH.
OR, AS I LIKE TO CALL IT, MAD COW AND MERCURY SOUFFLE.
© 2005 Aaron McGruder/Dist. by Universal Press Syndicate
11/22
www.ucomics.com
WELL, HOW ABOUT I JUST CANCEL THANKSGIVING ALTOGETHER?
ONLY IF YOU WANT TO LIVE TO SEE CHRISTMAS.

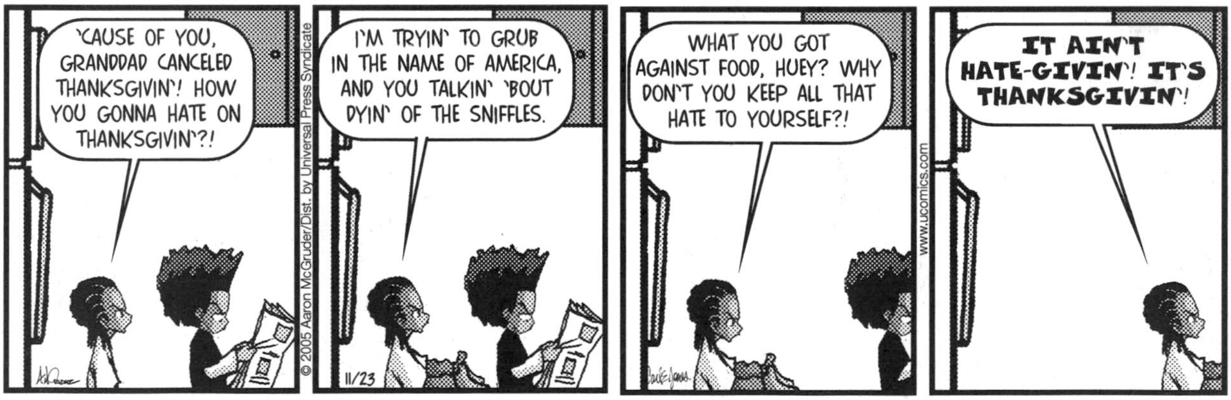
'CAUSE OF YOU, GRANDDAD CANCELED THANKSGIVIN'! HOW YOU GONNA HATE ON THANKSGIVIN'?!
© 2005 Aaron McGruder/Dist. by Universal Press Syndicate
I'M TRYIN' TO GRUB IN THE NAME OF AMERICA, AND YOU TALKIN' 'BOUT DYIN' OF THE SNIFFLES.
11/23
WHAT YOU GOT AGAINST FOOD, HUEY? WHY DON'T YOU KEEP ALL THAT HATE TO YOURSELF?!
www.ucomics.com
IT AIN'T HATE-GIVIN'! IT'S THANKSGIVIN'!

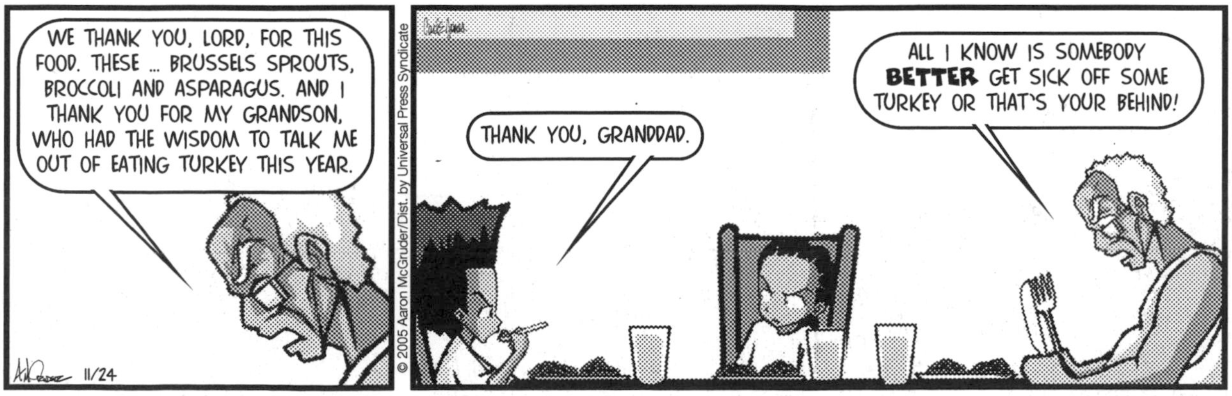
WE THANK YOU, LORD, FOR THIS FOOD. THESE ... BRUSSELS SPROUTS, BROCCOLI AND ASPARAGUS. AND I THANK YOU FOR MY GRANDSON, WHO HAD THE WISDOM TO TALK ME OUT OF EATING TURKEY THIS YEAR.
11/24
© 2005 Aaron McGruder/Dist. by Universal Press Syndicate
THANK YOU, GRANDDAD.
ALL I KNOW IS SOMEBODY BETTER GET SICK OFF SOME TURKEY OR THAT'S YOUR BEHIND!

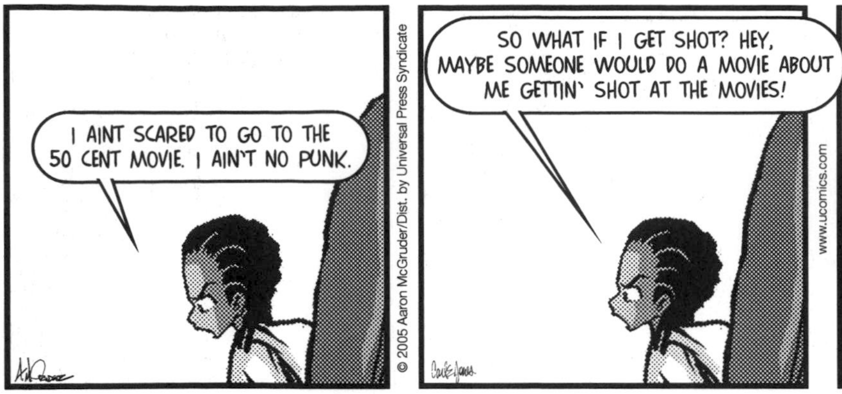
I AINT SCARED TO GO TO THE 50 CENT MOVIE. I AIN'T NO PUNK.
© 2005 Aaron McGruder/Dist. by Universal Press Syndicate
SO WHAT IF I GET SHOT? HEY, MAYBE SOMEONE WOULD DO A MOVIE ABOUT ME GETTIN' SHOT AT THE MOVIES!
www.ucomics.com
"GET POPCORN OR DIE TRYIN'"?
I CAN DO ALL MY OWN STUNTS!
11/25

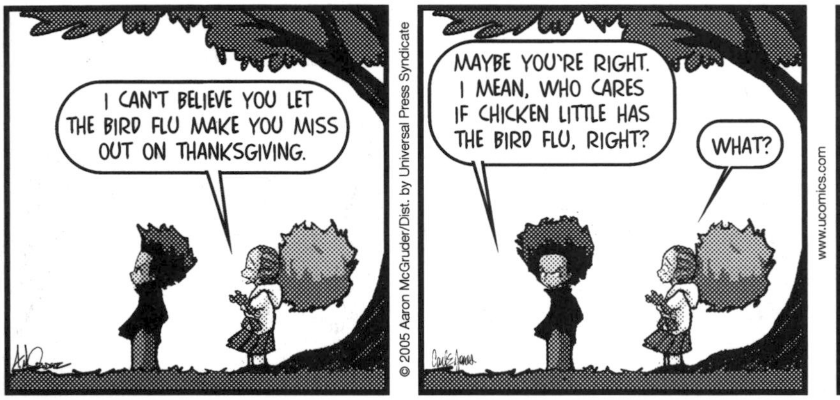
I CAN'T BELIEVE YOU LET THE BIRD FLU MAKE YOU MISS OUT ON THANKSGIVING.
© 2005 Aaron McGruder/Dist. by Universal Press Syndicate
MAYBE YOU'RE RIGHT. I MEAN, WHO CARES IF CHICKEN LITTLE HAS THE BIRD FLU, RIGHT?
WHAT?
www.ucomics.com
TOO BAD THEY DIDN'T CATCH IT BEFORE IT GOT DONALD DUCK ...
WHAT HAPPENED TO DONALD?!
11/26

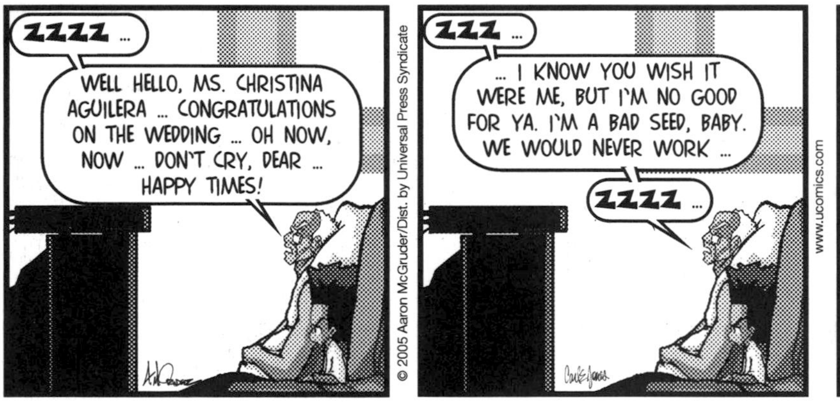
ZZZZ ...
WELL HELLO, MS. CHRISTINA AGUILERA ... CONGRATULATIONS ON THE WEDDING ... OH NOW, NOW ... DON'T CRY, DEAR ... HAPPY TIMES!
© 2005 Aaron McGruder/Dist. by Universal Press Syndicate
ZZZ ...
... I KNOW YOU WISH IT WERE ME, BUT I'M NO GOOD FOR YA. I'M A BAD SEED, BABY. WE WOULD NEVER WORK ...
ZZZZ ...
www.ucomics.com
NOW, NO MORE TEARS ... IT'S LIKE I'VE ALWAYS SAID — YOU ARE BEAUTIFUL IN EVERY SINGLE WAY ... OH, I LOVE YOU TOO, CHRISTINA ... CALL ME ...
ZZZ ...
11/28

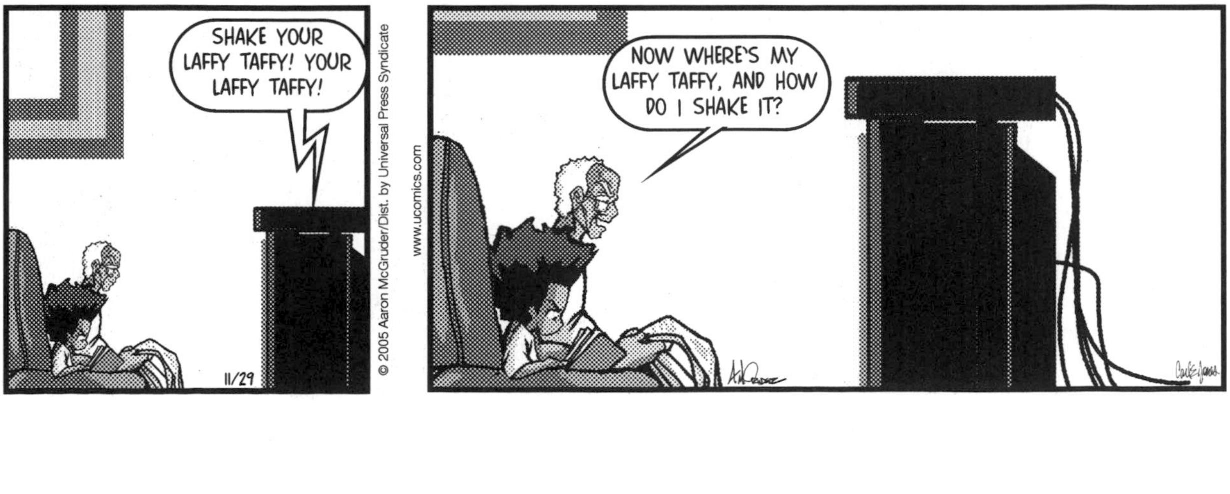
SHAKE YOUR LAFFY TAFFY! YOUR LAFFY TAFFY!
11/29
© 2005 Aaron McGruder/Dist. by Universal Press Syndicate
www.ucomics.com
NOW WHERE'S MY LAFFY TAFFY, AND HOW DO I SHAKE IT?

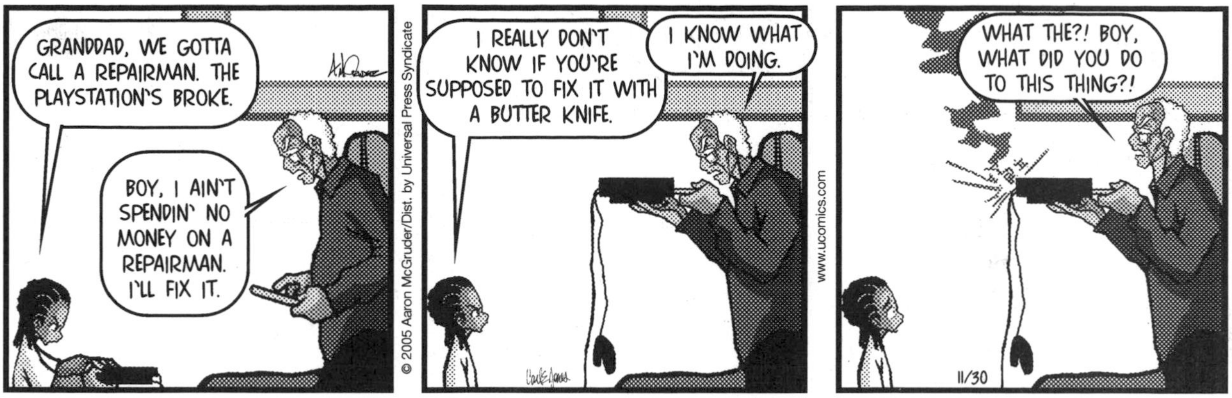
GRANDDAD, WE GOTTA CALL A REPAIRMAN. THE PLAYSTATION'S BROKE.
BOY, I AIN'T SPENDIN' NO MONEY ON A REPAIRMAN. I'LL FIX IT.
I REALLY DON'T KNOW IF YOU'RE SUPPOSED TO FIX IT WITH A BUTTER KNIFE.
I KNOW WHAT I'M DOING.
WHAT THE?! BOY, WHAT DID YOU DO TO THIS THING?!
11/30
© 2005 Aaron McGruder/Dist. by Universal Press Syndicate
www.ucomics.com

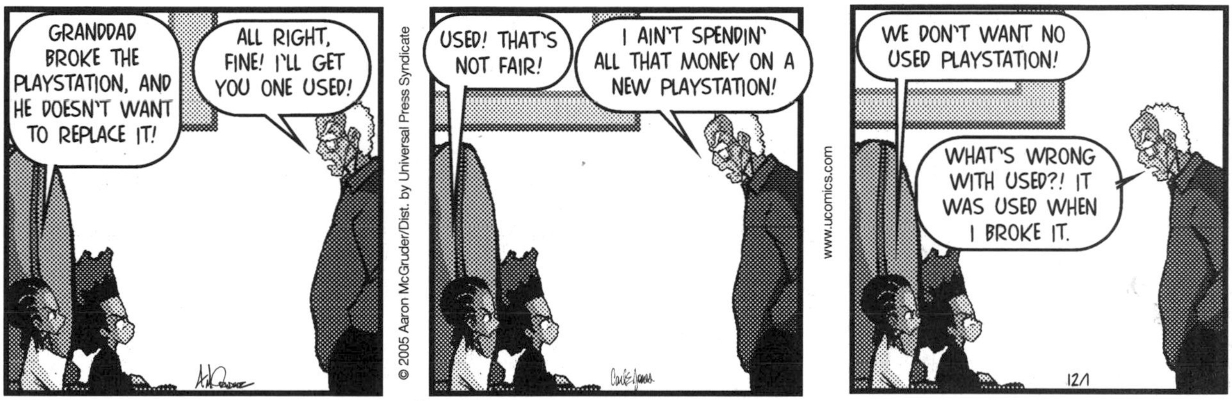
GRANDDAD BROKE THE PLAYSTATION, AND HE DOESN'T WANT TO REPLACE IT!
ALL RIGHT, FINE! I'LL GET YOU ONE USED!
USED! THAT'S NOT FAIR!
I AIN'T SPENDIN' ALL THAT MONEY ON A NEW PLAYSTATION!
WE DON'T WANT NO USED PLAYSTATION!
WHAT'S WRONG WITH USED?! IT WAS USED WHEN I BROKE IT.
12/1
© 2005 Aaron McGruder/Dist. by Universal Press Syndicate
www.ucomics.com

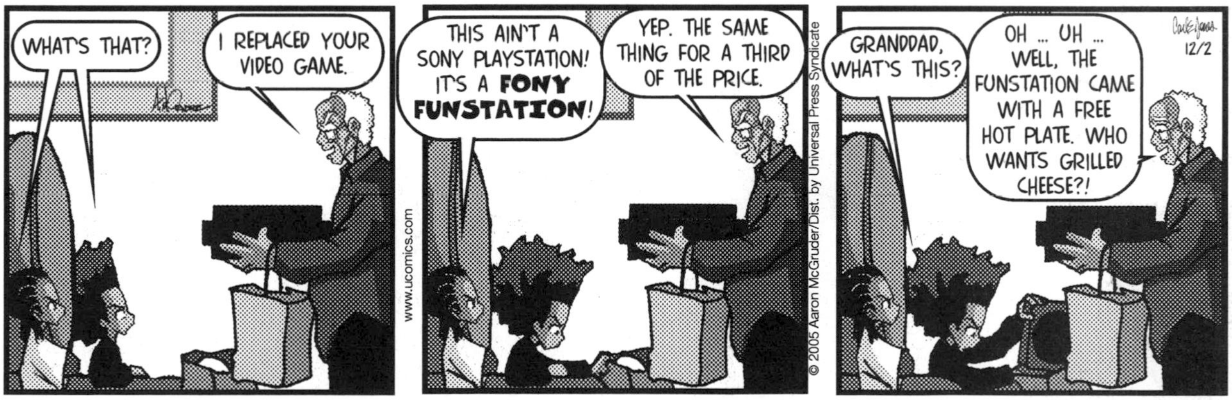
WHAT'S THAT?
I REPLACED YOUR VIDEO GAME.
www.ucomics.com
THIS AIN'T A SONY PLAYSTATION! IT'S A **FONY FUNSTATION**!
YEP. THE SAME THING FOR A THIRD OF THE PRICE.
© 2005 Aaron McGruder/Dist. by Universal Press Syndicate
GRANDDAD, WHAT'S THIS?
OH ... UH ... WELL, THE FUNSTATION CAME WITH A FREE HOT PLATE. WHO WANTS GRILLED CHEESE?!
12/2

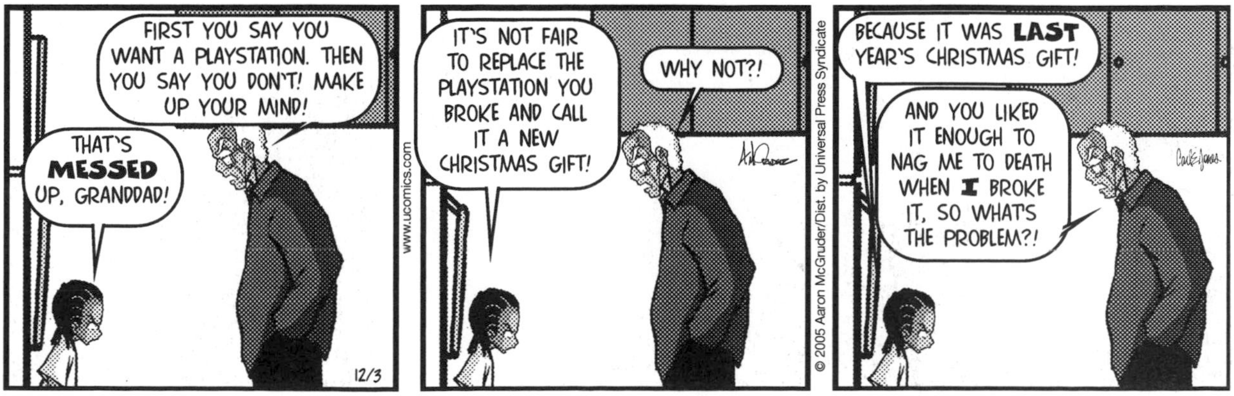
FIRST YOU SAY YOU WANT A PLAYSTATION. THEN YOU SAY YOU DON'T! MAKE UP YOUR MIND!
THAT'S **MESSED** UP, GRANDDAD!
12/3
www.ucomics.com
IT'S NOT FAIR TO REPLACE THE PLAYSTATION YOU BROKE AND CALL IT A NEW CHRISTMAS GIFT!
WHY NOT?!
© 2005 Aaron McGruder/Dist. by Universal Press Syndicate
BECAUSE IT WAS **LAST** YEAR'S CHRISTMAS GIFT!
AND YOU LIKED IT ENOUGH TO NAG ME TO DEATH WHEN **I** BROKE IT, SO WHAT'S THE PROBLEM?!

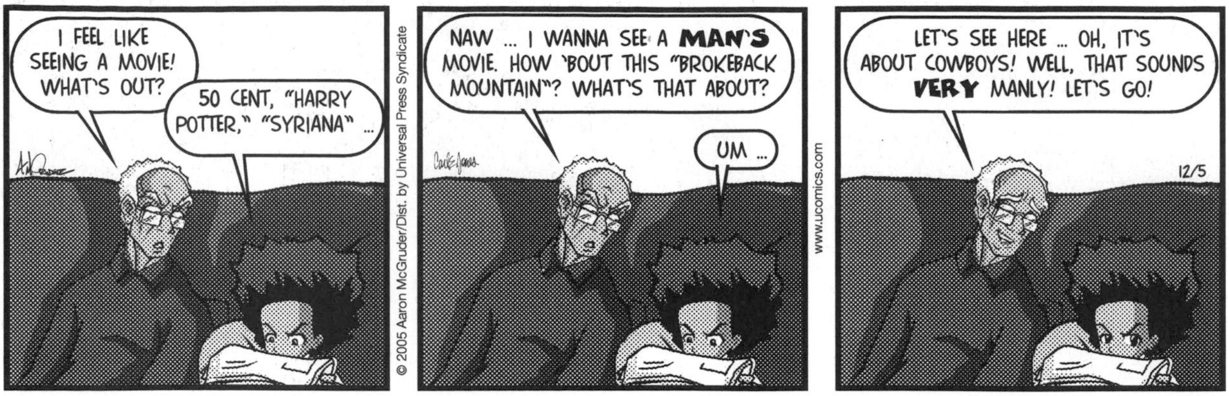
I FEEL LIKE SEEING A MOVIE! WHAT'S OUT?
50 CENT, "HARRY POTTER," "SYRIANA" ...
© 2005 Aaron McGruder/Dist. by Universal Press Syndicate
NAW ... I WANNA SEE A **MAN'S** MOVIE. HOW 'BOUT THIS "BROKEBACK MOUNTAIN"? WHAT'S THAT ABOUT?
UM ...
www.ucomics.com
LET'S SEE HERE ... OH, IT'S ABOUT COWBOYS! WELL, THAT SOUNDS **VERY** MANLY! LET'S GO!
12/5

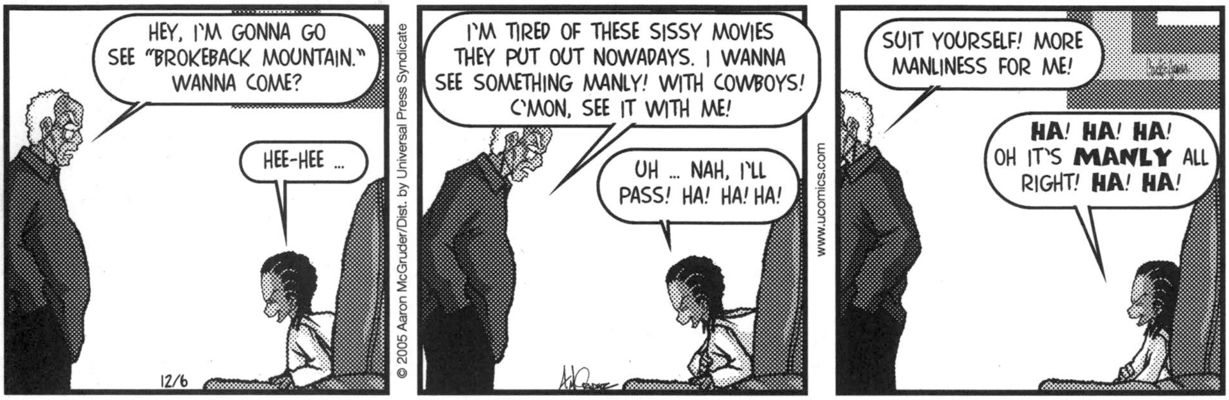
HEY, I'M GONNA GO SEE "BROKEBACK MOUNTAIN." WANNA COME?
HEE-HEE ...
12/6
© 2005 Aaron McGruder/Dist. by Universal Press Syndicate
I'M TIRED OF THESE SISSY MOVIES THEY PUT OUT NOWADAYS. I WANNA SEE SOMETHING MANLY! WITH COWBOYS! C'MON, SEE IT WITH ME!
UH ... NAH, I'LL PASS! HA! HA! HA!
www.ucomics.com
SUIT YOURSELF! MORE MANLINESS FOR ME!
HA! HA! HA! OH IT'S **MANLY** ALL RIGHT! **HA! HA!**

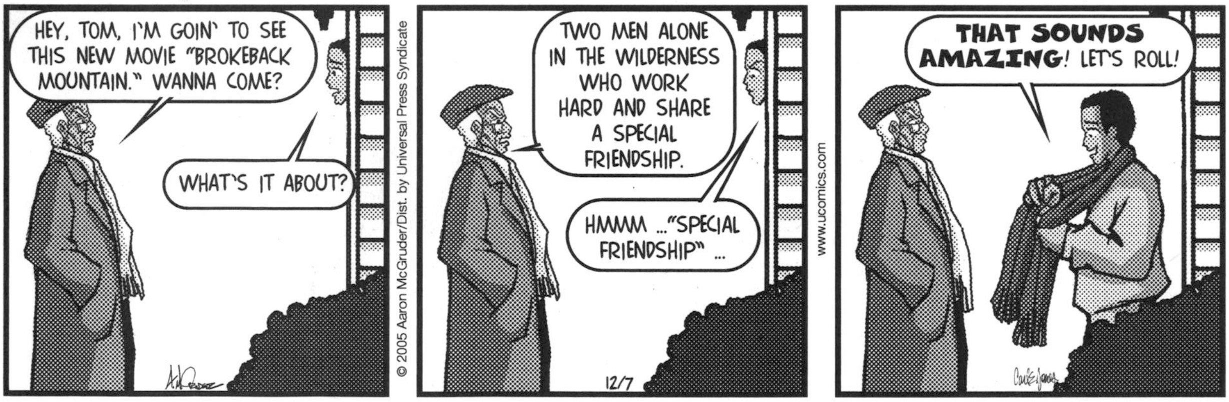
HEY, TOM, I'M GOIN' TO SEE THIS NEW MOVIE "BROKEBACK MOUNTAIN." WANNA COME?
WHAT'S IT ABOUT?
© 2005 Aaron McGruder/Dist. by Universal Press Syndicate
TWO MEN ALONE IN THE WILDERNESS WHO WORK HARD AND SHARE A SPECIAL FRIENDSHIP.
HMMM ..."SPECIAL FRIENDSHIP" ...
12/7
www.ucomics.com
THAT SOUNDS AMAZING! LET'S ROLL!

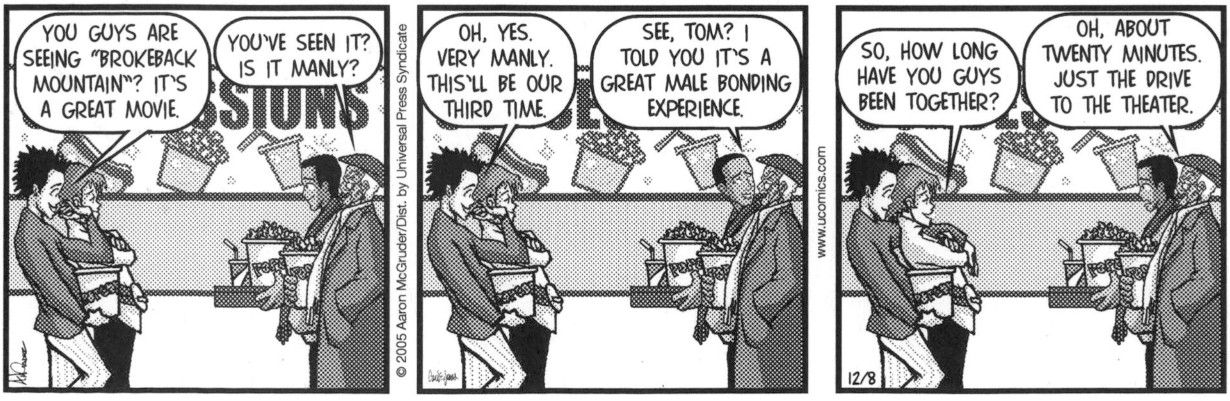
YOU GUYS ARE SEEING "BROKEBACK MOUNTAIN"? IT'S A GREAT MOVIE.
YOU'VE SEEN IT? IS IT MANLY?
© 2005 Aaron McGruder/Dist. by Universal Press Syndicate
OH, YES. VERY MANLY. THIS'LL BE OUR THIRD TIME.
SEE, TOM? I TOLD YOU IT'S A GREAT MALE BONDING EXPERIENCE.
www.ucomics.com
SO, HOW LONG HAVE YOU GUYS BEEN TOGETHER?
OH, ABOUT TWENTY MINUTES. JUST THE DRIVE TO THE THEATER.
12/8

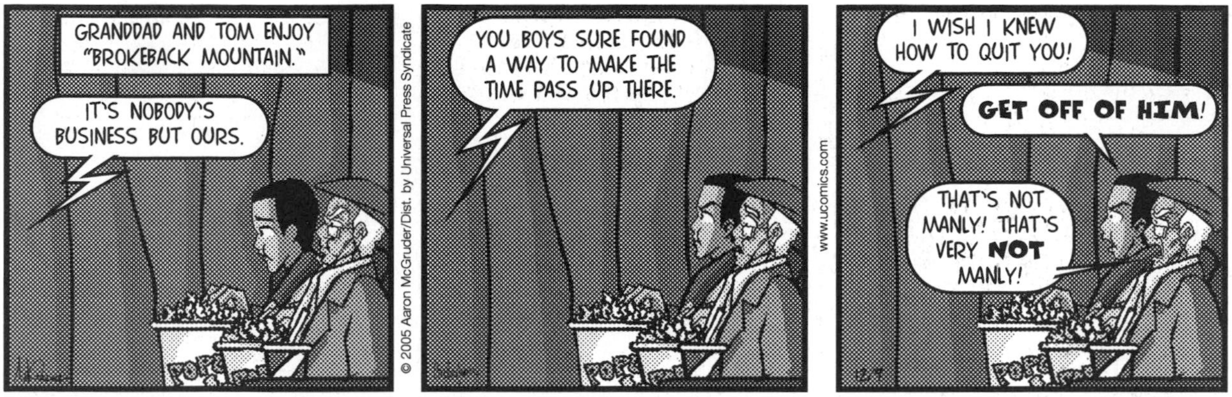
GRANDDAD AND TOM ENJOY "BROKEBACK MOUNTAIN."
IT'S NOBODY'S BUSINESS BUT OURS.
© 2005 Aaron McGruder/Dist. by Universal Press Syndicate
YOU BOYS SURE FOUND A WAY TO MAKE THE TIME PASS UP THERE.
www.ucomics.com
I WISH I KNEW HOW TO QUIT YOU!
GET OFF OF HIM!
THAT'S NOT MANLY! THAT'S VERY NOT MANLY!

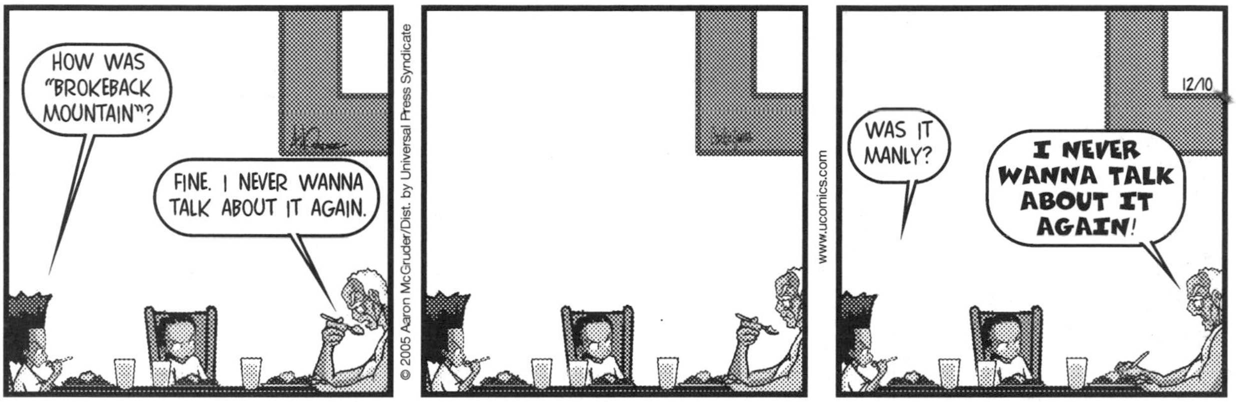
HOW WAS "BROKEBACK MOUNTAIN"?
FINE. I NEVER WANNA TALK ABOUT IT AGAIN.
© 2005 Aaron McGruder/Dist. by Universal Press Syndicate
www.ucomics.com
12/10
WAS IT MANLY?
I NEVER WANNA TALK ABOUT IT AGAIN!

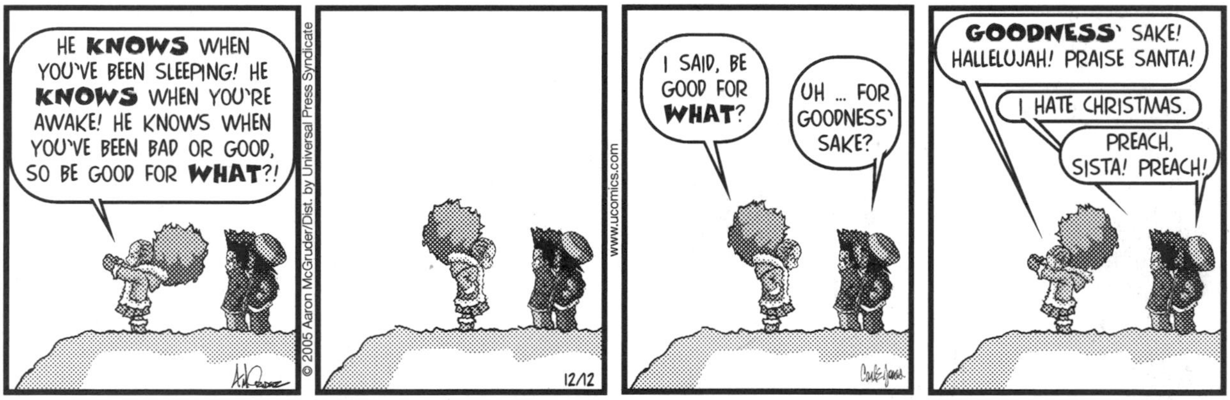
HE KNOWS WHEN YOU'VE BEEN SLEEPING! HE KNOWS WHEN YOU'RE AWAKE! HE KNOWS WHEN YOU'VE BEEN BAD OR GOOD, SO BE GOOD FOR WHAT?!
© 2005 Aaron McGruder/Dist. by Universal Press Syndicate
12/12
www.ucomics.com
I SAID, BE GOOD FOR WHAT?
UH ... FOR GOODNESS' SAKE?
GOODNESS' SAKE! HALLELUJAH! PRAISE SANTA!
I HATE CHRISTMAS.
PREACH, SISTA! PREACH!

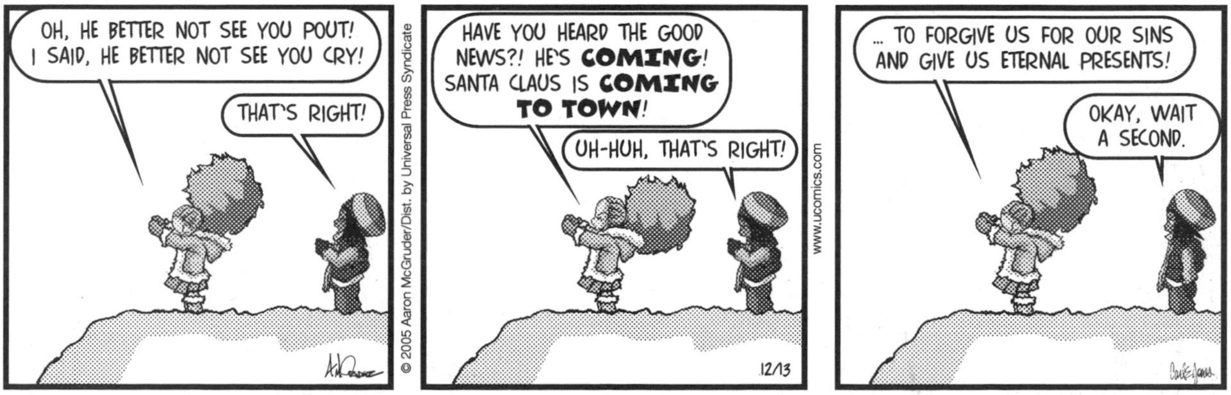
OH, HE BETTER NOT SEE YOU POUT! I SAID, HE BETTER NOT SEE YOU CRY!
THAT'S RIGHT!
© 2005 Aaron McGruder/Dist. by Universal Press Syndicate
HAVE YOU HEARD THE GOOD NEWS?! HE'S COMING! SANTA CLAUS IS COMING TO TOWN!
UH-HUH, THAT'S RIGHT!
12/13
www.ucomics.com
... TO FORGIVE US FOR OUR SINS AND GIVE US ETERNAL PRESENTS!
OKAY, WAIT A SECOND.

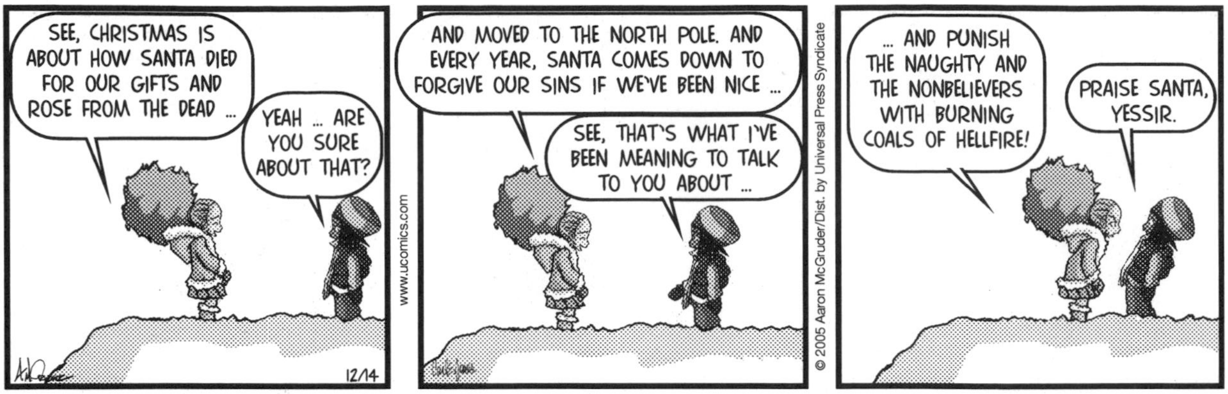
SEE, CHRISTMAS IS ABOUT HOW SANTA DIED FOR OUR GIFTS AND ROSE FROM THE DEAD ...
YEAH ... ARE YOU SURE ABOUT THAT?
12/14
www.ucomics.com
AND MOVED TO THE NORTH POLE. AND EVERY YEAR, SANTA COMES DOWN TO FORGIVE OUR SINS IF WE'VE BEEN NICE ...
SEE, THAT'S WHAT I'VE BEEN MEANING TO TALK TO YOU ABOUT ...
© 2005 Aaron McGruder/Dist. by Universal Press Syndicate
... AND PUNISH THE NAUGHTY AND THE NONBELIEVERS WITH BURNING COALS OF HELLFIRE!
PRAISE SANTA, YESSIR.

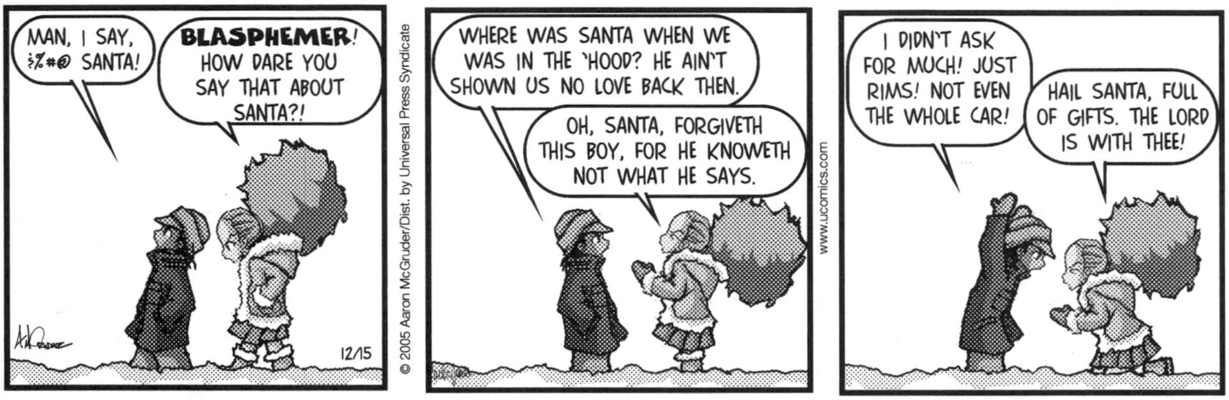
MAN, I SAY, $%#@ SANTA!
BLASPHEMER! HOW DARE YOU SAY THAT ABOUT SANTA?!
12/15
© 2005 Aaron McGruder/Dist. by Universal Press Syndicate
WHERE WAS SANTA WHEN WE WAS IN THE 'HOOD? HE AIN'T SHOWN US NO LOVE BACK THEN.
OH, SANTA, FORGIVETH THIS BOY, FOR HE KNOWETH NOT WHAT HE SAYS.
www.ucomics.com
I DIDN'T ASK FOR MUCH! JUST RIMS! NOT EVEN THE WHOLE CAR!
HAIL SANTA, FULL OF GIFTS. THE LORD IS WITH THEE!

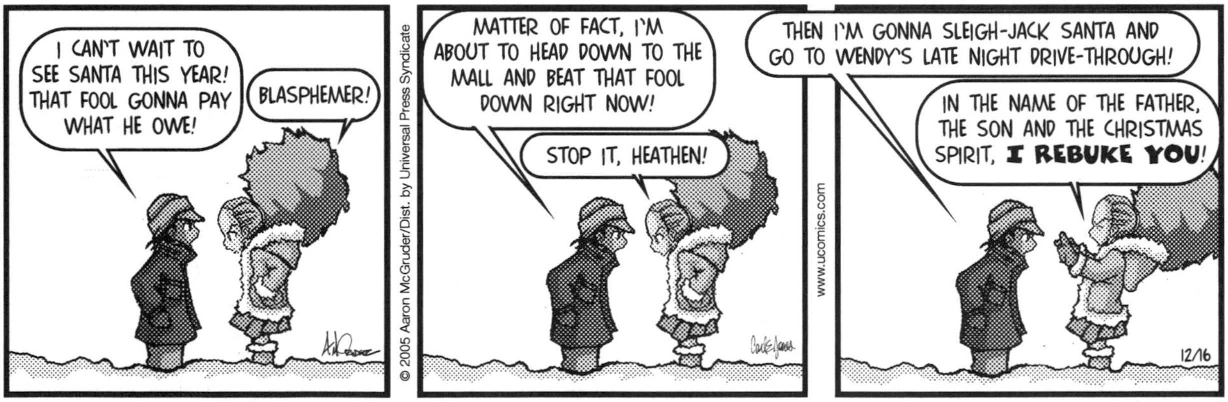
I CAN'T WAIT TO SEE SANTA THIS YEAR! THAT FOOL GONNA PAY WHAT HE OWE!
BLASPHEMER!
© 2005 Aaron McGruder/Dist. by Universal Press Syndicate
MATTER OF FACT, I'M ABOUT TO HEAD DOWN TO THE MALL AND BEAT THAT FOOL DOWN RIGHT NOW!
STOP IT, HEATHEN!
www.ucomics.com
THEN I'M GONNA SLEIGH-JACK SANTA AND GO TO WENDY'S LATE NIGHT DRIVE-THROUGH!
IN THE NAME OF THE FATHER, THE SON AND THE CHRISTMAS SPIRIT, I REBUKE YOU!
12/16

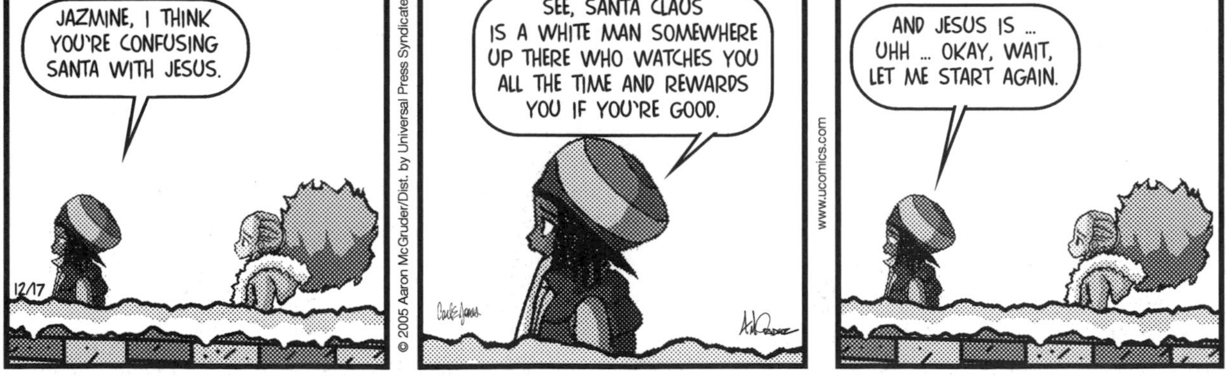
JAZMINE, I THINK YOU'RE CONFUSING SANTA WITH JESUS.
12/17
© 2005 Aaron McGruder/Dist. by Universal Press Syndicate
SEE, SANTA CLAUS IS A WHITE MAN SOMEWHERE UP THERE WHO WATCHES YOU ALL THE TIME AND REWARDS YOU IF YOU'RE GOOD.
www.ucomics.com
AND JESUS IS ... UHH ... OKAY, WAIT, LET ME START AGAIN.

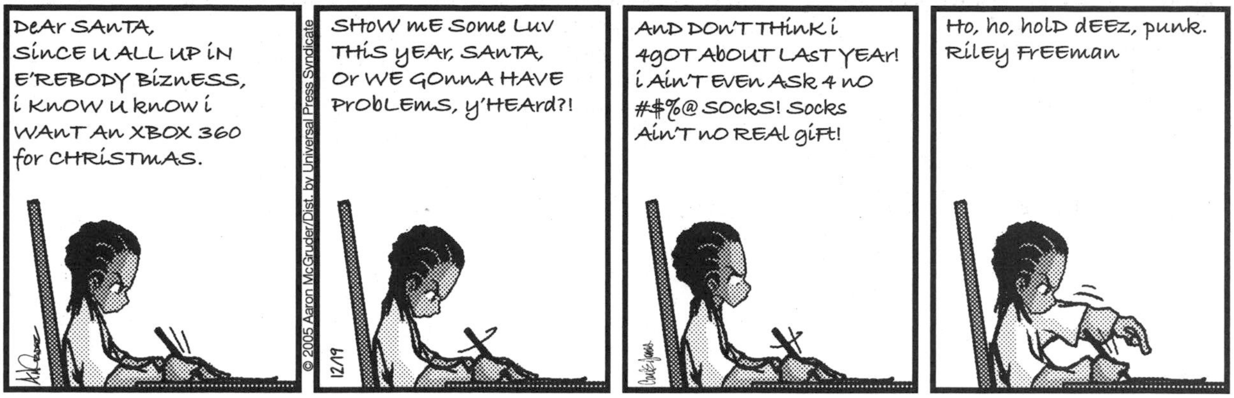

Dear Santa, since u all up in e'rebody bizness, i know u know i want an Xbox 360 for Christmas.
© 2005 Aaron McGruder/Dist. by Universal Press Syndicate
12/19
Show me some luv this year, Santa, or we gonna have problems, y'heard?!
And don't think i 4got about last year! i ain't even ask 4 no #$%@ socks! Socks ain't no real gift!
Ho, ho, hold deez, punk. Riley Freeman

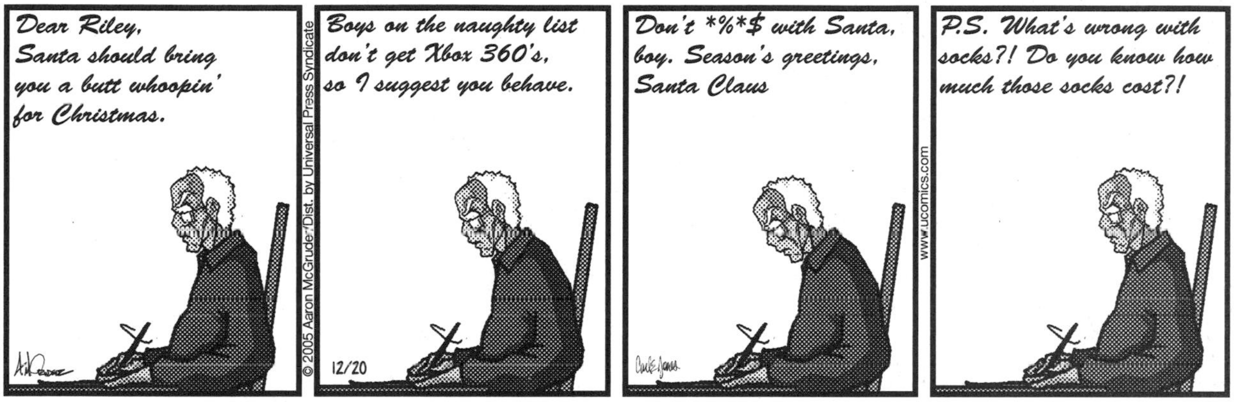

Dear Riley, Santa should bring you a butt whoopin' for Christmas.
© 2005 Aaron McGruder/Dist. by Universal Press Syndicate
12/20
Boys on the naughty list don't get Xbox 360's, so I suggest you behave.
Don't *%*$ with Santa, boy. Season's greetings, Santa Claus
www.ucomics.com
P.S. What's wrong with socks?! Do you know how much those socks cost?!

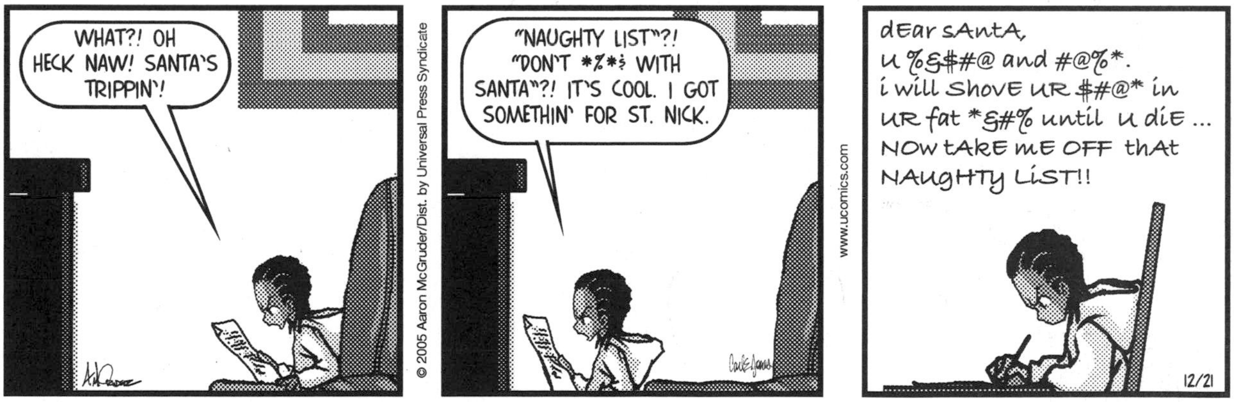

WHAT?! OH HECK NAW! SANTA'S TRIPPIN'!
© 2005 Aaron McGruder/Dist. by Universal Press Syndicate
"NAUGHTY LIST"?! "DON'T *%*$ WITH SANTA"?! IT'S COOL. I GOT SOMETHIN' FOR ST. NICK.
www.ucomics.com
dear santa, u %&$#@ and #@%*. i will shove ur $#@* in ur fat *&#% until u die ... now take me off that naughty list!!
12/21

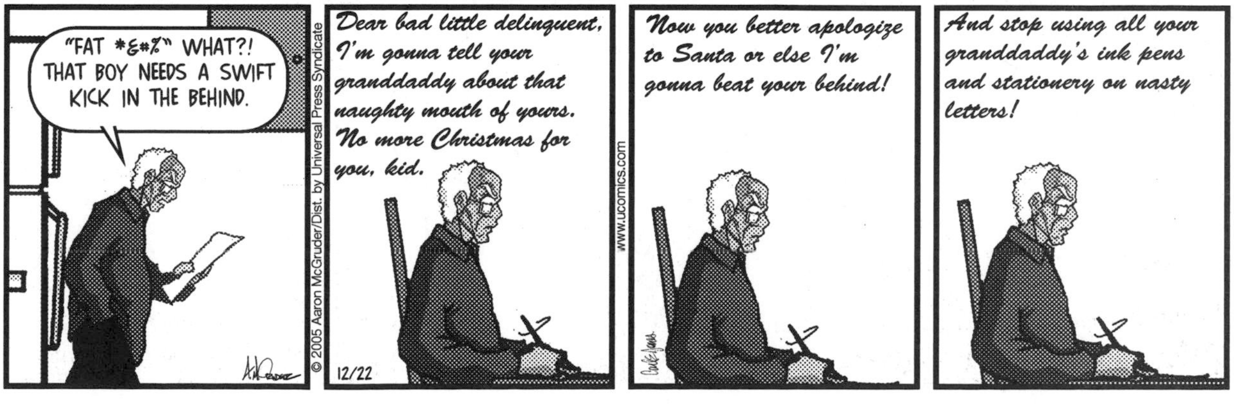

"FAT *&#%" WHAT?! THAT BOY NEEDS A SWIFT KICK IN THE BEHIND.
© 2005 Aaron McGruder/Dist. by Universal Press Syndicate
Dear bad little delinquent, I'm gonna tell your granddaddy about that naughty mouth of yours. No more Christmas for you, kid.
12/22
www.ucomics.com
Now you better apologize to Santa or else I'm gonna beat your behind!
And stop using all your granddaddy's ink pens and stationery on nasty letters!

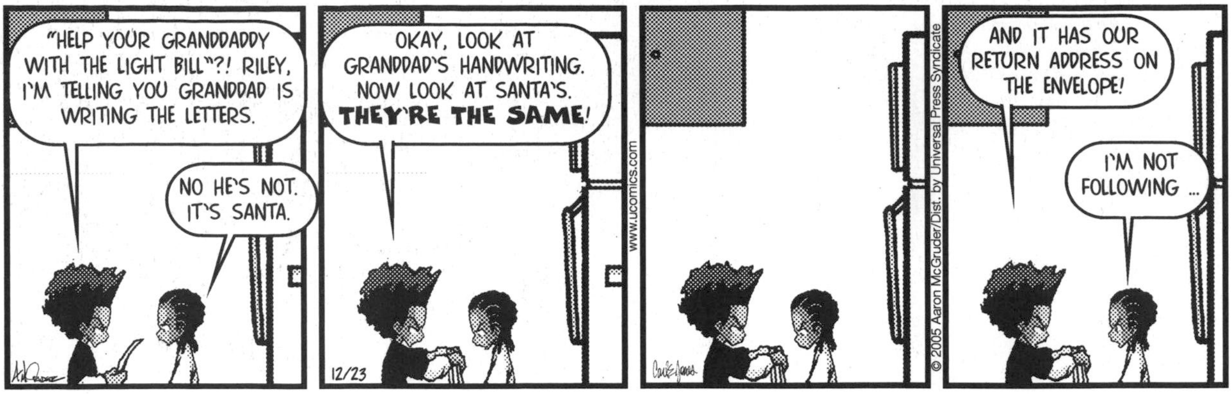
"HELP YOUR GRANDDADDY WITH THE LIGHT BILL"?! RILEY, I'M TELLING YOU GRANDDAD IS WRITING THE LETTERS.
NO HE'S NOT. IT'S SANTA.
12/23
OKAY, LOOK AT GRANDDAD'S HANDWRITING. NOW LOOK AT SANTA'S. THEY'RE THE SAME!
www.ucomics.com
© 2005 Aaron McGruder/Dist. by Universal Press Syndicate
AND IT HAS OUR RETURN ADDRESS ON THE ENVELOPE!
I'M NOT FOLLOWING ...

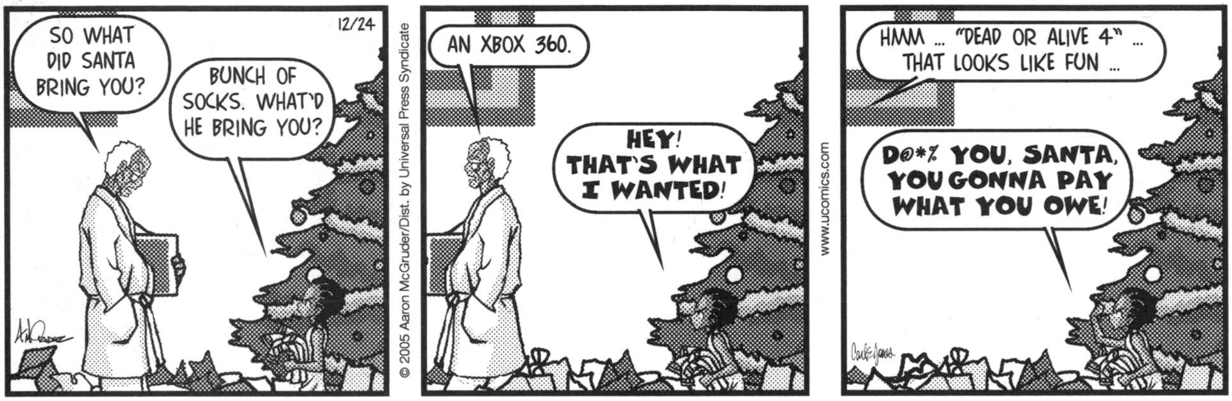
12/24
SO WHAT DID SANTA BRING YOU?
BUNCH OF SOCKS. WHAT'D HE BRING YOU?
© 2005 Aaron McGruder/Dist. by Universal Press Syndicate
AN XBOX 360.
HEY! THAT'S WHAT I WANTED!
www.ucomics.com
HMM ... "DEAD OR ALIVE 4" ... THAT LOOKS LIKE FUN ...
D@*% YOU, SANTA, YOU GONNA PAY WHAT YOU OWE!

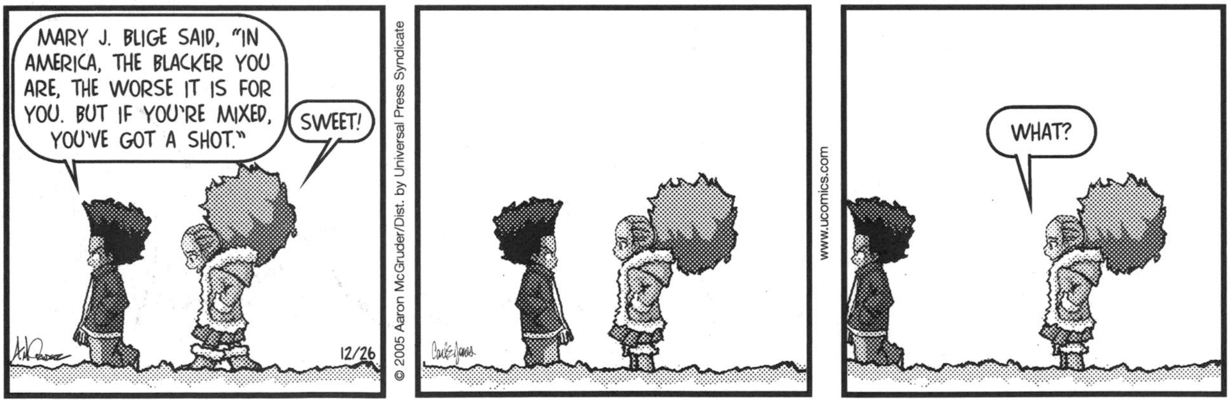
MARY J. BLIGE SAID, "IN AMERICA, THE BLACKER YOU ARE, THE WORSE IT IS FOR YOU. BUT IF YOU'RE MIXED, YOU'VE GOT A SHOT."
SWEET!
12/26
© 2005 Aaron McGruder/Dist. by Universal Press Syndicate
www.ucomics.com
WHAT?

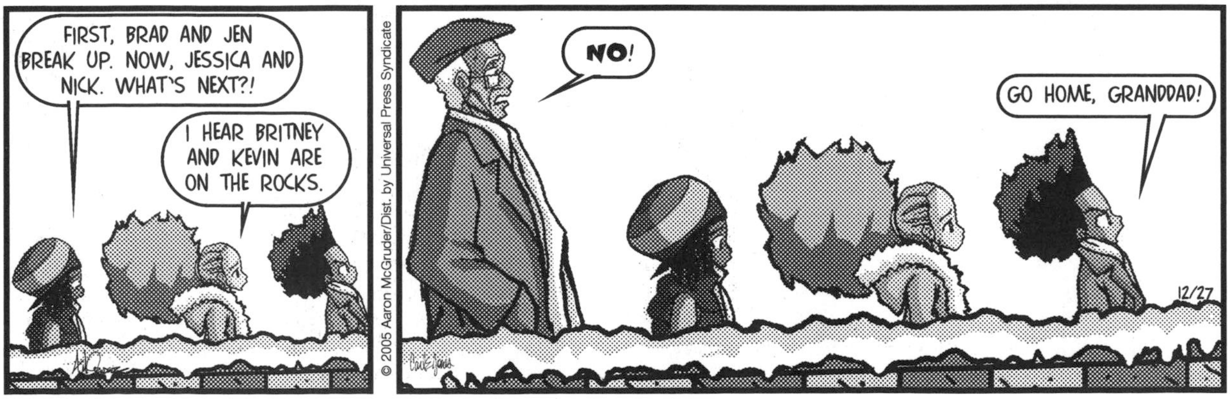
FIRST, BRAD AND JEN BREAK UP. NOW, JESSICA AND NICK. WHAT'S NEXT?!
I HEAR BRITNEY AND KEVIN ARE ON THE ROCKS.
© 2005 Aaron McGruder/Dist. by Universal Press Syndicate
NO!
GO HOME, GRANDDAD!
12/27

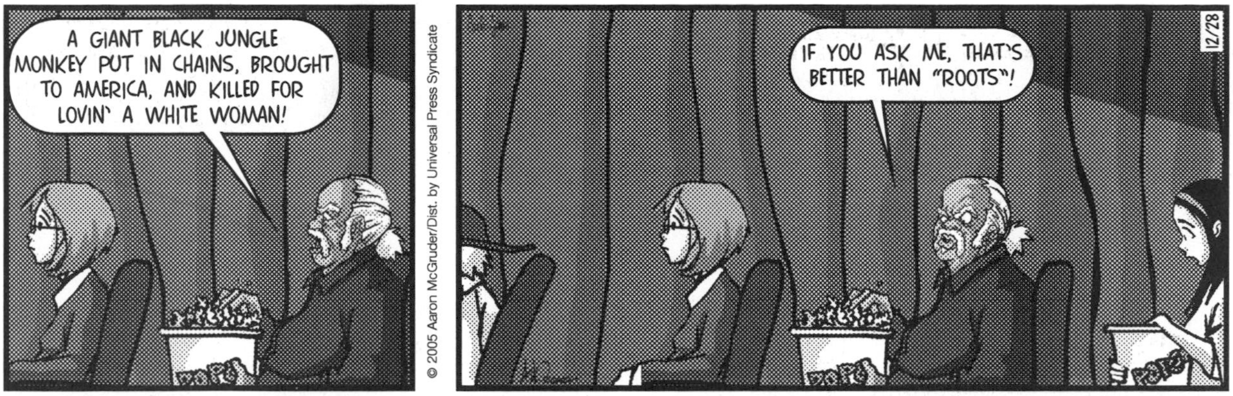
A GIANT BLACK JUNGLE MONKEY PUT IN CHAINS, BROUGHT TO AMERICA, AND KILLED FOR LOVIN' A WHITE WOMAN!
© 2005 Aaron McGruder/Dist. by Universal Press Syndicate
12/28
IF YOU ASK ME, THAT'S BETTER THAN "ROOTS"!

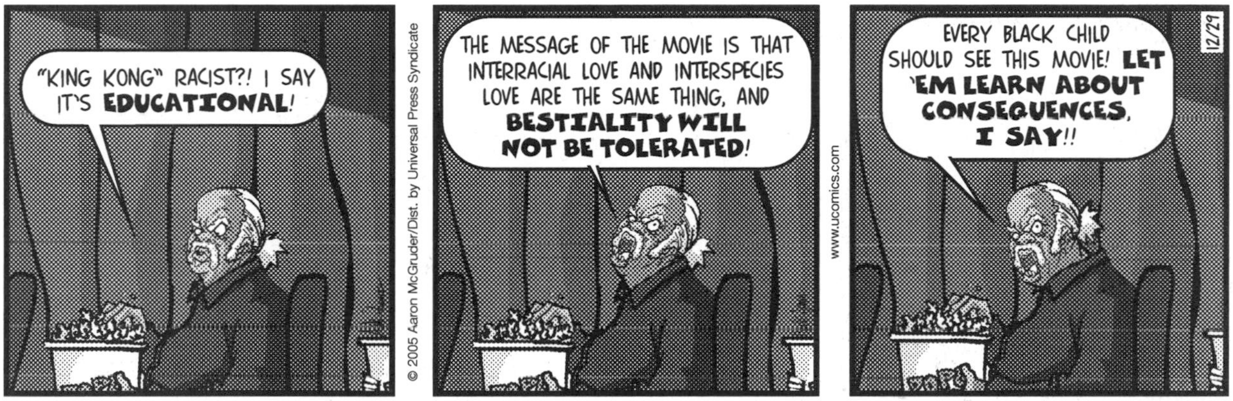
"KING KONG" RACIST?! I SAY IT'S **EDUCATIONAL**!
© 2005 Aaron McGruder/Dist. by Universal Press Syndicate
THE MESSAGE OF THE MOVIE IS THAT INTERRACIAL LOVE AND INTERSPECIES LOVE ARE THE SAME THING, AND **BESTIALITY WILL NOT BE TOLERATED**!
www.ucomics.com
12/29
EVERY BLACK CHILD SHOULD SEE THIS MOVIE! **LET 'EM LEARN ABOUT CONSEQUENCES, I SAY**!!

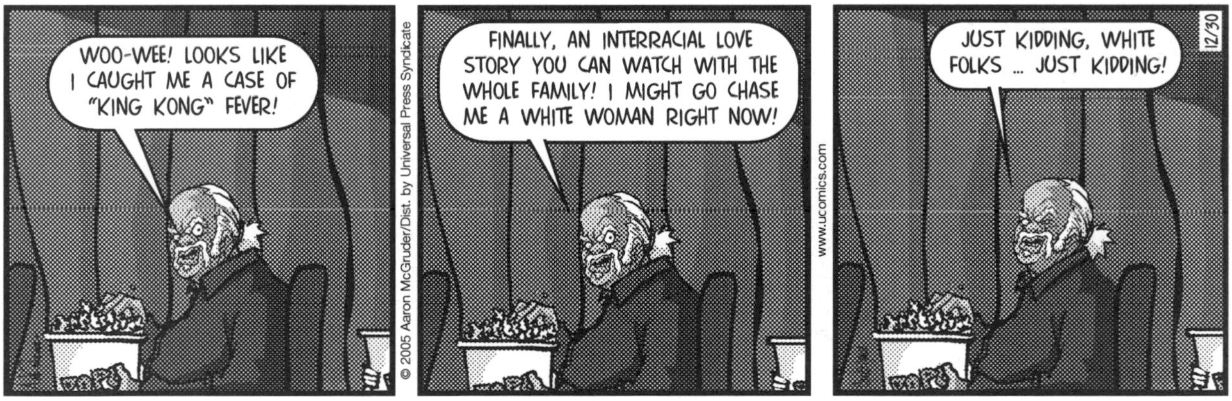
WOO-WEE! LOOKS LIKE I CAUGHT ME A CASE OF "KING KONG" FEVER!
© 2005 Aaron McGruder/Dist. by Universal Press Syndicate
FINALLY, AN INTERRACIAL LOVE STORY YOU CAN WATCH WITH THE WHOLE FAMILY! I MIGHT GO CHASE ME A WHITE WOMAN RIGHT NOW!
www.ucomics.com
12/30
JUST KIDDING, WHITE FOLKS ... JUST KIDDING!

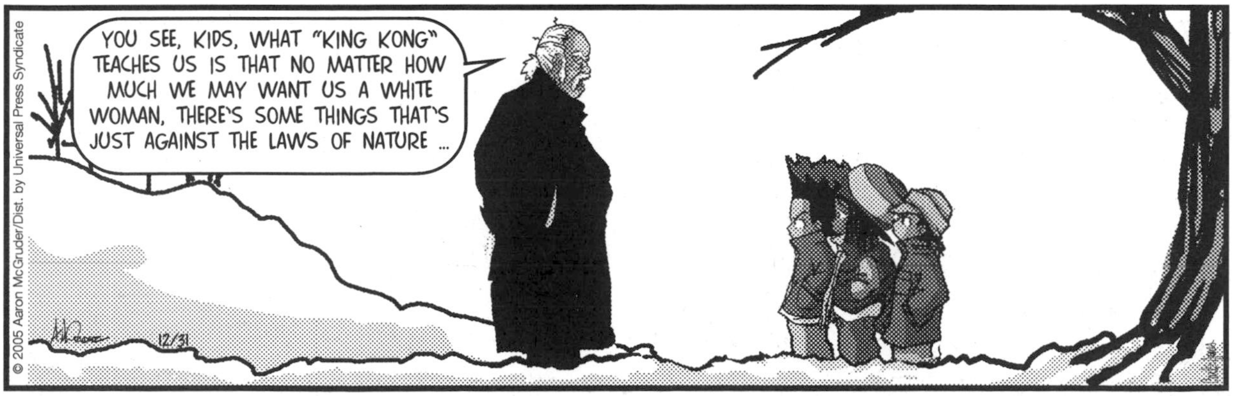
© 2005 Aaron McGruder/Dist. by Universal Press Syndicate
YOU SEE, KIDS, WHAT "KING KONG" TEACHES US IS THAT NO MATTER HOW MUCH WE MAY WANT US A WHITE WOMAN, THERE'S SOME THINGS THAT'S JUST AGAINST THE LAWS OF NATURE ...
12/31

PART

II

THE MEDIA

INTRODUCTION TO PART II

I'm often asked when I'm going to be on Bill Maher's show again or *Nightline* or whatever, but I think for the most part those days are behind me. I never really enjoyed going on television—I think I look goofy and the opportunity for catastrophic embarrassment on live TV was too much stress. I did all the press I could do early on in my career—it seemed to be the best way to help the strip find its audience. Later, after 9/11, I did a lot of interviews because I had a lot to say. Now, I kinda enjoy letting the work speak for itself. That's the great thing about notoriety . . . it's really easy to get rid of once you're sick of it. All you have to do is stop talking.

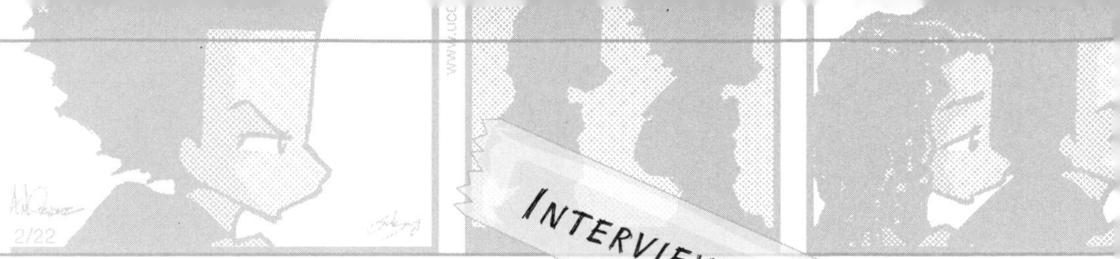

CBS News
AUGUST 31, 1999

INTERVIEW . . .

Aaron McGruder, Cartoonist, Talks About His Sometimes Controversial Strip, *Boondocks*

HATTIE KAUFFMAN, co-host: There's a new comic strip that challenges readers to laugh at their own prejudices. The strip, *The Boondocks*, features an African American kid who has no problem confronting racial issues, like this story line. Our star, Huey, chats online with director George Lucas about his movie, *Star Wars: The Phantom Menace.* He writes, "Mr. Lucas, I'm writing to commend you on your choice of Samuel L. Jackson to play the role of a Jedi Knight in the upcoming *Star Wars* film. Mr. Jackson is one of Hollywood's finest thespians, and I am confident that if any feature film is worthy of his immense talents, it will be your highly anticipated prequel. Hmm—but he had better not be the first one to die."

Twenty-five-year-old Aaron McGruder is the talent behind the comic that's been picked up by nearly 200 papers, and he joins us this morning.

Sounds like Huey doesn't take any crap.

Mr. AARON McGRUDER (cartoonist): No. No, he doesn't. Not much, no.

KAUFFMAN: First of all, congratulations on your success . . .

Mr. McGRUDER: Thank you.

KAUFFMAN: . . . 25 years old, 200 papers carrying it. Are—are you surprised at this?

Mr. McGRUDER: Yeah. It takes awhile for strips to gain an audience, so I—I was told I'd launch about 30 papers, and that would be a good launch.

KAUFFMAN: It takes awhile for the audience to—to connect with that character.

Mr. McGRUDER: Yeah.

KAUFFMAN: Tell us about Huey. Who is he?

Mr. McGRUDER: Huey is a—is the radical scholar. He's roughly nine, 10 years old. He's spent his first years of life in Chicago, recently moved to this fictional all-white suburb, and is sort of clashing with the—the folks who live there now, and he's got very strong militant beliefs, and . . .

KAUFFMAN: In fact, we've got another comic that shows him walking around the suburb there. Can we put that one up on the screen? He says, "Look, I just moved in across the"—oh, no, this is where he's talking to his neighbor, Jazmine.

Mr. McGRUDER: Right. And then Jazmine is a quote, unquote, "biracial girl." She has a black father and a white mother, and Huey and Jazmine clash as to the—the nature of black identity.

KAUFFMAN: Yeah. She says, "I moved in across the street. My name's Jazmine. What's yours?" "Huey. It's good to have more black people around." She says, "Ah, gee, why would you think I'm, ah, black?" And he says, "Well, first, Mariah, your Afro is bigger than mine." "I don't have an Afro. My hair's just a little frizzy." And he says, "Angela Davis's hair was a little freez—frizzy. You have an Afro." Now look at this: "I do not! And who is Angela Davis?" So you're poking fun at her and her lack of information?

Mr. McGRUDER: Yeah. In a—in a—in a—not in a cruel way, though. I—I just—you know, I think, you know, there's a lot of black people who don't know about ourselves.

KAUFFMAN: Uh-huh.

Mr. McGRUDER: And there's a lot of diverse opinions as to what it means to be black and—and exactly where you draw the color line.

KAUFFMAN: And you, as Huey, are not afraid to take on anybody. This is not just black and white.

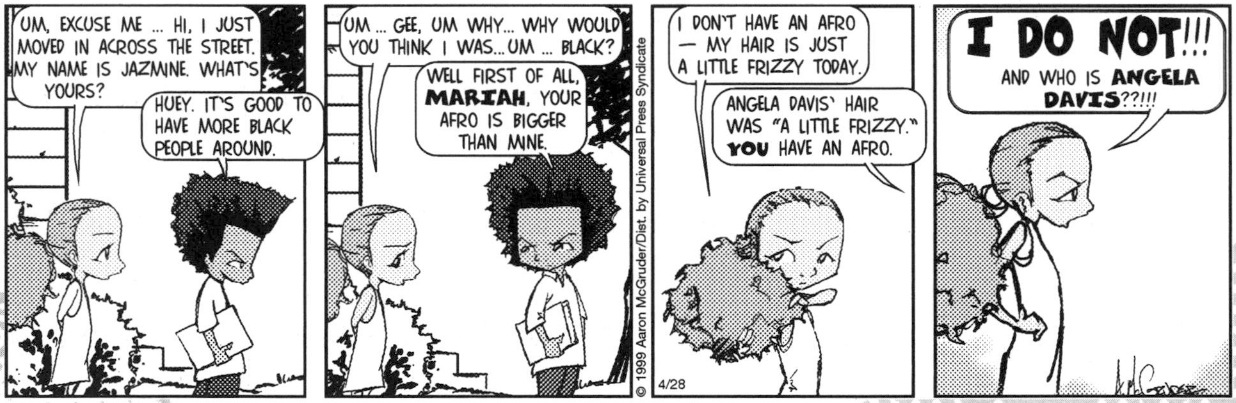
UM, EXCUSE ME ... HI, I JUST MOVED IN ACROSS THE STREET. MY NAME IS JAZMINE. WHAT'S YOURS?
HUEY. IT'S GOOD TO HAVE MORE BLACK PEOPLE AROUND.
UM ... GEE, UM WHY... WHY WOULD YOU THINK I WAS...UM ... BLACK?
WELL FIRST OF ALL, MARIAH, YOUR AFRO IS BIGGER THAN MINE.
© 1999 Aaron McGruder/Dist. by Universal Press Syndicate
I DON'T HAVE AN AFRO — MY HAIR IS JUST A LITTLE FRIZZY TODAY.
ANGELA DAVIS' HAIR WAS "A LITTLE FRIZZY." YOU HAVE AN AFRO.
4/28
I DO NOT!!!
AND WHO IS ANGELA DAVIS??!!!

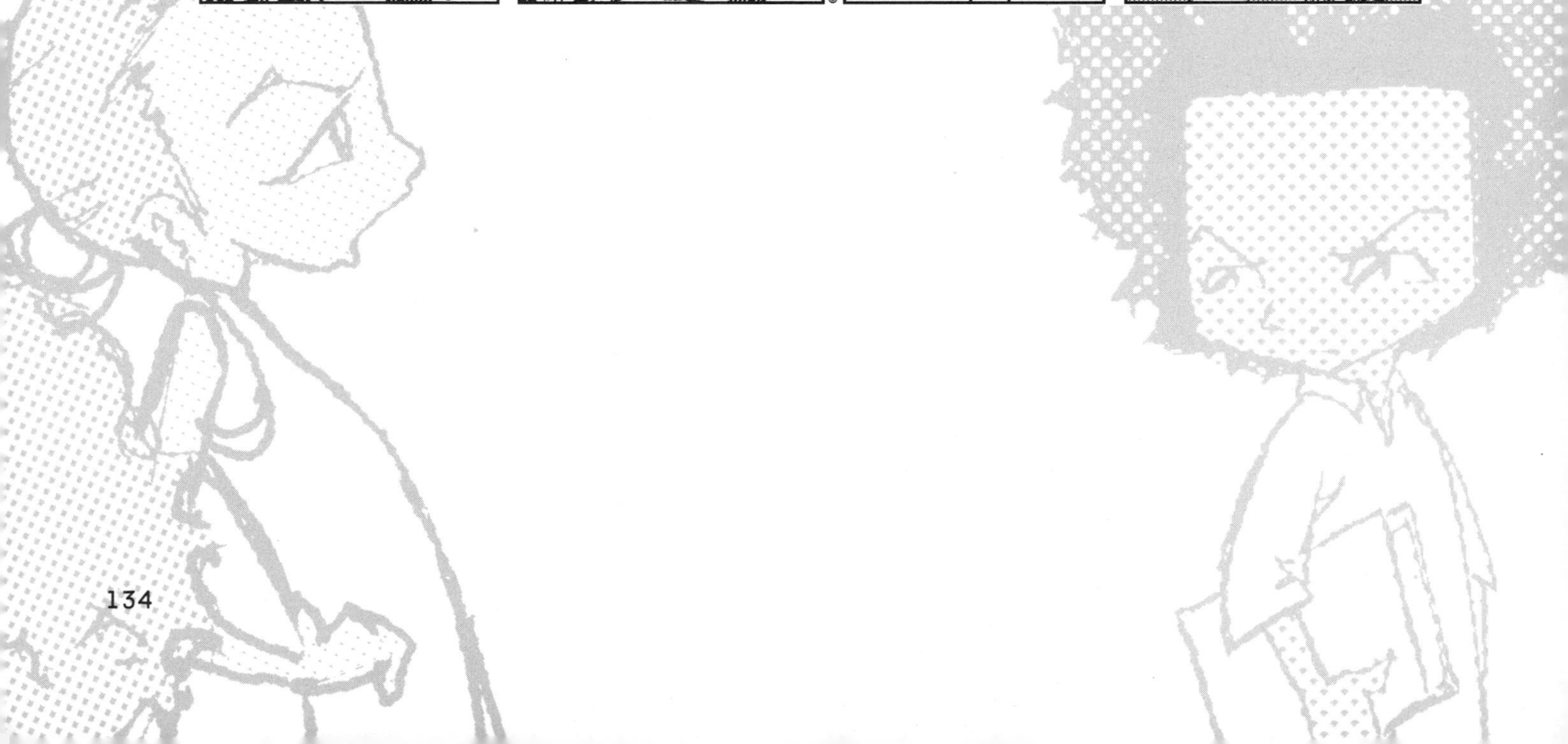

Mr. McGRUDER: Yeah. Well, I'm not Huey. I'm—I think I'm—I'm sort of all of the characters. I have to write for all of them every day.

KAUFFMAN: Uh-huh.

Mr. McGRUDER: And so they all have to really come from within the creator, I believe.

KAUFFMAN: OK. But, again, you're not afraid . . .

Mr. McGRUDER: No.

KAUFFMAN: . . . to offend . . .

Mr. McGRUDER: Well . . .

KAUFFMAN: . . . other members of the black community.

Mr. McGRUDER: . . . I—I—I don't think that's the right way to put it.

KAUFFMAN: No?

Mr. McGRUDER: I just think I'm not afraid to explore issues that have not been explored before. It is not my desire to offend anyone.

KAUFFMAN: Uh-huh. But . . .

Mr. McGRUDER: It happens, but—you know?

KAUFFMAN: The newspapers are getting lots of letters on this, supportive and—and detractors. What do some of your supporters say?

Mr. McGRUDER: Well, a lot of the supporters find that it—it truly represents their experiences that they've had. It—it deals with things they've never seen before that are very real to them, and—and a lot of those supporters, you know,

that—well, I should say that support really does transcend age and race categories. A lot of people have found that it—it makes them re-examine their own beliefs and their own perspectives on race in American society in general.

KAUFFMAN: Race is such a touchy issue. Do you think humor is a good way to address it?

Mr. McGRUDER: I think it is. I think it—it allows people to sort of let their guard down and—and rethink some issues. Certainly, it's been done effectively by stand-up comics. I mean, Chris Rock and Richard Pryor, you know, have—have addressed race in a—I think in a very effective way. I'm just doing it in a different medium.

KAUFFMAN: And you're the first one to do it as a comic strip.

Mr. McGRUDER: So overtly, yeah. Yeah.

KAUFFMAN: And next, will there be a Huey cartoon character on television?

Mr. McGRUDER: Television or film. I'm deciding on that right now.

KAUFFMAN: You're deciding and you're 25 years old! Great success. Congratulations.

Mr. McGRUDER: Thank you very much.

KAUFFMAN: Thank you for being with us this morning.

Mr. McGRUDER: Thank you.

The Sacramento Bee
JUNE 5, 2000

ARTICLE . . .

Artist Probes "Curious Parallel" in Gun Culture

FAHIZAH ALIM

Aaron McGruder's popular comic strip, *The Boondocks*, continues to plunge head-on into controversy. This time, he takes on the National Rifle Association as his young hip-hop character, Riley, explains his affinity for guns in a series of panels continuing today in papers across the country, including the *Bee*.

"This series is meant to draw a sort of curious parallel between black youth popular culture's current obsession with guns and the very white conservative cross-section of America that has the same obsession with gunplay," the 26-year-old McGruder says in a recent phone interview.

"These groups are very different, but both are celebrating firearms," he says, adding that he believes the NRA puts "a positive spin on (gun ownership) whereas young blacks (with guns) are just considered thugs. . . .

"It is very interesting where those philosophies agree and where they diverge. To me, that is what is interesting—what they have in common and what they don't."

Steve Helsley, a local spokesman for the NRA, denies there are similarities between his organization and what he calls "hip-hop culture."

"If hip-hop culture is what I see on TV, we share nothing with them. Everything I see in videos is the handling of guns incorrectly and irresponsibly. We believe the solution to America's gun problem is education. And we have no fascination with gunplay, although many people do collect firearms."

In the current storyline, Riley, who is fascinated with gang culture, tells his brother, Huey, a self-described "radical scholar," that he's joining the NRA because it supports kids having guns and is really "hard core."

McGruder says he initially started to do a series that suggested that the NRA teaches kids how to improve their aim so that when they go into schools to kill, they don't shoot any unintended victims.

He decided against it and penned the current series.

"Let me say that the strip pokes light fun at the NRA," McGruder says. "But I think it's fun within reason. It's not any more fun than I have poked at the NAACP (National Association for the Advancement of Colored People), and it is well within the normal range of the strip.

"I am not singling them out abnormally—only raising interesting questions. . . .

"I am not anti-gun," McGruder says. "And I don't believe guns should be banned. But the whole point is not to come down pro- or anti-gun; it's more the way . . . we look at those different cross-sections of America and their obsession with guns."

Certainly, *The Boondocks* has generated controversy since it was launched a year ago. But the controversy has not appeared to deter its success.

The strip chronicles the experiences of two young African American kids who recently moved to suburbia from the inner-city. It appears in more than 250 papers, with three or four papers having dropped it since its launch, according to Universal Press Syndicate, which distributes *The Boondocks*.

Subjects have touched on interracial marriage, racists, presidential candidates and explicit song lyrics. The strip also has taken sharp jabs at Black Entertainment Television's Bob Johnson and anti-affirmative action crusader Ward Connerly.

But its editors stand behind *The Boondocks*.

"I get a lot of calls," says Greg Melvin, associate editor at Universal and McGruder's editor. "However, we have found that most of the feedback is overwhelmingly positive. A lot of the calls are from people who say that, finally, there is something there for them.

"*Boondocks* is bringing something to the comic pages like nothing that's been there before. And newspapers keep saying that they want young readers."

However, some older readers feel that McGruder's hard-edged social and political commentary does not belong on the comic pages.

"I have always been offended by it. There's no humor in it. It seems to be attack, attack," says John Bowman, a retired schoolteacher who is now a criminal defense attorney in Sacramento. "It would solve the problem if *Boondocks* was placed on the editorial page."

Indeed, the *Atlanta Journal-Constitution* does run the strip on its editorial pages.

And in January, the *Washington Post* decided not to run a strip attacking the owner of Black Entertainment Television because it was deemed too personal.

Meanwhile, in February, the *Chicago Tribune* pulled a couple of strips that suggested that singer Whitney Houston abuses drugs, deeming them to be "inappropriate."

But McGruder and his editor maintain that the strip always has a joke or a punch line.

"I would say that *Boondocks* definitely entertains," Melvin says. "Aaron is well aware that he is writing and drawing a controversial strip, but he doesn't court controversy for the mere sake of it.

"It does mean, however, that his characters in the strip will probably say and do things that might not please all readers of newspapers."

McGruder, who moved to Los Angeles from a Maryland suburb in October to take advantage of opportunities in television broadcasting, says he's walking the tightrope of "self-censorship" by being true to the spirit of the strip and getting it into the nation's papers.

"There are things worth saying, but there are repercussions," he says. "I often have to ask myself, 'Is what I am saying more important than people never seeing the strip again?'"

Los Angeles Magazine
AUGUST 1, 2001

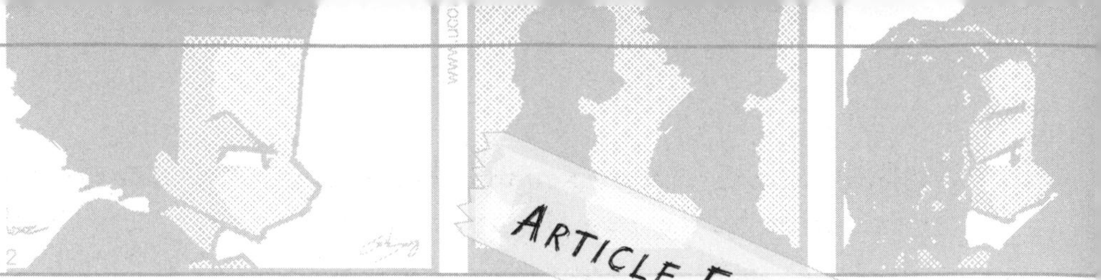

ARTICLE EXCERPT . . .

Down in the *Boondocks:* Cartoonist Aaron McGruder

Aaron McGruder Draws a World Where *Peanuts* and P-Diddy, Malcolm X and *X-Men* All Meet

STEPHANIE KANG

Uncompromising and caustically intelligent, *The Boondocks* crosses the conservative and even reactionary pages of the comics section and plants a flag where issues of racial identity, politics, and hip-hop music meet. . . .

Although he denies that Huey is his alter ego, **McGruder** admits that *The Boondocks* is "thematically autobiographical," echoing his experiences growing up in the predominantly white community of Columbia, Maryland. "I went through my periods," he says. "As a black kid in the suburbs, you had two choices: emphasize your blackness or blend in with the white kids." In his late teens McGruder drew from this conflict, envisioning a comic strip that satirized notions of black identity and combined his love of hip hop, politics, and race with art.

The Boondocks was first seen in 1996 on the Web site Hitlist. Soon came a brief stint at his alma mater, with the University of Maryland's independent newspaper, and in the hip-hop magazine *The Source.* A chance meeting in Chicago the next year at a National Association of Black Journalists convention led to a five-year, six-figure contract with Universal Press Syndicate.

Despite its brash tone, the strip's national debut in April 1999—in approximately 160 newspapers—was one of the biggest in comics history, surpassing the start-up numbers for such titans as *Doonesbury* and *Calvin and Hobbes*. Its success has spawned two books and negotiations for a television series. At 27 McGruder is a generation or two younger than most comic strip creators today. He's also one of no more than ten black cartoonists in syndication. But what makes *The Boondocks* unique—even more than its focus on middle-class black identity—is its youthful sensibility. . . .

"McGruder's made his mark and earned his readers by representing the hip-hop generation."

. . . there are a steady number of readers who appreciate McGruder's voice. "Finally a comic strip defines my place, my attitude, my life as a young black man," read one recent letter. Or as "Bobby" wrote on the *Boondocks* Web site, "He gives my thoughts a voice."

Some critics fail to see that rather than glorify gangsters, McGruder lampoons contemporary black culture, never more so than in his description of Riley as "shortsighted, ignorant, and concerned only with instant gratification." When

Riley contemplates turning to the straight path, he tallies up his options—playing pro ball, cutting a platinum album, or making blockbuster movies—only to stick to his thug life ambitions in the name of "keepin' it real."

McGruder has inadvertently stepped from obscurity into the impossible role of national spokesperson. "When you have so few black stories being told, each individual story has the pressure of representing more than it possibly can," he says. His success at criticizing black America has in turn made McGruder responsible for propagating a positive black image—ironic for someone who feels isolated from mainstream black culture. "I feel obsolete," he says. "I feel like an artifact among black people." . . .

"I've never seen him back down from a fight," says Tavis Smiley, former host of the talk show *BET Tonight*. "I told somebody, 'If you ever see Aaron McGruder in a fight with a bear, you help the bear.' ". . .

The cartoonist sums up his success by noting that money and fame notwithstanding, "at the end of the day, there's nothing like being an articulate, intelligent person who knows who they are and where they came from."

New York Newsday
OCTOBER 8, 2001

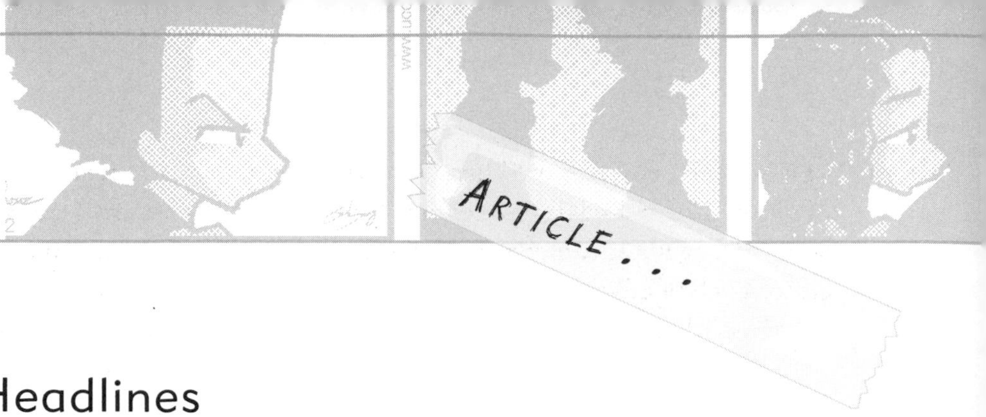
ARTICLE . . .

Drawing on the Headlines

Cartoonists take a stand, mixing tragedy and comedy in the comics

BETH WHITEHOUSE

When comic strip creators feel pain, they express it in their unique way, through the panes of their strips, through the words of their cartoon characters. And so a number of artists, some of whom have always tackled political issues, are taking on the World Trade Center attack.

Strips from *Doonesbury* to *The Boondocks* to *Mallard Fillmore* to *Hagar the Horrible* are delving into the events, emotions and politics of Sept. 11 and the aftermath. In *Doonesbury*, for instance, Mike will attend the funeral of a former boss who perished in the Twin Towers; on the flight to New York he'll struggle with ethnic profiling when he's seated next to a Muslim man.

In *The Boondocks*, the following exchange will occur this week: "Hasn't the president said over and over that we have to get back to normal?" "Yeah." "And what do I normally do?" "Criticize Bush." "So not criticizing Bush would kinda be like letting the terrorists win, right?"

It's natural that the terrorist attack would find its way into the comics, several strip creators said. It's taken until this week for the majority to address the attack because the artists normally submit their work several weeks in advance. "The cartoons you're seeing right now were done in the immediate aftermath," said Wiley Miller, who draws *Non Sequitur*. "This is a reflex act, a way of venting our emotions."

While some of the strips are political, others will focus on memorializing the fallen or embracing our country's newfound patriotism. "I have an inherent aversion to doing things that seem sappy," said *Mallard Fillmore* creator Bruce Tinsley of his uplifting strips, "but against the backdrop of what's happened . . . for one of the rare times in my career, I don't think I can be too positive."

Some of the strips will likely be controversial. Area newspaper editors are monitoring the comics to guard against offending New Yorkers who are particularly sensitive during this period. *Newsday*, for instance, pulled *The Boondocks* just after the attack because creator Aaron McGruder criticized previous U.S. support of Osama bin Laden when he fought the Soviet invasion of Afghanistan. "The points he made we've had in newspaper reports and editorials," said *Newsday* editor Anthony Marro. But because of the tone, it was replaced temporarily by previous *Boondocks* strips, he said.

The *New York Daily News* is still not running

The Boondocks weekdays. "There's a certain kind of heavy-duty political commentary that doesn't really belong in the funny pages," said *Daily News* editor in chief Edward Kosner.

Artist McGruder said *The Boondocks* has always been political, and that to draw about anything other than the attack right now would be a waste of time.

"I feel America started moving very quickly in a dangerous direction with the drumbeating and warmongering," McGruder said. "'They're evil and we're not'—that's such a fifth-grade way of looking at conflict. It is the responsibility of any thinking individual with a voice to say whatever they can say within their medium. You can't underestimate the power of one voice."

City Paper (Philadelphia)
NOVEMBER 5, 2001

INTERVIEW . . .

Boondocks Speaks: An Interview with Aaron McGruder

JENNIFER A. CARBIN

Aaron McGruder, creator of *The Boondocks* comic strip, is both older than his 27 years (pissed off, cynical and focused) and a big kid (he snacks on dry cereal, possesses a drawing style influenced by Japanese anime and is devoted to all things *Star Wars*). Reached at home on a recent morning, he's listening to the soundtrack of the original film, for which he has a special fondness—his first memory is of viewing it.

His job, which involves working from home and inking the adventures of a group of African-American kids adjusting to life in an integrated, predominantly white suburb and led by radical Huey Freeman, would be the envy of anyone who didn't understand the pressures of turning in seven strips each week, strips that take on the powers that be and that get pulled with some regularity.

In the wake of the events of Sept. 11, McGruder's strip was pulled from numerous newspapers because of its dissenting politics. Since then, he's been going beyond his usual *Boondocks* material—which includes discussion of political and societal hypocrisy—to take on censorship, U.S. policy and media lunacy. When he's not inking, he's writing scripts for the impending *Boondocks* TV show and screenplays, his latest being a political comedy.

Q: You started addressing the terrorist attacks on Sept. 24. You got to it faster than other strip creators. What influenced that?

A: One, I push my deadlines closer than anybody else, or let's say it this way: I'm really late. The only other cartoonist that would address it head on is Garry Trudeau, and being the better cartoonist, he gets his strips in a couple days earlier than I do . . . So I had more time to really think about it. [Also,] I think he didn't want to get into it that week. It was a big debate for me whether or not to do it so soon.

Q: Many papers have pulled your strips recently; the *New York Daily News* isn't running it weekdays. Does that flatter you or piss you off? Are you even aware of it?

A: I'm aware of it. It actually doesn't do either. I anticipated getting canceled by the *New York Daily News* while I was doing the strips . . . I figured given New York, the sensitivity there, it wouldn't go over well and I'd probably get dropped from the New York papers. But for me it was a worthwhile gamble. And there's still no guarantee that the *New York Daily News* will ever start running it again. . . . It's New York City . . . and they've gone through a lot, and you can't really expect them to take the jokes well. I've tried to be really careful to not make light at all of the death and suffering, which, like everybody else, I feel really bad about. But I have a different perspective on things than what the media's putting out, and I thought it was important to voice that, and if it meant losing the New York papers, I think it was worth it.

Q: Do you pull back from ideas that seem too inflammatory or controversial?

A: Yeah! That's not just now, that's always. . . . Especially when you're somebody that likes to talk about the president, there's just so much you can't say, for legal reasons . . . You have to be very careful to never threaten the president. There has been only once in the past few weeks that the wording of a strip had to actually be changed for that reason. The editors looked at it . . . it was one of the strips where Huey was calling the FBI [terrorist] hotline [to report George W. Bush] and the strip ended with, "Make sure you bring the really tight handcuffs." He was talking about going to the White House. It was originally written as, "Make sure you bring nightsticks." They said, "You know, that's not a good idea." And I said, "You're right."

Q: You get to address race, class and biracial issues, and the bullshit of politics. How satisfying is it to have a place to vent every day?

A: It's really satisfying sometimes, and sometimes you just don't have anything to talk about. You're like, "You know what? I'm not passionate about anything this week. I just want to relax." Certainly at a time like this, when you're sort of sitting home screaming at the television, you're

like, "Oh wait, I don't have to scream at the television. I actually have a big voice." . . . Then it's really, really good.

Q: How closely do Huey's opinions come to your own?

A: It would be inaccurate to say that Huey's opinions are my own. I think there's a broad opinion being put out through the strip with a combination of all the characters' voices, and it's really up to the reader to figure out what that is. Beyond that, I don't think the importance of the strip is about my own personal political agenda. I think the strip [challenges] people to think differently, and that to me is far more important than to have people thinking like me—[I want] to have people questioning what they're told on a daily basis.

Q: Huey and [the innocent, biracial] Jazmine DuBois—with their exchanges, there is just this whole other dimension to the Huey thing . . . It's almost sweet.

A. It's supposed to be kind of sweet . . . It's a really important dynamic. . . . I'm not really good at developing that type of stuff a lot in the tiny spaces of the strip. So most of that stuff's gonna get played out on television.

Q: An announcement?

A: It's not an official announcement yet, but it'll be 2002. Hopefully—it's Hollywood, so shit could fall through at any time.

Q: This must be exciting.

A: It's been a two-year process with several different networks, so at this point the excitement is way gone. It's been six- to eight-month negotiations at a time, having them fall through and starting again with another network.

Q: Are you going to explode into a merchandising bonanza?

A: It'll be tasteful. [Laughs]

Q: So you're going to be really rich.

A: You know, every time a summer movie comes out, people think they're gonna get rich off of the merchandise. Inspector Gadget didn't sell any toys. Yeah, we're gonna do it. We'll make some money. We could do it now, but we want to wait for the value to go up. It's going to be on television in a year . . . It'll be some type of clothing . . . It'll definitely be greeting cards.

Q: Do you have a fantasy strip?

A: It'll all be in the [TV] show. We're gonna be on a cable network and we're gonna be prime time, so there will be no limits. The show's gonna be more about the characters.

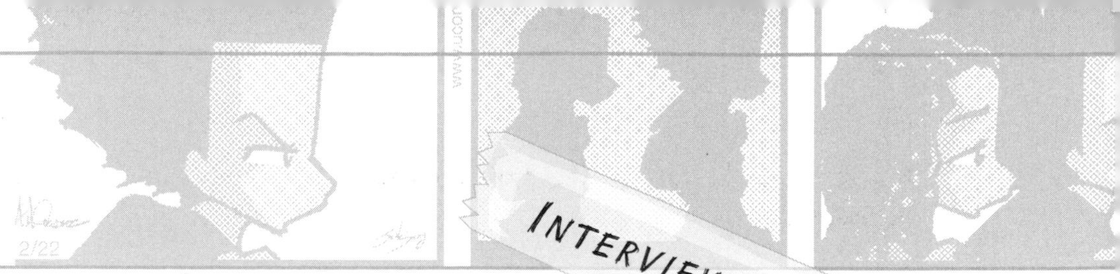

Salon.com
DECEMBER 7, 2001

INTERVIEW . . .

Aaron McGruder, Creator of *The Boondocks*

The controversial cartoonist calls Bush a moron, says Americans shouldn't worry about bin Laden and says he might leave the country.

STEPHEN LEMONS

Recently, [McGruder] tore himself away from ranting at the tube in his Los Angeles digs long enough to rant to *Salon* about the state of the nation.

Your strips post-9/11 have touched a raw nerve with some folks. Did you anticipate all the attention you've gotten because of them?

It's become a story because of timing. You know, the *New York Daily News* temporarily pulls the strip, and in the middle of this wartime situation, it became a story about freedom of speech and all that. The reality is I get pulled all the time from various newspapers for different reasons. And it's been that way since the strip started. Usually, it's a few strips here, a few strips there. Granted, this is the longest I've ever been removed from a major paper. But it wasn't that big of a deal, really. There's been everything from the National Rifle Association strips that got pulled in Dallas to some strips I did about Bob Johnson [of Black Entertainment Television] . . . You know, the newspapers make the call. They pull the strips that they don't want to run, and they put the strips back when they're comfortable. I've gotten used to it. I was somewhat surprised at how big of a story it became, because it's happened so often.

You don't feel like you're under siege, then?

No, because the syndicate has not asked me to do anything different. And I'm in 250 newspapers, and none of them have asked me to do anything different. So I've been doing exactly what I want, and I haven't felt any pressure to do otherwise.

What's the status of things now with the *Daily News* and the *Dallas Morning News*?

The *Daily News* said they were going to look at it on a daily basis and decide whether or not to run it. So I have no idea what they're doing. I heard about the *Dallas Morning News* moving it to a different section, but I don't know much about it. *Newsday* chose not to run a few strips, and I've heard some reports of some smaller papers. But I don't really keep track of stuff like that. With over 200 clients, it would be too time-consuming and more trouble than it was worth to worry about what each one was doing and why. I do the strip, send it out and what the newspapers want to do with it is up to them. It's between them and their readers.

Was there ever a doubt in your mind that you were going to address September 11 in the strip?

No, the only question was how soon? And that was the big decision that had to be made. My deadlines at the time were falling on Tuesdays. The day the attack happened was the deadline, and then I had a week to decide whether or not I was going to talk about it the following week. And I did.

I wanted to ask you specifically about the Thanksgiving strip where Huey compares President Bush to Osama bin Laden. Do you think that's crossing the line on a holiday like that after a major tragedy such as Sept. 11?

A couple of things about that: One, I stole that joke from an Internet forward that was going around. I don't even know who originated it. Two, the best thing about that strip is that it never says G. W. Bush. The reader has to make the connection. If the reader reads what I wrote and thinks about G.W. Bush, that means it's fucking true! So I didn't make it up; you came to the conclusion as well. And if it's true, why are you mad at me? If he's not all those things, then what are you mad at? (Laughs.)

Have there been strips you've pulled back on because of September 11?

It's always happening. It never happens because I send it in and the syndicate says we can't run it. It's always part of the creative process of me trying to walk that line and say the things I want to say without taking it too far and doing stuff that you're just not allowed to do in the newspapers. That's always a challenge.

Why did you decide to target the post–September 11 displays of patriotism in the strip, and essentially mock them with those two characters Flagee and Ribbon?

Because it wasn't genuine. I thought it was very faddish, and there was no real weight behind it. You know, we just came off an election that was a mess. We still don't know if the president won the election. We do know that he got less votes nationwide. There's no question about that. And he may not even have won, legitimately, the electoral contest. There were reports of the massive disenfranchisement of African Americans in Florida, which went totally unreported in this country, but was covered widely by the foreign press. There were black people in Florida yelling and screaming, trying to get somebody to pay attention to them. They were saying that they had their rights taken away from them, and they were not allowed to vote. And nobody in this country cared. Where was the flag then?

Where was this embracing of American ideals when people had their rights ripped from them so unjustly? We have a president who was appointed by the Supreme Court, and there was none of this talk about freedom and love of country at that time. So I feel like the deaths of 4,000 people had really nothing to do with love of country or not. This country made giant mistakes and failed to protect its people. We don't need to be rallying around the government and supporting it, we need to be holding it accountable and being very critical so this type of thing doesn't happen again. So there are a number of reasons why I was uncomfortable with the whole flag thing.

A lot of folks would argue that no matter what our disagreements are internally, if we're attacked from the outside, we have to come together and support the current administration even if we have problems with it. How do you respond to that argument?

I don't think that's true. Look, they're telling us these people are bad because they hate us, and they hate our way of life. And they hate our way of life because they hate freedom, and they hate the fact that we have freely elected officials. This is what the president said. Well, he wasn't elected! We really have to think about that. Considering that people around the world, other people, people "over there," "bad" people will always try to do bad things, that's kind of outside of your control. The only thing you can be responsible for is what goes on here. The American people have no control over what the military does. We have no say in American foreign policy. None. The only thing we can exercise some will on is what happens here domestically. So I think the focus is wrong.

I don't think the American people should be worried at all about Osama bin Laden or Saddam Hussein or anybody, because our government is going to do what it wants to do to them regardless of what we want them to do or not. All we can control is what happens here. And what happened here is what allowed those attacks to take place. The intelligence community failed. Security failed. The military failed. Everybody failed at the same time. I can be really nice to them and say, "You guys really messed up and need to check yourself." Or I could be not nice and say, "You know, I don't think it's really probable that all the systems can fail at the same time, which means something far more insidious took place." People are really afraid to get into that.

Are you suggesting some collusion on the part of our government in the September 11 attacks?

I'm not suggesting that. I'm saying I'm not going there. I'm going to give them the benefit of the doubt and assume they're idiots, and not that they had something far more nefarious in mind. However, history does teach us that the government has done things like that before, particularly with Pearl Harbor, where there's an overwhelming amount of evidence that [FDR] was aware of it and lured the Japanese to attack Pearl Harbor. He literally left it undefended. There's some new evidence that has just come out about the CIA planning terrorist attacks on U.S. soil in the '60s and how they were going to set up Castro for it in order to get America behind a war in Cuba. That's not even a conspiracy theory. The CIA drew up the plans, even though it never happened. So if I were to go that route, I wouldn't be crazy. But I'm not going to go that route. I'm just going to say that the American people need to be concerned about what happens here. Forget what happens overseas. That's out of your control. Be concerned with what happens here. Because honestly, if our game is tight here, we can't be attacked. If our intelligence community and airports and military are doing what they're supposed to do, then we should be relatively OK.

This reminds me of the strip where Huey calls the FBI terrorist hotline, tells them he's got a tip on someone who helped the terrorists, and it's Ronald Reagan. Do you think there's been enough coverage of the support our leaders have given the mujahedin in the past?

The media have reported on it. But it's not so much [that] they said it or not, it's the way they've said it. When the news wants to tell you something is important, they put dramatic theme music behind it. They scare you into watching the story. Like, anthrax—very, very important. Pay attention, it's scary. When they report on the U.S. creation of these people, these terrorists, it's all very matter of fact. Like, oh yeah, we gave them a whole bunch of money, and now on to sports. So a lot of it is not necessarily an issue of it being covered up. In fact, it can't be covered up—it's well known. But to me, it's not given the right emphasis. The question is to what extent is the government culpable for creating the people who have done this? And to what extent should they be held responsible for the actions of terrorists that they have supported in the past? That's what this is all about. I'm talking about Ronald Reagan, George Bush Sr., their whole crew, up until the crew that's in there today. After the embassy attacks in Africa, they were well aware of Osama bin Laden. They were well aware of his location in Afghanistan, his protection by the Taliban, and this Bush administration gave them $43 million this year! And nobody talks about it, and nobody holds them accountable, and that's wrong.

To be fair, though, I believe even the Clinton administration supported the Taliban in the beginning because they were viewed as a stabilizing force.

Well, to hell with Clinton, too. I'm not a Democrat. I don't give a damn about Clinton. Hold these people responsible! You know, Democratic and Republican administrations alike have supported individuals and regimes that have slaughtered millions across the globe. And they need to be held accountable for that.

Your depiction of the news media in your strip makes it out to be almost a cheerleader for the government. Is that a fair assessment of your opinion?

They've absolutely been playing cheerleader for the government, to the extent that even they've had to admit it. I watch news shows, and they're like, "Yeah, we're treating Bush differently now." I don't want the news to be patriotic. I don't want to see flags on the lapels of the anchors. I don't want any of that. I want the news delivered unbiased. I thought that was the whole point with journalism. They've thrown that out the window. And because they've all thrown it out the window at the same time, it's supposedly acceptable. No! It's ridiculous. I don't need to see that.

This is war. It's serious. People are dying on both sides. How dare the media just give in when the government says don't air any of Osama bin Laden's video messages! What is this? He's going to rub his nose and something is going to blow up over here? Like terrorists don't have satellite television, and they can't watch foreign news and get the same messages. That's insane. It's totally and thoroughly irresponsible behavior by the entire institution of the media.

Don't hold back, Aaron.

I won't. I was talking to some television journalists about this who gave me some interesting insight. Right now, they're scared to be critical of the government. Everything is about access. Reporters are afraid that the administration will cut them off. Decades ago, the mark of a good reporter was how much dirt you could dig up. Like the Watergate scandal. They were actively trying to find out what was going on and report the truth to people. Now it's the exact opposite. Nobody wants to say anything that makes the government mad, and that's ridiculous. Also, after the attacks, now people think it's unpatriotic to say anything critical of the government.

Come on, Bush is a moron. There is no doubt about it. And they really didn't have a problem going there before. But now, nobody wants to call him on it. People get excited because he can speak well. What world is this? When we're happy that the president can articulate well. That's something they only used to say about black men. "Oh, you speak so well." That's nuts. You don't say that about the president. We're supposed to have higher standards. The media are a big part of shaping the perception of the country, and right now, they're not asking the tough questions. They're not exploring, for example, the Bush administration's financial ties with Afghanistan. The fact that George Bush Sr. has financial investments in the area, and those investments become much more valuable when the Taliban government is removed. I'm not talking about getting into a whole bunch of conspiracies. Report what's actually happening, and challenge the government to explain itself. Why didn't they ask more questions? Like, how did this happen? How did four planes get hijacked in one day? And who got fired? That's the question I want to know the answer to, because a whole bunch of people should have gotten fired for what happened on Sept. 11. Report on the fact that G. W. Bush is sealing presidential papers. Indefinitely. His, his father's, Reagan's. It's totally unconstitutional. Why don't they talk about that?

On the topic of George W's I.Q., I think that idea is pretty threatening to people right now, because like it or not, we're stuck with him.

Yes, but living in denial doesn't help the situation. We have to confront the very scary fact that the president is a moron. He's really dumb. He's got some really smart people around him, and people weren't afraid to say that before. They said it in a nice way, but they said it. It was like, he's dumb, but he's got Cheney and he's got Powell, so we'll probably be OK. But now they act like he's done something great. You know, he's called [the terrorists] "evil." That's really some childish stuff. They're bad, we're good. That's the dumbest thing I've ever heard. That's so incredibly stupid. What do you think they do? They call us "evil." I just see so many parallels between both sides in this war, and it's really uncomfortable. You know, they kill civilians, we kill civilians. They say they're justified, we say the same thing. This is gang warfare on an international level. That's all it is. And when gang warfare happens in American cities, we say it's wrong. When somebody loads a gun, goes 20 blocks and kills the guy who killed his brother, it's not justifiable homicide or self-defense, it's murder and we put people in jail for it. Why is it acceptable that we do it now?

Do you support the war at all?

I don't support the killing of innocent people, and that's what's happening. What's worse is that we're killing innocent people out of retribution for the killing of innocent people. It's wrong. It's really wrong.

But assuming that Osama bin Laden and al-Qaeda are responsible, we have to go in and get them. How do we go in and get them without taking over that country?

I don't know. But I would ask, how many bombs can we drop to bring these people back? We can't drop enough bombs to bring 4,000 people back, and we can't drop enough bombs to ensure that it never happens again. Is it really about Osama bin Laden, or are we narrowing this? The people that hijacked the planes and crashed them are dead. If there's a terrorist network or a man responsible, yes, we should get them, but when you construct it like a police action or an investigation, and not like a war, then you're forced to respect the lives of innocents, even if it's a pain in the ass. I say it's not worth innocent people dying, even if it takes years and you have to keep sending SEAL teams or whatever in there. What the hell? That's what they're trained to do. That's why they exist. Drop them in there to get one guy. F-18s exist to wipe out towns. It may take longer the other way, but that's too bad.

But I'm sure you've seen pictures of Germany after World War II, and that country was flattened. Japan too. There were countless innocent lives lost.

World War II was 60 years ago. I mean, just in terms of technology, we're not fighting wars the same way. They had special ops, but it was the beginnings of special ops. They didn't have satellites that could listen to a conversation from space or pinpoint and read a newspaper headline from miles in the air. We didn't have that. You went to war, carpet-bombed and a whole lot of civilians died. And you know what? World War II was fucked up. How many millions of people died good and bad? Could World War II have been fought differently? I don't know.

There are few wars where innocent people don't die.

I don't know why this had to become a war. A war on whom? This feels like the war on drugs. When does it end? When you declare war on Japan or Germany, you know you can stop when those countries are flattened. When you declare war against the word "terrorism," when is that over? What does that mean? Stopping terrorism is like stopping rape or burglary, it's an individual action. Anyone with a gun can go out and commit an act of terrorism, even without a political affiliation. It never ends. So it's like the war on drugs, and what has that accomplished? Not a goddamn thing but a whole lot of black men in jail for nonviolent crimes, millions of dollars spent and nothing else. And that's what the war on terrorism is going to do—we're going to lose countless amounts of money, people are going to die and get locked up, but that's it. There's going to be no good coming out of it. We're going to lose our civil rights, and they're going to be gone forever.

You don't buy the argument that the curtailing of certain civil liberties is temporary, that it's been necessary in previous wars, and that eventually those rights will be restored?

It's not temporary. Once you give up rights, they're not going to give them back. This is a war that will never end. When are they going to say they've defeated terrorism? No one is stupid enough to say that. Because then when something blows up, they look like dickheads. They can never again come out and say America is

safe. They'd be idiots if they did. So given that they've set the situation up as a war they can't win, they're never giving the rights back. Literally, someone will have to be elected who doesn't agree with this shit and gives us our rights back. Someone, I don't know who, will have to get into power and say, "You know, this was all bullshit, and we're changing the laws."

What do you think we'll have to go through for that to happen?

America will really have to understand how corrupt its system is, and they'll have to get so fed up that they're ready to make change. And I don't think that'll happen because the media are so in line with the government and so invested in the status quo. We have, essentially, a worthless democracy. I hate to sound so extreme, but things are that bad. There's nothing we have to share with the rest of the world. We don't even have one man, one vote. And we have so much legal corruption in our political system that no one even thinks about it anymore.

You say that, but would you want to live anywhere else?

I tell you what, I visited Canada, and I liked it. I liked it a lot. This idea that there's no better place in the world to live, I don't buy that. The reality is this: Me, I'm comfortable. I make a lot of money. So I can say, America is OK, up until the point that the LAPD pulls me over and knocks out some teeth on some bullshit. That happens enough to black men that it's a legitimate concern for me. So I have to ask, even with my money, even though I've worked the American dream pretty well, is this really the best place for me to be? I don't know that's true. When you have money, anyplace is good. I could go to South Africa with what I'm making right now and live like a multimillionaire just off the currency exchange. I could live real well in a lot of different places. If you're broke, a lot of places suck. If you're broke in America or Brazil, it sucks.

Are you seriously considering that, or just talking? The reason I ask is that prior to Bush being elected, a lot of Hollywood types were talking about how they were going to move to Europe if Bush won and they're all still here.

You know, they're Hollywood types, fuck 'em. They're irrelevant to the conversation. Yes, I have thought about leaving. Right now, I can't even find the time to get an apartment in L.A. So when my life settles, and I have to think about where I'm going to raise my kids, when I have them, Canada will be the first place I look. I've never had the opportunity to go overseas because I was broke up until a couple of years ago. Now that I have money, I have to find time to really see the rest of the world. I can't say this is the best place on earth because I haven't been enough places. But I know that in Toronto and Vancouver there are all the comforts of America, and yet there's a difference in the people, and I had health care. When I visited Canada, I didn't have health care here. I go there, I have health insurance. And the air was cleaner—sparkling, even in downtown Toronto. People say Canada's just like America. No! I'm out of the country, and you know what? It ain't bad.

Yet what makes your strip successful, I think, is that it's going against the grain of American society. Don't you think you would lose that if you were living in some other country?

I don't need to live here to know how stupid this place is. I don't know G. W. Bush. What I know, I get from the television and the newspapers, and I can get that anywhere. I have been successful to a large degree because of controversy, but I have no intention of living my life mad. And I'm not so in love with making people mad that I want to live my life around it. Trust me, I would rather

the attacks had not happened and not have anything to talk about. Sure, the U.S. of A. gives me lots of material, but I would rather things be good. So in the abstract, I would leave. I haven't had the chance to seriously explore it. But I'm 27, so I have some time. This is just not the best place in the world for black people, even the U.N. knows that. They did some study ranking living conditions by ethnicity, and white American men were No. 1. I don't remember where black American men were, but they were a little bit further on down.

Do you think your strip reflects in any way a certain skepticism among black Americans toward the government?

I cannot be made into the commentator for the unspoken black masses. But I will say that the strip represents a political perspective that people black and white hold that is not being put out in the mass media. I just happen to have incredibly wide distribution in a medium that doesn't draw a lot of attention to itself. It's not like Bill Maher, where you say the wrong thing and the powers that be can just pull the plug. Comic strips don't really work that way. The message gets out there 20 million times a day, but it's still very subtle and very small. The medium itself, not just me.

I'd give you more credit than that. Because most comics don't deal with political issues, it makes you and *Doonesbury* pop out.

Yeah, we pop out, but it's not a dynamic medium. It's not TV, it's not movies. In that sense, it doesn't capture people's attention in the same way. What happened to Bill Maher is a good example. His show is done, I think.

What do you mean? You think *Politically Incorrect* is a goner?

I think it's going to be soon. I've heard things, but I don't want to say. I think they already know it's not [going to survive]. Maybe I'm wrong. I watched *Politically Incorrect* recently, and I felt like I was watching *Crossfire*. The jokes were gone. It was like, everybody was nervous. Nobody wanted to say anything. You can't have a show called *Politically Incorrect* and have everyone be afraid to be politically incorrect. It doesn't make sense. I mean, I've been on the show before back when the strip launched, and I think Bill Maher got a raw deal. But that's the difference between TV and comic strips.

You're working on a *Boondocks* TV show now. Will your show still retain the political flavor of the strip? Will this be on Comedy Central?

Well, it's going to be prime time cable as opposed to being network. I can't say the channel, because we've been through this with three networks and every time we think it's going to happen it falls through. But with a year lead time, you can't talk about current events. So the show's mainly going to be about the characters. It's still going to have a heavy political slant to it, but it's not going to talk about specific incidents.

Doesn't *South Park* do stuff that's timely?

Yeah, but we're talking about animation of a quality that's far superior to *South Park*, so it takes a long time. I love *South Park*, but it's animated very simply.

By the way, here's one vote for you not moving to Canada. Huey in Toronto just wouldn't be the same.

Thanks, but no matter where I live, it's more an issue of how much longer I want to do this. It's a very demanding job. How long am I going to feel like I have something relevant to say day in and day out? How long before I get bored with it or get fed up with the deadlines? A lot of guys who do this job do it for 50 years. That's not me. I don't feel like I'm going to be a lifer. There are weeks where I hate the strip more than anything. And then there are times, like recently, where everyone else is out of work, and I'm like yeah, I've got a job, woo-hoo! But am I going to do this another week, or am I just going to quit now and hope this Hollywood stuff pans out? It's always a debate.

This article first appeared in Salon.com, at http://www.Salon.com. An online version remains in the Salon archives. Reprinted with permission.

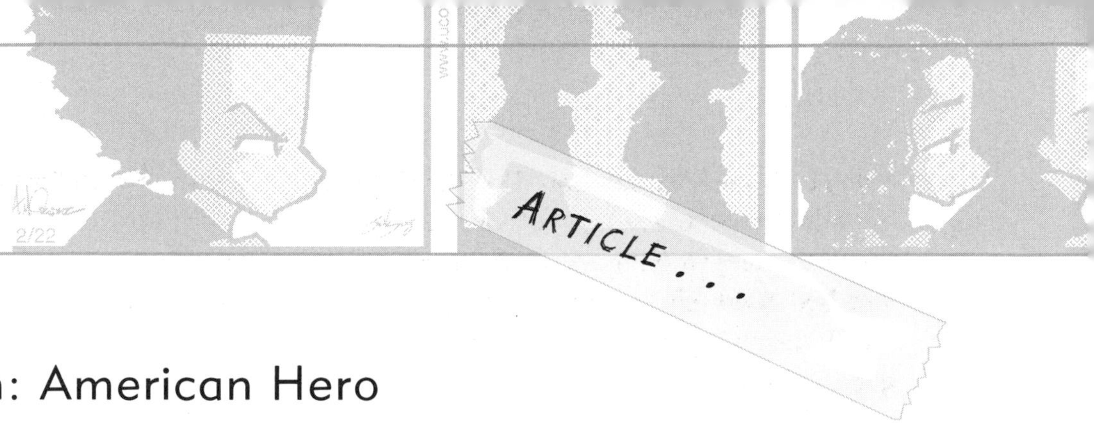
ARTICLE . . .

Huey Freeman: American Hero

Sure, he's a cartoon character,
but it still takes courage to speak out

JOHN NICHOLS

On Thanksgiving Day 2001, with the United States in the midst of what polls identify as one of the most popular wars in history and with President Bush's approval ratings hovering around 90 percent, more than 20 million American households opened their daily newspapers to see a little black kid named Huey Freeman leading the pre turkey prayer.

"Ahem," began the unsmiling youth. "In this time of war against Osama bin Laden and the oppressive Taliban regime, we are thankful that OUR leader isn't the spoiled son of a powerful politician from a wealthy oil family who is supported by religious fundamentalists, operates through clandestine organizations, has no respect for the democratic electoral process, bombs innocents, and uses war to deny people their civil liberties. Amen."

In the whole of American media that day, Huey's was certainly the most pointed and, no doubt, the most effective dissent from the patriotism that dare not speak its mind. And it was not the only day when the self-proclaimed "radical scholar" skewered George W. Bush, Attorney General John Ashcroft, the Defense Department, dithering Democrats, frenzied flag-wavers and scaremongering television anchors in what since September 11 has been the most biting and consistent critique of the war and its discontents in the nation's mass media.

The creation of 27-year-old cartoonist Aaron McGruder, Huey Freeman appears daily in *The Boondocks*, a comic strip featured in 250 of America's largest newspapers, including the *Washington Post*, *Dallas Morning News*, *Chicago Tribune*, *Los Angeles Times* and *Philadelphia Inquirer.* "There are a lot of newspapers where Aaron's comic strip probably is the only consistent voice of dissent," says Pulitzer Prize–winning cartoonist Joel Pett, whose editorial-page cartoons for the Lexington, Kentucky, *Herald-Leader* have raised tough questions about the suffering of Afghan civilians and the role the United States has played in spreading terror. "I think that not only is he doing good stuff, the fact that he is on those comics pages makes it important in a way that none of the rest of us could accomplish. He's hooking a whole group of people. He's getting ideas out to people who don't always read the opinion pages. And he's influencing a lot of young people about how it's OK to question their government and the media. When you think about it, what he has done since September 11 has just been incredible."

In recent weeks, McGruder's Huey has grumbled about how it may no longer be legal in John Ashcroft's America to ask whether George W. Bush was actually elected; hiked atop a mountain to yell, "For goodness sake people, it's a recession! Save money this Christmas!"; and repeatedly expressed the view that "Dick Cheney is just plain creepy." And he has listened in disbelief to an "announcement" from the Attorney General that went: "I would like to reassure Congress that my proposed Turban Surveillance Act, which would allow the FBI to covertly plant listening devices in the headgear of suspected terrorists, is in no way meant to single out Arab or Muslim Americans."

At a time when most comedians are still pulling their punchlines, McGruder has gotten plenty of laughs at the expense of the Bush Administration and its policies. But not everyone has been amused. In early October the cartoonist had Huey call the FBI's antiterrorist hotline to report that he had the names of Americans who trained and financed Osama bin Laden. When the FBI agent said that, yes, he wanted the names, Huey began, "All right, let's see, the first one is Reagan. That's R-E-A-G . . ." This series of strips was pulled from the New York *Daily News* and *Newsday* and shuffled off comics pages at other papers. Editors were quick to deny they were censoring *The Boondocks*, claiming they simply thought McGruder had gotten a little too political. McGruder played the controversy into more laughs. He produced an inane new strip featuring talking patriotic symbols, launching it with a satirical editor's note: "Due to the inappropriate political content of this feature in recent weeks, it is being replaced by 'The Adventures of Flagee and Ribbon,' which we hope will help children understand the complexities of current events. United we stand." Ribbon then declares, "Hey, Flagee, there's a lot of evil out there," to which his compatriot replies, "That's right, Ribbon. Good thing America kicks a lot of *@#!"

McGruder, whose cartoon began appearing nationally in April 1999, says he did not set out to make Huey the nation's No. 1 dissenter. Yes, *The Boondocks*—which recounts the experiences of Huey and his younger brother, Riley, inner-city youths who move with great trepidation to the suburbs—has always been controversial. Bitingly blunt in its examination of race and class issues, *The Boondocks* has made more waves more often than any nationally syndicated comic strip since Garry Trudeau's *Doonesbury* characters declared Nixon aides "Guilty! Guilty! Guilty!" in the Watergate era. "It even got pulled from the Buffalo paper for something involving Santa Claus," recalls McGruder, who grew up listening to rap artists Public Enemy and KRS-One, idolized Berkeley Breathed's politically pointed *Bloom County* comic strip, took an African American studies degree from the University of Maryland and started drawing cartoons for the hip-hop magazine *The Source*.

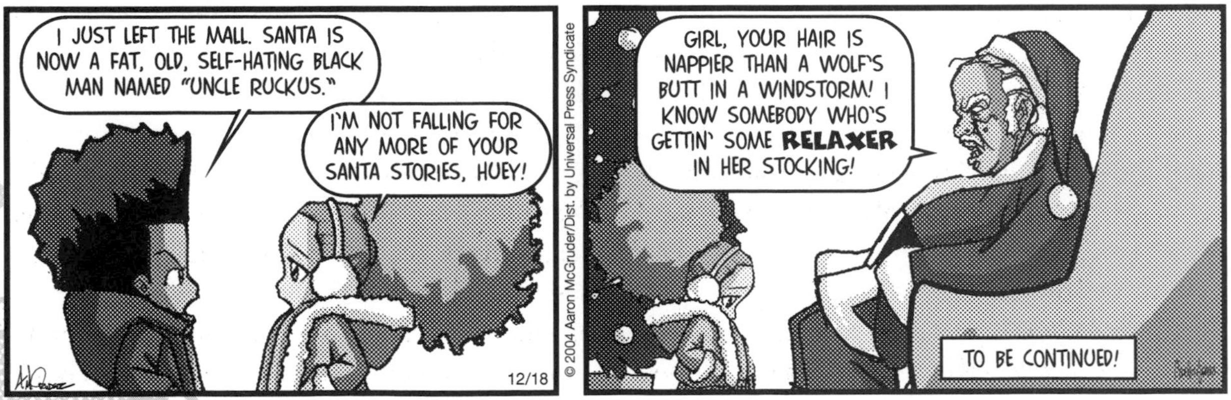
I JUST LEFT THE MALL. SANTA IS NOW A FAT, OLD, SELF-HATING BLACK MAN NAMED "UNCLE RUCKUS."
I'M NOT FALLING FOR ANY MORE OF YOUR SANTA STORIES, HUEY!
12/18
© 2004 Aaron McGruder/Dist. by Universal Press Syndicate
GIRL, YOUR HAIR IS NAPPIER THAN A WOLF'S BUTT IN A WINDSTORM! I KNOW SOMEBODY WHO'S GETTIN' SOME RELAXER IN HER STOCKING!
TO BE CONTINUED!

But the cartoonist knew that the controversy he would stir in the weeks after September 11 would be different from any he had provoked before. What he did not know was that, unlike Trudeau in the Watergate era, he and his preteen characters would challenge a popular President and his policies with little cover from allies in the media or Congress. "Sometimes, I do look around and say to myself, 'Gee, I'm the only one saying some of these things.' That can make you a little paranoid. But I don't think that's a reflection on me so much as it is a reflection on how narrow the discussion has become in most of the media today. The media has become so conglomerated that there really are very few avenues left for people to express dissent," says McGruder. Well aware that he is a young cartoonist—as opposed to a senator or veteran television commentator—McGruder is the first to note, "I should not be the guy right now. I should not be the one who is standing out here saying, 'Hold it. This doesn't make any sense.'. . . There are a lot of people who do this so much better than I do. I just have the distribution and the opportunity."

When the terrorist planes hit the World Trade Center and the Pentagon, McGruder was not thinking about the next turn in his career path, rather, he was doing what Huey and the other Boondocks kids do a lot of: watching television. "I watched five straight days of television. I was shocked by what happened. But I was also shocked by the simplistic nature of a lot of the commentary—this whole 'good' versus 'evil' analysis that sounded like something from fifth grade. And I started to recognize that this was going to be a defining moment in my career," recalls McGruder, who acknowledges that Huey tends to channel his most passionately held views. "I decided that I was going to risk throwing my career away. I absolutely thought that was the risk I was taking."

Why take the risk?

"*The Boondocks* is not an alternative weekly strip. This is not a Web site strip. This is in the *Washington Post*," he explains. "It just seemed like nobody else was going to say the things that needed to be said in the places where I had an opportunity to raise questions about the war—in newspapers that millions of people read every day."

McGruder is not the only cartoonist upholding the craft's honorable tradition of tweaking the powerful. Despite pressure from many editors to narrow the discourse—because, in the words of *Soup to Nutz* cartoonist and National Cartoonist Society spokesman Rick Stromoski, "Sales and subscriptions are down, and papers are afraid of offending their communities and losing even more readers"—a number of editorial-page cartoonists have poked and prodded more than most mainstream journalists. Pulitzer Prize-winner Steve Benson has created a tremendous stir in Phoenix, where his cartoons for the conservative *Arizona Republic* have attacked "war fever" and mocked superpatriots; angry readers have condemned Benson for what one described as "a vile tirade upon the people of the United States." Kentucky's Joel Pett has wondered aloud whether the antiterrorist cause might be better served by more food drops and fewer bombs. The *Philadelphia Inquirer*'s Tony Auth, the *Philadelphia Daily News*'s Signe Wilkinson and the *Sacramento Bee*'s Rex Babin have savaged the Bush Administration's assaults on civil liberties and decision to rely on military tribunals. And, though far gentler than in his heyday, Trudeau has used his *Doonesbury* strip—which often appears on editorial pages—to address anti-Arab stereotyping, slack media coverage and the dubious alliances made between the United States and Afghan warlords.

Gary Huck and Mike Konopacki, whose cartoons frequently appear in labor-union publications, have dissected war profiteering by corporations. Ted Rall, who is published in alternative weeklies and a growing number of daily papers, has exposed the excesses of corporate America (one of his cartoons, titled "America's business leaders consider their role in the war," features an executive crowing, "I laid off thousands of people and scored a bailout"); in addition, Rall has filed some of the best war reporting from Afghanistan by an American journalist. And no one has skewered the mindless patriotism of the media better than Dan Perkins, whose *Tom Tomorrow* strip coined the phrase "We must dismantle our democracy in order to save it."

But while many editorial cartoons are syndicated, none reach the audience that *The Boondocks* does daily. Thus when Huey started raising a ruckus, a lot of people noticed. One night last fall, when the L.A.-based cartoonist was visiting his parents in Maryland, McGruder sat down with Mom and Dad to watch a segment on ABC's *Nightline* portray him as one of America's most controversial commentators. Despite his off-message message, offers keep coming McGruder's way from Hollywood; he's developing an animated version of *The Boondocks* that's expected to show up as a network series this fall, and he's writing movie scripts—including one about George W. Bush's theft of the 2000 election. "If we can get it made, it will be a miracle," jokes McGruder, who calls Bush "our almost-elected leader." Weighing the continued success of *The Boondocks* and his Hollywood options against the recent controversy, McGruder says, "I can't say I've suffered. A few papers pulled [the strip] but most of them haven't. And the publicity has just drawn attention to what I'm doing."

Indeed, McGruder wonders why so few successful artists speak out about race, class, war and Bush's court-ordered presidency. "I understand that in a capitalist society, anger at the system is a luxury. But some people are on top of the system. Why don't they speak out?" he asks. "The only time I really get upset is when I see someone like Oprah [Winfrey], who has the money, who has the power, and I think, 'What is holding you back from changing the world, from changing the world in a drastic way?'" Adds McGruder, who has frequently used *The Boondocks* to criticize African American celebrities who take the cautious route, "Some of these people clearly decided, at some point, not to take any risks. I can't do that." So Huey Freeman refuses to shut up. "I'm going to stay cynical, resist this bandwagon war," the cartoon character told his pal Caesar in a recent strip. "Sure, my kind may be obsolete. But so what?"

Actually, McGruder says, he doesn't believe Huey's thinking—or his own—to be obsolete, or even all that radical. "I really think that what I am doing with *The Boondocks* is common sense. It's just that when no one in a position to be heard is speaking out, common sense seems radical," he says, sounding distinctly like Huey as he adds, "How's that for irony: We live in a time when commonsense statements seem radical."

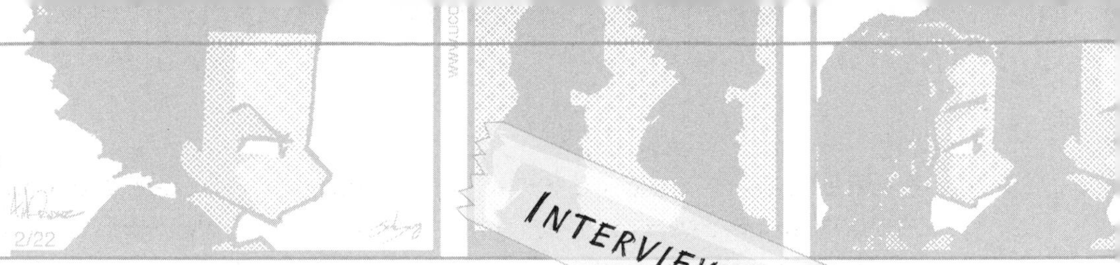

The Comics Journal
September 2003

Interview . . .

Encountering Aaron McGruder

R. C. Harvey

You wouldn't think, upon first seeing Aaron McGruder, that he was a bomb-throwing anarchist. A slight, brown-skinned man, he looked small and unthreatening in the middle of the lofty, barren stage at Foellinger Auditorium on the campus of the University of Illinois on Wednesday evening, Jan. 22, 2003. True, he was wearing sinister black, a sort of pea-coat, collar turned up, and turtleneck sweater (or was that a black scarf around his neck?), but after he was introduced and took possession of the microphone, a friendly smile lurked upon his lips as he looked out over the crowd of 500 or so who had come to listen to him give the keynote at the Martin Luther King Jr. Symposium, a feature of Black History Month on campus. He left the lectern right away and walked back and forth on the stage, not saying anything yet, just smiling at his audience.

"There's so much bad stuff going on," he said at last, "more bad stuff in the world than I have time to talk about. I'm not a motivational speaker," he continued. "I'm not here to make you feel good about yourself. I'm not here to convince you you can do it. You can't."

That was the first bomb. To any bunch of Americans, the idea that there's something they can't do to improve their lot in life is anathema. But McGruder's litany was long and insistent: The left is naive, the right is corrupt, the government has been hijacked and there's nothing you can do about it. Speaking entirely without notes, he kept on for well over an hour, pacing back and forth across the stage, smiling pleasantly all the while as he lobbed one bombshell after another at his listeners.

The Powers That Be have been given license to commit crimes no one could have imagined, he said. After lighting that fuse, he shouted, "Hey, I'm not a motivational speaker, remember? You should not be listening to someone under 30 anyway," he said, "with only one degree." He paused. "Barely."

McGruder's "lecture," as he called it, was laced with one-liners as well as incendiary calls to unspecified action. "Bush lost the election," he reminded us. "They took your vote away. They stole the election. Over half the voters voted for Gore, but he lost. They stole the election and nobody rioted!" After a pause, he continued: "If we lived up to our responsibilities as Americans—lived up to the ideals we profess as Americans—we'd overthrow the government."

Looking at his audience, he smiled. "They're

all depressed," he said to no one in particular, and to everyone. "You will know only what they want you to know," he said. "The left is naive. They've lost touch with reality. Progressives in this country still vote for Democrats as if they're not Republicans. They get money from the same people Republicans do," he cried, incredulous, "which is why they keep playing to the middle."

"Liberals are nice idealistic people," he said, "they like to laugh." But they're out of touch. "They won't play the game that needs to be played." Why are there no liberal radio talk shows? "The right is made up of mean, nasty people who scream on radio and other mean, nasty people who call in and say, 'Yeah!' Liberals are generally nice, realistic people. You can't yell at them. They get all hurt."

The invasion of Iraq was still two months in the future, but talk of war was everywhere, and McGruder was highly critical of the Bush League's bellicose intentions. "Beating up on Saddam Hussein is like the Rock beating up on a hungry, homeless man," he said. "That country was bombed into oblivion ten years ago, and they haven't done anything since. Iraq can't hurt anybody. Who are they going to attack? Israel? The Israelis will kill anybody in this room—just for fun."

McGruder saw little hope anywhere he looked. Hip hop as a force for revolution is dead, he said. Pop singers and performers? "They don't care, and they don't read," he declared. "How bad is political leadership on the left? The Green Party phoned and asked me to run for President! Me!" he said, incredulity radiating from every pore. "It won't work. First, I'm 28, I told them: you have to be 35 to run for President."

"I'm terrified," he went on, describing what he imagined as the Green Party selection process, going down a list of possible candidates until, at last, they reached him. "They had to work their way down a list to me!" he exclaimed.

As for black leadership, there is none: "There's a crisis in black leadership in this country. In progressive, leftist leadership, it's virtually nonexis-

tent. Most of the leftovers are from the civil rights movement, and they've done so much dirt, they've lost their moral authority." He criticized Jesse Jackson for making everything into a rhyming speech. "He's old," McGruder said. "He doesn't speak for me." As for Al Sharpton: "You'll never be taken seriously with a perm," he said, "unless you're Condi Rice. Al, get a haircut!"

Still, he urged action. "Get a plan. Win. Live. Black leaders have got to do one thing first: live! Stop dying." The crowd cheered.

Despite his exhortation, McGruder couldn't say what, exactly, an effective action should be. The nature of power has evolved but the nature of protest has not. "Marching isn't doing it," he shouted. "The government—the Powers—don't fear you anymore," he yelled at his audience. He couldn't suggest what form the appropriate protest for today might be, but if people can't think of something other than marching, he said, then do nothing. "They'll wonder what you're up to," he said. "If the best you can do is march on the Capitol 20-deep, they know you've got nothin' up your sleeve." But if you do nothing, they'll wonder and maybe worry. And that's better than marching. "The Right Wing lies, cheats, steals and kills," McGruder said, "and if you want to win, that's what you have to do. Do whatever it takes to win. They have no rules; you shouldn't." A white person in the audience, which was invited to interrupt him at any time with questions or comments, asked: "Are you violent?" McGruder grinned impishly: "Classic thing for a white person to say." The audience, mostly African American students, roared. "It's not about violence and non-violence," he said. "It's about winning and losing. It's hard to win. Marching is not hard: it's 'feel good.' " Use the tools of power, he counseled, the same tools, and—in answer to a question—"Yes, absolutely, you can use them for good."

The lesson, the message, seemed to be: Get outraged. Your rights and freedoms are being taken from you, so protest in some new and dramatic way. Find a strategy that works in this new power environment. Your foe is implacable and very powerful and doesn't care about you at all. Your adversary will do anything to maintain its power. You must be willing to do the same, to use the same weapons ruthlessly to unseat those who aim to take your rights away. Appearing at the University of Indiana later in the month, McGruder's presentation was a variation on the same schtick, according to the report filed by Steve Hinnefeld at the *Herald-Times:* "Americans have completely and totally lost control of their government," McGruder said, and his audience clapped. "You're applauding as if that ain't your fault," he said. The fact that George W. Bush is President despite losing the popular vote—and needed the Supreme Court to declare that he won Florida—is one sign Americans have lost control of their government. "We need a coup," he said. "If the exact same thing happened in Nigeria, we'd have looked at television and said, 'Look at the poor Nigerians.' "

"Republicans do what psychotic, power-hungry megalomaniacs are supposed to do," he continued. "But Democrats keep pretending they're Republicans. Worse, they're ineffectual." The Green Party? "You can't put Ralph Nader on television and expect people to vote for him. This is America. People don't like smart, nerdy guys. You don't run Ralph Nader. You run a real good-looking guy, and Ralph Nader tells him what to say." Jesse Jackson, McGruder said, successfully defied efforts by white conservatives to discredit him, then blew his credibility with young blacks by harping on the movie *Barbershop.* Al Sharpton has the best political ideas and speaking ability of any candidate for President, but he also has the worst hair. "In a million years, no black man with a perm is going to be sitting at the table of power. You can replace that perm with a big red clown nose—that's his image to the world."

McGruder's lectures are polished performances. He was entirely at ease on stage and in complete control of his audience. He's had plenty of practice, making speeches of this kind around the country for more than three years, since the spectacular launch of his comic strip, *The Boondocks.*

The strip started on a small urban-oriented Web site in February 1996. At the end of that year, it started in the campus newspaper, the *Diamondback,* at the University of Maryland where McGruder was enrolled. In the summer of 1998, he did the strip for three months in *The Source,* an urban-music magazine, but by then, he was already under contract with Universal Press.

McGruder had submitted his strip to several syndicates. "The return results were mixed," he said. "Some flat rejections, some promising phone calls, which eventually led to rejection, and some 'wait and see.' During the summer of 1997, I attended the National Association of Black Journalists' annual convention with the hope of making some newspaper contacts who would support the strip, and I actually met a Universal Press Syndicate executive there. I was offered a contract at the end of that summer."

UP's Executive Vice President and Editorial Director, Lee Salem, told McGruder that the strip might start with "only 30 to 50 papers," but a record-setting 160 papers signed up by the time the strip debuted April 19, 1999, and the subscription list topped 200 in less than six months. "The market was receptive," Salem said.

In an age in which real life and topicality in comic strips are prized, McGruder's strip pushes the envelope: his protagonists are African American kids from the inner city who have moved with their grandfather to the suburbs ("the boondocks") where they go through a wide range of adjustment situations in the almost all-white neighborhood. They encounter white America, which, in the fantasy of the inaugural series of strips, burns with curiosity about and cowers in fear before the surly scowls of the two inner city would-be tough guys. The two kids—grade-schoolers Huey Freeman, a self-described social agitator, and his brother Riley, a gangsta-wannabe—are passionately anti-system and promptly begin expounding in a very adult way on all sorts of subjects heretofore taboo in newspaper funnies: Race relations, biracial identity

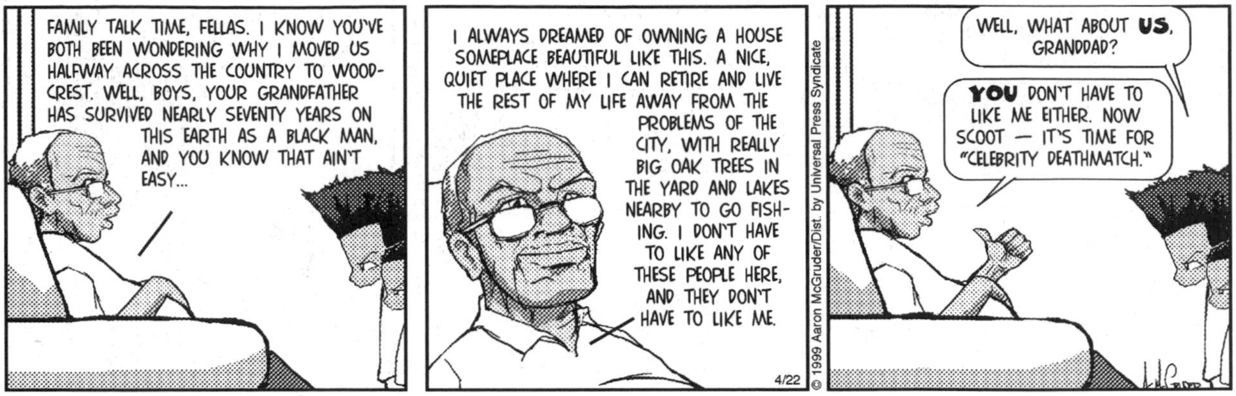
FAMILY TALK TIME, FELLAS. I KNOW YOU'VE BOTH BEEN WONDERING WHY I MOVED US HALFWAY ACROSS THE COUNTRY TO WOODCREST. WELL, BOYS, YOUR GRANDFATHER HAS SURVIVED NEARLY SEVENTY YEARS ON THIS EARTH AS A BLACK MAN, AND YOU KNOW THAT AIN'T EASY...
I ALWAYS DREAMED OF OWNING A HOUSE SOMEPLACE BEAUTIFUL LIKE THIS. A NICE, QUIET PLACE WHERE I CAN RETIRE AND LIVE THE REST OF MY LIFE AWAY FROM THE PROBLEMS OF THE CITY, WITH REALLY BIG OAK TREES IN THE YARD AND LAKES NEARBY TO GO FISHING. I DON'T HAVE TO LIKE ANY OF THESE PEOPLE HERE, AND THEY DON'T HAVE TO LIKE ME.
4/22
© 1999 Aaron McGruder/Dist. by Universal Press Syndicate
WELL, WHAT ABOUT **US**, GRANDDAD?
YOU DON'T HAVE TO LIKE ME EITHER. NOW SCOOT — IT'S TIME FOR "CELEBRITY DEATHMATCH."

and juvenile delinquency crop up in the first six months as the boys enroll in the all-white school whose all-white faculty views them as either a cosmic threat or a laboratory experiment. Racial myths brought up right and left are dispatched with sarcastic aplomb.

The comedy springs in part from the clash of cultures—hip-hop and soccer-mom—and in part from an awkwardness inherent in the ignorance about other races that is perpetuated in a society that keeps its races separate.

Asked why he chose to children to voice his opinions in the strip, McGruder explained that having adults do it would be too scary. Even so, people are scared of Huey. And in Hollywood, where the cartoonist now lives and works, "there are people who didn't want to be in a meeting with me because they thought I was Huey," he said.

His plan was to get a provocative point of view into newspapers by wrapping it in a cute package. "Media manipulation is a wonderful thing," he quipped. Sometimes, though, McGruder plays innocent: the strip is "just jokes," he said, "but people want to make it more than that." Even jokes are more than they seem. And, on occasion, McGruder acknowledges the existence in the strip of an agenda. *Boondocks* humor is about people not liking each other, he said—not liking themselves—and about African Americans, their world and how they (don't) get along.

Following its launch, a handful of papers canceled *The Boondocks* after only a few weeks because of reader complaints about its racial emphasis. One view came to me via a comics-scholars list on the Internet: "The strip doesn't offend me at all from the standpoint of my 'whiteness.' What turns me off about it are the blatantly stereotypical—and, to my caucasian sensibilities, unflattering—depictions of the black characters. Maybe I have my ethnic blinders on here, but does the average black person really not mind being depicted with hooded eyes and a hostile, surly, almost joyously threatening attitude? If that's not a stereotype for the '90s, I don't know what is. The strip centers around blacks and is drawn by a black, making it all very politically correct, I suppose, but it seems to present a very negative and hopeless picture over-all."

A white person, being melanin-challenged, is not equipped very well to say what black people might like or dislike. Aiming for "black readers generally and young people in general," McGruder is perfectly cognizant of the risk he's running: "I have a responsibility to the black community to represent us accurately, depicting us both in writing and art in such a way that black people will be proud to allow their children to read."

Judging from his growing list of subscribing papers in large cities with significant numbers of African American citizens, McGruder is achieving his goals. One reader wrote him: "Finally, a comic strip that defines my place, my attitude, my life as a black young man."

I've wondered whether a comic strip whose humor arises almost entirely from an explicitly acknowledged racial antagonism on both sides is a good thing for improving race relations. It is a

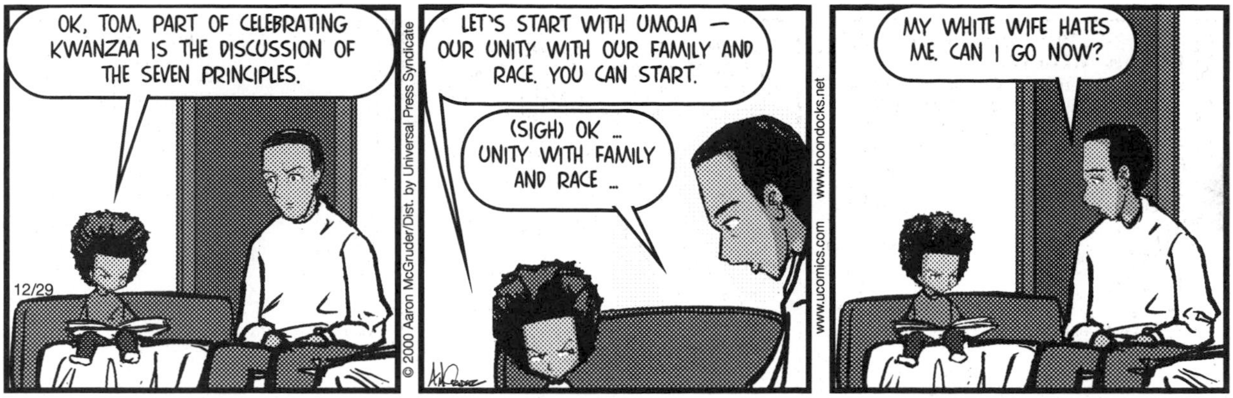
OK, TOM, PART OF CELEBRATING KWANZAA IS THE DISCUSSION OF THE SEVEN PRINCIPLES.
12/29
© 2000 Aaron McGruder/Dist. by Universal Press Syndicate
LET'S START WITH UMOJA — OUR UNITY WITH OUR FAMILY AND RACE. YOU CAN START.
(SIGH) OK ... UNITY WITH FAMILY AND RACE ...
www.ucomics.com www.boondocks.net
MY WHITE WIFE HATES ME. CAN I GO NOW?

matter of no little irony that the continued success of the strip would appear to depend upon perpetuating the racial conflicts that inspire its humor. But after wondering about it, I remembered that humor almost always elevates: It is, I've said, the spark of divinity in humankind. Moreover, as it turned out, McGruder soon annexed new topical territory to the boondocks, staking out all of popular culture as well as the realm of politics and government.

If the strip eases the racial tensions it seems based upon, McGruder won't mind: "To me, judging not only from the launch but the overwhelming response, I would say it's an indicator that while America has a long way to go before it tackles its racial issues, people from all walks of life are ready to start talking about things openly and addressing these taboo issues with candor and honesty. That's a good first step to solving problems."

The strip's grandfather keeps his politically motivated grandsons in check, but that doesn't prevent newspaper readers from rising up occasionally in protest against some offense against taste or decorum that McGruder commits with abandon. McGruder is an unabashed advocate for his demographic, but his sense of humor (albeit a somewhat grim one occasionally) keeps the strip from becoming too shrill—even during the 2000 presidential race when Huey started bashing Bush, thereby widening the focus of the strip to include politics. Other targets included the Ku Klux Klan, Jar Jar Binks, and Black Entertainment Television (BET) in addition to general hypocrisy and pomposity.

To keep the strip's satire as timely as possible, McGruder works with a deadline only a week in advance of publication, a shorter lead time than Garry Trudeau's on *Doonesbury*. McGruder produces the strip electronically, drawing on a Wacom tablet and transmitting the result to his syndicate via ether-mail. During an appearance on a radio talk show while in town for Black History Month, he astonished the show's host by bringing the tablet into the broadcast studio where he drew the strip as he was being interviewed. His syndicate trusts him, he said. Sometimes they even accept material they don't quite understand. "I'll say, 'Trust me—people will get this, people my age, black people.' And they trust me and send it out." Universal Press's cooperative posture with respect to its cartoonists is well-known in the profession, but in this case, the syndicate may be governed by pragmatism as much as principle: with only a week's lead time, there's not much room for revamping.

The Boondocks has frequently been omitted from subscribing newspapers' comics line-ups because it voices an unpopular (perhaps misanthropic) opinion—the kind of opinion I delight in finding anywhere these days but particularly on the funnies page. We need this sort of unvarnished reaction to our contemporary dilemmas in order to compensate for the pablum of political correctness on display in mass media everywhere. (Political correctness, according to Bill Maher—who should know—is defined as "the elevation of sensitivity over truth." Works for me.)

McGruder is not as much upset by being banned as he is fascinated by contemplating who bans the strip and for what. Sometimes a strip runs everywhere but in Chicago or Dallas or Atlanta. At the *Chicago Tribune*, where he speaks fairly often to the editor (who might say, "Great strip—we love it. But we're not running it this week"), he's dropped mostly for legal reasons. "God bless 'em," he says. He made a joke about Whitney Houston using pot, and the *Trib* dropped it. The story about Houston's infatuation with maryjane was all over the news, but the *Trib* didn't want to get sued over a comic strip. In Dallas, they dropped strips with jokes taking shots at the National Rifle Association. In Atlanta, it was Bush jokes. McGruder prefers that his client papers publish the strip, but he doesn't get bent if they don't. He feels he's lucky just being in the paper more often than not. And he's not very accessible to readers who want to complain. His Web site has been down for months. He doesn't like to respond to angry people; he waits until they cool down. And until he does, too. Sometimes, McGruder's offenses against decorum are inadvertent. One spring day, Huey spouts off about his teacher, who, Huey says, is "keeping the masses ignorant." He goes on to say that the man should enjoy his "ill-gotten riches" because "the day of reckoning fast approaches." Readers in Florida were outraged. The cause of their dismay? The strip, drawn a week earlier, was published just two days after a teacher was murdered by a student in Lake Worth, Fla. In response to the outcry, McGruder pointed out that Huey is just a comic-strip character whose readers know he's anti-system but not anti-people.

McGruder says he no longer tries to second-guess what upsets readers, hinting darkly at a racist double-standard: "Trudeau gets away with things, but I can't say the word *pimp*." He got in trouble saying the word *booty*, too, with a notorious strip that celebrated "booty" on BET with a close-up of a black woman's "gyrating rear end"—for which offense, as usual, the cartoonist was criticized by an uptight white readership.

During the radio broadcast, McGruder asked himself if he could continue doing the strip every day for 30 years. He doesn't know. "I didn't think I could do it for five years," he said. And then the strip started, and he didn't think he could do it for six months. It's the deadline pressure, day after day after day. It's wearing. Stalked by the relentless deadline, McGruder seriously considered giving up the strip two years ago. Then came Sept. 11, 2001, and McGruder, shocked, baffled, embarrassed and disgusted, decided to say some things in the strip that no one else, he believed, was saying. His reaction to the aftermath of the vileness of that day was both unconventional and satirical.

While everyone else was calling for terrorist scalps, Huey wondered why people from other nations hated Americans enough to turn themselves into lethal human missiles. While the news media beat the drum of patriotism, Huey carped about cable news turning the a-borning War on Terrorism into a miniseries with special logos and theme music. While everyone else saluted the

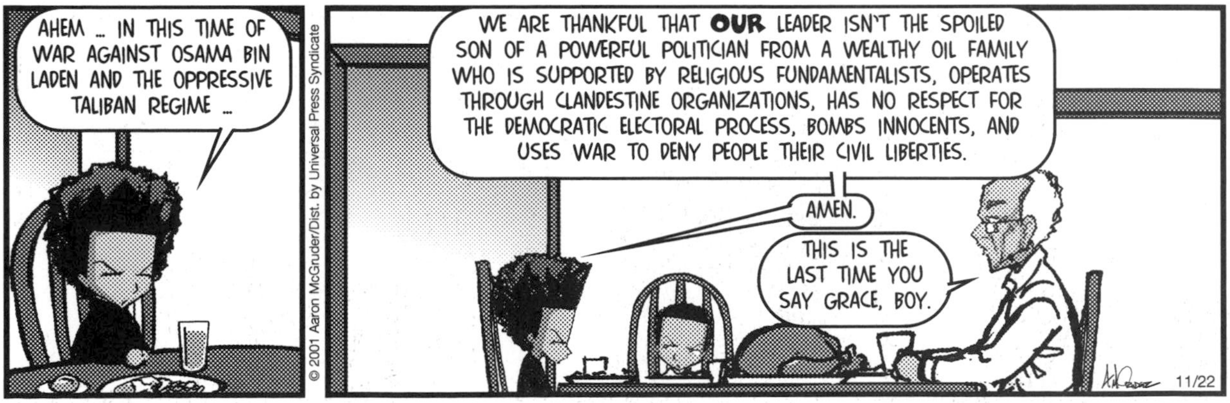
AHEM ... IN THIS TIME OF WAR AGAINST OSAMA BIN LADEN AND THE OPPRESSIVE TALIBAN REGIME ...
© 2001 Aaron McGruder/Dist. by Universal Press Syndicate
WE ARE THANKFUL THAT OUR LEADER ISN'T THE SPOILED SON OF A POWERFUL POLITICIAN FROM A WEALTHY OIL FAMILY WHO IS SUPPORTED BY RELIGIOUS FUNDAMENTALISTS, OPERATES THROUGH CLANDESTINE ORGANIZATIONS, HAS NO RESPECT FOR THE DEMOCRATIC ELECTORAL PROCESS, BOMBS INNOCENTS, AND USES WAR TO DENY PEOPLE THEIR CIVIL LIBERTIES.
AMEN.
THIS IS THE LAST TIME YOU SAY GRACE, BOY.
11/22

Commander in Chief and marched off to war, Huey remembered that Bush was only "almost elected" to the job.

The strip on Thanksgiving Day 2001 was a paean to divergent thinking with a deft finish, blunting the edge of the satire with a human touch but not softening its blow. It was, according to John Nichols writing in *The Nation*, "the most pointed and, no doubt, the most effective dissent from the patriotism that dare not speak its mind." Since 9/11, Nichols noted, *The Boondocks* "has been the most biting and consistent critique of the war and its discontents in the nation's mass media." For that, *The Nation* commended the strip by putting Huey's scowling visage on its cover (Jan. 28, 2002), proclaiming "Sure, he's a cartoon character, but it still takes courage to speak out."

Watching TV during the week of the attack, McGruder said he was shocked by what happened and shocked by "the simplistic nature of a lot of the commentary—this whole 'good' versus 'evil' analysis that sounded like something from fifth grade." In deciding to say something about his conviction, he said he knew he was going "to risk throwing my career away." But he did it anyhow because "it just seemed like nobody else was going to say the things that needed to be said in the places where I had an opportunity to raise questions about the war." Still, he says, "I should not be the guy right now. I should not be the one who is standing out here saying, 'Hold it: this doesn't make any sense.' There are a lot of people who do this so much better than I do."

David L. Ulin, writing in the *Los Angeles Weekly*, observed: "Were McGruder an older, more entrenched cartoonist, the risk of losing his career might have been stifling; even Garry Trudeau was strangely noncommittal for the first month or so after the attacks, as if he had to feel out the territory before he could react."

Sometimes, McGruder continued, he's amazed that he's the only one saying some of the things he says. "But I don't think that's a reflection on me so much as it is a reflection on how narrow the discussion has become in most of the media today. The media has become so conglomerated that there really are very few avenues left for people to express dissent."

But McGruder wasn't the only risk-taker in the equation. His syndicate joined him in the enterprise. Lee Salem explained that "we've always looked on our relationships with the cartoonists and writers we distribute as partnerships, from both a business perspective and from a creative one, too." When I asked Salem for comment on McGruder's crusade, he said: "Political humor—across the spectrum—helps fulfill the potential of comic strips in daily newspapers. Aaron has pushed out the boundaries a bit, but what he has done is well within the purview of *The Boondocks* and the art form."

Relatively few client newspapers objected, Salem said. "And that shows that when the nature of a strip is established, and that strip deals with issues that are part of our conversational currency, newspapers will give an artist some

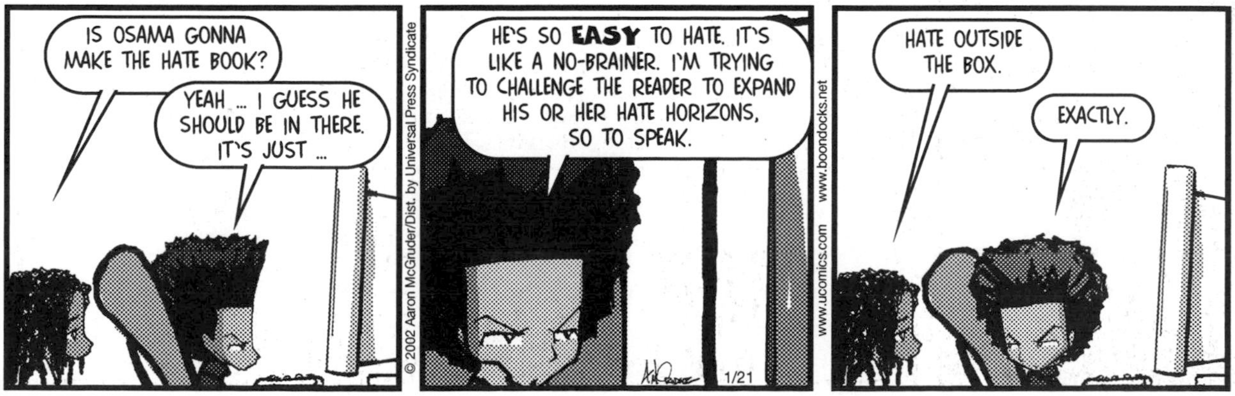
IS OSAMA GONNA MAKE THE HATE BOOK?
YEAH ... I GUESS HE SHOULD BE IN THERE. IT'S JUST ...
© 2002 Aaron McGruder/Dist. by Universal Press Syndicate
HE'S SO EASY TO HATE. IT'S LIKE A NO-BRAINER. I'M TRYING TO CHALLENGE THE READER TO EXPAND HIS OR HER HATE HORIZONS, SO TO SPEAK.
1/21
www.ucomics.com www.boondocks.net
HATE OUTSIDE THE BOX.
EXACTLY.

leeway. When *For Better or for Worse* introduced a gay character, or when *Doonesbury* toured Reagan's brain, many people lost track of the fact that despite the complaints, the vast majority of clients ran the material. I realize that didn't necessarily suggest support for the theme itself, but it did show a willingness to give artists (at least established artists) a bit of freedom. "It helps, too," he continued, "that Aaron is open to editing and suggestions and that when we think he's pushed a bit too much, he's cooperative."

Pulitzer-winning editorial cartoonist Joel Pett (*Herald-Leader*, Lexington, Kentucky) applauded McGruder. "There are a lot of newspapers where Aaron's comic strip probably is the only consistent voice of dissent," said Pett, who raised tough questions in his cartoons about the suffering of Afghan civilians and the role the U.S. has played in spreading terror, suggesting, on occasion, that we should have been dropping more food bundles and fewer bombs. And because *The Boondocks* is seen in so many more papers than the average syndicated editorial cartoonist, McGruder "is getting ideas out to people who don't always read the opinion pages," Pett went on. "He's influencing a lot of young people about how it's okay to question their government and the media. When you think about it, what he has done since September 11 has just been incredible."

A scant month later, McGruder was honored for his outspokenness, joining such luminaries as singer Janet Jackson, the late Secretary of Commerce Ron Brown, comedian Dick Gregory, singer Harry Belafonte and CNN newsman Bernard Shaw as a recipient of the NAACP Chairman's Award, an award for distinguished service and dignified representation of people of color. McGruder didn't seem particularly overwhelmed by NAACP's honor: During the week the award ceremony took place, Huey was lobbying NAACP to add to its roster of awards one for "the most embarrassing black person" and another for "the most ignorant black person." When, in actual life, Condoleezza Rice got an award, Huey thinks at first that NAACP has accepted his suggestion for a Most Embarrassing Black Person Award; then he finds out she received one of the prestigious Image Awards and is appalled: "I wonder if Pat Buchanan is getting a lifetime achievement award," he shouts in exasperation.

Naturally, not everyone thinks McGruder is God's Gift to Interracial Harmony. On Jan. 26, 2002, the *Washington Post* published a letter from a reader that began: "I cannot imagine what Martin Luther King Jr. would say if he were alive and read *The Boondocks* comic strip that ran on Monday [Martin L. King Day]. . . . a strip that referred to 'hating outside the box' and 'challenging the reader to expand his or her hate horizons.' Since when is racism funny? Where is your sense of responsible journalism? . . . I know that this comic strip offends readers. What are you trying to promote?"

Not one to lounge on his laurels, McGruder continued pecking away remorselessly in verbal assaults on BET and politics. And the strip continues to disappear every now and then in consequence. The Sunday strip for Oct. 13, 2002 was dropped at the *Washington Post* for its questionable taste, according to executive editor Len Downie. The strip played off comments made by a German official who compared Dubya's tactics on diverting public opinion with those of Adolf Hitler. "That's preposterous," says Huey, "even I would never compare Bush to Hitler—I mean, Hitler was democratically elected, wasn't he?"

At the *Chicago Tribune*, which ran the strip, the paper's ombudsman Don Wycliff noted after acknowledging complaints about it that many readers believe that McGruder is permitted to get away with saying objectionable things because he is black. Said Wycliff: "It would probably be more accurate to say that he is able to see the things he sees because he is black. Loath though many Americans are to accept it nowadays, having a different historical perspective . . . gives one a different perspective on life and issues. And that perspective, while not the sole determinant of a person's point of view, will assert itself in ways and places both expected and unexpected—even, sometimes, on the funny pages."

Earlier in the month, the *Orlando Sentinel*'s Scott Maxwell noticed that Florida politics had made it into *The Boondocks* soon after Governor Jeb Bush took a stance against a ballot proposal that would allow drug offenders to avoid jail by entering treatment programs. Huey phones Jeb to tell him how impressed he is with the Governor's position, "considering that his daughter, Noelle, has been arrested on drug charges." More significant than Huey's audaciousness, however, was reader reaction in Orlando. After observing that McGruder's strip frequently prompts tirades of outrage and disagreement from the *Sentinel*'s readers, Maxwell said the paper hadn't received a single letter of protest about Huey's comment in the four days since the strip ran.

Several client papers dropped McGruder's March 29, 2003 strip. Running just as the invasion of Iraq was getting underway, the strip consisted of what appeared to be a box of typeset text that had been superimposed upon the strip's panels. The text read: "In order to express the outrage and the disappointment at the situation in the Middle East, as well as an upcoming movie starring Cuba Gooding Jr. in which the actor will undoubtedly shame himself and his race, today's installment of *The Boondocks* will not be appearing. Seriously, folks—let's stop the madness. The Bush administration's hunger for war and Hollywood's continued production of movies starring Cuba Gooding Jr. must be stopped." McGruder has used this ruse before; a text message posing as a newspaper editor's comment. One of his most memorable deployments of the device was *Adventures of Flagee and Ribbon*, accompanied by a faux editor's note explaining that the regular *Boondocks* strip had been "replaced" for its unpatriotic point-of-view by "a hilariously patriotic new offering."

In Durham, N.C., at the *Herald-Sun*, one of the papers that dropped the March 29 strip,

executive editor Bill Hawkins said, "The issue is less about content than about someone going way out of bounds to express his personal political views outside the confines of the cartoon." He said he'd yank any strip that did the same— *Blondie*, for instance, even if the strip used the device in support of the invasion. A letter-writer took exception, saying McGruder's strip was "brilliant" and "acerbic": "Within the world that McGruder creates, his 'text' comic was consistent both in its form and content. The same tactic in *Blondie* would be ridiculous and out-of-character with that particular strip."

At the *Boston Globe*, which also pulled the offending strip, editor Martin Baron said, "What I saw was not a comic strip. It was a written statement on the war. For such commentary, we have the op-ed page and letters. We reserve the comics page for comics." The *Globe*'s ombudsman Christine Chinlund, responding to "dozens upon dozens" of readers who protested the paper's decision, said she'd hate to see the comics page turned into "a sea of text-based political messages" but, she continued, she sees little danger of that. "Allowing *Boondocks* the occasional use of a text note as one way to connect with readers would not threaten the integrity of the comics page." The outpouring of protest, she reported, was more concentrated and more passionate "than any that's been received by this office over the last year, probably longer."

From the beginning, *The Boondocks* has been a highly verbal enterprise. Very little of our comprehension of it depends upon understanding the pictures, which do little more than identify the speakers. At first, McGruder tended to embellish the parade of talking heads by depicting them in picturesque suburban landscapes, occasionally seen from above. And then Huey launched his online newspaper, and for days, we'd see the repetitive image of Huey facing his computer screen, typing something outrageous in a seemingly endless criticism of contemporary society, including sell-out African American entrepreneurs and celebrities.

Although excessively talky, McGruder's scathing take-no-prisoners wit is usually dead on, and the strip's circulation has climbed steadily: it's now in about 250 newspapers.

At the conclusion of his Martin Luther King Symposium keynote, which lasted over an hour, McGruder stood at the lectern on stage signing autographs for a long line of admirers. And when, at last, the line evaporated, we sat down in the first row of seats in the now deserted auditorium and talked. With me were two friends, John Bennett and Dan Yezbick. After about an hour or so, we climbed into John's car to take McGruder to a dinner engagement. What follows is a transcript of our peripatetic exchange, transcribed by Brian K. Morris and edited by me and Milo George.

R. C. HARVEY: Do you do comic strips because you had something to say or something you wanted to draw?

AARON McGRUDER: I love to draw. I loved to draw a lot more before I became a cartoonist.

HARVEY: Compared to how *Boondocks* appears now, there was a lot of drawing in [the] early strips.

McGRUDER: And it nearly killed me. I'm not joking. About spring of 2000, I was in the hospital, Johns Hopkins Emergency, because I had tremendous gastrointestinal disorders from stress. I'd experienced it earlier; it would come and go over the months. I never knew what it was. Then it got so intense that I literally just fell out and I had to go to the emergency room. I was told I might have cancer, and they did all these tests. I remember laying in Johns Hopkins, telling the doctors I could not have the cancer because I had a deadline [laughter] and even if the results of the tests were bad, I was going to make the deadline. I went back to L.A. and got all the tests back. Western doctors are not prone to attributing things to stress, but they said, "Look, if you don't do something about this,

you are going to die. You are going to get cancer. Something really bad is going to happen." I was in so much agony, I couldn't work. I mean, it was physically killing me because it was too much. I just hated trying to make that little space look good in that small an amount of time. I just couldn't do it any more. I said, "Nobody cares. There's five people who work for *The Comics Journal* who notice." [*Laughter.*]

HARVEY: I think that you got involved in this partly because you like to draw.

McGRUDER: Mm-mm.

HARVEY: But the storytelling part of it—the social and political criticism and humor—became as engaging to you as the drawing.

McGRUDER: Absolutely.

HARVEY: Then, with the deadline stress, when you realized that it was possible for you to create the social commentary that you wanted without having to do a lot of drawing, that's what you did.

McGRUDER: Yeah.

HARVEY: But at the beginning of it was drawing—before you became syndicated.

McGRUDER: Before that, I was trying to draw superhero comics. I learned a long time ago, when I used to try to draw superhero comics, that there was a very small percentage of people who could tell the difference between Jim Lee and Todd McFarlane and Art Thiebert and me, as an amateur. And nobody else cared. [*Laughter.*] It was just drawing to them. And if you pointed out the differences, maybe they would start to get it. But nobody cared. People don't read newspaper comics to marvel at beautiful art. They read comics to laugh. What's great about *Calvin and*

Hobbes is that they laughed and then marveled at the beautiful art.

There's no question, I loved to draw but it was easier for me to write than draw. I can write excellently and quickly with very little effort. I cannot do that with art; I have to work. Once I recognized that personal limitation, I could either keep fighting it, or I could keep my career. That's what the choice came down to. At a certain point, you're just being irresponsible by not turning it in, however it looks. That was something I had to learn. But had I continued to try to do what I was doing in the first year or so of the strip, the strip wouldn't even be around any more. And look, I didn't read comics a lot when I was a kid. I wanted to have a way to say something. I wanted a TV show, but realized, "Well, they're not going to just give away a TV show. Let me do a strip." [*Laughter.*] The number of opportunities that this strip has given me, it's astounding.

HARVEY: But before you get into that: I hope you don't give it up, because you're saying things that are rude and necessary to say to a lot of people every day.

McGRUDER: I know that. And the thing that you're doing now is pounding on me. I hear that all the time. John [*McMeel, chairman of Universal Press*] pounds that every time he talks to me. And he's right.

HARVEY: [*Laughter.*] OK, good for him. What are some of the things you're working on in Hollywood?

McGRUDER: Without being specific, the thing about Hollywood is you can make more money in failure [*laughter*] than you can make as a successful cartoonist—like in a weekend of failure. You can get a pilot script—they'll say, "Write a pilot script for us in a weekend." I have made more money doing that than I made in 365 strips, a year of work.

CUSTODIAN: Sorry to bother you, but the building is closing.

McGRUDER: Oh! So I guess we need to mosey someplace else. That's not good, considering it's not exactly warm outside.

HARVEY: [*Laughter.*] Well, let's go over to the student union. We can find a corner in the lounge there. [*They walk out of the building and across the campus.*] When you make money on the weekend writing something, are you writing a treatment or something like that?

McGRUDER: I can write a script in a weekend. Let me tell you, when I sat down to write my first movie, what scared me was that I realized what I was supposed to do for a living wasn't what I was doing. [*Laughter.*] I've never had more fun than when I wrote my first few movies. I was doing them as specs, so I wasn't getting paid, and I still did them on the side of seven days a week. It even made the strip more interesting, because I got to take my mind away from it to work on something else. Recently, I started actually getting paid. To see the amount of money they throw at people to just develop it—it's shocking. Cartooning, for me, is work—for a couple reasons. One, there's the art aspect of it, which is work. Two, it's never-ending, so you get sick of the characters; you have nothing else to say. You get tired and angry at it all. You know, movies end. [*Laughter.*] You get to the end and you get to start thinking about all-new things.

The craft of screenwriting came very, very easily. It was unexpected, but it was simple.

DAN YEZBICK: Remember, Bob, this is the guy who just said they don't just throw TV shows at you. [*Laughter.*] Now they're throwing movies at him.

McGRUDER: Well, not movies, actually. The TV show's being thrown. Let me tell you, I want that Image Award. I have three blind pilot offers, meaning, "We don't have the idea yet. We'll just put the money on the table, and we'll figure something out." [*Laughter.*] NBC, WB and Fox. NBC fell through because they didn't want us to do the ones on Fox and WB. [*Laughter.*] We ended up doing two pilots this season. We're still waiting on the early one for Fox to see if it's going to get shot or not. But even in just the writing of the script, it's tremendous money—you're talking about 22K for a screenplay. It's easy. I walk into meetings, and producers, studio heads, executives say, "Can you do two scripts a month?" [*incredulously*] "Oh no, I'm a cartoonist. [*Laughter.*] This is a breeze. You know, you guys, none of you know what work is." [*They enter the union and find a quiet corner of the lounge.*]

HARVEY: I suppose one of the things that makes scriptwriting come easy is that you're used to writing in that kind of a form—dialogue and so on.

McGRUDER: Oh, there's no question that the year and a half, two years of cartooning that I did before I started writing scripts is what made me a good screenwriter, because it's the ability to come up with jokes quick, especially sitcoms. There have to be a certain number of jokes per page, and that's real serious. Like, they *need* lots of jokes on each page. The ability to sort of conceive of set ups, execution and character development—all in a very short space—really came in handy.

JOHN BENNETT: To what extent does thinking visually play into that?

McGRUDER: It depends. Some writers like to direct on the page, but, generally, it's frowned upon. They don't like it too much when you start putting in too many visual cues on a page; that's really the work of directors. So the real question is to what degree would I be a good director, which I don't know and I'm not really interested in finding out just yet. [*Laughter.*]

BENNETT: What are these pilots called?

McGRUDER: Well, one which just died at WB was called *Milestone*. It was a one-hour action-drama, based on the comic-book universe. When I said that ten years ago I was trying to break into superhero comics, I was trying to get a job with Milestone. And when WB offered me this blind deal, I realized that WB is owned by Warner Brothers, Warner Brothers owns DC, they own the Milestone Universe. Everything, in a very interesting way, came full-circle, and we ended up developing this thing. It just died because it was a one-hour black drama.

Another is called *The Broke Diary*, which is based on a book an ex-girlfriend of mine wrote. It's very, very funny. She's this Philadelphia girl who didn't have any money and ended up going to UP [*University of Pennsylvania*]. *Diary* was a journal she kept about how she hustled her way through school just to pay her bills and buy books and eat. It was really, really funny. She kept a Web site. One day, Random House stumbled across the Web site, and offered her a book deal, so she expanded the journal into a book. She's no longer involved in the project, and I wrote the pilot script.

The real thing I'm actually very excited about, because this actually will be seen one day—well, it's a couple of things. We're doing animated shorts on Fox, like the *Simpsons* were on *Tracey Ullman*. We're doing one, an idea for a variety show on Fox. Fox asked me to create something they could do animated shorts on, like the *Simpsons* with Tracey. It's called *Super Bad*, a really funny comedy about a black superhero who nobody likes, even though he's a really good guy. And the other thing, which is going to be a graphic novel based on a movie script I wrote with Reggie Hudlin [*director of* House Party *and* Boomerang], called *Fight the Power*. It basically reimagines the Florida election mess in Illinois. [*Laughter.*] What happened in Florida was they paid four million dollars to have 50,000 names removed from the voter rolls, most of them black. So we had it take East St. Louis off the rolls. The Supreme Court does its thing, and the Mayor of East St. Louis is really depressed because he promised justice for his people. He gets a call from this guy who's basically the fictionalized version of Bob Johnson of the C.M.V.T. They get together and secede from the Union. [*Laughter.*] East St. Louis becomes its own country; they start an offshore bank in East St. Louis and get really rich, really quick. It ends with this escalation to war between the United States and East St. Louis. [*Laughter.*] It's just an amazing, amazing, amazing piece of satire. It's really a masterpiece. Anyway, we sold this graphic novel, which is going to come out, summer of 2004.

HARVEY: Who's drawing it?

McGRUDER: Not me. [*Laughter.*] I don't know yet. We're talking to Kyle Baker, but I don't think it's going to work out. He doesn't have the time.

HARVEY: Your syndicate obviously knows you're doing this kind of stuff.

McGRUDER: They know this and that, but they worry. I think they worry that my other commitments are why I'm still behind on deadlines, but I would be behind even if I was doing nothing else because it's hard. I think they also worry that I'm going to make so much money from these other projects that I will have no financial motivation to continue doing the strip, which I think is a legitimate concern. [*Laughter.*] But at the same time, the strip is literally the best and the worst thing. If I was just writing movies and just doing television, I would not be able to walk into a packed auditorium to give a lecture and have anybody care about what the hell I was saying. People recognize me on the street like a celebrity. It's not that I need that ego line, but it's a personal relation, a personal connection with people that there's no way to have in a movie or a TV show, where you've got all these different people working on it and your

voice gets changed and you don't really have a lot of say. In comics, that personal connection and voice are completely raw. Nobody stops me from doing anything.

HARVEY: It's about the only entertainment medium that that's true of.

McGRUDER: Yes, it is the absolute only one. I understand how rare it is. It's a really big deal, and it's not all about money for me. It's a weird thing. I want to quit every week. [*Laughter.*] I feel a burden to continue to do it, not that my life is richer. I've been doing the strip for two days out of a week. It's hard. It's so weird. On the one hand, I think, "So what? I can do this for five years." But I've been very close to quitting a number of times. I thought I had done so much damage to my career in terms of blowing deadlines that I was going to get dropped, and it never happened. And at one point, I think I even asked. [*Laughter.*] Lee Salem was trying to get me on time, and I said, "Lee, you know you can always drop me." He doesn't need an excuse. So if I get dropped, then I don't have to feel bad for quitting. [*Laughter.*] But no, I would not ever walk away from it lightly.

HARVEY: What comics did you like as a kid?

McGRUDER: When I was a kid, the *Peanuts* animated specials, to me, were always better than the *Peanuts* strip. But, understand when I was born and when I was reading, it was the later years of the strip. But I really got into comics. I got into *Bloom County* when I was in the seventh grade, and then *Calvin and Hobbes*. I never could get Garry. It just was too smart. I just didn't get the jokes. I wasn't that aware of current events to keep up. But *Bloom County* was accessible and *Calvin and Hobbes* was mostly philosophy. Those are the strips that made me want to do it, particularly *Bloom County*. That was really the one that was why I got into it.

HARVEY: [*Laughter.*] You were born in South Chicago. Where did you grow up?

McGRUDER: I lived here [*in Champaign, Ill.*] for a couple years. Then I moved to Louisville, Ky. for a couple years, but I grew up in Columbia, Md.

HARVEY: You said your dad worked here at the University of Illinois?

McGRUDER: No, he was going to the University. He's had a few jobs over the years. Now, he works for the N.T.S.B. [*National Transportation Safety Board, the federal department that investigates plane crashes*] of D.C. I lived at home when I went to college, commuted from home.

HARVEY: What other strips on the comics page do you admire these days?

McGRUDER: I'm still amazed that Garry Trudeau continues doing this.

HARVEY: And he's doing more elaborate drawings now than he was when he started.

McGRUDER: When I met Garry and sat down with him, it was a while ago—2000, 2001—he showed me the drawings that have been stripped. He has an inker, but he really does draw the hell out of that strip. The pencils are very tight. He loves to draw—I mean, he's doing it at this point because he wants to. I really feel I do it mostly out of a sense of obligation. There are very few times I sit down and think, "Oh, I've got this great joke I've got to tell."

HARVEY: You have a sense of obligation to whom?

McGRUDER: One, there's the financial obligation; until I'm set for life, I have to believe the comic job is a steady one. Once you're in there, you can—even after you die you'll still be getting paid. [*Laughter.*] And I do it out of a sense of obligation to my people.

HARVEY: Well, until you came along, I don't think any black cartoonist who did comic strips was critical of anything in the black community. Robb Armstrong isn't. Steve Bentley isn't.

McGRUDER: But here's the scary thing: before I came along, there were very few people in any medium that were critical of anything. Rap had become very apolitical by 1991, '92. All of black stand-up comedy was this Def Comedy Jam sex stuff—other than Chris Rock who, while his comedy was very political, he himself was not. He was very apolitical; he's strictly about the joke, and uses politics to get the joke across. I don't think he has very passionate political views. So you can look at a lot of media and see that no one was voicing these opinions anywhere. That's why it's such a heavy thing in terms of my responsibility to keep doing it. If I stop, the voice would not be there.

HARVEY: On the radio program today, you said that you didn't like some of the African American strips that have come along since you started. Your disapproval was a professional one; you said these were bad strips.

McGRUDER: Oh, they're bad, they're bad. I'm all for more black people working in any field, but I hate bad black art. If it's not funny, it's not creative. That's why I'm so critical of hip hop. Hip hop is not creative any more.

HARVEY: I was going to ask you about this. You've said that hip hop was a foundation for the humor in the strip—for the strip itself. Hip hop is an attitude, isn't it?

McGRUDER: Hip hop is the technical definition. It's a culture developed in the South Bronx, in New York City, in the mid-'70s. It's sometimes called a culture of collage, but basically, it is black people creating something out of nothing because the resources are not there: There was breakdancing, there's graffiti, MCing or rapping, and DJing. The kids in the ghetto don't have instruments; they got record players. Everyone's band got a record player but no one's got instruments, or you can turn a record player into an instrument. I think rhyming came out of a natural set of evolutions of a number of things, like The Last Poets, James Brown and Funkadelic. The attitude didn't really come out of nowhere. Like everything else, it was the natural evolution of black cultural expression. It's the spirituals, the rules of jazz, rock and roll, disco and funk. All that stuff brings us to hip-hop music. And it artistically stagnated around 1995, basically.

HARVEY: How would hip hop be important to you as a cartoonist on *The Boondocks*?

McGRUDER: My political perspectives as a young adult were shaped by hip hop's political era, which was 1987 to 1992, roughly when I was in junior high and high school. We had Public Enemy, KRS-One, X-Clan, Brand Nubian and all of these very overtly political groups.

HARVEY: Who were essentially saying "the Establishment lies to you."

McGRUDER: It was more than that: It was actual Black Nationalism; it was radical socialism. There was no black leadership supplying these political ideals to the next generation, and what few people there were, a lot of us—particularly those of us who grew up in the suburbs—discovered that through hip hop. We discovered who Louis Farrakhan was through hip hop. When the trends changed, most people changed with it, and a handful of us were put on this path to become politically oriented, because of hip hop. Everything about the strip, really—it's very much a friend of hip hop.

HARVEY: So when you say you found out about Louis Farrakhan and various other things in hip hop was it through song lyrics?

McGRUDER: Oh, yes. It was explicit song lyrics. There was a time when hip hop was very spiri-

tual, very political, and that had to be when I was in high school. It had a tremendous impact on me. It basically set me on the path that I've been on ever since.

HARVEY: Why did Huey, Riley and their grandfather have to go to the suburbs?

McGRUDER: White people are the backdrops in most black Americans' lives. It's basically just that simple. While most of our friends, our families, our ups, our downs all come from other black people, there's always that backdrop of white America— who we work for, who we pass on the way to the store and who we sit in classes with but don't really hang out with after class. That's our lives.

HARVEY: When the strip first started, there was a palpable sense of black kids in white America. But there isn't that sense, to me, anymore.

McGRUDER: It doesn't need to be. It was never—I made a conscious decision not to do the interracial story, but I had to set the story up and do the obvious jokes. But the strip has always been about the black perspective of the world, and that's what it is. There's not much more you can do with that space.

I look at what Garry does with his characters and think, "I haven't been reading the strip for ages, so I don't know these characters' backstories." I don't know them. At any given time, someone's going to pick this strip up on Tuesday and may not pick it up again till Friday. That wonderful story arc you worked out? No, it's all about hitting a solid joke every day. The easiest way for me to do that is to talk about what's going on in the world from this perspective that people don't ever hear, and that's uncomfortable. Telling stories about characters and all that stuff, to me, is better left to another medium.

HARVEY: A lot of Garry's effort is devoted to character development quite apart from whatever issues he's commenting on.

McGRUDER: Yes, yes. He'll do a week on politics and then a week on the characters, I guess because that's what [*Jim*] Andrews [*one of the founding partners of Universal Press*] told him when he was around. That's his and Lee's philosophy. You balance out. You do a week of heavy political stuff and a week of the character stuff. It's just not that easy for me.

HARVEY: Do you see any of Keith Knight's strip?

McGRUDER: I bought *Fear of a Black Marker*. It's clever, it's different, it's creative, and I like it. He's so very energetic. I look at guys like him and think, "They're real cartoonists. I'm just acting." [*Laughter.*] I'm just amazed at guys like him, who really are legitimate real-deal cartoonists. I'm just getting by. [*Laughter.*]

HARVEY: Who else do you admire on the funnies page?

McGRUDER: I like *Get Fuzzy*, actually. I like Garry and I admire Lynn Johnston just for being Lynn Johnston. That's never been my thing; the heartwarming, feely, touchy. But every single strip is just as unbelievable, this story that she's telling. I have a lot of respect for her. I like Wiley [*Non Sequitur*] because he wrote me a very nice e-mail the first day out. [*Laughter.*] It was the very first day and I was terrified.

HARVEY: Ah, good for Wiley. [*Laughter.*] You're going to be sharing wall space with Wiley at the Cartoon Art Museum in San Francisco pretty soon; they're running a show about controversial comics.

McGRUDER: I think Garry and Berkeley are also involved. That's how they sell me on the stuff. They say, "Garry's gonna do it." [*Laughter.*] "Berke's going to do it." [*Laughter.*]

HARVEY: Have you met Berke Breathed?

McGRUDER: No, I'm afraid to. All the stories I've heard, I'm afraid he'll be an asshole and I won't like him any more. [*Laughter.*] I just want to keep liking him. He just did a really interesting interview with *The Onion A.V.* I know he's doing a movie for Miramax—good luck dealing with Harvey Weinstein. [*Laughter.*]

HARVEY: What do you think of *Dilbert*?

McGRUDER: *Dilbert*'s really an amazing thing. To be that entertaining and be *soooo* crudely drawn.

HARVEY: You said today on the radio that you're always interested in why a newspaper dropped a strip. The strip would run in every paper in the country except one.

McGRUDER: Just one, and the reason's always a little different. It's a regional thing. I don't always know when stuff gets pulled. [*Laughter.*] It's not that big a deal, really. [*Laughter.*] They're still paying for it. Not that it happens a lot, but it happens enough for us. My worry about the deadlines basically eats up all the worry I got. [*Laughter.*] There's not a lot else to worry about. You can't even bring yourself to worry about other things like content issues because the deadlines are emptying. They take everything out of you.

EPILOGUE:

Later, as we were driving to take him to his dinner engagement, McGruder remarked, somewhat wistfully, that he deeply regretted that he never got a chance to find out what Charles Schulz thought of his strip.

COPYRIGHT R. C. HARVEY

172

The Crisis
SEPTEMBER/OCTOBER 2003

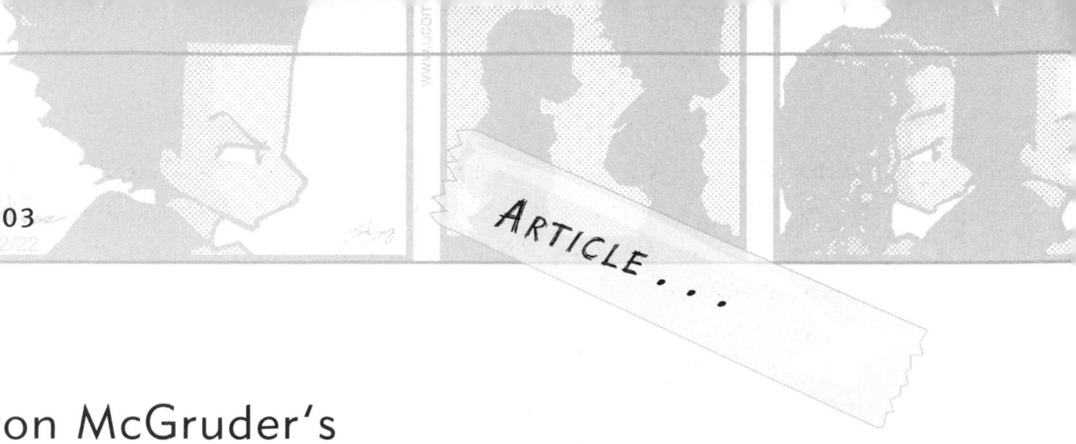
ARTICLE . . .

Free Huey: Aaron McGruder's Outer Child Is Taking on America

MICHAEL DATCHER

McGruder, Huey's creator, is in the running for American antihero.

"Marches are not gonna do it anymore," the bespectacled University of Maryland alum says, sitting on his living room couch. "We need guys who will change the world and no one will know their names. We need gangsters. We need people who have figured out what to do when you walk into the room of power and the only person in the room is the devil—because that's where we're at today."

Since Universal Press Syndicate (UPS) began syndicating *The Boondocks* in 1999, the 29-year-old free thinker has had something to say, and an audience of more than 20 million to say it to. And McGruder has not been shy. . . .

McGruder is a cartoonist who's making his readers laugh and pissing them off at the same time.

THREE RIVERS PRESS WISHES TO THANK THE CRISIS, THE PUBLISHER OF THE MAGAZINE OF THE NATIONAL ASSOCIATION FOR THE ADVANCEMENT OF COLORED PEOPLE, FOR THE USE OF THIS MATERIAL FIRST PUBLISHED IN THE SEPTEMBER/OCTOBER 2003 ISSUE OF *THE CRISIS*.

Africana
SEPTEMBER 30, 2003

INTERVIEW . . .

The Africana QA: Aaron McGruder

BOMANI JONES

"All I do is tell jokes for a living. I ain't a leader. This ain't the revolution," says Aaron McGruder. If only our leaders were as smart as this "entertainer"! . . .

When you look back at older strips, what are the biggest differences you notice in your work from now to then?

I try my best not to do that. It's one of the worst things you can do!

In your introduction, you said that doing the strip was beginning to burn you out before 9/11. What was so stressful about it?

Seven strips a week. It's a full-time job with no vacation. . . .

Last time I talked to you, you were adamant that your primary job is to be funny. But I turned to C-Span the other day, and I saw you giving an impassioned speech about how important it was for young black journalists to relay un-heard messages. Do you feel a stronger pull to making statements at this point than you did before?

What I was also telling those kids was that whatever message you want to get across, make sure that you're doing it effectively, and that's the whole point when I say the primary job is being funny. The reason that is, is because if I'm not funny no one pays attention to anything I'm saying. People who are trying to sort of counteract all of this negativity that we all talk about that's in the media can often shoot themselves in the foot by being ineffective communicators, meaning that if you're in the entertainment business and you're trying to get a message across, you have to be entertaining first. Or else, you'll end up like some of these underground rap groups that are "positive," but no one's listening to them. It really requires a sort of sophisticated understanding of how to walk that line between being entertaining and giving your audience what it wants, and then trying to sort of do something to sort of raise awareness at the same time. . . .

Do you think there will be a rise in black cartoonists?

There absolutely will be. As a matter of fact, there already has been. The question is, "are they gonna be good or are they gonna be knockoffs of me?" I personally don't wanna see any knockoffs of me. People have to be original. What I'm seeing so far are knockoffs of me, and that's not cool. Personally, I don't wanna see a bunch of black cartoonists if they're not good. That doesn't make me feel good that I opened the door for a bunch of untalented people who got on just because the other syndicates are trying to catch on with what Universal Press did.

That said, I know some very talented black cartoonists, and I'm hoping that they do get a shop. I try to help where I can, but I have no interests in seeing a bunch of bad *Boondocks* knockoffs turning up in newspapers.

The Washington Post
OCTOBER 19, 2003

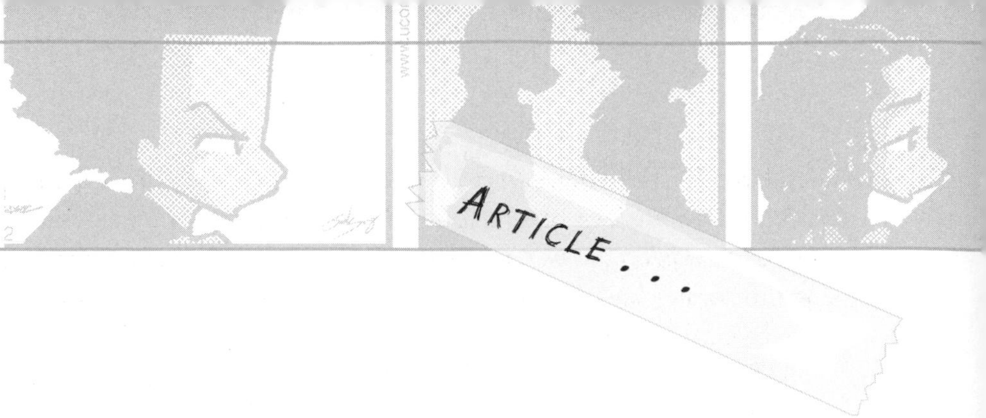
ARTICLE . . .

Putting *The Boondocks* in the Dock

MICHAEL GETLER

Followers of the comic strip *The Boondocks* were first puzzled and then angry last week. Sometimes this edgy, irreverent and controversial strip, drawn and written by a 29-year-old African American artist, Aaron McGruder, makes some readers mad, and they let the paper know.

But last week it was the many fans of McGruder, and of the clever collection of precocious youngsters he has created, who were mad at the *Post* when they realized the paper had killed six days of *Boondocks* strips and substituted reruns from 1999. On Monday and Tuesday, no notification ran that these were reruns. Beginning Wednesday, the paper printed a tiny line under the strip that said, "This strip has been previously published." No further explanation was given. The paper's Web site was a bit more forthcoming: "The *Washington Post* has decided not to publish this week's *Boondocks* strip. The comic will return to washingtonpost.com Oct. 19."

The *Post*, from time to time, decides not to publish a particular comic if it is deemed unsuitable for one reason or another. This can be a good thing; guardians of the news sections keep watch over everything, including the comics, that gets published. Some readers call this current act censorship. The *Post* calls it editing.

The *Post*, however, has never before killed an entire week's worth of one comic strip. Actually, because the strips dealt with a single theme, it would have made no sense to publish just some of them.

The unpublished strips focus on White House national security adviser Condoleezza Rice and a scheme cooked up by one of the kids in the strip. The idea is to save the world by getting Rice a boyfriend. "Maybe if there was a man in the world who Condoleezza truly loved, she wouldn't be so hellbent to destroy the planet," says one of McGruder's rambunctious youngsters. The strip's central character, Huey Freeman, who could be a 12-year-old, thinks this is a great idea and the strip ventures deeper into some touchy territory. McGruder knows this and pokes fun at his own characters, with Huey observing that what he really likes about the idea "is that it isn't the least bit sexist or chauvinistic."

Post Executive Editor Leonard Downie Jr. comes right to the point: "*The Boondocks* strips in question commented on the private life of the national security adviser and its relationship to her official duties in ways that violated our standards for taste, fairness and invasion of privacy." As for the lack of an explanation, he says: "We edit all parts of the paper every day, including the comics, and do not usually notify readers about what we are not publishing or why."

McGruder's strip is popular and about 250 newspapers publish it. An editor at Universal Press Syndicate, the distributor for *The Boondocks*, says that the *Post* was the only newspaper to kill this series of strips. There were no calls or complaints about it from other papers, he says.

Once *Post* readers caught on, and caught up with the strip in other papers and Web sites, plenty of complaints were made—against the paper. "We are grown-ups out here, not children," wrote one reader. "Pulling *Boondocks* was an insult to your readers and to Aaron McGruder," wrote another. "Has the *Post* become so timid as to refuse to run a comic strip that pokes fun at a member of the Bush administration?" another wrote. Many felt the *Post* was engaging in censorship, and that plenty of other comics and cartoons can be viewed as insulting to a public figure. "The *Post* has committed the cardinal sin of the humorless," added another. "It failed to recognize satire when it saw it. As the strip makes clear, we're laughing at the guy who suggested finding Condi a guy, not at Condi."

I may need a refresher course in sensitivity training, but I also found the sequence of strips within the bounds of allowable satire. I don't know a thing about Rice's personal life, nor do the characters in the strip, and I think readers understand that. The *Boondocks* characters, and their creator, were being mischievous and irreverent, in their mind's view of the world, about a high-profile public figure, and that seems okay to me.

Los Angeles Times
APRIL 25, 2004

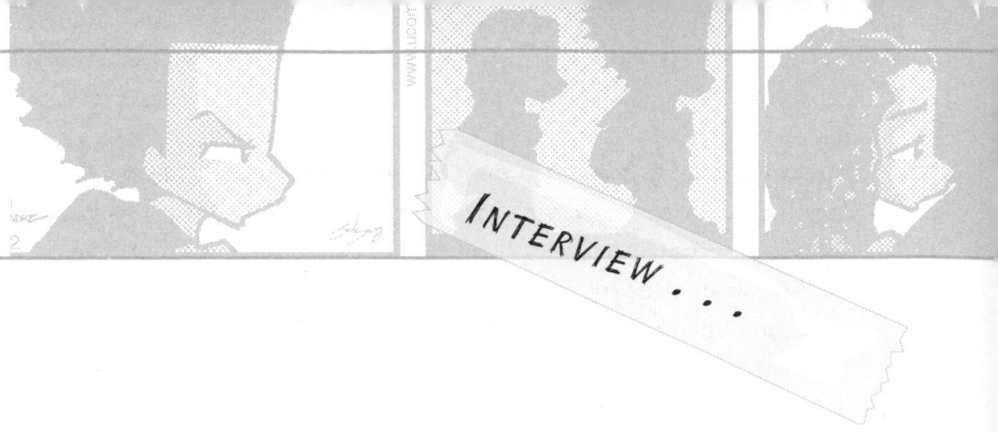
INTERVIEW . . .

He's Gotta Fight the Powers That Be

Aaron McGruder's In-Your-Face Cartoon Strip, *The Boondocks*, Takes No Prisoners—Black or White. How Did This Nice Young Man From the Suburbs Get So Mad?

GREG BRAXTON

The angriest black man in America sits in his living room, far from relaxed. As usual, he is engaged in battle.

As the sun disappears and the room grows darker, Aaron McGruder hunkers down on a plush couch that almost swallows his slight frame. The combative creator of *The Boondocks* comic strip is taking on his latest opponent, temporarily putting aside his usual targets—President Bush, Condoleezza Rice, Donald Rumsfeld, Puff Daddy, Will Smith, Whoopi Goldberg, Justin Timberlake, the BET and UPN networks, flag-wavers, black movies such as *My Baby's Daddy*, and the war in Iraq.

The cartoonist, writer, producer, unofficial prophet of the hip-hop generation is fighting a cold. And at this moment, on a chilly late winter evening, the cold is kicking his behind.

"I'm OK, I'm OK," says the warrior, who has little appetite but is forcing himself to snack. "Just trying to do too much, got run-down. It will be all right."

It's a battle the 29-year-old can't afford to lose. In a few days, McGruder will fly to Korea to oversee animated footage for a TV pilot based on his edgy comic strip about two black brothers from Chicago who reluctantly move to the suburbs with their gruff grandfather. The strip is syndicated in about 300 newspapers, including the *Los Angeles Times* and the *Washington Post*, making it one of the country's more popular syndicated strips. *A Right to Be Hostile*, a *Boondocks* collection from its first five years, was a recent bestseller.

There has never been a comic strip in American newspapers quite like *The Boondocks*—a blunt, critical remix of race relations, pop culture icons, black politics, rappers and racists. The strip mirrors much of McGruder's perspective about current affairs, as seen through the eyes of the militant 10-year-old Huey and the gangsta-wannabe Riley, who is "8-ish."

With his once-fashionably unkempt Afro now trimmed to a smoother shortness that highlights his subtly handsome features, McGruder may look like a young scholar more at home in the library than on the front lines of political discourse. But his low-key demeanor hides a passionate, plain-spoken activist who is seldom at a loss for words—particularly words that bite the powers that be. His college lectures often sell out, filled with fans who come to hear humorous commentary but wind up hearing an artist consumed by conspiracy theories and concern for his country.

And woe to the unsuspecting person who approaches McGruder at a party to challenge his views.

"I'm ready to fight outside work," he says. "If someone wants to come up and start a political conversation with me, it can quickly turn into an argument. People don't understand—a lot of this [expletive] is not funny to me."

If humor masks the pain of the comedian, then satire masks the indignation of the political cartoonist. But in the case of Aaron McGruder, it's not much of a disguise. Unlike his heroes, Garry Trudeau—whose once-radical *Doonesbury* lefties have lost their edge to middle age—and Berkeley Breathed—whose *Bloom County* has a playful, absurdist tinge—McGruder's *The Boondocks* is transparently cynical rage, filtered through an African American prism. It's no coincidence that one of the strip's protagonists shares a name with former Black Panther firebrand Huey Newton.

Just as hip-hop music, fashion and attitude dominate pop culture, McGruder's Afrocentric strip is read by cultural cognoscenti of all colors. Documentary filmmaker Michael Moore wrote the foreword to *A Right to Be Hostile*. Bill Maher frequently invites the cartoonist for his Real Time HBO discussion fest. Comedian Chris Rock featured projected images of Huey and Riley before each show on his recent tour.

And all this from a nice young man who grew up in Columbia, a middle-class Maryland suburb, with his stay-at-home mother, his father, who works for the National Transportation Safety Board, and an older brother, Dedric. Though the McGruder boys grew up in a suburban setting that mirrors Huey and Riley's, McGruder says politics "was not a big deal in our house," and he maintains his strip is not autobiographical.

"All the characters come from me, but they are not all me," he says. "They live in a household

without women, which was not my experience. Huey is not bound by limitations. He's more morally pure; he sees the world through 10-year-old eyes."

McGruder started drawing when he was a small child. Deciding in his late teens that he wanted to be a professional cartoonist, he started developing the strip while attending the University of Maryland. Early on, he focused on developing characters. The earliest *Boondocks* were less political, made distinctive by McGruder's simultaneous embrace and attack of black culture, and flavored by his dry wit. But the events of Sept. 11 changed him and his creation.

"I started seeing a problem," McGruder says. "Journalists stopped being journalists. All this cheerleading started. All of a sudden this lame president was being hailed as a bold national leader. No one was asking questions about how every system designed to protect this country failed. And where were all these flags coming from?

"I was disgusted by the whole thing. And I thought, 'What am I going to write about now? Puffy? That seems stupid now.' I suddenly knew what I wanted to do. And the material just wrote itself. It was then I became a political cartoonist."

The Boondocks has since raised hackles in political circles, mostly due to McGruder's attacks on the Bush administration and its policies. The *Washington Post* last October yanked a week of strips making fun of Rice and her love life. Previously, a few papers had pulled strips denouncing the wave of patriotism following the war.

But McGruder's public comments have brought him as much notoriety as his strip. He has bragged about calling Rice a "murderer" to her face. He has knocked the Democratic Party for not being aggressive or nasty enough to take back the White House, a declaration that earned him some boos at a dinner honoring *The Nation* magazine.

The aspiring cartoonist started sending out

packages of *The Boondocks* in 1997, a year before he graduated, to various newspaper syndicates. He wasn't getting much encouragement, but opportunity came at a National Association of Black Journalists convention.

Harriet Choice, who was then a vice president with Universal Press Syndicate, went to the convention looking for minority talent. As she sat in on a seminar on black cartoonists, someone handed her some papers over her shoulder. "I turned around and there was this young man there," she recalls. "He didn't say anything. He just smiled. I looked at what he had given me, and it was some strips. The first thing I noticed was his unique style. The drawings just had a different look. I knew the minute I saw them that this guy, with the proper nurturing, could be a major force in comics. I could see there was something biting about the comics, but it was also touching."

Lee Salem, executive vice president and editor of Universal Press Syndicate, adds that McGruder also came along at the right time, when there was a push for diversity among cartoonists. With the exception of the family-oriented *Curtis* and *Jump Start*, there were no black-themed strips. And only *Doonesbury* and *Mallard Fillmore* were taking bold political stances.

"We knew that *The Boondocks* was not a tried-and-true format, and that it would not sit well with a lot of people," Salem says. "It was not a slam dunk, because we knew some would love it and some would hate it."

McGruder laughs now when thinking back on his last school year, when he had postgraduate job security: "I was just intolerable. I did my undergraduate thesis on me!" More accurately, he says the thesis was about African American political cartoonists. The syndicate waited another year before launching *The Boondocks* in April of 1999. McGruder moved to Los Angeles that year.

The sensibility of the strip reflected the philosophies of McGruder's early heroes, musical acts such as KRS-One and Public Enemy, who used rap to convey political messages. He is disdainful of most contemporary hip hop. Sean Combs—a.k.a. Puff Daddy a.k.a. P. Diddy—was a frequent target of *The Boondocks* wrath.

Except for a sporty car and a Beverly Hills address, McGruder does not surround himself with the trappings of his success. He shuns celebrity and the party circuit, preferring to socialize with a small group of friends or write screenplays at home. He is an avid collector of *Star Wars* and other movie memorabilia.

He's also a bit awkward in crowds, particularly when he is the center of attention. When the American Civil Liberties Union honored him last year at a garden party in Brentwood, McGruder was visibly uncomfortable as he was shuttled from one famous member to another. When Los Angeles became the capital of Hip Hop Nation during the NBA All-Star Weekend in February, he left town.

"Aaron is not a loner by choice," says filmmaker Reginald Hudlin, one of McGruder's closest friends, who is co-developing the TV pilot for Fox and Sony Pictures Television. "He enjoys other people and enjoys collaborating. He just doesn't suffer fools. The nature of his work makes the stakes higher than just doing a comic strip or a TV series. The vacuum of political thought in black America adds to the pressure. Given his youth and the scale of pressure he has, he handles it very well."

Julian Bond, chairman of the National Association for the Advancement of Colored People, has called *The Boondocks* "one of the most distinctive comic strips in American history," comparing McGruder to Thomas Nast, the father of American editorial cartoons.

On the other side of the *Boondocks* fence is conservative radio talk-show host Larry Elder, who labels McGruder an artist out of control. Elder regularly rants about the cartoonist on his daily syndicated show.

"He's an obviously successful illustrator, and I find the strip sometimes quite funny," Elder says. "But he is ill-informed, childish and mean-spirited." Elder believes the strips about Rice and her love life "went over the line."

"Look at what she's accomplished: She's a concert pianist. She's fluent in Russian. She's a force of nature. And she's a figure that deserves a certain amount of respect.

"And when you say things such as Colin Powell is like Darth Vader, it's outrageous. The reason he gets less criticism is because he's black."

McGruder's response to Elder was to make him one of the potential suitors for Rice in the strip, making fun of the radio host's self-proclaimed title of "The Sage of South-Central." And the statuette for Huey's annual "Most Embarrassing Black People" award almost got a new name: "The Larry Elder."

As for Black Entertainment Television—a constant *Boondocks* target for what McGruder perceives as its over-reliance on booty-shakin', thug-lovin' music videos—network spokesman Michael Lewellen says: "Some of Aaron's commentaries have been shortsighted where the network is concerned. It's hard to tell whether he has a good understanding of what BET is all about. He certainly at times has sought to antagonize BET, and has made [founder Robert Johnson] a target. For reasons of his own, he's chosen to ignore the positive quality of BET. He's focused on the microcosms of the network, and has not seen it for what it's become."

The TV pilot is just the tip of the evolving McGruder empire. He, Hudlin and artist Kyle Baker are putting the final touches on their upcoming graphic novel *Birth of a Nation*, about the chaos that erupts when East St. Louis secedes from the country. A *Boondocks* movie, merchandise and a clothing line are planned.

And then there's the never-ending commitment of the strip. McGruder must come up with ideas to fill six daily installments, plus a Sunday edition. Even with assistance in drawing and writing *The Boondocks* McGruder laments, "It all basically comes back to me."

But, he admits, "The pressure I feel now with getting the show ready is nothing compared to the first four years of the strip, when I had two deadlines a week all by myself. Those years were all about getting the strip in on time. And I was always beating myself up about that."

McGruder regularly operated on panic mode with his deadlines. Prone to procrastination, he would look for inspiration from CNN, the newspaper, talks with friends. But inspiration was frequently elusive.

"A lot of people handle deadlines better, they have more experience," he explains. "But for me, it was a continual black cloud over my head. I aged 10 years in those first four years of the strip. And I grew to hate the strip."

According to his Universal Press Syndicate editor, Greg Melvin: "What compounded the situation was that drawing a comic strip, by its very nature, is a solitary profession. It's no bed of roses. It's one person looking at a blank computer, trying to come up with 365 good gags a year. And Aaron is his own worst critic."

There were times in those first years when McGruder was so distraught that he couldn't sleep and could barely eat. The mental stress manifested itself into a physical pain that racked the cartoonist day and night.

Hudlin witnessed McGruder's gradual meltdown: "It was horrific. He has this incredible job, but it's the job that never ends. And this was with a guy who had never left home before, and he had moved to the other side of the world. It all finally caught up to him. And it was the most scared I've ever seen him."

Other personal pressures weighed on him. His growing celebrity alienated him from longtime friends back home. "I felt very isolated during those first two years. I had just moved across the country. Some of my friends started buggin'. Everybody thought I had this glamorous life in Los Angeles; I was on TV and magazines. But they didn't know what I was going through. Egos got crazy. They anticipated change when there was none. I went back home to try and repair things, but there were shouting matches; irreparable damage was done.

"All this made me a very dark person. Friends would call me from parties, saying, 'Man, you should be here,' and I'd think, 'Yeah, but I'm working, trying to think up stuff.'

"I thought, 'What's the point of all this success if you're not having fun?'"

The angst manifested itself in the strip. Several installments of *The Boondocks* focused on Huey's procrastination about cutting the lawn, which was McGruder's way of illustrating his problems. And in one installment, Huey has difficulty coming up with an appropriate logo for the so-called "revolution." "I don't know why I gotta lead the revolution and illustrate it, too," he declared. "I don't even like drawing."

Then, one day in 2000, the panic became so severe that he suffered gastrointestinal pains that put him on the floor. During a visit home, he was rushed to Johns Hopkins Hospital. When he told emergency room doctors that he had a deadline to meet, one warned him that he might die if he didn't do something about his stress.

Says McGruder: "Things really changed at that point. I had to acknowledge that these deadlines were not worth my health. I came to accept that blowing a deadline would not mean the end of the world, or the end of my career."

September 11 changed the world forever. It also changed the world of *The Boondocks*, providing its creator with a newfound sensibility and making the strip more confrontational.

The regular characters were temporarily replaced at one point by "The Adventures of Flagee and Ribbon," featuring a talking American flag and a patriotic ribbon. But not everyone was laughing. Editors at several newspapers thought that the nation was still too raw to appreciate a sarcastic swipe at patriotism. Several papers refused to run them.

McGruder grew even more radical and critical of Bush and the government. The cartoonist

counts the period as one of his best, and believes it was award-worthy. Universal Press Syndicate nominated him for the Pulitzer Prize.

"I wasn't even a finalist," McGruder says. "I care little about awards, but I felt I deserved it. Other political cartoonists were saying how good my work was. It was a remarkable point in history, and it was really frustrating.

"That was my window, and I don't know if I'll ever get another opportunity to shine like that. That's why getting the NAACP Image Award made up for it."

In 2002, McGruder was to receive the Chairman's Award, the civil rights organization's highest honor. But even that was bittersweet due to another honoree—National Security Advisor Condoleezza Rice. The U.S. had just invaded Afghanistan, and Rice had become one of McGruder's chief nemeses. The two were to be feted at the same ceremony.

McGruder used the occasion to bite the hand that honored him.

"It was a delicate situation," he recalls. "I thought, 'How is that for crazy?' I started doing strips about the Image Awards honoring her."

The cartoonist says he contacted NAACP Chairman Julian Bond, "and told him I would have to address it in the strip, making fun of how they could honor her, but I wouldn't be inappropriate. But I had to not be hypocritical. I had to say something."

He would get his chance—in a way even he didn't anticipate.

At the ceremony, McGruder, who favors casual dress, was sitting in the front row of the Universal Amphitheatre in a suit—nervous and uptight. It was one of his first appearances at a ceremony that would be on national television.

But poise returned during his speech. "I'm not exactly sure what the NAACP was trying to start when they put me and Condoleezza Rice in the same row," he quipped, rubbing his chin. He then went into his real message. He said he created *The Boondocks* as "a radical black voice that the U.S. government could not kill." He said he didn't like the president, and he didn't like the war. He said, "If they decide to take me out, someone else can write for Huey, and his voice will go on." Near the end of his address, he told the audience to challenge what "they" tell you, "because they are lying."

The speech drew applause but also caused a bit of a stir in the audience. Some said afterward they thought McGruder went too far, especially in Rice's presence, and had been a bit ungracious in his speech.

After the show, he was talking with a friend when he felt a hand on his shoulder. He turned to see Rice's smiling face.

"I did not want to meet her, but there she was," McGruder says.

The crowd watched as the two engaged in hushed conversation. When they parted a few minutes there, some attendees applauded: "They thought we had a nice little exchange."

So what was said? McGruder is still a little uncomfortable discussing the meeting.

"She asked if she could be drawn into the strip," he finally says. "It was an indication of how little I mean to her. She couldn't have cared less about what I had said about her. She's not scared of me. I'm scared of her. I am not a threat to Condoleezza Rice. What I really wanted to do was call her 'murderer' to her face."

He still will not reveal precisely what he said to Rice, "but it was done in a clever way," he says. McGruder made even more of an impression with his acceptance speech.

"I had to say something," he insists.

One person in attendance that night was Fox Entertainment president Gail Berman.

"I was unaware of the strip at that time," she says. "I thought his statements were so cool, so wild. I thought, 'I've got to find out more about this guy.' I called him up, and it turns out we had a lot in common. We both grew up in Columbia.

"He wasn't ready to do anything in terms of

The Boondocks at that time, but it was the beginning of our creative relationship."

Rice got her wish—to a certain extent. In the following week's strip, Huey speculated that the real reason she was honored was because NAACP president and CEO Kweisi Mfume was not really Kweisi Mfume, but an evil twin cloned from strands of the real Mfume's hair.

As it turned out, McGruder was just getting started on Rice. Last October, Huey and Riley said they needed to find a boyfriend for Rice because, "if she had a man in her life, she wouldn't be so hellbent on destroying the world." The story line ran for a couple of weeks as the boys considered a list of candidates, including Elder, Ward Connerly and Montel Williams.

The *Washington Post* pulled the first week of strips, and *Post* executive editor Leonard Downie Jr. explained in a statement: " *The Boondocks* strips in question commented on the private life of the national security advisor and its relationship to her official duties in ways that violated our standards for taste, fairness and invasion of privacy."

McGruder's reaction?

"It's a mystery to me," he says with amusement. "Of all the stuff I've done on her, I thought this was really tame. And kinda cute."

Another Rice-flavored stir erupted in December during a Washington, D.C., dinner marking the 138th anniversary of *The Nation* magazine, which a few years before had put Huey on the cover. Referring to their NAACP Awards conversation, McGruder told the audience that he had called Rice "a murderer to her face." (Rice's office did not return phone calls regarding McGruder.) He drew boos when he proclaimed that Democrats had to be meaner if they wanted to take back the White House.

In January, on the syndicated TV show *America's Black Forum*, McGruder repeated his Rice denouncement, causing some on the panel, including syndicated columnist Armstrong Williams, to take issue: "I can't get over the fact you labeled Miss Rice a murderer," he said.

McGruder calmly replied: "She's a murderer because I believe she's a murderer."

Defining his confrontational comments, McGruder says: "I've always been aware that I have an opportunity to say things that nobody else is saying, or is afraid to say. And I don't want to waste a single opportunity."

McGruder should be exhausted. It is early March, and he has just arrived in New York from a trip to Asia. But there is no trace of fatigue in his voice.

"What I've seen is spectacular," he says, describing his visit to the studio that is doing the animation for the TV pilot.

McGruder and Hudlin have very specific ideas about how *The Boondocks* will look and feel on television. The style will be anime, a genre favored by many in the hip-hop generation.

They both are being meticulous about every detail. Endless casting and recasting sessions have been held for the voices of Huey, Riley and Grandpa. Because of the nine-month gap between script and finished animation, the show will not have the topical humor of the strip. But McGruder insists it will be edgy, and "most of all, it will be funny."

Outside of Comedy Central, Fox, which airs *The Simpsons* and *King of the Hill*, would seem like the perfect spot for *The Boondocks*. But Fox is also where *The PJs*, an animated series set in a housing project, failed to catch on, while catching fire for some of its depictions. McGruder is not expecting the animated *Boondocks* to be controversial.

McGruder, however, has decided to tone down his outspokenness and focus on his franchise. As *The Boondocks* moves uptown to Hollywood, McGruder feels it's time to cool out, at least for a while.

"The grand experiment of *The Boondocks* was to take on radical politics and make it cute," the cartoonist says. "I was able to package it as mainstream. At a certain point, when we live in a certain time where there are ramifications for saying things, I'm finding myself in a different position. Now I'm being judged. Until this show is picked up, it's time for me to take it down. I don't take back anything I've said. But strategically it's time to stop, at least for now. Theoretically, it could hurt the show. And I can do more with the show on the air than if it is off the air."

Plus, he adds, there are those rumors about White House calls to studios or networks to express concerns about a project, and the project's sudden disappearance.

"Right now, I want to err on the side of caution," he says with a slight laugh.

As Huey might say: Yo, Aaron, is The Man putting you under his thumb?

"If it gets on the air, I'll reevaluate things," he says. "And if it doesn't get on the air, I'll reevaluate things."

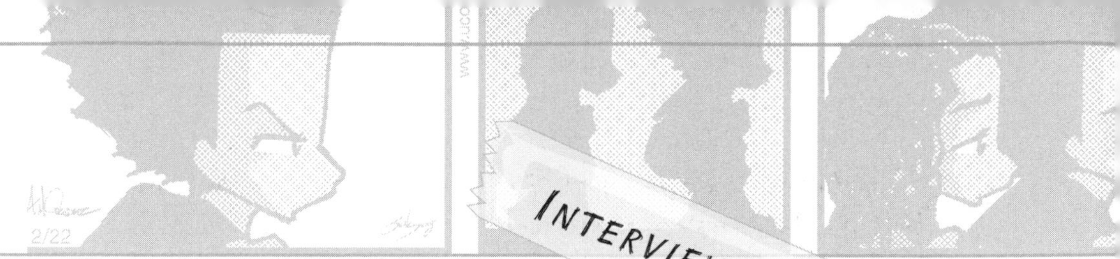

Tavis Smiley
AUGUST 2, 2004

INTERVIEW . . .

Aaron McGruder

TAVIS: Let's start. Let's start with Mr. Cosby. As you know, Mr. Cosby gave one big interview after his first foray into speaking about black America, and he came on this show, sat in that same seat. So, now here you are a few weeks later.

McGRUDER: It's an honor.

TAVIS: In that same chair as Mr. Cosby. But you've been ripping Mr. Cosby the last couple of weeks.

McGRUDER: Oh, I haven't been ripping him.

TAVIS: Oh, OK. What word would you use?

McGRUDER: I've been commenting. You know, it—I have to say what every black person has to say at the top of these discussions. I have a ton of respect for Bill Cosby. [Tavis laughs] You're not allowed to go any further until you say that, so let me just say it.

TAVIS: But having said that . . .

McGRUDER: Having said it, it was interesting. You know, I heard the controversy at first, which is "Cosby's saying things he's not allowed to say about black people in public." And I go, "well, go, Cos," 'cause that's—I'm all for that.

TAVIS: That's what you do, yeah.

McGRUDER: And then I kind of looked into the comments and go, "Ooh. Ooh. Ooh, Cos . . ." [Tavis laughs] "That's not right." And, look, the truth is really in the middle.

I sympathize with Bill's—with what he's trying to say. He's trying to say we need to be more responsible. He's trying to say we have to take better care of our kids. The problem is, you know, I hear people explaining what Bill was trying to say. And when they explain it—like Jesse or whatever—it makes sense. But it's not really what Bill said. What Bill said was kind of confusing and, I think, problematic on a number of levels. Now, you know, my take in the strip was that black people have just driven Bill Cosby out of his mind. [Tavis laughs]

TAVIS: He's a nice guy, but Negroes drove him crazy.

McGRUDER: On top of their pants being too low and not being able to speak proper English, now you can indict black America for driving a good man crazy. But I think really it just comes down to he's trying to say something, and he's the guy that's always been able to give the very insightful, clever, funny, witty take on life. And he's gotten that respect. And I just think as time goes on, he sort of passed the top of his game, which happens to all of us. I passed the top of my game several years ago. [Both laugh.]

TAVIS: And you're still not even 30 yet.

McGRUDER: So, I haven't accomplished nearly what he has, but it is to say—it's not coming across, I think, in the way he would want it to, and we can't allow anyone, even Bill Cosby, to publicly say things about us which are just flat-out not true.

TAVIS: What did Cosby say that was flat-out not true? And, by the way, you gotta—I mean, you gotta love the line. It was funny. It made a lot of people upset, but when he went to Chicago after coming on this show and said that, you know, he was tired of being chastised for people suggesting he was putting out dirty laundry. That was a great line. "Your dirty laundry gets out of school every day at 2:30." That was a funny line.

McGRUDER: It was.

TAVIS: That was funny!

McGRUDER: The problem with that statement was he was saying—I believe he was talking about poor blacks. "Your dirty laundry is coming out of the school at 2:30 and standing on the corner calling each other the 'N' word." So are rich blacks. So are poor whites. So are rich

whites. All their kids are out on the corner at 2:30 calling each other the "N" word. And that's because—you know, that has to do with youth culture today, rap culture today, which is partially the responsibility of the rappers, largely the responsibility of the corporations who distribute it.

TAVIS: So what did he say that was wrong?

McGRUDER: Well, the comment I kept hearing is that, you know, half of black kids are gonna drop out of school and the other half are gonna go to jail. So I go, "Wait a minute. That means if I get out of school, I go to jail?" That's not much of an incentive to read! You know, and it's like the point is maybe we have a higher dropout rate, but I don't know when he's joking. I don't know when he's exaggerating for comedic effect, and I don't know when he thinks he's telling the truth, but it's all being mushed up together into a mess, and the media is saying, "See, Cosby said you niggaz is out of control." Am I allowed to say the "N" word?

TAVIS: You said it already.

McGRUDER: OK. And it's not a productive conversation. But to me the most important thing is why do we care? He's a comedian.

TAVIS: Because he's Bill Cosby. You know why he cares. You just answered that question because when Cosby says it, the mainstream media covers it. That's why we care.

McGRUDER: But we have to not fall into this trap of having deep political discussions based around the musings of an entertainer.

TAVIS: We care what you say in *The Boondocks* every day. I care what you write every day.

McGRUDER: But I'll be the first person, and I've said this in public many times, to say I'm not a political leader. I'm an entertainer, and you should take what I do for what it is, but when you start talking about what black America should do, I'm not qualified to talk about that, not only because of my age, because of my profession. I'm an entertainer, and certainly I don't feel like it's my job or any rapper's job or any comedian's job to stand up and pretend to be a politician.

TAVIS: But there is an empowering—my word, not yours—there is an enlightening and an empowering and, often times, an encouraging component to what you do. You're not trying to shy away from that are you?

McGRUDER: No, but let's keep it in perspective. Let's keep it in perspective. You know, I was talking with Chuck D a couple days ago, and Chuck D—I've got my Chuck D T-shirt on. I love Public Enemy, and in 1987–88 when there was no black leader reaching me, those guys reached me, and they politicized me.

TAVIS: "Fight the power."

McGRUDER: Yes. But what they were, were conscious entertainers, and that's a great thing to be. What they were not was political leaders, and there's a difference.

TAVIS: When did Cosby cross the line then, to your point, from being a conscious entertainer to trying to be a quote "black leader"?

McGRUDER: It's a murky line. I think it's—To me there is a certain hypocrisy to what he's saying. As an entertainer, he created Mushmouth. You know, now when white people make fun of how black people talk, they do Mushmouth. He created that. Cosby has shown a very open hostility towards a lot of what black youth culture has been doing basically for the last 15 years or so, and I think there are some fair critiques to be made. I think you have to stop short of vilifying your own children and the younger generation. I think that's unhealthy, and I'm frustrated with a lot of what people my age and younger are doing, but it always has to be tempered with a certain amount of respect.

TAVIS: Let me move from Cosby then. Having said that, we still respect Mr. Cosby.

McGRUDER: We absolutely do.

TAVIS: After we said all that, we still have great respect for Bill Cosby!

McGRUDER: He's a great man and he's done more for me, and who am I to talk about Bill? I already feel bad for what I just said.

TAVIS: Ha ha ha! Not bad enough not to have said it.

McGRUDER: But I'm all ready to go apologize to Bill. I'm sorry. It was wrong. Who the hell am I? And my pants are hanging down way too low, and I need to pull 'em up.

TAVIS: Let me move from Mr. Cosby then. Pull your pants up, yeah! Ha ha ha! Let me move from Mr. C to the folk who many of us on the left argue were empowered by what he said, as you just made the point, the right, the political right, empowered in many respects by what Mr. Cosby is saying. What do you make of—what's Huey and Riley think—what do they think about George W. Bush these days?

McGRUDER: Same.

TAVIS: Same thing?

McGRUDER: He's lyin'. He's not that complicated, people. He's been lyin', he's gonna keep lyin', and, you know, it's amazing. It's—you know, the tough thing is you have . . . They've done an amazing job at selling poor-white America on an economic agenda which doesn't benefit them and on a foreign policy agenda that doesn't benefit them. And those people, um, I think, are largely being manipulated by race and xenophobia and ignorance. And religion, particularly religion.

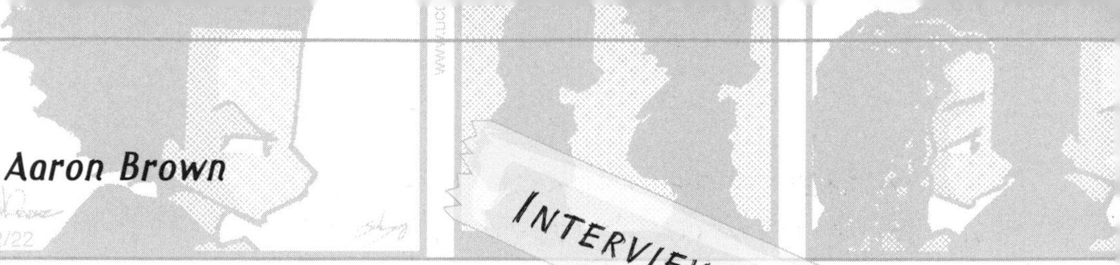

CNN Newsnight with Aaron Brown
October 1, 2004

INTERVIEW . . .

Analysis of First Presidential Debate

AARON BROWN, host: Good evening again, I guess. Well, the debates have debated, the spinners have spun and are continuing to spin. The pundits are about to go to work. And to our ear, at least, there was no clear knock-out punch thrown or landed tonight. So the question really is, Did the needle move? In part, that's a function of how you all saw the debate, and in part, it's a function of all the words that will be spoken, including ours, in the next hours.

We'll talk with Aaron McGruder, the cartoonist with an edge, to say the least. During the conventions, we used this space to explore a different point of view, a contrarian point of view, if you will. It's safe to say there's frequently no more contrarian view than a cartoonist.

We're joined by Aaron McGruder. His cartoon, *The Boondocks*, is syndicated most days in over 300 newspapers, but sometimes a few less, depending on the material.

Good to see you.

AARON McGRUDER, cartoonist, *The Boondocks*: Good to see you.

BROWN: All right. Two sentences: who won the debate? You're going to say this.

McGRUDER: Kerry. He got his ass whooped.

BROWN: Who did?

McGRUDER: Kerry. I'm sorry. No, I'm sorry. George Bush.

BROWN: You set that whole line up, and then you blew it.

McGRUDER: I did. No, it was—it was a very clear victory.

You know, what bothers me about shows like this, and all the news shows, after Bush talks I hear all these smart people completely ignoring the elephant in the room. And the elephant in the room, which nobody wants to say, is that Bush is not a smart man. He can't articulate well. He doesn't speak in complete sentences.

BROWN: Well . . .

McGRUDER: And everyone just ignores it, like that's OK.

BROWN: OK. So . . .

McGRUDER: But he's really dumb.

BROWN: OK. That's a different thing. Let's say he is not articulate. And I think they would concede he's not the most articulate guy on the planet. It doesn't mean he doesn't have convictions. It doesn't mean he believes in some things. It doesn't necessarily mean he's wrong. It just means he can't express himself.

McGRUDER: But beliefs don't mean anything if you're stupid. And not only that, but he—it's almost as though he's talking to the dumbest segment of society, whereas Kerry . . .

BROWN: Aaron, don't you think that's an incredibly arrogant way to look at the world?

McGRUDER: It's—you know, it's real, you know? It's just that nobody is saying the obvious, which is the man is not smart and he's the president.

BROWN: I wouldn't say that . . .

McGRUDER: Everybody knows it, but nobody is saying it.

BROWN: What does that say, then, about the 52 or three or one, or maybe it's 49.5 tonight, percent of the country that not only believes he is smart enough to run the country now but should be the guy to run the country for the next four years?

McGRUDER: I think they have been woefully misled. I think—I think Americans have a natural inclination, like all people around the world, to believe that their government is not corrupt, that the people are fair and smart and they're not lying to them.

And history doesn't prove that out. And current events doesn't prove that out. The American people have been lied to, and it's at the point now where I think that that percentage of people simply are not interested in the truth. They don't want to go down the road, the thought that the president, one, is not intelligent; and two, the people behind the president who are intelligent are deliberately lying and misleading the American people constantly.

BROWN: Let me see—let me see how cynical you are.

McGRUDER: OK.

BROWN: Do you believe that a Kerry presidency would be there—would be more honest, or is this a corruption, in your view, of the entire establishment?

McGRUDER: I—I don't blame it—I mean, to say the establishment is oversimplified. I think that the institution of journalism has failed in its responsibility to hold the government accountable. The government's doing what it's supposed to do when left unchecked.

I do think Kerry would be better than Bush. I think he would be more honest. I think he would be more intelligent. But that's—everybody knows that already. That's not really in anyone's debate. It's just people have picked a side.

It's—you know, it's like, you know—it's the kind of weird God people in the middle of America, the people that live on the coasts fly over. We don't talk to those people. We don't understand those people, and they don't understand us.

But nobody just says the obvious, that their president can't articulate himself and is dumb. And it drives me nuts.

BROWN: I got all that.

McGRUDER: There you go.

BROWN: Nice to meet you.

McGRUDER: It is a pleasure. Thank you for having me on.

BROWN: Come back, too.

McGRUDER: If you let me.

BROWN: I will. We're equal opportunity around here.

McGRUDER: There you go.

BROWN: In every respect. Thank you.

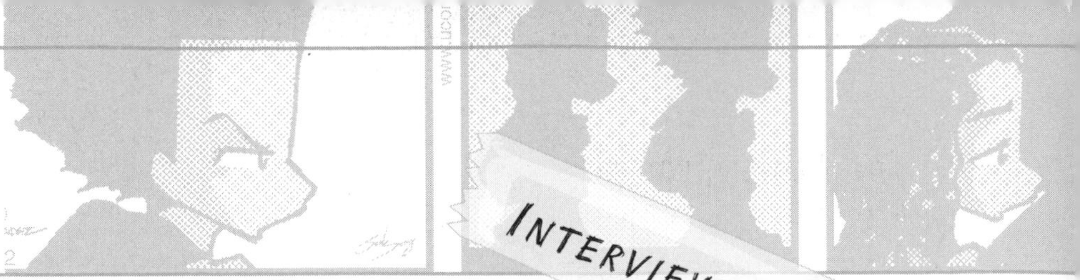

Interview . . .

Observer Magazine
OCTOBER 31, 2004

Talk of the Toon

PHIL HOAD

I ask [McGruder] if his brand of radicalism (and, with *Boondocks* merchandising on the way, a brand is what it will be) is in danger of becoming just another commodity for sale. He admits that, "Money has to be your focus, because money is the focus of everyone you're in business with." An ultra-bright, blinding admission of how traditional left/right polarities are meaningless in an era when bottom-line merchant Harvey Weinstein whips up a "coalition of the willing" to distribute *Fahrenheit 9/11*, after Disney bottled it, and Nike-wearing twentysomethings go to see documentaries like the forthcoming (and very good) *The Corporation* for their anti-corporate lifestyle tonic.

McGruder knows that with the *Washington Post* publishing his strip, Random House his books and Cartoon Network his TV show, he's as complicit as anyone. And he's getting rich without qualms. "I always wanted to get rich. I wanna live very, very well. The world sucks when you're poor. It's fucking deplorable. But I don't think it means you have to be part of the fucked-up system of oppressors and leaders just by virtue of making a lot of money."

Can he stay principled? He's already turned down offers to rope Huey and Co into commercials. "I don't spend a lot of time—moaning about what I can't get away with, because there's always other media. Rather than trying to be so radical, you just put yourself out of the game. Find the smart way to make the most out of these mass-media outlets. It still requires courage and it still requires pissing people off. You just have to know how to walk the tightrope . . . If you're not disciplined, it can be dangerous. You're literally dancing with the devil."

The News Tribune
NOVEMBER 6, 2005

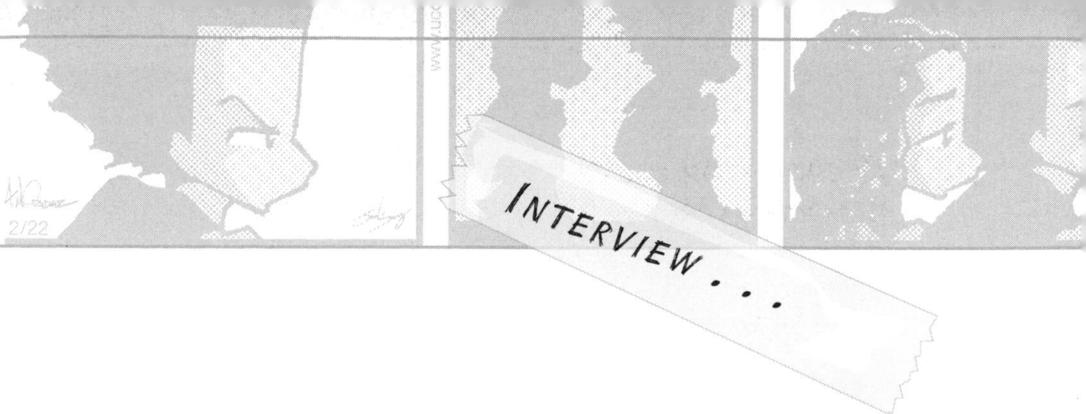
INTERVIEW . . .

Aaron McGruder Interview

BILL HUTCHENS

Aaron McGruder's popular and sometimes controversial comic strip *The Boondocks* turns into a TV cartoon at 11 p.m. Sunday, Nov. 6 on Cartoon Network's Adult Swim block of mature programming.

The 31-year-old talked to journalists recently during a conference call. Here's the complete transcript:

JOURNALIST: Describe a few of the upcoming plots. And also could you tell how much independence you had on the language? Were you able to use the words you wanted to use?

McGRUDER: In show four, Granddad gets in a physical fight with a blind old man and loses, and his ego won't let it die so he challenges him to a rematch. The one show, Tom, who is the assistant district attorney, is arrested for a murder he did not commit and has a limited number of hours before he is gonna be sent to jail and his worst fear of being anally raped will come true. He has to find the real killer. And then there's the episode where the entire episode is kind of a what-if Martin Luther King hadn't been assassinated but rather went into a coma after he got shot and wakes up in modern day and has difficulty sort of fitting into the modern political discourse and all of that. We did a bunch of 'em. There's one called "Let's Nab Oprah." Ed and Rummy, who are characters that we've met earlier in the season—they're international criminals, and with Riley tagging along decide to try and kidnap Oprah.

JOURNALIST: What about the language?

McGRUDER: Yeah, yeah, you know, I think we were given all the leeway we needed to say what we wanted to say.

JOURNALIST: *The Boondocks* has been popular for so long, I was wondering if there had been any other offers in the past to turn it into a TV series. And, if so, why those weren't pursued?

McGRUDER: Actually, I was trying to sell a show at the same time I was trying to sell the strip into syndication. I had been in talks with one entity or another for about six years now. The deals basically just didn't happen for a number of reasons, but most of them revolved around, you know, creative control issues and things like that. It's been kind of all over town, I guess, and we finally ended up here at Sony. And we did the pilot for Fox, and it didn't go at Fox. And then Adult Swim saved the day.

JOURNALIST: Do you still have hopes of maybe, sort of a reverse *Family Guy* type thing where *Family Guy* took off on Cartoon Network Adult Swim and Fox kind of picked it up again?

McGRUDER: There's no risk of Fox ever running this show.

JOURNALIST: I'm wondering if you're going to make use of all the resources you have available to you as a cartoon on Cartoon Network and Adult Swim, whether you feel you have to be more or less true to the strip—and I'm not referring specifically to profanity on that, but that's one of the things that would come up.

McGRUDER: I think that was one of the things I most wanted to do, which was kind of break the idea out of the very narrow confines of the comics page and sort of all these different places that my imagination wanted to go to. So we do greatly expand the world. We see, you know, Woodcrest, where they live, we see the sort of unnamed city that it's a suburb of, and we see obviously a number of different characters. We even flash back to different time periods and Granddad's younger life. And there's dream sequences. So, yeah, yeah, I certainly tried to take advantage of the medium.

JOURNALIST: Can you see yourself dropping dingbats for the real words or not?

McGRUDER: In the show, some words that we can't say in the strip, we can say without bleeps. And some words we still have to use bleeps. So there you go.

JOURNALIST: I wanted to get back to the use of the "N-word" in your episodes. We seem to be hearing it more in pop culture whether it's music or television. Do you think the word has lost some of its power to shock and offend?

McGRUDER: Um, probably not if we're still talking about it (*laughs*). I do think it's obviously been in pop culture and music a whole lot especially in the last 16, 17 years. You know, it doesn't seem to be a topic that ever goes a way. So I would guess it's still a touchy subject.

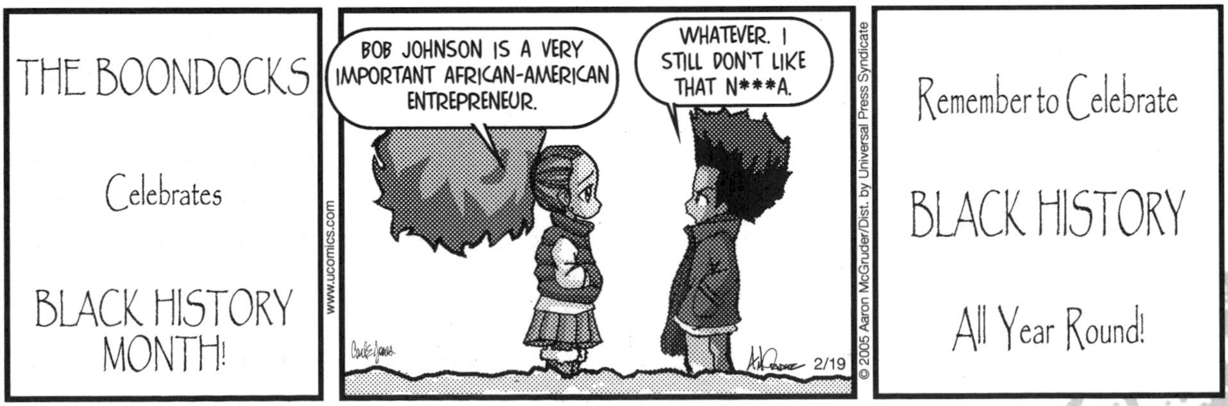
THE BOONDOCKS
Celebrates
BLACK HISTORY MONTH!
BOB JOHNSON IS A VERY IMPORTANT AFRICAN-AMERICAN ENTREPRENEUR.
WHATEVER. I STILL DON'T LIKE THAT N***A.
www.ucomics.com
2/19
© 2005 Aaron McGruder/Dist. by Universal Press Syndicate
Remember to Celebrate
BLACK HISTORY
All Year Round!

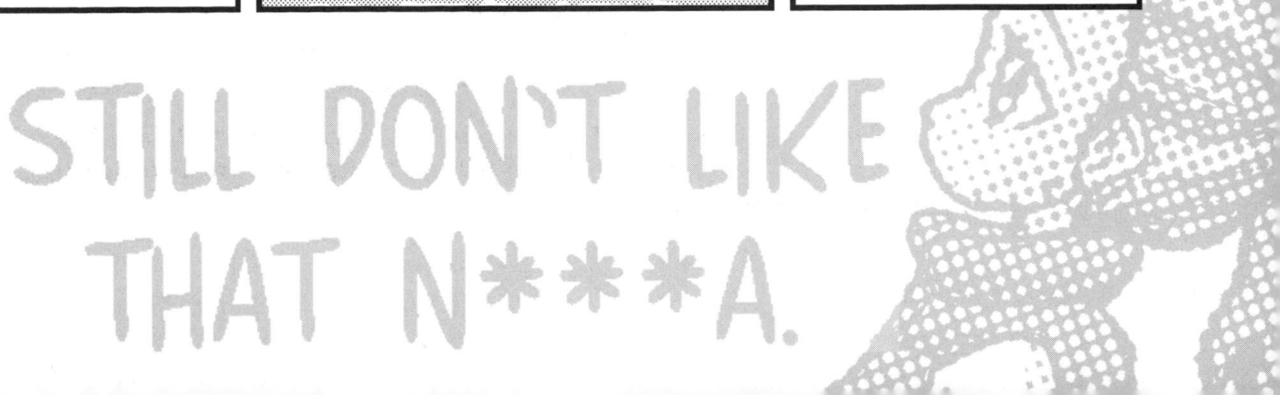
STILL DON'T LIKE THAT N***A.

JOURNALIST: So why is it important to you to be able to use it in this series?

McGRUDER: I think it's important for me to say a lot of things in the series. You know, it ain't *The Nigga Show* . . . You know, we do say a few other things, too. What I wanted to do was have the freedom to write the way I wanted to write and for the characters to be able to talk the way people actually talk.

JOURNALIST: Do you have the hope that there would be some time in the future when you could use the word without it causing so much of a stir. Or do you like the stir? Is that part of the attraction of using it?

McGRUDER: It's neither. I think I would look forward to the day where racial discourse has somehow evolved past the same conversations that we've been having for, like, 30 years. That's not to say that I don't want people to be upset about it anymore. It's not to say that I want people to deliberately be upset which is why I'm using it all the time. I just kind of wish that, at a certain point, the conversation would move forward and become, you know, more sophisticated. I just think we kind of stay stuck in a rut. We talk about the same things year in and year out and nothing ever changes.

JOURNALIST: Can I ask you who is doing the writing? 'Cause there were no writing credits in the press kit or on the screener. Are you doing the writing or collaborating with people with experience doing a half-hour animation?

McGRUDER: I am doing the writing, and I wrote most of the 15 episodes, but I do have a small team that's on to help out. Rodney Barnes . . . has been working on the show from very early in. And Yamara Taylor. There hasn't been much of a writing staff. It's really only a couple people as opposed to the full teams that other shows have. Ultimately, I still had to be the one to kind of show everybody what was in my head. So the vast majority of the writing duties did fall on me.

JOURNALIST: You didn't have a problem, you know, really structuring these stores, like, taking it, you know, from beginning to end?

McGRUDER: There was help. Again, for example, Rodney is an experienced writer on *Wife and Kids* for a few years. And I think he's currently also working on *Everybody Hates Chris*. There was some help there. I had developed a few pilots, some live action, in the years between when the strip launched and when this show actually went into production. Obviously, those didn't go very far. But, you know, I had been, you know, doing screen writing for a while and had written a few pilots. So it wasn't as dramatic a transition as you might think. But certainly I didn't come into it, you know, knowing everything I needed to know. And there fortunately were some experienced people on the team to help out.

JOURNALIST: I'm unclear. Was the pilot that we saw on the tape from Cartoon Network, is that the same thing that you shot for Fox? Or is this a completely different pilot?

McGRUDER: It's a completely different show. It's a completely different pilot. And there's very few similarities between the two shows. And the pilot that we did for Fox was only six minutes long. It was just a presentation. It was a different script, different everything.

JOURNALIST: Could you talk a little bit on the style of the animation? Did you have to go through different stages to find this style? And then as a corollary to that, I know you shipped this overseas the way a lot of shows do. Do you wish you could do what *South Park* does and just kind of go right up to the mat and six days ahead of time be very, very timely?

McGRUDER: I wanted it to be an anime show because I think as a medium anime is, Japanese style of animation is, the most cinematic and therefore I think gives you the most flexibility in terms of doing humor for adults. And also I wanted to do something very, very different from the style that Matt Groening basically set as the style for adult animation and, you know, and so I think *The Simpsons* is genius but I, obviously, I wanted to do something very different from that and so we did go in a very different direction and it took a while for us to get it right. You know, we're still working, cause there's still some stylistic things that we're going for that, you know, we're just learning. It's difficult because you can't find American artists that have worked on this type of show in the past. There's a lot of figuring-stuff-out-as-we-went kind of thing that we had to do.

JOURNALIST: Would you want to be more timely like *South Park?*

McGRUDER: What they have is just complete control because it's all done right under their noses. We have to send episodes halfway around the world (for production). And that inherently lessens the amount of control that you have over things. But there's a tradeoff, which is, you know, which is just, you know, the visual look of the show. *South Park* is a very simple show visually. And that's why they can turn it around fast. Our show is more complex, which requires more people, more artists, more time. It's a massive, massive undertaking. . . . I think the animation for *South Park* is absolutely perfect for *South Park.* But ours is a different show and we just didn't have that option to keep everything in house and in one place.

JOURNALIST: I've got a quote from you from the American Society of Newspaper Editors talk, back in 2002, where you said that your goal in creating *The Boondocks* was to challenge the way people thought about the norm of political thought and what's extremism, to get people to think more critically outside the standard liberal and conservative angles. Um, since the cartoon series can't be as topical on a political level or else it becomes dated too quickly, is there a different goal with the animated series? Is it still meant to have the same political punch?

McGRUDER: I don't think it can have the same political punch without being right up to the minute on the news. You know, I think that, you know, but I would also say that, um, you know, as important as any of those other lofty goals is entertaining. The television show and the strip offers pros and cons. I think that we have to do, you know, much, you know, kind of, broader satire. We can't stay sort of nailed down on specific people or specific issues because we're so far out. It just kind of makes you work a little harder to figure out how to get the same points across without dating the show. So, you know, to me, this is what it is. I think you make the best of the medium, but ultimately, you know any message, whether it's in the strip or whether it's in the show, if it ultimately isn't delivered in a very, very funny way, the message is somewhat irrelevant. . . . I think the show will challenge people and I think the show will make people think about things in a very different way. I don't think you necessarily have to be right on top of the news to do that.

JOURNALIST: One review I've read said that there might be more negative reaction to Robert's slapping up on Riley in the second episode than to the prominent use of the N-word. Do you agree with that?

McGRUDER: I've never had an ability to predict what people are going to be mad at. It always takes me by surprise. Anything is possible. We've had instances in the run of the strip where that exact kind of thing took place. Jokes that we thought were pretty harmless ended up taking us by surprise and people were really mad at us. So you really can't—I can't—predict it at least. I don't know.

JOURNALIST: I'm wondering how much creative control you had over the selection of voice talent, and are you pleased overall with the results?

McGRUDER: Yeah, I actually did have control over the voice talent, and I'm very happy. I think the cast is fantastic, and having worked with them now for close to two years, they've been very supportive and they've given a lot of their time.

JOURNALIST: Had you met John Witherspoon or Regina King before? Had you had a chance to talk to them?

McGRUDER: I think I had met Regina very briefly before casting, but just in passing. Had never met John. I don't think I had met any of the other cast members before casting.

JOURNALIST: Do they get what you're trying to do?

McGRUDER: They absolutely do. They really, they've been in it for a long, long time now and they have contributed a great deal to what the show is. They've really defined these characters in a way that a writer just can't do on his own. And so each of them has really spent a lot of time and thought and energy into getting these characters right. What we're doing is very difficult, and there's a lot of layers to it. But we were all exactly on the same page and that made it a lot easier.

JOURNALIST: How long has it been in the process for this show?

McGRUDER: We must have started the pilot in late 2003. And then in 2004, you know, we delivered to Fox in May and got dissed in May [*laughs*]. And then got our pickup from Adult Swim at the end of that summer. And we started October of last year on production of the season. And here we are now, so, yeah, it's been a long time.

JOURNALIST: Do you feel a need to maintain a certain plot continuity between the strip and the TV show?

McGRUDER: I do think certain things needed to remain consistent. I think the personality of the characters and who they are basically needed to be the same as the strip. Anything beyond that, I think it's dangerous to try to link up too much the show to the strip. I mean, I don't even try to link up the daily strips to the Sunday strips. They're in different papers, and you never know who's seeing what. So the characters are who they are, and they are who they've always been. But we really don't get into continuity issues and trying to make sure everything stays the same. Caesar, for example, who's in the strip very regularly, is not in the first season of the show at all.

JOURNALIST: Is there any concern that the strip will suffer because you're putting so much into the TV show?

McGRUDER: I think there's always concern about that. But that's ultimately passed. I think the most difficult period for me in maintaining both of them was this last year, this previous year where we were figuring out the show and trying to maintain the strip at the same time. We've got the show thing kind of figured out now, so that

197

makes it a lot easier on me. I presume that'll be less of a concern as time goes on actually.

JOURNALIST: We had a question from our site about how the second episode involves some music by Kanye West, "Gold Digger." How did that come about exactly and are there other plans to include current licensed music and how will that affect the budget of the show?

McGRUDER: We're actually now bankrupt because of Kanye West [*laughs*]. That's just jokes. It happened because I put it into a temp mix that was not for air. We were just trying to give the studio and the network a sense of what kind of music we would put in that spot. We do have a very modest music budget for the show. Basically, Mike Lazzo and Russ Krasnov, you know, Mike runs Adult Swim and Russ was heading up Sony television. They just decided they really wanted it and that it was (worth) spending the money for. So that's how it ended up in the show. We do plan on using licensed music. We do use other licensed music. But obviously we have budget constraints that we have to work around.

JOURNALIST: What do you want people to take away from the cartoon series, and also, you were recently quoted in this week's *Newsweek* saying black folks worry too much about what others think of them. What did you mean by that? And is that related toward expanding the discussion about race in our country?

McGRUDER: I think you have to first hope that they laugh. You just have to pray. That's the toughest job. If you've done that, at least you get to sort of survive to do it another day. But I think the stories kind of speak for themselves in a way. It's tough for me to sit here and explain the work because no explanation I give is gonna do it justice. It's kind of just all there and I think if I have to pinpoint anything it's that people [will] sort of be challenged and think about things a differ-

ent way and question and just kind of, you know, just be sort of introduced to a new idea, maybe a new thought. But really I think the shows kind of are what they are.

[Regarding the second question] I think that kind of speaks for itself, too. I think there's a fear amongst black people internally about how those outside of us judge us. I think it has very legitimate historical roots. But I think that fear can also be a somewhat paralyzing thing. I believe if you are equal and you truly believe that you're equal, well then you don't have anything to worry about in terms of what other people might think, and you'll speak your mind freely. That's basically it.

JOURNALIST: All these smart people have asked all my best questions. So I'll fall back on Plan B and ask you, will you be developing the personalities and characterizations of the characters that we know in the strip beyond what we know in the strip? And, as a follow up, will we see more characters from the strip like Caesar and Cindy, or will the show develop its own supporting cast like Uncle Ruckus No Relation?

McGRUDER: They do. And I think the best example of that is Granddad. Because we do get a chance to see Granddad at different stages in his younger life, including World War II where he's a fighter pilot, very, very young, young, like a teenager. And also in the Civil Rights Movement. That was a lot of fun because it's just something we just haven't done in the strip before. And, yeah, I mean, I think we get to get a lot into Huey's head and I think we really get to know the characters for the first time when you see 'em kind of walking and talking and moving and having these little adventures.

JOURNALIST: I was reading over some of the press material and it said that "In his own unique way, he uses Huey and Riley to open the lines of communication between adults and children on often unspoken topics." I was wondering [on] what specific topics you think you've been successful at doing that, and do you gauge your success at doing that?

McGRUDER: You mean in the show or in the strip?

JOURNALIST: In the strip or the show, I guess you wouldn't know about the show yet . . . but what topics you think have really come up between parents and children and how do you gauge your success in that area?

McGRUDER: I don't know how one would gauge success in something like that, but one of the central themes to the strip has always been the generation gap and the disconnect between Granddad and the boys. One of the major themes of the first episode of, well, is sort of the difference of opinion as to where they fit in to the new neighborhood and how they should behave. You know it's the Bill Cosby thing. The older generation being terrified that the younger generation is gonna make them look bad in front of white folks and that the young generation has got all types of moral issues. It's the music and the way they dress. I've always found that gap to be a very sort of interesting and entertaining place. Granddad in the strip and in the show has an obsession with Bill Cosby. I think I just try to mine it for as much humor as I can get out of [it]. Again I don't know if I'm actually bringing old folks and young people together in any way. I don't know how one would even judge that, but it is a part of the strip and a part of what the idea of what *The Boondocks* has always been.

JOURNALIST: What is involved in launching a strip? How did you get it syndicated and what kind of hassles were involved?

McGRUDER: Well, I'm gonna try to give you the quick answer because it's a pretty long story. Newspapers buy their features, crosswords, columns and cartoons and stuff from syndicates. . . . What you really have to do is come up with six weeks of the strip. You send it to the syndicate. They get a few thousand of those submissions a year. They just kind of pile up. . . . Every once in a while, a syndicate might find one out of those several thousands that it wants to syndicate. And then they offer you a contract and then they kind of, you know, clean you up and edit you and promote you, so all the cartoonist really has to do is worry about creating the strip. And they run around to the newspapers with their sales teams and try to sell it in as many papers as they can. And the tough job is, of course, the paper has to cut a strip every time it wants to buy a strip because generally papers aren't making a bunch of extra room for comics. . . . And that's basically, that's the very short, short version of it.

JOURNALIST: Do you have any thoughts about why there are so many adult-oriented cartoons these days?

McGRUDER: I think it's actually a medium that works pretty well for adults. We kind of associate animation with children's entertainment [in] this country and that's not really an association that takes place in other countries, particularly Japan. We've had obviously some big successes in adult animation with *The Simpsons* and *Family Guy* and *South Park*. So as long as it's something that people can make money off of, other people will be trying to figure out how to do it. If you look at Japan, they make every type of entertainment in an animated form from kids' shows to pornography and everything in between. Horror movies and action and comedies, whatever you can imagine, they do in animation. So I think it's kind of a natural thing. I don't see where it really needs to be just for kids.

JOURNALIST: Any update on the *Milestone* comics we talked about a few years go that you were trying to get up and running?

McGRUDER: That was one of the pilots I had mentioned earlier. It was the one-hour action drama called *Milestones* based on a comic book universe that was launched in the early 90s. It was black kids with super powers. It was a cool show. They never shot the pilot.

JOURNALIST: Any chance of it?

McGRUDER: Most shows don't survive their first rejection. We were lucky that *The Boondocks* was able to live on after being dissed at Fox. But that's not the norm usually. Once you've taken a shot at it, that's it.

JOURNALIST: I wanted to ask why you became attracted to making a mockery of the beleaguered Mr. R. Kelly. And is he aware of the mockery and has he reacted to you?

McGRUDER: I don't know if he's aware of it. If he is, he has not reacted to me. I think that episode was less about R. Kelly and more about what black audiences are willing to tolerate from their celebrities. We used R. Kelly to make a point. But I do think the episode is really about what we find acceptable versus what is unacceptable and where everyone draws that line.

JOURNALIST: I was just wondering if there is any facet of the criticism that comes your way that really does matter to you when you hear it.

McGRUDER: I try to insulate myself from as much of the feedback on the strip as possible because it makes it difficult to do the job. So I don't avoid it because I don't care and it's not like if I do read criticism it doesn't bother me. It's just ultimately you go into this knowing that some people are just going to not like what you do and you can't

let it interrupt the creative process. I think different artists have different ways of handling that. I just basically avoid it all. I try to avoid the fan mail and the hate mail, just to stay focused on what I have to do. I also think basically I'm my own worst critic. I don't think there's much that people can throw at me that I haven't already kicked myself in the ass for [*laughs*]. Like everyone, I get sensitive about my work and what you put out there. You just can't dwell on it, I guess. You just gotta stay focused on the job.

JOURNALIST: I really liked the shows, but I have to say, seeing the characters on the TV with voices and hearing them say the words as opposed to hearing them in my own head was kind of jarring a little. Did you take all that into consideration when you were creating the show, that it is going to be voices that people can hear, and maybe more of your interpretation of who the characters are than the readers' own?

McGRUDER: I think it's a challenge that every preexisting property that moves into television or movies has to face. *The Simpsons*, for example, did not exist in print for years and years and years before it showed up on TV. So the voices you heard were just the voices of those characters. With us we're battling against the voices that millions of people presumably have in their heads and each of them has a different voice. It's one of those things that it's just no escaping. I'm forced to live with a voice and everyone [*laughs*] has to live with it . . .

It's not just about the actual sound of the voice. You gotta go with who's gonna be able to pull off the performance, who's gonna be funny and who understands the characters and, you know, who can act. And it was a very, very challenging process to get all that right. You know going in that everyone who's a fan of the strip probably has a voice in their head already, probably not exactly the voice that's gonna come out the TV, but you just hope that pretty soon they get used to it. You gotta think, it was jarring for me [*laughs*] because I actually didn't have a clear voice in my head. And so it really was jarring but fun at the same time. And again it just brings so much more life to the character having the right person doing that voice.

JOURNALIST: What do you say to people when they compare your humor to Dave Chappelle's?

McGRUDER: I actually think it's a very high compliment. I have a tremendous amount of respect for Dave and what that show managed to accomplish in its two years.

JOURNALIST: I'm wondering if the comic strip sort of has lost its edge, and now that the show is coming if there's a possibility that it could become even more significant or gain renewed interest maybe from a couple years ago when the strip was at its peak?

McGRUDER: I think a political strip like mine, I think interest is going to grow and wane, not just based on what I do, even though obviously that's a big part of [it], but just the general mood of the country. A couple of years ago things were very, very different. I think the interest in politics was much higher leading up to Bush's reelection. I think there was the start of the Iraq war and 9/11 and all of those things is part of what made people's interest in the strip grow. I think after Bush's reelection, I think across the board, I got a sense that people were really a bit fatigued on politics and that perhaps it was time just for a break. Strips are judged in decades. There's gonna be periods where it's on fire and everyone's checking for it and times when, you know, I'm writing stuff and people just are a little bored with it. It's part of the perpetual nature of the job. How the show will ultimately affect the strip, I don't know, and I can't predict it. But . . . it is true that my focus has been mostly on the show this last year. Comic strips are a strange, strange thing. I honestly wish

I could just do it when I had the perfect joke to tell and really had something to say, but the job doesn't work like that. You gotta fill that space whether you got something to say or not, so we just do the best we can week in and week out.

JOURNALIST: Did you have any control over who your advertisers would be?

McGRUDER: I absolutely had no control over that at all. I was never involved in any of the discussions, and I would doubt that any show runner on earth would actually be involved in those discussions with the network.

JOURNALIST: Would you be opposed to, say, like, to Kentucky Fried Chicken or some possibly offensive advertiser?

McGRUDER: I think ultimately if a situation were to happen where an advertiser advertised on the show, I actually don't know. To be honest, once you decide to go into this business, and not just the business of television but in the business of entertainment, including the strip, you have to sometimes go into business with some unsavory corporations. The alternative is to just do it in your basement and just have it be something your family and friends enjoy. So, you know, this is one of those places where I have to sort of just say "Sorry, guys. If you want to see the show, this comes with the territory, and it's best that I actually not be involved [*laughs*], because, you know, this is where, there's no question that some of my political beliefs and own personal ideas and opinions could easily prevent any of this from ever seeing the light of day."

So you just kind of gotta grin and bear it. There's not really much I can do. I'm sorry gang, in order to see the show, someone has to market at you. It just has to happen. I feel guilty and ashamed about it [*laughs*]. . . . But just to answer your question specifically, no, I don't know of any specific sponsors at all. I'll probably learn when the show comes on like everybody else.

JOURNALIST: Are you gonna watch it?

McGRUDER: Of course I am! And everyone else should!

JOURNALIST: Is there any thought to removing one of the Rosa Parks jokes now that Ms. Parks has just passed?

McGRUDER: Yes, as a matter of fact, we've removed Rosa Parks from the trial of R. Kelly.

JOURNALIST: I know you said the strip doesn't particularly (reflect your own experience), but with the boys moving from an unnamed town to a suburb, is that in any way a reflection on your thoughts, moving from Chicago to suburban D.C. out there in Columbia?

McGRUDER: I never really spent a lot of time living in Chicago. Every time I read an article, the age at which I left Chicago is different . . .

JOURNALIST: For the record, what is it?

McGRUDER: My earliest memories are actually in Champagne, Illinois, so I must have been out of Chicago after maybe a year old or something like that. So I've lived in a bunch of different places. But I've never spent any amount of time in the inner city or anything like that. So, that was more of just a simple back story and its setup, but that wasn't sort of directly about my personal experience. I mean obviously, living out in the suburbs informed the strip and the writing of the show, but not necessarily being transplanted from someplace else.

JOURNALIST: First of all, you mentioned you had several attempts to get the show on the air. Did you learn anything from those attempts that

you're able to apply to *The Boondocks* [in] this current incarnation?

McGRUDER: Well, certainly, you learn a lot about entertainment law. I think you get a little bit better at the negotiating each time. I was able to walk away from deals that weren't right because the strip would keep the property alive and give it another chance at a later time. I've learned quite a bit about Hollywood in the past five or six years, and just a lot about writing. We've written a few different versions of this show, I have. And I think it got a lot closer to where it needed to be each time.

JOURNALIST: The different tries might have helped narrow it down to what it should have been.

McGRUDER: Absolutely. Absolutely. Even as much as—the Fox show wasn't what it needed to be. So that failure was quite critical.

JOURNALIST: What makes Adult Swim a good fit for the show?

McGRUDER: A couple things. One is that I think Mike Lazzo has a really smart idea of what a network should be and also works with creators really well and allows them to make the shows they want to make. And then the other thing is that Adult Swim has a genuine appreciation of art and animation. Other places we talked to looked at the Fox pilot and said, "We don't think it needs to be this pretty. Can't you make it simpler?" So I do think that's what make Adult Swim the very sort of ideal place for this because they really get it and appreciate everything I'm trying to do here.

JOURNALIST: Are you concerned at all about rich young white kids using this as a primer for urban development?

McGRUDER: Wow. I don't even know what that means.

JOURNALIST: Well, there's a lot of clueless little rich white kids around here.

McGRUDER: [*laughs*] Anything that starts out with, "Are you worried about, you know, white kids?" I generally go, "No" [*laughs*]. So even before you even get to the end of the sentence, "No." This show is what it is. Will it be misinterpreted? Absolutely. Will people take away terrible things from it and wrong things and all of that? Sure. I think it's the same with the strip. There's nothing I can really do about it other than not make the show. And I'd rather just make the show and make it for the people who get it and let the people who don't get it or misinterpret it just say, "Oh well, there's nothing I can really do."

JOURNALIST: Any thoughts on doing a *Birth of a Nation*–type animated film?

McGRUDER: I want to do *Birth of a Nation* live action, but it's tough. I think I need a hit show first.

JOURNALIST: What are your favorite animated works?

McGRUDER: Over time there's a bunch. But recently, and I think the shows that most inspired us on this show, is the show called *Fooly Cooly* and a show called *Samurai Champloo*.

JOURNALIST: I just wanted to ask about coming out of the box here, this first season, you're kind of going after sacred cows here. You've got Martin Luther King, Jesus and Oprah. Did you really want to just hit it hard and let people know where you were at right away?

McGRUDER: Well, for the record, we don't go after Martin Luther King or Jesus. We do go, the characters go, after Oprah, but in terms of me,

there [were] never any jokes against Oprah in any version of the let's-nab-Oprah script. And Martin Luther King appears very prominently in the show, but he's not, sort of, a target as much as a guest character. And Jesus actually does not appear [*laughs*] in the episode, but Huey does do a Christmas play called *The Adventures of Black Jesus*.

JOURNALIST: But just even any way of putting Martin Luther King into something, it's going to set people off.

McGRUDER: I look at it like this. You know, I got 15 episodes, and no one's promising any more than that, so any stories I want to tell, I better tell them now. And so, again, decisions aren't made, as hard as it may seem to believe, decisions aren't made with the thinking of "How many people is this going to piss off?" It really is about what's the funniest story and what am I only going to be able to do in the context of this show. And the MLK episode was one of those things, I think it's a story that, there's no other place to tell it other than this show. And I think it's a really interesting idea, and it's not done for the sake of controversy.

When we came up with the idea we just couldn't stop laughing, and we just thought it was not only very funny but a really interesting question to pose to America. You know, You celebrate Martin Luther King and yet how many people were behind this invasion of Iraq? And is there a contradiction there? That's kind of what we set out to explore. It's not done for shock value.

JOURNALIST: It sounds like creative control was part of what you wanted for this, and it sounds like you got it.

McGRUDER: Yeah, I did, actually. I was quite lucky.

JOURNALIST: Was that difficult to get?

McGRUDER: It wasn't difficult to get from Adult Swim. I think it was just difficult to eventually get to Adult Swim after years of being at other places.

JOURNALIST: It sounds like they kind of picked up on it quick after Fox.

McGRUDER: They absolutely did. They were very aggressive. They wanted to do the show real bad. And they've been completely supportive every day after that.

JOURNALIST: So I guess you had to go through all the other places to get to your destination.

McGRUDER: Such is life.

JOURNALIST: Do you miss drawing the strip? I understand you don't illustrate it anymore.

McGRUDER: That's correct. I don't illustrate it. And, no, I don't miss it.

JOURNALIST: But you do still write the strip?

McGRUDER: Yes.

JOURNALIST: You don't miss all that heavy hand-work, carpal tunnel or whatever?

McGRUDER: Not at all.

JOURNALIST: Aaron, could you talk about guest appearances on the show and the decision to draw Ed Asner as Ed Asner looks?

McGRUDER: Well, you know, I like Ed Asner. So I said "Well [*laughs*], why not use his likeness? You know, why not?" I don't know. It was just a cool thing, and I decided to do it from time to time.

It's kind of like what *The Simpsons* does. They draw real people into the show.

JOURNALIST: Will you be using it with anyone else, though?

McGRUDER: You know, it's interesting. Some—like, Ed plays a fictional character, but we use his likeness. We have—Xzibit, for example, does the show as himself. Quincy Jones does the show as himself. I'm trying to think about people where we also use them. We have other guest cast members. Like, Mike Epps did an episode. I'm trying to think about guys we actually drew that look like them. I don't know. I guess I just said "Oh, you know, let's make him look like Ed Asner," and that's how they drew him.

JOURNALIST: For those of us who didn't see the Martin Luther King episode, can you give us a quick synopsis.

McGRUDER: It starts with his assassination. And what we learn is that he doesn't die that day. He goes into a coma. He comes out of that coma in 2000. King mania starts to sweep the nation around 2001. He's got the book deal. He's got the movie coming out. Everything is going real good, and then September 11 happens. He goes on *Politically Correct* with Bill Maher, and Bill Maher asks him about what our response should be. And Martin Luther King says "Turn the other cheek and love thy enemy." And at that point he's deemed a traitor to the nation. No one goes to see his movie. He loses his book deal. And we fast forward to the present day where his book has finally come out on a tiny little independent publisher. And he's doing a signing in Woodcrest, and nobody shows up but Huey and Granddad to see him. And Granddad and MLK know each other from the movement. And it's a story where Huey and MLK kind of try to figure out where MLK fits in the modern day.

JOURNALIST: Can you tell us who illustrates your strip now?

McGRUDER: Carl Jones, who is also a producer on the show.

JOURNALIST MODERATOR: At this time there are no further questions. Do you have any closing remarks?

McGRUDER: Uh, gosh, uh, thank you very much. I didn't know I was gonna have to make closing remarks, but I appreciate everybody making the time and listening to me. And I hope I was able to answer all your questions. And enjoy the show, I guess. I don't know. Do any of them have any closing remarks for me? No? Okay, well . . .

JOURNALIST: I was just reading a lecture by Bill Watterson about the control the syndicates have over the comic strips and getting to own the creations and stuff like that. Did you face those kind of hurdles when you were starting out with selling the strip way back?

McGRUDER: No, and I'm with the same syndicate that Bill was with. But it's a different industry. And I think that those that paved the way like Schulz and Bill Watterson and those guys became such powerful creators that I think it changed the way the business dealt with creators. So when I came in quite late in the game, I was able to withhold a lot of rights that normally creators would have had to just give up outright a few years back.

JOURNALIST: That was because they liked the potential of your strip so much they sort of had to go along with what you wanted?

McGRUDER: I don't know. I don't know what would have happened if they had said, "No, we have to have everything." Fortunately they didn't.

JOURNALIST: Sort of like playing chicken, I guess.

McGRUDER: Hey, well, you know, it's just a negotiation. It's like any other negotiation. You have to—one, you have to be smart enough to ask for what you want. And, two, you have to hope that the other person is willing to give it up.

MODERATOR: At this time, any other remarks are welcome.

McGRUDER: [*whistles*]

JOURNALIST: Aaron, where are you living now?

McGRUDER: I live in L.A.

MODERATOR: At this time, there are no further remarks.

McGRUDER: [*whistles*] Actually, well thank you everybody. And I hope everyone does enjoy the show when it comes on November 6. Thank you.

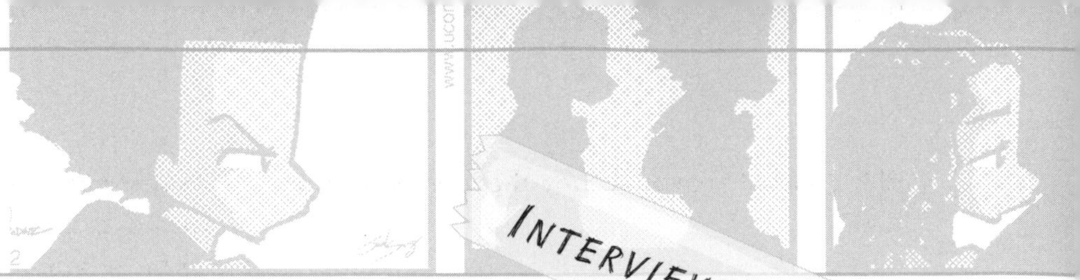

A.V. Club
NOVEMBER 23, 2005

INTERVIEW . . .

Aaron McGruder

NATHAN RABIN

In the sleepy, tranquil nursing home that is the daily comics page, Aaron McGruder's *The Boondocks* is a scowling B-boy with a boombox blaring Public Enemy.

AVC: Within the first minute and a half of the first episode I saw, Huey talks about Jesus being a black man, Ronald Reagan being the devil, and the government lying about September 11. Kind of throwing down the gauntlet there, eh?

AM: I think people were a little bit too concerned about what I would or would not be allowed to say. So let me just get that out of the way and get on to the business of telling, you know, a *story*, or two, or three, or 15. And also to say, "Okay, look. Here it is, don't worry about it. The restrictions and the watered-down and all the stuff that you thought was gonna happen really isn't the case." So we done got that out the way, and now we can just kind of move on.

AVC: On the show, Huey and Riley look and sound adorable. Do you think you can get away with more because they're so cute?

AM: I think that's always been part of the thinking behind the script, that—and I really tried really hard to impress that upon the staff of the show, the animation staff—to try to get them to understand that we would only be able to get away with what we were *writing* if the visuals were appealing enough that it was like a balance, and even people who didn't like what they were hearing would still not want to turn away because what they were *seeing* was so nice. So that was kind of my hunch, and I *think* it worked. I'm hoping it does.

AVC: What was the hardest part of adapting *The Boondocks* for television?

AM: I think it was going from working completely by myself to working with, not just a team of people, but really, *several* teams. Writers, producers, the artists, the illustrators, the designers, and, you know, overseas. I mean, it's small compared to what we would need to do the kind of show that we tried to do, but even at small numbers it's way more people than I'm used to working with. . . .

AVC: So what are you feeling angriest about these days?

AM: I'm actually kind of angriest about the fact that everybody keeps saying how angry I am.

AVC: You feel like you're kind of pigeonholed in that respect?

AM: I *do* the interviews and then I read about myself. I understand it and I get what it is. But there's so much stuff that I say, either jokingly or lightheartedly, that gets printed like I'm dead serious. I'm kind of conscious and aware of how ridiculous *everyone* involved with politics or talking about politics, especially on television, is—all the shouting matches and the screaming and the over-the-top personalities, and everyone's just playing. It's like WWF for news, almost. It's really ridiculous and I *really* don't want to be a part of it, and I'm not trying to put on this persona of this angry revolutionary to get people to follow me.

I just tell jokes, and I think a lot of people take it too seriously. It's not that I don't have things that I'm angry about in the world, and I think most decent human beings *are* upset about things, and even upset about things in their own country, but I'm not a particularly *unhappy* fellow. I think I'm happy with the show, and I think it's funny and I'm optimistic about it. What's on my mind, what's kind of bugging me, is clearly visible in the strip and in the show, but I still manage to joke about it. [*Laughs.*] I really get a little bit confused by all this "angry angry angry" talk when all I do is tell jokes and at least *some* people find it funny. . . .

AVC: You almost have a nostalgia for a time when the government was better at deceiving people, and was better . . .

AM: Yeah, we call those the Clinton years. . . .

AVC: How do you handle the pressure of doing both the show and the strip?

AM: You collapse a few times, and you put your head in your hands, and you say, "Oh my god, how am I gonna get through this?" You have a few of those nights, and then you get over it and you keep it moving. And those nights . . . As you get more used to the strain, I guess those nights are fewer and farther between. So that's the best you can hope for. It's a tough job and it's a lot to pull out of your brain. And then, on top of that, I think, being a public figure—which, I have to admit, I guess I'm largely responsible for, in terms of going out and putting myself out there—comes with its own burdens, and its own things that cause you stress, and its own worries. So it's been an interesting six years and I think I've learned a few things. But I'm glad I got through it, that I got to this point. Because I'm happy with the show, I'm really proud of what we've done, and I'm glad we made it this far.

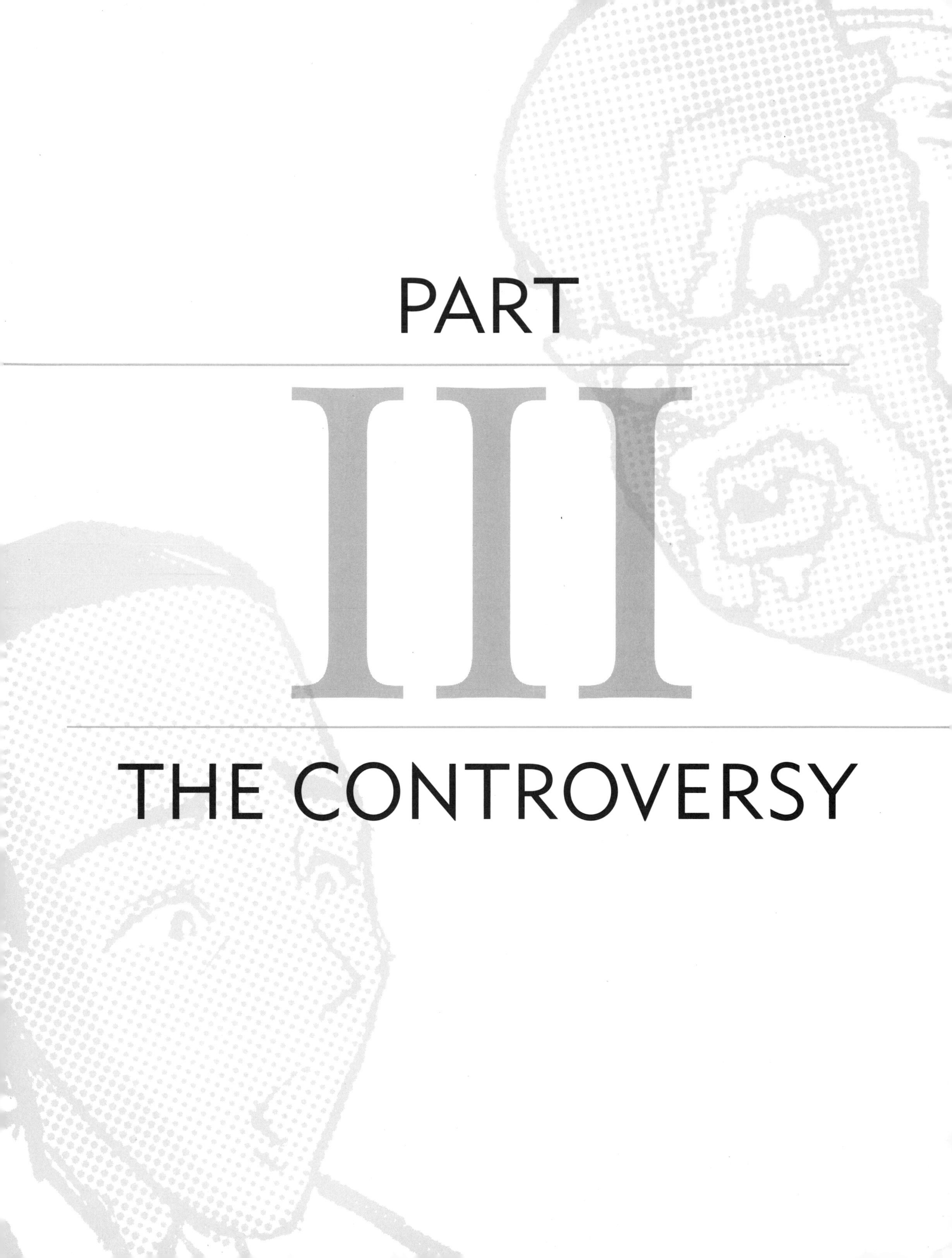

PART III

THE CONTROVERSY

Introduction to Part III

Looking at the sheer number of so-called "controversial" strips could perhaps leave the false impression that the strip was a constant battle with the syndicate to water things down. My relationship with the syndicate (deadline problems notwithstanding) stayed very positive through the entire run of the strip and through all the different controversies. For the most part Universal Press would just offer suggestions on how to make the strips a bit more palatable to the feature editors. If I was stubborn, they would gently remind me how many clients I would likely lose if a particular strip wasn't changed or cut. After that, they left the final decisions up to me . . . and they were happy to be on the front lines taking the heat for my juvenile decisions. They deserve thanks for that.

The Boondocks can keep a comics editor awake at night.

—Doug Sweet, *Montreal Gazette*

Week of

May 31, 1999

Violence has always been a part of comics because violence has always been a part of childhood. *Peanuts*, *Calvin & Hobbes*, and other classic comics have always shown kids knocking the shit out of one another. Even still, I gave in to the syndicate's request to keep the violence off-panel. Still didn't help.

I was a bit upset by the fallout of these strips, which was so ridiculously overblown. Some said it was the Columbine effect . . . I still believe it was racial double-standard . . . Racial, man . . . racial. . . .

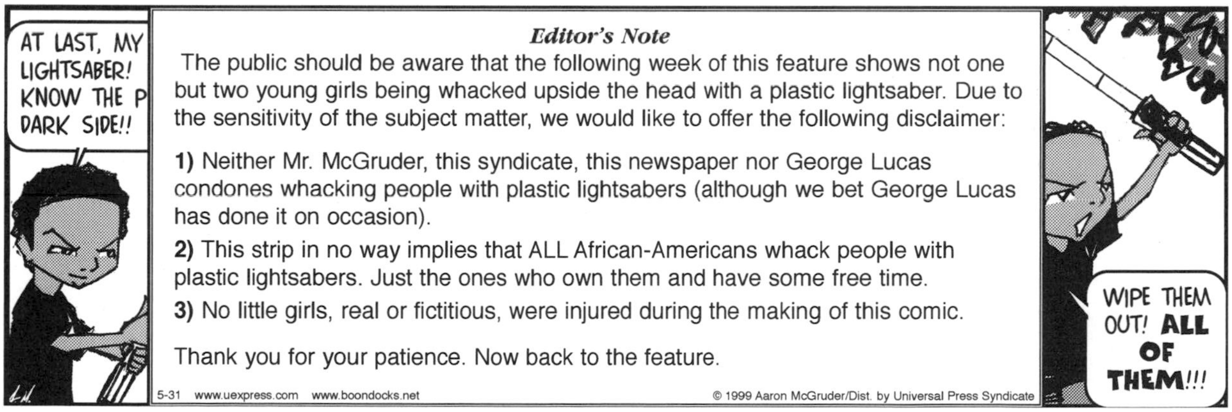

AT LAST, MY LIGHTSABER! KNOW THE P DARK SIDE!!
Editor's Note
The public should be aware that the following week of this feature shows not one but two young girls being whacked upside the head with a plastic lightsaber. Due to the sensitivity of the subject matter, we would like to offer the following disclaimer:
1) Neither Mr. McGruder, this syndicate, this newspaper nor George Lucas condones whacking people with plastic lightsabers (although we bet George Lucas has done it on occasion).
2) This strip in no way implies that ALL African-Americans whack people with plastic lightsabers. Just the ones who own them and have some free time.
3) No little girls, real or fictitious, were injured during the making of this comic.
Thank you for your patience. Now back to the feature.
5-31 www.uexpress.com www.boondocks.net
© 1999 Aaron McGruder/Dist. by Universal Press Syndicate
WIPE THEM OUT! ALL OF THEM!!!

JAZMINE DUBOIS, PEACEFUL CITIZEN OF EARTH, IS ABOUT TO FALL UNDER ATTACK.
© 1999 Aaron McGruder/Dist. by Universal Press Syndicate
HER ATTACKER, THE OMINOUS DARTH RILEY, IS IN FOR A BITTER DISAPPOINTMENT, HOWEVER.
6-1
WHACK!
www.boondocks.net
www.uexpress.com
OWWWWWWWWWWW!
HIS LIGHTSABER ISN'T REAL.
THIS THING CAN'T CUT?!! I WANT MY MONEY BACK!!!

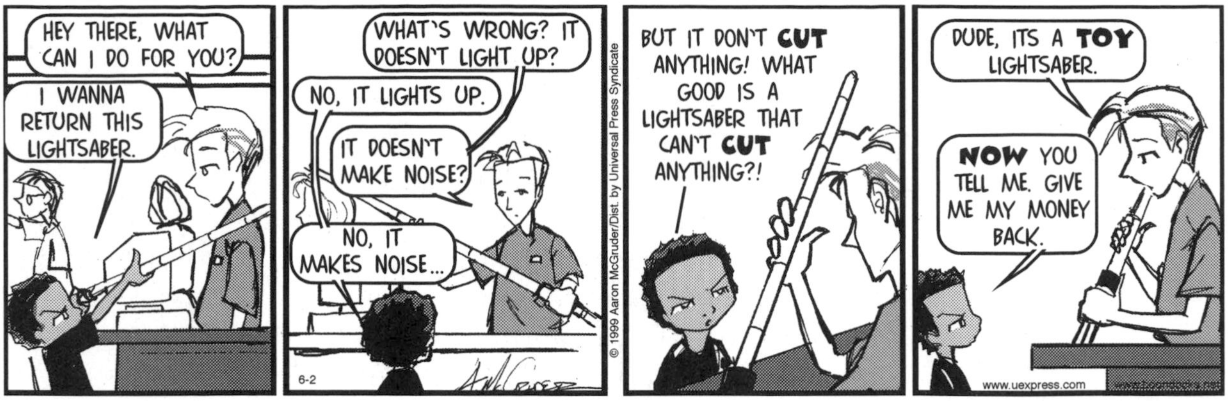
HEY THERE, WHAT CAN I DO FOR YOU?
I WANNA RETURN THIS LIGHTSABER.
WHAT'S WRONG? IT DOESN'T LIGHT UP?
NO, IT LIGHTS UP.
IT DOESN'T MAKE NOISE?
NO, IT MAKES NOISE...
6-2
© 1999 Aaron McGruder/Dist. by Universal Press Syndicate
BUT IT DON'T **CUT** ANYTHING! WHAT GOOD IS A LIGHTSABER THAT CAN'T **CUT** ANYTHING?!
DUDE, ITS A **TOY** LIGHTSABER.
NOW YOU TELL ME. GIVE ME MY MONEY BACK.
www.uexpress.com

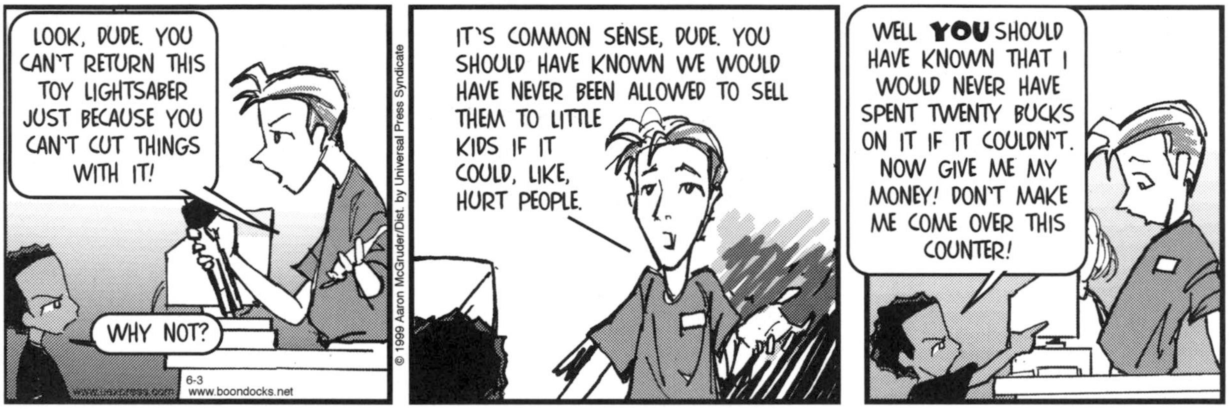
LOOK, DUDE. YOU CAN'T RETURN THIS TOY LIGHTSABER JUST BECAUSE YOU CAN'T CUT THINGS WITH IT!
WHY NOT?
www.uexpress.com
6-3
www.boondocks.net
© 1999 Aaron McGruder/Dist. by Universal Press Syndicate
IT'S COMMON SENSE, DUDE. YOU SHOULD HAVE KNOWN WE WOULD HAVE NEVER BEEN ALLOWED TO SELL THEM TO LITTLE KIDS IF IT COULD, LIKE, HURT PEOPLE.
WELL **YOU** SHOULD HAVE KNOWN THAT I WOULD NEVER HAVE SPENT TWENTY BUCKS ON IT IF IT COULDN'T. NOW GIVE ME MY MONEY! DON'T MAKE ME COME OVER THIS COUNTER!

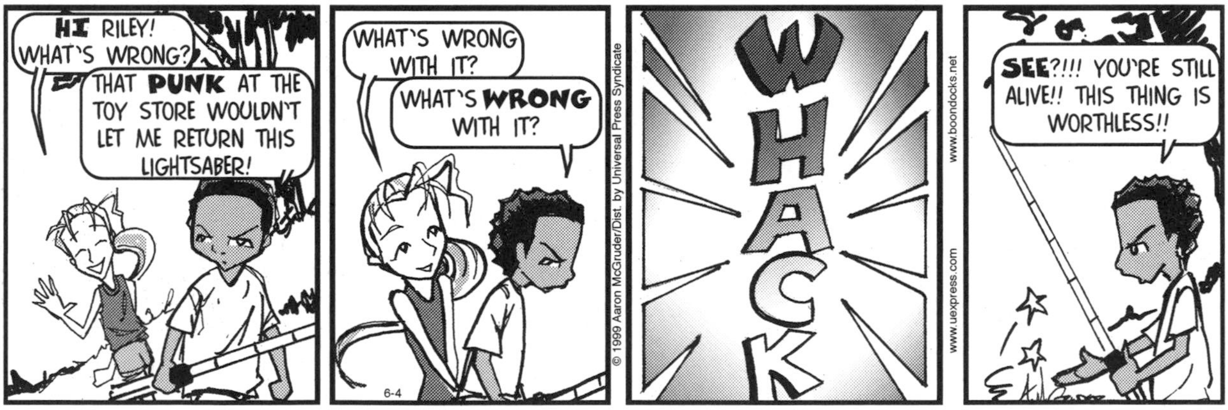
HI RILEY! WHAT'S WRONG?
THAT **PUNK** AT THE TOY STORE WOULDN'T LET ME RETURN THIS LIGHTSABER!
WHAT'S WRONG WITH IT?
WHAT'S **WRONG** WITH IT?
6-4
© 1999 Aaron McGruder/Dist. by Universal Press Syndicate
WHACK
www.boondocks.net
www.uexpress.com
SEE?!!! YOU'RE STILL ALIVE!! THIS THING IS WORTHLESS!!

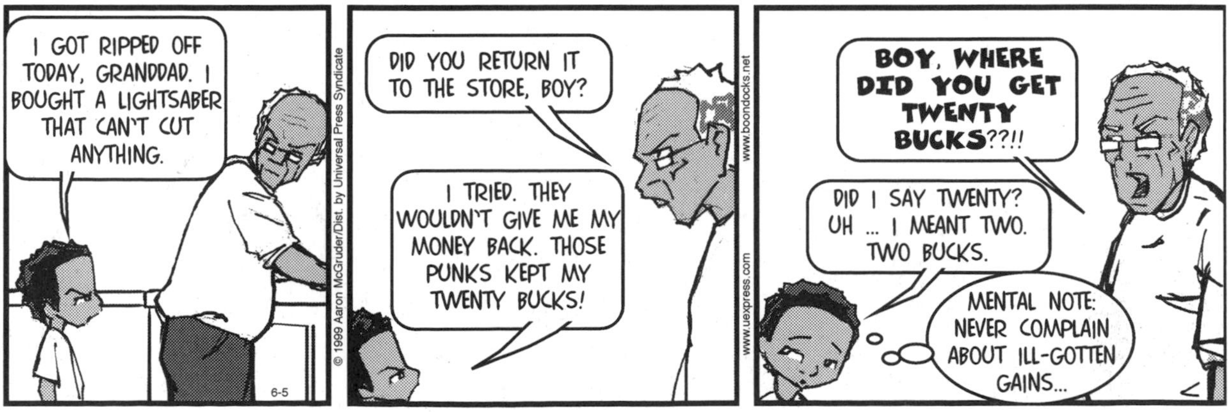
I GOT RIPPED OFF TODAY, GRANDDAD. I BOUGHT A LIGHTSABER THAT CAN'T CUT ANYTHING.
6-5
© 1999 Aaron McGruder/Dist. by Universal Press Syndicate
DID YOU RETURN IT TO THE STORE, BOY?
I TRIED. THEY WOULDN'T GIVE ME MY MONEY BACK. THOSE PUNKS KEPT MY TWENTY BUCKS!
www.boondocks.net
www.uexpress.com
BOY, WHERE DID YOU GET TWENTY BUCKS??!!
DID I SAY TWENTY? UH ... I MEANT TWO. TWO BUCKS.
MENTAL NOTE: NEVER COMPLAIN ABOUT ILL-GOTTEN GAINS...

Week of June 7, 1999

In doing a series where Huey decides to establish a neighborhood Klanwatch, I had him plan to stock an outrageous supply of weapons. My editor had me make Huey's weapon demands even more outrageous but less specific at the same time. Thus, I changed an "MP5 submachine gun" and a ".50 caliber Desert Eagle" to "flamethrowers" and "light artillery." The Columbine High School shootings had taken place less than two months previous (on April 20, 1999), and my syndicate was nervous about having guns in the comics.

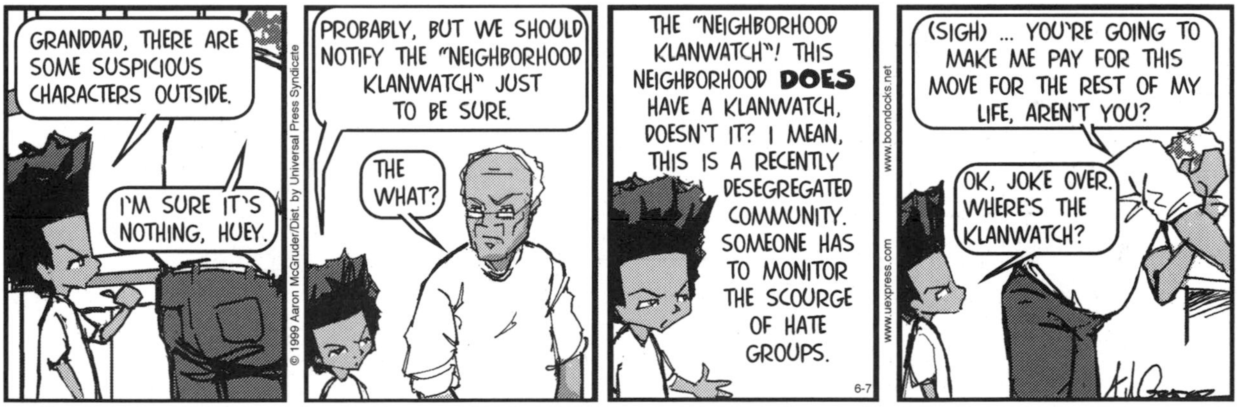
GRANDDAD, THERE ARE SOME SUSPICIOUS CHARACTERS OUTSIDE.
I'M SURE IT'S NOTHING, HUEY.
© 1999 Aaron McGruder/Dist. by Universal Press Syndicate
PROBABLY, BUT WE SHOULD NOTIFY THE "NEIGHBORHOOD KLANWATCH" JUST TO BE SURE.
THE WHAT?
THE "NEIGHBORHOOD KLANWATCH"! THIS NEIGHBORHOOD DOES HAVE A KLANWATCH, DOESN'T IT? I MEAN, THIS IS A RECENTLY DESEGREGATED COMMUNITY. SOMEONE HAS TO MONITOR THE SCOURGE OF HATE GROUPS.
www.boondocks.net
www.uexpress.com
6-7
(SIGH) ... YOU'RE GOING TO MAKE ME PAY FOR THIS MOVE FOR THE REST OF MY LIFE, AREN'T YOU?
OK, JOKE OVER. WHERE'S THE KLANWATCH?

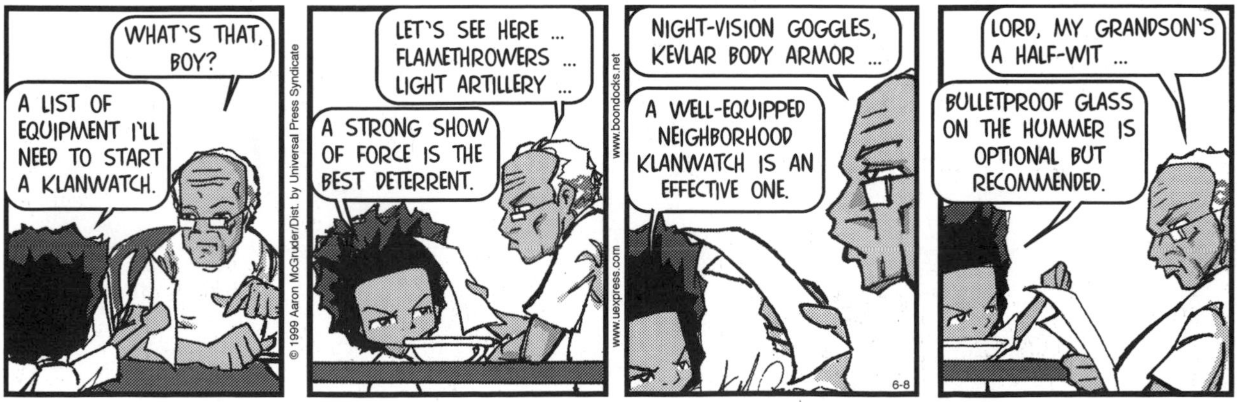
WHAT'S THAT, BOY?
A LIST OF EQUIPMENT I'LL NEED TO START A KLANWATCH.
© 1999 Aaron McGruder/Dist. by Universal Press Syndicate
LET'S SEE HERE ... FLAMETHROWERS ... LIGHT ARTILLERY ...
A STRONG SHOW OF FORCE IS THE BEST DETERRENT.
www.boondocks.net
www.uexpress.com
NIGHT-VISION GOGGLES, KEVLAR BODY ARMOR ...
A WELL-EQUIPPED NEIGHBORHOOD KLANWATCH IS AN EFFECTIVE ONE.
6-8
LORD, MY GRANDSON'S A HALF-WIT ...
BULLETPROOF GLASS ON THE HUMMER IS OPTIONAL BUT RECOMMENDED.

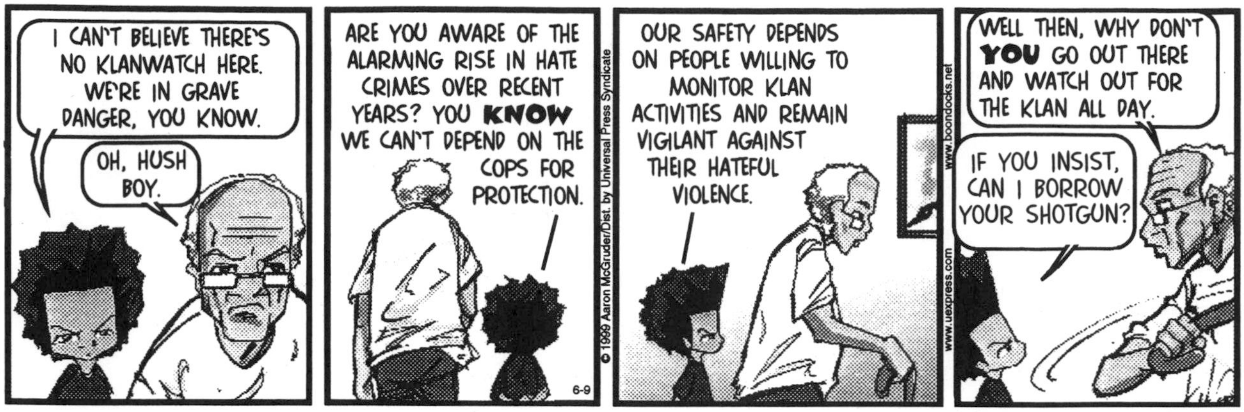
I CAN'T BELIEVE THERE'S NO KLANWATCH HERE. WE'RE IN GRAVE DANGER, YOU KNOW.
OH, HUSH BOY.
ARE YOU AWARE OF THE ALARMING RISE IN HATE CRIMES OVER RECENT YEARS? YOU **KNOW** WE CAN'T DEPEND ON THE COPS FOR PROTECTION.
6-9
© 1999 Aaron McGruder/Dist. by Universal Press Syndicate
OUR SAFETY DEPENDS ON PEOPLE WILLING TO MONITOR KLAN ACTIVITIES AND REMAIN VIGILANT AGAINST THEIR HATEFUL VIOLENCE.
www.boondocks.net
www.uexpress.com
WELL THEN, WHY DON'T **YOU** GO OUT THERE AND WATCH OUT FOR THE KLAN ALL DAY.
IF YOU INSIST, CAN I BORROW YOUR SHOTGUN?

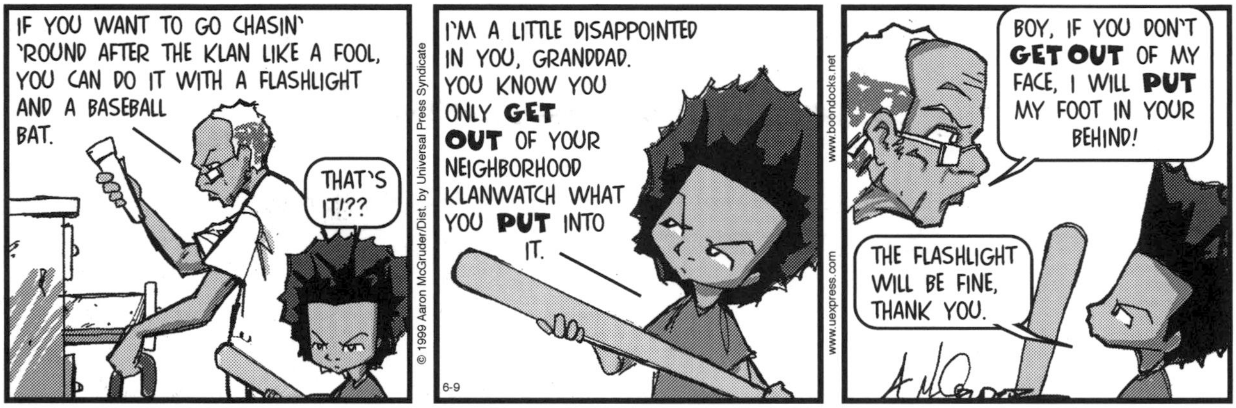
IF YOU WANT TO GO CHASIN' 'ROUND AFTER THE KLAN LIKE A FOOL, YOU CAN DO IT WITH A FLASHLIGHT AND A BASEBALL BAT.
THAT'S IT!??
© 1999 Aaron McGruder/Dist. by Universal Press Syndicate
6-9
I'M A LITTLE DISAPPOINTED IN YOU, GRANDDAD. YOU KNOW YOU ONLY **GET OUT** OF YOUR NEIGHBORHOOD KLANWATCH WHAT YOU **PUT** INTO IT.
www.boondocks.net
www.uexpress.com
BOY, IF YOU DON'T **GET OUT** OF MY FACE, I WILL **PUT** MY FOOT IN YOUR BEHIND!
THE FLASHLIGHT WILL BE FINE, THANK YOU.

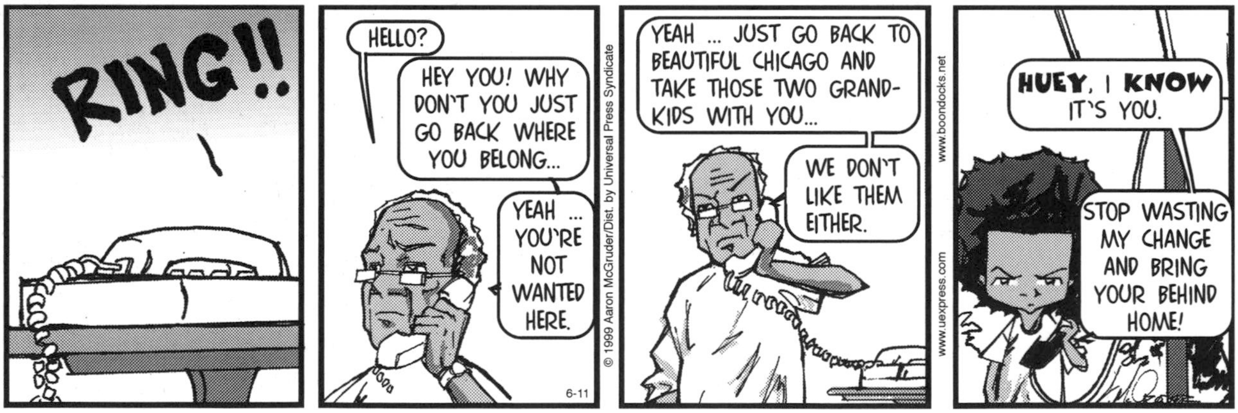
RING!!
HELLO?
HEY YOU! WHY DON'T YOU JUST GO BACK WHERE YOU BELONG...
YEAH ... YOU'RE NOT WANTED HERE.
6-11
© 1999 Aaron McGruder/Dist. by Universal Press Syndicate
YEAH ... JUST GO BACK TO BEAUTIFUL CHICAGO AND TAKE THOSE TWO GRAND-KIDS WITH YOU...
WE DON'T LIKE THEM EITHER.
www.boondocks.net
www.uexpress.com
HUEY, I **KNOW** IT'S YOU.
STOP WASTING MY CHANGE AND BRING YOUR BEHIND HOME!

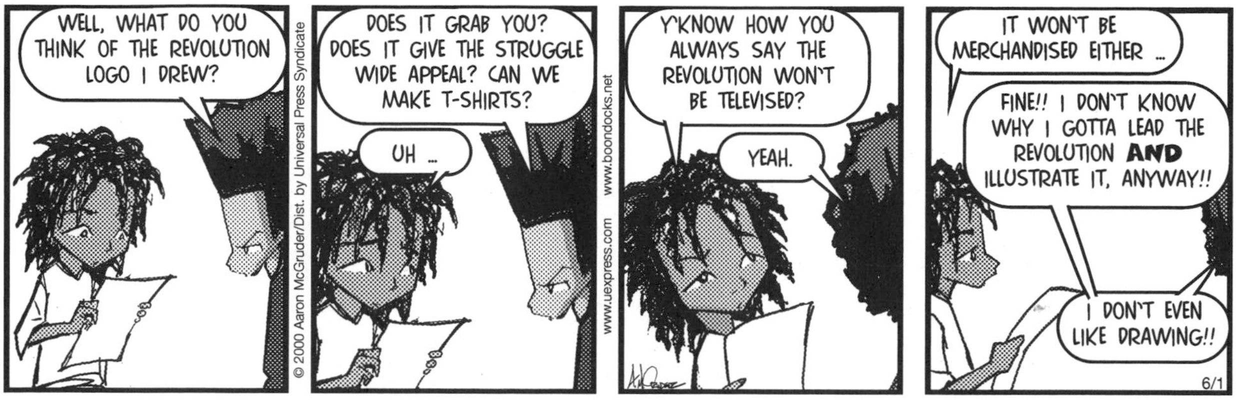
WELL, WHAT DO YOU THINK OF THE REVOLUTION LOGO I DREW?
© 2000 Aaron McGruder/Dist. by Universal Press Syndicate
DOES IT GRAB YOU? DOES IT GIVE THE STRUGGLE WIDE APPEAL? CAN WE MAKE T-SHIRTS?
UH ...
www.uexpress.com www.boondocks.net
Y'KNOW HOW YOU ALWAYS SAY THE REVOLUTION WON'T BE TELEVISED?
YEAH.
IT WON'T BE MERCHANDISED EITHER ...
FINE!! I DON'T KNOW WHY I GOTTA LEAD THE REVOLUTION **AND** ILLUSTRATE IT, ANYWAY!!
I DON'T EVEN LIKE DRAWING!!
6/1

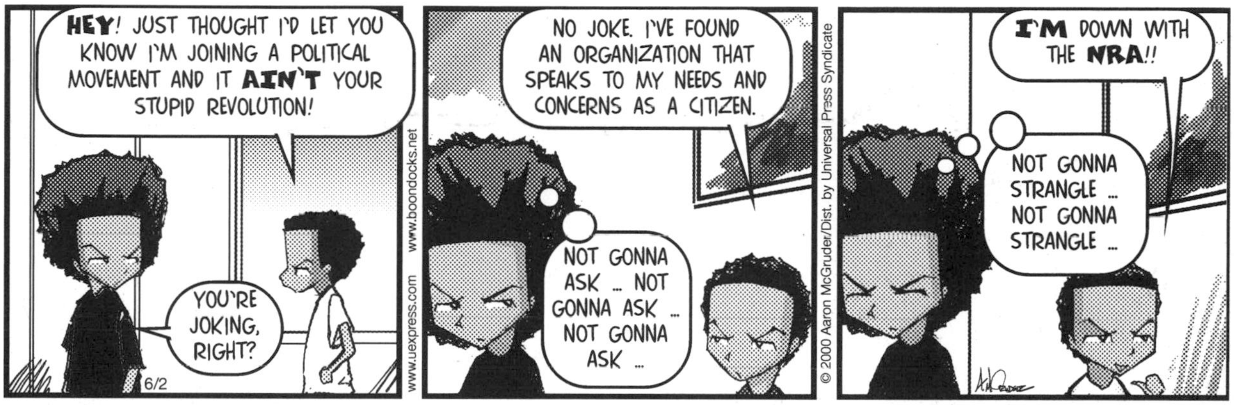
HEY! JUST THOUGHT I'D LET YOU KNOW I'M JOINING A POLITICAL MOVEMENT AND IT **AIN'T** YOUR STUPID REVOLUTION!
YOU'RE JOKING, RIGHT?
6/2
www.uexpress.com www.boondocks.net
NO JOKE. I'VE FOUND AN ORGANIZATION THAT SPEAKS TO MY NEEDS AND CONCERNS AS A CITIZEN.
NOT GONNA ASK ... NOT GONNA ASK ... NOT GONNA ASK ...
© 2000 Aaron McGruder/Dist. by Universal Press Syndicate
I'M DOWN WITH THE **NRA**!!
NOT GONNA STRANGLE ... NOT GONNA STRANGLE ...

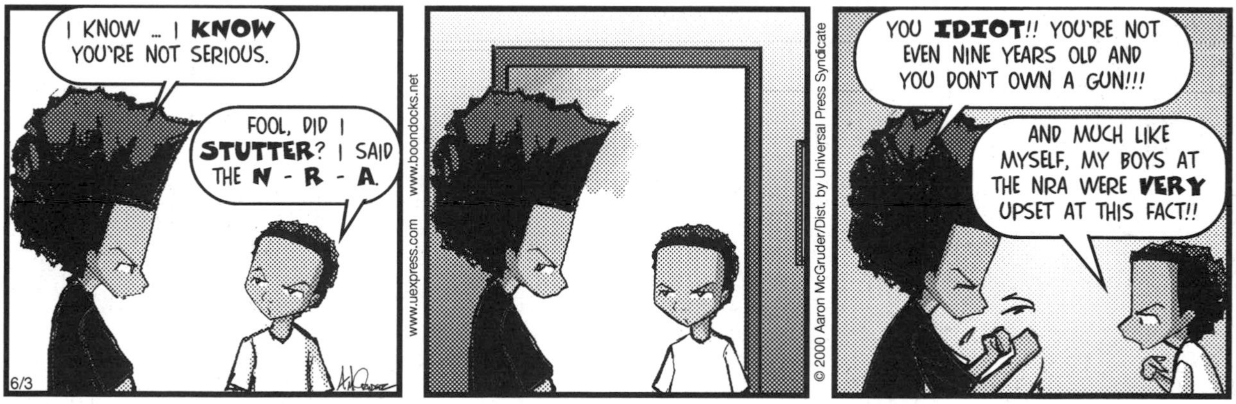
I KNOW ... I **KNOW** YOU'RE NOT SERIOUS.
FOOL, DID I **STUTTER**? I SAID THE **N - R - A**.
6/3
www.uexpress.com www.boondocks.net
© 2000 Aaron McGruder/Dist. by Universal Press Syndicate
YOU **IDIOT**!! YOU'RE NOT EVEN NINE YEARS OLD AND YOU DON'T OWN A GUN!!!
AND MUCH LIKE MYSELF, MY BOYS AT THE NRA WERE **VERY** UPSET AT THIS FACT!!

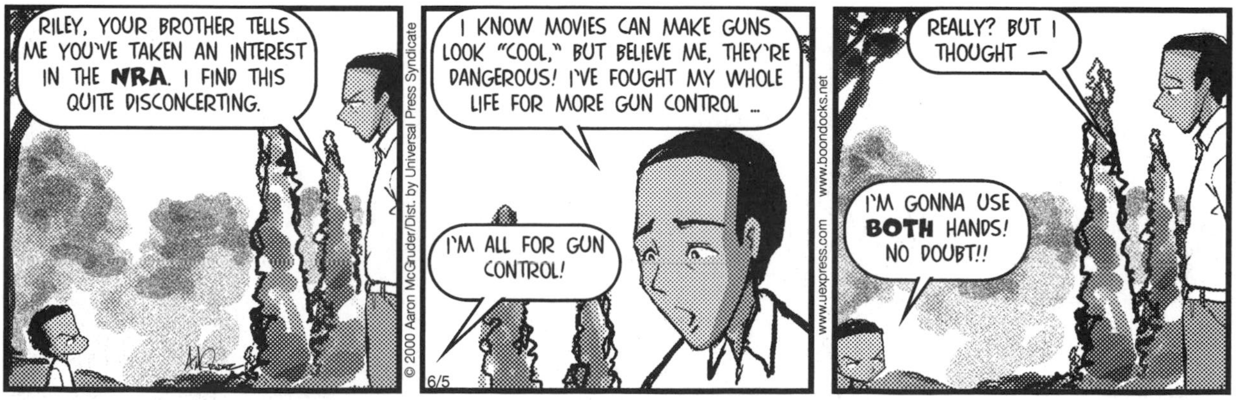
RILEY, YOUR BROTHER TELLS ME YOU'VE TAKEN AN INTEREST IN THE **NRA**. I FIND THIS QUITE DISCONCERTING.
© 2000 Aaron McGruder/Dist. by Universal Press Syndicate
I KNOW MOVIES CAN MAKE GUNS LOOK "COOL," BUT BELIEVE ME, THEY'RE DANGEROUS! I'VE FOUGHT MY WHOLE LIFE FOR MORE GUN CONTROL ...
I'M ALL FOR GUN CONTROL!
6/5
www.uexpress.com www.boondocks.net
REALLY? BUT I THOUGHT —
I'M GONNA USE **BOTH** HANDS! NO DOUBT!!

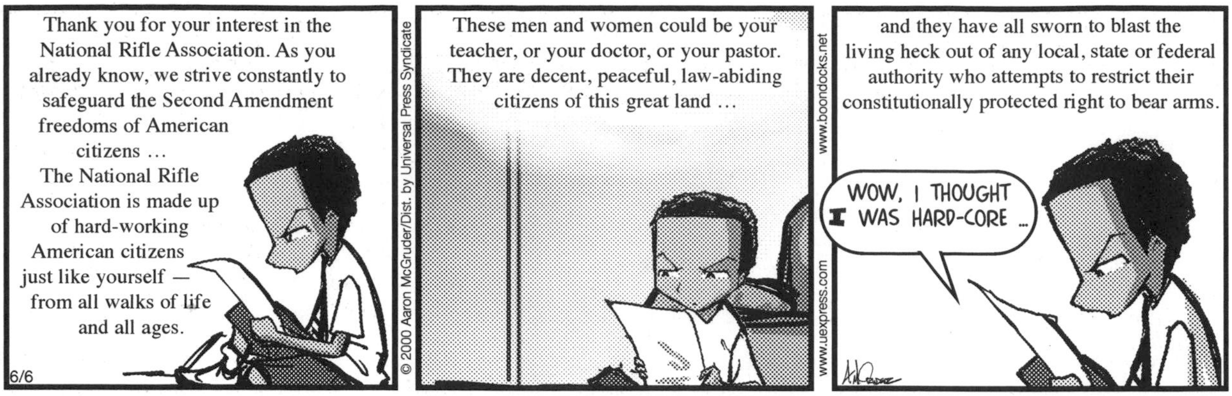
Thank you for your interest in the National Rifle Association. As you already know, we strive constantly to safeguard the Second Amendment freedoms of American citizens … The National Rifle Association is made up of hard-working American citizens just like yourself — from all walks of life and all ages.
6/6
© 2000 Aaron McGruder/Dist. by Universal Press Syndicate
These men and women could be your teacher, or your doctor, or your pastor. They are decent, peaceful, law-abiding citizens of this great land …
www.boondocks.net
www.uexpress.com
and they have all sworn to blast the living heck out of any local, state or federal authority who attempts to restrict their constitutionally protected right to bear arms.
WOW, I THOUGHT I WAS HARD-CORE …

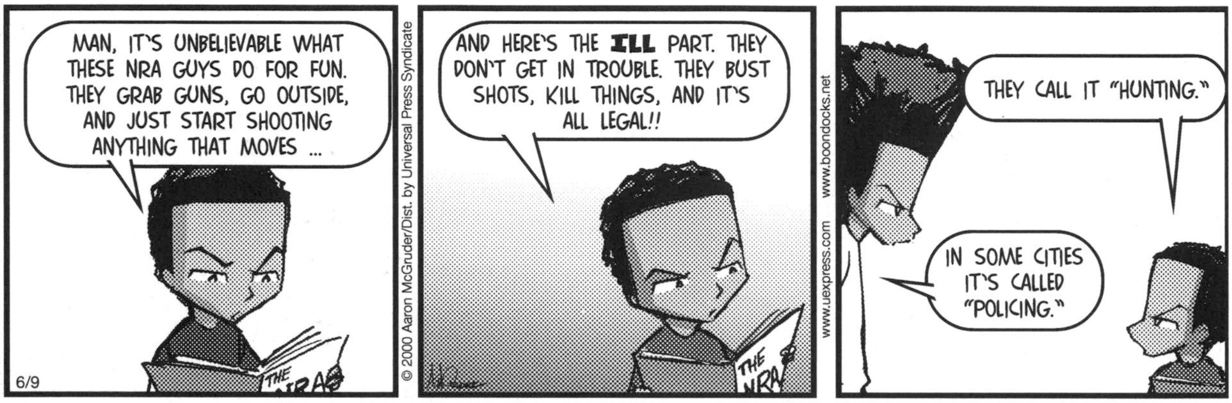
MAN, IT'S UNBELIEVABLE WHAT THESE NRA GUYS DO FOR FUN. THEY GRAB GUNS, GO OUTSIDE, AND JUST START SHOOTING ANYTHING THAT MOVES …
6/9
© 2000 Aaron McGruder/Dist. by Universal Press Syndicate
AND HERE'S THE ILL PART. THEY DON'T GET IN TROUBLE. THEY BUST SHOTS, KILL THINGS, AND IT'S ALL LEGAL!!
THE NRA
www.boondocks.net
www.uexpress.com
THEY CALL IT "HUNTING."
IN SOME CITIES IT'S CALLED "POLICING."

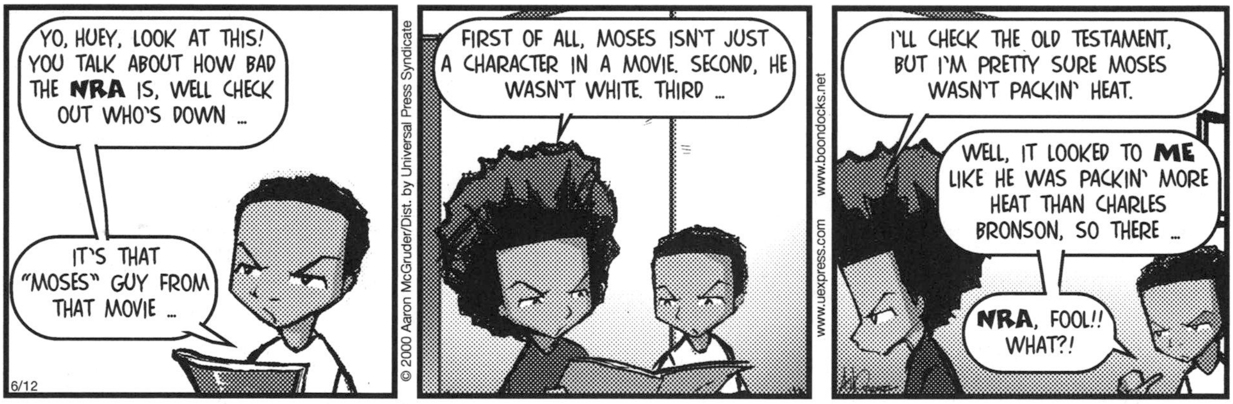
YO, HUEY, LOOK AT THIS! YOU TALK ABOUT HOW BAD THE NRA IS, WELL CHECK OUT WHO'S DOWN …
IT'S THAT "MOSES" GUY FROM THAT MOVIE …
6/12
© 2000 Aaron McGruder/Dist. by Universal Press Syndicate
FIRST OF ALL, MOSES ISN'T JUST A CHARACTER IN A MOVIE. SECOND, HE WASN'T WHITE. THIRD …
www.boondocks.net
www.uexpress.com
I'LL CHECK THE OLD TESTAMENT, BUT I'M PRETTY SURE MOSES WASN'T PACKIN' HEAT.
WELL, IT LOOKED TO ME LIKE HE WAS PACKIN' MORE HEAT THAN CHARLES BRONSON, SO THERE …
NRA, FOOL!! WHAT?!

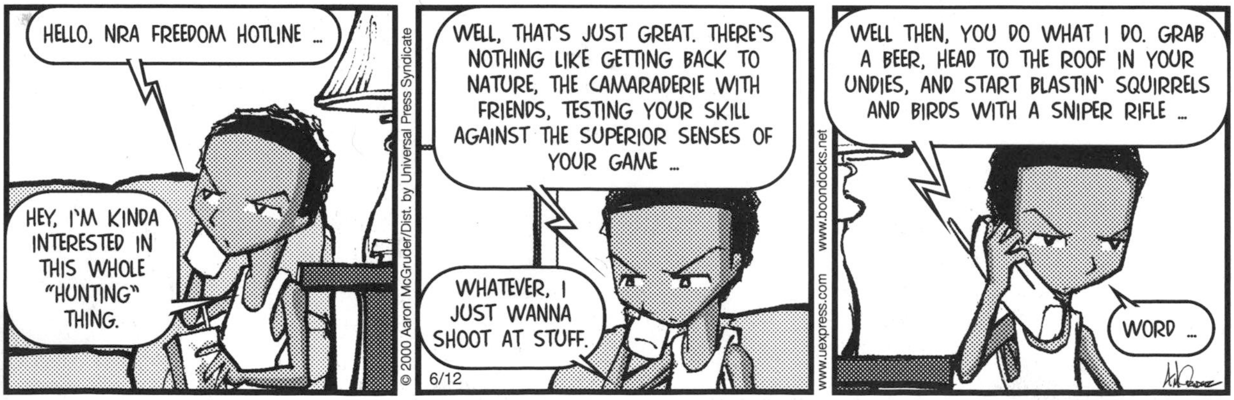
HELLO, NRA FREEDOM HOTLINE …
HEY, I'M KINDA INTERESTED IN THIS WHOLE "HUNTING" THING.
© 2000 Aaron McGruder/Dist. by Universal Press Syndicate
WELL, THAT'S JUST GREAT. THERE'S NOTHING LIKE GETTING BACK TO NATURE, THE CAMARADERIE WITH FRIENDS, TESTING YOUR SKILL AGAINST THE SUPERIOR SENSES OF YOUR GAME …
WHATEVER, I JUST WANNA SHOOT AT STUFF.
6/12
www.boondocks.net
www.uexpress.com
WELL THEN, YOU DO WHAT I DO. GRAB A BEER, HEAD TO THE ROOF IN YOUR UNDIES, AND START BLASTIN' SQUIRRELS AND BIRDS WITH A SNIPER RIFLE …
WORD …

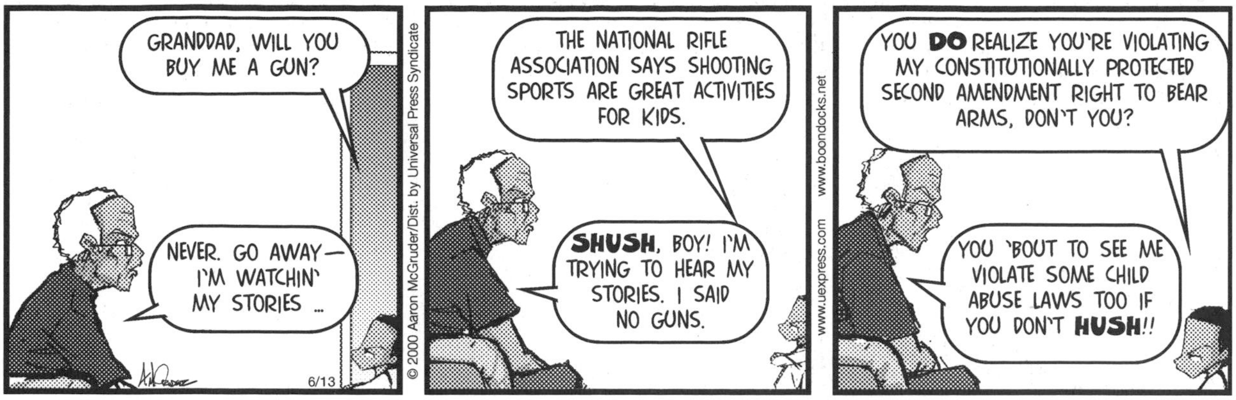
GRANDDAD, WILL YOU BUY ME A GUN?
NEVER. GO AWAY— I'M WATCHIN' MY STORIES ...
6/13
© 2000 Aaron McGruder/Dist. by Universal Press Syndicate
THE NATIONAL RIFLE ASSOCIATION SAYS SHOOTING SPORTS ARE GREAT ACTIVITIES FOR KIDS.
SHUSH, BOY! I'M TRYING TO HEAR MY STORIES. I SAID NO GUNS.
www.uexpress.com www.boondocks.net
YOU **DO** REALIZE YOU'RE VIOLATING MY CONSTITUTIONALLY PROTECTED SECOND AMENDMENT RIGHT TO BEAR ARMS, DON'T YOU?
YOU 'BOUT TO SEE ME VIOLATE SOME CHILD ABUSE LAWS TOO IF YOU DON'T **HUSH**!!

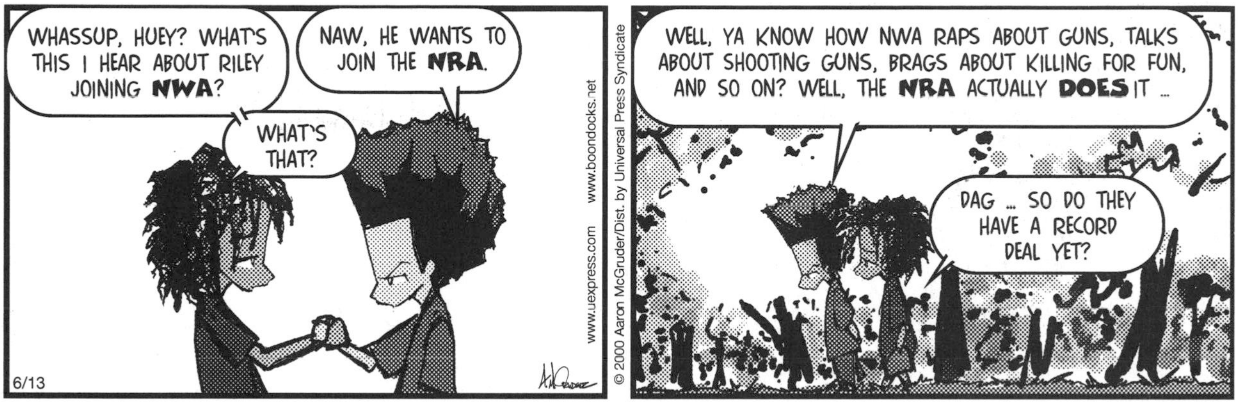
WHASSUP, HUEY? WHAT'S THIS I HEAR ABOUT RILEY JOINING **NWA**?
NAW, HE WANTS TO JOIN THE **NRA**.
WHAT'S THAT?
6/13
www.uexpress.com www.boondocks.net
© 2000 Aaron McGruder/Dist. by Universal Press Syndicate
WELL, YA KNOW HOW NWA RAPS ABOUT GUNS, TALKS ABOUT SHOOTING GUNS, BRAGS ABOUT KILLING FOR FUN, AND SO ON? WELL, THE **NRA** ACTUALLY **DOES** IT ...
DAG ... SO DO THEY HAVE A RECORD DEAL YET?

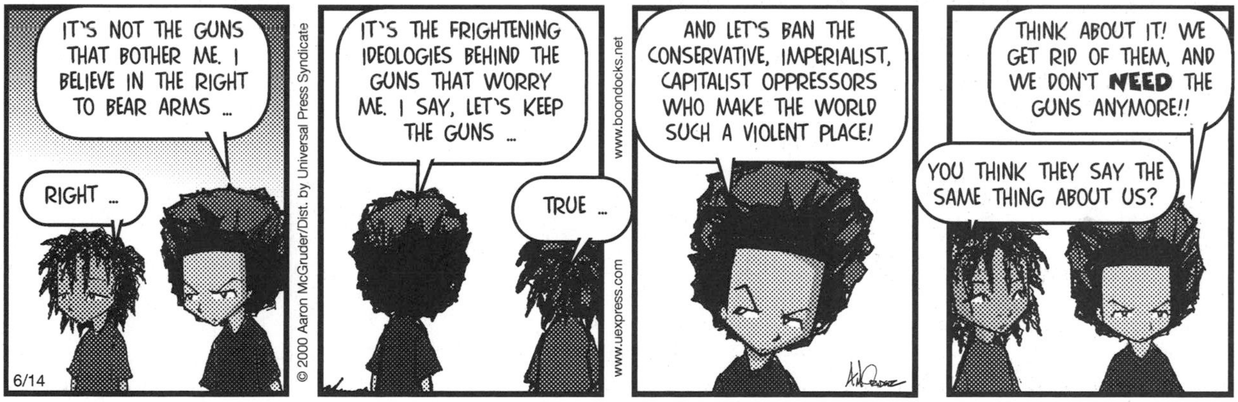
IT'S NOT THE GUNS THAT BOTHER ME. I BELIEVE IN THE RIGHT TO BEAR ARMS ...
RIGHT ...
6/14
© 2000 Aaron McGruder/Dist. by Universal Press Syndicate
IT'S THE FRIGHTENING IDEOLOGIES BEHIND THE GUNS THAT WORRY ME. I SAY, LET'S KEEP THE GUNS ...
TRUE ...
www.uexpress.com www.boondocks.net
AND LET'S BAN THE CONSERVATIVE, IMPERIALIST, CAPITALIST OPPRESSORS WHO MAKE THE WORLD SUCH A VIOLENT PLACE!
THINK ABOUT IT! WE GET RID OF THEM, AND WE DON'T **NEED** THE GUNS ANYMORE!!
YOU THINK THEY SAY THE SAME THING ABOUT US?

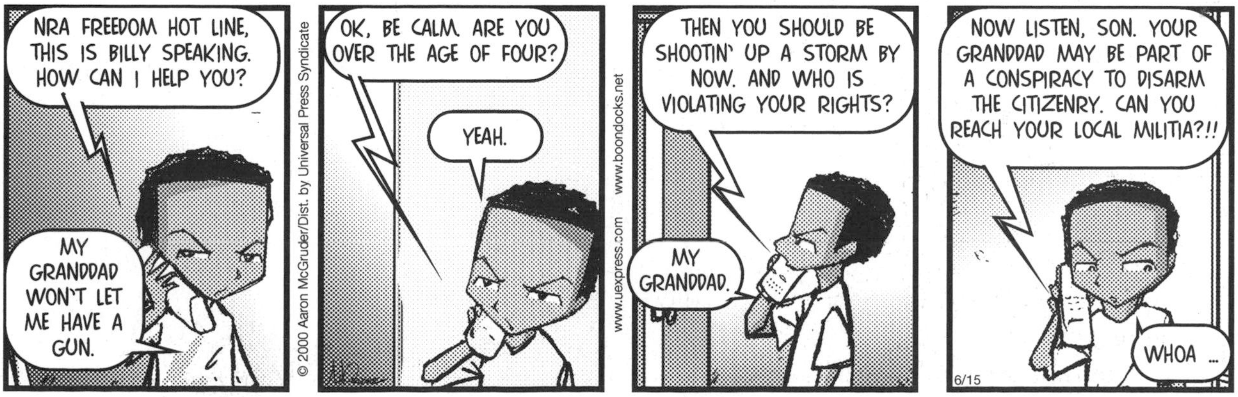
NRA FREEDOM HOT LINE, THIS IS BILLY SPEAKING. HOW CAN I HELP YOU?
MY GRANDDAD WON'T LET ME HAVE A GUN.
© 2000 Aaron McGruder/Dist. by Universal Press Syndicate
OK, BE CALM. ARE YOU OVER THE AGE OF FOUR?
YEAH.
www.uexpress.com www.boondocks.net
THEN YOU SHOULD BE SHOOTIN' UP A STORM BY NOW. AND WHO IS VIOLATING YOUR RIGHTS?
MY GRANDDAD.
NOW LISTEN, SON. YOUR GRANDDAD MAY BE PART OF A CONSPIRACY TO DISARM THE CITIZENRY. CAN YOU REACH YOUR LOCAL MILITIA?!!
WHOA ...
6/15

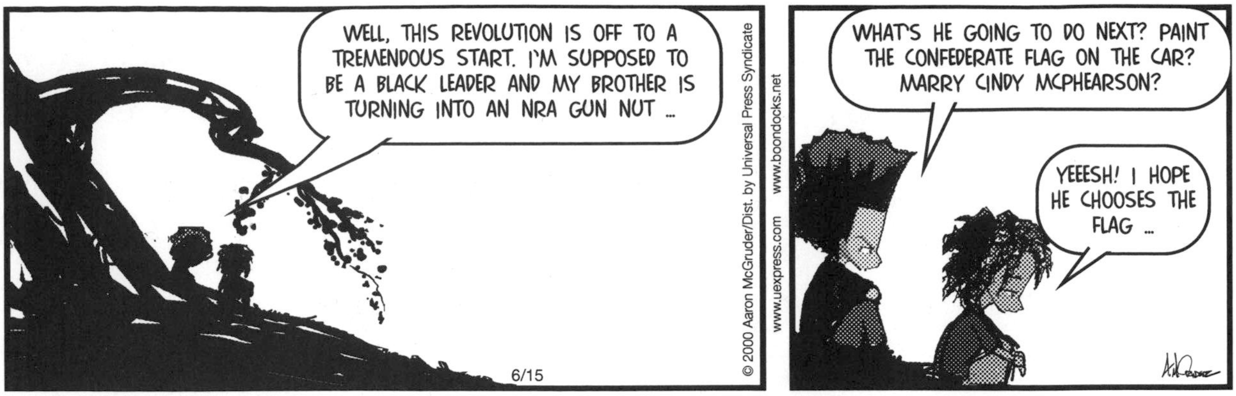
WELL, THIS REVOLUTION IS OFF TO A TREMENDOUS START. I'M SUPPOSED TO BE A BLACK LEADER AND MY BROTHER IS TURNING INTO AN NRA GUN NUT ...
6/15
© 2000 Aaron McGruder/Dist. by Universal Press Syndicate
www.uexpress.com www.boondocks.net
WHAT'S HE GOING TO DO NEXT? PAINT THE CONFEDERATE FLAG ON THE CAR? MARRY CINDY MCPHEARSON?
YEEESH! I HOPE HE CHOOSES THE FLAG ...

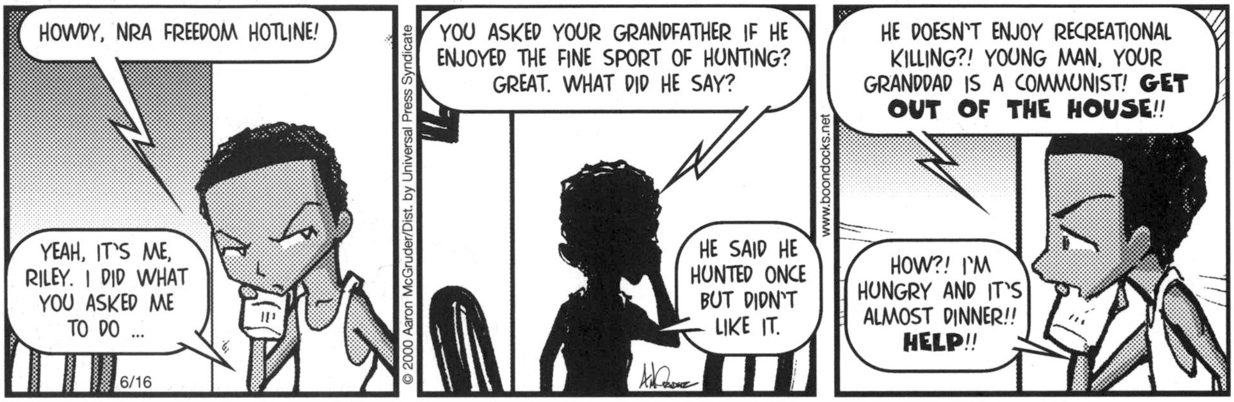
HOWDY, NRA FREEDOM HOTLINE!
YEAH, IT'S ME, RILEY. I DID WHAT YOU ASKED ME TO DO ...
6/16
© 2000 Aaron McGruder/Dist. by Universal Press Syndicate
YOU ASKED YOUR GRANDFATHER IF HE ENJOYED THE FINE SPORT OF HUNTING? GREAT. WHAT DID HE SAY?
HE SAID HE HUNTED ONCE BUT DIDN'T LIKE IT.
www.boondocks.net
HE DOESN'T ENJOY RECREATIONAL KILLING?! YOUNG MAN, YOUR GRANDDAD IS A COMMUNIST! **GET OUT OF THE HOUSE**!!
HOW?! I'M HUNGRY AND IT'S ALMOST DINNER!! **HELP**!!

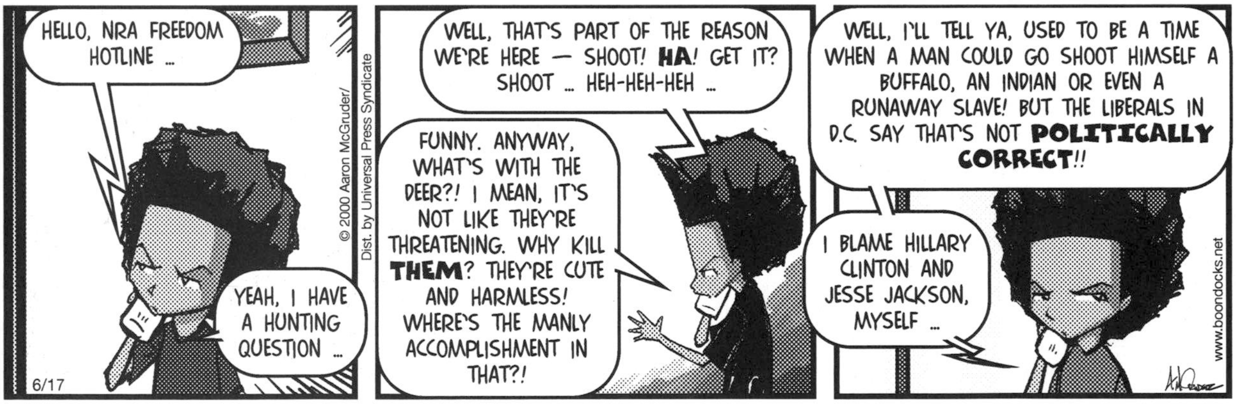
HELLO, NRA FREEDOM HOTLINE ...
YEAH, I HAVE A HUNTING QUESTION ...
6/17
© 2000 Aaron McGruder/ Dist. by Universal Press Syndicate
WELL, THAT'S PART OF THE REASON WE'RE HERE — SHOOT! **HA**! GET IT? SHOOT ... HEH-HEH-HEH ...
FUNNY. ANYWAY, WHAT'S WITH THE DEER?! I MEAN, IT'S NOT LIKE THEY'RE THREATENING. WHY KILL **THEM**? THEY'RE CUTE AND HARMLESS! WHERE'S THE MANLY ACCOMPLISHMENT IN THAT?!
WELL, I'LL TELL YA, USED TO BE A TIME WHEN A MAN COULD GO SHOOT HIMSELF A BUFFALO, AN INDIAN OR EVEN A RUNAWAY SLAVE! BUT THE LIBERALS IN D.C. SAY THAT'S NOT **POLITICALLY CORRECT**!!
I BLAME HILLARY CLINTON AND JESSE JACKSON, MYSELF ...
www.boondocks.net

September 27, 28, and 29, 2001

Much has already been said about the change in direction the strip took after 9/11. These strips started me down a path that would quickly have me banned in the New York *Daily News* for six weeks. I think that's a record!

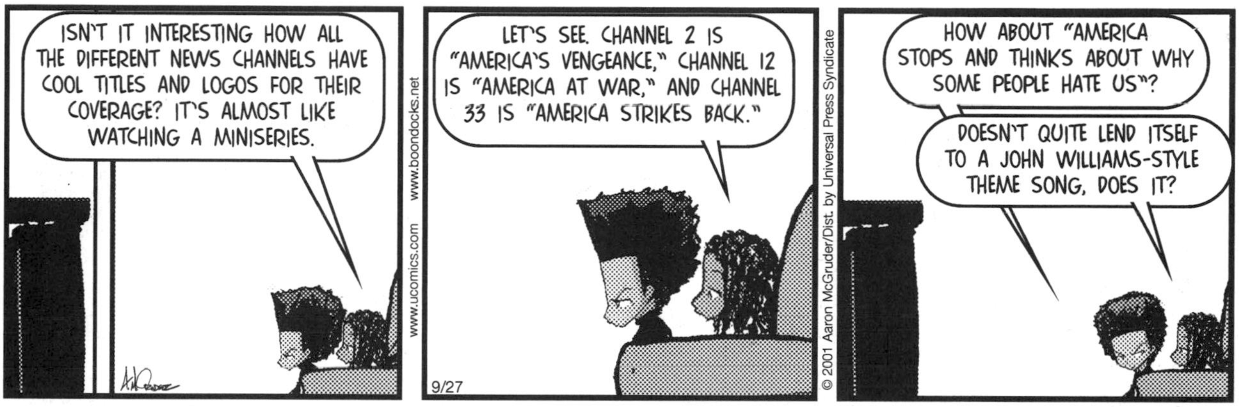
ISN'T IT INTERESTING HOW ALL THE DIFFERENT NEWS CHANNELS HAVE COOL TITLES AND LOGOS FOR THEIR COVERAGE? IT'S ALMOST LIKE WATCHING A MINISERIES.
www.ucomics.com www.boondocks.net
LET'S SEE. CHANNEL 2 IS "AMERICA'S VENGEANCE," CHANNEL 12 IS "AMERICA AT WAR," AND CHANNEL 33 IS "AMERICA STRIKES BACK."
9/27
© 2001 Aaron McGruder/Dist. by Universal Press Syndicate
HOW ABOUT "AMERICA STOPS AND THINKS ABOUT WHY SOME PEOPLE HATE US"?
DOESN'T QUITE LEND ITSELF TO A JOHN WILLIAMS-STYLE THEME SONG, DOES IT?

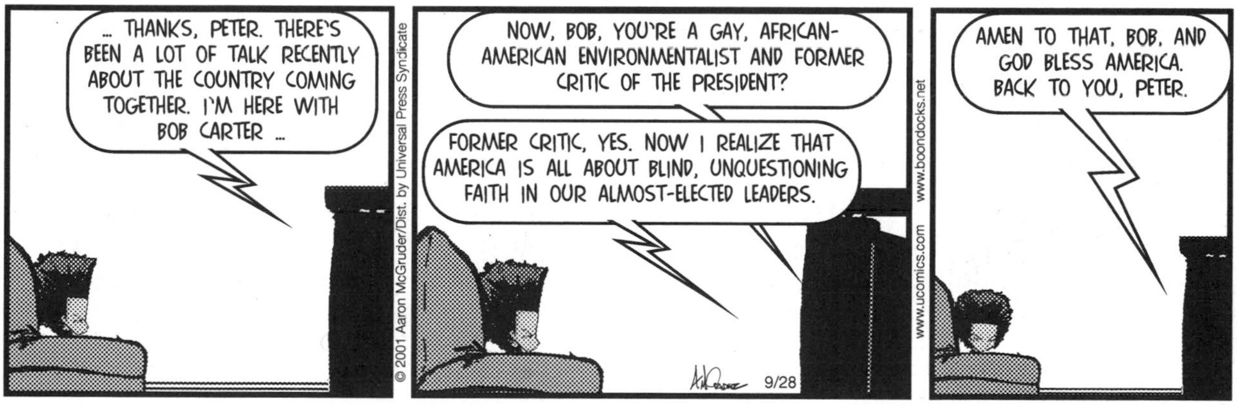
... THANKS, PETER. THERE'S BEEN A LOT OF TALK RECENTLY ABOUT THE COUNTRY COMING TOGETHER. I'M HERE WITH BOB CARTER ...
© 2001 Aaron McGruder/Dist. by Universal Press Syndicate
NOW, BOB, YOU'RE A GAY, AFRICAN-AMERICAN ENVIRONMENTALIST AND FORMER CRITIC OF THE PRESIDENT?
FORMER CRITIC, YES. NOW I REALIZE THAT AMERICA IS ALL ABOUT BLIND, UNQUESTIONING FAITH IN OUR ALMOST-ELECTED LEADERS.
9/28
www.ucomics.com www.boondocks.net
AMEN TO THAT, BOB, AND GOD BLESS AMERICA. BACK TO YOU, PETER.

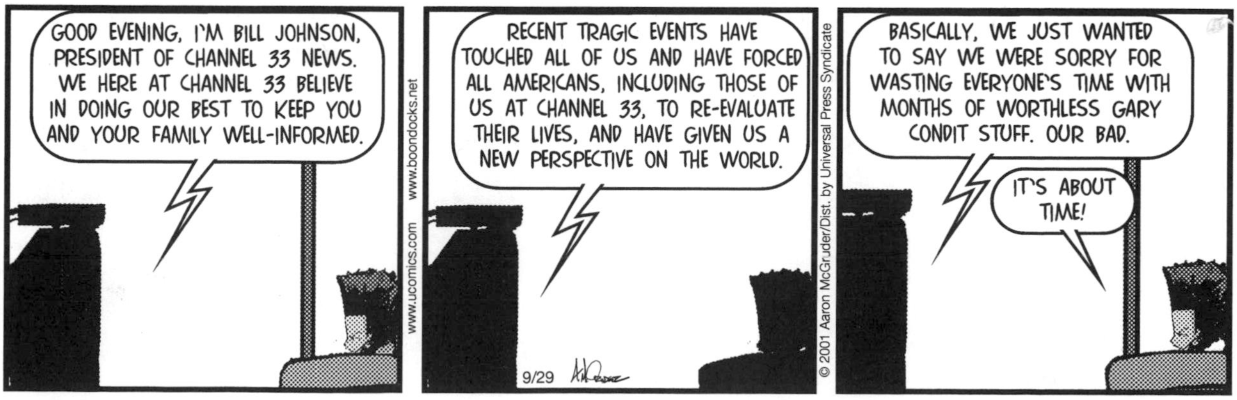
GOOD EVENING, I'M BILL JOHNSON, PRESIDENT OF CHANNEL 33 NEWS. WE HERE AT CHANNEL 33 BELIEVE IN DOING OUR BEST TO KEEP YOU AND YOUR FAMILY WELL-INFORMED.
www.ucomics.com www.boondocks.net
RECENT TRAGIC EVENTS HAVE TOUCHED ALL OF US AND HAVE FORCED ALL AMERICANS, INCLUDING THOSE OF US AT CHANNEL 33, TO RE-EVALUATE THEIR LIVES, AND HAVE GIVEN US A NEW PERSPECTIVE ON THE WORLD.
9/29
© 2001 Aaron McGruder/Dist. by Universal Press Syndicate
BASICALLY, WE JUST WANTED TO SAY WE WERE SORRY FOR WASTING EVERYONE'S TIME WITH MONTHS OF WORTHLESS GARY CONDIT STUFF. OUR BAD.
IT'S ABOUT TIME!

WEEK OF October 1, 2001

This four-day series where Huey calls the Terrorism Tip Line to turn in Reagan had editors throwing fits and ready to throw the strip on the op/ed pages.

In the years to come, if anyone ever remembers me or this strip, they will remember the 10/4/01 strip.

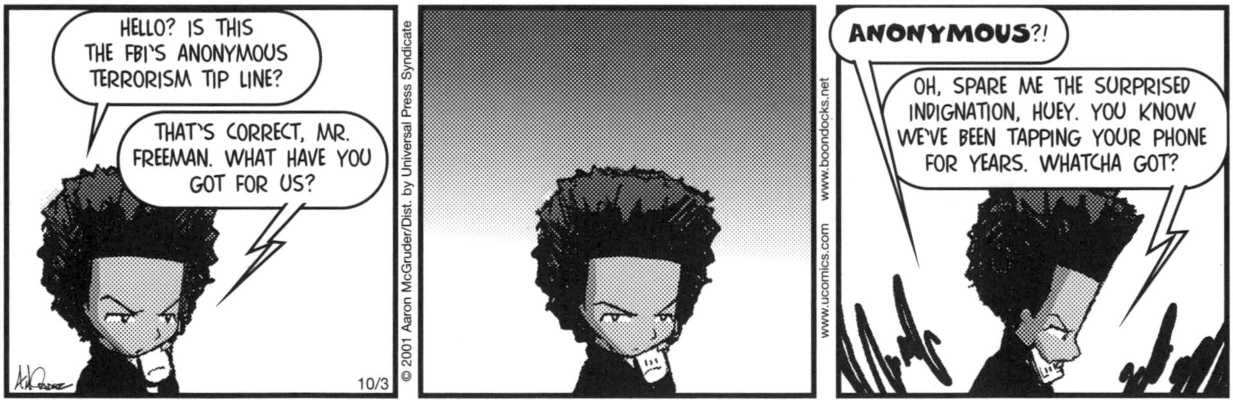
HELLO? IS THIS THE FBI'S ANONYMOUS TERRORISM TIP LINE?
THAT'S CORRECT, MR. FREEMAN. WHAT HAVE YOU GOT FOR US?
10/3
© 2001 Aaron McGruder/Dist. by Universal Press Syndicate
ANONYMOUS?!
OH, SPARE ME THE SURPRISED INDIGNATION, HUEY. YOU KNOW WE'VE BEEN TAPPING YOUR PHONE FOR YEARS. WHATCHA GOT?
www.ucomics.com www.boondocks.net

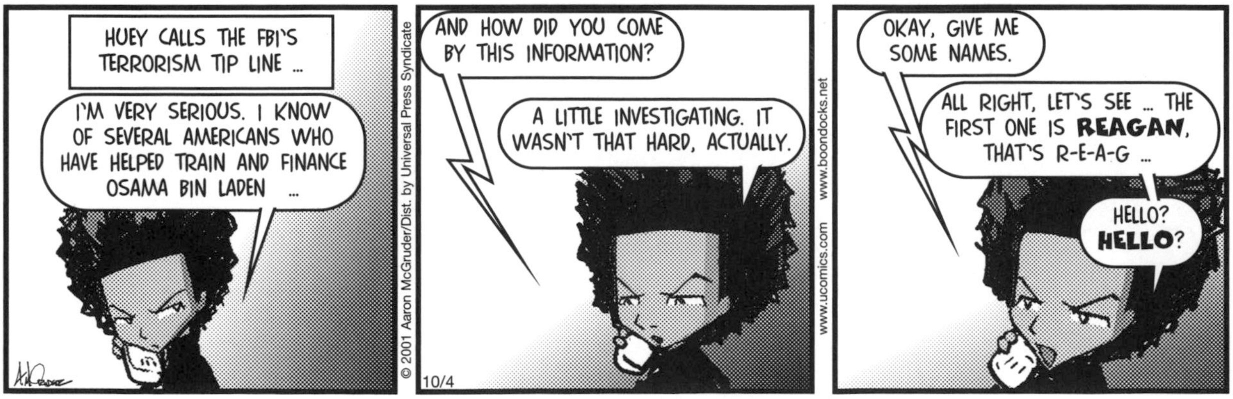
HUEY CALLS THE FBI'S TERRORISM TIP LINE ...
I'M VERY SERIOUS. I KNOW OF SEVERAL AMERICANS WHO HAVE HELPED TRAIN AND FINANCE OSAMA BIN LADEN ...
© 2001 Aaron McGruder/Dist. by Universal Press Syndicate
AND HOW DID YOU COME BY THIS INFORMATION?
A LITTLE INVESTIGATING. IT WASN'T THAT HARD, ACTUALLY.
10/4
OKAY, GIVE ME SOME NAMES.
ALL RIGHT, LET'S SEE ... THE FIRST ONE IS **REAGAN**, THAT'S R-E-A-G ...
HELLO? **HELLO**?
www.ucomics.com www.boondocks.net

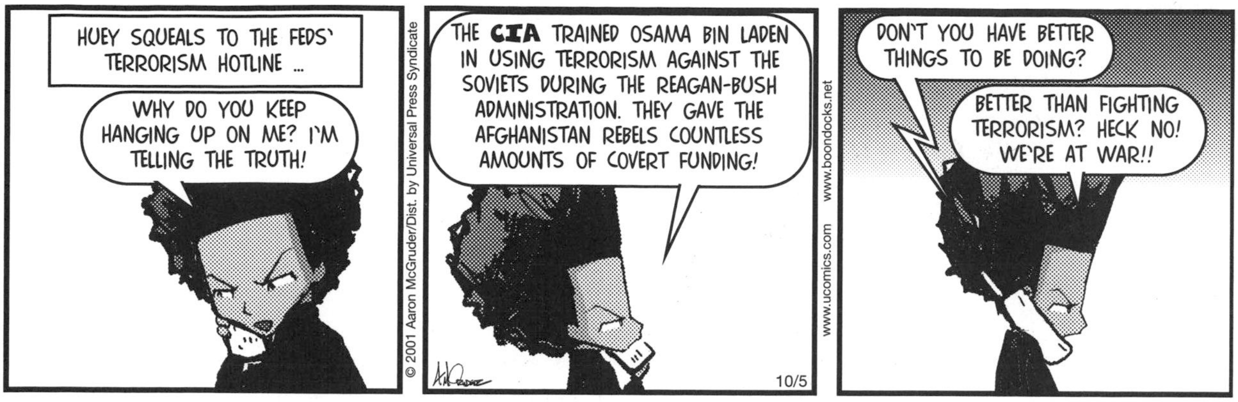
HUEY SQUEALS TO THE FEDS' TERRORISM HOTLINE ...
WHY DO YOU KEEP HANGING UP ON ME? I'M TELLING THE TRUTH!
© 2001 Aaron McGruder/Dist. by Universal Press Syndicate
THE CIA TRAINED OSAMA BIN LADEN IN USING TERRORISM AGAINST THE SOVIETS DURING THE REAGAN-BUSH ADMINISTRATION. THEY GAVE THE AFGHANISTAN REBELS COUNTLESS AMOUNTS OF COVERT FUNDING!
10/5
www.ucomics.com www.boondocks.net
DON'T YOU HAVE BETTER THINGS TO BE DOING?
BETTER THAN FIGHTING TERRORISM? HECK NO! WE'RE AT WAR!!

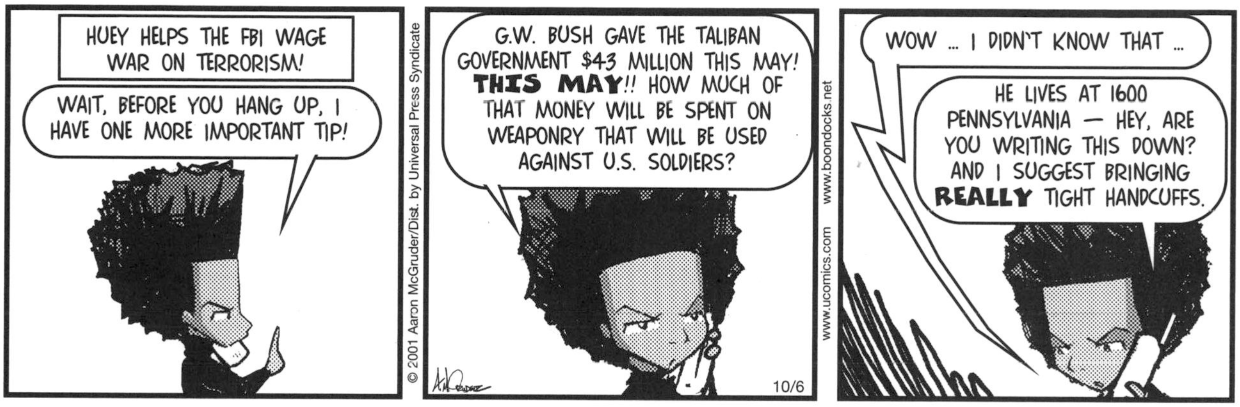
HUEY HELPS THE FBI WAGE WAR ON TERRORISM!
WAIT, BEFORE YOU HANG UP, I HAVE ONE MORE IMPORTANT TIP!
© 2001 Aaron McGruder/Dist. by Universal Press Syndicate
G.W. BUSH GAVE THE TALIBAN GOVERNMENT $43 MILLION THIS MAY! THIS MAY!! HOW MUCH OF THAT MONEY WILL BE SPENT ON WEAPONRY THAT WILL BE USED AGAINST U.S. SOLDIERS?
10/6
www.ucomics.com www.boondocks.net
WOW ... I DIDN'T KNOW THAT ...
HE LIVES AT 1600 PENNSYLVANIA — HEY, ARE YOU WRITING THIS DOWN? AND I SUGGEST BRINGING REALLY TIGHT HANDCUFFS.

September 21, 2002

AND THE WEEK OF

October 15, 2001

Very shortly after September 11, I found myself at lunch with Chris Rock and hit him up for strip ideas, and that's how Flagee and Ribbon were born. Of course, people assumed the "Editor's Note" was real and that the strip had really been pulled (which is half of the fun of doing strips like these). Eventually they made me stop calling them "Editor's Notes," I guess because editors around the country were being falsely accused of silencing me. I also had to change the address in the original version of the strip in case people actually sent money.

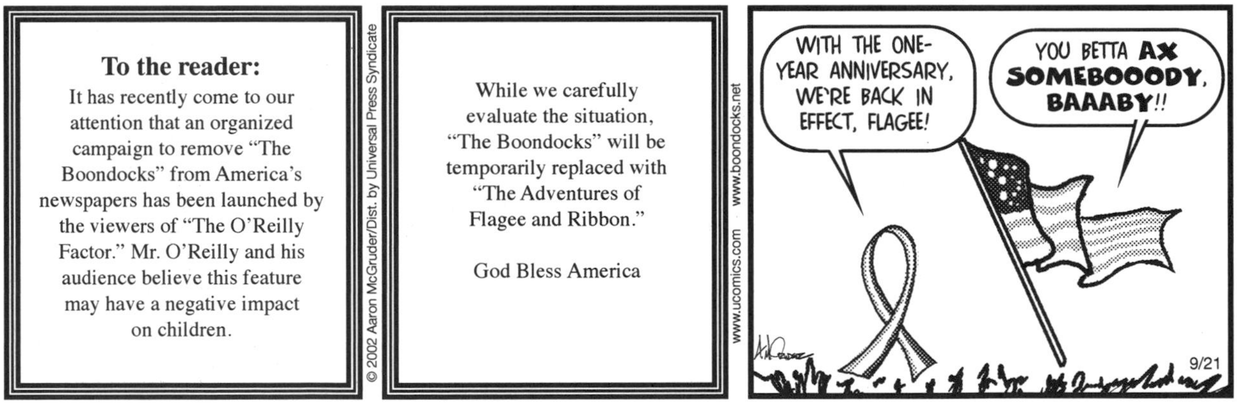
To the reader:
It has recently come to our attention that an organized campaign to remove "The Boondocks" from America's newspapers has been launched by the viewers of "The O'Reilly Factor." Mr. O'Reilly and his audience believe this feature may have a negative impact on children.
© 2002 Aaron McGruder/Dist. by Universal Press Syndicate
While we carefully evaluate the situation, "The Boondocks" will be temporarily replaced with "The Adventures of Flagee and Ribbon."
God Bless America
www.ucomics.com www.boondocks.net
WITH THE ONE-YEAR ANNIVERSARY, WE'RE BACK IN EFFECT, FLAGEE!
YOU BETTA AX SOMEBOOODY, BAAABY!!
9/21

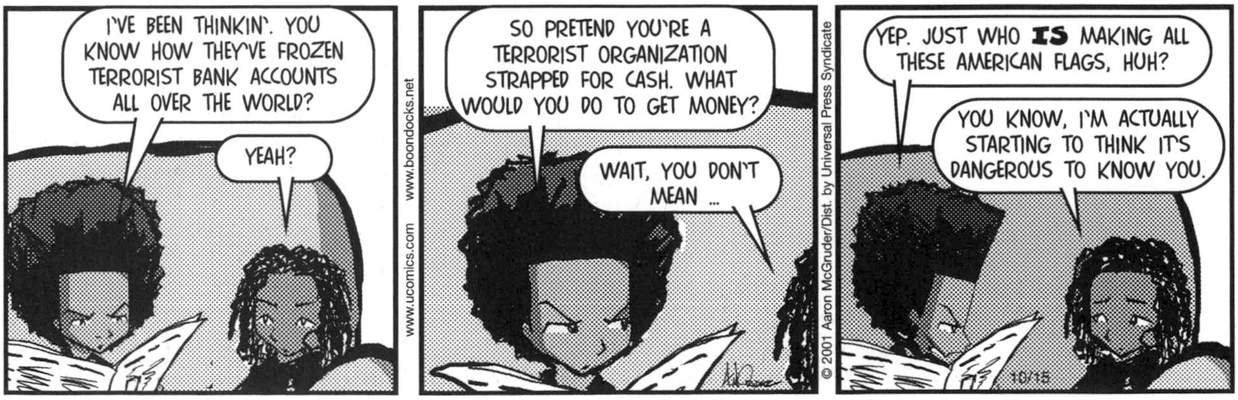
I'VE BEEN THINKIN'. YOU KNOW HOW THEY'VE FROZEN TERRORIST BANK ACCOUNTS ALL OVER THE WORLD?
YEAH?
www.ucomics.com www.boondocks.net
SO PRETEND YOU'RE A TERRORIST ORGANIZATION STRAPPED FOR CASH. WHAT WOULD YOU DO TO GET MONEY?
WAIT, YOU DON'T MEAN ...
© 2001 Aaron McGruder/Dist. by Universal Press Syndicate
YEP. JUST WHO IS MAKING ALL THESE AMERICAN FLAGS, HUH?
YOU KNOW, I'M ACTUALLY STARTING TO THINK IT'S DANGEROUS TO KNOW YOU.
10/15

Editor's Note

Due to the inappropriate political content of this feature in recent weeks, it is being replaced by "The Adventures of Flagee and Ribbon," which we hope will help children understand the complexities of current events.

United We Stand.

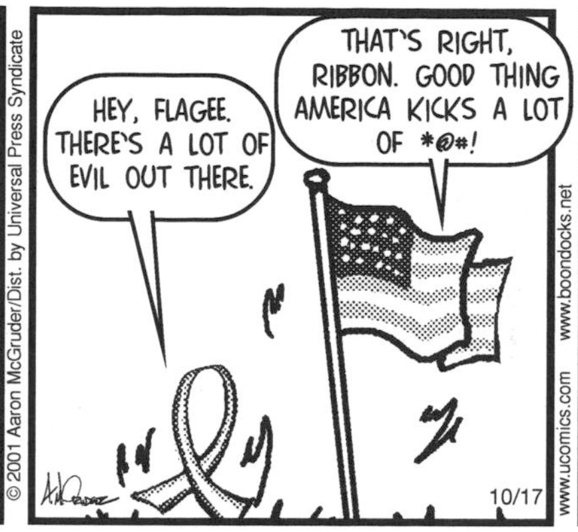
HEY, FLAGEE. THERE'S A LOT OF EVIL OUT THERE.
THAT'S RIGHT, RIBBON. GOOD THING AMERICA KICKS A LOT OF *@#!
10/17
© 2001 Aaron McGruder/Dist. by Universal Press Syndicate
www.ucomics.com www.boondocks.net

Editor's Note

"The Boondocks" is being replaced this week with "The Adventures of Flagee and Ribbon," a hilariously patriotic new offering.

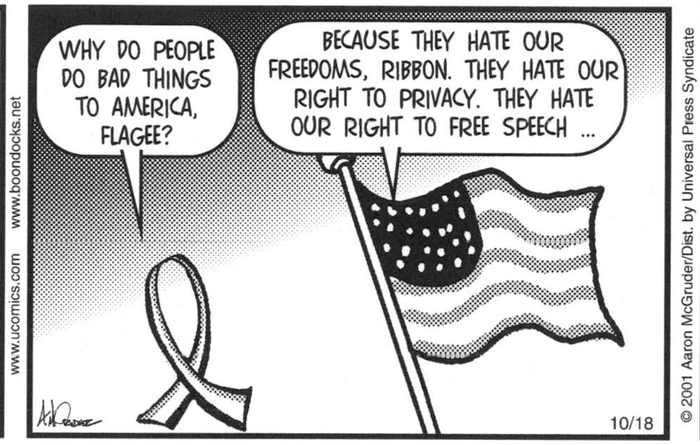
WHY DO PEOPLE DO BAD THINGS TO AMERICA, FLAGEE?
BECAUSE THEY HATE OUR FREEDOMS, RIBBON. THEY HATE OUR RIGHT TO PRIVACY. THEY HATE OUR RIGHT TO FREE SPEECH ...
10/18
www.ucomics.com www.boondocks.net
© 2001 Aaron McGruder/Dist. by Universal Press Syndicate

Editor's Note (Cont.)

Those of you who have written demanding the return of "The Boondocks," your names have been forwarded to the FBI.

Editor's Note

For the select few who are not daily readers of the comics, "The Boondocks" has been indefinitely replaced by the uproarious fun of "The Adventures of Flagee and Ribbon."

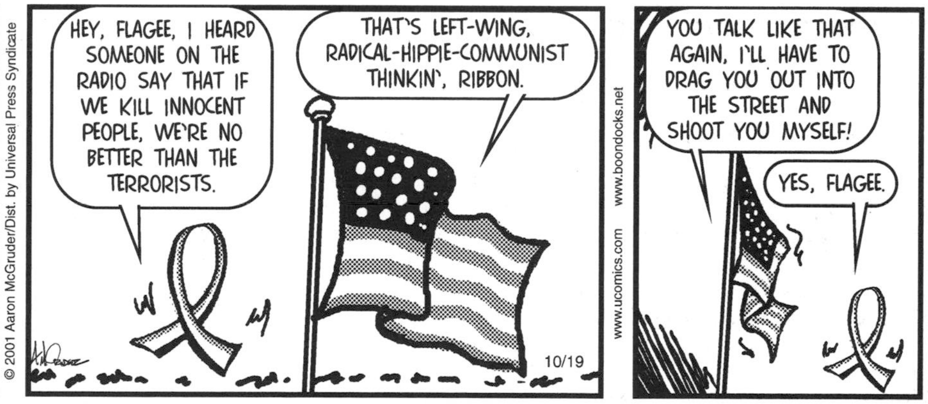
© 2001 Aaron McGruder/Dist. by Universal Press Syndicate
HEY, FLAGEE, I HEARD SOMEONE ON THE RADIO SAY THAT IF WE KILL INNOCENT PEOPLE, WE'RE NO BETTER THAN THE TERRORISTS.
THAT'S LEFT-WING, RADICAL-HIPPIE-COMMUNIST THINKIN', RIBBON.
10/19
www.ucomics.com www.boondocks.net
YOU TALK LIKE THAT AGAIN, I'LL HAVE TO DRAG YOU OUT INTO THE STREET AND SHOOT YOU MYSELF!
YES, FLAGEE.

Editor's Note

Welcome, Americans! As part of the efforts to support national unity, we are temporarily replacing "The Boondocks" with "The Adventures of Flagee and Ribbon."

Today, Flagee and his trusty sidekick, Ribbon, tackle the issue of "What can I do?"

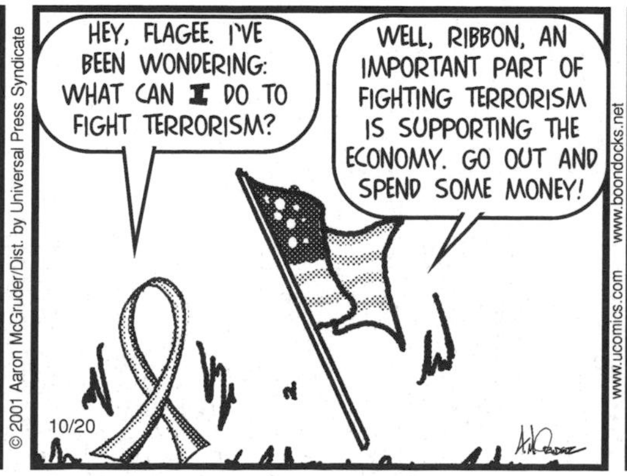
© 2001 Aaron McGruder/Dist. by Universal Press Syndicate
HEY, FLAGEE. I'VE BEEN WONDERING: WHAT CAN I DO TO FIGHT TERRORISM?
WELL, RIBBON, AN IMPORTANT PART OF FIGHTING TERRORISM IS SUPPORTING THE ECONOMY. GO OUT AND SPEND SOME MONEY!
10/20
www.ucomics.com www.boondocks.net

May 8, 2002

Here's Flagee and Ribbon again, correctly predicting the invasion of Iraq some ten months before it happened. Of course, one didn't need to be Ms. Cleo to see that one coming.

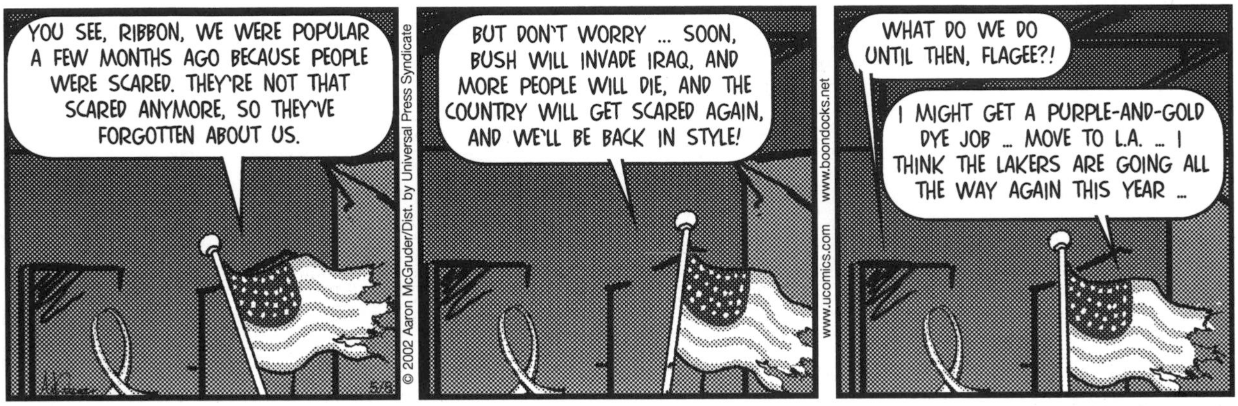
YOU SEE, RIBBON, WE WERE POPULAR A FEW MONTHS AGO BECAUSE PEOPLE WERE SCARED. THEY'RE NOT THAT SCARED ANYMORE, SO THEY'VE FORGOTTEN ABOUT US.
© 2002 Aaron McGruder/Dist. by Universal Press Syndicate
BUT DON'T WORRY ... SOON, BUSH WILL INVADE IRAQ, AND MORE PEOPLE WILL DIE, AND THE COUNTRY WILL GET SCARED AGAIN, AND WE'LL BE BACK IN STYLE!
www.ucomics.com www.boondocks.net
WHAT DO WE DO UNTIL THEN, FLAGEE?!
I MIGHT GET A PURPLE-AND-GOLD DYE JOB ... MOVE TO L.A. ... I THINK THE LAKERS ARE GOING ALL THE WAY AGAIN THIS YEAR ...

November 11, 2002

Sometimes, the issue of what I could and could not say made for a funny strip, as evidenced by the Jam Master Jay strip below. Readers who knew the actual song lyrics—"Goddamn, that DJ made my day!"—hopefully appreciated the irony of Caesar's response.

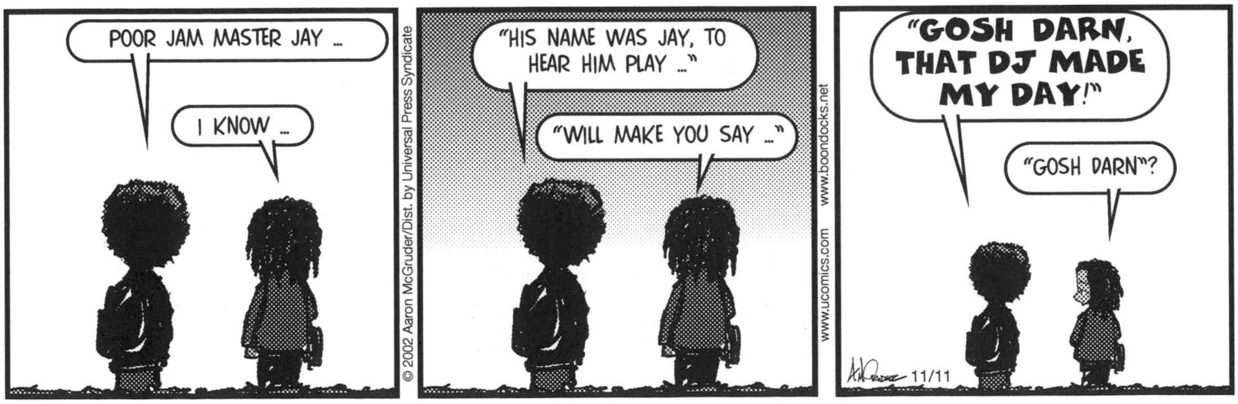
POOR JAM MASTER JAY ...
I KNOW ...
© 2002 Aaron McGruder/Dist. by Universal Press Syndicate
"HIS NAME WAS JAY, TO HEAR HIM PLAY ..."
"WILL MAKE YOU SAY ..."
www.ucomics.com www.boondocks.net
"GOSH DARN, THAT DJ MADE MY DAY!"
"GOSH DARN"?
11/11

March 29, 2003

It's not often that a cartoonist can pinpoint the exact moment when one particular strip gets you canceled from a newspaper. But my protest strip that ran in March 2004 got *The Boondocks* canceled from the *Herald-Sun* in Durham, North Carolina.

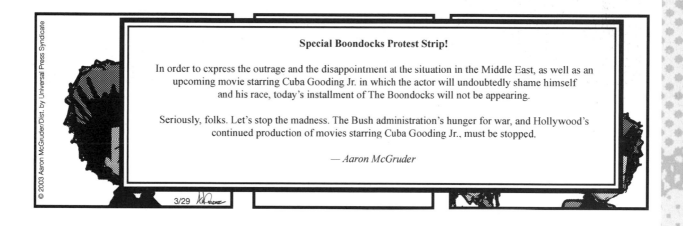

© 2003 Aaron McGruder/Dist. by Universal Press Syndicate
Special Boondocks Protest Strip!
In order to express the outrage and the disappointment at the situation in the Middle East, as well as an upcoming movie starring Cuba Gooding Jr. in which the actor will undoubtedly shame himself and his race, today's installment of The Boondocks will not be appearing.
Seriously, folks. Let's stop the madness. The Bush administration's hunger for war, and Hollywood's continued production of movies starring Cuba Gooding Jr., must be stopped.
— Aaron McGruder
3/29

We took a gamble when we became the first newspaper in North Carolina to pick up the controversial *Boondocks* strip. And over the months it has ran in our newspaper, we have heard more complaints from readers than we have plaudits.

But as long as the strip was in context and characters were doing the talking, we were content to allow McGruder to work out on the edge.

This time, however, he pushed us over it.

—Bill Hawkins, vice president and executive editor of *The Herald-Sun*

May 1, 2003

May 1, 2003, marks another turning point in *The Boondocks*—the first use of the "N-word," or as I like to say, "Nigga!" In this strip it was part of an acronym: H.N.I.C., which stands for "Head Nigger in Charge." The strip was pulled from four newspapers that day.

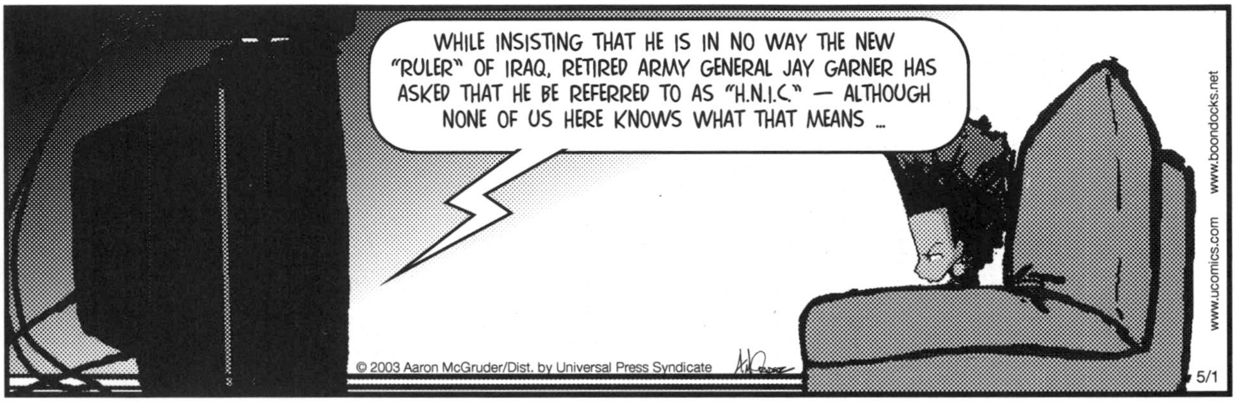
WHILE INSISTING THAT HE IS IN NO WAY THE NEW "RULER" OF IRAQ, RETIRED ARMY GENERAL JAY GARNER HAS ASKED THAT HE BE REFERRED TO AS "H.N.I.C." — ALTHOUGH NONE OF US HERE KNOWS WHAT THAT MEANS ...
© 2003 Aaron McGruder/Dist. by Universal Press Syndicate
www.ucomics.com www.boondocks.net
5/1

July 11, 2003

Two months later, the N-word appeared again. As would become common, only the first letter was used. Oddly enough, the strip wasn't pulled by any newspapers. Perhaps that was because of the Strom Thurmond strips that ran earlier in the week, which provoked their own strong reaction from a few southern newspapers. Or maybe because everyone just knows Strom Thurmond and the word *Nigger* go hand in hand.

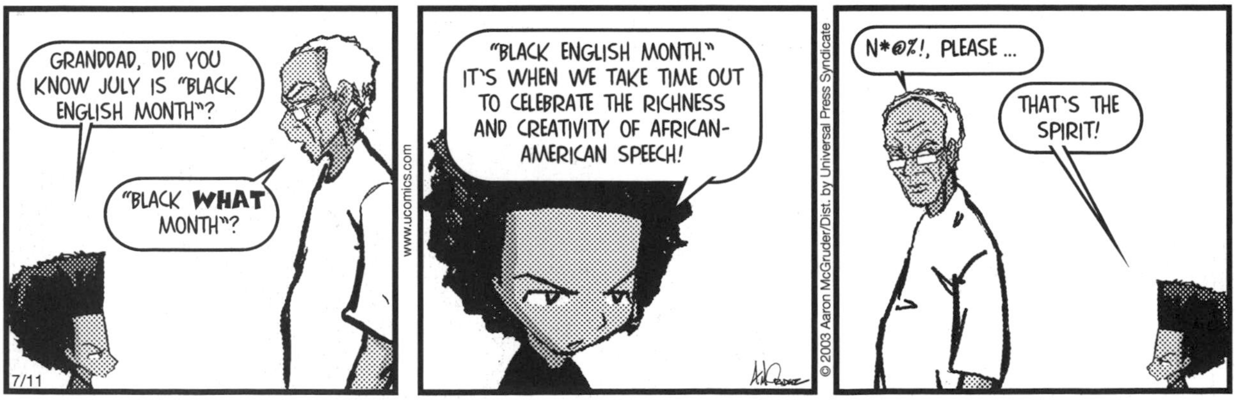
GRANDDAD, DID YOU KNOW JULY IS "BLACK ENGLISH MONTH"?
"BLACK **WHAT** MONTH"?
7/11
www.ucomics.com
"BLACK ENGLISH MONTH." IT'S WHEN WE TAKE TIME OUT TO CELEBRATE THE RICHNESS AND CREATIVITY OF AFRICAN-AMERICAN SPEECH!
© 2003 Aaron McGruder/Dist. by Universal Press Syndicate
N*@%!, PLEASE ...
THAT'S THE SPIRIT!

Weeks of

October 13 and 27
November 3, 10, and 17
December 1, 2003

(Sigh) Condi, Condi, Condi . . . these weeks are proof that you just can't predict what will set off newspaper editors. While I was writing these, I really believed they were much tamer than many of the other assaults I had made on Condi in the past. It shows what I know.

Oh, and I actually went out of my way to not do any lesbian jokes, but people still accused me of questioning her sexual orientation. Is it my fault we don't ever see her with a man?!

Now that I'm safely retired from the print world, I'd like to say that the *Washington Post* were some real bitches on this one.

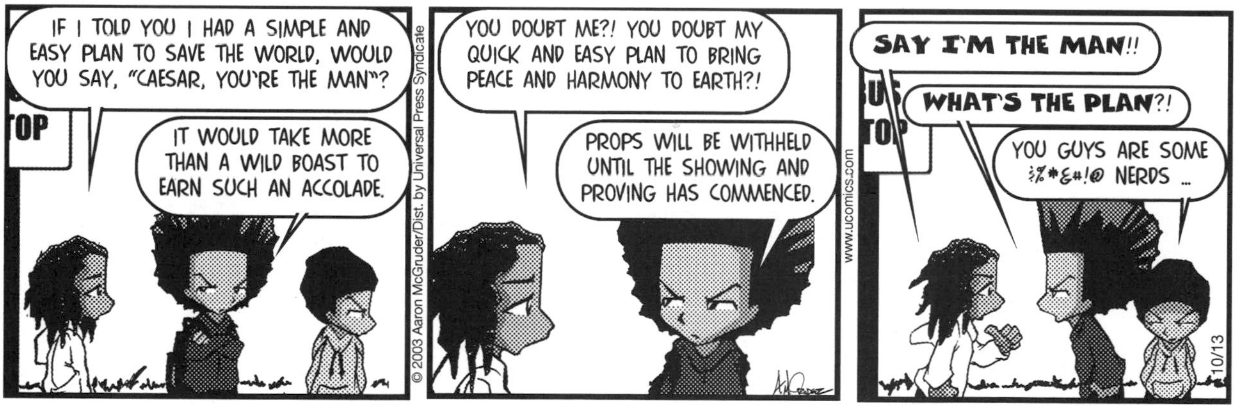
IF I TOLD YOU I HAD A SIMPLE AND EASY PLAN TO SAVE THE WORLD, WOULD YOU SAY, "CAESAR, YOU'RE THE MAN"?
IT WOULD TAKE MORE THAN A WILD BOAST TO EARN SUCH AN ACCOLADE.
© 2003 Aaron McGruder/Dist. by Universal Press Syndicate
YOU DOUBT ME?! YOU DOUBT MY QUICK AND EASY PLAN TO BRING PEACE AND HARMONY TO EARTH?!
PROPS WILL BE WITHHELD UNTIL THE SHOWING AND PROVING HAS COMMENCED.
www.ucomics.com
SAY I'M THE MAN!!
WHAT'S THE PLAN?!
YOU GUYS ARE SOME $%*&#!@ NERDS ...
10/13

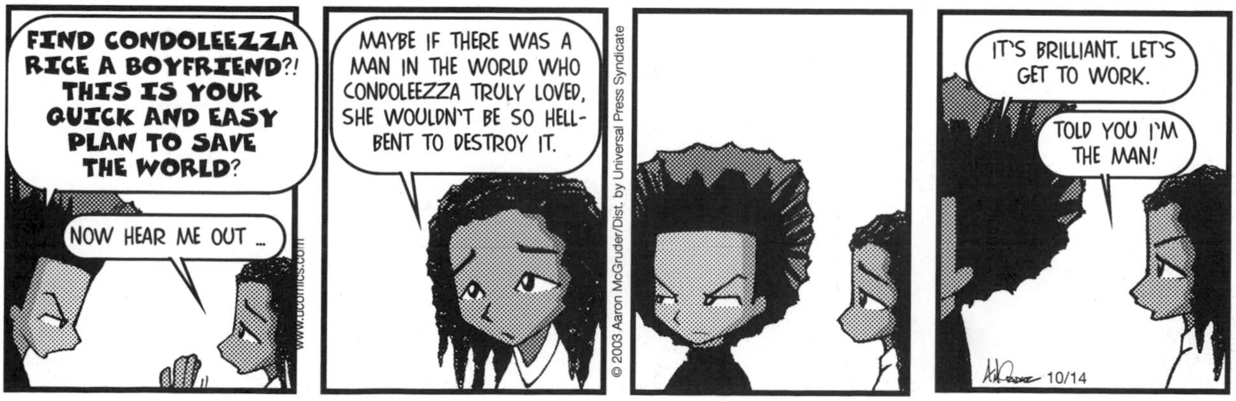
FIND CONDOLEEZZA RICE A BOYFRIEND?! THIS IS YOUR QUICK AND EASY PLAN TO SAVE THE WORLD?
NOW HEAR ME OUT ...
www.ucomics.com
MAYBE IF THERE WAS A MAN IN THE WORLD WHO CONDOLEEZZA TRULY LOVED, SHE WOULDN'T BE SO HELL-BENT TO DESTROY IT.
© 2003 Aaron McGruder/Dist. by Universal Press Syndicate
IT'S BRILLIANT. LET'S GET TO WORK.
TOLD YOU I'M THE MAN!
10/14

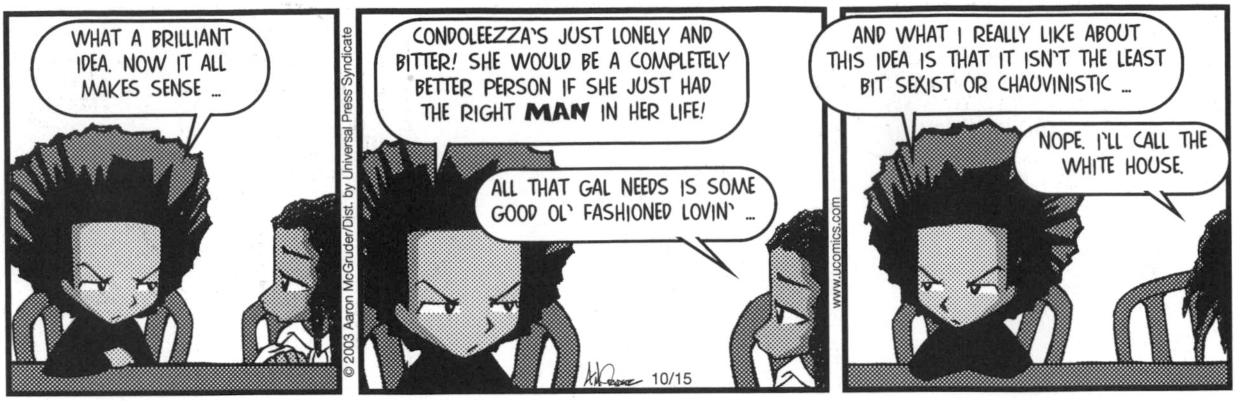
WHAT A BRILLIANT IDEA. NOW IT ALL MAKES SENSE ...
© 2003 Aaron McGruder/Dist. by Universal Press Syndicate
CONDOLEEZZA'S JUST LONELY AND BITTER! SHE WOULD BE A COMPLETELY BETTER PERSON IF SHE JUST HAD THE RIGHT **MAN** IN HER LIFE!
ALL THAT GAL NEEDS IS SOME GOOD OL' FASHIONED LOVIN' ...
10/15
www.ucomics.com
AND WHAT I REALLY LIKE ABOUT THIS IDEA IS THAT IT ISN'T THE LEAST BIT SEXIST OR CHAUVINISTIC ...
NOPE. I'LL CALL THE WHITE HOUSE.

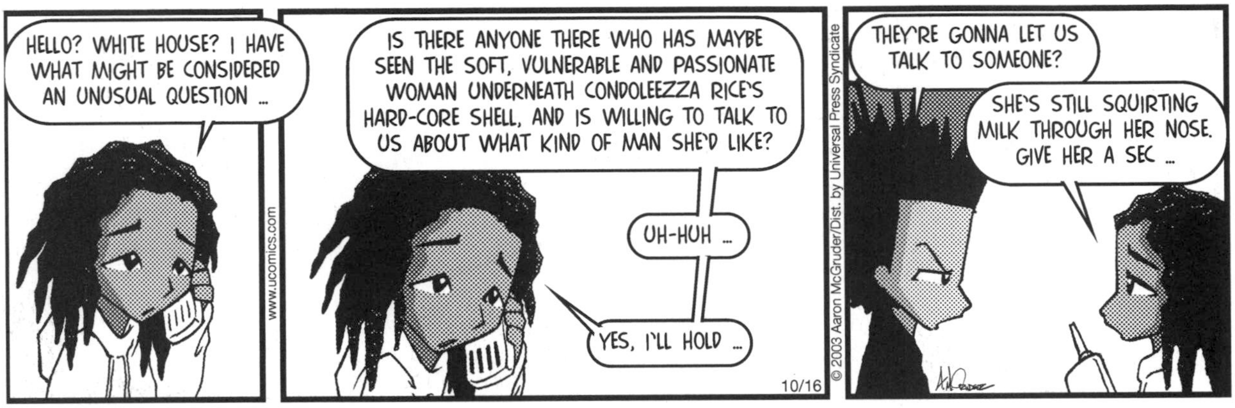
HELLO? WHITE HOUSE? I HAVE WHAT MIGHT BE CONSIDERED AN UNUSUAL QUESTION ...
www.ucomics.com
IS THERE ANYONE THERE WHO HAS MAYBE SEEN THE SOFT, VULNERABLE AND PASSIONATE WOMAN UNDERNEATH CONDOLEEZZA RICE'S HARD-CORE SHELL, AND IS WILLING TO TALK TO US ABOUT WHAT KIND OF MAN SHE'D LIKE?
UH-HUH ...
YES, I'LL HOLD ...
10/16
© 2003 Aaron McGruder/Dist. by Universal Press Syndicate
THEY'RE GONNA LET US TALK TO SOMEONE?
SHE'S STILL SQUIRTING MILK THROUGH HER NOSE. GIVE HER A SEC ...

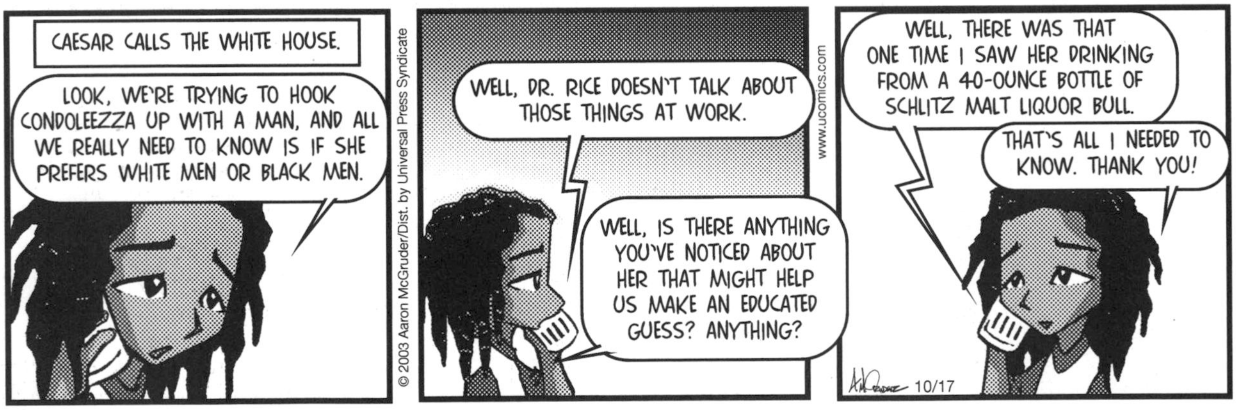
CAESAR CALLS THE WHITE HOUSE.
LOOK, WE'RE TRYING TO HOOK CONDOLEEZZA UP WITH A MAN, AND ALL WE REALLY NEED TO KNOW IS IF SHE PREFERS WHITE MEN OR BLACK MEN.
© 2003 Aaron McGruder/Dist. by Universal Press Syndicate
WELL, DR. RICE DOESN'T TALK ABOUT THOSE THINGS AT WORK.
WELL, IS THERE ANYTHING YOU'VE NOTICED ABOUT HER THAT MIGHT HELP US MAKE AN EDUCATED GUESS? ANYTHING?
www.ucomics.com
WELL, THERE WAS THAT ONE TIME I SAW HER DRINKING FROM A 40-OUNCE BOTTLE OF SCHLITZ MALT LIQUOR BULL.
THAT'S ALL I NEEDED TO KNOW. THANK YOU!
10/17

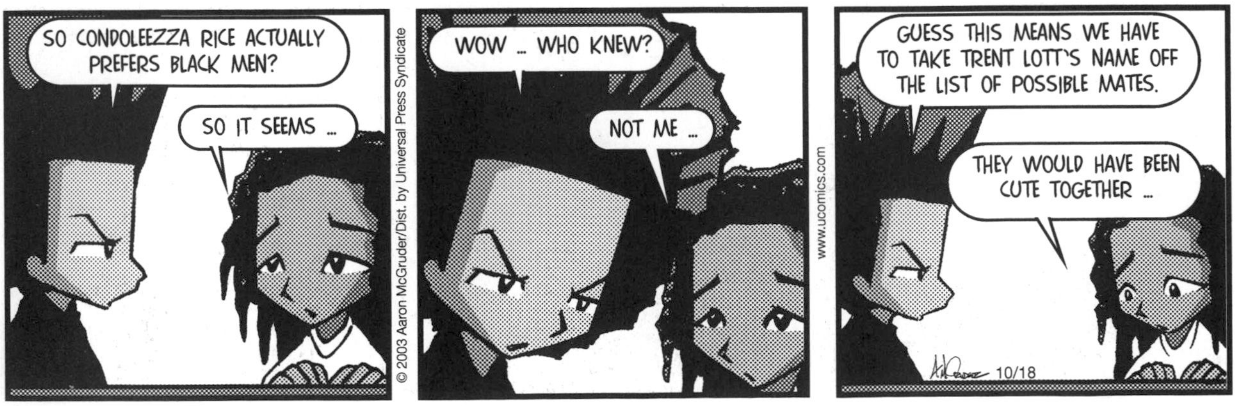
SO CONDOLEEZZA RICE ACTUALLY PREFERS BLACK MEN?
SO IT SEEMS ...
© 2003 Aaron McGruder/Dist. by Universal Press Syndicate
WOW ... WHO KNEW?
NOT ME ...
www.ucomics.com
GUESS THIS MEANS WE HAVE TO TAKE TRENT LOTT'S NAME OFF THE LIST OF POSSIBLE MATES.
THEY WOULD HAVE BEEN CUTE TOGETHER ...
10/18

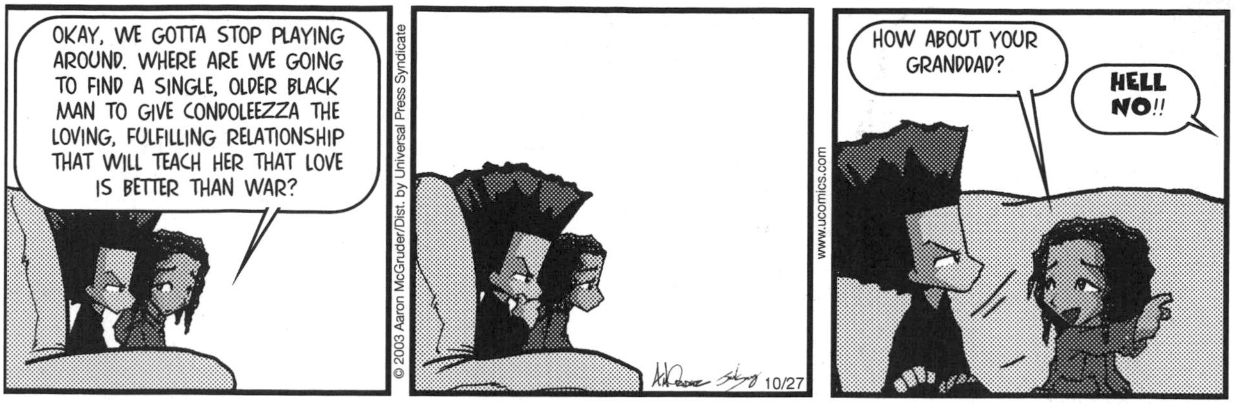
OKAY, WE GOTTA STOP PLAYING AROUND. WHERE ARE WE GOING TO FIND A SINGLE, OLDER BLACK MAN TO GIVE CONDOLEEZZA THE LOVING, FULFILLING RELATIONSHIP THAT WILL TEACH HER THAT LOVE IS BETTER THAN WAR?
© 2003 Aaron McGruder/Dist. by Universal Press Syndicate
10/27
www.ucomics.com
HOW ABOUT YOUR GRANDDAD?
HELL NO!!

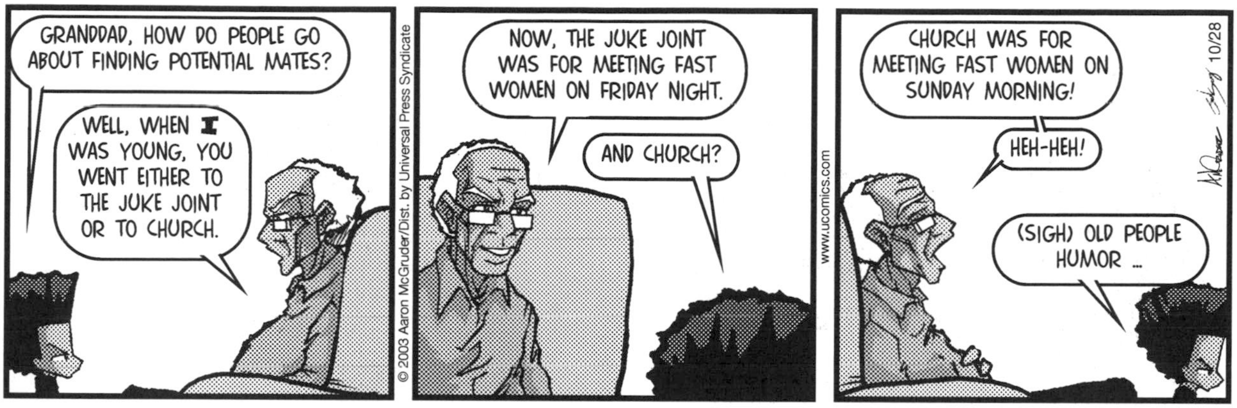
GRANDDAD, HOW DO PEOPLE GO ABOUT FINDING POTENTIAL MATES?
WELL, WHEN I WAS YOUNG, YOU WENT EITHER TO THE JUKE JOINT OR TO CHURCH.
© 2003 Aaron McGruder/Dist. by Universal Press Syndicate
NOW, THE JUKE JOINT WAS FOR MEETING FAST WOMEN ON FRIDAY NIGHT.
AND CHURCH?
www.ucomics.com
CHURCH WAS FOR MEETING FAST WOMEN ON SUNDAY MORNING!
HEH-HEH!
(SIGH) OLD PEOPLE HUMOR ...
10/28

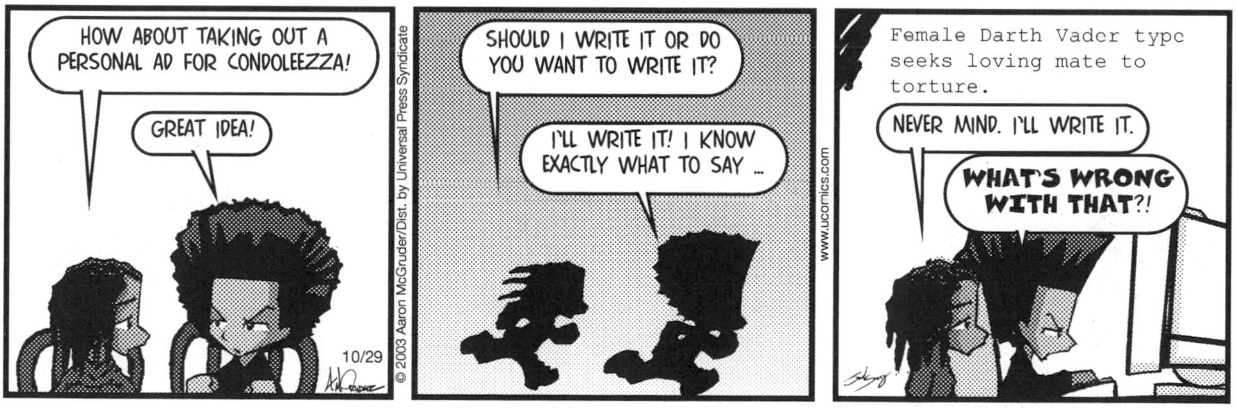
HOW ABOUT TAKING OUT A PERSONAL AD FOR CONDOLEEZZA!
GREAT IDEA!
10/29
© 2003 Aaron McGruder/Dist. by Universal Press Syndicate
SHOULD I WRITE IT OR DO YOU WANT TO WRITE IT?
I'LL WRITE IT! I KNOW EXACTLY WHAT TO SAY ...
www.ucomics.com
Female Darth Vader type seeks loving mate to torture.
NEVER MIND. I'LL WRITE IT.
WHAT'S WRONG WITH THAT?!

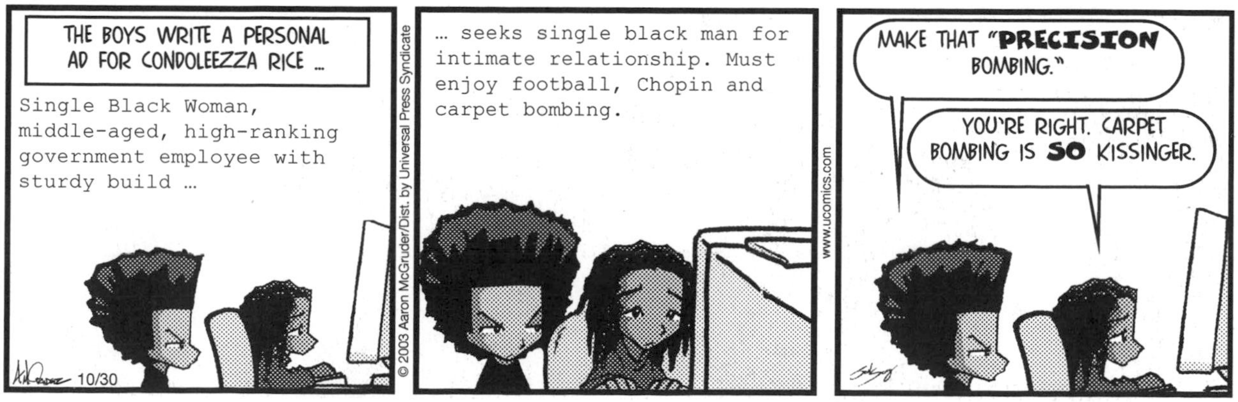
THE BOYS WRITE A PERSONAL AD FOR CONDOLEEZZA RICE ...
Single Black Woman, middle-aged, high-ranking government employee with sturdy build ...
10/30
© 2003 Aaron McGruder/Dist. by Universal Press Syndicate
... seeks single black man for intimate relationship. Must enjoy football, Chopin and carpet bombing.
www.ucomics.com
MAKE THAT "PRECISION BOMBING."
YOU'RE RIGHT. CARPET BOMBING IS SO KISSINGER.

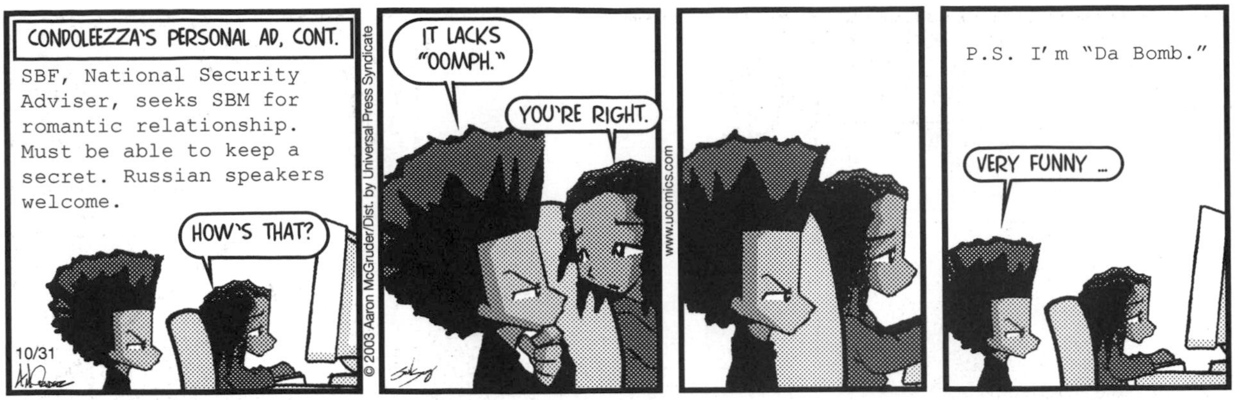
CONDOLEEZZA'S PERSONAL AD, CONT.
SBF, National Security Adviser, seeks SBM for romantic relationship. Must be able to keep a secret. Russian speakers welcome.
HOW'S THAT?
10/31
IT LACKS "OOMPH."
YOU'RE RIGHT.
© 2003 Aaron McGruder/Dist. by Universal Press Syndicate
www.ucomics.com
P.S. I'm "Da Bomb."
VERY FUNNY ...

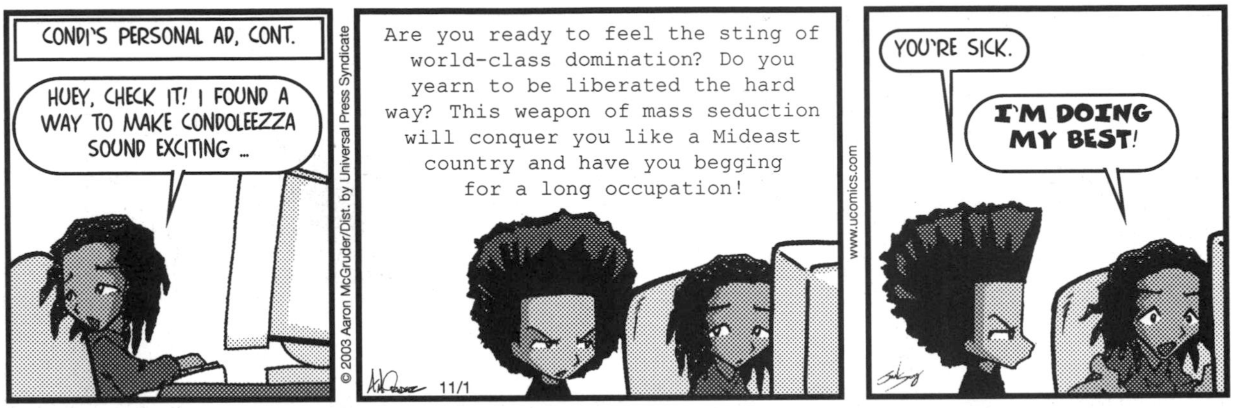
CONDI'S PERSONAL AD, CONT.
HUEY, CHECK IT! I FOUND A WAY TO MAKE CONDOLEEZZA SOUND EXCITING ...
© 2003 Aaron McGruder/Dist. by Universal Press Syndicate
Are you ready to feel the sting of world-class domination? Do you yearn to be liberated the hard way? This weapon of mass seduction will conquer you like a Mideast country and have you begging for a long occupation!
11/1
www.ucomics.com
YOU'RE SICK.
I'M DOING MY BEST!

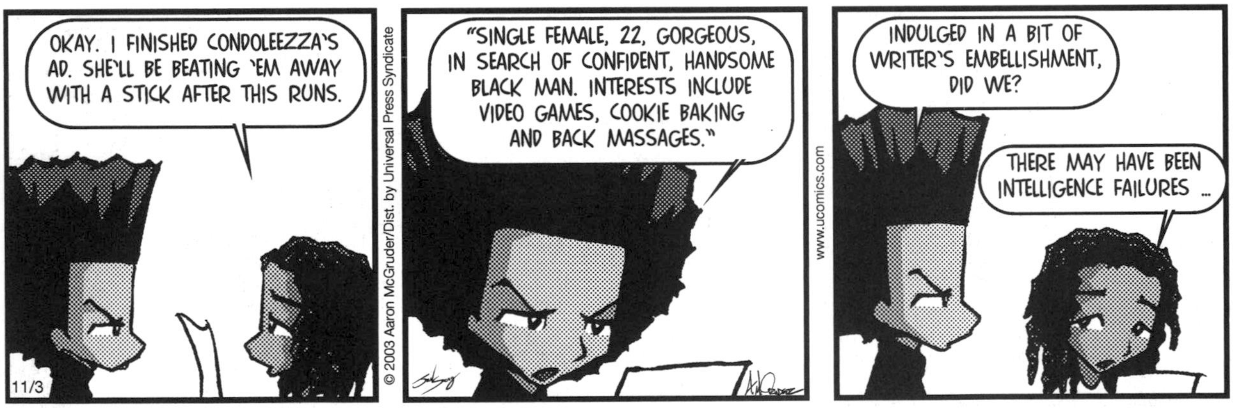
OKAY. I FINISHED CONDOLEEZZA'S AD. SHE'LL BE BEATING 'EM AWAY WITH A STICK AFTER THIS RUNS.
11/3
© 2003 Aaron McGruder/Dist. by Universal Press Syndicate
"SINGLE FEMALE, 22, GORGEOUS, IN SEARCH OF CONFIDENT, HANDSOME BLACK MAN. INTERESTS INCLUDE VIDEO GAMES, COOKIE BAKING AND BACK MASSAGES."
www.ucomics.com
INDULGED IN A BIT OF WRITER'S EMBELLISHMENT, DID WE?
THERE MAY HAVE BEEN INTELLIGENCE FAILURES ...

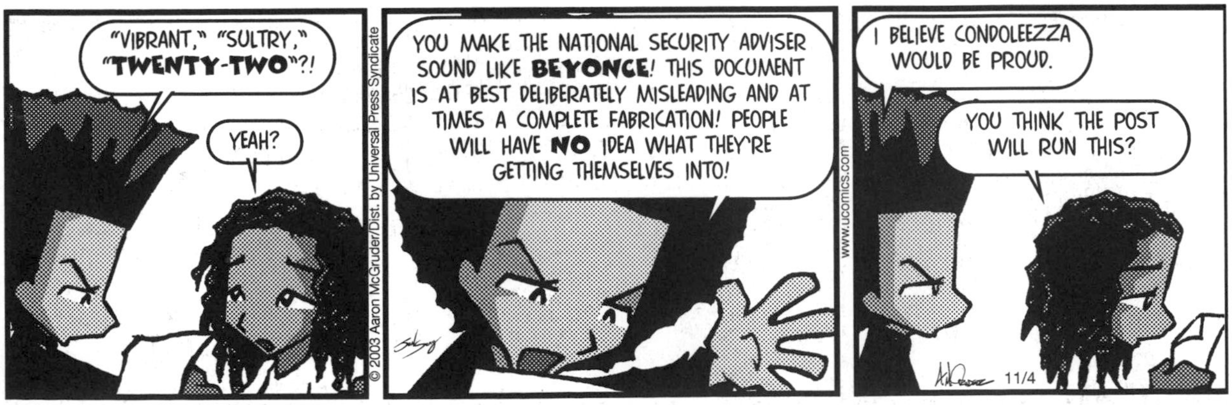
"VIBRANT," "SULTRY," "TWENTY-TWO"?!
YEAH?
© 2003 Aaron McGruder/Dist. by Universal Press Syndicate
YOU MAKE THE NATIONAL SECURITY ADVISER SOUND LIKE BEYONCE! THIS DOCUMENT IS AT BEST DELIBERATELY MISLEADING AND AT TIMES A COMPLETE FABRICATION! PEOPLE WILL HAVE NO IDEA WHAT THEY'RE GETTING THEMSELVES INTO!
www.ucomics.com
I BELIEVE CONDOLEEZZA WOULD BE PROUD.
YOU THINK THE POST WILL RUN THIS?
11/4

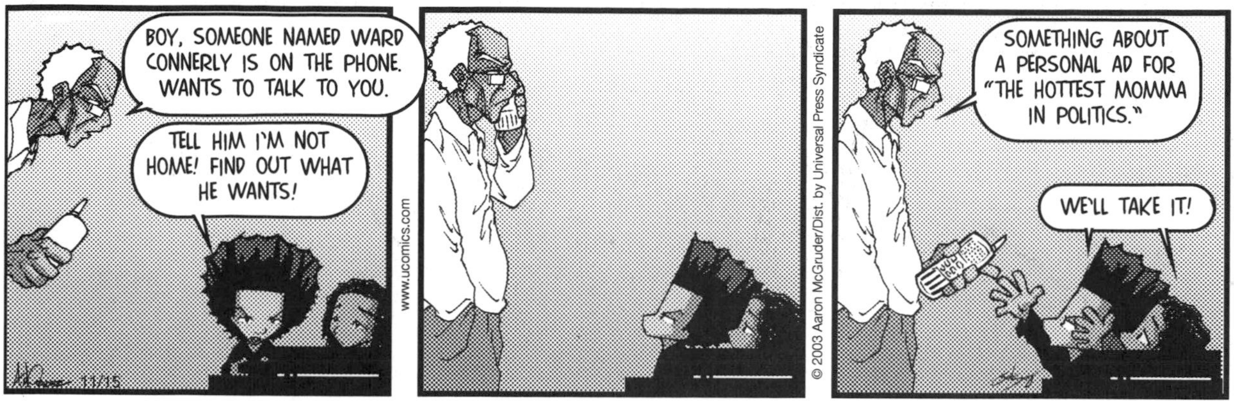
BOY, SOMEONE NAMED WARD CONNERLY IS ON THE PHONE. WANTS TO TALK TO YOU.
TELL HIM I'M NOT HOME! FIND OUT WHAT HE WANTS!
11/15
www.ucomics.com
© 2003 Aaron McGruder/Dist. by Universal Press Syndicate
SOMETHING ABOUT A PERSONAL AD FOR "THE HOTTEST MOMMA IN POLITICS."
WE'LL TAKE IT!

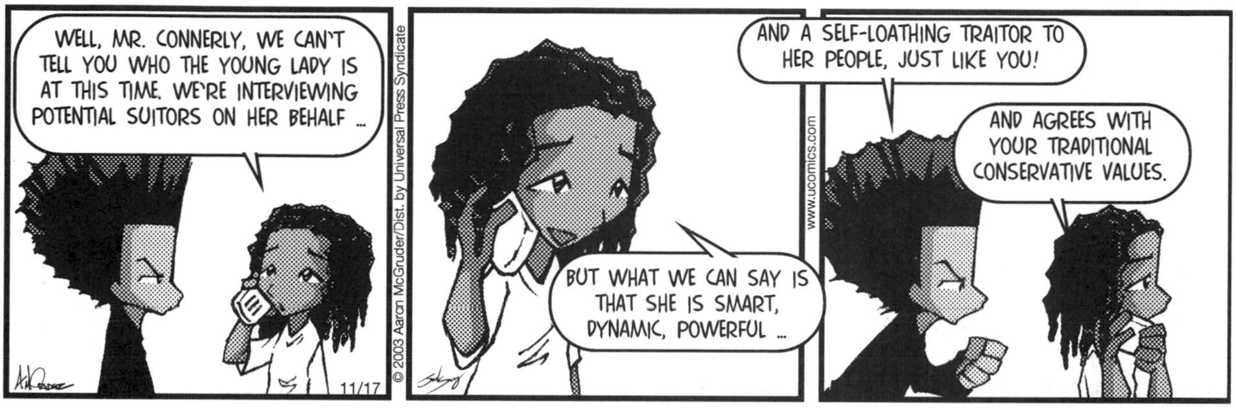
WELL, MR. CONNERLY, WE CAN'T TELL YOU WHO THE YOUNG LADY IS AT THIS TIME. WE'RE INTERVIEWING POTENTIAL SUITORS ON HER BEHALF ...
11/17
© 2003 Aaron McGruder/Dist. by Universal Press Syndicate
BUT WHAT WE CAN SAY IS THAT SHE IS SMART, DYNAMIC, POWERFUL ...
www.ucomics.com
AND A SELF-LOATHING TRAITOR TO HER PEOPLE, JUST LIKE YOU!
AND AGREES WITH YOUR TRADITIONAL CONSERVATIVE VALUES.

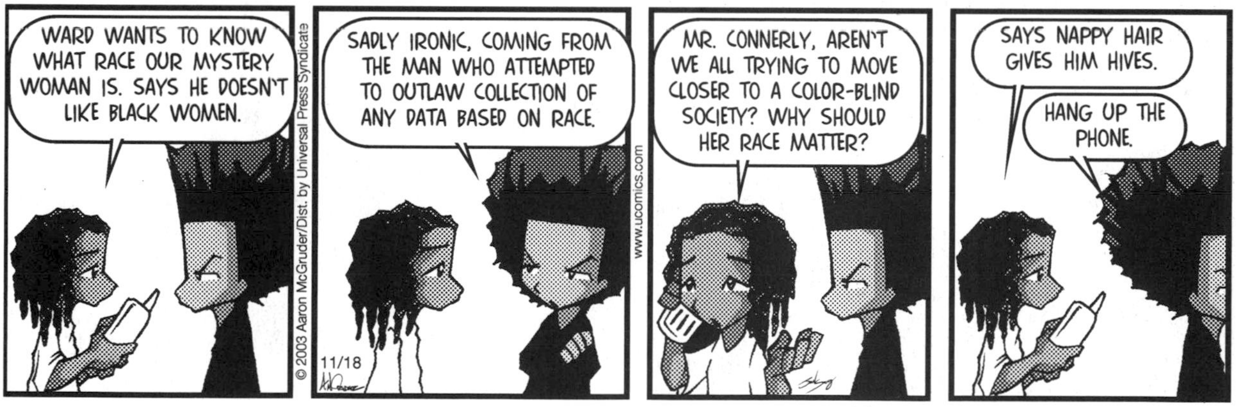
WARD WANTS TO KNOW WHAT RACE OUR MYSTERY WOMAN IS. SAYS HE DOESN'T LIKE BLACK WOMEN.
© 2003 Aaron McGruder/Dist. by Universal Press Syndicate
SADLY IRONIC, COMING FROM THE MAN WHO ATTEMPTED TO OUTLAW COLLECTION OF ANY DATA BASED ON RACE.
11/18
www.ucomics.com
MR. CONNERLY, AREN'T WE ALL TRYING TO MOVE CLOSER TO A COLOR-BLIND SOCIETY? WHY SHOULD HER RACE MATTER?
SAYS NAPPY HAIR GIVES HIM HIVES.
HANG UP THE PHONE.

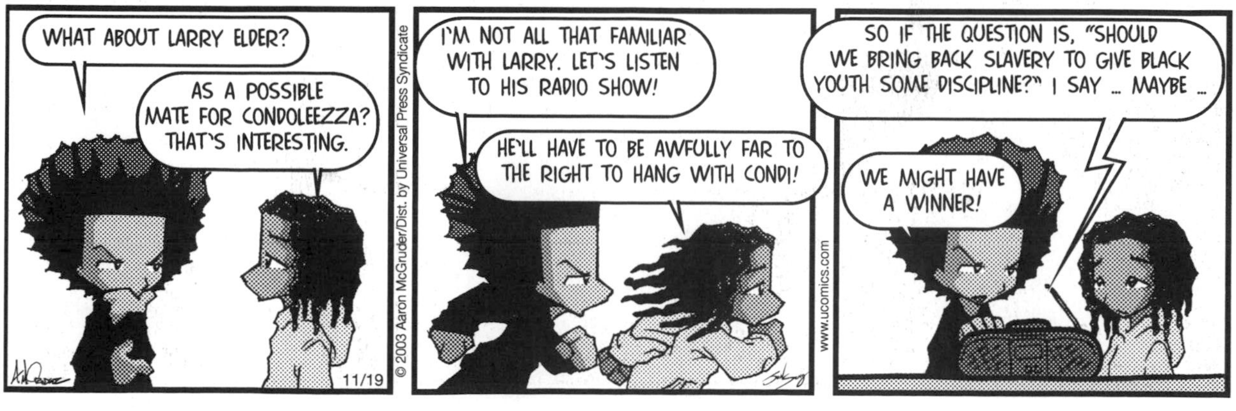
WHAT ABOUT LARRY ELDER?
AS A POSSIBLE MATE FOR CONDOLEEZZA? THAT'S INTERESTING.
11/19
© 2003 Aaron McGruder/Dist. by Universal Press Syndicate
I'M NOT ALL THAT FAMILIAR WITH LARRY. LET'S LISTEN TO HIS RADIO SHOW!
HE'LL HAVE TO BE AWFULLY FAR TO THE RIGHT TO HANG WITH CONDI!
www.ucomics.com
SO IF THE QUESTION IS, "SHOULD WE BRING BACK SLAVERY TO GIVE BLACK YOUTH SOME DISCIPLINE?" I SAY ... MAYBE ...
WE MIGHT HAVE A WINNER!

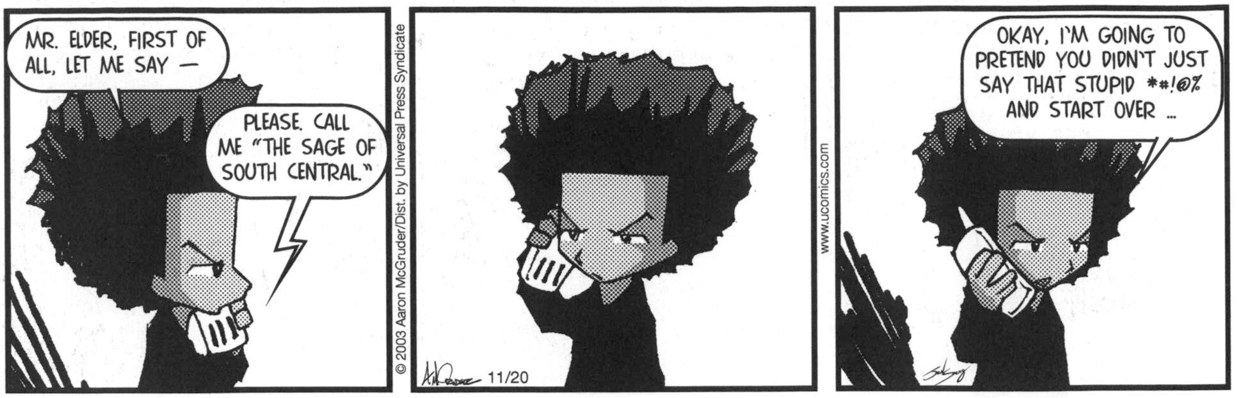
MR. ELDER, FIRST OF ALL, LET ME SAY —
PLEASE. CALL ME "THE SAGE OF SOUTH CENTRAL."
© 2003 Aaron McGruder/Dist. by Universal Press Syndicate
11/20
www.ucomics.com
OKAY, I'M GOING TO PRETEND YOU DIDN'T JUST SAY THAT STUPID *#!@% AND START OVER ...

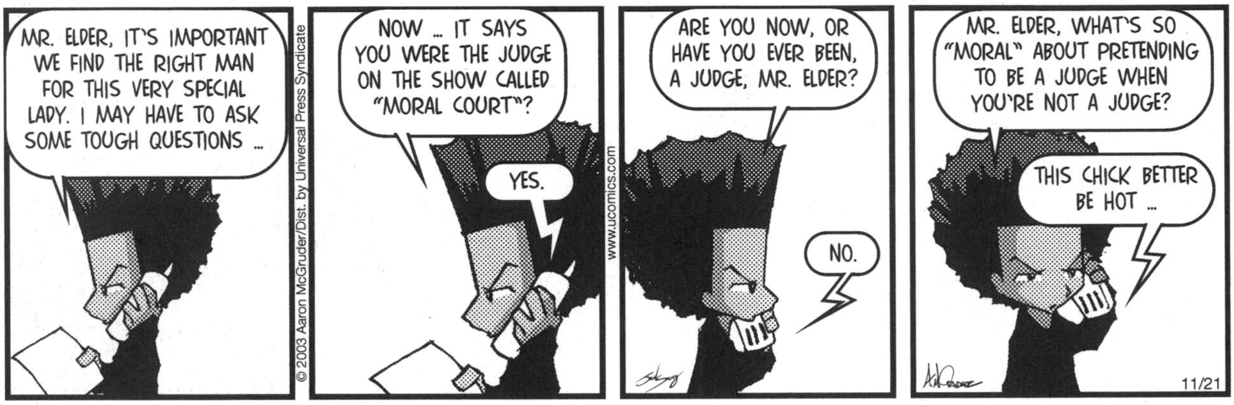
MR. ELDER, IT'S IMPORTANT WE FIND THE RIGHT MAN FOR THIS VERY SPECIAL LADY. I MAY HAVE TO ASK SOME TOUGH QUESTIONS ...
© 2003 Aaron McGruder/Dist. by Universal Press Syndicate
NOW ... IT SAYS YOU WERE THE JUDGE ON THE SHOW CALLED "MORAL COURT"?
YES.
www.ucomics.com
ARE YOU NOW, OR HAVE YOU EVER BEEN, A JUDGE, MR. ELDER?
NO.
MR. ELDER, WHAT'S SO "MORAL" ABOUT PRETENDING TO BE A JUDGE WHEN YOU'RE NOT A JUDGE?
THIS CHICK BETTER BE HOT ...
11/21

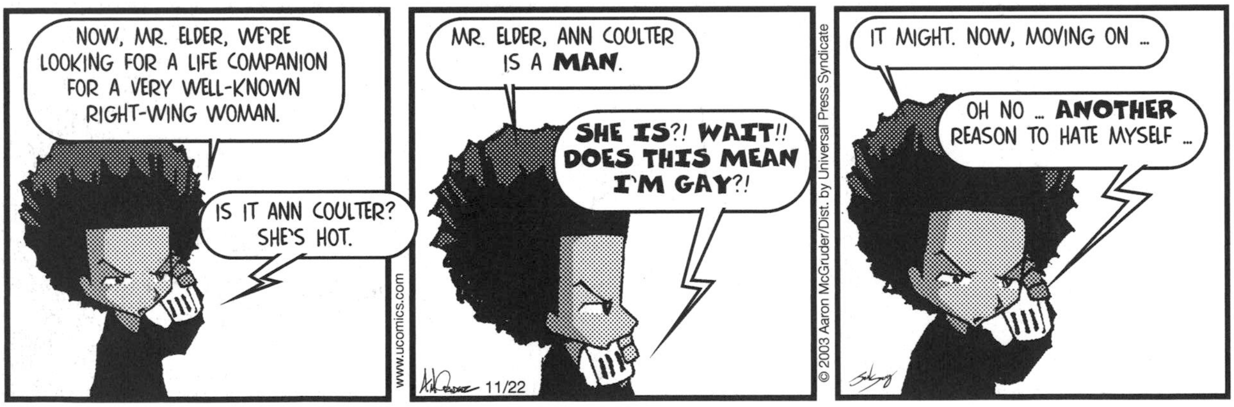
NOW, MR. ELDER, WE'RE LOOKING FOR A LIFE COMPANION FOR A VERY WELL-KNOWN RIGHT-WING WOMAN.
IS IT ANN COULTER? SHE'S HOT.
www.ucomics.com
MR. ELDER, ANN COULTER IS A MAN.
SHE IS?! WAIT!! DOES THIS MEAN I'M GAY?!
11/22
© 2003 Aaron McGruder/Dist. by Universal Press Syndicate
IT MIGHT. NOW, MOVING ON ...
OH NO ... ANOTHER REASON TO HATE MYSELF ...

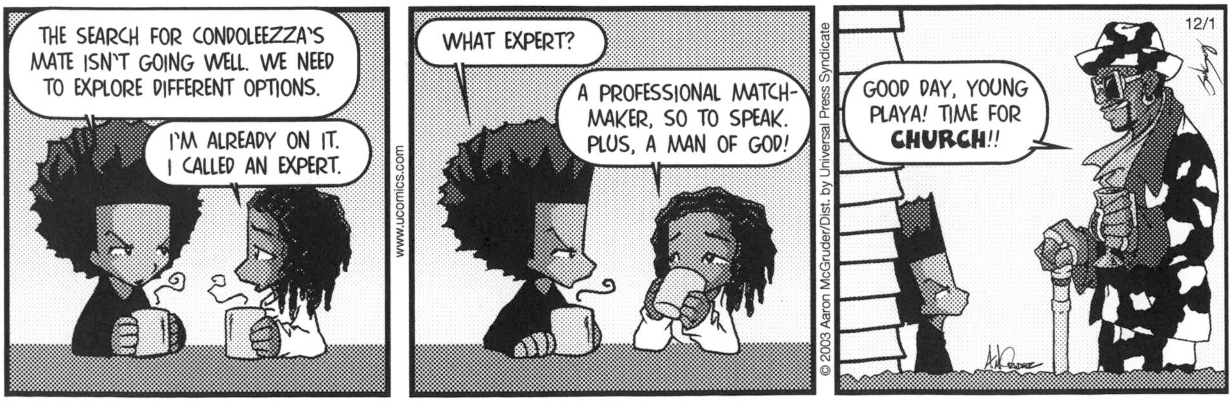
THE SEARCH FOR CONDOLEEZZA'S MATE ISN'T GOING WELL. WE NEED TO EXPLORE DIFFERENT OPTIONS.
I'M ALREADY ON IT. I CALLED AN EXPERT.
www.ucomics.com
WHAT EXPERT?
A PROFESSIONAL MATCH-MAKER, SO TO SPEAK. PLUS, A MAN OF GOD!
© 2003 Aaron McGruder/Dist. by Universal Press Syndicate
12/1
GOOD DAY, YOUNG PLAYA! TIME FOR CHURCH!!

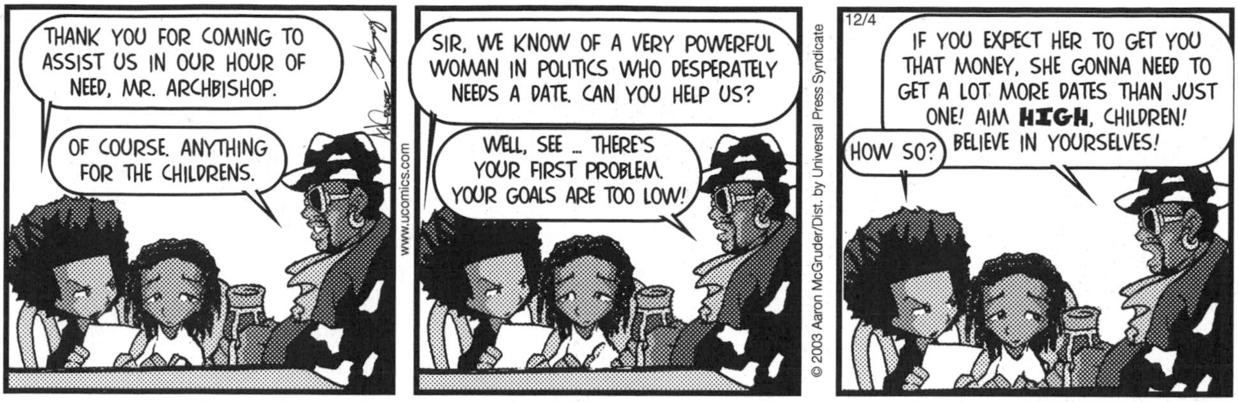
THANK YOU FOR COMING TO ASSIST US IN OUR HOUR OF NEED, MR. ARCHBISHOP.
OF COURSE. ANYTHING FOR THE CHILDRENS.
www.ucomics.com
SIR, WE KNOW OF A VERY POWERFUL WOMAN IN POLITICS WHO DESPERATELY NEEDS A DATE. CAN YOU HELP US?
WELL, SEE ... THERE'S YOUR FIRST PROBLEM. YOUR GOALS ARE TOO LOW!
© 2003 Aaron McGruder/Dist. by Universal Press Syndicate
12/4
HOW SO?
IF YOU EXPECT HER TO GET YOU THAT MONEY, SHE GONNA NEED TO GET A LOT MORE DATES THAN JUST ONE! AIM **HIGH**, CHILDREN! BELIEVE IN YOURSELVES!

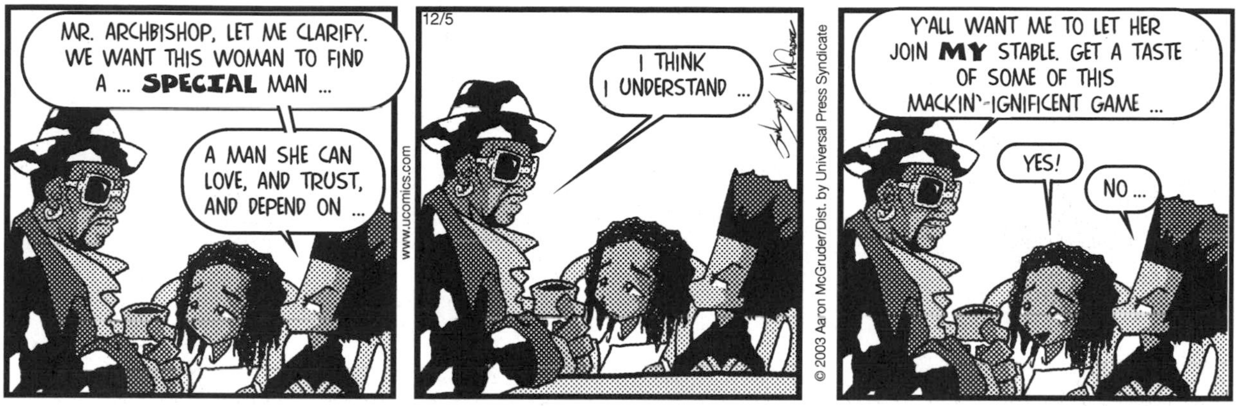
MR. ARCHBISHOP, LET ME CLARIFY. WE WANT THIS WOMAN TO FIND A ... **SPECIAL** MAN ...
A MAN SHE CAN LOVE, AND TRUST, AND DEPEND ON ...
www.ucomics.com
12/5
I THINK I UNDERSTAND ...
© 2003 Aaron McGruder/Dist. by Universal Press Syndicate
Y'ALL WANT ME TO LET HER JOIN **MY** STABLE. GET A TASTE OF SOME OF THIS MACKIN'-IGNIFICENT GAME ...
YES!
NO ...

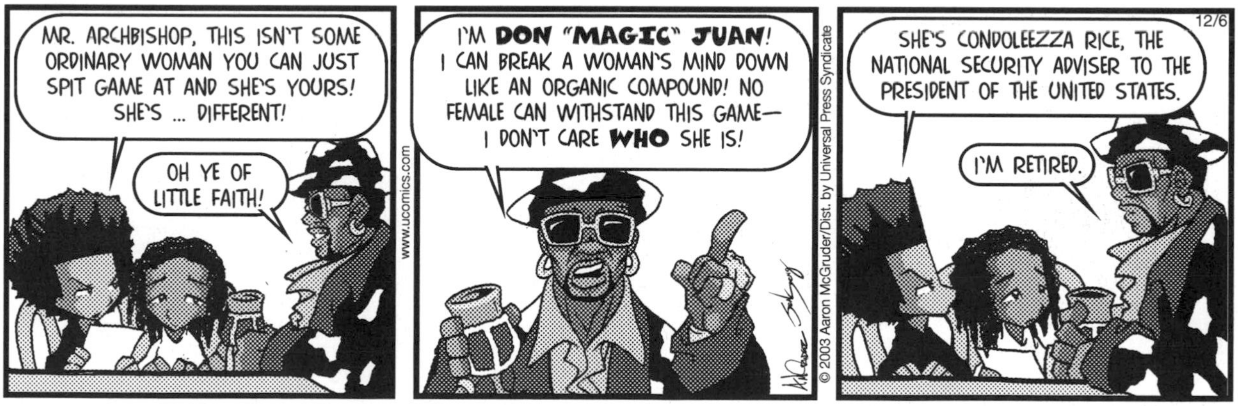
MR. ARCHBISHOP, THIS ISN'T SOME ORDINARY WOMAN YOU CAN JUST SPIT GAME AT AND SHE'S YOURS! SHE'S ... DIFFERENT!
OH YE OF LITTLE FAITH!
www.ucomics.com
I'M **DON "MAGIC" JUAN**! I CAN BREAK A WOMAN'S MIND DOWN LIKE AN ORGANIC COMPOUND! NO FEMALE CAN WITHSTAND THIS GAME— I DON'T CARE **WHO** SHE IS!
© 2003 Aaron McGruder/Dist. by Universal Press Syndicate
12/6
SHE'S CONDOLEEZZA RICE, THE NATIONAL SECURITY ADVISER TO THE PRESIDENT OF THE UNITED STATES.
I'M RETIRED.

Week of

November 24, 2003

For Thanksgiving week of 2003, I had Granddad find a pair of underwear on the kitchen table. The week proved "distasteful" to several newspapers, and one paper actually pulled the week. According to my editor, the phrase that did the week in was "crispy, funky drawz."

WELL, HOW DID IT GO WITH LARRY ELDER?
NOT GOOD. WE HAVE TO KEEP LOOKING.
© 2003 Aaron McGruder/Dist. by Universal Press Syndicate
WHO IN THE HELL LEFT THEIR UNDERWEAR ON MY KITCHEN TABLE?!
www.ucomics.com
11/24
SOUNDS LIKE A FAMILY ISSUE. YOU HAVE FUN WITH THAT.
AND THEY'RE DIRTY!!

BOYS, I WAS MAKING THANKSGIVING DINNER, AND I NOTICED SOMETHING ON MY TABLE. DO YOU KNOW WHAT THAT WAS?
TURKEY?
www.ucomics.com
YES, TURKEY ... AND A PAIR OF UNDERWEAR, SLIGHTLY SOILED.
WHY WOULD YOU PUT YOUR UNDERWEAR ON THE TABLE?
11/25
© 2003 Aaron McGruder/Dist. by Universal Press Syndicate
IT'S NOT MY UNDERWEAR!!
OH! RIGHT, GOT IT!

I DON'T MIND CRISPY BACON ON MY TABLE. I DON'T MIND CRISPY LETTUCE ON MY TABLE. I DO MIND SOMEBODY'S CRISPY, FUNKY DRAWZ!!
NOW I WANT TO KNOW WHOSE UNDERWEAR THIS IS!
www.ucomics.com
11/26
© 2003 Aaron McGruder/Dist. by Universal Press Syndicate
WHAT ... YOU CAN'T POSSIBLY THINK IT'S ME!
SNITCH!!

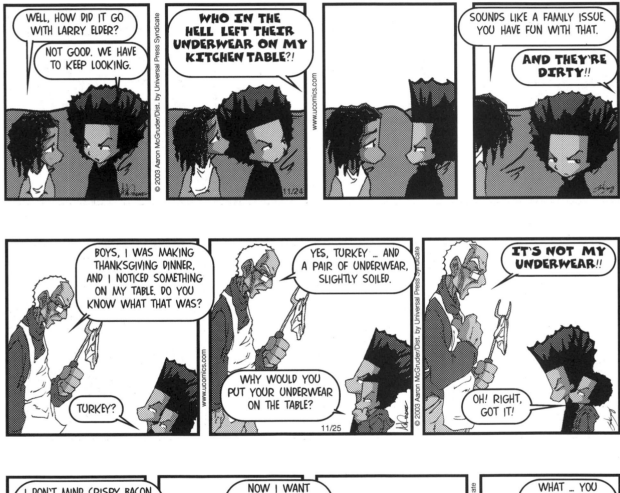

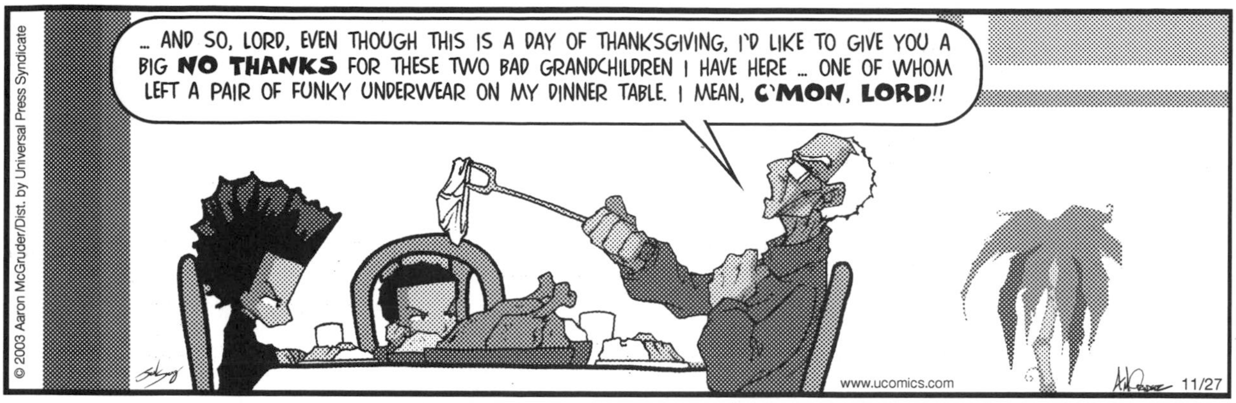
... AND SO, LORD, EVEN THOUGH THIS IS A DAY OF THANKSGIVING, I'D LIKE TO GIVE YOU A BIG **NO THANKS** FOR THESE TWO BAD GRANDCHILDREN I HAVE HERE ... ONE OF WHOM LEFT A PAIR OF FUNKY UNDERWEAR ON MY DINNER TABLE. I MEAN, **C'MON, LORD**!!
© 2003 Aaron McGruder/Dist. by Universal Press Syndicate
www.ucomics.com
11/27

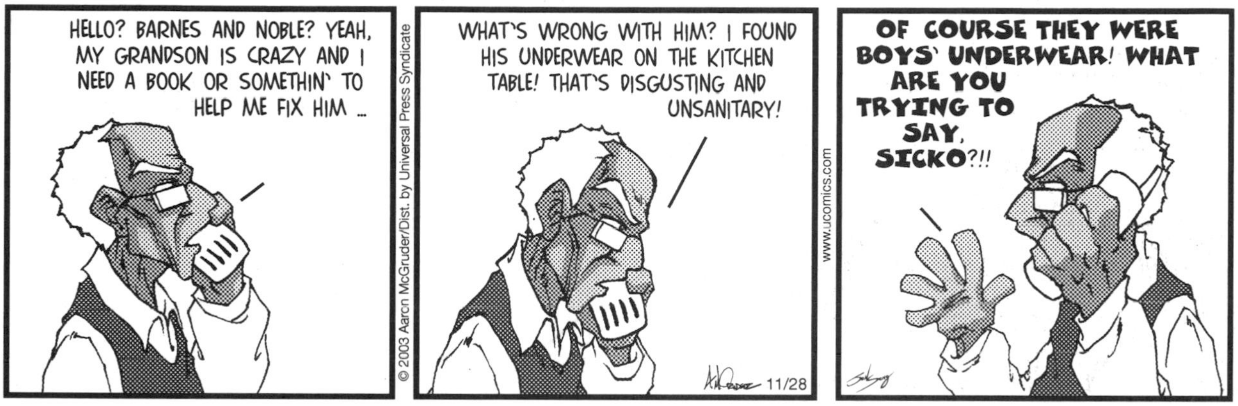
HELLO? BARNES AND NOBLE? YEAH, MY GRANDSON IS CRAZY AND I NEED A BOOK OR SOMETHIN' TO HELP ME FIX HIM ...
WHAT'S WRONG WITH HIM? I FOUND HIS UNDERWEAR ON THE KITCHEN TABLE! THAT'S DISGUSTING AND UNSANITARY!
11/28
OF COURSE THEY WERE BOYS' UNDERWEAR! **WHAT ARE YOU TRYING TO SAY, SICKO**?!!

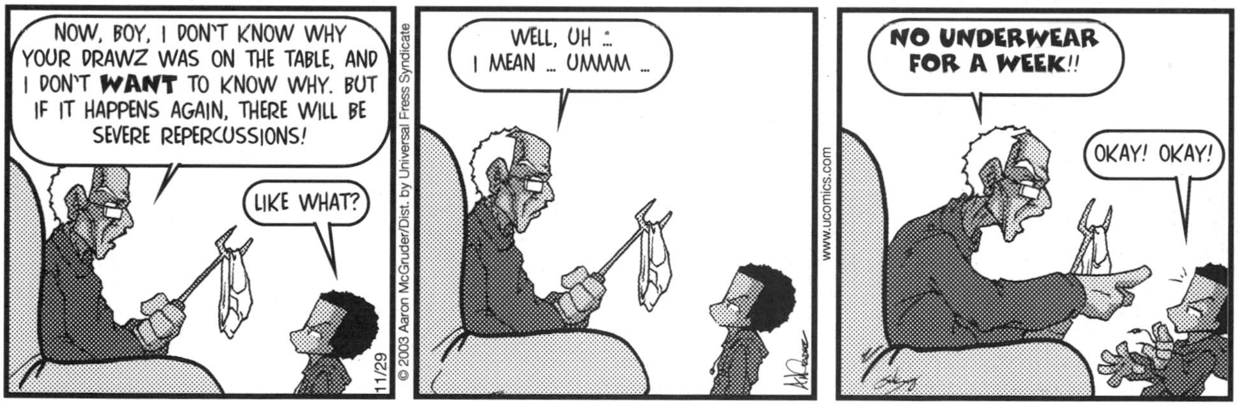
NOW, BOY, I DON'T KNOW WHY YOUR DRAWZ WAS ON THE TABLE, AND I DON'T **WANT** TO KNOW WHY. BUT IF IT HAPPENS AGAIN, THERE WILL BE SEVERE REPERCUSSIONS!
LIKE WHAT?
11/29
WELL, UH ... I MEAN ... UMMM ...
NO UNDERWEAR FOR A WEEK!!
OKAY! OKAY!

January 10, 2004

The strip below came in with the punchline originally being "Pork: The other white meat, b****!" The word *b****!* was then changed to "bee-yotch!" In the end, though, my syndicate sent out two versions, one where the final word was simply cut. Ironically, when I took a vacation week two years later, the same strip was sent out again with "Bee-Yotch!" in the punchline. This second time, it ran exactly that way in all the newspapers that carry *The Boondocks.*

THE NATIONAL PORK BOARD WOULD LIKE TO REMIND YOU SELF-RIGHTEOUS, HOLIER-THAN-THOU, BEEF-EATIN' SNOBS THAT THERE'S NEVER EVER BEEN A SINGLE CASE OF "MAD PIG" DISEASE.
PORK: THE OTHER WHITE MEAT, BEE-YOTCH!
www.ucomics.com
1/10 © 2004 Aaron McGruder/Dist. by Universal Press Syndicate

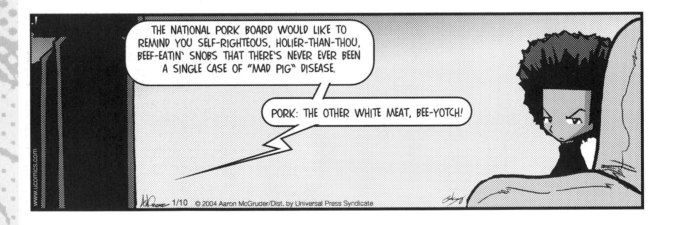

February 7, 2004

This particular strip never saw the light of day in its original form. Even though I tried to tone down the subject matter—R. Kelly's infamous video where he is shown urinating on a young girl—I ended up rewriting the second panel entirely. Here are both the original version, which has never been seen before, and the final version below:

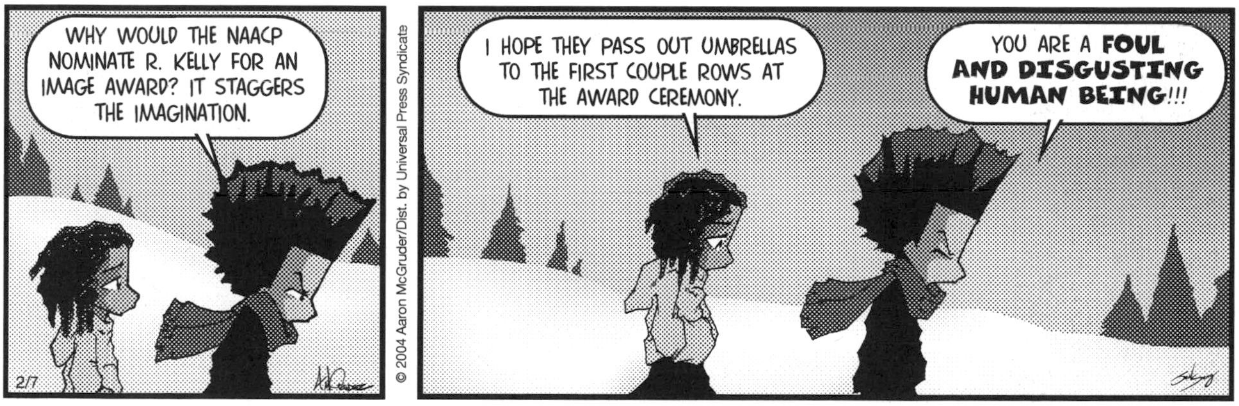
WHY WOULD THE NAACP NOMINATE R. KELLY FOR AN IMAGE AWARD? IT STAGGERS THE IMAGINATION.
2/7
© 2004 Aaron McGruder/Dist. by Universal Press Syndicate
I HOPE THEY PASS OUT UMBRELLAS TO THE FIRST COUPLE ROWS AT THE AWARD CEREMONY.
YOU ARE A **FOUL AND DISGUSTING HUMAN BEING!!!**

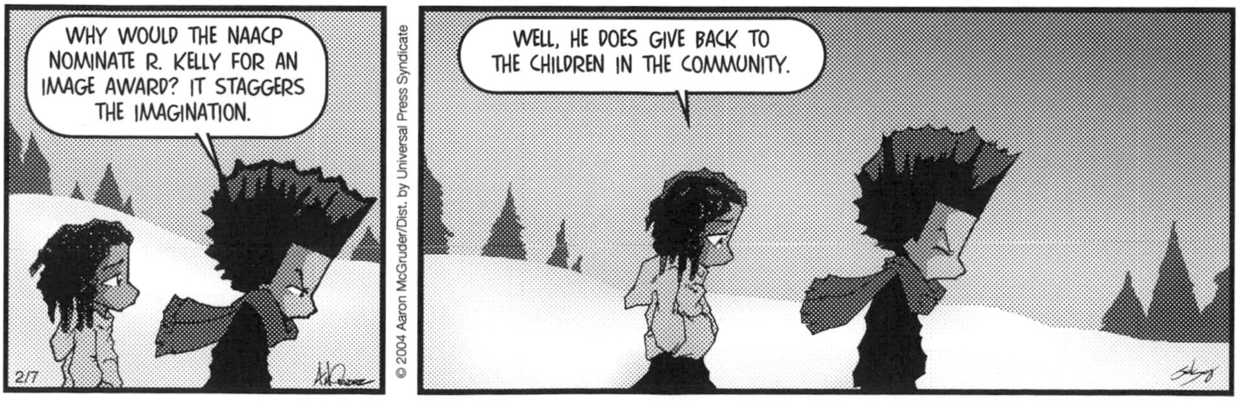
WHY WOULD THE NAACP NOMINATE R. KELLY FOR AN IMAGE AWARD? IT STAGGERS THE IMAGINATION.
2/7
© 2004 Aaron McGruder/Dist. by Universal Press Syndicate
WELL, HE DOES GIVE BACK TO THE CHILDREN IN THE COMMUNITY.

July 24, 2004

In a series of strips I did on Bill Cosby, the word *n***a* appeared again in *The Boondocks*. It wasn't pulled from any newspapers, either. This is noteworthy because of what came later . . .

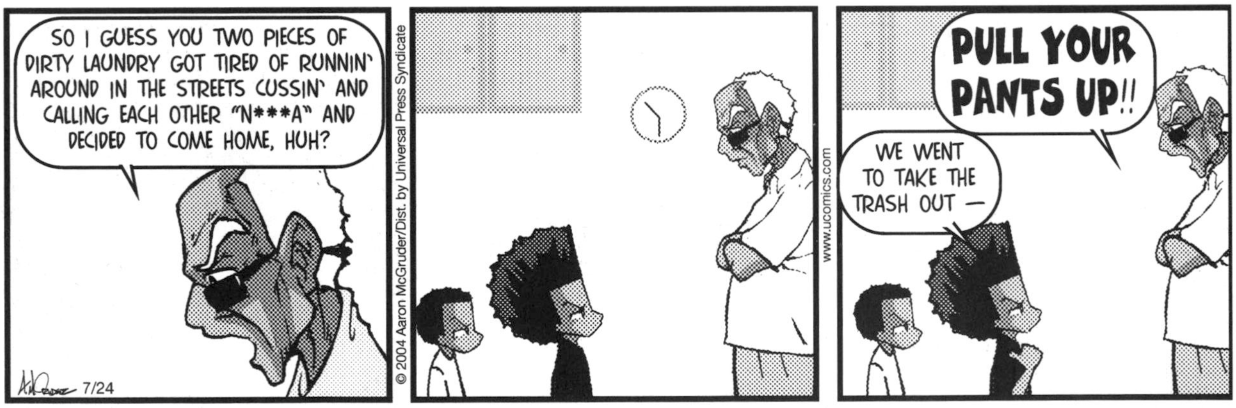
SO I GUESS YOU TWO PIECES OF DIRTY LAUNDRY GOT TIRED OF RUNNIN' AROUND IN THE STREETS CUSSIN' AND CALLING EACH OTHER "N***A" AND DECIDED TO COME HOME, HUH?
7/24
© 2004 Aaron McGruder/Dist. by Universal Press Syndicate
www.ucomics.com
WE WENT TO TAKE THE TRASH OUT —
PULL YOUR PANTS UP!!

September 20 and 25, 2004

I think I was watching the premiere of season 2 of *The Apprentice* when I was struck with this gem. I was really excited about these strips, but man were they a headache. "Can a nigga get a job" was changed to "Can a n***a get a job?" But even three asterisks weren't going to cut it. The syndicate had to send out two versions to all the newspapers. The alternate (or as I like to call "bitch-ass") version had many changes, the most notable of which was changing the various N-words to all asterisks. (Oddly enough, "b***h" was not changed to all asterisks in the alternate version and I don't think anyone complained.)

Furthermore, the violence in the 9/25 strip was toned down—knives were digitally erased in the third panel and some dialogue was changed.

And after all that, seven newspapers still chose not to run either version. On the flip side, none of this should have ever seen the light of day in an American newspaper, so I count myself lucky to have gotten past all but seven.

Epilogue: Within weeks of these strips running, I read a story that Russell Simmons was in talks for a reality show. Don't know what ever became of it. . . .

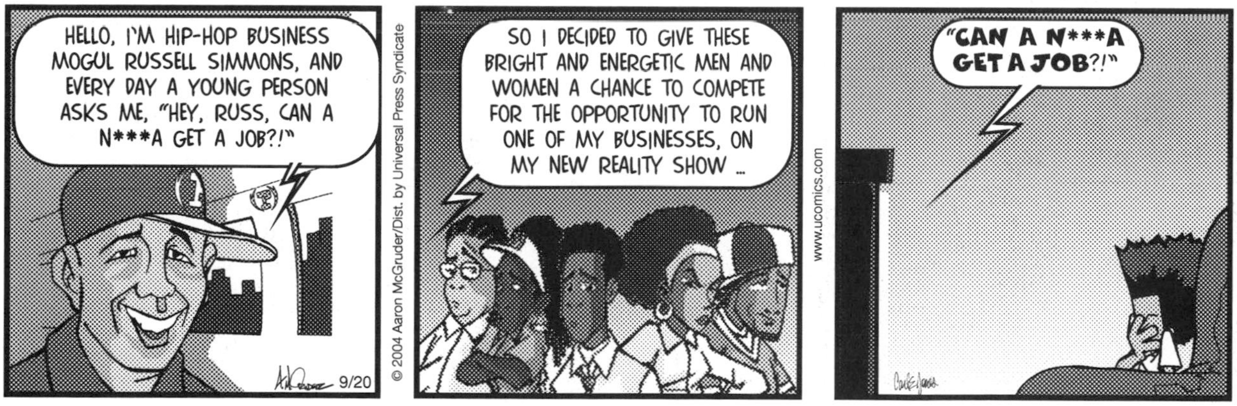
HELLO, I'M HIP-HOP BUSINESS MOGUL RUSSELL SIMMONS, AND EVERY DAY A YOUNG PERSON ASKS ME, "HEY, RUSS, CAN A N***A GET A JOB?!"
9/20
© 2004 Aaron McGruder/Dist. by Universal Press Syndicate
SO I DECIDED TO GIVE THESE BRIGHT AND ENERGETIC MEN AND WOMEN A CHANCE TO COMPETE FOR THE OPPORTUNITY TO RUN ONE OF MY BUSINESSES, ON MY NEW REALITY SHOW ...
www.ucomics.com
"CAN A N***A GET A JOB?!"

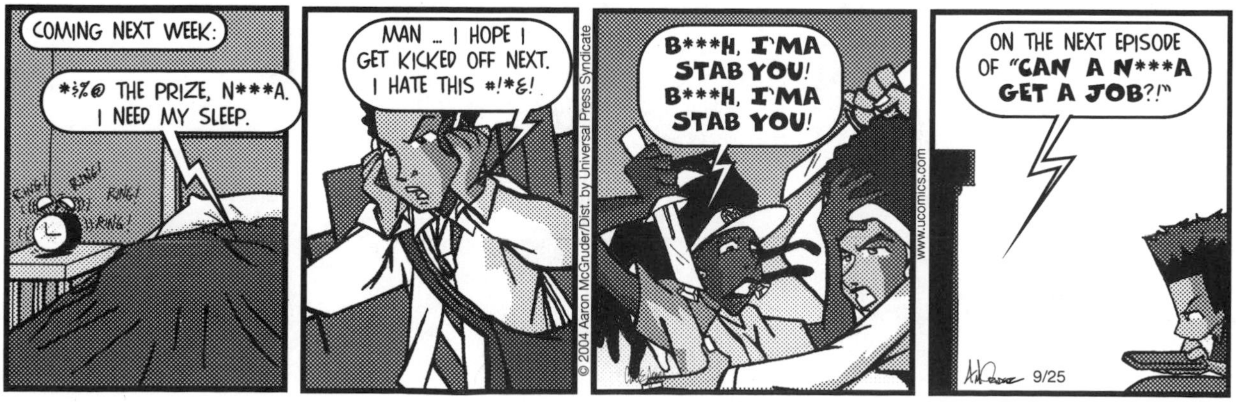
COMING NEXT WEEK:
*$%@ THE PRIZE, N***A. I NEED MY SLEEP.
MAN ... I HOPE I GET KICKED OFF NEXT. I HATE THIS *!*&!
© 2004 Aaron McGruder/Dist. by Universal Press Syndicate
B***H, I'MA STAB YOU! B***H, I'MA STAB YOU!
www.ucomics.com
ON THE NEXT EPISODE OF "CAN A N***A GET A JOB?!"
9/25

December 18, 2004

AND THE WEEK OF

December 20, 2004

Uncle Ruckus, the world's most self-hating Black man, was actually conceived of in the mid '90s. His debut in the strip was pushed off year after year, mostly because I didn't have the time to develop a new character—I was having enough trouble with the ones I was familiar with.

The first time I drew Uncle Ruckus was during the production of the Fox pilot.

Of course, the newspaper doesn't really do the character justice because even the most tame material we could come up with had folks up in arms (and it lacks the wonderful voice-work of Gary Anthony Williams).

Six newspapers pulled this whole week. Five more ran the week but cut two of the strips, the ones where Ruckus calls Huey and Caesar "chimpanzees" and "negro hooligans." But it's Ruckus, what are you gonna do?

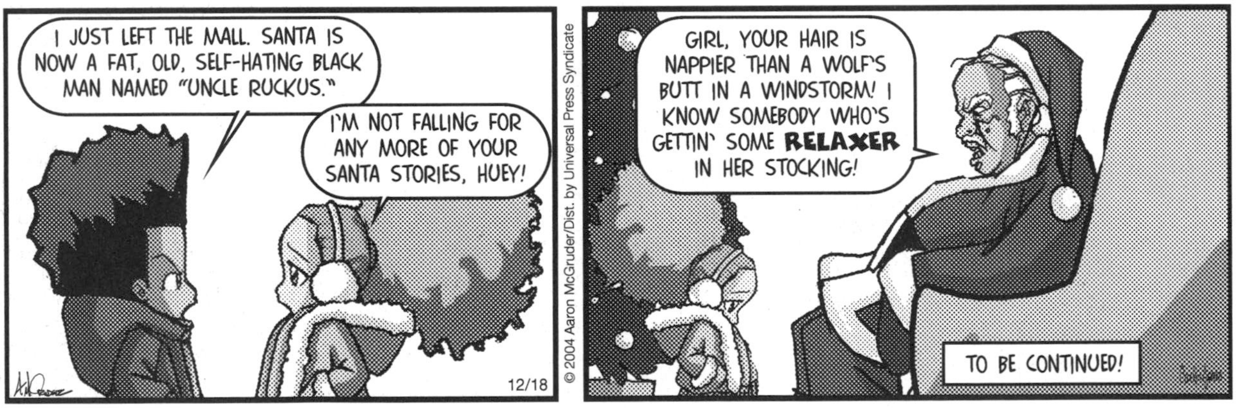
I JUST LEFT THE MALL. SANTA IS NOW A FAT, OLD, SELF-HATING BLACK MAN NAMED "UNCLE RUCKUS."
I'M NOT FALLING FOR ANY MORE OF YOUR SANTA STORIES, HUEY!
12/18
© 2004 Aaron McGruder/Dist. by Universal Press Syndicate
GIRL, YOUR HAIR IS NAPPIER THAN A WOLF'S BUTT IN A WINDSTORM! I KNOW SOMEBODY WHO'S GETTIN' SOME RELAXER IN HER STOCKING!
TO BE CONTINUED!

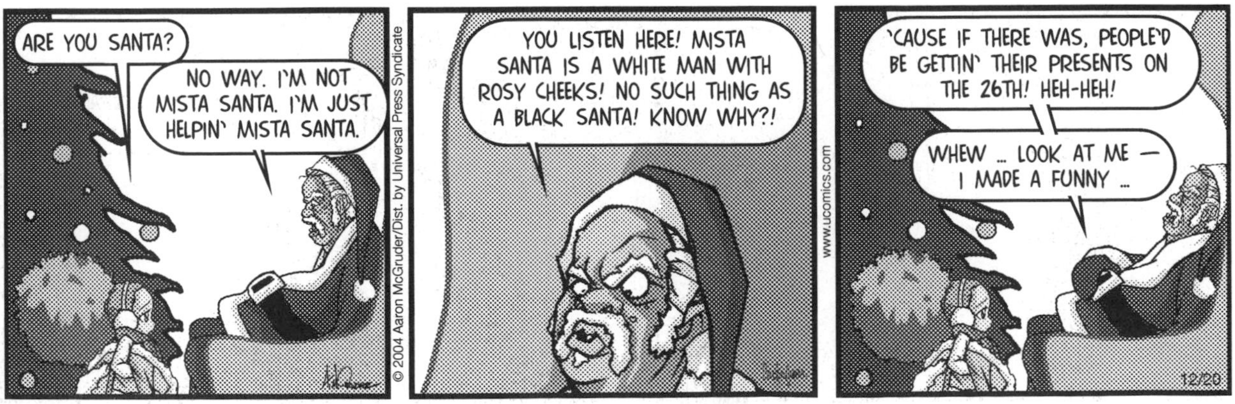
ARE YOU SANTA?
NO WAY. I'M NOT MISTA SANTA. I'M JUST HELPIN' MISTA SANTA.
© 2004 Aaron McGruder/Dist. by Universal Press Syndicate
YOU LISTEN HERE! MISTA SANTA IS A WHITE MAN WITH ROSY CHEEKS! NO SUCH THING AS A BLACK SANTA! KNOW WHY?!
www.ucomics.com
'CAUSE IF THERE WAS, PEOPLE'D BE GETTIN' THEIR PRESENTS ON THE 26TH! HEH-HEH!
WHEW ... LOOK AT ME — I MADE A FUNNY ...
12/20

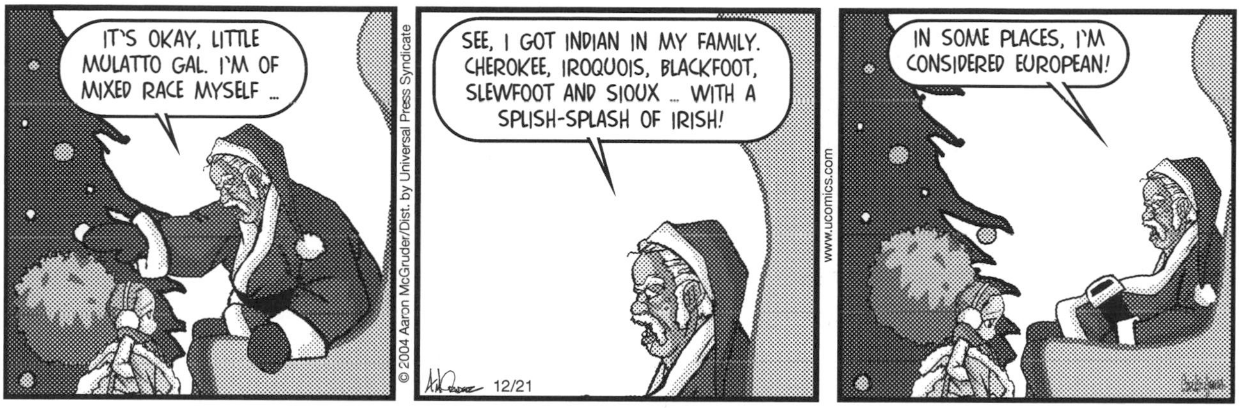
IT'S OKAY, LITTLE MULATTO GAL. I'M OF MIXED RACE MYSELF ...
© 2004 Aaron McGruder/Dist. by Universal Press Syndicate
12/21
SEE, I GOT INDIAN IN MY FAMILY. CHEROKEE, IROQUOIS, BLACKFOOT, SLEWFOOT AND SIOUX ... WITH A SPLISH-SPLASH OF IRISH!
www.ucomics.com
IN SOME PLACES, I'M CONSIDERED EUROPEAN!

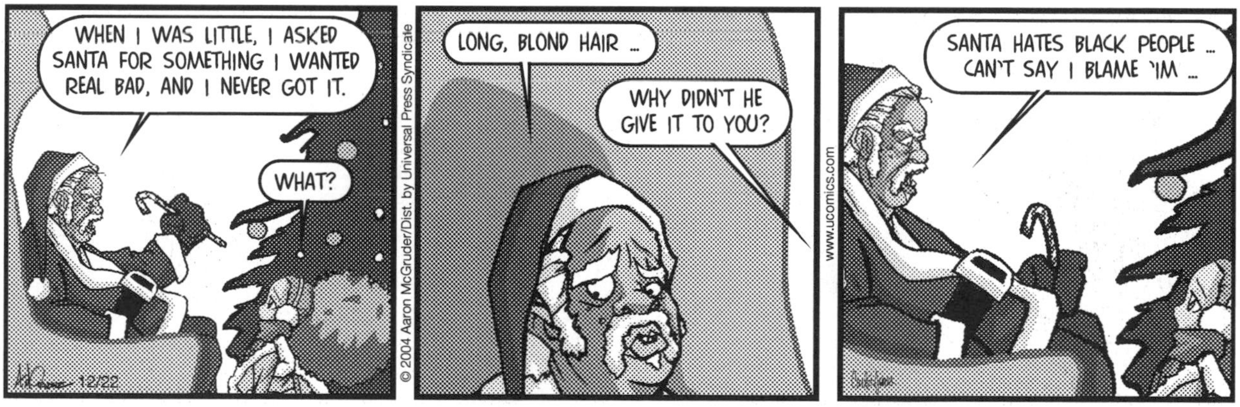
WHEN I WAS LITTLE, I ASKED SANTA FOR SOMETHING I WANTED REAL BAD, AND I NEVER GOT IT.
WHAT?
12/22
© 2004 Aaron McGruder/Dist. by Universal Press Syndicate
LONG, BLOND HAIR ...
WHY DIDN'T HE GIVE IT TO YOU?
www.ucomics.com
SANTA HATES BLACK PEOPLE ... CAN'T SAY I BLAME 'IM ...

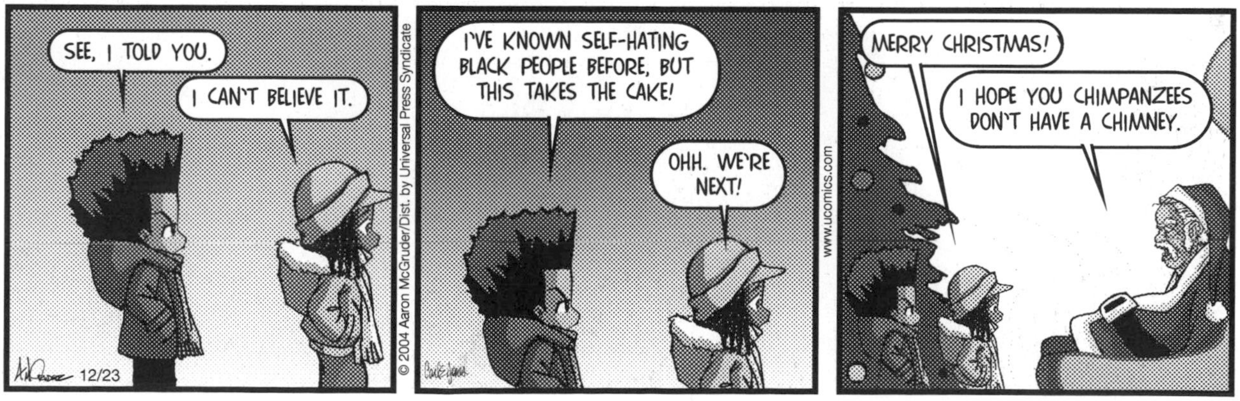
SEE, I TOLD YOU.
I CAN'T BELIEVE IT.
12/23
© 2004 Aaron McGruder/Dist. by Universal Press Syndicate
I'VE KNOWN SELF-HATING BLACK PEOPLE BEFORE, BUT THIS TAKES THE CAKE!
OHH. WE'RE NEXT!
www.ucomics.com
MERRY CHRISTMAS!
I HOPE YOU CHIMPANZEES DON'T HAVE A CHIMNEY.

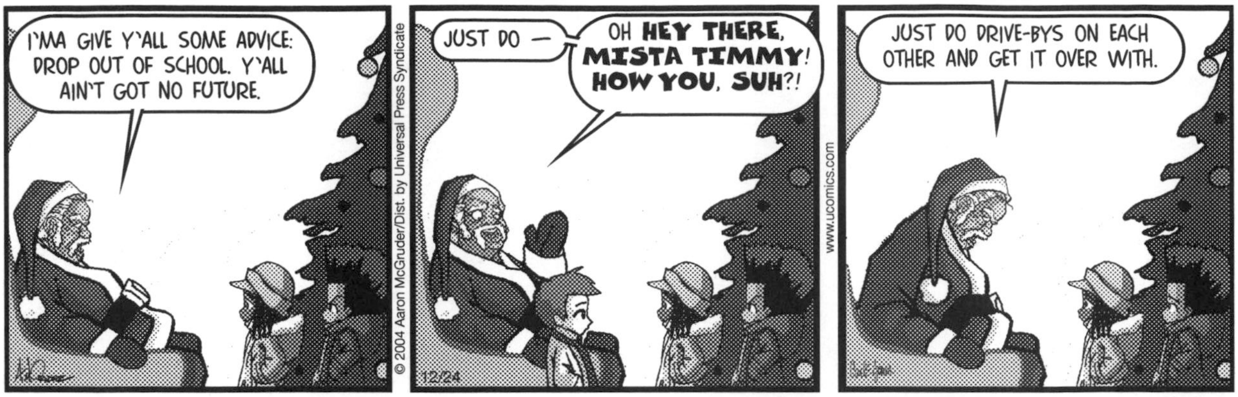
I'MA GIVE Y'ALL SOME ADVICE: DROP OUT OF SCHOOL. Y'ALL AIN'T GOT NO FUTURE.
© 2004 Aaron McGruder/Dist. by Universal Press Syndicate
12/24
JUST DO —
OH HEY THERE, MISTA TIMMY! HOW YOU, SUH?!
www.ucomics.com
JUST DO DRIVE-BYS ON EACH OTHER AND GET IT OVER WITH.

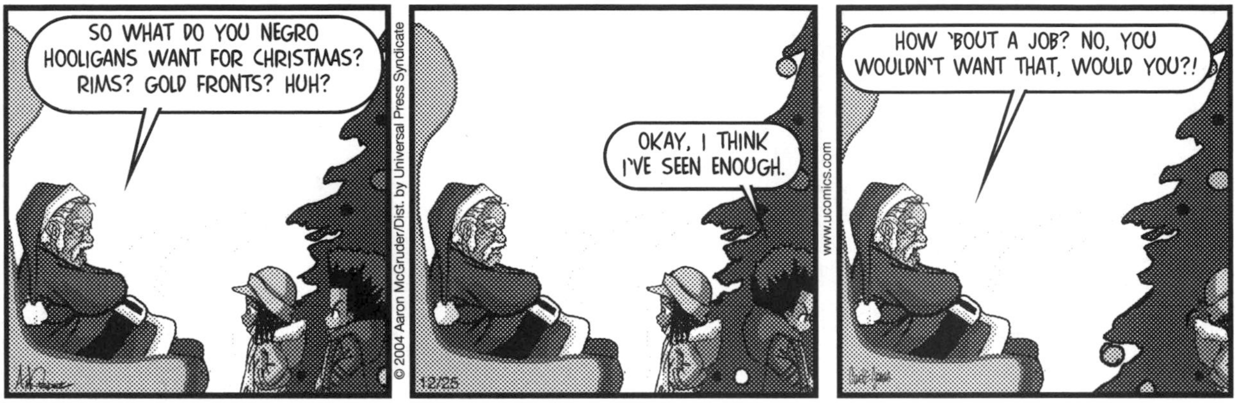
SO WHAT DO YOU NEGRO HOOLIGANS WANT FOR CHRISTMAS? RIMS? GOLD FRONTS? HUH?
© 2004 Aaron McGruder/Dist. by Universal Press Syndicate
12/25
OKAY, I THINK I'VE SEEN ENOUGH.
www.ucomics.com
HOW 'BOUT A JOB? NO, YOU WOULDN'T WANT THAT, WOULD YOU?!

SUNDAY

August 4, 2002

Here's a rare example of a before-and-after version of one of my strips.

BEFORE

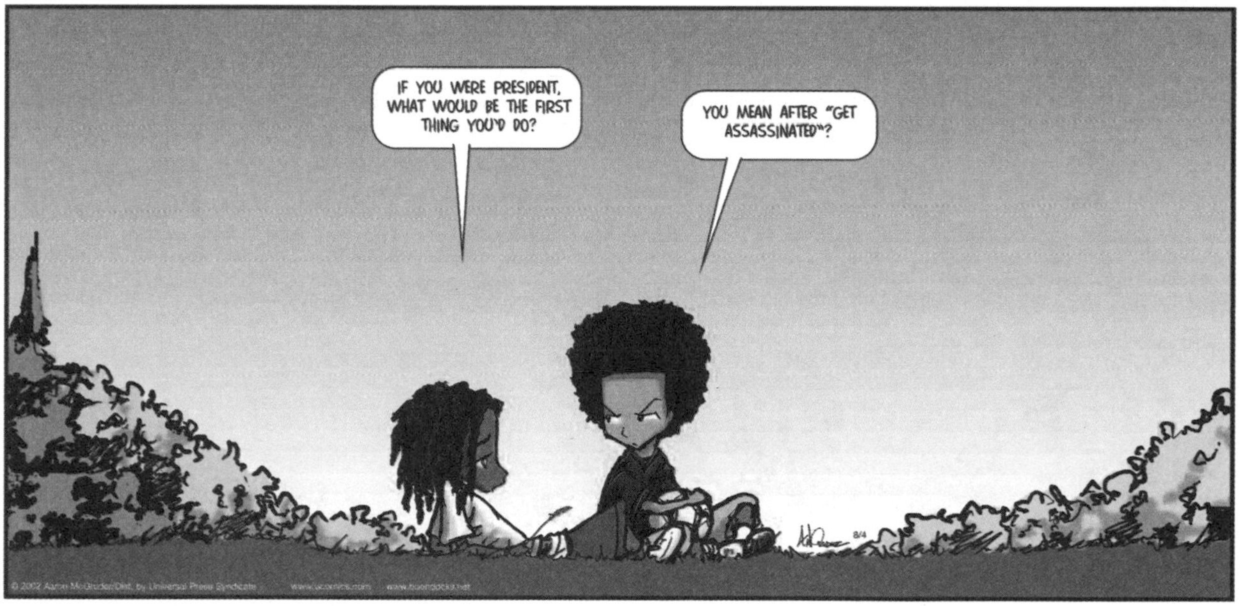
IF YOU WERE PRESIDENT, WHAT WOULD BE THE FIRST THING YOU'D DO?
YOU MEAN AFTER "GET ASSASSINATED"?

After

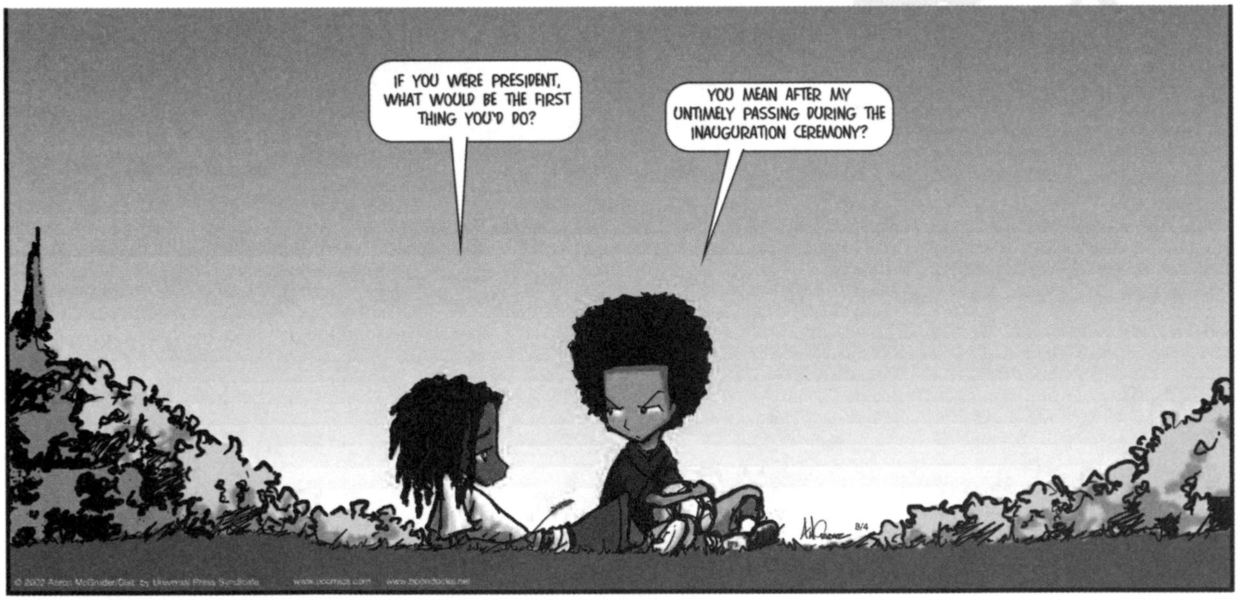
IF YOU WERE PRESIDENT, WHAT WOULD BE THE FIRST THING YOU'D DO?
YOU MEAN AFTER MY UNTIMELY PASSING DURING THE INAUGURATION CEREMONY?

SUNDAY

October 13, 2002

Note: People get mad when you compare the President to Hitler.

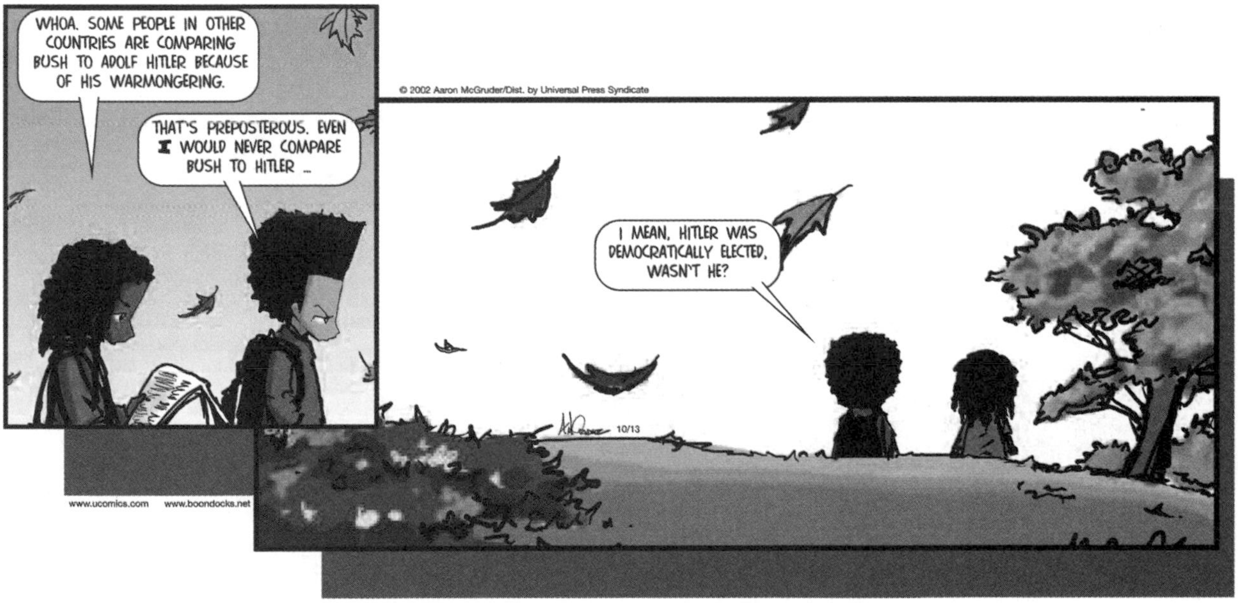
WHOA. SOME PEOPLE IN OTHER COUNTRIES ARE COMPARING BUSH TO ADOLF HITLER BECAUSE OF HIS WARMONGERING.
THAT'S PREPOSTEROUS. EVEN I WOULD NEVER COMPARE BUSH TO HITLER ...
I MEAN, HITLER WAS DEMOCRATICALLY ELECTED, WASN'T HE?
© 2002 Aaron McGruder/Dist. by Universal Press Syndicate
www.ucomics.com www.boondocks.net
10/13

SUNDAY

September 7, 2003

The syndicate asked me to draw rocks and grass so we could convincingly lie to the newspapers and tell them it was mud. It was, of course, not mud.

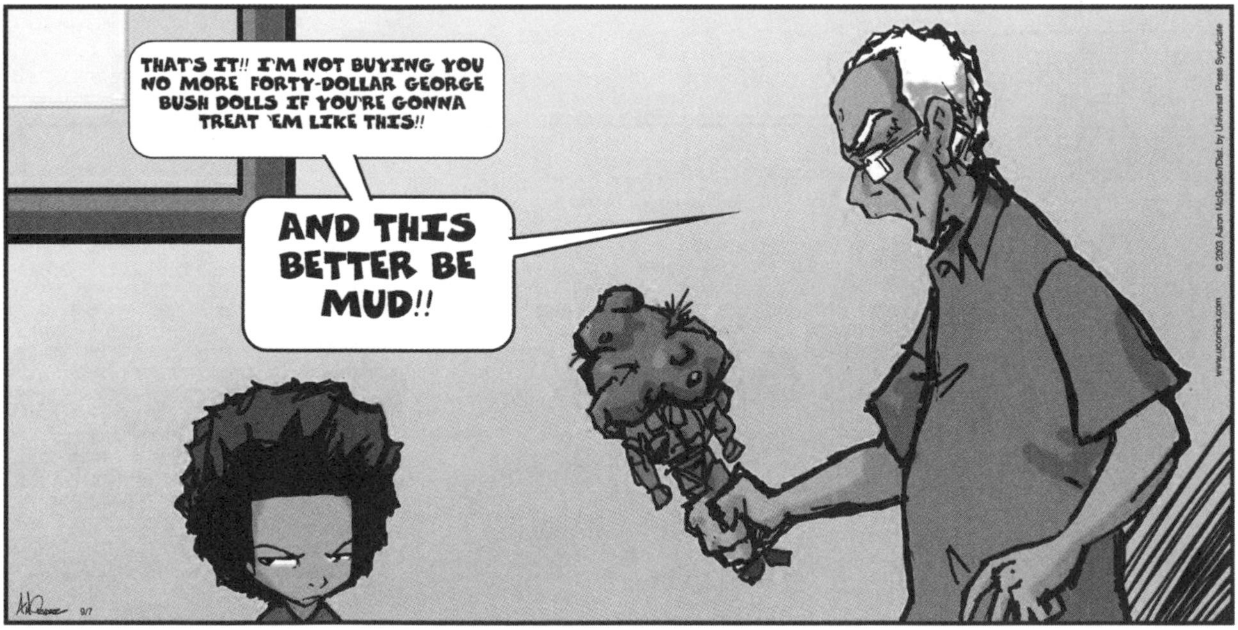
THAT'S IT!! I'M NOT BUYING YOU NO MORE FORTY-DOLLAR GEORGE BUSH DOLLS IF YOU'RE GONNA TREAT 'EM LIKE THIS!!
AND THIS BETTER BE MUD!!
© 2003 Aaron McGruder/Dist. by Universal Press Syndicate
www.ucomics.com

SUNDAY

January 9, 2005

OK, if you're mad at this you're just a hater.

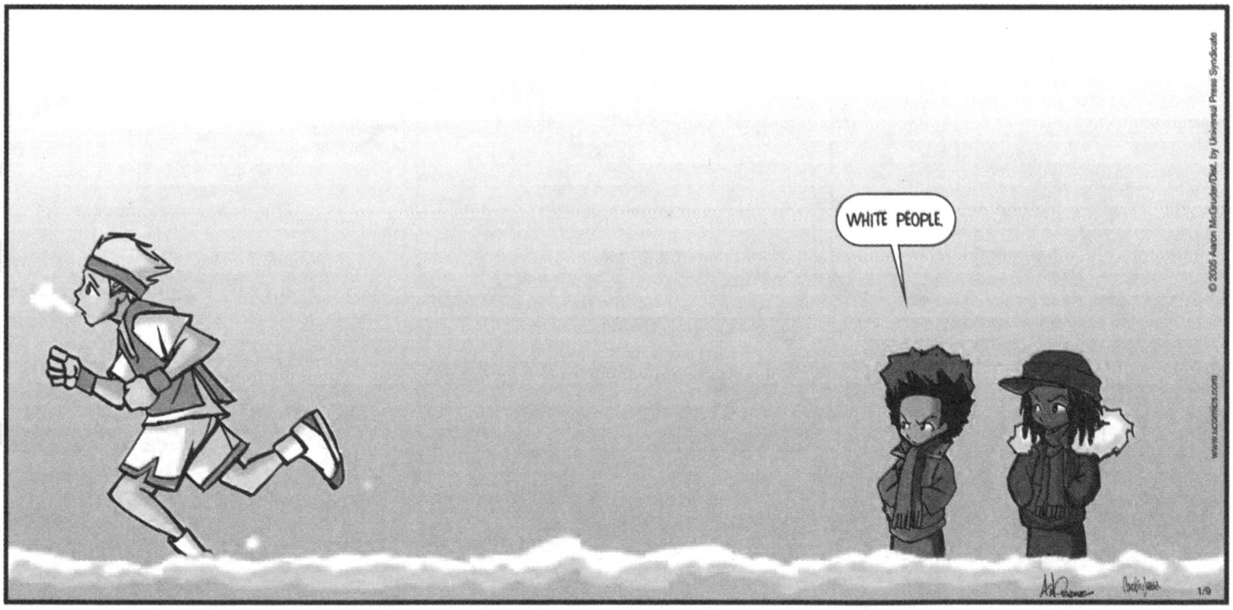
WHITE PEOPLE.

SUNDAY

September 18, 2005

Where Uncle Ruckus goes, trouble always follows. His turn as a bus driver got some heated responses from both readers and newspapers, especially when he called Huey and Riley "negro hooligans" (again!) in the third panel. One angry newspaper called my syndicate to let them know that the paper's "Diversity Committee" would be meeting to discuss complaints about this strip.

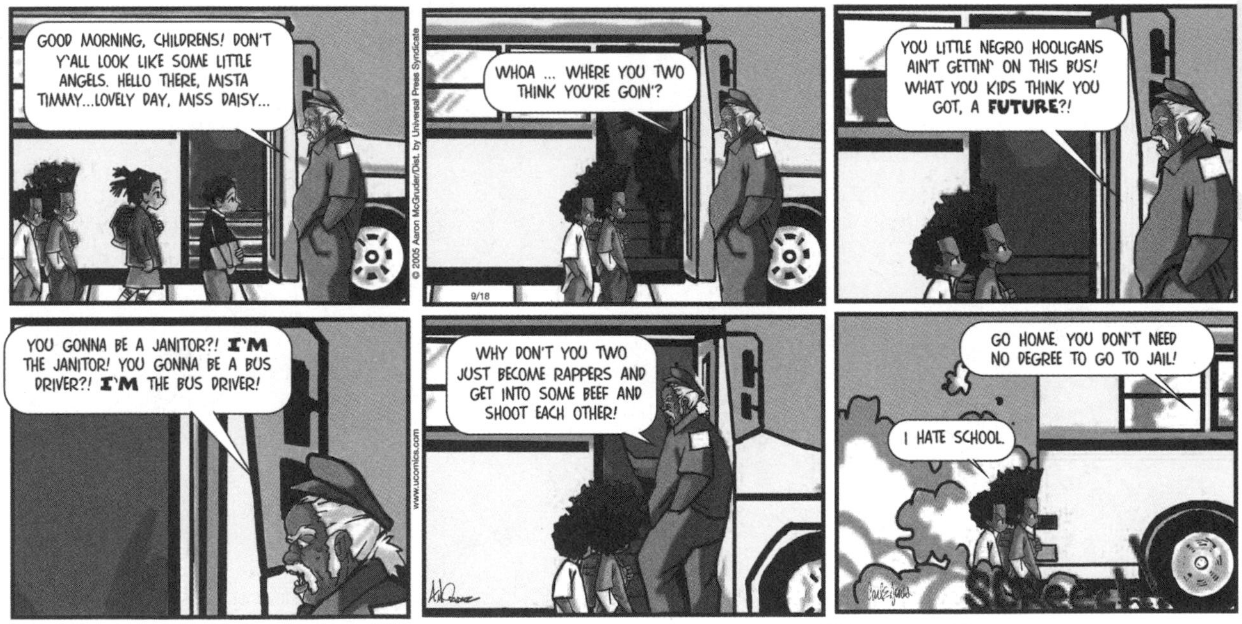
GOOD MORNING, CHILDRENS! DON'T Y'ALL LOOK LIKE SOME LITTLE ANGELS. HELLO THERE, MISTA TIMMY...LOVELY DAY, MISS DAISY...
© 2005 Aaron McGruder/Dist. by Universal Press Syndicate
WHOA ... WHERE YOU TWO THINK YOU'RE GOIN'?
9/18
YOU LITTLE NEGRO HOOLIGANS AIN'T GETTIN' ON THIS BUS! WHAT YOU KIDS THINK YOU GOT, A FUTURE?!
YOU GONNA BE A JANITOR?! I'M THE JANITOR! YOU GONNA BE A BUS DRIVER?! I'M THE BUS DRIVER!
www.ucomics.com
WHY DON'T YOU TWO JUST BECOME RAPPERS AND GET INTO SOME BEEF AND SHOOT EACH OTHER!
GO HOME. YOU DON'T NEED NO DEGREE TO GO TO JAIL!
I HATE SCHOOL.

SUNDAY

December 4, 2005

In this Sunday strip, it's easy to see where we digitally erased the automatic weapon from the hands of the crouching figure in the fourth panel.

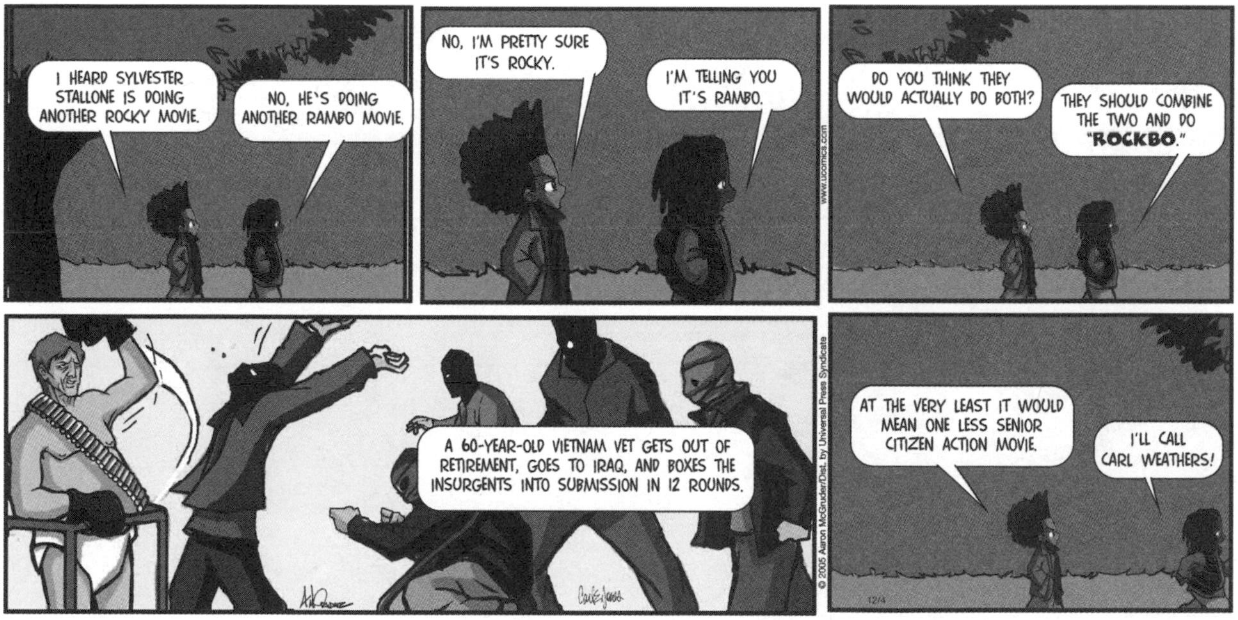
I HEARD SYLVESTER STALLONE IS DOING ANOTHER ROCKY MOVIE.
NO, HE'S DOING ANOTHER RAMBO MOVIE.
NO, I'M PRETTY SURE IT'S ROCKY.
I'M TELLING YOU IT'S RAMBO.
www.ucomics.com
DO YOU THINK THEY WOULD ACTUALLY DO BOTH?
THEY SHOULD COMBINE THE TWO AND DO "ROCKBO."
A 60-YEAR-OLD VIETNAM VET GETS OUT OF RETIREMENT, GOES TO IRAQ, AND BOXES THE INSURGENTS INTO SUBMISSION IN 12 ROUNDS.
© 2005 Aaron McGruder/Dist. by Universal Press Syndicate
AT THE VERY LEAST IT WOULD MEAN ONE LESS SENIOR CITIZEN ACTION MOVIE.
I'LL CALL CARL WEATHERS!
12/4

SUNDAY

March 26, 2006

My last Sunday in newspapers. And I couldn't say "Friggin'."

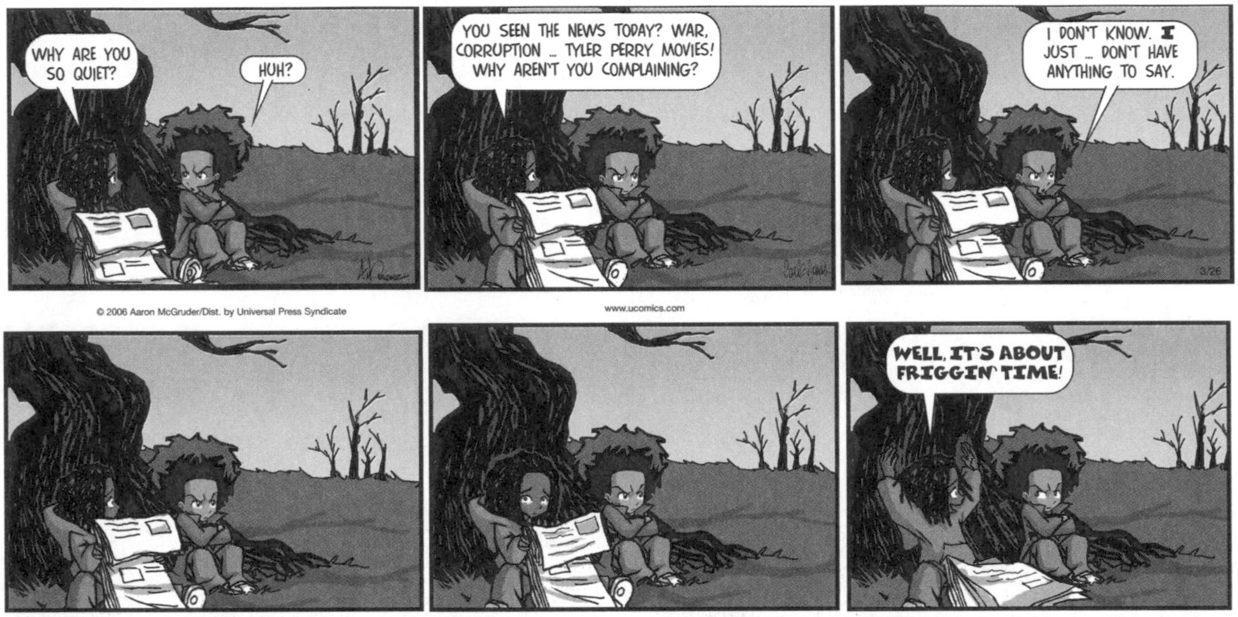
WHY ARE YOU SO QUIET?
HUH?
YOU SEEN THE NEWS TODAY? WAR, CORRUPTION ... TYLER PERRY MOVIES! WHY AREN'T YOU COMPLAINING?
I DON'T KNOW. I JUST ... DON'T HAVE ANYTHING TO SAY.
3/26
© 2006 Aaron McGruder/Dist. by Universal Press Syndicate
www.ucomics.com
WELL, IT'S ABOUT FRIGGIN' TIME!

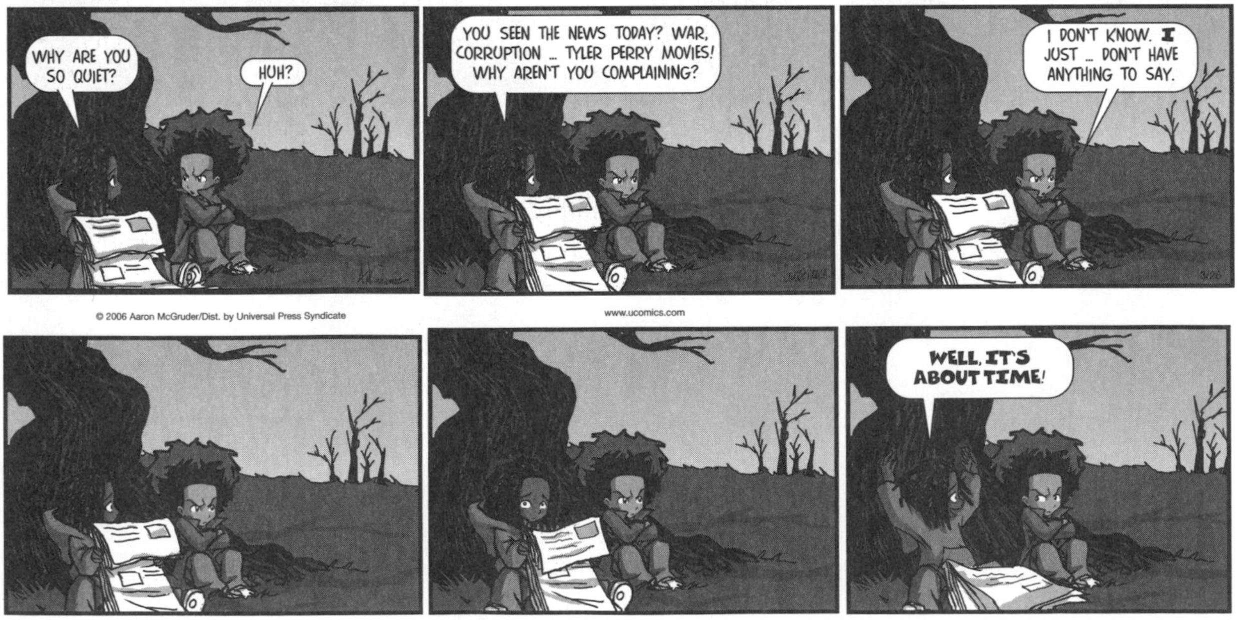
WHY ARE YOU SO QUIET?
HUH?
YOU SEEN THE NEWS TODAY? WAR, CORRUPTION ... TYLER PERRY MOVIES! WHY AREN'T YOU COMPLAINING?
I DON'T KNOW. I JUST ... DON'T HAVE ANYTHING TO SAY.
3/26
© 2006 Aaron McGruder/Dist. by Universal Press Syndicate
www.ucomics.com
WELL, IT'S ABOUT TIME!

February 1, 2005

My "*Boondocks* Black History Moment" about killing another human being for tennis shoes was pulled by several newspapers who found the strip "too negative for the first day of Black History Month." Oddly enough, no newspaper pulled the following day's strip, which shows newly retired FCC chairman Michael Powell saying, "I'm Michael Powell, b****! I'm retired."

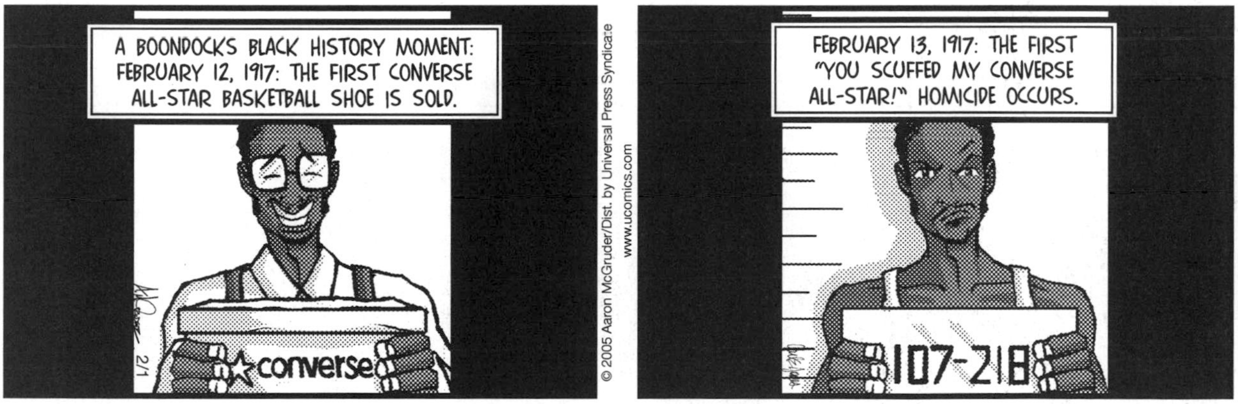
A BOONDOCKS BLACK HISTORY MOMENT: FEBRUARY 12, 1917: THE FIRST CONVERSE ALL-STAR BASKETBALL SHOE IS SOLD.
converse
2/1
© 2005 Aaron McGruder/Dist. by Universal Press Syndicate
www.ucomics.com
FEBRUARY 13, 1917: THE FIRST "YOU SCUFFED MY CONVERSE ALL-STAR!" HOMICIDE OCCURS.
107-218

February 19, 2005

Two versions of this strip about Bob Johnson were sent out to papers. I guess the one with all asterisks lets people pick their own bad word. I hope they picked well, I still don't like that n***a.

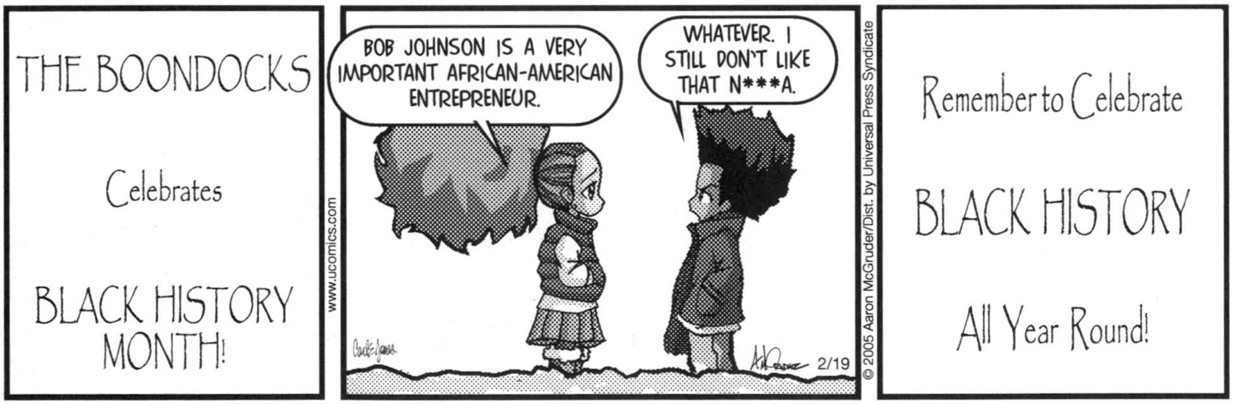
THE BOONDOCKS
Celebrates
BLACK HISTORY MONTH!
www.ucomics.com
BOB JOHNSON IS A VERY IMPORTANT AFRICAN-AMERICAN ENTREPRENEUR.
WHATEVER. I STILL DON'T LIKE THAT N***A.
2/19
© 2005 Aaron McGruder/Dist. by Universal Press Syndicate
Remember to Celebrate
BLACK HISTORY
All Year Round!

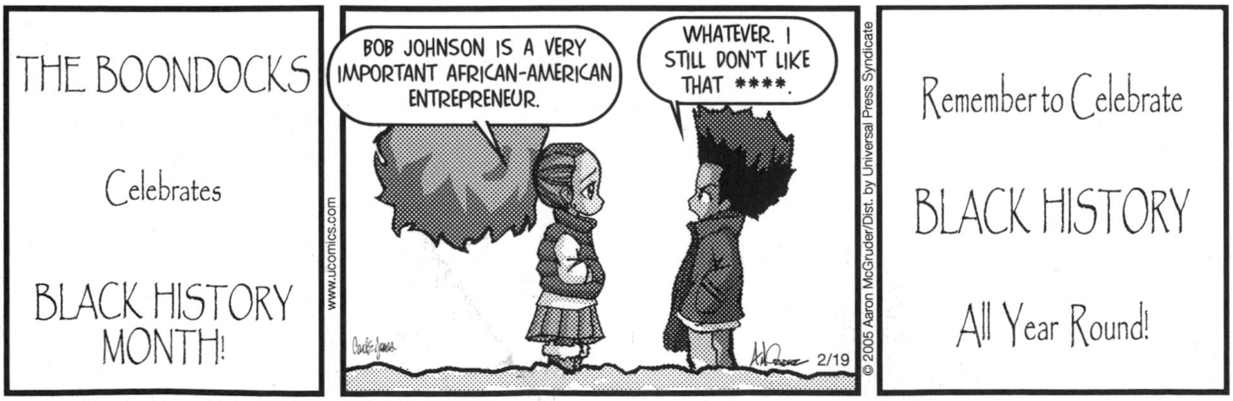
THE BOONDOCKS
Celebrates
BLACK HISTORY MONTH!
www.ucomics.com
BOB JOHNSON IS A VERY IMPORTANT AFRICAN-AMERICAN ENTREPRENEUR.
WHATEVER. I STILL DON'T LIKE THAT ****.
2/19
© 2005 Aaron McGruder/Dist. by Universal Press Syndicate
Remember to Celebrate
BLACK HISTORY
All Year Round!

WEEK OF

February 21, 2005

For the first time in six years my editor killed a partial week of strips. One eventually made it into print on March 4, 2005, but the remaining four never saw the light of day. I remember not being too upset about this, probably because I knew I had no business doing them in the first place.

To The Reader

Last Saturday's installment, of this featured, which included a character referring to BET founder Robert Johnson a "ni**a", was found to be distateful, ignorant, and downright offensive.

We offer our most sincere apologies.

We asssure you the word "ni**a" will never again appear in this feature. Instead, we will use the more acceptable social euphemism: " N-WORD".

We now return to our strip already in progress...

AND THEN THE n-word ON TV SAID WE SHOULDN'T USE THE WORD n-word!

UPPITY n-word!

WILL YOU n-wordS BE QUIET. I'M TRYING TO READ.

IT'S THE NEW MORE SOCIALLY RESPONSIBLE "BOONDOCKS"!

RILEY, GET IN HERE NOW!

I'M WATCHING TV, GRANDAD!

NOW!

THAT n-word' S TRIPPIN!

N-WORD **GET** YOUR A** IN HERE **NOW**!

n-word, YOU BETTER GO.

SHUT UP n-word!

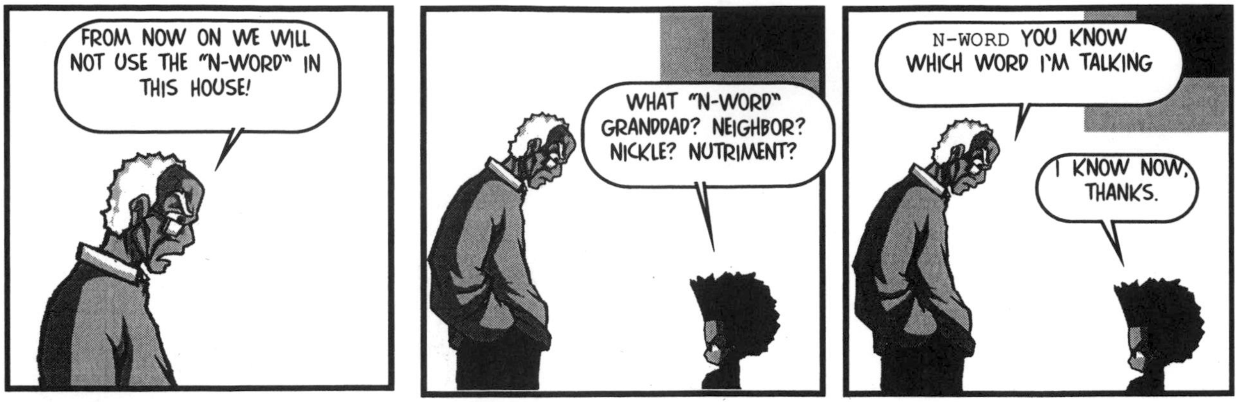
FROM NOW ON WE WILL NOT USE THE "N-WORD" IN THIS HOUSE!
WHAT "N-WORD" GRANDDAD? NEIGHBOR? NICKLE? NUTRIMENT?
N-WORD YOU KNOW WHICH WORD I'M TALKING
I KNOW NOW, THANKS.

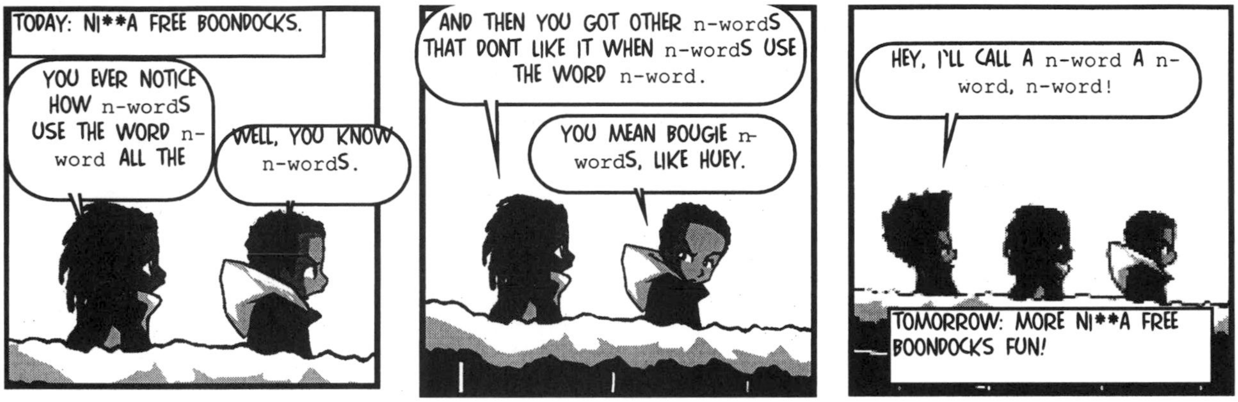
TODAY: NI**A FREE BOONDOCKS.
YOU EVER NOTICE HOW n-wordS USE THE WORD n-word ALL THE
WELL, YOU KNOW n-wordS.
AND THEN YOU GOT OTHER n-wordS THAT DONT LIKE IT WHEN n-wordS USE THE WORD n-word.
YOU MEAN BOUGIE n-wordS, LIKE HUEY.
HEY, I'LL CALL A n-word A n-word, n-word!
TOMORROW: MORE NI**A FREE BOONDOCKS FUN!

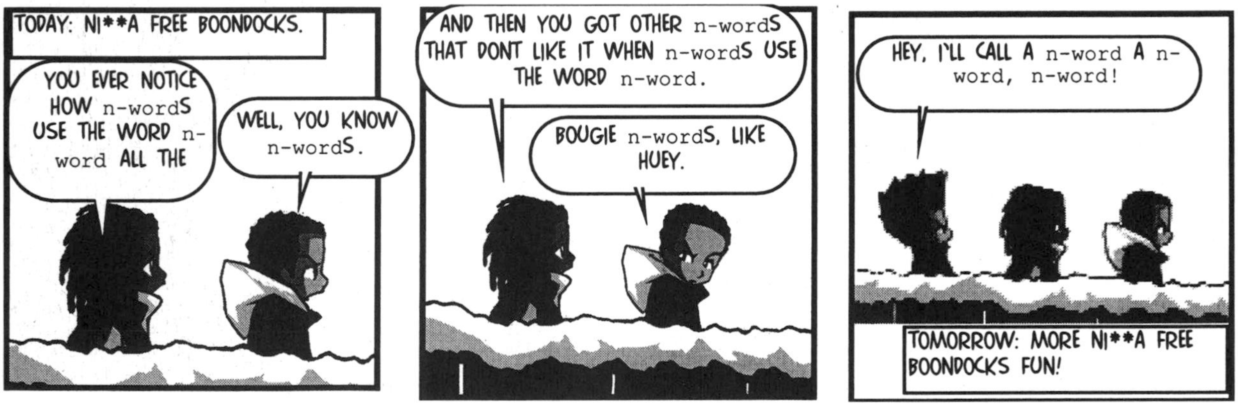
TODAY: NI**A FREE BOONDOCKS.
YOU EVER NOTICE HOW n-wordS USE THE WORD n-word ALL THE
WELL, YOU KNOW n-wordS.
AND THEN YOU GOT OTHER n-wordS THAT DONT LIKE IT WHEN n-wordS USE THE WORD n-word.
BOUGIE n-wordS, LIKE HUEY.
HEY, I'LL CALL A n-word A n-word, n-word!
TOMORROW: MORE NI**A FREE BOONDOCKS FUN!

WEEK OF

February 28, 2005

The week of strips for February 28, 2005, had something for everyone. Quite a few newspapers did not run my two strips with gags about George Bush admitting to smoking marijuana. And later in the week, several newspapers did not run my two N-word strips, one of which was recycled from the partial week that was killed by my editor.

March 17, 2005

This strip went out as two different versions, with changed dialogue in the final panel. In this instance, the alternate punch line holds up pretty well.

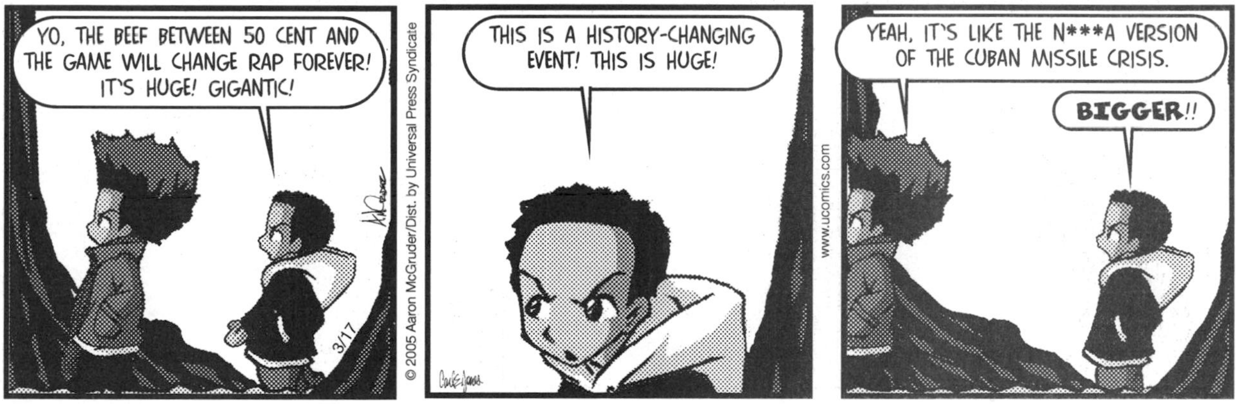
YO, THE BEEF BETWEEN 50 CENT AND THE GAME WILL CHANGE RAP FOREVER! IT'S HUGE! GIGANTIC!
3/17
© 2005 Aaron McGruder/Dist. by Universal Press Syndicate
THIS IS A HISTORY-CHANGING EVENT! THIS IS HUGE!
www.ucomics.com
YEAH, IT'S LIKE THE N***A VERSION OF THE CUBAN MISSILE CRISIS.
BIGGER!!

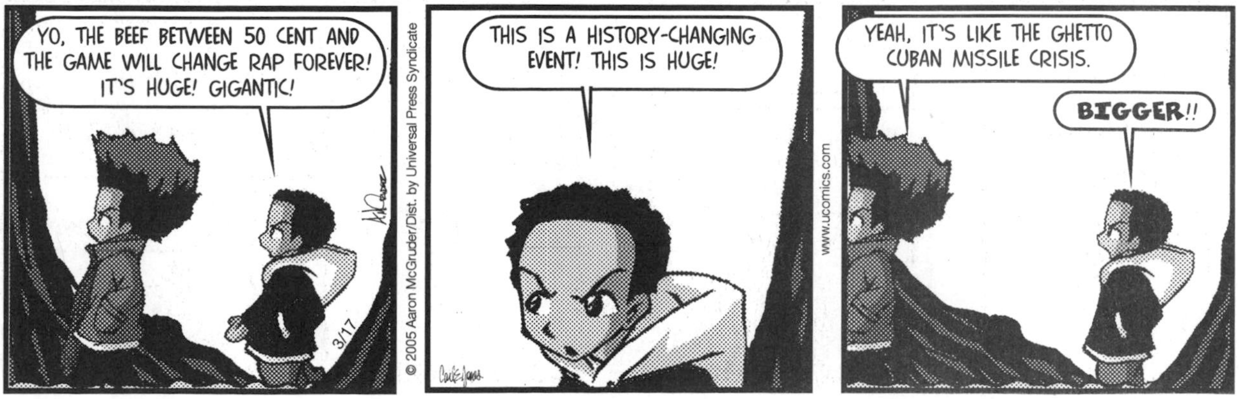
YO, THE BEEF BETWEEN 50 CENT AND THE GAME WILL CHANGE RAP FOREVER! IT'S HUGE! GIGANTIC!
3/17
© 2005 Aaron McGruder/Dist. by Universal Press Syndicate
THIS IS A HISTORY-CHANGING EVENT! THIS IS HUGE!
www.ucomics.com
YEAH, IT'S LIKE THE GHETTO CUBAN MISSILE CRISIS.
BIGGER!!

July 13, 2005

My strip about Oprah being turned away from the upscale shop Hermes in Paris went out as two versions. The phrase "For Christ's sake" was changed to "For Heaven's sake." Most papers ran the original version.

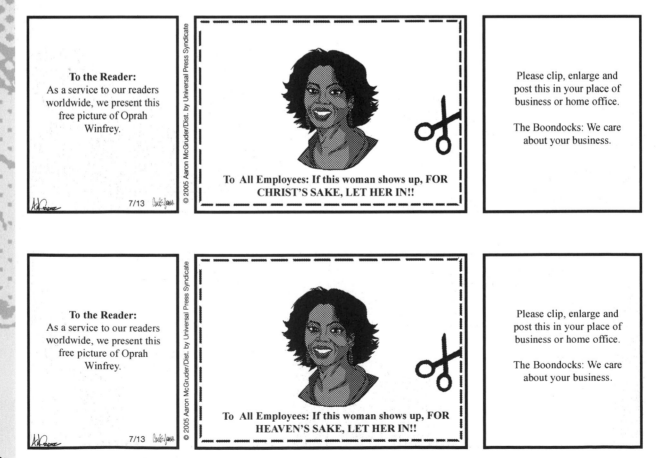

To the Reader:
As a service to our readers worldwide, we present this free picture of Oprah Winfrey.

7/13

© 2005 Aaron McGruder/Dist. by Universal Press Syndicate

To All Employees: If this woman shows up, FOR CHRIST'S SAKE, LET HER IN!!

Please clip, enlarge and post this in your place of business or home office.

The Boondocks: We care about your business.

To the Reader:
As a service to our readers worldwide, we present this free picture of Oprah Winfrey.

7/13

© 2005 Aaron McGruder/Dist. by Universal Press Syndicate

To All Employees: If this woman shows up, FOR HEAVEN'S SAKE, LET HER IN!!

Please clip, enlarge and post this in your place of business or home office.

The Boondocks: We care about your business.

WEEK OF July 18, 2005

My week of strips about the hip-hop makeover of McDonald's uniforms was not without some changes. In one strip, the *b* in "b#$%@" was changed to an asterisk, so no hint of the word *bitch* could be detected. In another strip, the *n* in "n**** " was also changed to an asterisk. But the biggest change was the digital erasing of the handgun being brandished by a scowling McDonald's patron on a billboard. My syndicate sent out both the original and the alternate versions to newspapers.

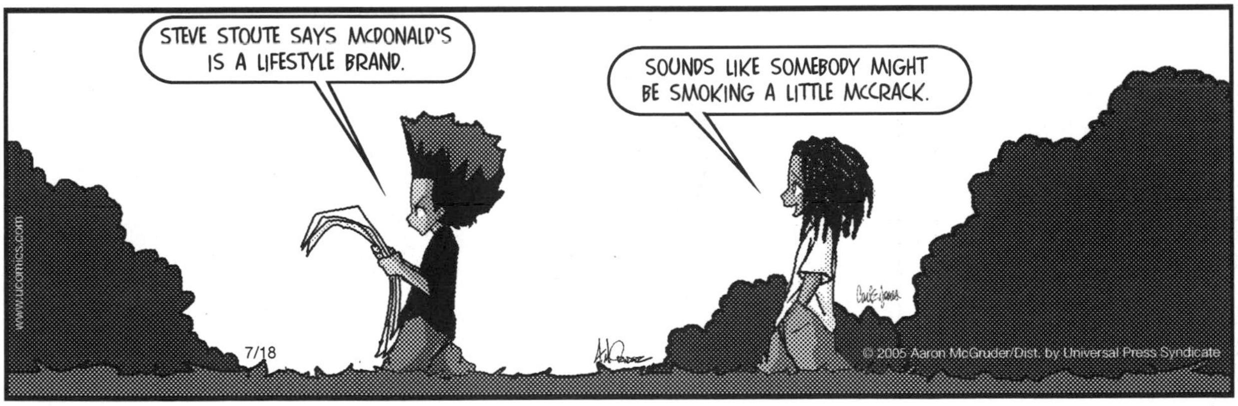
STEVE STOUTE SAYS MCDONALD'S IS A LIFESTYLE BRAND.
SOUNDS LIKE SOMEBODY MIGHT BE SMOKING A LITTLE MCCRACK.
7/18
www.ucomics.com
© 2005 Aaron McGruder/Dist. by Universal Press Syndicate

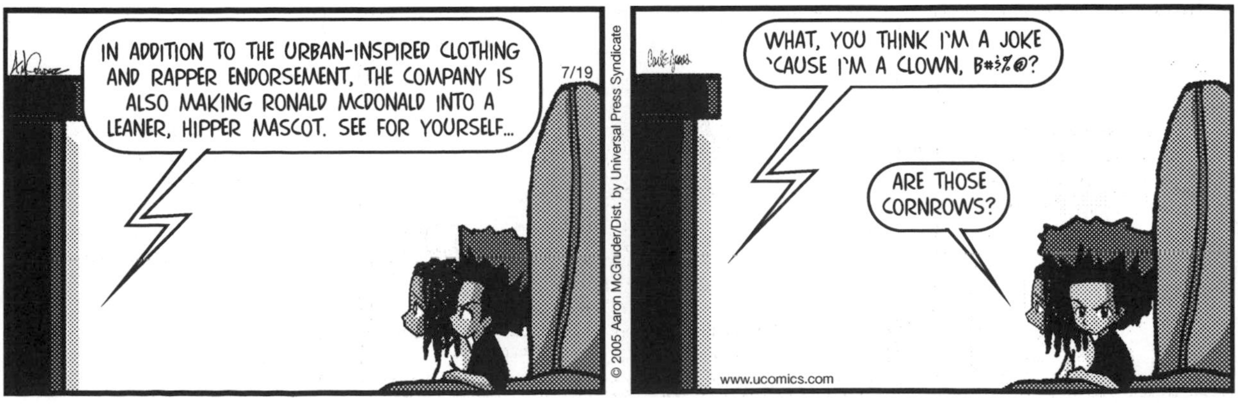
IN ADDITION TO THE URBAN-INSPIRED CLOTHING AND RAPPER ENDORSEMENT, THE COMPANY IS ALSO MAKING RONALD MCDONALD INTO A LEANER, HIPPER MASCOT. SEE FOR YOURSELF...
7/19
© 2005 Aaron McGruder/Dist. by Universal Press Syndicate
WHAT, YOU THINK I'M A JOKE 'CAUSE I'M A CLOWN, B#$%@?
ARE THOSE CORNROWS?
www.ucomics.com

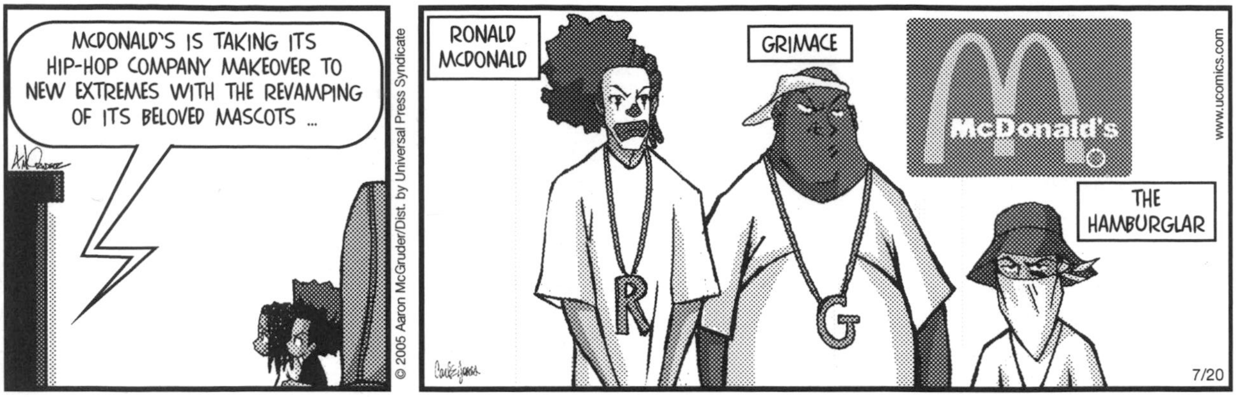
McDONALD'S IS TAKING ITS HIP-HOP COMPANY MAKEOVER TO NEW EXTREMES WITH THE REVAMPING OF ITS BELOVED MASCOTS ...
© 2005 Aaron McGruder/Dist. by Universal Press Syndicate
RONALD McDONALD
GRIMACE
McDonald's
THE HAMBURGLAR
www.ucomics.com
7/20

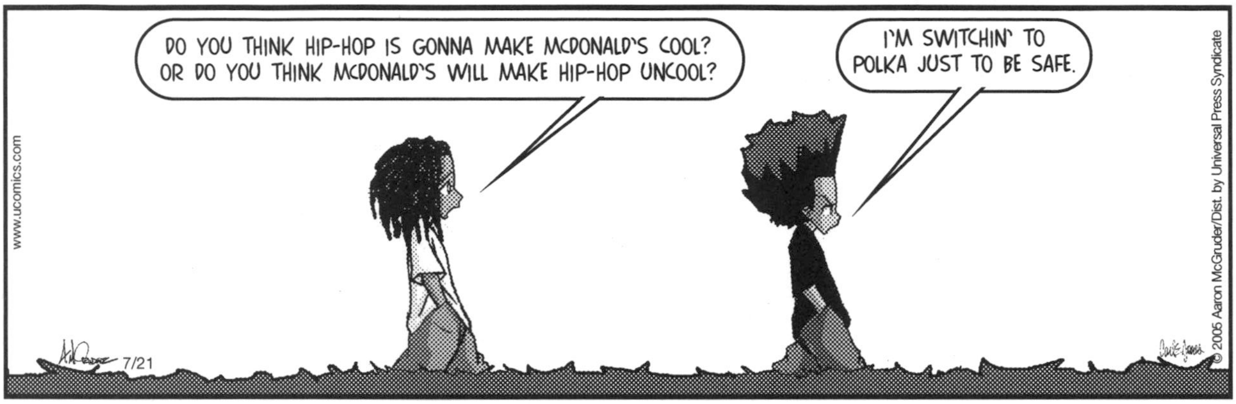
DO YOU THINK HIP-HOP IS GONNA MAKE McDONALD'S COOL? OR DO YOU THINK McDONALD'S WILL MAKE HIP-HOP UNCOOL?
I'M SWITCHIN' TO POLKA JUST TO BE SAFE.
www.ucomics.com
7/21
© 2005 Aaron McGruder/Dist. by Universal Press Syndicate

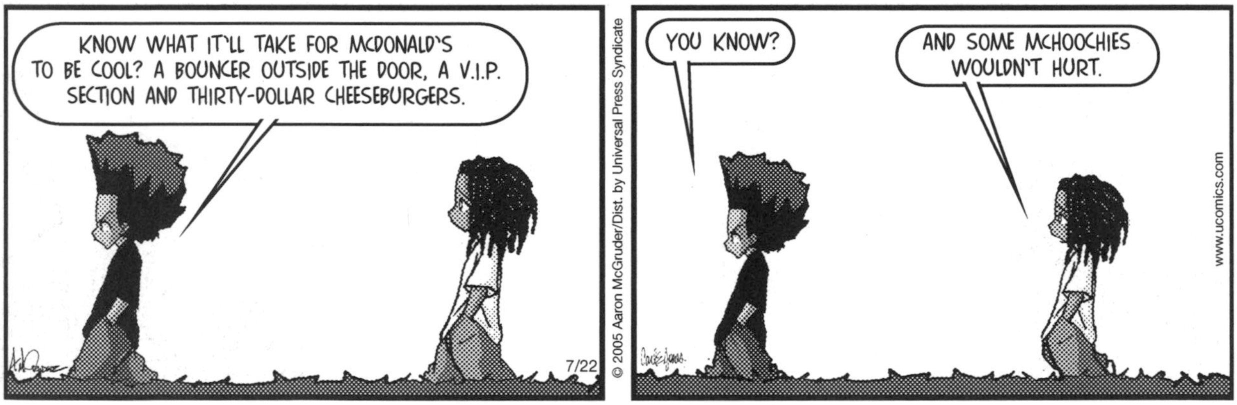
KNOW WHAT IT'LL TAKE FOR McDONALD'S TO BE COOL? A BOUNCER OUTSIDE THE DOOR, A V.I.P. SECTION AND THIRTY-DOLLAR CHEESEBURGERS.
7/22
© 2005 Aaron McGruder/Dist. by Universal Press Syndicate
YOU KNOW?
AND SOME McHOOCHIES WOULDN'T HURT.
www.ucomics.com

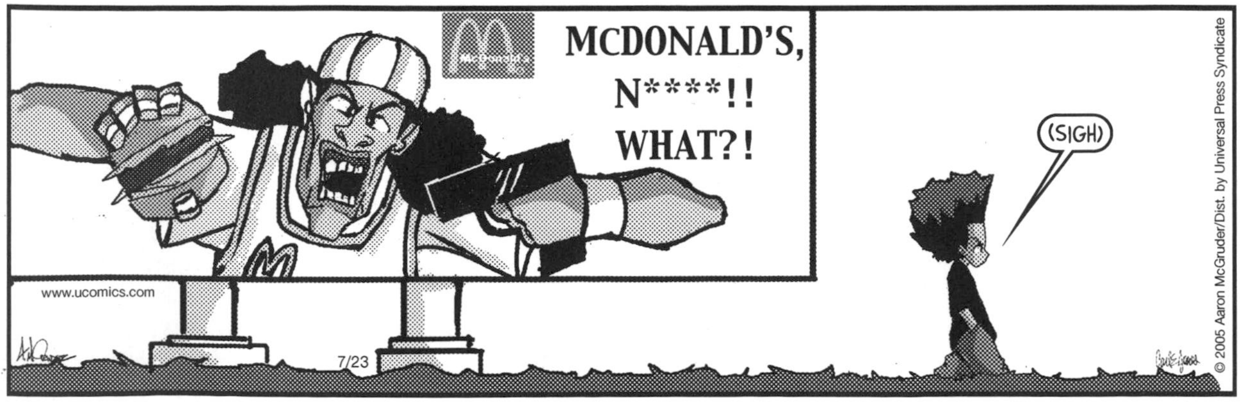
MCDONALD'S, N****!! WHAT?!
(SIGH)
www.ucomics.com
7/23
© 2005 Aaron McGruder/Dist. by Universal Press Syndicate

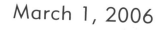

March 1, 2006

In order to prevent any possible offense to its readers, one major daily newspaper pulled this strip and ran an old one in its place because Granddad called some line-dancing cowboys "pansies."

© 2006 Aaron McGruder/Dist. by Universal Press Syndicate
GRANDDAD, ARE YOU WATCHING THE WILLIE NELSON COWBOY VIDEO? I THOUGHT YOU HATED THAT SONG?
I'M PRACTICING TOLERANCE, BOY. NOW MOVE ... THE PANSIES ARE LINE-DANCING.
3/1

FoxTrot Takes On The Boondocks

"When I announced my hiatus I ended up in *FoxTrot*. I suppose I had it coming . . ."

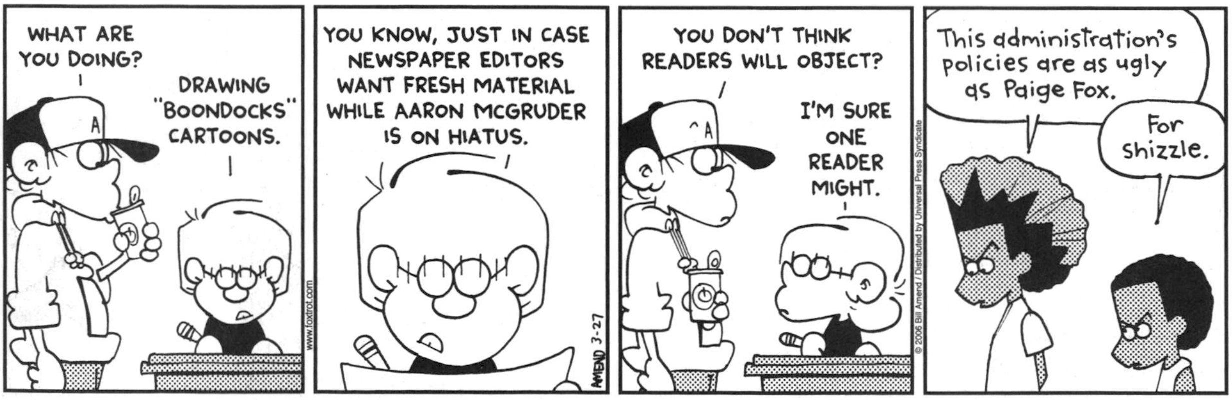
WHAT ARE YOU DOING?
DRAWING "BOONDOCKS" CARTOONS.
www.foxtrot.com
YOU KNOW, JUST IN CASE NEWSPAPER EDITORS WANT FRESH MATERIAL WHILE AARON MCGRUDER IS ON HIATUS.
AMEND 3-27
YOU DON'T THINK READERS WILL OBJECT?
I'M SURE ONE READER MIGHT.
© 2006 Bill Amend / Distributed by Universal Press Syndicate
This administration's policies are as ugly as Paige Fox.
For shizzle.

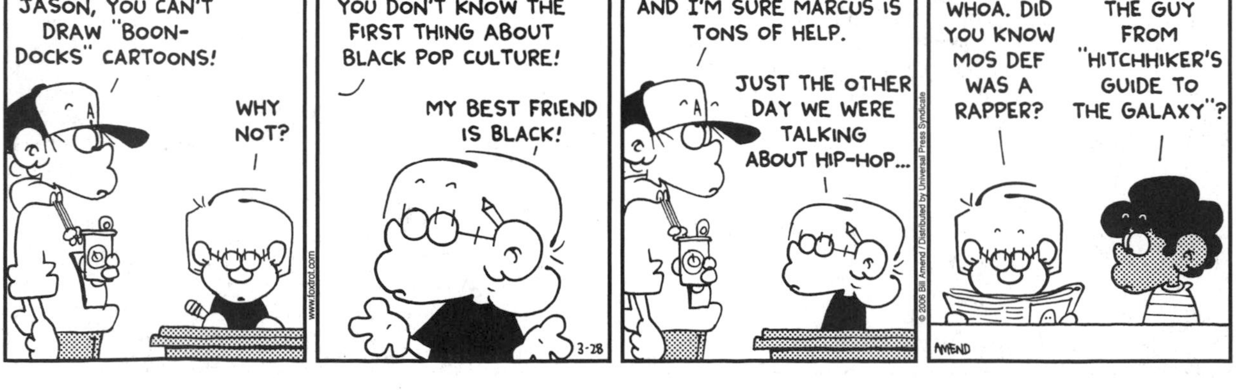
JASON, YOU CAN'T DRAW "BOON-DOCKS" CARTOONS!
WHY NOT?
www.foxtrot.com
YOU DON'T KNOW THE FIRST THING ABOUT BLACK POP CULTURE!
MY BEST FRIEND IS BLACK!
3-28
AND I'M SURE MARCUS IS TONS OF HELP.
JUST THE OTHER DAY WE WERE TALKING ABOUT HIP-HOP...
© 2006 Bill Amend / Distributed by Universal Press Syndicate
WHOA. DID YOU KNOW MOS DEF WAS A RAPPER?
THE GUY FROM "HITCHHIKER'S GUIDE TO THE GALAXY"?
AMEND

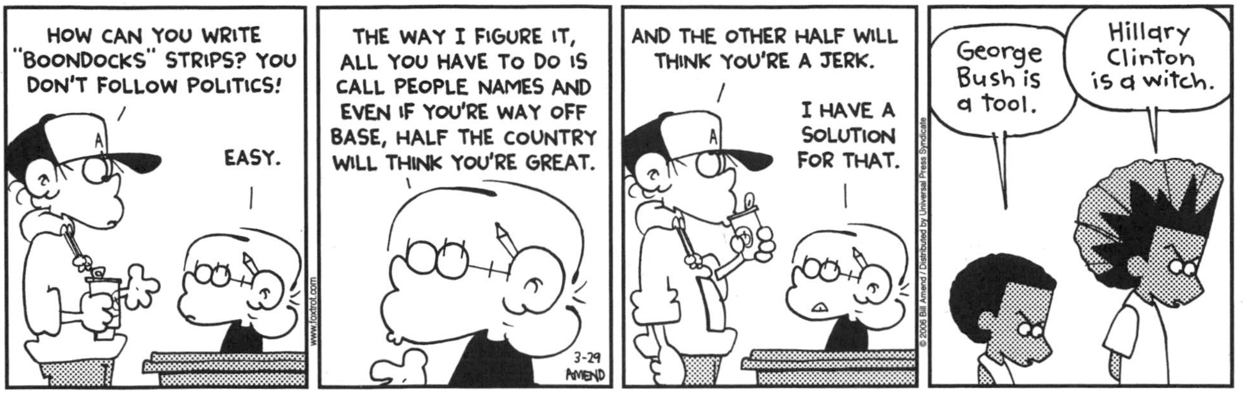
HOW CAN YOU WRITE "BOONDOCKS" STRIPS? YOU DON'T FOLLOW POLITICS!
EASY.
www.foxtrot.com
THE WAY I FIGURE IT, ALL YOU HAVE TO DO IS CALL PEOPLE NAMES AND EVEN IF YOU'RE WAY OFF BASE, HALF THE COUNTRY WILL THINK YOU'RE GREAT.
3-29 AMEND
AND THE OTHER HALF WILL THINK YOU'RE A JERK.
I HAVE A SOLUTION FOR THAT.
© 2006 Bill Amend / Distributed by Universal Press Syndicate
George Bush is a tool.
Hillary Clinton is a witch.

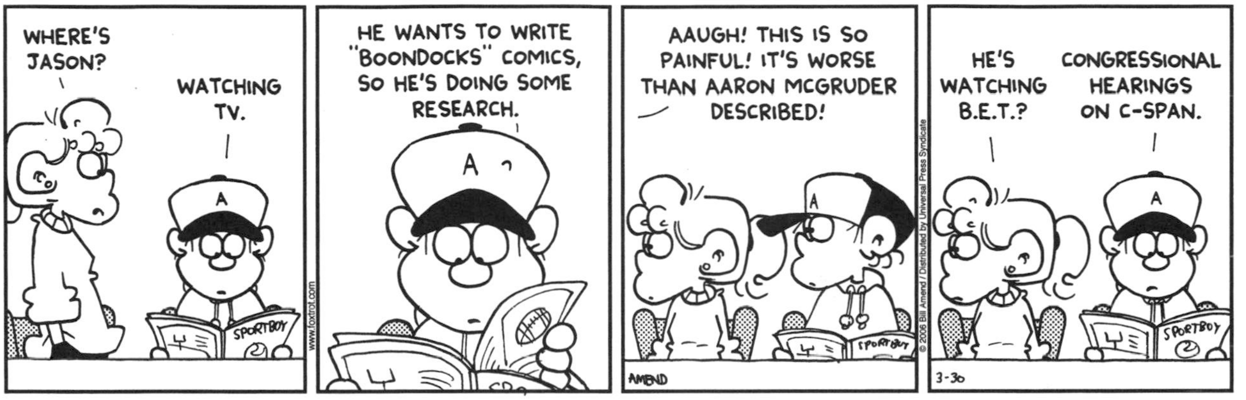
WHERE'S JASON?
WATCHING TV.
SPORTBOY
www.foxtrot.com
HE WANTS TO WRITE "BOONDOCKS" COMICS, SO HE'S DOING SOME RESEARCH.
AAUGH! THIS IS SO PAINFUL! IT'S WORSE THAN AARON MCGRUDER DESCRIBED!
AMEND
© 2006 Bill Amend / Distributed by Universal Press Syndicate
HE'S WATCHING B.E.T.?
CONGRESSIONAL HEARINGS ON C-SPAN.
3-30

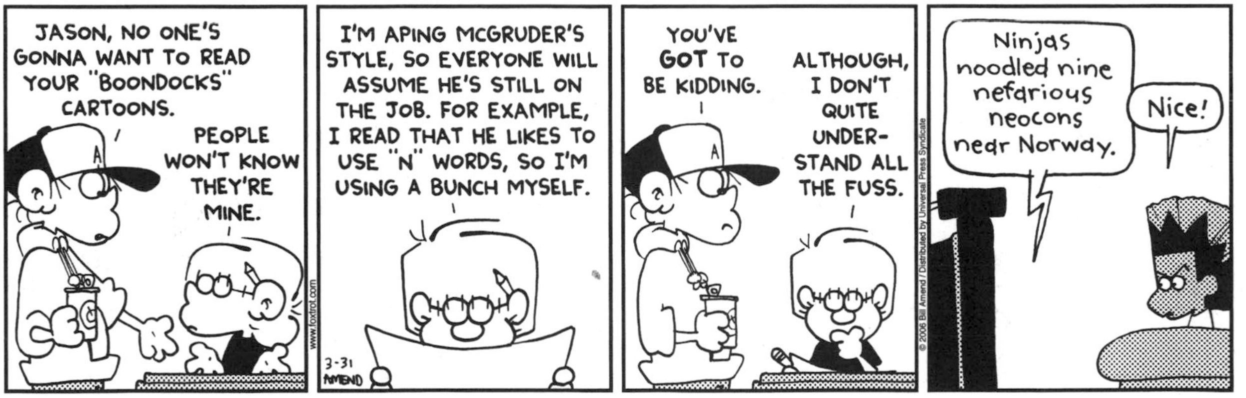
JASON, NO ONE'S GONNA WANT TO READ YOUR "BOONDOCKS" CARTOONS.
PEOPLE WON'T KNOW THEY'RE MINE.
www.foxtrot.com
I'M APING MCGRUDER'S STYLE, SO EVERYONE WILL ASSUME HE'S STILL ON THE JOB. FOR EXAMPLE, I READ THAT HE LIKES TO USE "N" WORDS, SO I'M USING A BUNCH MYSELF.
3-31 AMEND
YOU'VE **GOT** TO BE KIDDING.
ALTHOUGH, I DON'T QUITE UNDER-STAND ALL THE FUSS.
© 2006 Bill Amend / Distributed by Universal Press Syndicate
Ninjas noodled nine nefarious neocons near Norway.
Nice!

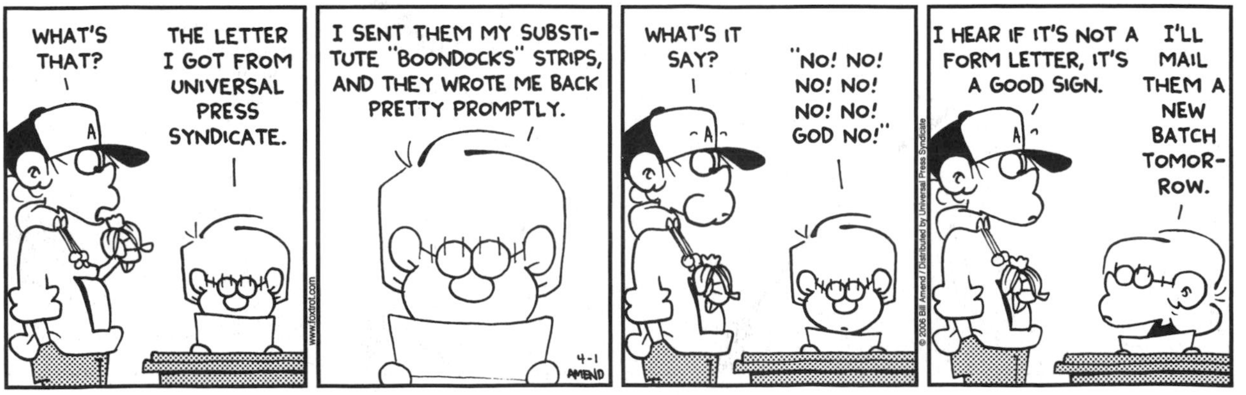
WHAT'S THAT?
THE LETTER I GOT FROM UNIVERSAL PRESS SYNDICATE.
www.foxtrot.com
I SENT THEM MY SUBSTI-TUTE "BOONDOCKS" STRIPS, AND THEY WROTE ME BACK PRETTY PROMPTLY.
4-1 AMEND
WHAT'S IT SAY?
"NO! NO! NO! NO! NO! NO! GOD NO!"
© 2006 Bill Amend / Distributed by Universal Press Syndicate
I HEAR IF IT'S NOT A FORM LETTER, IT'S A GOOD SIGN.
I'LL MAIL THEM A NEW BATCH TOMOR-ROW.

PRESENTED WITH SPECIAL THANKS TO BILL AMEND.

Also by **Aaron McGruder**

AARON McGRUDER • Foreword by Michael Moore
a RIGHT to be HOSTILE
THE BOONDOCKS TREASURY

The first big book of *The Boondocks*, with more than four years and 800 strips of one of the most influential, controversial, and scathingly funny comics ever to run in a daily newspaper.

A RIGHT TO BE HOSTILE
978-1-4000-4857-1
$16.95 PAPER (CANADA: $25.95)

PUBLIC ENEMY #2
AN ALL-NEW BOONDOCKS COLLECTION
AARON McGRUDER
Author of the Bestselling RIGHT TO BE HOSTILE

The next big collection of *The Boondocks*, with more than 500 previously uncollected strips—including those banned from newspapers around the country.

PUBLIC ENEMY #2
978-1-4000-8258-2
$16.95 PAPER (CANADA: $21.95)

BIRTH OF A NATION
A COMIC NOVEL
AARON McGRUDER
CREATOR OF THE BOONDOCKS
REGINALD HUDLIN
Writer/Director of House Party
Illustrated by KYLE BAKER
Author/Illustrator of Why I Hate Saturn

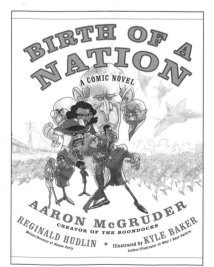

A hilarious political satire that answers the burning question: Would anyone care if East St. Louis seceded from the Union?

BIRTH OF A NATION
978-1-4000-8316-9
$14.95 PAPER (CANADA: $21.00)

Sources

Aaron McGruder
By Nathan Rabin
© A.V. Club
November 23, 2005

Aaron McGruder, Cartoonist,
Talks About His Sometimes
Controversial Strip, *Boondocks*
The Early Show on CBS:
August 31, 1999
© CBS Worldwide Inc., 1999.
All Rights Reserved.

Aaron McGruder, Creator of
The Boondocks
By Stephen Lemons
This article first appeared
in Salon.com,
at *http://www.salon.com*.
An online version remains in the
Salon archives. Reprinted with
permission.

The Africana QA: Aaron McGruder
by Bomani Jones
© Bomani Jones, 2003
c/o Africana.com,
September 30, 2003

Artist Probes "Curious Parallel"
in Gun Culture
By Fahizah Alim
© The Sacramento Bee, 2000

Boondocks Speaks: An Interview
with Aaron McGruder
By Jennifer A. Carbin
© City Paper (Philadelphia),
November 5, 2001
www.citypaper.net.
Jennifer Carbin.

CNN Newsnight with Aaron Brown
© CNN, October 1, 2004
Reprinted with permission

Color It Controversial
By Kathy Boccella
© Philadelphia Inquirer, 1999
Reprinted with permission from The
Philadelphia Inquirer

Down in the *Boondocks*
By Stephanie Kang
© Stephanie Kang, 2001
c/o Los Angeles Magazine,
August 2001

Drawing on the Headlines
by Beth Whitehouse
© 2001, Newsday
Reprinted with permission

Encountering Aaron McGruder
By R. C. Harvey
© R. C. Harvey (www.RCHarvey.com)
c/o The Comics Journal,
September 2003

The Equal Opportunity Offender:
Aaron McGruder's 'Boondocks' is
the Anti-'Family Circus'
By John Simpkins
© John Simpkins, 2001
c/o The New York Times Magazine,
June 2001

Foxtrot
© 2006 Bill Amend.
Reprinted with permission of
UNIVERSAL PRESS SYNDICATE.
All rights reserved.

Free Huey: Aaron McGruder's Outer
Child Is Taking on America
By Michael Datcher
© The Crisis,
September/October 2003

From *The Boondocks:*
An Interview with Aaron McGruder
By Nicole Mosley
© The Spokesman, April 13, 2001
Independent Newspaper of
Morgan State University

He's Gotta Fight the Powers
That Be
by Greg Braxton © 2004,
Los Angeles Times
Reprinted with permission

Huey Freeman: American Hero
by John Nichols
Reprinted with permission
from the January 28, 2002, issue
of *The Nation*. For subscription
information, call 1-800-333-8536.
Portions of each week's *Nation*
magazine can be accessed at
http://www.thenation.com.

Putting *The Boondocks* in the Dock
by Michael Getler
© 2003, The Washington Post,
reprinted with permission

Talk of the Toon
By Phil Hoad
© Phil Hoad, 2004
c/o Observer Magazine,
October 2004

Tavis Smiley
August 2, 2004
Aaron McGruder